DUMBARTON OAKS
MEDIEVAL LIBRARY

*Daniel Donoghue, General Editor*

# THE
# OLD ENGLISH AND ANGLO-LATIN
# RIDDLE TRADITION

DOML 69

# The
# Old English and Anglo-Latin
# Riddle Tradition

WITHDRAWN

Edited and Translated by

## ANDY ORCHARD

DUMBARTON OAKS
MEDIEVAL LIBRARY

HARVARD UNIVERSITY PRESS
CAMBRIDGE, MASSACHUSETTS
LONDON, ENGLAND
2021

First Printing

*Library of Congress Cataloging-in-Publication Data*
Names: Orchard, Andy, editor, translator.
Title: The Old English and Anglo-Latin riddle tradition / edited and
    translated by Andy Orchard.
Other titles: Dumbarton Oaks medieval library ; 69.
Description: Cambridge, Massachusetts : Harvard University Press, 2021. |
Series: Dumbarton Oaks medieval library; 69 | See also the
    complementary companion volume: A commentary on The Old
    English and Anglo-Latin Riddle Tradition (Washington, DC :
    Dumbarton Oaks Research Library and Collection, 2021), issued as
    Dumbarton Oaks medieval library, 69 supplement. | Includes
    bibliographical references and index. | Texts in Old English or Anglo-
    Latin with English translations following; introduction and
    commentary in English.
Identifiers: LCCN 2020038373 | ISBN 9780674055339 (cloth)
Subjects: LCSH: Riddles, English (Old) | Riddles, Latin—England. |
    English poetry—Old English, ca. 450–1100.
Classification: LCC PR1762 .O73 2021 | DDC 829/.8009—dc23
LC record available at https://lccn.loc.gov/2020038373

# Contents

# CONTENTS

# Introduction

Riddles, wordplay, and enigmatic utterance have been at the heart of English literature for many centuries: if the crossword as a form is only a hundred years old, the principles that underlie its successful solution go back more than a millennium, when anagrams, acrostics, and a variety of word and sound games both within and beyond Old English and Latin, the two literary languages of Anglo-Saxon England, are attested both widely and well.[1]

At first glance, the Old English and Anglo-Latin riddle tradition might seem a frivolous, obscure, and irrelevant subject for serious discussion in learned circles, a quaint coda to a sober field. But in fact not so: close study of the intellectual and material aspects of the riddles, composed for the most part by some of the most literate Anglo-Saxons whose names we know, and in both Latin and Old English, reveals a good deal of what we can ever hope to recover of the Anglo-Saxon world, its interests and opinions and, perhaps most important, its ties to those other worlds (the deep and beguiling seas of the classical, Continental, and Christian spheres) that it sought variously both to supplement and to supplant. The intimate connections between the learned and the lewd, the lay and the devout, the Latin and the vernacular, the inherited and the imported, and the oral and the literary provide contrasting perspectives. Such alternative insights into both the extraordinary and the everyday offer additionally a useful lens through which to perceive the past and the perceptions of others, as well as an appreciation of how wondrous the world can seem, and how marvelous the mundane.

In that sense, the Old English and Anglo-Latin riddle tradition can only aid us in solving the riddle of the Anglo-Saxons themselves, and how they chose to understand a wider world to which they perhaps inevitably felt peripheral, and not just geographically. Literate (which in the context of the surviving written record mostly meant Latinate) and therefore learned Anglo-Saxons would have known that the Mediterranean was quite literally the center of the world, but they did not simply surrender thereby their own space. However much the inherited and alien traditions of Latin and even Byzantine Greek impinged on their world view, not to mention analogues from the culturally closer Norse and Celtic regions, Anglo-Saxon riddlers seem to have sought from the start to make the genre their own.

There are, of course, riddles in the Bible, notably those posed by Samson (Judges 14:14) and the Queen of Sheba (1 Kings 10:1). In the classical world it was the Greeks who made most use of the form. Oedipus answers the famous riddle of the Sphinx: "What walks on four feet in the morning, two in the afternoon, and three in the evening?" The answer is "man," with a clue potentially enshrined in his very name, if we focus on the last syllable, which means "foot." The encyclopedic and highly bookish *Deipnosophistae* (Δειπνοσοφισταί; the title might be translated as *Dons at Dinner, Fellows Feasting,* or *Learned Banqueters,* as in Olson's edition) of Athenaeus, who flourished in the first quarter of the third century, demonstrates in Book 10 that riddles and problems were bandied about during banquets and drinking parties by the learned. Likewise, Book 14 of the sprawling collection of Greek poems from across several centuries now known as the *Palatine Anthology* comprises around 150 riddles, problems, and oracles. It is surely noteworthy that Latin speakers simply took over into their own tongue the two main Greek words for "riddle," namely αἴνιγμα (Latin *aenigma*) and γρῖφος (Latin *griphus*). Certainly, there seems no great indigenous Latin tradition of verse riddles (the native term *scirpus*, literally, "bullrush," but designating a riddle as complex as basketry, seems to have been used only in very specialized settings), although in an echo of the practice of the *Deipnosophistae*, we are told by Aulus Gellius in his *Noctes Atticae* of how well-educated Romans in Athens in the second century spent the feast of the Saturnalia, which took place in December each year. The chapter heading says it all (18.2):

*Cuiusmodi quaestionum certationibus Saturnalicia ludicra Athenis agitare soliti simus; atque inibi expressa quaedam sophismata et aenigmata oblectatoria.*

What kind of questions we used to ask in competition as Saturnalian amusements in Athens; and some entertaining puzzles and riddles that were produced there.

Latin riddlers evidently identified primarily with Greek contexts and Greek contests of learned emulation too, and it is no surprise to find that the esteemed rhetorician and poet

Ausonius, who died around the year 395, should imitate the studied frivolity so evident here. Indeed, he even uses the term *frivola* (trifles) to describe his own enigmatic composition in the introduction to his *Griphus ternarii numeri (Riddle on the Number Three)*, just before going on to emphasize the association of riddling and drink:

> *Ac ne me gloriosum neges, coeptos inter prandendum versiculos ante cenae tempus absolvi, hoc est dum bibo et paulo ante quam biberem. Sit ergo examen pro materia et tempore. Sed tu quoque hoc ipsum paulo hilarior et dilutior lege; namque iniurium est de poeta male sobrio lectorem abstemium iudicare.*

And just so that you don't deny that I am boastful: I began these little verses over lunch and finished before suppertime; that is to say, I began while drinking and then a bit before I was drinking again. Let that be your scale for the theme and the timing. Read them too while a bit merrier and more drenched; for it is unfair for a sober reader to pass judgment on a poet in his cups.[2]

It is against this background that we should turn to the *aenigmata* of Symphosius, the verse preface of which explicitly states that his own *frivola* were composed, perhaps even extemporaneously, at a drinking party as entertainment during the Saturnalia; it concludes with a chirpy request for indulgence from a readership less drunk than the poet himself. The author's own name (which does not seem to be attested before the fourth century), indeed, with its clear parallels to the common noun *symposium* (drinking party), connects this collection of one hundred riddles back directly to those of his Greek predecessors. Symphosius laments the fact that he has brought nothing with him, presumably in the way of the kind of mechanical and memorized words that stud the sayings of the *Deipnosophistae,* and claims that his *aenigmata* either came to him quite spontaneously or were worked up on the basis of then-cited tropes. The preface to Symphosius's *Aenigmata* (here SYM PR) is itself of course a carefully contrived conceit: an opening pair of lines that does not appear in all manuscripts addresses an unknown teacher and points the way to the later use of these and other *aenigmata* in classroom contexts, while the final line addresses an anonymous "reader" (*lector,* another term that appears to be deliberately echoed by the Anglo-Saxon Aldhelm), perhaps pointing to a conscious literary collection. Certainly, the framing tale offered by Symphosius provides a secular echo of the reported inspiration of the pious cowherd Cædmon in late seventh-century Northumbria at a drinking party: Bede calls the gathering Cædmon attended a *convivium* (party); the Old English Bede adds the interesting extra detail that it was a *gebeorscipe* (beer-drinking party).

Suggested dates for Symphosius's texts range from the fourth to the sixth centuries, in the same milieu as, for example, Ausonius, Macrobius, and Martianus Capella, with tradition placing his origins in North Africa. Such a suggestion is all the more tantalizing given Symphosius's demonstrable and explicitly acknowledged influence on Aldhelm (who died 709/10), the first Anglo-Saxon author to have composed extensively in Latin verse, and who chose the genre of *aenigmata* for his earliest compositions (ALD). Ald-

helm was educated at the celebrated Canterbury school of
Theodore and Hadrian, where among the subjects he tells us
he studied was Latin metrics. Theodore, a Greek-speaking
monk from Tarsus, may have introduced Aldhelm to the
Greek tradition of riddling, but it was most likely the Latin
scholar Hadrian, coming from North Africa, who introduced Aldhelm to the Symphosian style of riddling in a classroom context. It is striking that in the prose preface to his
own collection of one hundred *aenigmata* Aldhelm is silent
about any vernacular riddle traditions, but instead points
very carefully to three major influences, namely Symphosius, Aristotle, and the Bible. This gesture may indicate his
wider knowledge (presumably via Theodore, and certainly
in translation) of the kind of Greek and Byzantine riddles
preserved in the *Palatine Anthology,* and certainly downplays
Symphosius as his only influence. Indeed, Aldhelm goes out
of his way to surpass Symphosius, both in explicitly using
Christian themes and language, and in composing lengthier
riddles of between four and eighty-three lines (all of Symphosius's are strictly three lines long).

While Symphosius was certainly a major influence on the
Anglo-Saxon riddle tradition well beyond Aldhelm, and in
both Latin and Old English, it is harder to assess the impact
(not to mention the provenance) of another anonymous
collection of *aenigmata* variously called the *Bern Riddles,
Aenigmata Hexasticha,* or the *Enigmata Tullii* (BER). These
sixty-two *aenigmata* are uniformly composed in six lines
of rhythmical rather than metrical hexameters and have a
clear link to Symphosius (consistently doubling in scale the
scope of his three-line *aenigmata*); their connection to the
Anglo-Latin riddle tradition is less clear cut. The earliest

manuscript (Bern, Burgerbibliothek 611, dating to the early eighth century), which does not contain solutions, derives from an Irish monastic foundation on the Continent; hence the much-disputed attribution of the whole collection to a seventh-century Irishman, although conjectures concerning the collection's age range from the fourth century on. A closing acrostic spelling out *PAULUS* (ps-BER 1) may, allowing for scribal error in transmission, underlie the attribution to "Tullius," presumably saddling Cicero, via his full name of Marcus Tullius Cicero, with material he would more likely disclaim than willingly declaim. Since the collection is given the title *Quaestiones* (questions, challenges) in some manuscripts, it is tempting to identify the author or compiler with the otherwise unknown "Paulus Quaestor" (another form of *quaesitor,* "seeker," "questioner"?) named and quoted by Aldhelm in the two metrical treatises (*De metris* and *De pedum regulis*) that accompany his *aenigmata.* If so, the metrical verses attributed to Paulus may have been appended to the existing collection of rhythmical verses: the *aenigmata* themselves are purely rhythmical, except for the final acrostic. Whatever one's views on the literary merit and influence of BER, the judgment of their first editor, Riese, that these are "six-line rhythmical poems, horrid in their roughness" *(hexasticha rhythmica barbarie horrida)* seems a tad harsh.[3]

The educational impact and potential of Latin *aenigmata,* hinted at by Symphosius, notably in an opening distich to the preface that may in fact be an interpolation (SYM P. 1–2), is very clearly developed in several of the Bern *aenigmata,* and implicit in the at times somewhat obscure allusions of *Versus cuiusdam Scotti de alfabeto* (*The Verses of a Certain Irishman on the Alphabet,* ALF). Such didactic aspects are also explicit in the book learning combined with firsthand observation that characterizes ALD. It is seen still more starkly in the *aenigmata* of Boniface (BON), whose general debt to Aldhelm (especially ALD) is widely acknowledged. So, just as Aldhelm sought to outdo Symphosius in his use of longer poems treating more serious, more learned, and more Christian topics, as well as Greek-influenced acrostics in his preface, likewise Boniface took the model still a stage further by embedding the solutions in a series of acrostics and by moving the whole riddle tradition away from concrete objects, real or imagined, to abstract ones. In an implicit homage to the ending of the verse version of Aldhelm's longest and most serious work, *De virginitate (On Virginity)*, which, unlike its earlier prose counterpart, features a description of the battle of the Vices and the Virtues inspired by Cassian (who died in 435), Boniface produces for an unnamed "sister" (perhaps to be identified with Leofgyth or Leoba, abbess of Bischofsheim, who died in 782) twenty *aenigmata* dealing with the Virtues and Vices.

It is in any case clear that several senior, learned, and highly influential Anglo-Saxon churchmen all chose in the course of their busy lives to compose *aenigmata,* including Aldhelm, who became bishop of Malmesbury; Boniface, who became bishop of Mainz; Tatwine, who became archbishop of Canterbury (TAT); Hwætberht, who became abbot of Wearmouth–Jarrow (716–747), if the "Eusebius" addressed by Bede is to be identified with the author of EUS; and Alcuin, the most influential Anglo-Saxon at the court of Charlemagne (ALC). It is perhaps inevitable, therefore, that the Venerable Bede (673–735) should be credited with two series of Latin *aenigmata,* in both verse and prose; the former

(BED) may be his, but the latter (ps-BED) seems more likely spurious.

There are also a number of anonymous collections of Anglo-Latin *aenigmata,* and indeed individual *aenigmata,* that can be closely associated with these six named and strikingly prominent and prolific authors. It is tempting to connect the so-called "Lorsch Riddles" (LOR) with Boniface too, given the fact that these twelve *aenigmata* are preserved uniquely in a single eighth-century manuscript, U, that also contains not only ALD and SYM but also Boniface's highly derivative *De metris (On Meters).* Moreover, the dozen *aenigmata* of LOR have, embedded with them, a thirty-six-line epitaph for the Anglo-Saxon priest Domberht, who was apparently taught by Boniface and accompanied his mission. Also to be closely associated with this learned and literate Anglo-Latin tradition of *aenigmata* is the collection of twelve poems that make up the *Bibliotheca magnifica (The High-Minded Library,* BIB), all of which deal with abstract scholarly topics, with much of the material drawn directly from Isidore's *Etymologiae.* Once again, the manuscript context is important: BIB is found uniquely in an important mid-eleventh-century compilation generally known as the "Cambridge Songs" manuscript (Cambridge, University Library, Gg. 5.35; here designated G). It fits well within the wider tradition, just as the single *aenigma,* the Abingdon Riddle (ABI), with its double solution and association with the learned Bishop Æthelwold of Winchester (904/9–984), fits in well with the by then more than two-hundred-year-old Anglo-Saxon riddle tradition.

Against such a pious and learned background, it is perhaps less surprising that yet another learned Anglo-Saxon churchman, Bishop Leofric of Exeter (1050–1072), should present to the cathedral at Exeter a late tenth-century manuscript (here designated E) containing at present around ninety Old English riddles and one Latin *aenigma* (EXE) — the precise number will likely never be known — some of which are clearly risqué. Several Latin models for such a combination of secular and educational verse texts survive from Anglo-Saxon England, and two of the more extensive contain riddles, notably the late tenth-century Royal manuscript (London, British Library, Royal 12. C. XXIII; here designated L) and the "Cambridge Songs" manuscript (G) already mentioned. The constant corrections and alterations made by the Exeter Book scribe suggest a scribe striving to be accurate, even when evidently uncomprehending of his copy. The fact that he fails to implement his own oversight consistently only engenders a kind of confidence in his endearing incompetence and his apparent willingness to adjust and invent when bafflement kicks in. Such imaginative nimbleness must have been essential for all medieval readers and copiers of manuscripts, and it is a skill sadly lost or at least diminished today, when spell-checkers and proofreaders have tended to smooth over both scribal and authorial infelicities. But of course such challenges of transmission are particularly acute in the case of those texts that are by their very nature enigmatic and obscure, and it is unclear how far we can trust a scribe whose work we can show is far from perfect.

The sheer size, diversity, and occasional brilliance of EXE have tended not only to overshadow other riddles in Old English, but somehow to relegate the Latin *aenigma* tradition, and that in Anglo-Latin in particular, to a lower rung on the literary ladder, an unfortunate development exacerbated only by the fact that, outside EXE (which itself has closer parallels than often acknowledged, and indeed includes a Latin riddle, EXE 86), many of the other Old English riddles have very clear links with the Latin tradition in general, and indeed with specific Latin texts. So, for example, a very early translation of ALD 33 appears as the so-called *Leiden Riddle* (LEI) and again later as EXE 33, while the Old English material relating to the dialogue between Solomon and Saturn (here SOL) clearly derives from a variety of Latin texts, if not necessarily from a single source. Likewise, the *Old English Prose Riddle* (OEP), whether composed or simply written down by Abbot Ælfwine of Winchester, also fits into the same bilingual scheme, since similar incest riddles are again found both in Latin (in the tale of Apollonius of Tyre, which includes versions of several of the *aenigmata* of SYM, although the Old English version has a lacuna at this point, where the quire containing the vernacular versions appears to have been physically removed) and in Old English in the biblically inspired EXE 44 (*LOTH OND HIS BEARN*, "Lot and his children"). At first glance, the so-called *Old English Rune Poem* (OER) may seem to run counter to this trend, but in fact the late date of the now-lost manuscript source, as well as the learned and literary nature of the analogues (ALF in Latin, OIR in Icelandic, and ONR, given here in the notes to OIR) undermine considerably any idea of independence; further analogues (including some very specific parallels) also connect the much later collection of Old Norse–Icelandic riddles found in *Heiðreks saga* (GES) with the wider Anglo-Saxon riddle tradition in both Latin and Old English. The early riddle (plus solution) carved in runes on the Franks Casket and describing the origin of the box (FRA) also shows a complex relationship to the Latin tradition. The fact that the Casket juxtaposes scenes from Roman history, Germanic legend, and the Bible, containing inscriptions not only in common but in encrypted runes, alongside Latin texts in the Roman alphabet, means that the physical context of FRA only highlights and underlines the hybrid nature of the Anglo-Saxon riddle tradition as a whole, and the perils of perceiving it in a merely monoglot manner.

## MANUSCRIPT CONTEXTS

FRA also offers a further useful corrective in reminding us that the written word in Anglo-Saxon England was not confined to manuscripts, a trope witnessed in other texts where objects seem to speak, whether the Alfred Jewel or the Ruthwell Cross, and one well explored within the riddles themselves: see, in particular, EXE 47 (*HUSEL-DISC,* "paten") and 57 (*HUSEL-FÆT,* "chalice"). The (at first glance) chaotic context of FRA has been elucidated as part of a wider plan, and the same might be said for the texts in an impressive range of manuscripts within the wider riddle tradition. For an example, we might turn to the two major Anglo-Saxon manuscripts containing *aenigmata* already mentioned, namely G and L. Both manuscripts are heavily glossed, in the same hand as the text, and appear to go back to a common stock. In G, the titles/solutions appear in the margin, while in L the titles/solutions are likewise given in the same hand, but in capitals above each *aenigma.* Both manuscripts share a common core of material, which might be schematically arranged to show the order of the relevant texts as follows, with L (the older manuscript) presented first:

L1: ALD PR, 79v–82v
L2: ALD, 83r–103v
L3: SYM, 104r–13v
L4: EUS, 113v–21v          G1 (= L4): EUS, 370r–75v
L5: TAT, 121v–27r          G2 (= L5): TAT, 375v–77v
      \* \* \*                      \* \* \*
L6: ALF, 137v–38v          G3 (= L6): ALF, 381r–82r
                                   G4 (*not in* L): BON, 382r–89r
                                   G5 (= L3): SYM, 389r–94r
                                   G6 (= L2): ALD, 394v–407r
                                            \* \* \*
                                   G7 (*not in* L): BED, 418v–19r
                                   G8 (*not in* L): BIB, 423v–25r

ALF comes at the end of L, with clear damage to the final folio, and it is possible that the manuscript also originally contained BON and perhaps even BIB too. Both manuscripts also share two poems of advice for princes wrongly attributed to Alcuin, and more usually known as *Versus quos Smaragdus ad unum de filiis Ludovici Pii misit* (*Verses Which Smaragdus Sent to One of the Sons of Louis the Pious,* SK 7810) and *Versus cuiusdam ad Ludovicum Pium* (*Verses by Someone for Louis the Pious,* SK 10988). In both manuscripts these monitory poems appear in the same order between TAT and ALF (L, fols. 132r–37v, and G, fols. 378r–80v); at first glance, although these poems are by no means enigmatic, they are divided into subsections, which in the manuscripts contain brief titles such as *DE TIMORE* (on fear), *DE SAPIENTIA* (on wisdom), and *DE PACE* (on peace), and may therefore have seemed appropriate additions to the broader collection. Perhaps the best lesson to be drawn from these two large and varied manuscripts, which evidently have both an encyclopedic and a didactic intention, is the sense in which riddles (in this case *aenigmata,* but the same basic argument holds for EXE) were recognized as a genre, and tended to circulate alongside what might be termed like-minded texts: as modern readers, we extract them from those contexts at our peril, even if, as successive scribes and compilers did, we realign, reconfigure, and recontextualize them as we will.

## Sources and Analogues

For an extensive discussion of sources and analogues, consult the complementary companion volume, *A Commentary on "The Old English and Anglo-Latin Riddle Tradition"* (Washington, D.C., 2021; abbreviated throughout this volume as *COEALRT*). In keeping with DOML series conventions, this section gives only the most salient details.

Several debts to the Bible are noted at particular moments in the Notes to the Translations below, but perhaps the greatest single source for the Anglo-Saxon riddle tradition is the *Etymologiae* ("etymologies"; the work is also often known by the alternative title *Origines,* "origins") written by Isidore, bishop of Seville, which was published soon after its author's death in 636 by his close friend and colleague Braulio, bishop of Zaragoza (who himself died in 651). In drawing deeply on the classical encyclopedic tradition, Isidore attempts to encompass the sum of human knowledge in twenty volumes and a total of 448 chapters. The significant degree of overlap between the Anglo-Saxon riddle tradition and the *Etymologiae* is indicated broadly in the Notes to the Translations below, and in more detail elsewhere (in an Index of Parallels in *COEALRT*): all twenty of the volumes are witnessed in one way or another, and nearly one hundred chapters. The raw figures are certainly misleading, however, for a number of reasons, not least of which is the unevenness of the distribution. Some books are disproportionately represented in individual collections: most of the parallels to ALF are in Book 1, *De grammatica (Grammar),* for example, and most of those to BIB are in Book 2, *De rhetorica et dialectica (Rhetoric and Dialectic).* Meanwhile, others are themselves vastly overrepresented, such as Book 12, *De animalibus (Animals),* which accounts for more than a third of the overlapping entries and has parallels in many of the collections discussed here (see especially SYM, ALD, BED, EUS, EXE, and BER). Here again, the distribution is extremely uneven: almost all of the parallels come from just three collections, namely SYM, ALD, and EUS, with many of those from the last collection coming from EUS 41–60. That said, what is most striking about the relevant entries is the extent to which there seems strikingly little duplication or overlap, almost as if the authors of the successive collections consciously sought to avoid repetition.

Still more intriguing in this connection is the curious set of apparently seventh-century Hiberno-Latin texts known by the combined title of the *Hisperica famina* (the hybrid flavor of the title's forms is perhaps best suggested by a translation such as *Westernly Speakifications*), at least some version of which seems to have been known to Aldhelm. These texts, composed in extraordinarily arcane and allusive language, are evidently the product of a high degree of learning, albeit perhaps misapplied, and offer considerable insight into the daily experience of what is apparently a wandering band of scholars, presumably in Ireland. The so-called A-text of the *Hisperica famina* contains a number of passages that are in terms of style and concept very like riddles (including titles/solutions for several in the manuscript) and address a number of topics that can be matched in the Anglo-Saxon riddle tradition.[4] For the background and possible influence of the *Hisperica famina* on the Anglo-Saxon riddle tradition, see the notes to EXE 1 and ALD 2 below. Likewise, other potential sources and analogues for individual texts and discussions are considered in the relevant headnotes.

Against such a complex background, it will be clear that the precise choice of sources and analogues presented here (SYM, BER, ALF, OIR, GER, and XMS) is a somewhat impressionistic and ragged affair, dictated in large part by reasons of space and overlap: the parallel publication *COEALRT,* along with texts and translations of the various collections of Byzantine riddles, to take just two examples, will certainly revolutionize attitudes toward the Anglo-Saxon tradition; in the meantime, the connections between these various texts from different periods and diverse manuscripts in dissimilar languages remain, encouraging further comparison.

## Use of Titles

The old notion that the Anglo-Latin *aenigmata* traveled with their solutions, while the Old English riddles did not, is doubly misleading. Perhaps the earliest Old English riddle, that engraved in runes on the seventh-century Franks Casket

(FRA) gives the answer, a description of the material from which the casket is carved (*HWÆLES BAN*, "whale's bone"), while several of the manuscripts of ALD, including some of the earliest, circulate the solutions as a separate item. Elsewhere in Old English, EXE 21, 34, and 73 (for example) use a variety of cryptic strategies in all three cases to offer solutions that may well be interpolations, and where the "solutions" in the last two are almost certainly wrong. Similarly cryptic is the use of anagrams in EXE 22 and 40, using runes in the first case and rune names in the second, but in both these cases the embedded solutions seem correct.

Likewise, several Anglo-Latin *aenigmata* have clearly corrupt, imprecise, or otherwise highly questionable titles/solutions, as (for example) the notes on TAT 3–4, 35, and 39 make clear. Moreover, in those riddles where answers are given, there is disagreement in the manuscripts as to the grammatical form of any supposed solution: some offer nominatives, as is implied in the frequent vernacular challenge to "say what I am called," while others in Latin have the more bookish prepositional *DE* (about, concerning) followed by an ablative, which probably reflects a secondary development and the increased use of riddles in a classroom context, and was perhaps influenced by the use of that formulation in encyclopedic and didactic works, notably in the chapter headings of Isidore's *Etymologiae*. Certainly, such niceties seem to distinguish the so-called first and second recensions of ALD, a collection where, as has been mentioned, it is evident that the titles/solutions also sometimes circulated independently. In a similar vein, it is clear that several of the *aenigmata* in particular offer broad hints or clues to their solutions embedded within the text, often as part of the opening line or two (or, in the case of BON, via acrostics): see further the note to ALD 7.

The opposite device, namely adding a further riddle-within-a-riddle, is less common, but is also attested, most widely in ALD and EXE, as the note to ALD 44 indicates. In a somewhat parallel but characteristically idiosyncratic treatment, in ALC D76–83 Alcuin has his respondent answer the riddles with a string of knowingly cryptic comments that hint at a solution, including: *Hoc coqui nostri norunt* (Our cooks know that one) . . . *Rusticorum est haec venatio* (That's poor people's hunting) . . . *Pueri in schola hoc sciunt* (The boys in school know this one). Such extra clues surely testify to some currency and vibrancy for the tradition as a whole.

## SHARED THEMES ACROSS THE COLLECTIONS

Other evidence for shared connections within the riddle tradition, whether in Latin or in Old English, is supplied by the many overlaps of treatment and theme. The widely found "biter bitten" motif stems from the opening line of SYM 44 (*CAEPA,* "onion": "I bite the biters, yet of my own accord I bite no one," *mordeo mordentes, ultro non mordeo quemquam*) and is clearly echoed by Aldhelm in the opening line of ALD 46 (*URTICA,* "nettle": "I trouble those who trouble me, but I trouble no one of my own accord," *torqueo torquentes, sed nullum torqueo sponte*), as well as in BER 37.5 (*PIPER,* "pepper": "I bite the biter with a bite, but I don't wound with teeth," *mordeo mordentem morsu, nec vulnero dente*). The thematic connection of the vegetable solutions only strengthens the link between these *aenigmata,* but other riddles can also be associated with the motif, and so underline the importance of conceiving of the Anglo-Saxon riddle tradition as a whole. Verbal parallels ally this motif with an *aenigma* on an apparently unrelated theme in BER 41.3–4 (*VENTUS*, "wind": "I have no mouth, and do not harm anyone with my teeth, / though I bite everyone loitering in woods and in fields," *Os est mihi nullum, dente nec vulnero quemquam, / mordeo sed cunctos silvis campisque morantes*), and so striking is the notion of the biting tooth of the wind that it is repeated in a "riddle-within-a-riddle" in EXE 83.5a (*BLÆST-BELG*, "bellows": "with heaven's tooth," *heofones toþe*), one of the more risqué of the double-entendre riddles. Further verbal parallels with the "biter bitten" motif connect it very clearly to TAT 7.6 (*TINTINNUM*, "bell": "I am toothless, but with my lips soon bite the one who bites me," *mordeo mordentem labris mox dentibus absque*), BON 13.67 (*CUPIDITAS*, "greed": "for biting, his quivering limbs would shudder under my teeth," *mordendo trepidi tremerent sub dentibus artus*), and perhaps less so in TAT 1.10 (*SAPIENTIA*, "wisdom": "I embrace the one who gnaws me; I shall bereave the one who spares me," *mordentem amplector; parcentem me viduabo*). Other *aenigmata* that seem to share the theme include ALD 69 (*TAXUS*, "yew"), BED 17 (*CETUS*, "whale"), and EUS 51 (*SCORPIO*, "scorpion"). The legacy of SYM 44 is still more obvious in one of two closely connected Old English riddles with the same solution: EXE 63.5–6 (*CIPE*, "onion": "I bite no man, unless he bites me; / there are many of those who bite me," *monnan ic ne bite, nymþþe he me bite; / sindan þara monige þe mec bitað*) even seems to quote in translation the punning Latin of Symphosius. The second of the Old English "onion" riddles, EXE 23, is evidently heavily reliant on EXE 63, but owes little or nothing to SYM 44, again developing instead into a highly sexualized double-entendre riddle. That the "biter bitten" motif can be detected in various manifestations in no fewer than eight of the riddle collections considered here is striking enough; that it developed in ways that take it far from the simple wordplay of its ultimate source Symphosius, considering an onion, demonstrates the extent to which the Anglo-Saxon riddle tradition matured and grew sometimes far from its roots. As Mary Jane Williams, who considers the motif in detail, concludes:

> It seems significant that we do not find this moti[f] among the Greek enigmas, nor does Taylor cite any folk riddles which utilize it. Rather it seems restricted to those few Latin enigmas and the Anglo-Saxon one which imitates them. The close verbal parallels and the limited currency of the moti[f] strongly suggest that here we have a case of direct transmission from a single literary source.[5]

Also highlighted here is a perceived and often repeated dichotomy between "folk riddles" on the one hand and "literary riddles" on the other, a dichotomy that has perhaps been as pernicious to the full appreciation of the Anglo-Saxon riddle tradition as that which seeks to keep strictly separate compositions in Latin and in Old English.

The "biter bitten" motif is but one of many: several of the riddles in the Anglo-Saxon tradition focus on shared themes, for example, that of the mother/daughter paradox, where each gives birth to the other (in the original Latin form, ice/water): such is the underlying theme of ps-SYM 1, quoted directly by Aldhelm in the prose introduction to ALD that appears in *De metris (On Meters)* at the beginning of the tradition, and also found at ps-BED 6, LOR 4.6–7, EXE 33.9–10, and especially prominently in BER, notably BER 8, 31, 32, and 38.3–4.[6] The theme, which in Anglo-Saxon England appears both in Latin and in Old English, can be traced directly back to Greek material witnessed in both *Deipnosophistae* 10.452a and *Palatine Anthology* 14.41:

Μητέρ᾽ ἐμὴν τίκτω καὶ τίκτομαι εἰμὶ δὲ ταύτης
ἄλλοτε μὲν μείζων ἄλλοτε μειοτέρη.

I bear my mother, and am born from her; sometimes I'm bigger than her, sometimes smaller.

What is intriguing here is that while the Anglo-Latin focuses firmly on the relationship between Latin *glacies* (ice) and *aqua* (water), both of which are grammatically feminine, the Greek riddles have a different given solution, namely "night and day," since both the nouns νύξ (night) and ἡμέρα (day) are grammatically feminine. Further developments of the theme in Old English (where *wæter,* "water," and *is,* "ice," are both neuter) are found in EXE 35 (*BLÆST-BELG,* "bellows") and EXE 44 (*LOTH OND HIS BEARN,* "Lot and his children"), so demonstrating the ubiquity of the basic theme, and how the tradition continued to develop and diversify.

Many other themes and devices connect the various collections considered here. Several texts in the tradition focus on the hard life and multiple afterlives of draft animals, specifically oxen: clear connections can be drawn between, for example, ALD 83, EUS 37, ps-BED 7, LOR 11.1–5, and EXE 12.1–4 and 38, as the notes there show. There are other texts which, at a first glance at their titles/solutions, might look as if they should be associated with this tight grouping, but on closer examination seem to have little in the way of common themes, namely SYM 32 (*TAURUS*, "bull") and EUS 12 (*BOS*, "bull") and 13 (*VACCA*, "cow"). A further group of texts, likewise spanning the various collections, clusters round the description of a quill pen writing: clear examples are found in ALD 59, TAT 6, EUS 35, BED 18, ps-BED 11, LOR 9, and EXE 51.

Similarly, a significant number of the riddles in EXE more or less openly invite erroneous sexual solutions, and indeed while there is considerable critical commentary on the so-called double-entendre riddles, the description "single entendre" might well be more appropriate. At least twenty-two riddles may be relevant here, covering a wide variety of tame solutions, with little correspondence.[7] Where there is overlap in terms of solutions, it is striking to note that the linked riddles generally occur in the first (EXE 1–57) and third (EXE 59–91) of the groupings in E, as the pairings 9 and 61, 23 and 63, 35 and 83 (and 85), and 42 and 87 clearly show. It is often assumed and indeed asserted that the presence of such double entendres distinguishes EXE from the Latin collections, but notes to individual *aenigmata*, notably BER 5 (*MENSA*, "table"), 37 (*PIPER*, "pepper"), and 47 (*CONCHA*, "conch"); BED 6 (*SEGES*, "field of grain"); and TAT 30 (*ENSIS ET VAGINA*, "sword and sheath") make plain the connection. In the same vein, the double-entendre riddles in many cases seem to spring directly from the idea of a creature rendered useful to mankind through suffering—

what is termed here as the "suffering servant" motif—a notion developed particularly in TAT, though it is also attested several times in EXE and BER, as the note to TAT 5 makes clear. Further thematic links between collections are evident when one considers such themes as the enumeration of body parts, on which see, for example, ALD 20, 43, 84, and 95; TAT 10; EUS 40 and 45; and ALC D 10–37 in Latin; and EXE 37, 56, 77, and 82 in Old English, or the idea of the mock heroic, explored, for instance in ALD 26 (*GALLUS,* "cockerel"), 56 (*CASTOR,* "beaver"), 75 (*CRABRO,* "hornet"), and 82 (*MUSTELA,* "weasel"); TAT 17 (*SCIURUS,* "squirrel"); EXE 13 (*IGIL,* "hedgehog"); and SYM 93 (*MILES PODAGRICUS,* "gouty soldier"). The very range of such connecting themes implies the broad interface that links the various riddles of the Anglo-Saxon tradition, which share not only themes, but also aspects of language.

## STYLE

Many rhetorical techniques are apparent throughout the Anglo-Saxon riddle tradition, and while some are more prominent in one language or another, there are several that are borrowed across the linguistic boundaries of Latin and Old English. Anaphora, the successive repetition of identical words at the beginning of clauses, is one of the hallmarks of SYM (there are particularly striking examples at SYM 16, 24, 53, 59, and 90) and is also a sporadic feature of some of the other Latin collections (for example, ALD 33 and 72, EUS 10, BON 11, ALC 1, BER 55). But anaphora is also a significant feature of several of the vernacular riddles of EXE (see, for example, EXE 12, 20, 22, 33, 37, 56, and 89); of these, only EXE 33 derives from a Latin original. The envelope pattern is a different kind of structuring feature, as witnessed by ALC D as a whole, but it is also found elsewhere in individual riddles and *aenigmata,* such as, for example, ALD 9 and EXE 10, 19, 37, 45–47, and 57. Polyptoton, the close repetition of words formed from the same root, is a prominent feature of SYM (there are examples in SYM 4, 5, 9, 20, 22, 56, 59, and 72) but is also found sporadically elsewhere (notably ALD 7; TAT 18 and 22; EUS 15, 42, and 44; BON 8). The parallel close repetition of similar-sounding elements that are etymologically unrelated (a punning effect generally known as paronomasia or parechesis) is a further feature of several of the same Latin collections (for example, TAT 25, 26, and 32; EUS 18 and 31; SYM 36, 57, and 71). Another notable aspect of the language of the Anglo-Saxon riddle tradition in both Latin and Old English is the fondness for compound nouns and adjectives, many of which in Old English are so-called *hapax legomena* (the ultimately Greek term for "things that are said only once"), unique in the vernacular verse tradition. Since the distribution of such compounds in both languages seems a useful indicator of links between texts, as well as offering clues to the idiosyncratic style of individual authors and texts, I have drawn systematic and specific attention to such forms throughout the notes.

## This Text and Translation

With such a necessarily wide-ranging purview, it is perhaps inevitable that much of the material here will have been derived from secondary sources. Nonetheless, the texts and translations here are based wherever possible on firsthand analysis of the manuscripts, especially those written or owned in England before 1100 (as noted in G-L), and I have tried to consult as broad a range as possible of existing translations. For details with regard to individual texts and collections, see the relevant headnotes below. The solutions to the riddles are provided, along with other basic commentary, in the Notes to the Translations. The prefatory note there explains in more detail the conventions that I have adopted for distinguishing, where necessary, solutions provided in the manuscripts by the medieval authors or scribes from those proposed, with varying degrees of confidence, by modern readers; where these differ, I have explained the choice of preferred solution in the Notes to the Translations, and often more fully in the companion commentary, *COEALRT*. One other convention employed widely in the texts and notes should be noted here, namely the practice of printing what I consider interpolations or added material (often in the form of formulaic additions or embedded solutions) in *italics*. I have also used *italics* for letters that contribute to acrostics or telestics and for runic transcriptions, but I trust that context will always make clear the distinction in usage. In a few cases, I have used <u>underlining</u> to emphasize wordplay or other kinds of correspondence in the original languages.

The Anglo-Saxon riddle tradition is rich and reaches back: the demonstrable connection between the Old English material and a literate and learned Latinate tradition only emphasizes the importance of investigating such a link in closer focus. But it also reaches across, connecting what might otherwise seem somewhat trivial texts to a broader tradition that transcends national, temporal, cultural, and linguistic boundaries. Anglo-Saxons evidently wanted to understand the world, to explain it, and perhaps above all, to marvel at its myriad ways. The Anglo-Saxon riddle tradition poses many questions and seems to be comfortable with the fact that for each and all of those questions there is not necessarily a single or simple and unanswerable solution. Sometimes just asking is apparently enough, and in picking a path through the question at hand the respondent seems encouraged to wander. In the spirit of the multilingual Anglo-Saxon riddle tradition, this book aims not only to ask more questions than it can possibly answer but also to keep an eye on the benefits of wandering in wonder, as well as the grave dangers of error.

This volume has been many years in the making, and I am deeply grateful to successive generations of students at Cambridge, Toronto, and Oxford who have helped to hone and improve it. During the editorial process for the Dumbarton Oaks Medieval Library, many excellent improvements and suggestions have been made by several members of the editorial board, especially Dan Donoghue, Drew Jones, and Katherine O'Brien O'Keeffe, as well as by others, especially Rafael Pascual and Nicole Eddy. This volume is dedicated to the memory of my mother, Paddy Orchard, who sadly did not live to see the final form.

## Notes

1 Throughout this work, "Anglo-Saxon" is used in specific reference to the history and culture of the English-speaking people in what is now England from the sixth to the eleventh century CE.

2 Green, *The Works of Ausonius,* p. III, lines 22–28; translation mine. The term *frivola* is found in line 9.

3 Alexander Riese, ed., *Anthologia Latina,* part 1, fasc. 1 (Leipzig, 1874; repr., Amsterdam, 1964), xlvii.

4 See, among others, *Hisperica famina* A358–80 (*DE CAELO,* "on the sky"): compare BER 60 (*CAELUM*); A381–425 (*DE MARI,* "on the sea"): compare BED 15 and ALC D48 (both *MARE*); A426–51 (*DE IGNE,* "on fire"): compare ALD 44, TAT 33, ALC D51, ALC D73 (all *IGNIS*), EXE 48 (*FYR,* "fire"), and GES 29 (*ELDR,* "fire"); A479–496 (*DE VENTO,* "on the wind"): compare ALD 2, ALC D46, BER 41, ps-BED 5 (all *VENTUS*), and EXE 1 (*WIND OND GOD,* "wind and God"); A513–30, (*DE TA-BERNA,* "on a book container"): compare ALD 89 (*ARCA LIBRARIA,* "bookchest") and EUS 33 (*SCETHUM,* "book satchel"); A531–46 (*DE TA-BULA,* "on a writing tablet"): compare ALD 32 and XMS S3 (both *PUGIL-LARES,* "writing tablets"). See too Orchard, "*Hisperica famina* as Litera-ture"; Gabriele Knappe, "On Rhetoric and Grammar in the *Hisperica famina,*" *The Journal of Medieval Latin* 4 (1994): 130–62; and Sarah Corrigan, "Hisperic Enigma Machine: Sea Creatures and Sources in the *Hisperica famina,*" *Peritia* 24–25 (2014): 59–73.

5 Williams, "The Riddles of Tatwine and Eusebius," 77, where she alludes to a series of important studies by Archer Taylor, notably *English Riddles from Oral Tradition, The Literary Riddle Before 1600,* and "The Varieties of Riddles."

6 Ehwald, *Aldhelmi Opera,* p. 75, line 21 (where Symphosius, in the form *Simfosius,* is named), and p. 77, line 12 (where ps-SYM 1 is quoted).

7 See further the notes to EXE 2 (*BELLE,* "bell"), 9 (*WIN-FÆT,* "cup of wine"), 10 (*OXA,* "ox"), 18 (*SECG,* "sword," "man"), 19 (*SULH,* "plow"), 23 (*CIPE,* "onion"), 35 (*BLÆST-BELG,* "bellows"), 40 (*HANA OND HÆN,* "cock and hen"), 42 (*CÆG,* "key"), 43 (*DAG,* "dough"), 44 (*LOTH OND BEARN,* "Lot and his children"), 51 (*GEALGA,* "gallows," "cross"), 52 (*CYRN,* "churn"), 59 (*CYRTEL,* "shirt," "garment"), 60 (*BOR,* "borer"), 61 (*GLÆS-FÆT,* "glass beaker"), 63 (*CIPE,* "onion"), 77 (*WEDER-COC,* "weathercock"), 83 (*BLÆST-BELG,* "bellows"), 85 (*BLÆST-BELG,* "bel-lows"), 87 (*CÆG,* "key"), and 88 (*BOC,* "book," "beech").

# THE ANGLO-LATIN
# TRADITION

# Aldhelm

## ALD PR

*A*rbiter, aethereo iugiter qui regmine sceptr*A*
*L*ucifluumque simul caeli regale tribuna*L*
*D*isponis moderans aeternis legibus illu*D*—
*H*orrida nam multans torsisti membra Vehemot*H*,
5     *E*x alta quondam rueret dum luridus arc*E*—
*L*impida dictanti metrorum carmina praesu*L*
*M*unera nunc largire, rudis quo pandere reru*M*
*V*ersibus enigmata queam clandistina fat*V*:
*S*ic, Deus, indignis tua gratis dona rependi*S*.
10     *C*astalidas nimphas non clamo cantibus istu*C*,
*E*xamen neque spargebat mihi nectar in or*E*;
*C*ynthi sic numquam perlustro cacumina, sed ne*C*
*I*n Parnasso procubui nec somnia vid*I*.
*N*am mihi versificum poterit Deus addere carme*N*
15     *I*nspirans stolidae pia gratis munera ment*I*;
*T*angit si mentem, mox laudem corda rependun*T*.

# Aldhelm

## ALD PR

You, judge, who always govern with heavenly rule
both the scepters and the starry royal judgment-seat of the
    sky,
controlling it all with eternal laws —
for in punishment you tortured the grim limbs of
    Behemoth,
when that dread one once fell headlong from the lofty     5
    citadel —
now, protector, lavish clear gifts on the one composing
poems in meter so that, even unskilled,
I may through speech be able to reveal in verse the masked
    mysteries of things:
in this way, God, do you freely give your gifts to the
    unworthy.
    I do not summon here with songs the Castalian nymphs,   10
nor did any swarm trickle nectar into my mouth;
so, I never wander over the peaks of Cynthus,
nor yet did I ever fall asleep upon Parnassus, nor see
    dreams.
For God can bestow on me verse-inducing song,
freely breathing pious gifts into a dull mind;   15
if he touches a mind, soon do hearts reverberate in praise.

*M*etrica nam Moysen declarant carmina vate*M*
*I*amdudum cecinisse prisci vexilla trope*I*,
*L*ate per populos illustria, qua nitidus So*L*
20  *L*ustrat ab oceani iam tollens gurgite cepha*L*;
*E*t psalmista canens metrorum cantica voc*E*,
*N*atum divino promit generamine nume*N*
*I*n caelis prius exortum, quam Lucifer orb*I*
*S*plendida formatis fudisset lumina saecli*S*.
25  *V*erum si fuerint bene haec enigmata vers*V*,
*E*xplosis penitus naevis et rusticitat*E*,
*R*itu dactilico recte decursa nec erro*R*
*S*eduxit vana specie molimina menti*S*,
*I*ncipiam potiora, sui Deus arida serv*I*,
30  *B*elligero quondam qui vires tradidit Io*B*,
*V*iscera perpetui si roris repleat haust*V*.
*S*iccis nam laticum duxisti cautibus amne*S*
*O*lim, cum cuneus transgresso marmore rubr*O*
*D*esertum penetrat, cecinit quod carmine Davi*D*.
35  *A*rce poli, genitor, servas qui saecula cunct*A*,
*S*olvere iam scelerum noxas dignare nefanda*S*.

# ALD 1

Altrix cunctorum, quos mundus gestat, in orbe
nuncupor (et merito, quia numquam pignora tantum

For metrical songs declare that the prophet Moses
once, long ago, sang of the trophies of an ancient victory,
widely famous throughout the nations, wherever the
    brilliant sun,
lifting its head from the depths of the sea, shines;         20
likewise the Psalmist, singing metrical songs out loud,
proclaims a godhead born through divine generation,
brought forth in the heavens when the universe was
    created,
before the morning star had shed its shining light upon the
    world.
But if these mysteries in verse have been well traversed,    25
with flaws and roughness utterly expunged,
in correct dactylic style, and error has not corrupted
the efforts of the mind with its empty appearance,
I shall begin something better, if God,
who once gave strength to battling Job, were to fill up    30
the dry innards of his servant with a draft of eternal dew.
For you drew streams of water from dry rocks
once, when the host, having crossed the Red Sea,
entered the desert, as David sang in song.
You, father in the citadel of heaven, who guard the whole    35
    universe,
deign now to disperse the wicked blight of sins.


# ALD 1


I am called she who nourishes everything on the globe
that the world produces (and deservedly so, since wicked
    offspring

improba sic lacerant maternas dente papillas).
Prole virens aestate; tabescens tempore brumae.

## ALD 2

Cernere me nulli possunt nec prendere palmis;
argutum vocis crepitum cito pando per orbem.
Viribus horrisonis valeo confringere quercus;
nam superos ego pulso polos et rura peragro.

## ALD 3

Versicolor fugiens caelum terramque relinquo;
non tellure locus mihi, non in parte polorum est.
Exilium nullus modo tam crudele veretur;
sed madidis mundum faciam frondescere guttis.

## ALD 4

Crede mihi, res nulla manet sine me moderante,
et frontem faciemque meam lux nulla videbit.
Quis nesciat dicione mea convexa rotari
alta poli solisque iubar lunaeque meatus?

never gnaw with their teeth mother's nipples as much as
    this).
In summer I am burgeoning with progeny; languishing in
    wintertime.


## ALD 2

No one can see me or hold me in their hands;
I swiftly spread the piercing sound of my voice throughout
    the world.
I can smash oak trees, with my grim-sounding strength;
for I strike the high skies and pass through the fields.


## ALD 3

Fleeing in many colors, I leave heaven and earth behind;
there is no place for me on the ground, nor in the sphere of
    the sky.
No one else so dreads such a fearful exile;
but with moist drops I shall make the world grow green.


## ALD 4

Believe me, there is nothing beyond my control,
and no eye sees my face and form.
Who does not know that at my command the high vaults of
    heaven,
    and the sunbeams, and the motions of the moon, all spin?

## ALD 5

Taumantis proles priscorum famine fingor,
ast ego prima mei generis rudimenta retexam:
sole ruber genitus sum partu nubis aquosae;
lustro polos passim, solos non scando per austros.

## ALD 6

Nunc ego cum pelagi fatis communibus insto,
tempora reciprocis convolvens menstrua cyclis:
ut mihi lucifluae decrescit gloria formae,
sic augmenta latex cumulatus gurgite perdit.

## ALD 7

Facundum constat quondam cecinisse poetam:
"Quo Deus et quo dura vocat Fortuna; sequamur!"
Me veteres falso dominam vocitare solebant,
sceptra regens mundi dum Christi gratia regnet.

## ALD 5

I am alleged to be the child of Thaumas, according to the
    ancients,
but I shall reveal the first beginnings of my birth myself:
I was born red from the sun through a watery cloud;
I brighten the sky by my wanderings, and only in the wind
    do I not rise up.

## ALD 6

Now I am involved in the shared fate of the sea,
rolling out monthly patterns in alternating cycles:
for just as the brightness of my light-shining form grows
    less,
so too does the water, piled up, lose the increase of its swell.

## ALD 7

It is said that once a skillful poet sang:
"Where God and harsh Fortune summon us, let us go!"
Falsely our ancestors used to call me mistress,
when in fact Christ's grace should govern, ruling the
    thrones of the world.

## ALD 8

Nos Athlante satas stolidi dixere priores;
nam septena cohors est, sed vix cernitur una.
Arce poli gradimur necnon sub Tartara terrae;
furvis conspicimur tenebris et luce latemus,
5    nomina de verno ducentes tempore prisca.

## ALD 9

En ego non vereor rigidi discrimina ferri,
flammarum neu torre cremor; sed sanguine capri
virtus indomiti mollescit dura rigoris:
sic cruor exsuperat, quem ferrea massa pavescit.

## ALD 10

Sic me iamdudum rerum veneranda potestas
fecerat, ut domini truculentos persequar hostes;
rictibus arma gerens bellorum praelia patro,
et tamen infantum fugiens mox verbera vito.

## ALD 8

Plodding predecessors have said that we were the children
    of Atlas;
we are indeed seven, though one is hard to see.
We walk in the summit of the sky, as well as in the depths of
    the earth;
we can be seen in the deepest darkness, but disappear in
    light,
taking our ancient names from the time of spring.      5

## ALD 9

Look: I do not fear the dangers of hard iron,
nor do I burn in a furnace of fire; but in goat's blood
the hard force of my unconquerable strength is made soft:
so gore defeats what a mass of iron trembles to take on.

## ALD 10

In this way did the fearsome force of things make me long
    ago
to chase after my master's enemies when they attack;
wearing weapons in my jaws I engage in the conflicts of war,
though by fleeing I am quick to avoid the blows of children.

## ALD 11

Flatibus alternis vescor cum fratre gemello;
non est vita mihi, cum sint spiracula vitae.
Ars mea gemmatis dedit ornamenta metallis:
gratia nulla datur mihi, sed capit alter honorem.

## ALD 12

Annua dum redeunt texendi tempora telas,
lurida setigeris replentur viscera filis;
moxque genestarum frondosa cacumina scando,
ut globulos fabricans tum fati sorte quiescam.

## ALD 13

Quamvis aere cavo salpictae classica clangant,
et citharae crepitent strepituque tubae modulentur,
centenos tamen eructant mea viscera cantus;
me praesente stupet mox musica chorda fibrarum.

## ALD 14

Pulcher et excellens specie, mirandus in orbe,
ossibus ac nervis ac rubro sanguine cretus;

## ALD 11

Along with my twin brother I am fed by alternate breaths;
I have no life, although the air of life is in me.
My skill has given decoration to bejeweled metals:
I have no thanks, but another takes the credit.

## ALD 12

When the annual time for weaving silk thread returns,
my pale innards overflow with bristly fibers;
and soon I climb up the leafy peaks of broom,
so that once I have made small drops I can rest, as is my
     fate.

## ALD 13

Though trumpeters may blow hollow brass battle trumpets,
and harps vibrate and horns resound with clamor,
still my insides breathe out a hundred melodies;
when I am around, the musical sound of strings is soon
     struck dumb.

## ALD 14

Fair and gorgeous to look at, I am a wonder to the world,
even if I am made of flesh and red blood and bone;

cum mihi vita comes fuerit, nihil aurea forma
plus rubet et moriens mea numquam pulpa putrescit.

## ALD 15

Ignibus in mediis vivens non sentio flammas,
sed detrimenta rogi penitus ludibria faxo.
Nec crepitante foco nec scintillante favilla
ardeo, sed flammae flagranti torre tepescunt.

## ALD 16

Nunc cernenda placent nostrae spectacula vitae:
cum grege piscoso scrutor maris aequora squamis,
cum volucrum turma quoque scando per aethera pennis,
et tamen aethereo non possum vivere flatu.

## ALD 17

E geminis nascor per ponti caerula concis,
vellera setigero producens corpore fulva;
en clamidem pepli necnon et pabula pulpae
confero: sic duplex fati persolvo tributum.

as long as I live, no gold glows more golden,
and when I die, my flesh fails to rot.


## ALD 15

Living in the midst of fire I feel no flames,
and I reckon incendiary damage a total joke.
When the furnace crackles and the sparks do fly
I do not burn, but flames fade in the blazing pyre.


## ALD 16

The must-see spectacle of my life is a wonder:
with a school of fish I examine the deep with scales,
and with a flock of birds I climb the skies with wings,
and yet I cannot live by breathing air.


## ALD 17

I am born from a double shell in the blue waters of the
      deep,
producing tawny coverings from my hairy body;
see how I produce the covering of cloaks as well as the food
      of flesh:
twice over I pay out the debt of fate.

## ALD 18

Dudum compositis ego nomen gesto figuris:
ut leo, sic formica vocor sermone Pelasgo
tropica nominibus signans praesagia duplis,
cum rostris avium nequeam rescindere rostro.
5  Scrutetur sapiens, gemino cur nomine fungar.

## ALD 19

Dudum limpha fui squamoso pisce redundans,
sed natura novo fati discrimine cessit,
torrida dum calidos patior tormenta per ignes:
nam cineri facies nivibusque simillima constat.

## ALD 20

Mirificis formata modis, sine semine creta
dulcia florigeris onero praecordia praedis;
arte mea crocea flavescunt fercula regum.
Semper acuta gero crudelis spicula belli,
5  atque carens manibus fabrorum vinco metalla.

## ALD 18

For a long time I have been carrying a compounded name:
in Greek, I am called both a lion and an ant,
meaning something metaphorical by a double designation,
since with my own beak I cannot cut off the beaks of birds.
Let someone wise work out why I have a double name.      5

## ALD 19

I used to be liquid, teeming with scaly fish,
but that state stopped, as fate newly decreed,
when I suffered searing torments through scorching flames:
indeed, it is a fact that my appearance most resembles ash
    or snow.

## ALD 20

I was created in amazing ways; produced without any seed,
I stock my sweet insides with what I take from flowers;
by my skill the yellow platters of kings grow golden.
I always carry the sharp weapons of cruel war,
and even without hands I surpass the smiths' metallic craft.      5

## ALD 21

Corpore sulcato necnon ferrugine glauca,
sum formata fricans rimis informe metallum.
Auri materias massasque polire sueta;
plano superficiem constans asperrima rerum;
5  garrio voce carens rauco cum murmure stridens.

## ALD 22

Vox mea diversis variatur pulcra figuris;
raucisonis numquam modulabor carmina rostris.
Spurca colore tamen, sed non sum spreta canendo:
sic non cesso canens fato terrente futuro;
5  nam me bruma fugat, sed mox aestate redibo.

## ALD 23

Nos geminas olim genuit natura sorores,
quas iugiter rectae legis censura gubernat;
temnere personas et ius servare solemus.
Felix in terra fieret mortalibus aevum,
5  iustitiae normam si servent more sororum.

# ALD 21

With my furrowed frame, with its grayish iron rust,
I was shaped for smoothing unshaped metal with my teeth.
I am used to polishing the matter and material of gold;
being myself the roughest thing there is, I smooth a surface;
voiceless, I prattle piercingly with a harsh shriek.                    5

# ALD 22

My beautiful voice is varied in different ways;
I never shall sing songs with a harsh-sounding beak.
Although I am dull in color, I am not despised in singing:
so I do not stop singing even when the future is frightening;
winter chases me away, but I shall return as soon as summer.    5

# ALD 23

Nature produced us once as a pair of sisters,
whom the stricture of proper law always controls;
and it is our practice to uphold justice and disregard the
          status of individuals.
The life of mortals would be happy on earth,
if they observed the rule of justice just as we sisters do.         5

## ALD 24

Me caput horrentis fertur genuisse draconis;
augeo purpureis gemmarum lumina fucis,
sed mihi non dabitur rigida virtute potestas,
si prius occumbat squamoso corpore natrix,
5  quam summo spolier capitis de vertice rubra.

## ALD 25

Vis mihi naturae dedit, immo creator Olimpi,
id, quo cuncta carent veteris miracula mundi.
Frigida nam chalibis suspendo metalla per auras,
vi quadam superans sic ferrea fata revinco,
5  mox adamante Cypri praesente potentia fraudor.

## ALD 26

Garrulus in tenebris rutilos cecinisse solebam
augustae lucis radios et lumina Phoebi.
Penniger experto populorum nomine fungor;
arma ferens pedibus belli discrimina faxo
5  serratas capitis gestans in vertice cristas.

# ALD 24

The head of a dreadful dragon is supposed to have given
    birth to me;
I increase the brightness of jewels by my crimson coloring,
but no strength firm in power will be granted to me,
if that serpent with scaly body should die before
I am snatched, bright red, from the very top of its head.       5

# ALD 25

The force of nature, or rather the creator of heaven,
granted me what is missing from all the wonders of the
    ancient world.
I cause cold metallic steel to hang in air,
and by some force I conquer and control iron fates,
but am robbed of powers at once, faced with a Cyprian       5
    diamond.

# ALD 26

Chatty in the dark, I used to sing about
red rays of splendid light and the brightness of the sun.
I wear feathers and bear the name of a famous folk;
on my feet I carry weapons, and fight hazardous battles,
wearing a jagged crest on the crown of my head.       5

## ALD 27

Frigidus ex gelido prolatus viscere terrae;
duritiem ferri quadrata fronte polibo,
atque senectutis vereor discrimina numquam,
Mulcifer annorum numerum ni dempserit igne:
5   mox rigida species mollescit torribus atris.

## ALD 28

Sum mihi dissimilis vultu membrisque biformis,
cornibus armatus, horrendum cetera fingunt
membra virum; fama clarus per Gnossia rura,
spurius incerto Creta genitore creatus;
5   ex hominis pecudisque simul cognomine dicor.

## ALD 29

Quis non obstupeat nostri spectacula fati,
dum virtute fero silvarum robora mille,
ast acus exilis mox tanta gestamina rumpit?
Nam volucres caeli nantesque per aequora pisces
5   olim sumpserunt ex me primordia vitae:
tertia pars mundi mihi constat iure tenenda.

# ALD 27

I am brought forth frozen from the chilly innards of the
    earth;
I shall polish iron's hardness with my square form,
and never fear the dangers of old age,
as long as Vulcan does not diminish the tally of my years by
    fire:
my stiff form soon softens in dark flames.         5

# ALD 28

I have two forms, with unmatched face and limbs,
being armed with horns, while my other limbs make me
a shaggy man; I am well known throughout the land of
    Knossos,
a bastard born in Crete by an unknown father;
my name derives from that of man and beast as one.     5

# ALD 29

Who is not amazed at the sight of my lot,
since by my strength I carry a thousand oaks of the forests,
but a slender point soon sinks such burdens?
The birds of the air and the fishes swimming in the seas
once took their lives' beginnings out of me:     5
it is clear that a third of the world is under my control.

## ALD 30

Nos denae et septem genitae sine voce sorores;
sex alias nothas non dicimus annumerandas.
Nascimur ex ferro rursus ferro moribundae,
necnon et volucris penna volitantis ad aethram;
5  terni nos fratres incerta matre crearunt.
Qui cupit instanter sitiens audire docentes,
tum cito prompta damus rogitanti verba silenter.

## ALD 31

Candida forma nitens necnon et furva nigrescens
est mihi, dum varia componor imagine pennae;
voce carens tremula nam faxo crepacula rostro.
Quamvis squamigeros discerpam dira colubros,
5  non mea letiferis turgescunt membra venenis;
sic teneros pullos prolemque nutrire suesco
carne venenata tetroque cruore draconum.

## ALD 32

Melligeris apibus mea prima processit origo,
sed pars exterior crescebat cetera silvis;

## ALD 30

We were born voiceless, seventeen sisters;
there are six other bastards that we do not speak of to be
      included in our number.
We are produced through iron and in turn are to die
      through iron,
or through the feather of a bird that soars swiftly up to the
      sky;
three brothers produced us with an unknown mother.     5
Whoever, earnestly thirsting to hear, wants our teaching,
we quickly give them ready words in silence when they ask.

## ALD 31

I have a shining, bright-white form, but also dusky black,
since I am made up of different-colored feathers;
I do not have a melodious voice, but I make a rattling sound
      with my beak.
Although I cruelly tear to pieces scaly snakes,
my limbs never swell with deadly venom;     5
so, I tend to feed my delicate chicks and children
with serpents' venomous flesh and vicious blood.

## ALD 32

My main parts came from honey-laden bees,
though my other part, the exterior one, grew in the woods;

calciamenta mihi tradebant tergora dura.
Nunc ferri stimulus faciem proscindit amoenam,
5  flexibus et sulcos obliquat adinstar aratri.
Sed semen segiti de caelo ducitur almum,
quod largos generat millena fruge maniplos.
Heu! Tam sancta seges diris extinguitur armis!

## ALD 33

Roscida me genuit gelido de viscere tellus;
non sum setigero lanarum vellere facta;
licia nulla trahunt nec garrula fila resultant;
nec crocea Seres texunt lanugine vermes;
5  nec radiis carpor duro nec pectine pulsor;
et tamen en vestis vulgi sermone vocabor:
spicula non vereor longis exempta faretris.

## ALD 34

Quamvis agricolis non sim laudabilis hospes,
fructus agrorum viridi de cespite ruris
carpo, catervatim rodens de stipite libros,
iamdudum celebris spolians Nilotica regna,
5  quando decem plagas spurca cum gente luebant.

shoe-leather furnished my tough spine.
Now a point of iron scars my pretty face,
and, like a plow, carves out furrows as it turns this way and        5
    that.
Yet the nourishing seed is brought to the field from heaven,
and produces fertile sheaves with a thousandfold crop.
Alas, that such a holy harvest should be destroyed by sharp
    weapons!


## ALD 33

The dewy ground gave me birth from chilly innards;
I was not produced from a shaggy fleece of wool;
no yarn draws me, nor sounding threads leap about;
nor do Chinese worms weave me from their saffron floss;
nor am I drawn from wheels, nor beaten with the harsh             5
    comb;
yet still will I be called "clothing" in common speech:
I fear no darts drawn forth from lengthy quivers.


## ALD 34

Although I may not be a praiseworthy guest to farmers,
I pluck the fruits of their fields from the green sod of the
    farm,
munching away in swarms at the stalks' inner core,
long since notorious for ravaging the kingdoms of the Nile,
when they, along with their impure people, suffered ten          5
    plagues.

Cor mihi sub genibus, nam constat carcere saeptum;
pectora poplitibus subduntur more rubetae.

# ALD 35

Duplicat ars geminis mihi nomen rite figuris,
nam partem tenebrae retinent partemque volucres.
Raro me quisquam cernet sub luce serena,
quin magis astriferas ego nocte fovebo latebras.
5  Raucisono medium crepitare per aethra suescens,
Romuleis scribor biblis, sed voce Pelasga,
nomine nocturnas dum semper servo tenebras.

# ALD 36

Corpore sum gracilis, stimulis armatus acerbis;
scando catervatim volitans super ardua pennis,
sanguineas sumens praedas mucrone cruento;
quadrupedi parcens nulli; sed spicula trudo
5  setigeras pecudum stimulans per vulnera pulpas,
olim famosus vexans Memphitica rura,
nam toros terebrans taurorum sanguine vescor.

My heart lies under my knees: where it stands locked in
    prison;
like a toad's, my chest is lower than my knees.

## ALD 35

Design has properly given a double name to my twin form,
since both birds and darkness have a share in me.
Seldom will anyone see me in the bright day,
but instead I favor starry hiding places by night.
I am described in Latin books as croaking in midair     5
with a harsh-sounding cry, but in the tongue of Greece,
according to my name I always keep to the darkness of
    night.

## ALD 36

I am slight in form, though armed with piercing points;
I travel in swarms, flitting with wings above the heights,
acquiring bloody booty with a gory sword;
sparing no four-footed creature; I thrust out my darts,
pricking with wounds the bristled flesh of cattle,     5
gaining fame once for plaguing the Egyptian land,
for I drill into the brawny flesh of bulls and taste their
    blood.

## ALD 37

Nepa mihi nomen veteres dixere Latini:
humida spumiferi spatior per litora ponti;
passibus oceanum retrograda transeo versis,
et tamen aethereus per me decoratur Olimpus,
5   dum ruber in caelo bisseno sidere scando;
ostrea quem metuit duris perterrita saxis.

## ALD 38

Pergo super latices plantis suffulta quaternis
nec tamen in limphas vereor quod mergar aquosas,
sed pariter terras et flumina calco pedestris;
nec natura sinit celerem natare per amnem,
5   pontibus aut ratibus fluvios transire feroces;
quin potius pedibus gradior super aequora siccis.

## ALD 39

Setiger in silvis armatos dentibus apros
cornigerosque simul cervos licet ore rudentes,
contero nec parcens ursorum quasso lacertos;
ora cruenta ferens morsus rictusque luporum

## ALD 37

The ancient Romans called me *Nepa* by name:
I travel along the damp shores of the foaming sea;
I cross the ocean backward with backward steps,
and yet the ethereal heaven is adorned by me,
when I climb into the heavens, ruddy, along with twelve        5
     constellations;
the oyster, frightened by hard stones, fears me.

## ALD 38

Supported on four feet I travel over fluids
and yet I do not fear that I'll be drowned in the watery
     liquid,
but I tread on foot equally on land and streams;
nor does nature allow me to swim in swift rivers,
nor to cross ferocious waterways by bridge or boat;        5
instead, I go with dry feet over calm waters.

## ALD 39

I am a shaggy beast in the forest and defeat boars
armed with tusks and stags with antlers, though they bellow
     loud,
nor do I refrain from crushing the limbs of bears;
because I have a bloody maw, I do not fear the snapping and
     biting

5   horridus haud vereor regali culmine fretus;
    dormio nam patulis, non claudens lumina, gemmis.

## ALD 40

Sum niger exterius rugoso cortice tectus,
sed tamen interius candentem gesto medullam.
Dilicias, epulas regum luxusque ciborum,
ius simul et pulpas battutas condo culinae:
5   sed me subnixum nulla virtute videbis,
    viscera ni fuerint nitidis quassata medullis.

## ALD 41

Nolo fidem frangas, licet irrita dicta putentur;
credula sed nostris pande praecordia verbis.
Celsior ad superas possum turgescere nubes,
si caput aufertur mihi toto corpore dempto.
5   At vero capitis si pressus mole gravabor,
    ima petens iugiter minorari parte videbor.

## ALD 42

Grandia membra mihi plumescunt corpore denso;
par color accipitri, sed dispar causa volandi,
nam summa exiguis non trano per aethera pennis,

of wolves, being fearsome myself, and relying on my regal        5
    status;
I sleep with gemlike eyes wide open, and never close them.

## ALD 40

I am black on the outside, enclosed in wrinkled rind,
but on the inside I have a bright-white core.
I season delicacies, kings' banquets, and the finest of foods,
as well as the kitchen's soups and ground meats:
but you will find that I am endowed with no power at all,        5
unless my innards with their shining core are ground down.

## ALD 41

Please do not disbelieve me, although what I say may seem
    worthless;
rather, keep your heart open to my words.
I can swell up rather high toward the clouds above,
if a head is taken off me and the whole body removed;
but if I am pressed down by the weight of a head,               5
sinking, I seem to be diminished somewhat.

## ALD 42

My massive limbs sprout feathers on a thick body;
I am similar in color to the falcon, but dissimilar in flying,
since I do not pass through the upper air on my tiny wings,

sed potius pedibus spatior per squalida rura,
5   ovorum teretes praebens ad pocula testas;
Africa Poenorum me fertur gignere tellus.


# ALD 43

Lurida per latices cenosas lustro paludes;
nam mihi composuit nomen fortuna cruentum,
rubro dum bibulis vescor de sanguine buccis.
Ossibus et pedibus geminisque carebo lacertis,
5   corpora vulneribus sed mordeo dira trisulcis,
atque salutiferis sic curam praesto labellis.


# ALD 44

Me pater et mater gelido genuere rigore,
fomitibus siccis dum mox rudimenta vigebant,
quorum vi propria fortunam vincere possum,
cum nil ni latices mea possint vincere fata;
5   sed saltus, scopulos, stagni ferrique metalla
comminuens penitus naturae iura resolvam;
cum me vita fovet, sum clari sideris instar,
post haec et fato victus pice nigrior exsto.

but rather I wander through scrubby fields on my feet,
producing smooth eggshells suitable for goblets;                5
the African land of the Phoenicians is said to have produced
    me.

## ALD 43

Horrid, I lurk in the waters of stinking fens;
for fate has given me a bloody name,
since I feed in thirsty gulps on bright-red blood.
I lack bones and pairs of feet and arms,
yet I cruelly gnaw bodies with three-forked gashes,             5
and with my health-bringing lips I offer a cure.

## ALD 44

My father and mother gave me birth from frigid hardness,
and soon my beginnings began to flourish in dry kindling,
whose fortune I can conquer by my own strength,
since nothing except water can conquer my fate;
but, diminishing forests, rocks, and tin, and iron metals,     5
I will destroy the laws of nature utterly;
when life is warm within me, I am like a shining star,
yet after I am defeated by fate, I am blacker than pitch.

## ALD 45

In saltu nascor ramosa fronde virescens,
sed fortuna meum mutaverat ordine fatum;
dum veho per collum teretem vertigine molam:
tam longa nullus zona praecingitur heros.
5  Per me fata virum dicunt decernere Parcas;
ex quo conficitur regalis stragula pepli:
frigora dura viros sternant, ni forte resistam.

## ALD 46

Torqueo torquentes, sed nullum torqueo sponte;
laedere nec quemquam volo, ni prius ipse reatum
contrahat et viridem studeat decerpere caulem.
Fervida mox hominis turgescunt membra nocentis;
5  vindico sic noxam stimulisque ulciscor acutis.

## ALD 47

Absque cibo plures degebam marcida menses,
sed sopor et somnus ieiunia longa tulerunt.
Pallida purpureo dum glescunt gramine rura,
garrula mox crepitat rubicundum carmina guttur.

## ALD 45

I was born in the woodland, growing green on a leafy
    branch,
but fortune has changed my fate in due course;
in my twirling I carry a smooth weight around my neck:
no hero wears so long a belt as I.
They say that through me the Fates decree men's lot;     5
from me is made the covering of a royal robe:
harsh cold would lay men low, unless I strongly resisted it.

## ALD 46

I trouble those who trouble me, but I trouble no one of my
    own accord;
I don't want to hurt anyone, unless he first incurs the blame
and tries to pluck the bright-green stalk.
Soon the hot limbs of the one who harms me swell;
that's how I repay injury and take revenge with sharp stings.   5

## ALD 47

Languishing, I used to spend many months without food,
but sleep and slumber helped me bear long periods of
    fasting.
When the pale fields swell with purple growth,
my ruddy throat soon sounds out fulsome songs.

5   Post teneros fetus et prolem gentis adultam,
sponte mea fugiens umbrosas quaero latebras;
si vero quisquam pullorum lumina laedat,
affero compertum medicans cataplasma salutis
quaerens campestrem proprio de nomine florem.

## ALD 48

Sic me formavit naturae conditor almus:
lustro teres tota spatiosis saecula ciclis
latas in gremio portans cum pondere terras;
sic maris undantes cumulos et caerula cludo.
5   Nam nihil in rerum natura tam celer esset,
(quod pedibus pergat, quod pennis aethera tranet
accola neu ponti volitans per caerula squamis
nec rota, per girum quam trudit machina limphae),
currere sic posset, ni septem sidera tricent.

## ALD 49

Horrida, curva, capax, patulis fabricata metallis
pendeo nec caelum tangens terramve profundam,
ignibus ardescens necnon et gurgite fervens;

After my delicate offspring and the brood of my kin grows    5
    up,
of my own accord I fly off to find a shady hiding place;
but if indeed someone should harm the eyes of my chicks,
to cure them I bring a healing poultice that I found
looking for a flower of the field that shares my name.


## ALD 48

The kindly creator of nature made me as follows:
I am smooth, and travel round the whole world in vast
    cycles,
carrying in my lap the spacious earth and its weight;
so too I encompass the billowing expanses and blue depths
    of the sea.
For there is nothing in the nature of things that would be so    5
    swift to run
(nothing that walks on foot, or sails through the sky on
    wings
neither the inhabitant of the sea, flying through the blue
    depths with fins,
nor even the wheel that a water mill drives in circles),
as I would be, if the seven planets did not slow me down.


## ALD 49

I am ugly, round, and vast, forged from metal sheets,
and I hang, touching neither the sky nor the deep earth,
burning with fire and boiling with water;

sic geminas vario patior discrimine pugnas,
5  dum latices limphae tolero flammasque feroces.


## ALD 50

Prorsus Achivorum lingua pariterque Latina,
mille vocor viridi folium de cespite natum.
Idcirco decies centenum nomen habebo,
cauliculis florens quoniam sic nulla frutescit
5  herba per innumeros telluris limite sulcos.


## ALD 51

Sponte mea nascor fecundo cespite vernans;
fulgida de croceo flavescunt culmina flore.
Occiduo claudor, sic orto sole patesco:
unde prudentes posuerunt nomina Graeci.


## ALD 52

Materia duplici palmis plasmabar apertis:
interiora mihi candescunt: viscera lino
seu certe gracili iunco spoliata nitescunt;
sed nunc exterius flavescunt corpora flore
5  quae flammasque focosque laremque vomentia fundunt,
et crebro lacrimae stillant de frontibus udae.

in this way I suffer a double attack with different trials,
as I endure flowing liquids and ferocious flames.     5


## ALD 50

In short, in the language of the Greeks, and also in Latin,
I am called the thousand-leafed one, sprung from bright-
    green turf.
So I have a name that is ten times a hundredfold,
flourishing with tiny stalklets, as no other grassy plant
burgeons throughout the countless furrows in the expanse     5
    of the earth.


## ALD 51

I am born of my own accord, budding in the fertile soil;
my bright heads turn golden on the saffron bloom.
At evening I close, and open with the rising sun:
and that is where the wise Greeks took my name from.


## ALD 52

I was made by open hands from a double substance:
my guts glow bright white: my innards shine,
stripped from flax or from the slender rush;
but now my outer body turns golden from the bloom
as it pours forth belching flames and heat and warmth,     5
and liquid teardrops drip constantly from my face.

Sic tamen horrendas noctis extinguo latebras;
reliquias cinerum mox viscera tosta relinquunt.

## ALD 53

Sidereis stipor turmis in vertice mundi;
esseda famoso gesto cognomina vulgo;
in giro volvens iugiter non vergo deorsum,
cetera ceu properant caelorum lumina ponto.
5  Hac gaza ditor: quoniam sum proximus axi,
qui Ripheis Scithiae praelatus montibus errat,
Vergilias numeris aequans in arce polorum,
cui pars inferior Stigia Letheaque palude
fertur et inferni fundo succumbere nigro.

## ALD 54

Credere quis poterit tantarum foedera rerum
temperet et fatis morum contraria fata?
Ecce larem, laticem quoque gesto in viscere ventris,
nec tamen undantes vincunt incendia limphae,
5  ignibus aut atris siccantur flumina fontis,
foedera sed pacis sunt flammas inter et undas;
malleus in primo memet formabat et incus.

But that is how I extinguish the dread shadows of night;
my burned-up innards soon leave the remains of ashes.


# ALD 53

I am packed in with bands of stars at the top of the world;
I carry the name "war chariot" in common speech;
wheeling in a continual circle, I never sink below,
like the other stars in the sky, in headlong flight into the
    sea.
I am empowered by this benefit, since I am closest to the     5
    pole,
which wanders manifest above the Rhipaean mountains of
    Scythia,
equaling in number the Pleiades in the summit of the sky,
and the lower part of which is said to languish
in the swamps of the Styx or Lethe, or in the dark pit of
    Hell.


# ALD 54

Who could credit the union of such great things,
and harmonize destinies that are usually opposed?
See how I combine warmth and water in the innards of my
    belly,
and yet the welling liquid cannot quench the blaze,
nor are the waters of the fountain dried out by the dark     5
    fires,
but the flames and the waves have made a pact of peace;
it was the hammer and the anvil that first formed me.

# ALD 55

Alma domus veneror divino munere plena,
valvas sed nullus reserat nec limina pandit
culmina ni fuerint aulis sublata quaternis;
et licet exterius rutilent de corpore gemmae,
5   aurea dum fulvis flavescit bulla metallis,
sed tamen uberius ditantur viscera crassa
intus, qua species flagrat pulcherrima Christi:
candida sanctarum sic floret gloria rerum;
nec trabis in templo, surgunt nec tecta columnis.

# ALD 56

Hospes praeruptis habitans in margine ripis
non sum torpescens, oris sed belliger armis,
quin potius duro vitam sustento labore,
grossaque prosternens mox ligna securibus uncis;
5   humidus in fundo, tranat qua piscis, aquoso,
saepe caput proprium tingens in gurgite mergo.
Vulnera fibrarum necnon et lurida tabo
membra medens pestemque luemque resolvo necantem;
libris corrosis et cortice vescor amara.

# ALD 55

I am honored as a house that nourishes, filled with a divine
    gift,
though no one opens my door or lays bare my threshold
unless the roof is first removed from my fourfold hall;
and although gems shine red on the outside of my body,
while an aureate boss in tawny metal grows golden,                    5
nonetheless my dense innards are worth richly more
inside, where there blazes the most ravishing beauty of
    Christ:
that is how the bright-white glory of what is holy burgeons;
and there is no beam in this temple, no roof rising up on
    columns.

# ALD 56

As a guest living on the edge of steep banks
I am not sluggish, but a warrior, with weapons in my mouth;
rather I maintain my life by hard toil,
soon felling mighty trees with curved axes;
damp in the watery depths, where the fish swim,                       5
I often dip my own damp head, steeped in the flood.
I am a healer both of injuries to the vocal cords and of limbs
    blighted by infection,
and dispel both pestilence and deadly disease;
I eat both bitter pith and gnawed inner bark.

## ALD 57

"Armiger infausti Iovis" et "raptor Ganimidis":
quamquam pellaces cantarent carmine vates,
non fueram "praepes," quo fertur "Dardana proles";
sed magis in summis cicnos agitabo fugaces
5   arsantesque grues proturbo sub aetheris axe.
Corpora dum senio corrumpit fessa vetustas,
fontibus in liquidis mergentis membra madescunt;
post haec restauror praeclaro lumine Phoebi.

## ALD 58

Tempore de primo noctis mihi nomen adhaesit;
occiduas mundi complector cardine partes;
oceano Titan dum corpus tinxerit almum,
et polus in glaucis descendens volvitur undis,
5   tum sequor, in vitreis abscondens lumina campis,
et fortunatus, subito ni tollar ab aethra,
ut furvas lumen noctis depelleret umbras.

# ALD 57

"Weapon-Bearer of accursed Jove" and "Snatcher of
    Ganymede":
despite what deceptive poets might sing in song,
I never was the "speedy one" who took the "Trojan youth";
instead, I'll stir up swans escaping in the sky
and disturb screeching cranes under heaven's pole.        5
When tired old age undoes my body with the weight of
    years,
my limbs are freshened when dipped in liquid streams;
and afterward I am restored by the bright light of the sun.

# ALD 58

My name stuck to me from the early hours of the night;
I enfold the western regions of the world's axis;
when the sun has dipped his nourishing body in the ocean,
and the diving polestar is immersed in blue-green waves,
then do I follow on, hiding my light in glassy plains,        5
and I am happy, unless I am suddenly snatched from the
    sky,
so that light might drive off the dusky shadows of the night.

# ALD 59

Me dudum genuit candens onocrotalus albam,
gutture qui patulo sorbet de gurgite limphas.
Pergo per albentes directo tramite campos,
candentique viae vestigia caerula linquo,
5   lucida nigratis fuscans anfractibus arva.
Nec satis est unum per campos pandere callem:
semita quin potius milleno tramite tendit,
quae non errantes ad caeli culmina vexit.

# ALD 60

Collibus in celsis saevi discrimina Martis,
quamvis venator frustra latrante moloso,
garriat arcister contorquens spicula ferri
nil vereor; magnis sed fretus viribus altos
5   belliger impugnans elefantes vulnere sterno.
Heu! Fortuna ferox, quae me sic arte fefellit:
dum trucido grandes et virgine vincor inermi!
Nam gremium pandens mox pulchra puerpera prendit
et voti compos celsam deducit ad urbem.
10  Indidit ex cornu nomen mihi lingua Pelasga;
sic itidem propria dixerunt voce Latini.

48

## ALD 59

Once upon a time it was the bright-white pelican that made
    me white,
swallowing with gaping throat the waters of the deep.
I wander through whitened fields in a direct path,
and on that bright-white trail I leave dusky traces,
darkening light plains with black wanderings.                    5
But it is not enough to open a single line through these
    fields:
instead, the way proceeds by a thousandfold course,
and has taken to the heights of heaven those who do not
    stray.

## ALD 60

On high hills I do not fear the contests of cruel Mars,
although the hunter, with a hound barking in vain,
chatters on, an archer shooting iron darts;
instead, warlike, relying on my great strength,
attacking lofty elephants I lay them low with a wound.          5
Ah, cruel fortune, which has craftily fooled me so:
when I cut down mighty creatures, but am overtaken by an
    unarmed maid!
For the beautiful girl, by spreading out her lap, captures me
and, getting her wish, takes me down to the soaring city.
The Greek language gave me my name from my horn;              10
the Romans have named me likewise in their tongue.

49

## ALD 61

De terrae gremiis formabar primitus arte;
materia trucibus processit cetera tauris,
aut potius putidis constat fabricata capellis.
Per me multorum clauduntur lumina leto,
5   qui domini nudus nitor defendere vitam.
Nam domus est constructa mihi de tergore secto
necnon et tabulis, quas findunt stipite, rasis.

## ALD 62

De madido nascor rorantibus aethere guttis,
turgida concrescens liquido de flumine lapsu,
sed me nulla valet manus udo gurgite nantem
tangere, ni statim rumpantur viscera tactu,
5   et fragilis tenues flatus discedat in auras.
Ante catervatim per limphas duco cohortes,
dum plures ortu comites potiuntur eodem.

## ALD 63

Dum genus humanum truculenta fluenta necarent
et nova mortales multarent aequora cunctos
exceptis raris gignunt qui semina saecli,

## ALD 61

From the bosom of the earth I was first formed by craft;
the rest of my material came from fierce bulls,
or maybe was produced instead from stinking goats.
Because of me the eyes of many are closed in death
when, unsheathed, I strive to defend my lord's life.                    5
My house is built of leather cut to fit,
as well as shaved strips taken from a tree.

## ALD 62

I am born from the damp sky in dewy drops,
growing swollen as I fall from the clear flood,
but no hand can touch me as I float in the wet stream,
unless my innards are straightaway burst by a touch,
and my fragile breath disappears into thin air.                        5
Until then, I lead my colleagues in crowds through the
        waters,
since many comrades are produced by the same beginning.

## ALD 63

When cruel floods were killing the human race
and fresh-made oceans were laying every mortal creature
        low,
excepting only those few who bore the seeds of the world,

primus viventum perdebam foedera iuris,
5  imperio patris contemnens subdere colla;
unde puto dudum versu dixisse poetam:
"Abluit in terris, quidquid deliquit in undis."
Nam sobolem numquam dapibus saturabo ciborum,
ni prius in pulpis plumas nigrescere cernam.
10  Littera tollatur: post haec sine prole manebo.


# ALD 64

Cum Deus infandas iam plecteret aequore noxas
ablueretque simul scelerum contagia limphis,
prima praecepti complevi iussa parentis,
portendens fructu terris venisse salutem.
5  Mitia quapropter semper praecordia gesto,
et felix praepes nigro sine felle manebo.


# ALD 65

Fida satis custos conservans pervigil aedes,
noctibus in furvis caecas lustrabo latebras,
atris haud perdens oculorum lumen in antris.
Furibus invisis, vastant qui farris acervos,
5  insidiis tacite dispono scandala mortis,
et vaga venatrix rimabor lustra ferarum,
nec volo cum canibus turmas agitare fugaces,

I was the first of all living things to break the legal
    covenants,
refusing to submit to patriarchal authority;                    5
that's why I reckon that a poet once announced in song:
"It atones on land for what it committed on water."
I shall never stuff my offspring with feasts of food,
unless I first see feathers grow black on their flesh.
Take away a letter: then I'll be left childless.                10

## ALD 64

When God was smiting unspeakable sins with a flood
and was cleansing the blight of evils with water,
I fulfilled the first orders of what the Father commanded,
showing by vegetation that salvation had come to the earth.
Because of that, I always have a gentle heart,                  5
and shall remain a blessed bird, free from black gall.

## ALD 65

Always alert, I am a pretty good guard for the house,
and I shall wander round its dusky corners in the dark of
    night,
and not lose the light of my eyes even in black caves.
When there are unseen thieves who raid the stores of grain,
I silently set deadly obstacles with traps                      5
and, as a roaming huntress, I sniff out the lairs of beasts,
but do not want to join with the dogs in chasing them as
    they flee.

qui mihi latrantes crudelia bella ciebunt:
gens exosa mihi tradebat nomen habendum.

## ALD 66

Nos sumus aequales communi sorte sorores,
quae damus ex nostro cunctis alimenta labore.
Par labor ambarum, dispar fortuna duarum,
altera nam cursat, quod numquam altera gessit;
5  nec tamen invidiae stimulis agitamur acerbis:
utraque, quod mandit, quod ruminat ore patenti,
comminuens reddit famulans sine fraude maligna.

## ALD 67

Sicca pruinosam crebris effundo fenestris,
candentemque nivem iactans de viscere furvo;
et tamen omnis amat, quamvis sit frigida nimbo
densior et nebulis late spargatur in aula.
5  Qua sine mortales grassantur funere leti
(sic animae pariter pereunt, dum vita fatescit)
et qua ditati contemnunt limina Ditis.
Liquitur in prunis numquam torrentibus haec nix,
sed, mirum dictu, magis indurescit ad ignem.

They, barking, will turn their cruel attacks on me:
the race I hate once gave me the name I hold.

## ALD 66

We are sisters, equal in our shared fate,
and by our work we provide food for everyone.
We two share the same work, but not the same
    circumstance:
one runs around, and the other never did;
but we are not driven by the bitter sting of envy:      5
what each of us eats and chews over, openmouthed,
we serve up made smaller, with no wicked trick.

## ALD 67

Though dry, I pour out snowy powder through many
    openings,
bright white and frosty, tossing it out from dusky innards;
and yet everyone loves it though it is cool and sprinkled
all around the hall, thicker than a cloud or misty vapor.
Without it, mortals are laid low by death's termination      5
(and their souls perish too, when life grows faint),
but when they have it in plenty they despise death's door.
This is a snowy powder that never melts on the toasting
    coals,
but, amazingly, grows even harder in the flames.

## ALD 68

Sum cava, bellantum crepitu quae corda ciebo,
vocibus horrendis stimulans in bella cohortes.
Idcirco reboans tanto clamore resulto,
quod nulla interius obtundant viscera vocem;
5 spiritus in toto sed regnant corpore flabra.
Garrula me poterit numquam superare cicada
aut arguta simul cantans luscinia ruscis
quam lingua propria dicunt *acalantida* Graeci.

## ALD 69

Semper habens virides frondenti in corpore crines,
tempore non ullo viduabor tegmine spisso,
Circius et Boreas quamvis et flamina Chauri
viribus horrendis studeant deglobere frontem;
5 sed me pestiferam fecerunt fata reorum,
cumque venenatus glescit de corpore stipes,
lurcones rabidi quem carpunt rictibus oris,
occido mandentum mox plura cadavera leto.

## ALD 70

De terris orior candenti corpore pelta,
et nive fecunda, Vulcani torre rigescens,

## ALD 68

I am hollow, and shall stir the hearts of warriors with my
    noise,
rousing fighting-men to battle with frightening sounds.
So, resounding, I reverberate with so great a racket,
because no innards dull my voice inside;
the blasts of breath reign right through my body.      5
No chirping grasshopper could ever surpass me
or the lively nightingale singing along in the thickets,
that bird the Greeks call *acalanthis* in their own tongue.

## ALD 69

I always have a green crown atop my leafy body;
I shall not lack a thick covering at any time,
though Circius and Boreas and the blasts of Caurus
strive with frightening force to make my brow bare;
but the fate allotted to sinners has made me venomous,      5
and when there swells from my body a poisonous stem,
which ravenous gluttons snatch in their jaws,
I soon strike down in death many corpses of my chewers.

## ALD 70

I arise from the earth as a shield with bright-white body,
and with a life-giving whiteness, growing hard by Vulcan's
    heat,

carior et multo quam cetera scuta duelli;
nec tamen in medio clipei stat ferreus umbo.
5 Me sine quid prodest dirorum parma virorum?
Vix artus animaeque carerent tramite mortis,
ni forsan validis refrager viribus Orco.

## ALD 71

Me pedibus manibusque simul fraudaverat almus
arbiter, immensum primo dum pangeret orbem;
fulcior haud volitans veloci praepetis ala,
spiritus alterno vegitat nec corpora flatu;
5 quamvis in caelis convexa cacumina cernam,
non tamen undosi contemno marmora ponti.

## ALD 72

Omnia membra mihi plasmavit corporis auctor,
nec tamen ex isdem membrorum munia sumpsi;
pergere nec plantis oculis nec cernere possum,
quamquam nunc patulae constent sub fronte fenestrae;
5 nullus anhelanti procedit viscere flatus
spicula nec geminis nitor torquere lacertis.
Heu! Frustra factor confinxit corpus inorme,
totis membrorum dum frauder sensibus intus.

and far more valuable than other battle bucklers;
but no iron boss stands in the middle of the board.
Without me what is the use of a fierce fighter's defense?     5
Scarcely would the limbs and souls escape the path of
        death,
if I did not resist deadly Hades with my mighty strength.


# ALD 71

The kindly judge, when first he laid out the vast world,
had robbed me of hands and feet together;
I do not fly supported on the swift wings of a bird,
nor does breath make me live with alternating blasts;
although I see the vaulted heights of heaven,          5
I do not scorn the billows of the wavy sea.


# ALD 72

The maker of my body molded all my limbs,
but I do not have from them the benefit of limbs;
I cannot walk on feet nor use my eyes to see,
although beneath my forehead there are now open
        windows;
no breath emerges from panting innards,                5
nor do I try to cast darts from my twin arms.
Alas, my creator made my vast body in vain,
since I am robbed inside of all feeling from my limbs.

## ALD 73

Per cava telluris clam serpo celerrimus antra,
flexos venarum girans anfractibus orbes;
cum caream vita sensu quoque funditus expers,
quis numerus capiat vel quis laterculus aequet,
5  vita viventum generem quot milia partu?
His neque per caelum rutilantis sidera sperae,
fluctivagi ponti nec compensantur harenae.

## ALD 74

Glauca seges lini vernans ex aequore campi,
et tergus mihi tradebant primordia fati.
Bina mihi constant torto nam brachia filo,
ex quibus immensum trucidabam mole tirannum,
5  cum cuperent olim gentis saevire falanges.
Plus amo cum tereti bellum decernere saxo
quam duris pugnans ferrata cuspide contis.
Tres digiti totum versant super ardua corpus;
erro caput circa tenues et tendor in auras.

# ALD 73

I secretly snake most swiftly through the hollow chambers
    of the ground,
twisting in supple circles through the winding of veins;
although I lack life, and am also utterly free of feeling,
what number can express, or what counting board calculate,
how many thousands of living creatures I give life and     5
    birth?
Their number is matched neither by the stars of the sphere
that shines in the sky, nor by the sands of the wave-driven
    sea.

# ALD 74

The blue-gray crop of flax, burgeoning on the plain of the
    field,
and a hide together granted me the beginnings of my lot.
For I have twin arms made out of twisted thread,
and with them I once felled a mighty-sized tyrant,
when once hosts of heathens sought to rage.     5
I far prefer to decide wars with a smooth stone
rather than with hard iron-tipped spears.
Three fingers swing my whole body up in the air;
I wander about the head and stretch out in thin air.

# ALD 75

Aera per sudum nunc binis remigo pennis,
horridus et grossae depromo murmura vocis,
inque cavo densis conversor stipite turmis
dulcia conficiens propriis alimenta catervis,
5  et tamen humanis horrent haec pabula buccis.
Sed quicumque cupit disrumpens foedera pacis
dirus commaculare domum sub culmine querno,
extemplo socias in bellum clamo cohortes,
dumque catervatim stridunt et spicula trudunt,
10  agmina defugiunt iaculis exterrita diris.
Insontes hosti sic torquent tela nocenti
plurima, quae constant tetris infecta venenis.

# ALD 76

Fausta fuit primo mundi nascentis origo,
donec prostratus succumberet arte maligni;
ex me tunc priscae processit causa ruinae,
dulcia quae rudibus tradebam mala colonis.
5  En iterum mundo testor remeasse salutem,
stipite de patulo dum penderet arbiter orbis,
et poenas lueret soboles veneranda Tonantis.

# ALD 75

I row my way now through clean air on double pairs of
     wings,
a frightening thing, as I spread the buzzing of my loud
     voice,
and in thick swarms I congregate in a hollow stump,
producing sweet food for our own throngs,
even though such nutrition is terrible to human taste.     5
But if anyone, breaking the bonds of peace, has an urge
savagely to disturb our home beneath its oaken roof,
at once I call all our allied forces to battle,
and while they buzz in swarms and press their points,
the attackers withdraw, fearful of our savage stings.     10
Blameless, they cast against the harmful foe their darts
in vast numbers, darts infected with harmful poisons.

# ALD 76

Blessed was the first beginning of the world when it was
     born,
until by the cunning of the wicked one it was laid low;
it was from me that the cause for the ancient Fall first came,
since I provided sweet apples to those fresh inhabitants.
But I bear witness that salvation came again to the globe,     5
when the judge of the world was hanged from a spreading
     tree,
and the glorious Son of the Thunderer washed away our
     sins.

## ALD 77

Quis prior in mundo deprompsit tegmina vestis,
aut quis clementer miserum protexit egenum?
Irrita non referam verbis nec frivola fingam;
primitus in terra proprio de corpore peplum,
5   ut fama fertur, produxi frondibus altis;
Carica me curvat, dum massis pabula praestat,
sedulus agricola brumae quas tempore mandit.

## ALD 78

En, plures debrians impendo pocula Bacchi,
vinitor expressit quae flavescentibus uvis
pampinus et viridi genuit de palmite botris,
nectare cauponis complens ex vite tabernam.
5   Sic mea turgescunt ad plenum viscera musto,
et tamen inflatum non vexat crapula corpus,
quamvis hoc nectar centenis hauserit urnis.
Proles sum terrae glescens in saltibus altis;
materiam cuneis findit sed cultor agrestis,
10  pinos evertens altas et robora ferro.

# ALD 77

Who before me gave the covering of clothes to the world,
or who graciously wrapped up a wretch in need?
I shan't speak empty words or fake frivolities;
in the beginning of the earth I produced a cloak
from my own body, out of lengthy leaves, as the story goes;     5
the Carian fruit weighs me down, when it offers food in
      bunches
that the careful farmer consumes at wintertime.

# ALD 78

Well, there are many that I make drunk, doling out
      Bacchus's cups,
ones that a vintner has pressed out from golden grapes
and the vine stem bore in bunches from the bright-green
      stalk,
filling the stall of the wine seller with nectar from the vine.
So my innards are swollen to fullness from the must,     5
but no hangover troubles my bulging body,
even if it were to drain this nectar from a hundred jars.
I am a child of the earth, growing in tall groves;
yet the country farmer splits my substance with wedges,
toppling tall pines and oak trees with an iron ax.     10

## ALD 79

Non nos Saturni genuit spurcissima proles
Iupiter, immensum fingunt quem carmina vatum,
nec fuit in Delo mater Latona creatrix;
Cynthia non dicor nec frater Apollo vocatur,
5  sed potius summi genuit regnator Olimpi,
qui nunc in caelis excelsae praesidet arci.
Dividimus mundum communi lege quadratum,
nocturnos regimus cursus et frena dierum.
Ni soror et frater vaga saecula iure gubernent,
10  heu! Chaos immensum clauderet cuncta latebris,
atraque nunc Erebi regnarent Tartara nigri.

## ALD 80

De rimis lapidum profluxi flumine lento,
dum frangant flammae saxorum viscera dura,
et laxis ardor fornacis regnat habenis;
nunc mihi forma capax glacieque simillima lucet.
5  Nempe volunt plures collum constringere dextra
et pulchre digitis lubricum comprendere corpus;

# ALD 79

Not by that most wicked offspring of Saturn,
Jupiter, whom the songs of poets feign to be great,
were we produced, nor did mother Latona bring us forth on
    Delos;
I am not called Cynthia, nor is my brother named Apollo,
but rather our father is the ruler of highest Olympus,     5
who now presides over a lofty citadel in the sky.
We divide with a common jurisdiction the four-cornered
    world,
controlling the courses of night and the constraints of the
    day.
Unless sister and brother were properly governing the
    wandering universe,
alas, vast chaos would engulf everything in darkness,    10
and the black shadows of dark Erebus would now be in
    command.

# ALD 80

I seeped out in a slow stream from cracks in the rock,
when flames split the hard innards of the stones,
and, with all restraint removed, the heat of the furnace
    prevails;
now my capacious form shines most like ice.
In truth, many want to enclose my neck with their right    5
    hand
and grasp my beautifully smooth form with their fingers;

sed mentes muto, dum labris oscula trado,
dulcia compressis impendens basia buccis,
atque pedum gressus titubantes sterno ruina.

## ALD 81

Semper ego clarum praecedo lumine lumen;
signifer et Phoebi, lustrat qui limpidus orbem;
per caelum gradiens obliquo tramite flector;
eoas partes amo, dum iubar inde meabit
5  finibus Indorum, cernunt qui lumina primi.
O felix olim servata lege Tonantis!
Heu! Post haec cecidi proterva mente superbus;
ultio quapropter funestum perculit hostem.
Sex igitur comites mecum super aethera scandunt,
10  gnarus quos poterit per biblos pandere lector.

## ALD 82

Discolor in curvas deflecto membra cavernas,
pugnas exercens dira cum gente draconum.
Non ego dilecta turgesco prole mariti,
nec fecunda viro sobolem sic edidit alvus,
5  residuae matres ut sumunt semina partus;
quin magis ex aure praegnantur viscera fetu.
Si vero proles patitur discrimina mortis,
dicor habere rudem componens arte medelam.

but I alter their minds by kissing on their lips,
doling out sweet kisses to puckered mouths,
and their teetering steps I trip up in a fall.

## ALD 81

I always come before that clear light with my light;
I am the standard-bearer of Phoebus, who brightly wanders
    the world;
going through the sky, I travel a slanting path;
I love the Eastern regions, since there my beam will ramble
at the very edge of India, and the folk who first see the     5
    light.
I was so happy once, when the law of the Thunderer was
    observed!
Alas, I fell after that, made proud by an arrogant mind;
so punishment put down the deadly enemy.
Six companions therefore travel through the skies with me,
and a learned reader can explain from books who they are.     10

## ALD 82

Motley colored, I curl my limbs in curving hollows,
waging war against savage serpent-kind.
I am not made swollen with a husband's darling brood,
nor does my womb, made fertile by a male, offer offspring
in the way that other mothers receive their babies' seed;     5
instead, my innards conceive children through my ear.
Indeed, if my brood endures the shock of death,
I'm said to have a basic remedy craftily concocted.

## ALD 83

Arida spumosis dissolvens faucibus ora,
bis binis bibulus potum de fontibus hausi.
Vivens nam terrae glebas cum stirpibus imis
nisu virtutis validae disrumpo feraces;
5  at vero linquit dum spiritus algida membra,
nexibus horrendis homines constringere possum.

## ALD 84

Nunc mihi sunt oculi bis seni in corpore solo,
bis ternumque caput, sed cetera membra gubernant.
Nam gradior pedibus suffultus bis duodenis,
sed decies novem sunt et sex corporis ungues,
5  sinzigias numero pariter similabo pedestres.
Populus et taxus, viridi quoque fronde salicta
sunt invisa mihi, sed fagos glandibus uncas,
fructiferas itidem florenti vertice quercus
diligo; sic nemorosa simul non spernitur ilex.

## ALD 85

Iam referam verbis tibi, quod vix credere possis,
cum constet verum fallant nec frivola mentem.

## ALD 83

I moisten my dry mouth with dripping jaws,
when, drinking, I have taken a sip from four springs.
When alive, by straining my mighty strength,
I break up the fertile clods of earth with their roots below;
but when the breath leaves my chilly limbs,                    5
I can bind men with terrible bonds.

## ALD 84

Now I have twice-six eyes in a single body,
and twice-three heads, which govern other limbs.
For I travel supported on twice-twelve feet,
but my body has ten times nine plus six nails.
I am equal in number in that way to the total tally of          5
    metrical feet.
The poplar and the yew and the willow tree with bright-
    green leaves
are hateful to me, but I adore the bending beech tree with
    its nuts
and likewise the acorn-bearing oaks with verdant crown;
and in the same way the bushy holm oak is not despised.

## ALD 85

Now I will tell you in words what you can hardly believe,
although it is true, and no trickery beguiles the mind.

Nam dudum dederam soboli munuscula grata,
tradere quae numquam poterat mihi quislibet alter,
5   dum Deus ex alto fraudaret munere claro,
in quo cunctorum gaudent praecordia dono.

## ALD 86

Sum namque armatus rugosis cornibus horrens;
herbas arvorum buccis decerpo virentes,
et tamen astrifero procedens agmine stipor,
culmina caelorum quae scandunt celsa catervis.
5   Turritas urbes capitis certamine quasso
oppida murorum prosternens arcibus altis.
Induo mortales retorto stamine pepli;
littera quindecima praestat quod pars domus adsto.

## ALD 87

De salicis trunco, pecoris quoque tergore raso,
componor patiens discrimina cruda duelli.
Semper ego proprio gestantis corpore corpus
conservabo, viri vitam ne dempserit Orcus.
5   Quis tantos casus aut quis tam plurima leti
suscipit in bello crudelis vulnera miles?

For I had once given a welcome offering to my offspring,
something no one else had ever been able to offer me,
since God on high robbed me of that brilliant gift,                    5
and the hearts of everyone rejoice in that reward.


## ALD 86

I am frightening, armed with wrinkled horns;
I graze on bright-green grass of the fields in mouthfuls,
and yet, as I travel, I am pressed in by a starry troop
that crosses the heights of heaven in crowds.
I shatter the towers of towns with an attack of my head,              5
laying low city walls with their lofty citadels.
I clothe mortals with the twisted thread of a cloak;
add the fifteenth letter in front, and I am part of a house.


## ALD 87

From willow wood, and also from the scraped hide of cattle,
I am formed to endure the rough trials of battle.
I shall always guard the body of the one that holds me
with my own body, so that Orcus will not take away the
    man's life.
What warrior endures such great misfortunes                          5
or so very many wounds of cruel death in war?

# ALD 88

Callidior cunctis aura vescentibus aethrae,
late per mundum dispersi semina mortis;
unde horrenda seges diris succrevit aristis,
quam metit ad scelera scortator falce maligna;
5   cornigeri multum vereor certamina cervi.
Namque senescenti spoliabor pelle vetustus,
atque nova rursus fretus remanebo iuventa.

# ALD 89

Nunc mea divinis complentur viscera verbis
totaque sacratos gestant praecordia biblos;
at tamen ex isdem nequeo cognoscere quicquam:
infelix fato fraudabor munere tali,
5   dum tollunt dirae librorum lumina Parcae.

# ALD 90

Sunt mihi sex oculi, totidem simul auribus hausi,
sed digitos decies senos in corpore gesto;
ex quibus ecce quater denis de carne revulsis
quinquies at tantum video remanere quaternos.

# ALD 88

More cunning than all the creatures that breathe the breath
    of air,
I scattered the seeds of death widely throughout the world;
and from them frightening crops grew up with a dreadful
    harvest,
which the whoremonger reaps with his scythe for wicked
    sins;
I greatly fear conflict with the antler-bearing stag.        5
When I am old, I shall be deprived of my aging skin,
but I shall once again remain, sustained by fresh youth.

# ALD 89

Now my innards are filled with sacred words
and my whole insides carry holy volumes;
and yet I cannot learn anything from them:
unlucky, I shall be robbed of such a gift by destiny,
since the dreadful Fates deprive me of the illumination of    5
    books.

# ALD 90

I have six eyes: I listen at the same time with as many ears,
but look: I have six times ten digits on the body;
when four times ten of these have been taken from my flesh
I seem to retain only four times five.

## ALD 91

Omnipotens auctor, nutu qui cuncta creavit,
mi dedit in mundo tam "victrix" nomen habendum.
Nomine nempe meo florescit gloria regum,
martiribus necnon, dum vincunt proelia mundi:
5  edita caelestis prensant et praemia vitae;
frondigeris tegitur bellantum turma coronis,
et viridi ramo victor certamine miles.
In summo capitis densescit vertice vellus,
ex quo multiplicis torquentur tegmina pepli;
10  sic quoque mellifluis escarum pasco saginis,
nectare per populos tribuens alimenta ciborum.

## ALD 92

Rupibus in celsis, qua tundunt caerula cautes,
et salis undantes turgescunt aequore fluctus,
machina me summis construxit molibus amplam,
navigeros calles ut pandam classibus index.
5  Non maris aequoreos lustrabam remige campos
nec ratibus pontum sulcabam tramite flexo,
et tamen immensis errantes fluctibus actos
arcibus ex celsis signans ad litora duco,
flammiger imponens torres in turribus altis,
10  ignea brumales dum condunt sidera nimbi.

# ALD 91

The all-powerful creator, who formed everything by his
    command,
gave me the name "victorious woman" in the world.
For assuredly the glory of kings flourishes in my name,
and likewise for martyrs, when they win the wars of the
    world:
they gain the lofty prize of heavenly life;                          5
the band of warriors is covered with leafy crowns,
and the fighter, victorious in the fray, with a bright-green
    branch.
At the crown of my own head the covering grows thick,
and from it the layers of a manifold cloak are woven;
so too I provide the sweet nourishment of food,                     10
offering provisions of foodstuff as nectar to the people.

# ALD 92

On high cliffs, where the billows pound the rocks,
and salty waves surging grow swollen in the flood,
a crane built me large with my soaring structure,
so that as a guide I can point out paths for sailing to ships.
I never traveled the watery plains of the sea with oars             5
nor did I ever plow the deep in boats on a bending course,
but instead I lead to shore those wandering and buffeted
by vast waves, by sending out a signal from high peaks,
flame-bearing, setting torches on lofty towers,
when wintry clouds conceal the shining stars.                       10

## ALD 93

Quae res in terris armatur robore tanto,
aut paribus fungi nitatur viribus audax?
Parva mihi primo constant exordia vitae,
sed gracilis grande soleo prosternere leto,
5 quod letum proprii gestant penetralia ventris.
Nam saltus nemorum densos pariterque frutecta,
piniferosque simul montes cum molibus altos,
truxque rapaxque capaxque feroxque sub aethere spargo,
et minor existens gracili quam corpore scnifes,
10 frigida dum genetrix dura generaret ab alvo,
primitus ex utero producens pignora gentis.

## ALD 94

Sambucus, in silva putris dum fronde virescit,
est mihi par foliis; nam glesco surculus arvis,
nigros bacarum portans in fronte corimbos;
quem medici multum ruris per terga virentem,
5 cum scabies morbi pulpas irrepserit aegras,
lustrantes orbem crebro quaesisse feruntur;
cladibus horrendae, dum vexat viscera tabo,

## ALD 93

What thing on earth is armed with strength so great,
or bravely strives to exert powers equal to mine?
At first the beginnings of my life are small,
but although I am slight I tend to lay low in death the great,
a death the inmost parts of my own belly hold.                    5
Indeed, the dense woods of the grove, also shrubs,
and likewise pine-covered, lofty, massive mountains,
I, savage, greedy, hungry, and fierce, raze them all under the
        sky,
even though I am tinier than the slight body of a gnat,
when my chilly mother in generating me out from her hard    10
        belly,
producing from the first the offspring of her kin out of her
        womb.

## ALD 94

The elder tree, as it flourishes in the wood with its rank
        foliage,
is like me in its leaves; for I grow as a shrub in the fields,
bearing the black bunches of berries on my crown;
and doctors, frequently wandering the world,
are said to have sought me, sprouting thickly in the            5
        countryside,
when the illness of disease has spread through sick flesh;
for I can help, so that the virus of leprosy, frightening in its
        devastation

ne virus serpat, possum succurrere, leprae,
sic olidas hominum restaurans germine fibras.

## ALD 95

Ecce, molosorum nomen mihi fata dederunt
(Argolicae gentis sic promit lingua loquelis),
ex quo me dirae fallebant carmina Circae,
quae fontis liquidi maculabat flumina verbis:
5  cruraque cum coxis, suras cum poplite bino,
abstulit immiscens crudelis verba virago.
Pignora nunc pavidi referunt ululantia nautae,
tonsis dum trudunt classes et caerula findunt
vastos verrentes fluctus grassante procella,
10  palmula qua remis succurrit panda per undas,
auscultare procul, quae latrant inguina circum.
Sic me pellexit dudum Titania proles,
ut merito vivam salsis in fluctibus exul.

## ALD 96

Ferratas acies et denso milite turmas,
bellandi miseros stimulat quos vana cupido,
dum maculare student armis pia foedera regni,

when it torments the innards with its taint, does not
    spread,
restoring with my seed the stinking guts of men.


# ALD 95

See: the Fates have given me the name of dogs
(since that is how the language of the Greek race renders it
    in speech)
ever since the time when the charms of dreadful Circe
    deceived me,
she who once polluted the waters of the liquid stream with
    her words:
as for my hips and shins and calves and twin knees,        5
the cruel witch snatched them when she wove her words.
Now fearful sailors say that they hear from afar—
as they drive their ships with oars and in the raging storm
cleave the seas, sweeping the vast waves,
while the curved blade helps the oar through the swell—   10
the wailing of puppies barking round my loins.
So Titan's offspring tricked me once,
and so I deserve to live as an exile in the salty waves.


# ALD 96

As for the ironclad troops and group of massed warriors,
the wretches whom the empty lust for fighting stirs,
when they seek to stain the fine covenants of the kingdom
    with arms,

salpix et sorbet ventosis flatibus auras,
5  raucaque clangenti resultant classica sistro;
cernere non pavidus didici trux murmura Martis.
Quamquam me turpem nascendi fecerit auctor,
editus ex alvo dum sumpsi munera vitae,
ecce tamen morti successit gloria formae,
10  letifer in fibras dum finis serpat apertas;
bratea non auri fulvis pretiosa metallis,
quamvis gemmarum constent ornata lucernis,
vincere, non quibunt falerarum floribus umquam.
Me flecti genibus fessum natura negavit,
15  poplite seu curvo palpebris tradere somnos,
quin potius vitam compellor degere stando.

## ALD 97

Florida me genuit nigrantem corpore tellus,
et nil fecundum stereli de viscere promo,
quamvis Eumenidum narrantes carmine vates
tartaream partu testentur gignere prolem.
5  Nulla mihi constat certi substantia partus,
sed modo quadratum complector caerula mundum.
Est inimica mihi, quae cunctis constat amica,
saecula dum lustrat, lampas Titania Phoebi.
Diri latrones me semper amare solebant,
10  quos gremio tectos nitor defendere fusco.
Vergilium constat caram cecinisse sororem:

and while the battle trumpet sucks the air with windy blasts
and the loud horns of battle resound with a strident cry:    5
fierce, I have learned to look without fear upon these
    rumblings of war.
My maker created me ugly at birth,
when, having emerged from the womb, I took on the gifts
    of life,
but look: the glory of beauty follows my death,
when the death-bringing end snakes into my open guts;    10
no precious sheets of gold with tawny metal,
although they are adorned with the illumination of gems
and flowery trappings, can ever surpass me.
Nature has prevented me from kneeling down when I am
    tired,
or on bent knee from closing my eyelids in sleep;    15
instead, I am obliged to spend my life standing up.

# ALD 97

The fertile earth bore me, black in body,
and I bring forth nothing fruitful from my sterile womb,
although the poets, telling in song of the Furies,
may claim that I spawned in birth that race of Tartarus.
I do not have any certain offspring,    5
but, dusky, now I enfold the four corners of the world.
The Titan torch of Phoebus, which is a friend to all
while it traverses the world, is an enemy to me.
Cruel robbers always used to love me,
and I strive to keep them covered in my dark embrace.    10
Virgil is known to have sung this of my dear sister:

"Ingrediturque solo et caput inter nubila condit,
monstrum horrendum, ingens, cui quot sunt corpore
      plumae,
tot vigiles oculi subter, mirabile dictu,
15  tot linguae, totidem ora sonant, tot subrigit auris;
nocte volat caeli medio terraeque per umbras."

## ALD 98

Ostriger en arvo vernabam frondibus hirtis
conquilio similis: sic cocci murice rubro,
purpureus stillat sanguis de palmite guttis.
Exuvias vitae mandenti tollere nolo,
5  mitia nec penitus spoliabunt mente venena;
sed tamen insanum vexat dementia cordis,
dum rotat in giro vecors vertigine membra.

## ALD 99

Consul eram quondam, Romanus miles equester,
arbiter imperio dum regni sceptra regebat;
nunc onus horrendum reportant corpora gippi,
et premit immensum truculentae sarcina molis.

"She walks on the ground and hides her head in the
    clouds,
a huge and dreadful monster, on whose body the feathers
are matched in number by watchful eyes beneath,
    marvelous to tell,
and as many tongues and mouths sound forth, just as many    15
    ears prick up;
she flies at night through the shadows, midway between
    heaven and earth."

## ALD 98

Look: I used to grow in the field, purple and with furry
    leaves,
a little like a whelk, so that with reddened dye of scarlet
purple blood drips in drops from my tip.
I do not want to take away the spoils of life from whoever
    eats me,
nor will my gentle venom make him completely lose his    5
    mind;
and yet a madness of spirit torments him in a frenzy
as, out of his wits, he twists his limbs in a whirling circle.

## ALD 99

I was once a consul, when the noble Roman knight,
like a judge in authority, ruled the scepters of power;
now my body supports the dreadful burden of a hump,
and a load of deadly weight presses down my bulk.

5  Terreo cornipedum nunc velox agmen equorum,
qui trepidi fugiunt mox quadripedante meatu,
dum trucis aspectant immensos corporis artus.


## ALD 100

Conditor, aeternis fulcit qui saecla columnis,
rector regnorum, frenans et fulmina lege,
pendula dum patuli vertuntur culmina caeli,
me varium fecit, primo dum conderet orbem.

5    Pervigil excubiis: numquam dormire iuvabit,
sed tamen extemplo clauduntur lumina somno;
nam Deus ut propria mundum dicione gubernat,
sic ego complector sub caeli cardine cuncta.
Segnior est nullus, quoniam me larbula terret,

10  setigero rursus constans audacior apro;
nullus me superat cupiens vexilla triumphi
ni Deus, aethrali summus qui regnat in arce.
Prorsus odorato ture flagrantior halans
olfactum ambrosiae, necnon crescentia glebae

15  lilia purpureis possum conexa rosetis
vincere spirantis nardi dulcedine plena;
nunc olida caeni squalentis sorde putresco.
Omnia, quaeque polo sunt subter et axe reguntur,
dum pater arcitenens concessit, iure guberno;

20  grossas et graciles rerum comprenso figuras.

Now I terrify the swift column of hoofed horses     5
that immediately flee, frightened, escaping on four feet
when they catch sight of the vast limbs of my fierce body.

# ALD 100

The creator, who set up the universe on eternal columns,
the king of kingdoms, reining in even lightning by law,
while the hanging heights of spacious heaven turn,
made me manifold, when he first created the world.
    I am very vigilant in watching: it will never please me to     5
        sleep,
and yet my eyes close suddenly in sleep,
since, just as God governs the globe by his own authority,
just so do I embrace everything beneath the hinge of
        heaven.
No one is more timid, since a ghost terrifies me,
but again I stand bolder than a bristling boar;     10
no one who wants the banners of victory conquers me
except for God, who reigns supreme in the citadel of the
        sky.
    I am more fragrant than scented incense
as I exude the perfume of ambrosia, and I can surpass
the lilies, filled with the sweetness of the scented nard,     15
growing in the field alongside red rosebushes;
but now I rot with the putrid filth of the squalid mire.
    All things that are governed beneath the axis and pole of
        the sky,
as the citadel-ruling Father has granted, I rightly control;
I comprise both fat and fine figures of things.     20

Altior, en, caelo rimor secreta Tonantis,
et tamen inferior terris tetra Tartara cerno;
nam senior mundo praecessi tempora prisca,
ecce, tamen matris horno generabar ab alvo.
25    Pulchrior auratis, dum fulget fibula, bullis,
horridior ramnis et spretis vilior algis.
Latior, en, patulis terrarum finibus exto,
et tamen in media concludor parte pugilli;
frigidior brumis necnon candente pruina,
30    cum sim Vulcani flammis torrentibus ardens;
dulcior in palato quam lenti nectaris haustus;
dirior et rursus quam glauca absinthia campi.
Mando dapes mordax lurconum more Ciclopum,
cum possim iugiter sine victu vivere felix.
35    Plus pernix aquilis, Zephiri velocior alis,
necnon accipitre properantior, et tamen horrens
lumbricus et limax testudo tarda palustris,
atque fimi soboles sordentis cantarus ater
me dicto citius vincunt certamine cursus.
40    Sum gravior plumbo: scopulorum pondera vergo;
sum levior pluma, cedit cui tippula limphae;
nam silici, densas quae fudit viscere flammas,

Look: higher than heaven, I explore the secrets of the
    Thunderer,
and yet, lower than the earth, I see foul Tartarus;
since I am older than the world I preceded ancient times,
but behold, I was produced from my mother's womb this
    year.
    More beautiful than golden bosses, when a brooch is       25
    gleaming,
I am more bristly than brambles, viler than discarded
    seaweed.
Look: I stand broader than the spreading limits of the
    lands,
and yet I can be contained inside someone's fist;
colder than winter and bright-white frost,
even though I may be burning in Vulcan's searing flames;    30
I am sweeter on the palate than a taste of smooth nectar;
again I am more bitter than the gray wormwood of the
    field.
I gobble food greedily like the gluttonous Cyclops,
although I can equally live happily without eating.
I am swifter than eagles, faster than the wings of the    35
    Zephyr,
more speedy than the hawk, and yet that ugly
earthworm, and the snail, and the sluggish swamp turtle,
and the black beetle born of stinking dung,
quicker than it can be told, surpass me in a race.
    I am heavier than lead: I approach the weight of rocks;    40
I am lighter than a feather: to me even a water strider
    yields;
indeed I am harder than flint, which has produced dense
    flames

durior aut ferro, tostis sed mollior extis.
Cincinnos capitis nam gesto cacumine nullos,
45   ornent qui frontem pompis et tempora setis;
cum mihi caesaries volitent de vertice crispae,
plus calamistratis se comunt quae calamistro.
    Pinguior, en, multo scrofarum axungia glesco,
glandiferis iterum referunt dum corpora fagis,
50   atque saginata laetantur carne subulci;
sed me dira famis macie torquebit egenam,
pallida dum iugiter dapibus spoliabor opimis.
    Limpida sum, fateor, Titanis clarior orbe,
candidior nivibus, dum ningit vellera nimbus,
55   carceris et multo tenebris obscurior atris,
atque latebrosis, ambit quas Tartarus, umbris.
Ut globus astrorum plasmor teres atque rotunda,
spherula seu pilae necnon et forma cristalli;
et versa vice protendor ceu Serica pensa,
60   in gracilem porrecta panum seu stamina pepli.
    Senis, ecce, plagis, latus qua panditur orbis
ulterior multo tendor, mirabile fatu;
infra me suprave nihil per saecula constat,
ni rerum genitor mundum sermone coercens.
65   Grandior in glaucis ballena fluctibus atra,
et minor exiguo, sulcat qui corpora, verme,

from its innards, or iron, but I am more tender than roasted
     flesh.
I do not have any curly locks on the top of my head
to adorn my forehead with a fringe or my temples with          45
     tresses,
although a crimped hairdo tumbles down from my crown,
and makes my coiffure more curled than any curling tongs.
     Look: I grow fatter by far than the grease of sows,
as they heave their bodies back from the nut-bearing beech
     trees,
and the swineherds smile at the fattened flesh;               50
but a terrible hunger will torture me with thinness in my
     need,
when, pale, I will be continually robbed of fine feasts.
     I am good-looking, I confess, and more shining than the
     sphere of the sun,
more bright white than the snow, when the cloud produces
     a fleecy fall,
and much darker than a dungeon's black shadows,               55
and those dusky shades that Tartarus encompasses.
I was made smooth and round like the globe of the stars,
or the orb of a ball, or like a crystal sphere;
and on the other hand I am stretched out like Chinese silk,
drawn out into a thin thread or the fibers of a cloak.        60
     See: I reach far further than the six zones by which
the breadth of the earth is divided, amazing to say;
nothing exists in the universe below or above me,
except the Father of all things, controlling the world with
     his Word.
I am greater than the shiny-black whale in the gray waves,    65
and smaller than the puny worm that burrows into bodies,

aut modico, Phoebi radiis qui vibrat, atomo;
centenis pedibus gradior per gramina ruris
et penitus numquam per terram pergo pedester.

70    Sic mea prudentes superat sapientia sofos,
nec tamen in biblis docuit me littera dives,
aut umquam quivi, quid constet sillaba, nosse.
Siccior aestivo torrentis caumate solis,
rore madens iterum plus uda flumine fontis;

75    salsior et multo tumidi quam marmora ponti,
et gelidis terrae limphis insulsior erro,
multiplici specie cunctorum compta colorum,
ex quibus ornatur praesentis machina mundi,
lurida cum toto nunc sim fraudata colore.

80    Auscultate mei credentes famina verbi,
pandere quae poterit gnarus vix ore magister,
et tamen infitians non retur frivola lector;
sciscitor inflatos, fungar quo nomine, sofos.

or the tiny mote that shimmers in the rays of the sun;
I go on a hundred feet through the grass of the field
and truly never travel through the land as a pedestrian.

    Thus is my wisdom beyond wise learned men,      70
and yet no precious letter in books taught me,
nor was I ever able to know from what a syllable is made.
I am drier than the summer heat of the burning sun,
yet again, dripping with dew, I am damper than a fountain's
      stream;
I am saltier by far than the billows of the swelling sea,      75
though I wander blander than the icy waters of the land.
Painted with the manifold beauty of all colors,
with which the fabric of the current world is adorned,
yet I am now pale and drained of all color.

    Listen, you who have faith in the utterances of my word,      80
which even a clever teacher could scarcely explain in
      speech,
and yet a skeptical reader should not think them frivolous
      things;
I challenge the puffed-up sages to say what name I use.

# Bede

## BED 1

Nil herebo melius, celo nil peius habetur;
vilius aut potius quam quod pretio caret est quid?
Bis titivicilium plumbum numerat trutinando,
ter sese cedit prope peiori meliusque;
5  plus oneris hoc est, quod iam minus aggravat orcam.

## BED 2

Littera quae mutata saporem mutat acerbum?

## BED 3

Quae sensum vertit monosillaba grammata servans?

# Bede

## BED 1

Nothing is better than hell, nothing is worse than heaven:
what is more worthless, or more valuable, than that which
    is inestimable?
A scintilla counts twice as much as lead does when you add
    it up;
the better one yields itself to the worse nearly three times;
the one that now weighs less in the scale counts more.     5

## BED 2

What letter, when changed, changes the bitter taste?

## BED 3

What monosyllable switches its meaning while keeping its
letters?

## BED 4

Vel quae pars urbem dissillaba versa patrabit?

## BED 5

Nemo supinum non amat omnipotens nec amantes.

## BED 6

Quid dat hac illacque meanti pabula panis?

## BED 7

Gramma pedem tollit sine sanguine quod copulatum.

## BED 8

Quae res sola manet stans recta sodalibus uncis?

## BED 4

Or what two-syllable word, turned round, will form a city?

## BED 5

The almighty does not love "nobody" *(nemo)* backward, nor those that love that backward one.

## BED 6

What renders bread's sustenance going in either direction?

## BED 7

There is a letter that, when added, bloodlessly takes away a foot.

## BED 8

What thing alone can stand straight while its companions are bowed over?

## BED 9

Littera queque culum facit ut videat velut oclus?

## BED 10

Si bonus amittit caput admittens onus artat.

## BED 11

Perversus bonus est, brevitatis si caput absit.

## BED 12

Quid capite et cauda sicca meat in mare natans?

## BED 13

Tres proles nantes iuncte genuere sorores;
rursus easdem post he mature pepererunt.
Manducasse nocent somno; prosunt bene mensa.

## BED 9

What letter makes an anus see like an eye?

## BED 10

If a good man loses his head, he contracts, allowing a burden.

## BED 11

A good man (*bonus*) is stubborn, if the beginning of "brevity" disappears.

## BED 12

What wanders swimming in the sea with dry head and tail?

## BED 13

Three sisters, when joined, produced swimming offspring;
then these, when grown up, gave birth to the same.
They are harmful to have eaten in sleep, but they are very
    good at table.

## BED 14

Vidi cornutam in celo petiisse volantem,
quam minime peteret si non hanc ipse iuvaret.

## BED 15

Quid iugiter cedit cum siverit omen habebit?

## BED 16

Quid quanto crescit tanto mage curtior extat?

## BED 17

Quis nolens hospes maris illustrat tenebrosa?
A nullo pastus pascit populum numerosum;
unius arte hominis perit at non fauce valebit,
una namque die nunquam consumptus abibit.

# BED 14

I saw that a flying thing chased after a beaked one in the
  sky,
which it would hardly have chased if the other did not aid
  it.

# BED 15

What travels constantly, and will be considered an omen
when it ceases?

# BED 16

What is the shorter, the more it increases?

# BED 17

What sojourner of the sea unwillingly lights the shadows?
Fed by no one, it feeds numerous people;
it dies through a single man's skill; but that one will not
    succeed in swallowing him,
for the creature will never pass away by being consumed in
    a single day.

## BED 18

Tres gemini repunt stimulati marmore pellis;
hac illacque vias geminas monstrant vagitando,
atque docent muti fantes cecique videntes.
Sepe moventem se fallunt quod it haud ubi mandant;
5   a se sepe etiam falluntur torta colendo.

\* \* \*

## ps-BED 1

Dic mihi, quaeso, quae est illa mulier, quae innumeris filiis
ubera porrigit, quae quantum sucta fuerit, tantum inundat?
*Mulier ista est sapientia.*

## ps-BED 2

Vidi filium cum matre manducantem, cuius pellis pendebat
in pariete.

## BED 18

Three siblings, being prodded, creep over a bright surface
    of skin;
wandering here and there, they indicate twin paths,
and, though mute, they teach those who speak; though
    blind, those who see.
Often they deceive the one that moves them, because he
    does not go where they ask;
they are also often deceived by themselves, cultivating what    5
    is wrong.

\*   \*   \*

## ps-BED 1

Tell me, please, who is that woman, who offers her breasts
to unnumbered children, but as much as she is sucked she
supplies still more? *That woman is wisdom.*

## ps-BED 2

I saw a son eating alongside a mother, and the skin of one of
them was hanging on a wall.

## ps-BED 3

Sedeo super equum non natum, cuius matrem in manum teneo.

## ps-BED 4

Dic mihi quae est illa res, quae, cum augetur, minor erit; et dum minuitur, augmentum accipit.

## ps-BED 5

Dic mihi quae est illa res quae coelum totamque terram replevit, siluas et surculos confringit, omniaque fundamenta concutit; sed nec oculis videri, aut manibus tangi potest?

## ps-BED 6

*Quid est quod* mater me genuit, et mox eadem gignetur a me?

## ps-BED 7

Vidi filium inter quatuor fontes nutritum; si vivus fuit, disrupit montes; si mortuus fuit, alligavit vivos.

## ps-BED 3

I am sitting on a horse that has not been born, and I am holding its mother in my hand.

## ps-BED 4

Tell me: what is that thing that as it grows, will become less; and as it diminishes, is augmented?

## ps-BED 5

Tell me, what is that thing that has filled up the sky and the whole earth, smashes trees and shrubs, buffets all foundations, but it cannot be seen by eye not touched by hand?

## ps-BED 6

*What is it?* A mother produced me, and soon the same will be produced from me.

## ps-BED 7

I saw a son reared among four springs; if he was alive, he broke up mountains; if he was dead, he bound the living.

## ps-BED 8

Vidi bipedem super tripodem sedentem; cecidit bipes, corruit tripes.

## ps-BED 9

Vidi filium non natum, sed ex tribus personis suscitatum, et eum nutritum, donec vivus vocaretur.

## ps-BED 10

Vidi mortuum super vivum sedentem, et ex risu mortui moriebatur vivus.

## ps-BED 11

Vidi virginem flentem et murmurantem: viae eius sunt semitae vitae.

## ps-BED 12

Vidi mulierem cum sex oculis, cum sexaginta digitis, cum tribus linguis, cum uno ore loquentem.

## ps-BED 8

I saw a two-footed thing sitting on a three-footed thing; the two-footed thing fell, the three-footed thing collapsed.

## ps-BED 9

I saw a son not born but brought forth from three persons, and fed until he might be called living.

## ps-BED 10

I saw a dead thing sitting on a live thing, and the live thing was dying from the burbling of the dead thing.

## ps-BED 11

I saw a girl weeping and muttering; her ways are the paths of life.

## ps-BED 12

I saw a woman with six eyes, with sixty digits, with three tongues, speaking with one mouth.

## ps-BED 13

Vidi unum hospitem stantem super pedem, corpus eius de terra, sanguis eius de cervisia.

## ps-BED 13

I saw a host standing on a foot, his body of earth, his blood of beer.

# Tatwine

## TAT PR

Sub deno quater haec diverse enigmata torquens,
stamine metrorum exstructor conserta retexit.

## TAT 1

*S*eptena alarum me circumstantia cingi*T,*
vecta per alta poli quis nunc volitare solesco,
abdita nunc terrae penetrans atque ima profundi.
Sum Salamone sagacior et velocior euro,
5  clarior et Phoebi radiis, pretiosior auro,
suavior omnigena certe modulaminis arte,
dulcior et favo gustantum in faucibus eso.
　　Nulla manus poterit nec me contingere visus;
cum praesens dubio sine me quaerentibus adsto.
10  Mordentem amplector; parcentem me viduabo.

# Tatwine

## TAT PR

By turning these riddles backward after the fortieth,
their compiler unravels how they are linked by a thread of
    verses.

## TAT 1

Seven encompassing wings surround me,
supported by which I am growing accustomed to flying,
        now through the heights of heaven,
now plumbing the earth's secrets and the lowest regions of
        the deep.
I am wiser than Solomon and swifter than the east wind,
and brighter than Phoebus's rays, more precious than gold,     5
more pleasant surely than all kinds of musical craft,
and sweeter than honey tastes in the mouths of those who
        eat it.
   No hand can touch nor eye fall upon me;
when present, I am without doubt at hand to those who
        seek me.
I embrace the one who gnaws me; I shall bereave the one     10
        who spares me.

Est felix mea qui poterit cognoscere iura;
quemque meo natum esse meum sub nomine rebor.

## TAT 2

*U*na tres natae sumus olim ex matre sagac*I;*
est felix, eius liceat cui cernere formam
reginae, fausto semper quae numine regnat,
solifero cuius thalamus splendore nitescit.
5    Cernere quae nullus nec pandere septa valebit,
maternis quis nec poterit fore visibus aptus,
nostris ni fuerit complexibus ante subactus.

## TAT 3

*B*is binas statuit sua nos vigiles dominatri*X*
thesauri cellaria conservare sorores,
diversis quae intus fulgent ornata metallis,
omnigena et florum dulcedine serta virescunt.
5   Gaudentes nostris hec mox reseramus amicis,
ingratisque aditum sed iure negamus apertum.

Happy the one who can learn my laws;
and everyone born under my name I shall think of as my
    son.

## TAT 2

We three ladies were once born from one wise mother;
happy the one who is allowed to see the form
of the queen who reigns forever with goodwill,
whose bower shines with sunny splendor.
    No one will be able to see or open up those enclosures,    5
nor will anyone be fit for our mother's eyes,
unless first he has been caught up in our embraces.

## TAT 3

Our lady set the four of us up as guardian sisters
to keep watch on the storehouses of her treasure,
which are decorated and gleam inside with various metals,
and flourish wreathed with the sweetness of every kind of
        flower.
These we soon reveal happily to our friends,                  5
but rightly we deny clear entrance to the unwelcome.

## TAT 4

Dulcifero pia nos genitrix ditavit honor*E*
dulcia quod bibulis praestamus pocula buccis,
tosta ministrantes nitidis et fercula mensis;
sed tamen apta damus cunctis responsaque certa.
5    Littera tollatur, non fulget nominis ortus.

## TAT 5

Efferus exuviis populator me spoliavi*T;*
vitalis pariter flatus spiramina dempsit;
in planum me iterum campum sed verterat auctor.
    Frugiferos cultor sulcos mox irrigat undis;
5    omnigenam nardi messem mea prata rependunt,
qua sanis victum et lesis prestabo medelam.

## TAT 6

Nativa penitus ratione heu fraudor ab host*E;*
nam superas quondam pernix auras penetrabam,
vincta tribus nunc in terris persolvo tributum.
    Planos compellor sulcare per aequora campos;

## TAT 4

Our doting mother enriched us with an honor that brings
    sweetness,
since we offer sweet cups to freely drinking lips,
as we serve cooked dainties on snow-white tables;
yet we grant sure and suitable responses to all.
    Take a letter away, and the word's beginning does not      5
    shine.

## TAT 5

A fierce ravager has robbed me of what I once wore,
and also taken away the spirit of the breath of life;
but an artisan made me a level plain in turn.
    Soon a cultivator irrigates fruitful furrows with what
    flows;
my meadows yield a varied crop of balsam,             5
through which I shall offer nourishment for the healthy and
    a cure for the injured.

## TAT 6

Alas, I am completely cheated by an enemy of the purpose I
    was born to;
since once I used to dart swiftly through the lofty air,
but now, thrice bound, I render tribute on the ground.
    I am compelled to furrow level fields on flat surfaces;

5  causa laboris amor; is tum fontes lacrimarum
   semper compellit me aridis infundere sulcis.

## TAT 7

*O*lim dictabar proprio sub nomine caesa*R*,
Optabantque meum proceres iam cernere vultum.
   Nunc aliter versor superis suspensus in auris,
   et cesus cogor late persolvere planctum,
5  cursibus haut tardis cum ad luctum turba recurrit.
   Mordeo mordentem labris mox dentibus absque.

## TAT 8

*Q*uadripedis pulchri quamvis constat mihi form*A*,
sponte tamen nullus me usquam lustrare videbit.
   Bis binis certe per quadrum cornibus armor;
   quosque meis dapibus dignos satiare solesco;
5  indignis potumque cibumque referre negabo.
   Ex alta clarum merui re nomen habere.

the cause of the labor is love: that then always drives me    5
to pour out floods of tears into dry furrows.

## TAT 7

Once I was called by my own name, Caesar,
and noblemen used to be keen to see my face.
   But now, suspended in the upper air, I am turned into
      something else,
and, once struck, I am made to spread my complaint wide,
as a crowd comes together with unsluggish steps to lament.    5
   I am toothless, but with my lips soon bite the one who
      bites me.

## TAT 8

Although my form is that of a beautiful quadruped,
no one will ever see me walk about on my own.
   Square shaped, I am certainly armed with four horns;
and I habitually satisfy the deserving with my food,
and I shall refuse to offer the undeserving food and drink.    5
   From my lofty task I have earned the right to have a
      famous name.

## TAT 9

*V*ersicolor cernor nunc, nunc mihi forma nitesci*T;*
lege fui quondam cunctis iam larbula servis,
sed modo me gaudens orbis veneratur et ornat.
    Quique meum gustat fructum iam sanus habetur,
5  nam mihi concessum est insanis ferre salutem;
propterea sapiens optat me in fronte tenere.

## TAT 10

*A*ngelicas populis epulas dispono frequente*R,*
grandisonisque aures verbis cava guttura complent.
    Succedit vox sed mihi nulla aut lingua loquendi,
et bino alarum fulci gestamine cernor,
5  quis sed abest penitus virtus iam tota volandi,
dum solus subter constat mihi pes sine passu.

## TAT 11

*T*orrens me genuit fornax de viscere flamma*E,*
conditor invalido et finxit me corpore luscam;
sed constat nullum sine me iam vivere posse.
    Est mirum dictu cludam ni lumina vultus,
5  condere non artis penitus molimina possum.

## TAT 9

Sometimes I seem changeable in color, sometimes my
    shape shines.
Once, by law, I was a terrifying specter for all slaves,
but now the world, rejoicing, honors and adorns me.
    Whoever tastes my fruit is now considered healed,
for it has been given to me to bring health to the unhealed;    5
and so the wise man chooses to bear me on his brow.

## TAT 10

Frequently I offer folk angelic food,
as my hollow throat fills ears with thunderous words.
    A voice emerges, though I have none, nor tongue to talk,
and I seem to be supported by a twin foundation of wings,
in which there is absolutely and entirely no power of flight,    5
while a single foot stands underneath, unable to move.

## TAT 11

A burning furnace produced me from a womb of flame,
and my maker made me one-eyed and with a frail body;
yet it turns out that no one can live without me.
    Strange to say, unless I obstruct the eye in my face,
I am wholly unable to produce a skillful undertaking.    5

## TAT 12

*E*xterius cernor pulcher formaque decoru*S;*
interius minus haut mulcent mea viscera caros;
quotque diei horae sunt tot mihi lumina lucent,
et sena comptus potior sub imagine crurum,
5   unius sed amoena quidem pedis est mihi forma.

## TAT 13

*R*eginae cupiunt animis me cernere necno*N*
reges mulcet adesse mei quoque corporis usus;
nam multos vario possum captare decore.
   Quippe meam gracilis faciem iugulaverat hospes,
5   nobilior tamen adcrescit decor inde genarum.

## TAT 14

*H*aut tristis gemino sub nexu vincula gest*O;*
vincta resolvo ligata iterumque soluta ligabo.
   Est mirum dictu ardent quod mea viscera flammis,
nemo tamen sentit fera vinctus dampna cremandi;
5   sed mulcent ea plus vinctum quam dulcia mella.

## TAT 12

Outside, I seem beautiful and fair of form;
inside, no less do I delight my friends;
just as many eyes gleam on me as the hours of a day,
and I possess legs, being adorned by a sixfold likeness,
although my lovely form has but a single foot.          5

## TAT 13

Queens desire in their hearts to see me, and likewise
the use of my body is also a delight to kings,
for I can charm many with my varied fairness.
    Since a slender guest has previously pierced my face,
the fairness of my cheeks grows nobler still.          5

## TAT 14

Without sadness I bear fetters that are doubly binding;
I loosen tight bonds, and shall bind them up again.
    Strange to say, my innards burn with flames,
though no one bound by me feels the wild wounds of
      burning,
but instead they delight that bound one more than sweet          5
      honey.

## TAT 15

*A*ethereus ternas genitor nos iam peperit ho*C*
sub miserae fato legis de matre sorores;
invida namque patris cogit sors frangere fatum,
una tamen spes est tali sub lege retentis:
5  quod mox regalem matris remeamus in alvum.

## TAT 16

*E*merita gemina sortis sub lege tenemu*R.*
nam tollenti nos stabiles servire necesse est,
causanti contra cursus comitamur eundo;
sicque vicissim bis binae coniungimur ambis
5  quippe sorores; decreta stat legibus urna.

## TAT 17

*C*elsicolae nascor fecunda matris in alv*O*
quae superas penitus sedes habitare solescit.
    Sum petulans agilisque, fera insons; corporis astu
ardua ceu pennis convecta cacumina scando,
5  veloci vitans passu discrimina Martis.

## TAT 15

A father from above has already produced us three ladies,
sisters of one mother, under the fate of this sad decree;
for malicious fortune causes our father's fate to fracture,
but there is one hope for those of us held back under such a
    decree:
that soon we may return to our mother's royal womb.      5

## TAT 16

We are governed under lot's proper double laws:
for when we are subject to the one removing we must stand
    still,
but on the contrary when we go traveling we accompany
    the one accusing;
thus in turn we four sisters are joined to both:
our lot stands firmly determined by laws.      5

## TAT 17

I am born from the fertile womb of my lofty-living mother
who tends to live entirely in dwellings on high.
    I am pert and agile, harmless, wild; with bodily skill
I climb towering heights as if borne on wings,
avoiding with swift steps the perils of conflict.      5

## TAT 18

*D*iscernens totum iuris natura locavi*T*
nos pariter geminos una de matre creatos;
divisi haut magno parvi discrimine collis,
ut numquam vidi illum, nec me viderat ipse;
5  sed cernit sine me nihil, illo nec sine cerno.

## TAT 19

*I*nter mirandum cunctis est cetera, quod nun*C*
narro quidem: nos produxit genitrix uterinos,
sed quod contemplor, mox illud cernere spernit,
atque quod ille videt secum mox cernere nolo.
5  Est dispar nobis visus, sed inest amor unus.

## TAT 20

*U*us sum genitus lucifer fratris sine fruct*U*
eius sed propriam post ditabor comitatu
mortem, una vitam deinceps sine fine tenemus;
in vita, natum nullus quem creverat umquam,
5  hoc qui non credit verum tunc esse videbit.

## TAT 18

Nature, overseeing the whole of the law, has positioned
the pair of us born together from a single mother,
divided by the narrow space of a small hill,
so that I have never seen him, nor he me;
but he sees nothing without me, nor do I see without him.     5

## TAT 19

Among all other things, there is one to be marveled at by all
      people
which I describe now: a mother bore us brothers,
but what I gaze at, he soon refuses to see,
and what he sees, I soon don't want to see.
Our sight is not the same, but our desire is one.     5

## TAT 20

I was born a lonely light-bearer, without benefit of brother,
but I shall share his company after my own death,
and then we will have a life together without end;
there will be born to life the one that no one had ever seen,
and he who does not think this true will then see that it is so.     5

## TAT 21

*E*st mirum ingrato cunctis quod nomine dico*R,*
cum rarum aut dubium qui me sine vivere constat,
nec ego privatim constare bono sine possum;
certum namque bonum si dempseris omne, peribo:
5   iam mihi nulla boni innata est substantia veri.

## TAT 22

*R*egem me quondam gnari et dominum vocitaban*T,*
sceptri dum solus tunc regmen in orbe tenebam.
    Pro dolor! Heu, socia virtute redactus inermem
hostilis subito circum me copia cinxit,
5   ac deinceps miserum servis servire coegit.

## TAT 23

*S*aucio loetiferis omnes cum morsibus intu*S:*
iam rabidi trino capitis sub dente perimo;
sed multi evadunt binorum vulnera dentum,
tertius est nullus quem devitare licebit;
5   sed binorum alter mordet quemcumque perimit.

## TAT 21

It is amazing that I am called by an ungracious name by all,
when it is rare or doubtful that anyone can live without me,
nor can I exist by myself, without the good;
for it is certain that if you took away all good, I would die:
yet there is no aspect of true good innate in me.                    5

## TAT 22

Clever creatures once used to call me king and lord,
while at that time I alone used to wield the scepter in the
    world.
  Oh woe! Alas, reduced by the power of my mate,
an enemy force on an instant entirely surrounded me when
    unarmed,
and then compelled me, wretched, to be a slave to slaves.            5

## TAT 23

I wound everyone inwardly with deadly bites:
for I destroy with the threefold teeth of my raging head;
though many escape the wounds of two of my teeth,
no one is allowed to avoid the third;
but one of the other two destroys anyone it bites.                   5

## TAT 24

Egregius vere nullus sine me est neque feliX;
amplector cunctos quorum me corda requirunt,
qui absque meo graditur comitatu morte peribit,
et qui me gestat sospes sine fine manebit.
5  Inferior terris et celis altior exsto.

## TAT 25

Eximiae quondam sedis sum nata parentE,
quem diris vinctum dampnis regna spoliavi;
septenas pariter mihi deservire parabam
reginas, comitum septas cum prole maligna.
5  Parvulus ast obiens me iam prostraverat armis.

## TAT 26

Nos quini vario fratres sub nomine templuM
concessum nobis colimus constanter ab ortu.
Nam thuris segetem fero, fercula et ille saporis,
hic totum presens affert tangi, ille videndum,
5  ast laetam quintus famam tristemque ministrat.

## TAT 24

No one is truly outstanding or blessed without me;
I embrace all those whose hearts seek me out,
and whoever walks without my company will die the death,
and whoever goes with me will remain forever.
I am lower than the ground and higher than the sky.          5

## TAT 25

I was born from a father whose abode was once lofty,
whom, after he was bound by dreadful punishments, I
    deprived of those realms;
I likewise prepared seven queens to serve under me,
encircled with a wicked brood of companions.
Yet a little boy, standing against me, has laid me low with          5
    arms.

## TAT 26

We five, brothers with various names,
constantly tend the temple granted to us from the first.
For I bring the crop of incense; he the tasty dish;
this one, what it takes to be touched; that one, what needs
    to be seen;
while the fifth provides both sad and happy tales.          5

## TAT 27

*I*amque meum tibi quod narro mirabile dict*V*
fatum, nam geminis constat mihi robur in armis;
captandi sub rictibus est fiducia grandis.
   Non praedura vel aspera neu me fervida terrent;
5   rictibus intrepidis sed cuncta capessere tempto.

## TAT 28

*G*rande caput collo consertum sumere cerno*R,*
cui penitus nulli constant in vertice crines;
heu! Fato miser, inmobili qui sto pede fixus,
cedere tantundem siniturus verticis arcem;
5   insons vindictam sed nolo referre nocenti.

## TAT 29

*M*ultiferis omnes dapibus saturare solesc*O;*
quadripedem hinc felix ditem me sanxerat aetas
esse tamen pulchris fatim dum vestibus orner.
   Certatim me praedones spoliare solescunt,
5   raptis nudata exuviis mox membra relinquunt.

## TAT 27

Now the fate I tell you may seem strange to say,
for my strength abides in twin weapons;
I have great confidence in snatching with my jaws.
 Not hard, nor harsh, nor hot things do I fear;
but I try to grab everything in my fearless jaws.                    5

## TAT 28

I seem to bear a big head stuck on my neck,
on the top of which no hair stands at all;
alas, my lot is wretched, who stand fixed on a steady foot,
and will not allow the top of my crown to budge at all;
innocent, I won't pay back the harm I'm done.                       5

## TAT 29

I am used to satisfying everyone with sumptuous food;
therefore a blessed age decided that my four-footed self
be made lavish, while I am abundantly adorned with pretty
     coverings.
 Robbers are accustomed to plunder me eagerly,
and when what covers me is snatched away, my naked form    5
     remains.

## TAT 30

*A*rmigeri dura cordis compagine fingo*R*,
cuius et hirsuti extat circumstantia pepli;
pangitur et secto cunctum de robore culmen,
pellibus exterius strictum, quae tegmina tute
5  offensam diris defendunt imbribus aulam.

## TAT 31

*T*estor quod crevi, rarus mihi credere sed vul*T*,
iam nasci gelido natum de viscere matris,
vere quae numquam sensit spiramina vitae;
ipse tamen mansi vivens in ventre sepultus.

## TAT 32

*A*rmigeros inter Martis me bella subir*E*
obvia fata iubent et corpora sternere leto,
insidiasque gregi cautas inferre ferino,
nunc iuvenum laetos inter discurrere coetus.

## TAT 30

I am created with the hard frame of a weapon-bearing
    heart,
surrounded by the covering of a shaggy cloak;
the whole tip is driven in between split oaken strength,
tight with hide outside, and those coverings safely
shield the penetrated chamber from dread wetness.     5

## TAT 31

I bear witness that I emerged, but few want to trust me,
that I was born from a mother's chilly innards,
and she never really felt the breath of life;
though I myself remained living, buried in her womb.

## TAT 32

Opposing fates urge me to enter the battles of Mars
alongside weapon-bearing men, and to lay bodies low in
    death;
to set well-laid ambushes for the wild herd,
and now to fly among happy gatherings of young men.

## TAT 33

*T*estatur simplex triplicem natura figura*M*
esse meam, haut mortales qua sine vivere possunt;
multiplici quibus en bona munere grata ministro,
tristia non numquam; tamen haut sum exorsus ab illis.

## TAT 34

*O*mnia enim dirae complent mea viscera flamma*E,*
nam me flamma ferox stimulis devastat acervis
ut pacis pia mox truculenter foedera frangam,
non tamen oblectat me sponte subire duellum.

## TAT 35

*R*ubricolor flammor flagrat ceu spargine lume*N*
scintillans flammae seu ridet gemma rubore.
Nominis intus apex medium si nonus haberet,
gemma rubens iam non essem sed grando nivalis.

## TAT 36

*Q*uae me fata manent iuris testor rogitant*I*:
nam geminis captum manibus persolvere cogor

## TAT 33

My single nature bears witness that I have
a triple form, without which mortals cannot live;
to them I grant good services with a multifaceted gift,
yet sometimes sad ones too; but then I don't derive from
    them.

## TAT 34

Terrible flames fill my entire innards,
since a wild flame lays me waste with sharp stings
so that soon I shall savagely break the holy bonds of peace,
yet of my own accord it doesn't delight me to enter conflict.

## TAT 35

All red, I am enflamed, just as light sparkling
with a scattering of flame blazes, or as a jewel glows with
    redness.
If the ninth letter is added halfway in my name,
I would not be a ruddy jewel, but snowy hail instead.

## TAT 36

To anyone who asks, I declare what fates of duty keep me:
gripped by twin hands, I am forced to do my duty

ius sinuamine complexas et spargere sordes,
semina quod vitae pululent in pectore sola.

## TAT 37

*V*era loquor: quamvis fatum dubitabile finga*M*,
quod bona thesauri que condere destino perdam,
ut moriantur; quae vero perdenda reservo,
ceu dulcissima sint auri sub monte metalla.

## TAT 38

*E*xul sum generis factus mutante figur*A*,
postquam me perdendo ferox invaserat hostis,
expertem penitus vita formaque relinquens,
officinae servum deinceps me iussit haberi.

## TAT 39

*N*atam me gelido terrae de viscere dicun*T,*
inclita Romanis sed et urbs dudum vocitabar.
Sordida calcantum pedibus nunc sternor inermis,
ridet acumine qui rodens me lingit habunde.

and to scatter the sordid shells with my swinging,
so that only the seeds of life thrive in the heart.

## TAT 37

I tell the truth: although I fashion a doubtful fate,
I throw away the good things from my hoard, which I
    intend to preserve,
so that they die; and I keep what really ought to be thrown
    away,
as if those things were the sweetest nuggets of gold under a
    mountain.

## TAT 38

I have become an exile from my kind, when my form
    changed,
after a fierce enemy had invaded, destroying me,
leaving me entirely deprived of life and form,
then had me made a slave in a workshop.

## TAT 39

They say that I was born from the chilly innards of the
    earth,
but to the Romans I was also once called a famous town.
   Now soiled and helpless I am trodden underfoot,
but the one who repeatedly bites and licks me smiles keenly.

## TAT 40

Summa poli spatians dum lustro cacumina laetuS,
dulcibus allecti dapibus sub culmine curvo
intus ludentem sub eodem temporis ortu
cernere me tremulo possunt in culmine caeli
5  corporis absens plausu: quid sum pandite, sophi!

## TAT EP

*Conclusio poetae de
supra dictis enigmatibus*

Versibus intextis vates nunc iure salutat,
litterulas summa capitum hortans iungere primas;
versibus extremas hisdem ex minio coloratas
conversus gradiens rursum perscandat ab imo!

# TAT 40

While I wander, happily traversing the lofty heights of the
    sky,
those who are allured by sweet food under the curving vault
can see me playing inside and at the same point of time
also in the shimmering vault of heaven,
far from a body's touch: you sages, reveal what I am!        5

# TAT EP

*Conclusion of the poet concerning the*
*aforementioned riddles:*

With a woven thread of verses the poet now duly offers
    greetings,
urging the reader to join together the first letters at the
    head of each section;
then again, reversing direction from the bottom, let the
    reader make his way back up
through the rubricated letters at the ends of the same
    verses.

# Hwætberht, *The Riddles of Eusebius*

## EUS 1

Cum sim infra cunctos, sublimior omnibus adsto:
nullus adestque locus in quo circumdatus essem;
alta domus mea cum sit sedes semper in imis:
agmina devastans avertor laesus ab uno.

## EUS 2

Nuntius emissus discurro more ministri:
non labor ac tedium, iam nulla molestia cursum
tardat et intrantis vestigia nulla videntur;
cautior effectus casu quo corruit anguis.

# Hwætberht, *The Riddles of Eusebius*

## EUS 1

Although I am beneath everything, I am higher than all
   things:
there is no space in which I might be encompassed;
my home is lofty, although I always have a dwelling in the
   depths:
I crush whole armies, but am thwarted and wounded by an
   individual.

## EUS 2

Sent as a messenger, I run around like a servant:
no work nor boredom nor interference slackens my pace,
and there are no traces to be seen when I enter;
I have been made more wary by the fall through which the
   serpent fell.

## EUS 3

Incola sum patriae, cum sim miserabilis exul;
vinco viros fortes sed rursum vincor ab imis:
abiectoque potenter sunt mihi regna, potestas.
Est locus in terris sed ludo in sedibus altis.

## EUS 4

Haec mea materiae substantia bina creata est:
sed gravis una videtur quae tamen ipsa peribit,
cuius et ipse fugax defectum gessit helidrus;
tenuior est alia et quae semper fine carebit.

## EUS 5

Quaerite vos ipsi causam qua vendor avaris;
si me quique tenet nunc, postea semper habebit,
meque tenere tenax terrae sublime nequibit,
cum me nullus habet nisi qui fuit imus in illa.

## EUS 3

I am a native of a homeland, though I am a miserable exile;
I overcome strong men, but again I am overcome by the
    lowest:
and although I was powerfully cast down, I possess both
    kingdom and power.
I have a place on earth, though I play in deep abodes.

## EUS 4

This substance of my matter was created twofold:
one seems heavy, which, however, will perish,
a defect which the fugitive serpent has caused;
the other is finer, and will never have an end.

## EUS 5

Seek for yourselves the reason why I am sold to the greedy;
if anyone holds me now, he will afterward always hold me,
but the one who clings to earth cannot keep me, who am
    sublime,
since no one holds me who has not been the lowest there.

## EUS 6

Quos alo nascentes, crescentes scindor ab illis;
pascunturque bonis etsi me calce subigunt;
unde seducam nunc multos et supprimo natos,
nam perdent quod amant et nulli morte carebunt.

## EUS 7

Innumerae sumus, et simul omnes quaeque sonamus:
una loqui nequit: nos tetrae ludimus albis,
et licet alta loquamur, non sonus auribus instat.
Praeteritum loquimur praesens et multa futura.

## EUS 8

Dissimiles sumus et mos non similis tenet ambos;
unus contingi patitur nec forte videri;
sed prope aspicitur pulcher nec tangitur alter:
subvolat unus per caelos stat et alter in imis.

## EUS 6

The ones I nourish when newborn are the same ones I am
      torn apart by;
they are fed on good things even though they trample me
      underfoot;
for that reason I shall now lead many astray, and press upon
      my children,
for they will lose what they love, and none shall escape
      death.

## EUS 7

We are innumerable, and we all make sounds together:
one cannot speak alone: we black ones play on white,
and although we speak profoundly, no sound enters the
      ears.
We speak of the past, the present, and much to come.

## EUS 8

We are different, and a dissimilar nature maintains us both;
one can be touched, but does not happen to be seen;
but the other is lovely to look at up close, but can't be
      touched:
one flies through Heaven, the other stands in Hell.

## EUS 9

Dux ego linguarum resonans et prima per orbem,
dicor et unum, quingentos, vel mille figuro;
atque vocari primus per me coepit Adamus;
do domina linguae pueris me vim resonare.

## EUS 10

Omnis quaque via pergit, venit ut requiescat:
non mea sic via, non mihi sedes subditur ulla,
sed iuge restat iter, quod non finitur in annis;
non populi et reges cursum prohibere valebunt.

## EUS 11

Non labor est penitus pergenti in lumine Phoebi,
sed mihi difficilis longas discurrere noctes;
umbriferis varias in noctibus intro figuras,
postea deficiens; tunc offert lumina frater.

## EUS 9

I am called the leader of languages, sounding first
    throughout the world,
and I form the figures one and five hundred and one
    thousand;
Adam began to be called first by means of me;
as the lady of language I give children the power to make
    my sound.

## EUS 10

Every road, wherever it wanders, ends in rest:
my road is not like that, nor is there any resting place for
    me,
but my journey remains continuous, never finished in years;
neither nations nor kings will be able to check my course.

## EUS 11

There is no hardship at all for one traveling in the light of
    Phoebus,
but mine is difficult: to traverse long nights;
I enter various phases in dark nights,
afterward fading; then my brother grants his light.

## EUS 12

Nunc aro, nunc operor, consumor in omnibus annis;
multae sint cereres, semper desunt mihi panes;
et segetes colui, nec potus ebrius hausi.
Tota urbs pallebat quo signo verba sonabam.

## EUS 13

Sunt pecudes multae mihi quas nutrire solebam,
meque premente fame non lacteque carneve vescor,
cumque cibis aliis et pascor aquis alienis,
ex me multi vivunt: ex me et flumina currunt.

## EUS 14

Post alias reliquas augustus me creat auctor;
utor vi alterius nam non specialis imago
concessa est mihi, cum pro denis sola videbor,
unaque sum forma sed vim retinebo duarum.

## EUS 12

Now I plow, now I toil, exhausted through all the years;
there are many harvests, but I never have bread;
and I have cultivated crops, but have not drained drinks
    when drunk.
The whole city grew pale at that sign, when I sounded out
    words.

## EUS 13

I have many herds of cattle that I used to nourish,
but when hunger presses on me I feed on neither milk nor
    meat,
and whenever I consume different food and other drink
many live from me: streams flow from me.

## EUS 14

My august creator made me after the others;
I use the power of another, since no special function
is granted to me: although alone, I shall seem to be ten,
and while I have one form, I shall retain the power of two.

## EUS 15

Proelia nos gerimus cum iungimur ambo rebelles,
sed tamen ut multis bene prosint bella peracta;
non facie ad faciem conflictu belligeramur:
murus inest medius ne statim corruat unus.

## EUS 16

Me terrent proprii quos vobis confero mores;
vinum laetificans homines non laeta bibebam,
osque reducit de ventre que suscipit ore,
claudendi oris vel reserandi est vis mihi numquam.

## EUS 17

Per me mors adquiritur et bona vita tenetur;
me multi fugiunt, multique frequenter adorant;
sumque timenda malis, non sum tamen horrida iustis;
dampnavique virum, sic multos carcere solvi.

# EUS 15

We wage war, when we warlike ones are both brought
        together,
but nevertheless our battles are fought to be of use to many;
we do not fight in conflict face to face:
there is a buffer in between, so that neither of us
        immediately comes to ruin.

# EUS 16

My own habits, which I am describing to you, frighten me;
I never drank gladly the wine that brings men joy,
my mouth brings back from the stomach what it took in
        through the mouth,
and I never have the power to open or close my mouth.

# EUS 17

Through me death is gained and the good life is attained;
many run from me, and many frequently worship me;
I am to be feared by the wicked, but I am not fearsome to
        the just;
I condemned one man, and so freed many from bondage.

## EUS 18

Tempore quo factae fuimus pugnare solemus;
quaerimus armatos post nosque venire rogamus;
seque sequentibus una solet sub melle venenum
largiri, altera dat sub tristi tegmine vinum.

## EUS 19

Quinta vocor princeps vocum; est mihi trina potestas:
nam nunc sola sonans loquor aut nunc consono verbis,
nunc medium pactum retinens nil dicor haberi.
Me malus Arrius expellit de iure fidei.

## EUS 20

Nunc tego quosque viros a quis et retro tegebar,
ac durum frigus miserans hiememque repello;
tempore luciferi solis movebo calorem,
stans tamen, haec faciam; succumbens utraque numquam.

## EUS 18

From the time that we were created, we have always fought:
we seek out armed men, and ask them to follow us;
one of us showers those who follow her with poison decked
    in honey,
the other offers wine cloaked in misery.

## EUS 19

I am called the fifth of the vowels and the first; I have a
    triple power:
for at times I speak sounding alone, and at times I am
    consonant in words,
and at times, keeping a middle route, I am said to be
    considered nothing.
Wicked Arius banishes me from the rule of faith.

## EUS 20

Now I cover those men by whom I was covered back then,
and in pity I repel hard frost and wintry cold;
in the time of bright sunshine, I shall keep out the heat,
but I shall do that while standing; when flattened I shall
    never do either.

## EUS 21

Pacificari non volumus sed nec viduari:
continuum bellum geritur, non stantibus armis;
cum pax perficitur subter vel pugna quiescit,
unumque ex alio semper decerpitur insons.

## EUS 22

Pervolo valde celer currens per inania missus:
qui me mittit habet venturus sicubi mittor.
Ensibus igne securus sic penetrabo reclusa;
non videor volitans, oculorum adspectibus adstans.

## EUS 23

Motor, curro, fero velox, nec desero sedem;
tenue vagumque manens, tam grandia pondera porto;
Nix neque me tegit aut grando premit aut gelu vincit,
desuper aut multis sternor sed pluribus intus.

# EUS 21

We are unwilling either to make peace or to be parted:
perpetual war is waged, but there are no weapons;
when peace is completed below, or fighting ceases,
one of us, innocent, is always destroyed by the other.

# EUS 22

I fly very quickly, sent forth running through emptiness:
the one who sends me keeps me, though I shall go wherever
    I am sent.
Safe from fire and sword, in this way I shall penetrate closed
    places;
I am unseen as I fly, though I am there in the sight of eyes.

# EUS 23

I am stirred up, I run, I flow quickly, but I never leave my
    place;
remaining fine and wavering, I convey rather mighty loads;
no snow covers me, no hail crushes me, no frost defeats me,
nor am I strewn with many things above, but with many
    more within.

## EUS 24

Binae nos sumus: una est flens maesta tenebris;
altera perseverat tam lucida laetaque semper;
cum me plus homines instant conquirere tristem,
illa laetifica pereunt quae lumine ridet.

## EUS 25

Unus inest homo, qui tantum in me clausa videbit,
quique suis me non oculis conspexerat umquam.
Non sum magna domus, cum pervenit accola magnus;
nulla est ianua, cum tamen omnes me simul implent.

## EUS 26

Cum proprii generis viginti quattuor horis
unusquisque creatur, non ego solus adesse
possum; sed neque perficiar nec forte creabor
semper decursis nisi in ordine quattuor annis.

# EUS 24

We two are sisters: one is sad and weeping in darkness;
the other endures, rather bright and happy always;
whenever men insist more on pursuing me, the sad one,
they are destroyed by that happy one who smiles in the
    light.

# EUS 25

There is someone inside, who alone will see the secrets in
    me,
but who had never gazed on me with their own eyes.
I am not a mighty house, when a mighty guest comes along;
there is no door, yet everyone fills me all at once.

# EUS 26

Whenever each one of my own kind is created
with twenty-four hours, I alone am able to be absent;
yet I cannot be completed or created by chance
except when every fourth year has been fulfilled in
    sequence.

## EUS 27

Curva licet maneam vel strata soloque depressa,
me tamen hinc omnes nunc exaltabo tenentes.
Effera stans inimica mea sustollitur alta,
atque suos sternit vel comprimit illa sequaces.

## EUS 28

Quod reliquis in me libet, hoc mihi vile defectum
praebet, et extinguor quo multis lumina praesto.
Cumque aliis possim splendescere non mihi lux sum;
pars quoque quae multis lucet haec taetra videtur.

## EUS 29

Rite vicenis quadragies octies una
quaeque sororum formatur de more mearum
nempe momentis; tunc ego sola peracta videbor,
cicli nondecimus cum deficit extimus annus.

## EUS 27

Although I remain bowed down or laid low and forced to
the ground,
yet I shall later raise up those who hold to me now.
My enemy stands unrestrained, and is raised up high,
and she lays low or forces down those who follow her.

## EUS 28

What pleases others in me leaves me a poor remnant;
and I am destroyed by the very thing by which I offer
brightness to many.
Although I can illuminate others, I am no light to me;
likewise, the part that shines for many appears black.

## EUS 29

Each and every one of my sisters is properly formed,
appropriately, from exactly twenty times forty-eight
intervals;
but I alone will seem completed,
when the cycle's final nineteenth year is done.

## EUS 30

Armorum fueram vice meque tenebat in armis
fortis et armigeri gestabar vertice tauri.
Vas tamen intus habens sum nunc intestina amara,
viscera, sed ructans bonus ibit nitor odoris.

## EUS 31

Aequalem facie scindit me vomer acutus,
at sulcata manens semper sum seminis expers;
scissa premor post haec sed sum speciosior inde.
Nunc ego verba tenens, nunc saepe repello tenebras.

## EUS 32

Antea per nos vox resonabat verba nequaquam;
distincta sine nunc voce edere verba solemus.
Candida sed cum arva lustramur milibus atris,
viva nihil loquimur, responsum mortua famur.

# EUS 30

I once stood instead of weapons, and one strong in weapons
    used to keep me,
and I was carried on the head of a weapon-wielding bull.
But now, a vessel, I have inside me bitter gall as my innards,
but when I belch, a fine brilliance of scent will be sent
    forth.

# EUS 31

A sharp plowshare cuts me when I am smooth of face,
but, though furrowed, I am always without seed;
once cut, I am afterward pressed, but after that I am more
    fair.
Now I retain words; now I often drive out the dark.

# EUS 32

Previously, no voice produced words through us in any way;
but now we often broadcast words without a separate voice.
We are white fields, but are traversed by thousands of black
    things;
alive, we say nothing, but, dead, we utter an answer.

## EUS 33

In me multigena sapientia constat habunde,
nec tamen illud scire quid est sapientia possum.
Cum prudentia forte meo processerit ore,
tunc quod ab internis venit intus habere nequibo.

## EUS 34

Pergo per innumera flexis discursibus arva,
sed locus et specialis habet me semper et unus;
cum duo nomina praecedat mea sillaba eadem
*(incipit hoc una nomen qua sillaba et illud),*
5   nomine cur isto brevis est et longa per illud?
*Littera subtrahitur: post haec fulgebo per orbem.*

## EUS 35

Natura simplex stans non sapio undique quicquam,
sed mea nunc sapiens vestigia quisque sequetur.
Nunc tellurem habitans, prius aethera celsa vagabar;
candida conspicior, vestigia tetra relinquens.

## EUS 33

In me, wisdom of many kinds is contained in abundance,
yet I am unable to know what wisdom is.
Although by chance knowledge may come forth from my
    mouth,
I shall not then be able to retain within what emerges from
    inside.

## EUS 34

I travel through innumerable fields with winding routes,
but one special place always keeps me there;
although the same syllable begins my two names
*(both this noun and that begins with the same syllable),*
why is it short in one and long in the other?                    5
*A letter is taken away, and afterward I shall shine throughout the*
    *world.*

## EUS 35

I am simple in nature, and have no wisdom in any way,
but now every wise man will follow my tracks.
Now I live on the earth, but once I wandered through lofty
    skies;
I appear bright white, but leave behind black tracks.

## EUS 36

Sanguinis humani reus et ferus en ero vindex:
corpora nunc defendere nunc cruciare vicissim
curo; sed haec ago non nisi cum me quinque cohercent;
partibus attingor tribus et nece †tot pene† possum.

## EUS 37

Post genitrix me quam peperit mea saepe solesco
inter ab uno fonte rivos bis vivere binos
progredientes; et si vixero, rumpere colles
incipiam; vivos moriens aut alligo multos.

## EUS 38

Cum corio ante meo tectus vestitus et essem,
tunc nihil ore cibi gustabam, oculisque videre
non potui; pascor nunc escis, pelle detectus;
vivo, sed exanimis transivi viscera matris.

# EUS 36

Guilty of human bloodshed, look, I shall also be a wild
    avenger:
my concern is sometimes to defend bodies, sometimes to
    punish in turn;
but I cannot do these things unless five enclose me;
I am touched by three parts, and I can almost kill the same
    number.

# EUS 37

After my mother bore me, I often used to live
among four trickles streaming from the same source;
and if I should live, I shall begin to break the fields;
or dead, I bind many of the living.

# EUS 38

When I was previously covered and concealed in clothing,
then I tasted no food with my mouth, nor could I
see with my eyes; now I eat food,
stripped of my covering; I live, but I passed lifeless from my
    mother's womb.

## EUS 39

Effigie gracilis sum usurpans famina regum;
nempe mearum grossior est me quaeque sororum,
sed me vis sequitur maior: nam sola duarum
et regimen hominis aliaque sceptra patrabo.

## EUS 40

Non volo penniger aethram, non vago rura pedester;
sic manibus pedibusque carens me pennula fulcit.
Trano per undisonas ac turgida cerula limphas,
astriferumque polum et sublime peragro tribunal.

## EUS 41

Argolici me dixerunt septena cephala
olim habuisse, vocorque inmitis "scedra" latine;
ex quibus unum cum caput esset ab ense peremptum,
illius extemplo vice trina manare solebant;
5   sic mihi tunc nullus poterat confligere miles,
sed me ardente gigas combusserat Hercules igne:
sum pululans locus ex limphis vastantibus urbem.

# EUS 39

Slight in form, I assume the words of kings;
indeed, each of my sisters is larger than I,
but a greater power follows me, for alone of two letters,
I shall assume the governance of man and other dominions.


# EUS 40

I have no wings to fly through the air, nor feet to tread the
    fields;
but, lacking hands and feet, a winglet supports me.
I swim through the wave-booming waters and the billowing
    blue sea,
and I pass through the starry sky and the lofty judgment-
    throne.


# EUS 41

The Greeks said that I once had seven heads,
and in Latin I am called a fierce *scedra;*
if one of those heads were to be cut off by a sword,
immediately, three more would spring up in its place;
in that way no warrior could contend with me then,      5
but Hercules the giant burned me with a fiery flame:
I am a place teeming with waters that devastate a city.

## EUS 42

Horridus horriferas speluncae cumbo latebras;
concitus aethereis volitans miscebor et auris,
cristatusque volans pulcher turbabitur aether.
Corpore vipereas monstra vel cetera turmas
5    reptile sum superans gestantia pondus inorme.
Inmanisque ferus perparvo pascitur ore,
atque per angustas assumunt viscera venas
aethereum flatum; nec dentibus austera virtus
est mihi, sed mea vim violentam cauda tenebit.

## EUS 43

Cursu pennigeros celeri similabo volucres;
nunc fera sum maculis furvi stellata coloris,
nunc fluvius rapido dicendus valde meatu;
nomine nempe meo Persi dixere sagittam.

## EUS 44

Foedera multigenis reddens animantibus orbis,
trux ero valde draconi: sic erit aemulus ipse.
Me genitrix gestans alium generare nequibit;
et genitor dicor, si littera tertia cedat.

## EUS 42

Fearsome, I rest in the fearful haunts of a cave;
when stirred, I shall fly around, mingled with the lofty air;
soaring, crested, the beautiful air will be disturbed.
As a crawling thing I surpass in size the nests of vipers
and other monsters carrying vast weight.                        5
This huge and wild creature is fed through a tiny mouth,
and its innards draw the breath of air
through narrow pipes; nor does my pungent power
rest in my teeth, but my tail will show deadly force.

## EUS 43

In my quick flight I shall mimic the feathered birds;
at one time, a wild beast speckled with dark-colored
    markings,
at another, reckoned a river with a very swift stream;
the Persians, indeed, called the arrow by my name.

## EUS 44

Though I keep the peace with many kinds of the world's
    creatures,
I shall be very fierce toward the dragon, and likewise he will
    be a rival.
Once my mother has borne me, she will not be able to have
    another;
I too am called a father, if the third letter goes away.

## EUS 45

Muneror orbiculis ut pardus discolor albis;
lucror equo collum par forte pedesque buballo,
et cephal aptatum tuberosi more cameli:
respectaeque rei cuiusque resumo colorem.

## EUS 46

Saeva mihi genitrix atroxque est lena decreta;
crudelisque pater pardus pardaeque maritus.
Hinc velox, ferus; hinc trux atque robustus et audax:
nascitur ex ipsis coniunctum nomen habendo.

## EUS 47

Aspera orbiculis tergo scutalibus hirtis
dorsa stupescentes trucidare solesco venenis;
quos celeres cursu non cepi, capto colore.
Fervida natura pressis hiemeque pruinis
5  exuvias positura meas, brumalia calcans
frigora; continuis lucrabor nomina notis.

# EUS 45

Like the parti-colored leopard, I am adorned with light
    spots;
by chance I am granted a neck like a horse, and feet like a
    buffalo,
and a head like that of the humpbacked camel:
I adopt the color of whatever thing I see.

# EUS 46

A fierce and savage mother, a seductress, was ordained for
    me;
my father is the cruel panther, the she-panther's proper
    mate.
She is born swift and wild from the one, harsh and strong
and bold from the other, taking from them a compound
    name.

# EUS 47

I am coarse, with small, rounded scales rough on my back;
I often kill with venom those who are dazzled by my back:
the swift I could not catch with speed, I capture by my
    coloration.
Being hot by nature, I am about to shed my skin,
spurning wintry cold, when the frosts and winter are          5
    oppressive;
I shall take my name from my uninterrupted markings.

## EUS 48

Non sumus aequales quamvis ambaeque sorores:
tetrica nam facie est una stans, altera pulchra;
horrida sed requiem confert et grata laborem.
Non simul et semper sumus at secernimur ipsi.

## EUS 49

Flexosis geminum contractibus in caput errans
curro, caput nam trux aliud mea cauda retentat,
flammigeros gestans oculos ex more lucernae;
viperei generis solam me confero brumae.

## EUS 50

Porro senectutis fugiens discrimina ferre,
lumina fuscantur mihi sicque foramina tecti
illa parte domus quae solis spectat in ortum
intro, ac Titanis radiis inluminor ipsis.

## EUS 51

Vermibus ascriptus necnon serpentibus atris,
quislibet utrorum sociatus ab ore solesco

## EUS 48

Though we are both sisters, we are not alike:
one is gloomy faced, while the other stands fair;
the unsightly one brings rest, the lovely one labor.
We never appear at the same time, nor continuously, but we
    keep ourselves apart.

## EUS 49

Wandering in winding forms, I travel with a twin head,
since my tail contains a second fierce head,
bearing fiery eyes that look like lanterns;
alone of the serpentine kind do I entrust myself to winter.

## EUS 50

Later, escaping the burden of the problems of old age,
my eyes grow dim, and so I crawl inside a hole in the roof,
in that part of the house that faces the rising sun,
and so am brightened by Titan's very rays.

## EUS 51

I am counted among the worms but also among the black
    serpents,
but whichever of the two I belong to I am generally armed

armari bino; quod vulnere corpora caudae
inficiens virus diffundo hinc Graece vocabar,
5  et reliquos mordens artus non vulnero palmas.

## EUS 52

Porro triforme ferum vel monstrum fingor inorme:
setiger aptavit leo rictibus ora nefandis,
postremas partes draco diras indidit atrox,
cetera formae membra dedit fera caprea velox.
5  Cum filologi me dicunt consistere montem
nunc Cilicum, capreasque leones atque chelidros
gignentem: studio virtuteque Bellerofontis
sic velut occisus dicor cum nunc habitari
illius ingenio possum fortique labore.

## EUS 53

Nomen imago dedit servandum voce Pelasga:
narratur mihi quod dorsum, iuba, hinnitus aeque
assimilatur equo, sed rostrum vertit aduncum
ad frontem versus, mordens ceu dentibus apri.
5  Rorifluo cunctos degens in gurgite phoebos,
rura per umbriferas depascor florida noctes.

with a double bite; the fact that I spread venom by
    infecting bodies
with a wound from my tail is the source of my Greek name,
and, while I bite other limbs, I never wound the palms.     5


## EUS 52

In the end, I am fictionalized as a three-part beast and a
    great monster:
the shaggy lion gave me my mouth with its unspeakable
    maw,
the savage dragon added my dread hind parts,
and the swift wild goat gave to my body its other limbs.
Scholars now say that I am a mountain     5
in Cilicia, one that spawns goats and lions and serpents:
and that I am said to have been slain by the zeal and effort
of Bellerophon, since now I have been made habitable
by the shrewdness and strong labor of that man.


## EUS 53

My appearance gave me a name always to be preserved in
    the Greek tongue:
it is said that my back and mane and whinnying alike
resemble a horse, but my hooked muzzle turns
twisted upward to my brow, biting with tusks like a boar.
I spend every day in the flowing waters,     5
and in the dusky nights I graze the flourishing groves.

## EUS 54

Forma manet tenuis cum semipedalis imago est,
et tamen inmensas solus retinebo liburnas
sic tantum herendo; licet irruat aequora ventus,
saeviat aut pelagus validis motabile flabris,
5    ceu radicata ratis perstans at cernitur undis:
inde meumque moram nomen dixere Latini.

## EUS 55

Corpora si viva tangam, torpescere faxo;
propter hoc opus infandum mihi nomen adhesit.
Quin magis Indicus etsi me generamine pontus
ediderit, validi qui tunc me forte lacerti
5    longius attigerint contis seu qualibus astis,
torpuerint, et veloces vincire pedestres
possum, vel potius sic vis mea tanta videtur
aura mea afficiat sanos quo corporis artus.

## EUS 56

Porro soni crepitus proprii me fecit habere
nomen, nam quatiente ferensque crepacula rostro

## EUS 54

My form remains slight, since I am half a foot in size,
and yet unaided I shall hold back vast merchant ships
solely by sticking to them; although the wind should stir up
    waves,
or the inconstant ocean seethe from mighty breezes,
the vessel seems transfixed as if rooted to the water:    5
from that, the Romans gave me the name "delay."

## EUS 55

If I touch living creatures, I cause them to become numb;
because of this unspeakable deed a name has stuck to me.
Worse still: even if the Indian Ocean gave me birth,
and then by chance strong arms touch me
from afar with oars or any kind of poles,    5
they become numb, and I can cause the swift of feet to
    stand still,
or rather my power seems so great that
my very aura affects a body's healthy limbs.

## EUS 56

In the end, the particular noise of my sound gave me my
    name,
since with my creaking beak I produce a shattering cry

nuntia sum veris, multis stipata catervis;
hostis chelidrorum, nullum vitabo venenum,
5   quin potius pulli pascentur carne colubri.
Aequora transcendens me ducet praevia cornix,
lata cibabit multigenas has Asia turmas,
quas ego rorifluis collecta per agmina limphis
ut comites iteris habeo; sic sollicitudo
10   circa communis cunctis stat tam pia multos
natos, sic ut alentes hos vestimine carnes
nostras nudemus; sed quanto tempore nostras
progenies nutrimus, sic et alemur ab illis.

# EUS 57

Infandus volucer sum et nomen habebo Pelasgum,
et pennas velut usurpans avis advolo numquam
altius a terra et conceptum neglego foetum
forte fovere meum, sed fotu pulveris ova
5   sparsa foventur vel potius animantur in illo.

and announce the arrival of spring, surrounded by mighty
    throngs;
I am an enemy of serpents, and shall not shun their venom,
but rather my chicks will be fed on the flesh of the snake.          5
A crow traveling in front will lead me as I traverse the
    waves,
and broad Asia will feed these varied flocks,
which I have as traveling companions in groups
brought together from every watery way; so there is
for all a common care so supportive for so many young          10
    ones,
so that in raising them in this way we strip our own flesh
of its outer covering; but for just as much time as we
    nurture
our offspring, we will be equally cared for by them.


# EUS 57


I am an unspeakable bird and I shall have a Greek name,
yet although I take on the wings of a bird, I never fly
too high from the ground; and by chance I neglect to keep
    warm
my offspring once conceived, but by the warmth of the
    earth
my scattered eggs are kept warm, or are rather brought to          5
    life there.

## EUS 58

Garrula nigriferas noctis discurro per umbras,
vitans luciflui suffundi lumine Phoebi;
nomen habens furvum; visus hebetatur ob ortam
Titanis lucem, at Cretensis tellus habere
5    sola nequibit me: potius aliunde relata
extemplo austriferi patior discrimina loeti.

## EUS 59

India litoribus propriis me gignit amoenum;
collum nam torques ruber emicat; ala colore
tam viridi decorata est; et mea latior instat
lingua loquax reliquis avibus; hinc verba sonabo,
5    nomina et humanae reddam de more loquelae;
nam natura mihi "ave" est vel iam dicere "χαῖρε":
cetera per studium depromam nomina rerum.

## EUS 60

Ignava volucris, venturi nuntia luctus,
pigraque perseverans vertor prae pondere plumae,
noctibus et phoebis latitans tam foeda sepulchris,
furva per umbriferas semper constabo cavernas,
5    atque sono vocis nomen tractabo vocandum.

## EUS 58

Chattering, I dash through the darkening shadows of the
    night,
avoiding being flooded by the light of bright Phoebus;
I have a dark name; my sight is dulled by Titan's rising light;
the land of Crete alone won't be able to keep me:
in fact, if I am brought there from elsewhere,        5
I immediately suffer the dangers of a death brought by the
    south wind.

## EUS 59

India bears my charming self on its own shores;
my neck shines like a red collar, and my wing
is decorated in a bright green color; and my tongue
is more broadly talkative than that of other birds; so I shall
    speak
words and render names just like in human speech;        5
for it is in my nature to say "farewell" or "welcome":
I shall put out other words with further effort.

## EUS 60

I am a lazy bird, a harbinger of grief to come,
and I become persistently sluggish on account of the weight
    of my plumage,
lurking, so loathsome, day and night in tombs,
and I shall always stand, dusky, in gloomy caverns
and shall take the name I'm known by from the sound of    5
    my own voice.

# Boniface

## BON PR

Aurea nam decem transmisi poma sorori,
quae in ligno vitae crescebant floribus almis,
illius et sacris pendebant dulcia ramis,
cum lignum vitae pendebat in arbore mortis.
5 Cum quibus et ludens conprendas gaudia mentis,
et tibi venturae conplearis dulcedine vitae;
manducans mulso inspireris nectaris haustu:
spirantes nardi repleat flagrantia nares.
Cum quibus et malis conpares regna futura:
10 dulcia sic quondam celebrabis gaudia caeli.
    Sunt alia alterius ligni acervissima mala,
pestifero vernant quae in ligno mortis amarae,
quae Adam manducans dira est cum morte peremptus,
antiqui infecta et flatu et felle draconis,
15 vipereo ut dudum saeve perlita veneno.
Nitatur palmis haec numquam tangere virgo,
mandere quae nefas est et gustare profanum,
ne dentes strideant fuscati peste maligna,

# Boniface

## BON PR

So, I have sent ten golden apples to my sister,
which used to grow from fine flowers on the tree of life
and used to hang sweetly on its holy boughs,
when the tree of life once hung upon the beam of death.
Toying with these, may you gain the joys of the mind          5
and be filled with the sweetness of the life that will come to
      you;
chewing them, may you be suffused with a sweet draft of
      nectar;
may the fragrance of nard fill your breathing nostrils.
With these apples may you also gain the kingdom to come:
so one day you will celebrate the sweet joys of heaven.          10
   There are other very sharp apples on another tree,
which grow on the harmful tree of bitter death,
and chewing these, Adam died a dreadful death,
infected as they were with the breath and bile of that
      ancient serpent,
having just been wickedly smeared with the venom of the          15
      snake.
Let a virgin try never to touch these with her hands,
to eat these is a crime and to taste them profane;
may teeth not gnash, blackened by a vile disease,

talibus aut malis frangantur foedera sancta,
20  vel superi incassum perdantur praemia regni.


## BON 1

*V*incere me nulli possunt, sed perdere multi,
*E*st tamen et mirum, Christi quod sedibus adsto,
*R*egnans et gaudens superis cum civibus una
*I*ncola, sed quaerens germanam rura peragro,
5  *T*erras quas stolidi fantur liquisse nefandas.
*A*mplius in sceptris mundi iam degere nolo,
*S*anctam merendo tristis non nancta sororem:
*A*ntiquus vates cecinit quod carmine David,
*I*n terris vanos homines me virgine dempta,
10  *T*rans, ubi semper eram, fugiens nunc sidera scandam.


## BON 2

*F*ecunda et fortis vernans virtutibus altis,
*I*psius altithroni ductrix et nuntia dicor,
*D*um Christi populo per mundum labara porto,
*E*t virtute mea viventes legibus aequis
5  *S*acrantur Christo et demuntur crimina prisca;
*C*lamor cuncta dei cernentis praevia legis,
*A*ccola sum terris, sed caeli ad gaudia plures

184

nor holy bonds be broken by such apples,
nor the prizes of the kingdom above be lost in vain.    20


## BON 1

None can conquer me, though many can lose me,
and it is amazing that I live, an inhabitant, in the estates of
    Christ,
reigning and rejoicing together
with heaven's citizens, but also seeking a sister,
as I roam the earth, wicked lands that fools say I have left.    5
I don't want to live any longer in the realm of the world,
grieving sadly that I didn't find a holy sister.
As the ancient poet David sang in song,
men are empty on the earth when I, a virgin, am snatched
    away,
but, fleeing, I shall now reach the stars, where I always was.    10


## BON 2

Strong and fertile, burgeoning with high virtues,
I am called the guide and messenger of the high-throned
    one himself,
since I carry Christ's cross to people throughout the world,
and those living by my virtue under measured laws
are made sacred to Christ, and their ancient sins are purged.    5
I am proclaimed the herald of the law of the God who sees
    all things;
I live on earth, but I send many to the joys of heaven,

*T*ransmitto inlustres superis et sedibus aptos.
*H*ic sine me nullus Petri consortia sancti,
10 *O*mnibus aut Pauli captat qui finibus orbis
*L*uciflua promunt fuscis mea lumina saeclis.
*I*nclita me nullus relicta ad praemia regni
*C*onscendit Christi, misero nec gratia fulget.
*A*st tamen, heu miserae, non scando regna polorum.

## BON 3

*S*ancta comes faustos omnes comitata perhortor
*P*erpetuam meritis caelo comprendere vitam,
*E*t sine me scandit nullus per culmina caeli,
*S*ed tristem ac miseram post illinc fata secernunt.
5    *F*ortunata nimis, si non mentita fuissem,
*A*urea promittens starent ut ludicra mundi.
*T*errigenas iugiter duco ad caelestia regna,
*V*iribus ut freti tradant ad corpora poenas,
*R*egmina venturi captantes aurea saecli.

the splendid ones who are fit for the kingdom on high.
Without me, no one here gains the companionship
of Saint Peter or Paul, who, in every corner of the earth,                    10
spread my brilliant light throughout the dark world.
No one ascends to the famed gains of Christ's kingdom,
if they abandon me, nor does grace shine on the wretch.
Nonetheless (poor me!) I do not myself ascend to the
      kingdom on high.


## BON 3

As a sacred companion, I stand by everyone fortunate
and urge them to take hold by their merits of eternal life in
      heaven,
and without me no one ascends through the heights of
      heaven,
but, afterward, from then on fates keep me, sad and
      wretched, from that place.
   Oh, excessively fortunate, if I had not told an untruth,      5
promising that the golden deceptions of the world might
      stand.
I constantly lead those who live in the world to the
      kingdom above,
so that, relying on my strength, they may give their bodies
      over to punishments,
so gaining the golden realms of the world to come.

# BON 4

*M*oribus en geminae variis et iure sorores,
*I*nstamus domini cunctis in callibus una.
*S*ed soror in tenebras mortales mergeret atras,
*E*t poenas Erebi luerent per devia Ditis,
5 *R*egmina si saecli tenuisset sola per orbem,
*I*llius adversas vires ni frangere nitar,
*C*lamans atque: "Soror" dicens "carissima parce."
  *O* genus est superum felix, me virgine nancta,
*R*egmine nempe meo perdono piacula terris,
10 *D*o vitae tempus, superi do lumen Olympi,
*I*ngentem mundi variis cum floribus arvum,
*A*urea gens hominum scandat quod culmina caeli.
  *A*st tamen altithroni non sacris finibus absum,
*I*mpetrans miseris veniam mortalibus aevi,
15 *T*ranando iugiter Christi per saecla ministra.

# BON 4

Look: as twin sisters with different habits and jurisdiction,
we walk together on all the paths of the Lord.
But my sister would sink mortals into black darkness,
and make them pay the punishments of hell through the
     byways of Dis,
if she had had sole control of the world throughout the    5
     earth,
unless I strove to shatter her opposing force,
calling out and saying "dearest sister, have mercy."
   Oh, those folk on high are blessed since they have me, a
     virgin,
because under my authority I pardon sins on earth;
I grant a time for living: I grant the light of heavenly    10
     Olympus,
the vast plain of the world with its various flowers,
so that the golden race of men may scale heaven's heights.
   Nonetheless, I do not leave the holy borders of the high-
     throned one,
obtaining forgiveness for the wretched mortals of this
     world,
traveling always as Christ's servant forever.    15

# BON 5

Cernere quis poterit, numero aut quis calculo aequat,
    Splendida quae stolidis praestavi munera saeclis?
A qua praesentis moderantur dogmata vitae,
    Atque futura novi praestantur praemia regni;
5   Ritibus atque meis conplentur iussa superna,
    Talibus humanum semper miserebor in aevum.
Iuvavi mortale genus virtutibus almis
    Imperiis domino superis famularier alto,
Tetrica mundani calcant ut ludicra luxus.
10    Regina clamor, caelorum filia regis;
Ad requiem ut tendant animae, pulsabo tonantem,
    Actus vel dicti sensus seu ut vincla resolvant.
Sedibus e superis soboles nempe architenentis,
    Cuncta meis precibus restaurat saecla redemptor.
15   Arbiter aethereus condit me calce carentem,
In qua nec metas aevi nec tempora clausit,
    Tempora sed mire sine tempore longa creavit.

# BON 5

Who could surmise, or who could equal in number of
    reckoning,
  the splendid gifts I have bestowed upon the stupid
    world?
The teachings of the present life are controlled by me,
  and the future prizes of the new kingdom are bestowed;
heavenly biddings are fulfilled by my practices,         5
  with which I shall always show pity to humanity forever.
I have helped the mortal race with sustaining powers
  to serve the high Lord and his heavenly decrees,
so that they may spurn the filthy pleasures of worldly
    luxury.
  A queen I'm called, the daughter of the king of the    10
    heavens;
I shall press the Thunderer, so that souls may head to their
    rest,
  so that they may loosen the bonds of thought or word or
    deed.
Indeed, from the realms above, the son of the master of
    heaven,
  the redeemer, restores all ages at my request.
The heavenly judge establishes me without a curb,     15
whom he did not curtail by time or the limits of age,
but, outside time himself, he wondrously made vast periods
    of time.

## BON 6

*I*gneus en genitor fertur mihi Iuppiter esse,
*V*ocibus et virgo stolidorum famine dicor,
*S*ed scelus ob varium terras liquisse nefandas;
*T*errigenis raro facies mea cernitur usquam,
5 *I*nclita caelorum fuerim cum filia regis,
*T*alibus ut genitor moderans cum legibus orbem,
*I*n gremio gaudens et figens oscula patris.
*A*urea gens hominum semper gauderet in aevo,
*D*atam si normam servarent virginis almae.
10 *I*ncubuit populis, spreta me, turba malorum,
*X*risti dum iugiter calcarent iussa tonantis;
*I*dcirco penetrant Erebi sub tristia nigri,
*T*artara Plutonis plangentes ignea regis.

## BON 7

*P*er me probantur veri falsique prophetae,
*A*tque mali expulsi sanctorum a limite longe;
*T*empora non perdunt per me pia facta peracta.
*I*n proprium meritum pressuras verto reorum,
5 *E*t miro exemplo scaevorum dira piacla

## BON 6

Listen: Jupiter is said to be my fiery sire,
and in the speech and saying of fools I am called a virgin,
and it's said I left the wicked world because of various sins;
my face is rarely ever seen by those who dwell on earth,
since I remain the famous daughter of the king of the          5
     heavens,
controlling the world with laws, just like my father,
rejoicing in his embrace and fixing my father with kisses.
The golden race of men would always rejoice forever
if they kept the rule granted by the kindly virgin.
A crowd of evils has settled on people when I have been        10
     scorned,
since they continually spurned the commands of Christ the
     Thunderer;
and so they are thrust beneath the sad depths of black
     Erebus,
bemoaning the hellish fires of Pluto the king.

## BON 7

Prophets true and false are tested through me,
and the wicked driven far from the borders of the saints;
time does not diminish the fine acts performed through
     me.
I turn the blows of the guilty to their just deserts,
and, by my wondrous example, I change the dreadful            5
     punishments

*N*isibus eximiis commuto in praemia sancta.
*T*etrica multorum per me conpescitur ira,
*I*gneus atque furor rixae cum torribus ardens.
*A*ltrix virtutum, custos et sancta vocabor.
10     *A*rte mea iugiter conplentur iussa superna,
*I*n caeli cuneo Christi quia sedibus adsto;
*T*ranquilla aeternum regem comitabor in aevum.

## BON 8

*P*acificum passim fieret mortalibus aevum,
*A*eternum imperium regerem si sola per orbem.
*X*risticolis quondam e caelo sum carmine missa,
*V*era dei soboles ortu dum saecla beavit.
5  *E*n regnatoris saeclorum nomine dicor,
*R*egno inter Christi semper vernacula vernans,
*A*t terras iustorum habitans regina vocabor;
*C*aelicolaeque tenent iugiter me in culmine caeli:
*R*egmina quaecumque inlustro mea gaudia gestant,
10  *I*n quibus et non sum, precibus iam rogor adesse.
    *S*piritus et corpus, si digner servier ipsis,
*T*etrica pugnarum non torquent bella proterva;
*I*nfames fugio discordias semper ubique:
*A*rbiter aethralis iussit me semper habere.
15  *N*isibus infringor scaevorum et mente maligna,
*A*urea mira mihi sed parta est aula polorum.

of the evildoers to holy rewards by extraordinary efforts.
The foul anger of many is constrained through me,
and the fiery wrath, burning with flames of quarreling.
I shall be called the nourisher of virtues, and their holy
  guardian.
  By my skill heavenly commands are constantly fulfilled,      10
since I stand in Christ's estates in the host of heaven;
I shall quietly attend the eternal king forever.


# BON 8

There would be everywhere an age of peace for mortal men
if I alone controlled eternal power throughout the world.
Once I was sent down with song from heaven to Christians,
when the true son of God blessed the world with his birth.
Look, I am called by the name of the king of the ages,       5
a maidservant flourishing always in the midst of Christ's
  kingdom,
but, living in the lands of the just, I shall be named a queen;
heaven dwellers keep me constantly in the heights of
  heaven:
whatever realms I wander through bear my joys,
and in those in which I am not, I am asked in prayer to be.   10
  Body and soul, if I ever deign to be served by them,
do not engage in the cruel and fierce battles of conflicts;
I always and everywhere flee from wicked disputes.
The heavenly judge has commanded that I be kept always.
I am spoiled by the efforts and evil hearts of the wicked,   15
but the wondrous golden palace of the skies has been made
  ready for me.

Heu miseris longe quis sum mortalibus aegris,
qui in proprio tecto me dedignantur habere:
clauditur his superum caeli sub cardine regnum;
20  quapropter populi talem non spernite sponsam:
qua sine non caeli penetratur virgine templum.

# BON 9

*H*ic inter numeror sacras vix sola sorores,
*V*estibus in spretis specie quia nigrior exsto;
*M*ulti me spernunt, cunctis dispectior en sum;
*I*n terris nusquam similatur vilior ulla,
5  *L*ibertatis opem dominus sed dabit in aethra;
*I*ma solo quantum, tantum fio proxima caelo:
*T*erras indutus me Christus sanguine salvat.
*A*rdua caelorum conscendet culmina nullus,
*S*i me forte caret, propria nec sorte sororum,
10  *C*um domino Christo una sim carissima sponsa.
    *R*uricolae et reges, pueri innuptaeque puellae,
*I*nnumeri heroes nati melioribus annis,
*S*anctorum excellens martyrum pulchra corona,
*T*erribilesque viri meritis cum matribus almis,
15  *I*n tanto numero, excepta me, viribus audax:
*A*ltithroni nullus capiet pia gaudia regis,

Alas for those sick mortal wretches for whom I am far away,
who disdain to keep me under their own roof:
to them the kingdom above is closed beneath heaven's
    expanse;
wherefore, you peoples, do not spurn such a bride:       20
without that virgin the temple of heaven cannot be entered.

# BON 9

Here I alone am barely numbered among the holy sisters,
because I am blacker in appearance, standing in scorned
    clothing;
many scorn me; look, I am more looked down upon than
    all;
none meaner ever looked like me on earth,
though the Lord will grant the gift of freedom in the sky;     5
for just as I am lowest on earth, I have become closest to
    heaven:
Christ, clothed in me, saves the world by his blood.
No one will ascend the lofty heights of heaven,
who happens to be without me, nor my sisters, by their own
    lot,
since I alone am the dearest spouse of Christ the Lord.     10
    Rustics and kings, boys and unmarried girls,
heroes unnumbered born in better years,
the fine and fair circle of holy martyrs,
and men to be feared for their talents, along with
    nourishing mothers,
in such a number, without me, however bold in strength:     15
not one will gain the fine delights of the high-throned king,

*N*i iugiter nutrix et tutrix omnibus adsim,
*A*eterni placans et mulcens pectora regis.
   *F*lebilis et vacuus vocitatur mente monarchus,
20   *A*cta mea pravo tumidus si corde refutat.
   *T*errigenis paucis conprobor amabilis hospes,
   *E*t tamen altithroni nato lectissima virgo.
   *T*rano comes plures ducens super aethra phalanges,
   *V*iribus et sponsi fidens sum sancta virago;
25   *R*egi regnorum mea simplex foedera servo.

# BON 10

*V*itae perpetuae vernans cum floribus almis,
*I*nclita cum sanctis virtutum gesto coronam,
*R*egis saeclorum matrem comitata Mariam,
*G*audens quae genuit proprium paritura parentem,
5   *I*mpia qui proprio salvavit sanguine saecla.
*N*uncupor angelicis et sum germana ministris,
*I*gnea conculcans spernendo ludicra luxus;
*T*ollitur in caelum rumor meus ante tribunal,
*A*lmae martyrii dum gestant serta sorores.
10   *S*anctorum frontem praecingens floribus orno,
*A*urea flammigeris tranent ut ad astra coronis.

unless I am constantly the nurse and protectress of them
    all,
placating and soothing the heart of the eternal king.
   A monarch is called pitiful and empty headed
if he turns from my deeds, swollen in his heart.         20
I shall be proven a popular guest for few who dwell on
    earth,
and yet I am the choicest virgin to the son of the high-
    throned one.
I travel as a companion, leading many companies above the
    skies,
and I am a holy heroine, trusting in the strength of my
    spouse;
in simplicity I keep my pacts with the king of kingdoms.   25

# BON 10

Burgeoning with nourishing flowers of eternal life,
I wear the crown of virtues famously with the saints,
accompanying Mary, mother of the king of the ages,
who, rejoicing in her pregnancy, gave birth to her own
    parent,
the one who saved the wicked world by his own blood.     5
I am and am called the sister to angelic servants,
spurning and scorning the fiery pleasures of luxury;
my fame is raised up into heaven before the judgment seat,
while nourishing sisters carry the crowns of martyrdom.
I adorn the foreheads of the saints with flowers,        10
so that they may pass to the golden stars with flaming
    crowns.

*I*gneus ut Phoebus splendentia sidera supra,
*T*angor non pullis maculis speciosa virago.
   *H*ac auri vinco specie gemmata metalla;
15 *V*irgine me facie quia non est pulchrior ulla.
*M*e cives caeli clamant: "Carissima virgo
*I*n terris longe fueras, soror inclita, salve!
*L*ucida perpetuae exspectant praemia vitae
*I*nternusque dies atque inmutabile tempus."
20 *V*ivida quique mei proiecit foedera iuris,
*M*entis eius non ingredior habitacula demum.

## BON EP

Agmine post iuncto multis cum milibus una,
carmen selectum dicemus famine miro,
cetera quod numquam modulatur turma piorum,
aetherium dulci laudantes carmine regem,
5 qui proprio nostram mundavit sanguine vitam;
cui merito grates sanctas sine fine canemus.

## BON 11

*N*on est in terris me virgo stultior ulla,
*E*xistens cunctis neglectu audacior una.
*G*rates dedignor domino persoluere dignas
*L*impida quoque modo perlustrent lumina terras,
5 *E*t caeli speciem depingent sidera pulchram,

Like fiery Phoebus, above the shining stars,
as a beautiful virgin I am untouched by impure stains.
　With this kind of gold I surpass metaled jewelry,
since there is no virgin more beautiful in appearance than　　15
　　me.
The inhabitants of heaven cry out to me: "Dearest virgin,
you have been long on earth, famed sister, greetings!
The shining rewards of perpetual life await you:
a light within and a time without change."
And whoever has broken the living bonds of my law,　　20
never again do I enter the dwellings of his heart.


# BON EP

After the company has been joined, together with many
　　thousands,
we will utter a special song in wonderful speech,
one that the rest of the band of the pious never sings,
praising in sweet song the heavenly king,
who cleansed our lives with his own blood;　　5
to whom we shall rightly sing holy thanks without end.


# BON 11

There is no virgin on earth more foolish than me,
alone, existing more reckless in neglect than all.
I do not deign to offer the thanks that are due to the Lord
for the way that bright lights illuminate the earth
and stars adorn the lovely face of heaven;　　5

*G*entis humanae aut dominus quis conditor esset,
*E*x qua re varias voluisset fingere formas.
*N*on ignara mali, recti sed nescia vivens,
*T*ot hominum leges et iussa altissima Christi
10  *I*nfringens semper spernendo quaerere nolo,
*A*ut quid praeciperet mortalibus arbiter orbis.
    *A*rdua non cupio, vereor non ima profundi;
*I*n terra mortem timeo, non vivere curo:
*T*alibus exuberans dicor stultissima virgo.

## BON 12

*I*gnea sum fervens, turbo praecordia bellis,
*R*ixarum iactans iugiter per corda venenum,
*A*ntiquos scaeve lacerando dissipo amicos,
*C*aram iustitiamque dei mox dissico demens.
5  *V*iribus atque meis valeo depellere sensus,
*N*esciat ut ratum mens vano errore decepta.
*D*extera namque mea tradet fera corpora leto,
*I*nscia baccatur quando vertigine caeca:
*A*rdentes agito sermones ordine stulto.
10    *L*urida rixarum populis fera semina spargo;

or offer thanks for what sort of creator the Lord of the
    human race is,
or for the reason why he wanted to create various forms.
I am not ignorant of evil, but, living without knowledge of
    what is right,
I refuse to seek, but rather break and scorn,
the laws of so many men and the highest commandments of   10
    Christ,
or whatever the judge of the world has ordained for mortal
    men.
    I don't seek the heights, nor do I fear the deepest depths;
I'm scared of death on earth, but take no care to live:
teeming with such things, I'm called the most foolish
    virgin.


## BON 12

I am both fiery and burning; I stir up minds for war,
continually casting the poison of conflicts throughout
    hearts,
by wickedly attacking them I split up ancient friends,
and swiftly slice up in my madness God's dear justice.
With my powers I can also drive out sense,            5
so that the mind, deceived by empty error, does not
    recognize what is reasonable.
So my crazed right hand will deliver bodies to death,
when it rages, senseless, in a blind whirl:
I stir up enflaming words in a foolish way.
    I spread the wild and ghastly seeds of conflicts among   10
    peoples;

Omnipotens mandat sanctis me absistere templis:
Quae me circumstent non deinde pericula cerno.
Vox mea terrificis vaga personat alta loquelis,
Inrita dicta ferens et raro sentio vera.
15 Talibus in rebus spatior retrograda vivens,
Vana superstitione mea volo semper adesse;
Ritibus angelicis expellor ab aethere summo.

## BON 13

Cernebam tetrum lustrans per saecula monstrum,
Visibus horrendum nec dictu effabile ulli,
Pignora purpureo maculet quod sanguine terrae,
In varias caedes mortalia pectora cogens,
5 Dira fremens saevo passim cum murmure Martis
Ignea inferni animabus Tartara complet,
Terrigenasque tamen demulcet mente dolosa,
Auri materiem et fulvo splendore metalla
Sumant ut pretium, trucidato fratre gemello;
10 Aut gnatus auro bibat, genitore perempto.
Insane sapiunt homines, quia belua maligna est,
Tot tantosque viros multans cum matribus una,

the Almighty commands me to be absent from holy
    temples;
finally, I do not see the dangers that surround me.
My loud voice travels and resounds with awful words,
carrying inflammatory speech, and rarely do I sense the
    truth.
Living in such a manner, I travel looking back,          15
and wish always to be present, empty with my delusion;
I am cast out from highest heaven through the services of
    angels.

## BON 13

I used to see a foul monster wandering through the world,
dreadful in aspect and unutterable in any speech,
and it stains the children of the earth with its bright-red
    blood,
forcing mortal hearts to various slaughters,
roaring out dreadful things everywhere with the cruel    5
    clamor of war,
it fills the fiery depths of hell with souls,
and yet deludes the earthborn with a cunning mind,
so that gold objects and metals of shining splendor
they accept as payment, once they have cut to pieces their
    twin brother;
or so that a son drinks from a golden vessel, having killed    10
    his father.
Mankind completely loses its mind, because the beast is
    wicked,
destroying so many men so great, along with their mothers,

tetrica crudelis trudens ad limina Ditis.
Haud secus alloquitur mortales ore superbo
15  bestia pinnipotens dominans sub finibus orbis:
"Horrendum dicunt omnes, sed famine ficto;
carior at multis conprobor lumine vitae.
Ast ego infesta crudelior hostibus omnes
invisos habeo, et cum strofa sternere nitor.
20      "Non quisquam in terris numerus aut calculus aequat
milia quot passim strofosa morte peremi.
Reges et proceres docui temerare premendo
foedera at leges patrias propriosque propinquos,
haud secus ut populi perdant sua iura minores.
25  Pontifices multos temptans per devia duxi,
candida ut meritis non scandant atria caeli;
presbiterosque simul vastans per lucra peremi:
ordinibus sacris degentes sterno phalanges,
cum semel adgrediens comitabor fraude monarchos.
30  Cetera feminei sexus seu turma virorum,
si mihi consentit mortalia grana serenti,
perpetuo perdet mercedis lucra perennis,
horrida pestiferis cumulat tormenta maniplis.
        "Divitis et cuius propria dominabor in aula:
35  sollicitus pauper fit rebus semper egenus,

and, thrusting them over the dreadful threshold of cruel
    hell,
that beast with mighty wings addresses mortal men
just this way, with a proud mouth, beneath the edges of the    15
    earth:
"They all call me dreadful, but they don't mean it:
I prove to be more precious to many than the light of life;
but I, being dreadful and crueler than enemies,
hold everyone hateful, and strive to lay folk low through
    fraud.
   "No number or reckoning on earth can match    20
the thousands who here and there I have destroyed in
    deceitful death.
I have led nobles and kings to violate with oppression
pacts and the laws of the land and their own family and
    neighbors,
and likewise that lesser folk lose their own rights.
By tempting many bishops I have led them astray,    25
so that they do not deserve to ascend into the bright halls
    of heaven;
just so I have destroyed priests, crushing them with love of
    cash:
I lay low the ranks of those living in holy orders,
as soon as I approach their leaders and join them in
    falseness.
As for the remaining band of women or of men,    30
if they fall in with me as I sow deadly seeds,
they will forever lose the benefits of an eternal reward,
and pile up dreadful torments in deadly bundles.
   "As for the rich man in whose own hall I shall reign:
that one turns into a needy soul always requiring things,    35

nequicquam dapibus saecli saturatur opimis,
et mentis longa merendo pace carebit,
omnes magnanime spernit virtutis amicos.
Iustitiaeque fidem et pacem depello serenam,
40   et Christi humilitas longe disperditur a me;
sanctorum mansit numquam patientia mecum;
misericordia non umquam mea tecta videbat;
semper me horrescens fugiet dilectio sancta.
    "Natas priscorum clamant has carmina vatum
45   regis caelorum summa qui regnat in arce,
quas ego invisas damnando semper habebam.
Qui me bachantem sua subter tecta recondit,
concito caede furens, irarum maxima mater,
alter ut alterius fratres sua viscera rumpant.
50     "Conditor excelsus, dudum qui saecla creavit,
non me formavit pariter sub lege creandi,
sed priscus dudum in paradiso viscere natrix
edidit invisam superis sub fraude maligna.
Inlicio plures stolidos me amare ferocem,
55   dulcius ut mulsum quaerant quam nectaris haustum.
Quique tenet strictim strofosis actibus unam,
amplius in sceptris mundi invitatur habere;
non quod cernit habet caecatis mentibus errans,
nec suus est proprius, sed mihi servus habetur.
60     "Anthletis Orci dicor dulcissima virgo;

in no way sated by the splendid feasts of the world,
and someone who will in sorrow lack much peace of mind,
and arrogantly scorn every friend of virtue.
I also drive out the faith of justice and calm peace,
and Christ's humility is dispersed far from me;                    40
the patience of the saints has never stayed with me;
mercy never used to see the walls of my house;
and holy charity, horrified at me, will always run away.
   "The songs of ancient poets proclaim these daughters
of the king of the heavens, who reigns in the highest citadel,    45
while I always used to condemn them and consider them
     hateful.
The one who hides me, raving, beneath his own roof,
I egg him on, raging in slaughter, the mightiest mother of
     furies,
so that one brother spills the guts of another.
   "The lofty creator, who once fashioned the world,              50
did not form me through the same rule of creation,
but the ancient serpent in paradise brought me forth from
     its guts,
a thing hateful to those on high, through a wicked trick.
I seduce more fools to love me, even though I am fierce,
so that they seek a honeyed mead sweeter than a swig of           55
     nectar.
Whoever tightly holds only me with my tricky deeds
is incited to live more fully in the kingdom of the world;
he does not have what he sees, wandering with darkened
     mind,
nor is he his own man, but is reckoned my own slave.
   "I am called the sweetest virgin by those who strive in       60
     Hell;

caelicolae econtra vocitant me pessima belua,
quod plures populos mordens sub Tartara trusi.
Audivi quendam procerum dixisse priorum,
inlustrem factis, famoso nomine Paulum,
65 cunctorum stirpem et causam me esse malorum.
Prendere hunc mihi si traderet arbiter orbis,
mordendo trepidi tremerent sub dentibus artus."


# BON 14

Serpens angelicus genuit me in culmine caeli,
Viperea spirans et crimina noxia cordi;
Pellexi et populi insidiando milia multa,
E superis regnis trudens in Tartara nigra.
5 Regina et mater peccati et praevia dicor,
Bella movens animis, caste qui vivere malunt;
Irasque insidiasque et mille crimina trado;
Altera in terris non est crudelior ulla.
      Luciferum ut dudum seduxi fraude malignum,
10 Omnes sic passim mortales perdere tempto:
Qui me sub sinu gestant, se sternere tendent.
Viribus infestis alias convinco sorores;
In terris gradior, sed nubila vertice tango;
Terrificas grassans germanas subsequor una;
15 Viribus invisis sanctos in calce perimo;
Rectos ex armis propriis prosternere nitor.

by contrast, heaven dwellers dub me worst of beasts,
since, sinking my teeth into many folk, I have buried them
    in the depths.
I have heard that one of the ancient great ones,
outstanding in deeds, by the famous name of Paul,
said once that I was the fount and cause of all ills.      65
If the world's judge were to hand him over to me to take
for biting, his quivering limbs would shudder under my
    teeth."

# BON 14

The angelic serpent produced me in the heights of heaven,
breathing sins that were viperous and harmful to the heart;
by being cunning I have coaxed many thousands of folk,
thrusting them from the kingdom above into the black
    depths.
I am called sin's queen, its mother, and its guide,      5
causing battles in spirits who prefer to live in innocence;
I introduce anger and cunning and a thousand crimes;
no other on earth is crueler than me.
    Just as I once beguiled Lucifer, wicked in trickery,
so now I try in many ways to destroy all mortals:      10
the ones who keep me in their breasts will tend to lay
    themselves low.
In hostile force I surpass my other sisters;
I walk on earth, but touch the clouds with my top;
attacking, I follow my terrifying sisters together;
with hateful force I strike the holy in the heel;      15
I strive to defeat the righteous with their own weapons.

## BON 15

Clara fui quondam, sodomae dum farra manebant,
Regmina foeda tenens, donec pius ultor ab alto,
Ardentes flammas multans et sulphura misit.
Praevia sum luxus petulantis foetore carnis,
5  Viribus aequalis bibulae perfecta sorori.
Lurida nam dudum frangebam moenia sancta,
Aurea dum Solymae famosae templa ruebant:
Grandia nam populus mordax quondam idola fecit.
Vivere iam docui mediocres mente superba,
10  Lectos et proceres iustos quoque spernere victus.
Arte mea plures submersi faucibus Orci,
Externi ut superis miscentur civibus ignis.


## BON 16

Ex bibulis semper dinoscor condita buccis;
Blandius inliciens stultis sum cara virago.
Rixas irarum iugiter conturbo feroces;
Ignavos oculos et linguam famine trico,
5  Et pedibus tardis somnos et somnia dira
Toto infirmato mollescens corpore trado.
Aurea faustorum fugiet sapientia longe,
Stultorum passim persultant gaudia mecum.
Dulcem semper amat me sic luxoria matrem,

# BON 15

I was once famous, when the seed of Sodom still remained,
ruling their foul realms, until a conscientious avenger from
    on high,
in destructive mood sent down burning flames and sulfur.
I lead the way to wanton luxury in the foulness of the flesh,
being a full-blown equal in power to my bibulous sister.     5
For once, I, ghastly, shattered sacred walls,
when the golden temples of famed Jerusalem tumbled:
for once, the voracious nation constructed mighty idols.
I have already taught the mediocre to live with a proud
    heart,
and the wellborn and noble to despise right food.     10
By my skill I have drowned many in the maw of Hell;
like exiles from on high, they are mingled with flame
    dwellers.

# BON 16

Aromatic, I am always recognized by my guzzling cheeks;
enticing them rather smoothly, I am a maiden dear to fools.
I constantly stir up the ferocious conflicts of wrath;
I confound sluggish eyes and the tongue in speech,
granting sleep to slow legs and planting dire dreams     5
in the whole enfeebled body as I make it soft.
The golden wisdom of the fortunate will flee far away,
the joys of fools prance here and there with me.
So lust always loves me as her own sweet mother,

10    *I*llius in gremio iugiter nutrimina porto,
     *C*rudelis animas urens cum torribus atris,
     *E*dita stelligeri ut non scandant culmina caeli,
     *B*aratri repetant lustrantes ima profundi.
     *A*uferat humanis deus istum mentibus hydrum,
15    *T*ale homines ut non vastet per saecula monstrum!


# BON 17

     *L*impida sum, fateor, saeva sed fraude maligna,
     *V*sibus humanis dulcis ceu nectaris haustus,
     *X*risticolas passim perdens per tetra venena.
     *O*mnia pertemptabo ardendo viscera febre;
5    *R*uricolam rarum quemquam sine vulnere linquo.
     *I*gnibus internis animas ad Tartara duco,
     *A*urea luciferi ut non tranent culmina caeli.
     *A*rs mea escarum et vini nutrimine crescit.
     *I*nfelix mortale genus, quod bestia talis
10    *T*etrica mulcendo tradit per Tartara mortis!
     Heu miseri, talem, mortales, spernite gypsam
     quae matres maresque simul disperdere temptat!
     Parcite sumptuosos victus et sumere potus,
     quo solet antiquus serpens nutrimine pasci,

into whose lap I constantly bring nourishment,                                    10
cruelly burning spirits with black flames,
so that they may not climb to the lofty heights of starry
      heaven,
but, wandering, they seek again the depths of deep hell.
May God remove that snake from human hearts,
so that such a monster does not destroy mankind forever.          15


# BON 17

I am good-looking, I must say, but wicked with cruel
      trickery,
just as a draft of nectar is sweet in human usage,
and I destroy Christians here and there with terrible
      poisons.
I shall thoroughly tempt all the inner parts of man with
      feverish burning;
it is rare that I leave an inhabitant of earth unscathed.              5
By the fire I stoke within, I lead souls to the depths,
so that they may not travel to the golden heights of brilliant
      heaven.
My skill increases from the nourishment of food and wine.
Unhappy mortal race, that such a foul beast,
by softening them, should send them to the depths of                10
      death!
O wretched mortals, scorn such a serpent
that seeks to destroy both men and mothers alike!
Leave off taking sumptuous food and drink,
the nourishment on which the ancient serpent usually
      feeds;

15  qui Sodomae princeps quondam dum regna vigebant,
    igniferum rapuit dum cives sulphur ab aethra.

## BON 18

*I*mpia gignendo sum filia demonis atri:
*N*on sum satoris superi moderamine creta;
*V*iribus atque meis mors introivit in orbem,
*I*n paradisi hortos quondam dum vipera repsit.
5  *D*um fratrum aspiciam sanctorum facta tabesco:
*I*nfelix fatum tanta me fraude fefellit,
*A*c bona sic propria frendendo perdo dolose.
    *A*tque ego virtutum vastatrix impia dicor;
*I*gnea si pariter sum nec martyria prosunt,
10  *T*artareum macerans et torquens corde venenum.

## BON 19

*I*am dudum nutrix errorum et stulta vocabor:
*G*ermine nempe meo concrescunt pignora saeclis
*N*oxia peccati late per limina mundi.
*O*b quod semper amavit me Germanica tellus,

he was the prince of Sodom once, when those realms were     15
    strong,
until the fiery brimstone from the sky snatched its citizens
    away.

## BON 18

I am the daughter of a black demon, and wicked from birth:
I was not created at the dispensation of the heavenly
    Father;
by my powers death made an entry into the world,
when once the serpent slithered into the gardens of
    paradise.
While I observe the deeds of holy brothers, I wither away:     5
an unlucky fate has deluded me by such fraud,
and I gnash my teeth over their very goods, which I
    cunningly destroy.
    I am called the wicked devastator of virtues;
nor do even fiery martyrdoms avail, if I am also there:
a hellish poison in the heart, weakening and tormenting.     10

## BON 19

For a long time now I shall be described as a fool and nurse
    of errors:
indeed, from my seed there springs up in the world
the harmful offspring of sin widely throughout the expanse
    of the earth.
For that reason the German soil has always loved me,

5 *R*ustica gens hominum Sclaforum et Scythia dura;
  *A*dsum si gnato, genitor non gaudet in illo.
  *N*on caelum terramve, maris non aequora salsa
  *T*ranantem solem et lunam, non sidera supra
  *I*gnea contemplans quaero, quis conderet auctor;
10 *A*ltrix me numquam docuit, sapientia quid sit.
    *A*ltera sordidior saeclis non cernitur usquam.
  *I*dcirco, "invisam" vocitat me Grecia prudens,
  *T*etrica quod numquam vitans peccamina curo.

## BON 20

*V*ersicolor varie migrans per saecula lustro,
*A*uribus atque oculis serviens per devia duco.
*N*on una specie, varia sed imagine ludo
*A*uri flaventis passim argentique micantis.
5 *G*emmiferas species, ut ament, mortalibus apto,
*L*uciflua ut perdant venturae praemia vitae.
*O*mnigeno iugiter mortales agmine vasto:
*R*urigenas animas perdens per vulnera sterno;
*I*ncautis semper furtim mea spicula mitto:
10 *A*rte mea perdunt multi pia facta laboris.
*I*eiunium pariter, solamina et pauperis aegri,
*A*lmisonaeque preces claris cum laudibus una
*C*lam pereunt, factor si non est cautus in actu.

harsh Scythia, and the rustic race of Slavs;                                  5
if I am in a son, his father has no pleasure in him.
As I look at the heaven or earth, or at the sun and moon
traveling over the salty expanse of the sea,
or at the fiery stars above, I do not ask who their creator
       was:
no mother ever taught me what wisdom is.                                      10
    Nowhere in the world is another more sordid seen,
and so wise Greece calls me "unperceived,"
because I never take pains to avoid filthy sins.


# BON 20


I wander flitting through the world, variously changeable in
      hue,
ministering to ears and eyes, and leading them astray
      through byways.
I do not toy with a single form, but with a multiple likeness
of tawny gold and shining silver in turns.
I fit jeweled forms to mortals to make them love them,                       5
so that they lose the brilliant rewards of the life to come.
I continually devastate mortals in every kind of conflict:
I lay low worldly spirits, destroying them with wounds;
I always cast my darts cunningly at the unwary:
by my craft many lose the pious deeds won by labor.                          10
In equal measure, fasting and the comfort of the poor and
      sick,
consoling prayers, together with bright praise, quietly fail,
if the one who does them is not cautious in the act.

*T*alia patrantem vocitant me "virgo maligna,"
15  *A*urea venturae qui quaerunt munera vitae.
*N*on cesso spolians plures mercede futura;
*T*errigenas Christi pererrans omnia tempto,
*I*ntemerata fides nusquam ut videatur in orbe,
*A*eterna et felix perdet habitacula miles.
20      Et gemma et aurum et vestis, lanugine texunt
quam Seres vermes, propria ad mea iura recurrunt.
Omnia humanis non necessaria rebus,
quae homines longe lateque habere videntur:
usibus ecce meis serviunt sub mente superba;
25  falsior inter nos probatur nulla sororum.

For bringing about such things they name me "a wicked
    virgin,"
those who seek the golden rewards of the life to come.       15
I never cease depriving more folk of future reward;
wandering among Christ's worldly ones, I try all things,
so that pure faith may never be seen in the world,
and the blessed warrior lose eternal dwellings.

   The gem and the gold and the garment that       20
Chinese worms weave from their floss: they keep coming
    under my sway.
Everything unnecessary to human needs,
which mankind seems to possess both far and wide:
look, they serve my purposes inside a proud heart;
none of us sisters is proved to be more false.       25

# Alcuin

## ALC 1

Bestia nam subito nostras subrepserat aedes,
in qua imago fuit capitum miranda duorum,
quae maxilla tamen pariter coniunxerat una,
bis ternis decies sed dentibus horruit illa.
5  Esca fuit crescens illis de corpore vivo
nec caro, nec fruges. Fructus nec vina bibentum
dentibus edebat; patulo non tabuit ore.
Scis, Damoeta meus, quae sit haec bestia talis?

## ALC 2

Causa necis fueram, tamen et nil nuncupor esse;
ordine quisque legat recto me, comedet et me;
me super ille equitet, transverso qui legat ore.

# Alcuin

## ALC 1

A beast had all of a sudden crept into our house,
a creature on which there was the amazing spectacle of two
      heads,
which, however, a single jaw connected,
though it bristled with sixty teeth. Their food, which grew
from a living body, was neither meat nor produce;     5
it used to bring forth for the teeth neither fruits nor wines
      for drinking.
Yet that creature, with its gaping mouth, did not fade away.
Do you know, my Damoetas, what kind of beast is this?

## ALC 2

I was the cause of death, although I am also said to be
      nothing;
and whoever reads me in the right order will eat me;
he may ride me, who reads me in reverse.

## ALC 3

Sex mihi litterulae sunt et praeclara potestas;
disrumpis nomen medio de tramite totum,
pars colet una deum, hominem pars altera signat;
littera tollatur faciet mox quarta venenum.

## ALC 4

Est vir iam totus canuto vertice sanus,
matrona effectus prima pereunte figura;
post primam binae pereunt, erit horrida scrofa.

## ALC 5

Presbyter integro celebravit nomine missam;
littera tollatur, praestat convivia paschae.
Atque minister erit, tollatur tertia, mensae;
quartaque tollatur, miscet mala verba venenis;
5  fur erit, addatur extremis prima duabus;
tertia cum prima tollatur littera, mirum;
decrepita adcurrit nixa dolabra per aedes.

## ALC 3

I have six letters and a splendid power:
if you split my whole name in the middle
one part will worship God, the other means "man";
take away the fourth letter, and soon it will produce poison.

## ALC 4

There is a whole man healthy with a hoary head,
made an old woman when the first letter disappears;
when the two after the first disappear, there will be a
      bristling sow.

## ALC 5

A priest celebrated mass with name intact;
take away a letter, and it offers the Easter feast.
When the third is taken away, there will be the table's
      servant;
take away the fourth: one mixes wicked words with poison;
there will be a thief, when the first is added to the two last;    5
when the first and third are taken away, amazingly,
a decrepit, struggling slave woman dashes up through the
      hall.

## ALC 6

Tu qui pergis iter per celsa palatia, lector:
dic duo quae moveant totas monosyllaba lites;
dic duo quae sanctam rumpunt pronomina pacem;
dic duo quae faciunt pronomina nomina cunctis;
5  omnia dic, quae sunt verbi, quae syllaba signet,
qualiter et tecum loquitur, qui non fuit umquam.
Haec lege, solve cito, aut aurum persolve poetae.

## ALC 7

Si mea dona tibi cupias, nimbose viator,
    da prior ecce tua, sic tibi prende mea.
Est mihi venter edax, calido qui pascitur igne;
    vertice sub quadro fumidus exit odor.
5  Ad me mox hospes gelido fugit imbre Decembri,
    a me qui Augusto florida in arva fugit.

## ALC 8

En, ego pulcra foras sum, sed magis utilis intus,
est calidus venter, feritur dum frigore vertex.

## ALC 6

You, reader, as you wander through the lofty palaces:
tell me the two monosyllables that cause all conflicts;
tell me the two pronouns that disturb the holy peace;
tell me the two pronouns that produce nouns for all;
tell me everything about the word, what the syllable means,  5
and how the one who never was speaks with you.
Read these lines, solve them quickly, or give the poet gold.

## ALC 7

If you want my gifts for yourself, drenched wanderer,
    look: first give yours, then take mine to yourself.
My belly is greedy, fed by blazing fire;
    a smoky smell emerges from the corners of my head.
A guest soon rushes to me from the chilly December storm,  5
    and shuns me in August for the burgeoning fields.

## ALC 8

I am beautiful on the outside, but much more useful within,
my belly is hot, even when my head is stricken with cold.

## ALC 9

Avidus hospes amat gelidae me tempore brumae,
    qui calida aestate spernit adesse mihi.
Os in ventre mihi est, quadrato in gutture nares,
    qui spirat fumum, dum calet ille foco.

## ps-ALC 1

Grammatibus duplici mutata descripta vocali:
indico factorem caeli terraeque marisque;
littera, littera, littera, nexae parte sub una:
sic Pater et Genitus necnon cum Flamine Sancto
5   creditur esse Deus unus qui sidera torquet.

*Pippini regalis et nobilissimi iuvenis*
*disputatio cum Albino scholastico*

## ALC D1

*Pippinus* Quid est littera?    *Albinus* Custos historiae.

## ALC D2

*P.* Quid est verbum?   *A.* Proditor animi.
*P.* Quis generat verbum?   *A.* Lingua.

# ALC 9

The keen guest loves me in the time of cold winter,
　　and scorns to be with me in the hot summer.
My mouth is in my belly, my nostrils in my square throat,
　　that breaths out smoke, while it warms at the hearth.

# ps-ALC 1

When I am written out in letters and the two vowels are
　　changed,
I indicate the creator of heaven and earth and the sea;
letter, letter, letter, joined in one part:
just as the Father and Son, along with the Holy Spirit
are believed to be the one God who turns the stars.　　5

*Debate between the Royal and Most Noble Youth
Pippin and the Scholar Alcuin*

# ALC D1

*Pippin* What is a letter?　*Alcuin* The keeper of story.

# ALC D2

*P.* What is a word?　*A.* The betrayer of the mind.
*P.* What produces a word?　*A.* The tongue.

## ALC D3

*P.* Quid est lingua?　*A.* Flagellum aeris.

## ALC D4

*P.* Quid est aer?　*A.* Custodia vitae.

## ALC D5

*P.* Quid est vita?　*A.* Beatorum laetitia, miserorum maesti-
tia, exspectatio mortis.

## ALC D6

*P.* Quid est mors?　*A.* Inevitabilis eventus, incerta peregri-
natio, lacrimae viventium, testamenti firmamentum, latro
hominis.

## ALC D7

*P.* Quid est homo?　*A.* Mancipium mortis, transiens viator,
loci hospes.
*P.* Cui similis est homo?　*A.* Pomo.
*P.* Quomodo positus est homo?　*A.* Ut lucerna in vento.
*P.* Ubi est positus?　*A.* Intra sex parietes.

## ALC D3

*P.* What is the tongue?   *A.* The beater of breath.

## ALC D4

*P.* What is breath?   *A.* The guardian of life.

## ALC D5

*P.* What is life?   *A.* The joy of the blessed, the sorrow of the wretched, the expectation of death.

## ALC D6

*P.* What is death?   *A.* An inevitable outcome, an uncertain journey, the tears of the living, the foundation of a testament, the robber of mankind.

## ALC D7

*P.* What is mankind?   *A.* The slave of death, a traveler passing through, a guest in the house.
*P.* What is mankind like?   *A.* A fruit tree.
*P.* How is mankind placed?   *A.* Like a lantern in the wind.
*P.* Placed where?   *A.* Within six walls.

*P.* Quos?    *A.* Supra, subtus; ante, retro; dextra laevaque.
*P.* Quot habet socios?    *A* Quattuor.
*P.* Quos?    *A.* Calorem, frigus, siccitatem, humorem.
*P.* Quot modis variabilis est?    *A.* Sex.
*P.* Quibus?    *A.* Esurie et saturitate; requie et labore; vigiliis et somno.

## ALC D8

*P.* Quid est somnus?    *A.* Mortis imago.

## ALC D9

*P.* Quid est libertas hominis?    *A.* Innocentia.

## ALC D10

*P.* Quid est caput?    *A.* Culmen corporis.

## ALC D11

*P.* Quid est corpus?    *A.* Domicilium animae.

## ALC D12

*P.* Quid sunt comae?    *A.* Vestes capitis.

*P.* Which?    *A.* Above, below; before, behind; right and left.
*P.* How many partners has he or she?    *A.* Four.
*P.* Which?    *A.* Heat, cold, dryness, moisture.
*P.* Liable to change in how many ways?    *A.* Six.
*P.* Which?    *A.* From hunger and from fullness, from rest and from labor, from wakefulness and from sleep.


## ALC D8

*P.* What is sleep?    *A.* The semblance of death.


## ALC D9

*P.* What is the freedom of mankind?    *A.* Absence of harm.


## ALC D10

*P.* What is the head?    *A.* The top of the body.


## ALC D11

*P.* What is the body?    *A.* The dwelling of the soul.


## ALC D12

*P.* What is hair?    *A.* The clothing of the head.

## ALC D13

*P.* Quid est barba?    *A.* Sexus discretio, honor aetatis.

## ALC D14

*P.* Quid est cerebrum?    *A.* Servator memoriae.

## ALC D15

*P.* Quid sunt oculi?    *A.* Duces corporis, vasa luminis, animi indices.

## ALC D16

*P.* Quid sunt nares?    *A.* Adductio odorum.

## ALC D17

*P.* Quid sunt aures?    *A.* Collatores sonorum.

## ALC D18

*P.* Quid est frons?    *A.* Imago animi.

## ALC D13

*P.* What is a beard?    *A.* A distinguisher of gender, a badge of age.

## ALC D14

*P.* What is the brain?    *A.* The keeper of memory.

## ALC D15

*P.* What are the eyes?    *A.* The rulers of the body, a vessel of light, the indicators of the mind.

## ALC D16

*P.* What are the nostrils?    *A.* The conduit for smells.

## ALC D17

*P.* What are the ears?    *A.* The collectors of sounds.

## ALC D18

*P.* What is the face?    *A.* The semblance of the mind.

## ALC D19

*P.* Quid est os?    *A.* Nutritor corporis.

## ALC D20

*P.* Quid sunt dentes?    *A.* Molae morsorum.

## ALC D21

*P.* Quid sunt labia?    *A.* Valvae oris.

## ALC D22

*P.* Quid est gula?    *A.* Devorator cibi.

## ALC D23

*P.* Quid manus?    *A.* Operarii corporis.

## ALC D24

*P.* Quid sunt digiti?    *A.* Chordarum plectra.

## ALC D19

*P.* What is the mouth?　*A.* The feeder of the body.

## ALC D20

*P.* What are teeth?　*A.* The millstones of morsels.

## ALC D21

*P.* What are the lips?　*A.* The doorways of the mouth.

## ALC D22

*P.* What is the throat?　*A.* The swallower of food.

## ALC D23

*P.* What are the hands?　*A.* The workers of the body.

## ALC D24

*P.* What are the fingers?　*A.* The pluckers of strings.

## ALC D25

*P.* Quid est pulmo?    *A.* Servator aeris.

## ALC D26

*P.* Quid est cor?    *A.* Receptaculum vitae.

## ALC D27

*P.* Quid est iecur?    *A.* Custodia caloris.

## ALC D28

*P.* Quid est fel?    *A.* Suscitatio iracundiae.

## ALC D29

*P.* Quid est splenis?    *A.* Risus et laetitiae capax.

## ALC D30

*P.* Quid est stomachus?    *A.* Ciborum coctor.

## ALC D25

*P.* What is a lung?   *A.* The keeper of breath.

## ALC D26

*P.* What is the heart?   *A.* The coffer of life.

## ALC D27

*P.* What is the liver?   *A.* The guardian of heat.

## ALC D28

*P.* What is the gallbladder?   *A.* The arousal of rage.

## ALC D29

*P.* What is the spleen?   *A.* What holds laughter and happiness.

## ALC D30

*P.* What is the stomach?   *A.* The cook of food.

## ALC D31

*P.* Quid est venter?    *A.* Custos fragilium.

## ALC D32

*P.* Quid sunt ossa?    *A.* Fortitudo corporis.

## ALC D33

*P.* Quid sunt coxae?    *A.* Epistylia columnarum.

## ALC D34

*P.* Quid sunt crura?    *A.* Columnae corporis.

## ALC D35

*P.* Quid sunt pedes?    *A.* Mobile fundamentum.

## ALC D36

*P.* Quid est sanguis?    *A.* Humor venarum, vitae alimentum.

## ALC D31

*P.* What is the belly?    *A.* The keeper of crumbs.

## ALC D32

*P.* What are the bones?    *A.* The strength of the body.

## ALC D33

*P.* What are the hips?    *A.* The architraves of the columns.

## ALC D34

*P.* What are the legs?    *A.* The columns of the body.

## ALC D35

*P.* What are the feet?    *A.* A moving foundation.

## ALC D36

*P.* What is blood?    *A.* What flows through the veins, the nourishment of life.

## ALC D37

*P.* Quid sunt venae?   *A.* Fontes carnis.

## ALC D38

*P.* Quid est caelum?   *A.* Sphera volubilis, culmen immensum.

## ALC D39

*P.* Quid est lux?   *A.* Facies omnium rerum.

## ALC D40

*P.* Quid est dies?   *A.* Incitamentum laboris.

## ALC D41

*P.* Quid est sol?   *A.* Splendor orbis, coeli pulchritudo, naturae gratia, honor diei, horarum distributor.

## ALC D37

*P.* What are the veins? *A.* The fountains of the flesh.

## ALC D38

*P.* What is the sky? *A.* The revolving sphere, an immense height.

## ALC D39

*P.* What is light? *A.* The appearance of all things.

## ALC D40

*P.* What is day? *A.* The spur to work.

## ALC D41

*P.* What is the sun? *A.* The glory of the world, the beauty of the sky, the grace of nature, the adornment of the day, the distributor of hours.

## ALC D42

*P.* Quid est luna? *A.* Oculus noctis, roris larga, praesaga tempestatum.

## ALC D43

*P.* Quid sunt stellae? *A.* Pictura culminis, nautarum gubernatores, noctis decor.

## ALC D44

*P.* Quid est pluvia? *A.* Conceptio terrae, frugum genitrix.

## ALC D45

*P.* Quid est nebula? *A.* Nox in die, labor oculorum.

## ALC D46

*P.* Quid est ventus? *A.* Aeris perturbatio, mobilitas aquarum, siccitas terrae.

## ALC D42

*P.* What is the moon?  *A.* The eye of night, dispenser of dew, the prophetess of storms.

## ALC D43

*P.* What are the stars?  *A.* A painting of the vault, the steerers of sailors, the ornament of night.

## ALC D44

*P.* What is the rain?  *A.* The fertilizer of earth, the spawner of produce.

## ALC D45

*P.* What is a cloud?  *A.* Night in the daytime, work for the eyes.

## ALC D46

*P.* What is the wind?  *A.* The disturbance of the air, the moving of the waters, the drying up of the earth.

## ALC D47

*P.* Quid est terra?    *A.* Mater crescentium, nutrix viventium, cellarium vitae, devoratrix omnium.

## ALC D48

*P.* Quid est mare?    *A.* Audaciae via, limes terrae, divisor regionum, hospitium fluviorum, fons imbrium, refugium in periculis, gratia in voluptatibus.

## ALC D49

*P.* Quid sunt flumina?    *A.* Cursus indeficiens, refectio solis, irrigatio terrae.

## ALC D50

*P.* Quid est aqua?    *A.* Subsidium vitae, ablutio sordium.

## ALC D47

*P.* What is the earth?   *A.* The mother of growing things, the nurturer of living things, the storehouse of life, the devourer of all.

## ALC D48

*P.* What is the sea?   *A.* The path of audacity, the edge of the earth, the divider of territories, the resting place of rivers, the source of showers, a haven in dangers, a blessing in delights.

## ALC D49

*P.* What are rivers?   *A.* An unceasing motion, the refreshment of the sun, the watering of the earth.

## ALC D50

*P.* What is water?   *A.* The foundation of life, the cleanser of stains.

## ALC D51

*P.* Quid est ignis?    *A.* Calor nimius, fotus nascentium, maturitas frugum.

## ALC D52

*P.* Quid est frigus?    *A.* Febricitas membrorum.

## ALC D53

*P.* Quid est gelu?    *A.* Persecutio herbarum, perditio foliorum, vinculum terrae, fons aquarum.

## ALC D54

*P.* Quid est nix?    *A.* Aqua sicca.

## ALC D55

*P.* Quid est hiems?    *A.* Aestatis exsul.

## ALC D56

*P.* Quid est ver?    *A.* Pictor terrae.

## ALC D51

*P.* What is fire?    *A.* An excessive heat, the warming of the newborn, the ripening of fruit.

## ALC D52

*P.* What is cold?    *A.* A shuddering of the limbs.

## ALC D53

*P.* What is ice?    *A.* The persecution of plants, the destruction of leaves, the binding of the earth, a source of waters.

## ALC D54

*P.* What is snow?    *A.* Dry water.

## ALC D55

*P.* What is winter?    *A.* An exile from summer.

## ALC D56

*P.* What is spring?    *A.* The painter of the earth.

## ALC D57

*P.* Quid est aestas?    *A.* Revestio terrae, maturitio frugum.

## ALC D58

*P.* Quid est autumnus?    *A.* Horreum anni.

## ALC D59

*P.* Quid est annus?    *A.* Quadriga mundi.
*P.* Quis ducit eam?    *A.* Nox et dies, frigus et calor.
*P.* Quis est auriga eius?    *A.* Sol et luna.
*P.* Quot habet palatia?    *A.* Duodecim.
*P.* Qui sunt praetores palatiorum?    *A.* Aries, Taurus, Gemini, Cancer, Leo, Virgo, Libra, Scorpius, Sagittarius, Capricornus, Aquarius, Pisces.
*P.* Quot dies habitant in unoquoque palatio?    *A.* Sol xxx dies et decem semis horas. Luna duos dies et octo horas, et bisse unius horae.

## ALC D60

*P.* Magister, timeo altum ire.    *A.* Quis te duxit in altum?
*P.* Curiositas.    *A.* Si times, descendamus. Sequar quocunque ieris.

# ALC D57

*P.* What is summer?  *A.* The recovering of the earth, the ripening of fruits.

# ALC D58

*P.* What is autumn?  *A.* The storehouse of the year.

# ALC D59

*P.* What is the year?  *A.* The chariot of the world.
*P.* Who pulls it?  *A.* Night and day, cold and heat.
*P.* Who is its charioteer?  *A.* Sun and moon.
*P.* How many palaces does it have?  *A.* Twelve.
*P.* Who are the heads of the palaces?  *A.* Aries, Taurus, Gemini, Cancer, Leo, Virgo, Libra, Scorpio, Sagittarius, Capricorn, Aquarius, and Pisces.
*P.* How many days do they stay in each palace?  *A.* Sun for thirty days and ten half hours. Moon for two days and eight hours and two-thirds of an hour.

# ALC D60

*P.* Master, I am afraid to go on high.  *A.* What has led you on high?
*P.* Curiosity.  *A.* If you are afraid, let us go down. I shall follow you wherever you go.

## ALC D61

*P.* Si scirem quid esset navis, praepararem tibi, ut venires ad me.  *A.* Navis est domus erratica, ubilibet hospitium, viator sine vestigiis, vicinus arenae.

## ALC D62

*P.* Quid est arena?  *A.* Murus terrae.

## ALC D63

*P.* Quid est herba?  *A.* Vestis terrae.

## ALC D64

*P.* Quid sunt olera?  *A.* Amici medicorum, laus coquorum.

## ALC D65

*P.* Quid est, quod amara dulcia facit?  *A.* Fames.

## ALC D61

*P.* If I knew what a ship was, I should have made one ready for you, so that you might come to me.   *A.* A ship is a wandering home, a lodging anywhere, a traveler without tracks, a neighbor to the sandy shore.

## ALC D62

*P.* What is the sandy shore?   *A.* The wall of the earth.

## ALC D63

*P.* What is grass?   *A.* The clothing of the earth.

## ALC D64

*P.* What are herbs?   *A.* The friends of doctors, the glory of cooks.

## ALC D65

*P.* What is it that makes bitter things sweet?   *A.* Hunger.

## ALC D66

*P.* Quid est, quod hominem non lassum facit?    *A.* Lucrum.

## ALC D67

*P.* Quid est vigilanti somnus?    *A.* Spes.

## ALC D68

*P.* Quid est spes?    *A.* Refrigerium laboris, dubius eventus.

## ALC D69

*P.* Quid est amicitia?    *A.* Aequalitas animorum.

## ALC D70

*P.* Quid est fides?    *A.* Ignotae rei et mirandae certitudo.

# ALC D66

*P.* What is it that no one wearies of?   *A.* Wealth.

# ALC D67

*P.* What is sleep to the wakeful?   *A.* Hope.

# ALC D68

*P.* What is hope?   *A.* A relief from labor, an uncertain outcome.

# ALC D69

*P.* What is friendship?   *A.* The equality of minds.

# ALC D70

*P.* What is faith?   *A.* The certainty of something unknown and wonderful.

## ALC D71

*P.* Quid est mirum? *A.* Nuper vidi hominem stantem, molientem, ambulantem, qui nunquam fuit. *P.* Quomodo potest esse, pande mihi? *A.* Imago in aqua. *P.* Cur hoc non intellexi per me, dum toties vidi hunc ipsum hominem? *A.* Quia bonae indolis es iuvenis et naturalis ingenii, proponam tibi quaedam alia mira; tenta, si per teipsum possis coniicere illa. *P.* Faciemus; tamen ita: si secus quam est dicam, corrigas me.

## ALC D72

*A.* Faciam, ut vis. Quidam ignotus mecum sine lingua et voce locutus est, qui nunquam ante fuit, nec postea erit; et quem non audiebam, nec novi. *P.* Somnium te forte fatigavit, magister?

## ALC D73

*A.* Etiam, fili. Audi et aliud: Vidi mortuos generare vivum, et aura vivi consumpti sunt mortui. *P.* De fricatione arborum ignis natus est, consumens arbores.

## ALC D71

*P.* What is a wonder? *A.* I recently saw a person who was never there standing, moving, and walking. *P.* How can this happen? Tell me. *A.* It was a reflection in water. *P.* Why did I not understand this myself, even though I saw the very same person so often? *A.* Since you are a young man of fine talent and natural wit, I shall describe to you some other wonders; see if you are able to interpret them yourself. *P.* Let us do that; but with this condition: that you put me straight if I make a mistake.

## ALC D72

*A.* I shall do as you wish. Someone I did not know spoke with me without tongue or voice, one who had never been, nor shall be again and whom I was not used to hearing and did not recognize. *P.* Perhaps a dream disturbed you, master?

## ALC D73

*A.* Quite right, son. Hear another: I saw dead things produce something living, and the dead were consumed by the breath of one living. *P.* Fire is produced from the rubbing of wood, and it devours wood.

## ALC D74

*A.* Verum est. Audivi mortuos multa loquentes.  *P.* Nunquam bene, nisi suspendantur in aere.

## ALC D75

*A.* Vere. Vidi ignem inexstinctum pausare in aqua.  *P.* Silicem in aqua significare vis, reor.

## ALC D76

*A.* Ut reris, sic est. Vidi mortuum sedentem super vivum, et in risu mortui moritur vivus.  *P.* Hoc coqui nostri norunt.

## ALC D77

*A.* Norunt. Sed pone digitum super os, ne pueri hoc audiant, quid sit. Fui in venatione cum aliis, in qua si quid cepimus, nihil nobiscum portavimus; quem non potuimus capere, domum portavimus nobiscum.  *P.* Rusticorum est haec venatio.

## ALC D74

*A.* That's true. I heard dead ones speaking aloud.    *P.* Never a good thing, unless they are hanging in the air.

## ALC D75

*A.* True. I saw fire that had not been put out sitting in water.    *P.* You mean flint in water, I reckon.

## ALC D76

*A.* It is what you reckon. I saw a dead thing sitting on top of a living thing, and the living dies from the laughter of the dead thing.    *P.* Our cooks knew that one.

## ALC D77

*A.* They do. But put your finger to your lips, so that the boys don't hear this one. I was out hunting with others, and if we caught anything we carried nothing with us; what we carried home with us is what we couldn't catch.    *P.* That's poor people's hunting.

## ALC D78

*A.* Est. Vidi quemdam natum, antequam esset conceptus.   *P.* Vidisti, et forte manducasti.

## ALC D79

*A.* Manducavi. Quis est, qui non est, et nomen habet et responsum dat sonanti?   *P.* Biblos in silva interroga.

## ALC D80

*A.* Vidi hospitem currentem cum domo sua; et ille tacebat, et domus sonabat.   *P.* Para mihi rete, et pandam tibi.

## ALC D81

*A.* Quis est, quem videre non potes, nisi clausis oculis?   *P.* Qui stertit, tibi ostendit illum.

## ALC D82

*A.* Vidi hominem octo in manu tenentem, et de octonis subito rapuit septem, et remanserunt sex.   *P.* Pueri in schola hoc sciunt.

# ALC D78

*A.* It is. I saw something born before it was conceived.   *P.* You did, and perhaps you ate it.

# ALC D79

*A.* I did eat it. Who is it who does not exist, who has a name, and answers whoever calls?   *P.* Ask the reeds in the forest.

# ALC D80

*A.* I saw a traveler running with his house, and he was silent, while his house was rowdy.   *P.* Give me a net, and I'll show you.

# ALC D81

*A.* Who is it that you can't see except with closed eyes?   *P.* That guy snoring shows you.

# ALC D82

*A.* I saw a man with eight in his hand, and from eight he suddenly took seven, and six were left.   *P.* The boys in school know that one.

# ALC D83

*A.* Quis est, cui, si caput abstuleris, altior surgit?    *P.* Vade ad lectum tuum et ibi invenies.

# ALC D84

*A.* Tres fuere; unus nunquam natus et semel mortuus. Alter semel natus, nunquam mortuus. Tertius semel natus et bis mortuus.    *P.* Primus aequivocus terrae meae; secundus Deo meo; tertius homini pauperi.    *A.* Dic tamen primas litteras nominum.    *P.* I. V. XXX.

# ALC D85

*A.* Vidi feminam volantem, rostrum habentem ferreum, et corpus ligneum et caudam pennatam, mortem portantem.    *P.* Socia militum.

# ALC D86

*A.* Quid est miles?    *P.* Murus imperii, timor hostium, gloriosum seruitium.

## ALC D83

*A.* What is it that gets taller when you take away the head?   *P.* Go to your bed, and you'll find it there.

## ALC D84

*A.* Three they were: one never born and once dead. Another once born, never dead. The third once born and twice dead.   *P.* The first has the same name as the earth; the second as my God; the third as a pauper.   *A.* Tell me the first letters of their names.   *P.* I, V, XXX.

## ALC D85

*A.* I saw a female flying, with an iron beak, a wooden body, and a feathery tail, carrying death.   *P.* She is the soldiers' friend.

## ALC D86

*A.* What is a soldier?   *P.* The protection of the realm, the terror of enemies, service with glory.

## ALC D87

*A.* Quid est quod est et non est?   *P.* Nihil.   *A.* Quomodo potest esse et non est?   *P.* Nomine est, et re non est.

## ALC D88

*A.* Quis est tacitus nuntius?   *P.* Quem manu teneo.   *A.* Quid tenes manu?   *P.* Epistolam tuam.   *A.* Lege feliciter, fili.

# ALC D87

*A.* What is it that is and is not?    *P.* Nothing.    *A.* How can it be and not be?    *P.* It exists in name but not in fact.

# ALC D88

*A.* What is a silent messenger?    *P.* What I'm holding in my hand.    *A.* What are you holding in your hand?    *P.* Your letter.    *A.* Enjoy reading it, son.

# The Lorsch Riddles

## LOR 1

Sunt mihi diverso varia sub tempore fata:
me pater in primis fecit sine matre supremus,
postque per alterius genitoris semen in orbem
consatus egrediens matris de ventre processi.

5    Ecce sub ancipiti saeclo cum fine timendo
ultima nunc trepide vereor iam fata superstes,
quando miser nimium gelida sub morte rigescens
matris et in propriae gremium deponar ibique,
usque quo mortalis claudantur tempora vitae,

10   abditus exspectem sub morte novissima fata,
per genitorem iterum recreandus in ordine primo
in regione poli aut mortis sine fine manendus.

## LOR 2

Dum domus ipsa mea dormit, vigilare suesco
atque sub angusto tenear cum carcere semper,
liber ad aetheream transcendo frequentius aulam,

# The Lorsch Riddles

## LOR 1

I have changing fates at different times:
the supreme Father made me in the beginning without a
    mother,
and then, once sown through the seed of a second sire,
out of a mother's belly I have emerged into the world.
  So now, surviving in this doubtful world,               5
with its dreadful end, I nervously fear my final fate.
When, utterly wretched, growing stiff in chilly death,
I will be placed in my own mother's lap, and there,
right up to when the time of mortal life has ended,
when, hidden, I await my final fate in death:              10
to be reformed again, through my father, just as I was at
    first,
to remain forever, either in heaven's realm or that of death.

## LOR 2

While my house itself sleeps, I am used to being awake,
and although I am continually kept under narrow
    confinement,
I cross freely rather frequently to the heavenly hall,

alta supernorum scrutans secreta polorum.
5  Omnia quin potius perlustro creata sub orbe,
rura peragro salumque peto, tunc litora linquens
finibus immensum fundum rimabor abyssi;
horriferae minime pertranseo claustra Gehennae,
ignea perpetue subeo sed tartara Ditis.
10  Haec modico peragro speleo si claudar in arvis
mortifero concussa ruant ni ergastula casu.
Sin vero propria dire de sede repellor,
mortis in occasu extimplo fit pulpa putrescens;
sic sunt fata mea diversa a patre creata.

## LOR 3

De mare velivolo consurgo, per aethera trano,
aurea luciflui cedunt cui sidera caeli;
postea horrifera ventorum mole revincor,
sicca peto subito terrarum terga resolvens;
5  atque sub ingenti repeto sic murmure pontum,
ast tamen imbrifero perfundo gurgite mundum,
unde valet populis spissam producere messem.

surveying the deep secrets of the skies above.
 Still yet do I pass through all creation under the sun,   5
traversing fields, I seek out the sea; then, leaving the shores,
I shall roam the mighty ocean to the edge of the abyss;
not at all do I pass through the prison of dreadful Gehenna,
but I do eternally endure the enflamed pits of Hell.
 I traverse these places from inside my tiny cave, if I am  10
  enclosed in earth,
unless by a deadly disaster that prison house collapses.
But if I am cruelly ripped from out of my proper place,
it immediately becomes rotting flesh in the ruin of death;
in this way, separate fates have been created for me by my
  father.


# LOR 3

I rise up from the sail-decked sea, I soar across the skies,
I am the one to whom the golden stars of the light-
  flickering heaven yield;
afterward, I am beaten back by the shuddering weight of
  the winds,
and, relaxing, suddenly seek the dry back of lands;
so then with a mighty murmur I rush again to the ocean,  5
yet drench the world with a shower-bringing downpour,
from which it can produce a burgeoning harvest for folks.

## LOR 4

Me pater ex gelido generat dum tergore matris,
quamdiu horriferis ipsam complectitur alis;
magna sub ingenti mihimet patre corpora surgunt,
donec ipse prius fato terrente recedat
5   aestibus aethereis sole vaporante fugatus.
Tunc ego morte cadens propriam progigno parentem;
tempore post iterum haut multo gignenda per ipsam.

## LOR 5

Lucidus et laetus quinis considere ramis
saepe solent pariter splendentes, laeta iubentes
aedibus in mediis fieri non tristia corda.
    Dumque simul ludunt ramisque tenentur apertis,
5   dulcia quin bibulis tradunt et bassia buccis;
multifer egreditur tantumque remanet adhaerens
lucidus in ramis, quibus antea sedit uterque.

# LOR 4

My father produces me from my mother's chilly surface,
when he embraces her with shuddering wings;
great masses surge from me beneath their vast father
until, in the face of terrifying fate, he first recedes,
routed by the sun steaming with summery heat.                5
Then, as I sink in death, I spawn my own mother;
and not much later in time I shall be born again through
    herself.

# LOR 5

Two things, one bright, one bringing cheer, equally
    resplendent,
are used to reclining often in five branches, bidding hearts
be joyful and not gloomy in the middle of the hall.
   And while they play together and are held in open
    branches
they exchange sweet kisses with mouths that drink them in;   5
the bountiful one goes forth, and only one remains behind,
bright still among the branches, where they both reclined
    before.

## LOR 6

Nubibus e tetris vidi dilabere quandam:
ipsa velox cecidit super ardua tecta domorum.
Mollis erat visu necnon lenissima tactu;
inde cadens iosumque manavit leniter asprum
5    dura super torum sibimet qui terga cadenti
praebuit, infixus terrae stabilisque manendo.

## LOR 7

Scribitur octono silvarum grammate lignum;
ultima terna simul tuleris si grammata demens,
milibus in multis vix postea cernitur una.

## LOR 8

En video sobolem propria cum matre morantem,
mandre cuius pellis in pariete pendet adhaerens.

## LOR 9

Candida virgo suas lacrimas dum seminat atras,
tetra per albentes linquit vestigia campos
lucida stelligeri ducentia ad atria caeli.

## LOR 6

From dark clouds I saw some woman slip:
she fell swiftly onto the high roofs of houses.
She was soft to the sight and most gentle to the touch;
falling from there, she gently poured downward
upon a harsh bed, which offered its hard surface to her          5
as she fell; a bed fixed in the ground by remaining stable.

## LOR 7

A tree among the woods is written with eight letters;
but if in folly you were to take away the last three letters at
     once,
then scarcely is a single such girl seen among many
     thousands.

## LOR 8

Look: I see an offspring dallying with its own mother,
and its skin was hanging stuck to the wall of its cell.

## LOR 9

A bright-white virgin, while she sows her own black tears,
leaves throughout whitish fields dark tracks
that lead to the bright halls of the starry sky.

## LOR 10

Saeva nefandorum non gessi furta latronum
nec diro humanum fudi mucrone cruorem,
sed tamen in laqueo reus ut fur pendeo longo.
    Si quis at ardenti tangit mea viscera flamma,
5   mox simul egregiam lumen dispergo per aulam;
sicque meo noctis tetras depello tenebras
lumine, clarifica perfundens luce sacellum.

## LOR 11

Quando fui iuvenis bis binis fontibus hausi;
postquam consenui montes vallesque de imis
sedibus evertens naturae iura rescidi.
Post misero fato torpenti morte tabescens,
5   mortuus horrende vivorum stringo lacertos,
necnon humanis praebens munimina plantis,
frigoris a rigidis inlaesas reddo pruinis:
sic mea diversis variantur fata sub annis.

## LOR 12

Silva fui dudum crescens in sentibus aspris,
lymfa velut fueram decurrens clara per amnem;
tertia pars mihimet tradenda est arte reperta.

## LOR 10

I have not performed the cruel thefts of wicked thieves,
nor have I poured human blood with a dreadful blade,
yet I dangle like a guilty bandit from a stretching noose.
   But if anyone touches my innards with a burning flame,
I soon spread light all at once throughout the fine hall;               5
and so with my light I scatter the black shadows of night,
drenching the little room with brilliant radiance.

## LOR 11

When I was young I drank from twice two streams;
after I grew old I turned over hills and dales
from their deepest foundations, and tore apart the laws of
      nature.
Later, by a miserable fate, rotting in numbing death,
when dead I grimly bind the arms of the living,                          5
and also, by providing protection to human feet,
I render them unharmed by the hard frosts of cold:
so my fates are varied throughout the changing years.

## LOR 12

Once I was a wooded thing, growing among harsh thorns,
just as once I was clear water, flowing in a stream;
my third part shall be given me through cunning skill.

Lucifica nigris tunc nuntio regna figuris,
late per innumeros albos si spargas agellos;
necnon horrifera soleo tunc tartara trusum
grammate terribili narrare vitanda relatu.

At one time I proclaim the kingdom of light with dark
    marks,
if you scatter me widely through unnumbered little white     5
    fields;
at other times, when forced out in the form of letters, I am
    accustomed to tell,
in a terrible account, what hellish terrors are to be avoided.

# The Abingdon Riddle

## ABI

Bis binae fialae caritatis nos vocitamur
nosque duae natu maiores dicimur esse.
Si vos maiores nobis modo vultis adesse,
non nos peiores similes tamen esse videmur.

# The Abingdon Riddle

## ABI

We are called twice two cups of love,
and the two of us are said to be the greater in status.
If you who are bigger than us now wish to be here,
we, however, do not equally seem to be the worse.

# The High-Minded Library

## BIB 1

Me sine matre pater genuit pariente puellam,
   sed genita prole non erat ille prior.
Virgine virgo forem quanquam de perpete perpes,
   non mihi abest nullo coniuge matris honor.
5  Sunt mihi nam ternae patrio sine semine natae,
   sed mea virginitas semper in aeva manet.
Terna mihi est species, oculi tot fronte sub una,
   ubera tot niveo pectore sacra tument,
totque meo latices turgent de ventre manantes,
10    lota, sophistarum pro quibus quisque nitet.

## BIB 2

Innuba me genuit genitrix de coniuge nullo,
   dum sit patris amor est mihi matris honor;

# The High-Minded Library

## BIB 1

A father produced me, a young woman, without a pregnant
    mother,
  but once that offspring was born, he was not the senior.
Although I shall be a perpetual virgin, produced from a
    perpetual virgin,
  I don't lack the honor of being a mother, far from any
    partner.
For three daughters are born to me, without a father's seed,    5
  although my virginity always remains forever.
I have a threefold appearance, and three eyes under a single
    forehead,
  three holy breasts swell on a snowy chest,
and just as many streams course flowing from my belly,
  those breasts are glorious, before which each of the wise    10
    ones shines.

## BIB 2

An unmarried mother produced me, without any spouse;
  while I have my father's love, I have my mother's honor,

mater enim constat mea patris origine sola,
    ast ego de sola sum genitrice sata.
5  Sed quanquam genitrix mea virgo perenniter instet,
    foemineae sobolis pignora trina tulit.
Sunt mihi bis binae species, tot lumina lucent,
    pignora tot genui virgo sed ipsa manens,
inque meo turgent niveo tot pectore mammae,
10    tot quibus aeterno fonte fluenta manant.


## BIB 3

Me sterilem genuit patrio sine semine mater,
    sed mihi sunt propria proles in aeva manens.
Sunt mihi germanae genitae de virgine trinae,
    quae sine me nequeunt numina habere sua.
5  Bina patet species duplici sub fronte tot ora;
    ubera tot niveo pectore sacra tument.
Una mihi species hilaris ut lumine trino,
    altera sic triplici munere lucis ovat.


## BIB 4

Sunt mihi tres mirae species, sunt lumina sena,
    quaelibet ut species lumina bina ferat.
Unus eorum oculus vigilans in celsa tuetur;
    rite suum visum alter ad ima premit,

for my mother exists solely from a father's beginning,
    but I come from my mother's seed alone.
But although my mother remains a virgin forever,     5
    she has borne three offspring in female form.
I have four forms, and four eyes shine;
    I have produced four offspring, while remaining a virgin,
and four teats swell on my snowy breast,
    from where four streams drip in an eternal flow.     10

## BIB 3

Without a father's seed my mother produced me sterile ,
    but I have offspring of my own that remain forever.
I have three sisters produced from a virgin,
    who cannot have their own powers without me.
I have two faces, and the same number of mouths beneath a    5
      double frontage,
    and the same number of holy nipples swell on my snowy
      breast.
One of my faces is happy, as with a triple eye;
    the other rejoices with a threefold gift of light.

## BIB 4

I have three amazing faces, and six eyes,
    since every face has two eyes.
One of those eyes looks vigilantly to the skies,
    the other properly casts its sight to the depths,

5   Tertius ante videt, quartus sed retro retorquet;
     quintum sextumque dextra sinistra tenent.
  Metior at radio coelum pelagumque solumque,
     terra tamen tribuit nomen in aeva mihi.

## BIB 5

Vox mea non sonuit penitus non atque sonabit,
    nulla canora tamen vox sine me resonat.
Sunt mihi tres mirae species, sunt lumina trina,
    ubera tot niveo pectore sacra tument.
5  Me sine dulce nihil tubicen, citharista, poeta,
    clangore, fidibus, carmine ferre queunt.
Nescio quid fuerit resonant cum carmina vatum,
    quippe mihi nullus sensus inesse potest.

## BIB 6

In terris mihi grata domus, sed pascor Olympo,
    tot mihi sunt oculi quot polus astra vehit,
ast mea sceptra manent sese dum tempora volvunt,
    dumque suas moveant lux tenebraeque vices.
5  Ipse sed extinguar, mea gloria cuncta peribit,
    luxerit aeterne dum sine nocte dies.

the third looks ahead, but the fourth turns backward;     5
    left and right direct the fifth and sixth.
In a circuit I measure land and sea and sky,
    but the earth has granted me my name always.


## BIB 5

My voice has not sounded inside, nor will it sound,
    yet no singing voice resounds without me.
I have three amazing faces, three eyes,
    and the same number of holy nipples swell on my snowy
        breast;
without me the trumpeter, harpist, or poet     5
    can do nothing sweet in sounding, strings, or singing.
I do not comprehend what it is when the songs of singers
        resonate,
    since for sure no understanding can remain in me.


## BIB 6

I have a welcome home on earth, yet I nourish myself on
        the heavens;
    I have as many eyes as the sky bears stars,
yet my powers remain for as long as time wheels,
    for as long as light and dark ring their changes.
But I shall be snuffed out myself, and my whole glory will     5
        fail,
    when day grows bright forever, without night.

## BIB 7

Sunt mihi germanae genitae de virgine binae;
    una secunda meo est, altera honore prior;
una creaturas ego ritus tertia linguas,
    Ordinat in species, dividit atque suas,
5  prima secunda tacent, loquitur sed tertia sola,
    Pro nobis etenim sunt sibi verba data.
Sunt mihi bis binae species, bis lumina bina:
    pignora tot genui virgo sed ipsa manens.

## BIB 8

Sunt mihi germanae patrio sine semine ternae:
    nam genitrix nostra virgo per aeva manet.
E quibus una modos humanis moribus optat,
    ne plus quisque petat quam sibi sorte datur.
5  Altera prudentum defendit ab hoste catervas,
    insidiae cunctae cui sine nube patent.
Tertia Christicolis vires largitur enormes,
    cuncta quibus facile ferre pericla queant.
Quarta, tenens geminam lancem moderaminis aequi,
10    sedibus in summis iudicat ante Deum.

## BIB 7

I have two sisters produced from a virgin;
 one is second to me in honor, the other is ahead;
one is governor of creatures, I of customs, the third of
  tongues,
 and we divide up each into their own aspects.
The first and second sisters are silent, and only the third   5
  speaks,
 but her words are given to her for us.
I have twice-two faces, and twice-two eyes:
 I have produced the same number of offspring, but
  remain a virgin myself.


## BIB 8

I have three sisters, born without a father's seed,
 for our mother remains a virgin forever.
One of us sisters wants to set limits on human behavior,
 so that no one seeks more than he is granted by fate.
The second defends the ranks of the sensible from an   5
  enemy,
 and to her all treacheries are cloudlessly clear.
The third provides great strength to Christians,
 so that they can bear all dangers with ease.
The fourth, holding a twin balance of equal poise,
 gives judgment in the highest courts before God.   10

Illa, nuens iustis coelestia scandere regna,
    imperat iniustis Ditis adire domos.

## BIB 9

Est mihi sola parens, geminae sine patre sorores,
    quarum notitia me pereunte perit.
Tres mihi sunt species, fulgent tot fronte sub una
    lumina; tot genui pignora virgo manens.
5  Imperio quorum cunctae per secula linguae
    expediunt vitam, quae sine labe nitent.

## BIB 10

Littera distribuit mihi nomen Graeca perenne;
    nescio sed quid sit littera, quidve potest.
Grammata cuncta meae ditioni et singula verba
    subdita, sed nota grammata nulla mihi.

## BIB 11

Ast mihi tradiderat nomen foecunda loquela:
    singula despiciens plurima verba fero.
Me veneranda phalanx reveretur in aeva rethorum,
    dum sine me nequeunt quae referenda loqui.

She, signaling to the just that they ascend to the heavenly
    kingdom,
    commands the unjust to go to the halls of Hell.


## BIB 9

I have one parent and two sisters, without a father,
    and knowledge of them dies when I do.
I have three faces, and as many eyes shine underneath a
    single brow:
    I produced the same number of offspring, while
        remaining a virgin.
By mastering my offspring that shine immaculately,                    5
    all tongues throughout the ages open the way to life.


## BIB 10

The Greek for letter has granted me an eternal name;
    but I do not know what a letter is, or what it can do.
All letters and single words are subject to my authority,
    but no letters are known to me.


## BIB 11

For my part, fertile speech had offered me a name:
    scorning single words, I bring forth very many.
A venerable band of rhetoricians reveres me always,
    since without me they cannot say what needs to be said.

# BIB 12

Sunt mihi germanae genitae de virgine binae,
  nominibus quarum sacra sophia viget.
Grammatibus cunctis variaverat una figuras,
  altera dicendi ferre perita modos.
5  Ast ego mente sollers breviter discrimina rerum
  segrego quam nulla fallere menda queunt.
Omne sylogismis dubium manifesto repertis:
  quippe sophistarum mens mihi Graeca domus.
Sed mihi dum pauci praestant habitacula digna,
10  mens sine me dubia multa relinquit inops.

## BIB 12

I have twin sisters, both born of a virgin,
    and holy wisdom grows strong in their names.
One had varied figures using all letters;
    the other was skilled in using different modes of speech.
As for me, sharp minded, I parse out in brief order     5
    the distinctions among things; no errors can deceive me.
I reveal everything that is doubtful in detected syllogisms:
    the Greek mind of the sophists is my dwelling.
But while few provide me with suitable habitation,
    without me, the helpless mind leaves many things     10
        doubtful.

# THE OLD ENGLISH
# TRADITION

# The Franks Casket Riddle

## FRA

Fisc flodu ahof    on fergen-berig;
warþ gas-ric grorn    þær he on greut giswom.
*Hronæs ban.*

# The Franks Casket Riddle

## FRA

The sea raised up the fish onto the towering beach;
the king of terror became sorrowful, when he swam onto
    the shingle.
*Whale's bone.*

# The Leiden Riddle

## LEI

Mec se ueta uong,   uundrum freorig,
ob his innaðae   aerest cændæ.
   Ni uaat ic mec biuorthæ   uullan fliusum,
herum ðerh heh-craeft,   hygi-ðoncum min.
5   Uundnae me ni biað ueflæ,   ni ic uarp hafæ,
ni ðerih ðreatun giðraec   ðret me hlimmith.
   Ne me hrutendo   hrisil scelfath,
ne mec ouana   aam sceal cnyssa.
   Uyrmas mec ni auefun   uyrdi craeftum,
10  ða ði geolu godueb   geatum fraetuath.
   Uil mec huethrae suae   ðeh uidæ ofaer eorðu
hatan mith hẹliðum   hyhtlic giuæde.
   Ni anoegun ic me aerig-faerae   egsan brogum,
ðeh ði numen siæ   niudlicae ob cocrum.

# The Leiden Riddle

## LEI

The wet ground, wondrously chilly,
first gave me birth from its innards.
   I know that I was not produced from woolly fleeces,
or hairs, through lofty skill in thoughts.
   There are no twisted wefts for me, nor do I have warps,     5
nor through a threat of violence does a thread resound in
      me,
   nor do humming shuttles shiver in me,
nor does a slay beat me about;
   nor did worms weave me with the skills of fate,
those who craftily decorate fine yellow cloth.               10
   Nonetheless, I will be called a desirable garment
widely over the earth among heroes;
   nor do I fear the flight of arrows with the terrors of awe,
even though it be drawn purposefully from quivers.

# The Exeter Book Riddles

## EXE 1

Hwylc is hæleþa þæs horsc    ond þæs hyge-cræftig
þæt þæt mæge asecgan    hwa mec on sið wræce
þonne ic astige strong,    stundum reþe,
þrym-ful þunie,    þragum wræcca
5 fere geond foldan,    folc-salo bærne,
ræced reafige?    Recas stigað,
haswe ofer hrofum;    hlyn bið on eorþan,
wæl-cwealm wera,    þonne ic wudu hrere,
bearwas bled-hwate,    beamas fylle.
10 Holme gehrefed,    heahum meahtum
wrecen on waþe,    wide sended,
hæbbe me on hrycge    þæt ær hadas wreah
fold-buendra,    flæsc ond gæstas,
somod on sunde.
                              Saga hwa mec þecce,
15 oþþe hu ic hatte,    þe þa hlæst bere.

    Hwilum ic gewite    (swa ne wenaþ men),
under yþa geþræc    eorþan secan,
gar-secges grund.    Gifen biþ gewreged,
. . .    famge wealcen;
20 hwæl-mere hlimmeð,    hlude grimmeð,
streamas staþu beataŏ,    stundum weorpaþ

298

# The Exeter Book Riddles

## EXE 1

What man is so brisk and so crafty in mind
that he can tell who drives me on my way
when I rise up strong, angry at times,
thunder full of power, occasionally as an exile
pass over the land, burn the folk's homes,             5
plunder the buildings? Fumes rise,
gray over the rooftops; there is tumult on earth,
grave slaughter of men, when I shake up the woods,
the fruitful groves, fell the trees.
Roofed with water, driven afar,                        10
forced into wandering by lofty powers,
I have on my back what once cloaked the kinds
of earth's inhabitants, flesh and spirits,
together in the stream.
                              Say who covers me,
or how I am called, who carries that load.             15
    Sometimes I travel (unexpectedly to men)
beneath the thrash of waves, seeking the ground,
the bottom of the deep. The ocean is roused,
. . . the foamy billows;
the whale-sea growls, loudly howls,                    20
tides batter cliffs, at times cast up

on stealc hleoþa    stane ond sonde,
ware ond wæge,    þonne ic winnende,
holm-mægne biþeaht,    hrusan styrge,
25  side sæ-grundas.    Sund-helme ne mæg
losian ær mec læte    se þe min latteow bið
on siþa gehwam.

             Saga, þoncol mon,
hwa mec brægde    of brimes fæþmum,
þonne streamas eft    stille weorþað,
30  yþa geþwære,    þe mec ær wrugon.

    Hwilum mec min frea    fæste genearwað,
sendeð þonne    under sal-wonges
bearm þone bradan,    ond on bid wriceð,
þrafað on þystrum    þrymma sumne,
35  hæste on enge,    þær me heard siteð
hruse on hrycge.    Nah ic hwyrft-weges
of þam aglace,    ac ic eþel-stol
hæleþa hreru;    horn-salu wagiað,
wera wic-stede,    weallas beofiað,
40  steape ofer sti-witum.

             Stille þynceð
lyft ofer londe    ond lagu swige,
oþþæt ic of enge    up aþringe,
efne swa mec wisaþ    se mec wræde on
æt frum-sceafte    furþum legde,
45  bende ond clomme,    þæt ic onbugan ne mot
of þæs gewealde    þe me wegas tæcneð.

    Hwilum ic sceal ufan    yþa wregan,
streamas styrgan    ond to staþe þywan
flint-grægne flod.    Famig winneð
50  wæg wið wealle,    wonn ariseð

on steep shore-slopes stone and sand,
weed and water, when I, contending,
wrapped in water-power, churn up the ground,
the broad sea-deeps. My covering of liquid                    25
I cannot lose, before he lets me, who is my leader
on every expedition.
                Say, learned man,
who draws me from the wave's embrace,
when the streams again grow still,
the breakers calm, that concealed me before.                 30
  Sometimes my lord tethers me tight,
sends me then beneath the lush land's
broad bosom, and forces me to a standstill,
confines in darkness a certain one of powers,
with harsh restraint, where hard upon me                     35
the soil sits on my back. I have no escape
from that awful attack, but instead I shake up
the homesteads of men; shiver hall-gables,
the people's buildings; walls shake,
high over householders.                                      40
              The sky seems still
over the earth, and the sea is silent,
until from constraint I catapult up,
even as he leads me who first laid on me
shackles from the very start,
bonds and bindings, so I might not budge                     45
from the power of him who guides my paths.
  Sometimes I must whip up waves from on high,
stir the streams and force to the shore
the flint-gray flood. Foamy swell contends
against cliff wall, there rises up dim                        50

dun ofer dype;   hyre deorc on last,
eare geblonden,   oþer fereð,
þæt hy gemittað   mearc-londe neah,
hea hlincas.
            Þær bið hlud wada,
55  brim-giesta breahtm,   bidað stille
stealc stan-hleoþu   stream-gewinnes,
hop-gehnastes,   þonne heah geþring
on cleofu crydeþ.
               Þær bið ceole wen
sliþre sæcce,   gif hine sæ byreð
60  on þa grimman tid,   gæsta fulne,
þæt he scyle rince   birofen weorþan,
fere bifohten   fæmig ridan
yþa hrycgum.
           Þær bið egsa sum
ældum geywed,   þær þe ic yrnan sceal
65  strong on stið-weg.   Hwa gestilleð þæt?
    Hwilum ic þurhræse   þæt me on bæce rideð,
won wæg-fatu,   wide toþringe
lagu-streama full,   hwilum læte eft
slupan tosomne.
           Se bið swega mæst,
70  breahtma ofer burgum,   ond gebreca hludast,
þonne scearp cymeð   sceor wiþ oþrum,
ecg wið ecge;   eorpan gesceafte,
fus ofer folcum,   fyre swætað,
blacan lige,   ond gebrecu ferað
75  deorc ofer dreorgum   gedyne micle,
farað feohtende,   feallan lætað
sweart swinsendu   seaw of bosme,

a mountain over the deep; dark in its track,
suffused with the sea, another comes,
so that they collide close by the land's edge,
lofty ridges.

            Then there is a loud sound of waters,
the clamor of sea spirits; the steep stone slopes      55
await unmoved the tidal contest,
the bay-crash of waves, when the towering surge
crowds down on the cliffs.

              Then a ship can expect there
a cruel conflict, if the sea carries it
at that fierce time, filled with souls,      60
so that it becomes bereft of men,
beset by danger, to ride foaming
on the breakers' backs.

           Then there is real terror
revealed to men, when I must run
strong on a stern path. Who keeps that calm?      65
Sometimes I rush through what rides on my back,
dark water vessels, scatter wide
the cup of liquid streams, sometimes allow them
to slip back together again.

            That is the mightiest of sounds,
of clamoring over townships, and the loudest of collisions,   70
when one shower sharply connects with another,
edge against edge; the murky creatures,
striving forward over folk, stream with fire,
bright flame, and sounds of clashing pass
dark over the afflicted with a mighty din;      75
they travel battling, they let fall
dark moisture roaring from their bosom,

wætan of wombe.
              Winnende fareð
atol eored-þreat,    egsa astigeð,
80    micel mod-þrea    monna cynne,
brogan on burgum,    þonne blace scotiað
scriþende scin    scearpum wæpnum.

    Dol him ne ondrædeð    ða deað-speru,
swylteð hwæþre,    gif him soð meotud,
85    on geryhtum ryne    þurh regn ufan,
of gestune læteð    stræle fleogan,
færende flan.    Fea þæt gedygað,
þara þe geræceð    ryne-giestes wæpen.
Ic þæs orleges    or anstelle,
90    þonne gewite    wolcen-gehnaste,
þurh geþræc þringan    þrimme micle,
ofer brunra bosm.    Biersteð hlude
heah hloð-gecrod;    þonne hnige eft,
under lyfte helm,    londe near,
95    ond me on hrycg hlade    þæt ic habban sceal,
meahtum gemagnad    mines frean.

    Swa ic þrymful þeow    þragum winne:
hwilum under eorþan,    hwilum yþa sceal
hean underhnigan,    hwilum holm ufan
100    streamas styrge,    hwilum stige up,
wolcn-fare wrege,    wide fere,
swift ond swiþ-from.           Saga hwæt ic hatte,
oþþe hwa mec rære,    þonne ic restan ne mot,
oþþe hwa mec stæðþe,    þonne ic stille beom.

juice from their belly.

                    Contending, there travels
a dread troop of horsemen; horror mounts,
mighty panic for the race of men,                                                    80
terror for the townships, when black gliding ghosts
shoot down with sharp weapons.

    The fool does not fear those deadly spears,
but he still dies, if the true God,
as it is running straight down through the rain above,                               85
lets fly a shaft from the whirlwind,
terrifying arrows. Few survive,
whom that running-spirit's weapon reaches.
I bring about that battle's beginning,
when I pass in a clash of cloud,                                                      90
squeezing through the press with a mighty force,
over the bosom of the dark ones. There loudly bursts
a lofty tumult of troops; then I sink back,
under the cover of the sky, nearer the land,
and heave on my back what I must have,                                                95
strengthened by the powers of my lord.

    So I, a mighty servant, occasionally contend:
sometimes under earth, sometimes I sink low
under the waves, sometimes above the sea
I stir up streams, sometimes mount up,                                               100
rouse the drifting clouds, travel wide,
swift and aggressive.

                    Say what I am called,
or who raises me up, when I may not rest,
or who makes me steady, when I stand still.

## EXE 2

Ic sceal þrag-bysig     þegne minum,
hringum hæfted,     hyran georne,
min bed brecan,     breahtme cyþan
þæt me hals-wriþan     hlaford sealde.
5     Oft mec slæp-werigne     secg oðþe meowle
gretan eode;     ic him grom-heortum
winter-ceald oncweþe.     Wearm lim
gebundenne bæg     hwilum bersteð;
se þeah biþ on þonce     þegne minum,
10     med-wisum men,     me þæt sylfe,
þær wiht wite,     ond wordum min
on sped mæge     spel gesecgan.

## EXE 3

Ic eom an-haga     iserne wund,
bille gebennad,     beado-weorca sæd,
ecgum werig.
          Oft ic wig seo,
frecne feohtan;     frofre ne wene,
5     þæt mec geoc cyme     guð-gewinnes,
ær ic mid ældum     eal forwurðe;
ac mec hnossiað     homera lafe,
heard-ecg heoro-scearp     hond-weorc smiþa,
bitað in burgum;     ic abidan sceal
10     laþran gemotes.
          Næfre læce-cynn

## EXE 2

Busy at times, fettered by rings,
I must eagerly obey the one who serves me,
break my bed, loudly proclaim
that my lord gave a neck ring to me.
   Often a man or woman went to greet me,     5
when I was sleep-weary; those fierce-hearted ones
I answer winter-cold. A warm limb
sometimes bursts the bound circlet;
yet it is pleasing to the one who serves me,
a man middling wise, and also myself,     10
who knows a jot and can in words
successfully say my story.

## EXE 3

I am a loner, wounded with iron,
battered by a blade, with battle-deeds sated,
tired out by swords.
            Often I see war,
a dangerous fight; I expect no comfort,
that help should come to me in the conflict of war,     5
before I am entirely destroyed among men;
but the hammers' leavings hack at me,
the hard-edged, highly sharp handwork of smiths,
bites me in townships; I must await
a crueler clash.                  10
      I could never find

on folc-stede    findan meahte,
þara þe mid wyrtum    wunde gehælde,
ac me ecga dolg    eacen weorðað
þurh deað-slege    dagum ond nihtum.

## EXE 4

Mec gesette soð    sigora waldend,
Crist, to compe.    Oft ic cwice bærne,
unrimu cyn,    eorþan getenge,
næte mid niþe,    swa ic him no hrine,
5    þonne mec min frea    feohtan hateþ.
   Hwilum ic monigra    mod arete;
hwilum ic frefre    þa ic ær winne on
feorran swiþe;    hi þæs felað þeah,
swylce þæs oþres,    þonne ic eft hyra
10    ofer deop gedreag    drohtað bete.

## EXE 5

Hrægl min swigað,    þonne ic hrusan trede,
oþþe þa wic buge,    oþþe wado drefe.
   Hwilum mec ahebbað    ofer hæleþa byht
hyrste mine,    ond þeos hea lyft,
5    ond mec þonne wide    wolcna strengu
ofer folc byreð.
            Frætwe mine
swogað hlude    ond swinsiað,

any kind of doctors in the dwelling place,
of those who might heal wounds with herbs,
but the scars of edges increase on me
through deadly blows day and night.

## EXE 4

Christ, the true ruler of victories,
set me up for conflict. Often I burn the living,
countless kinds, close to the earth;
I afflict them with ill, even though I do not touch them,
when my lord summons me to fight.                               5
   Sometimes I gladden the minds of many;
sometimes I succor those I once assailed
from very far off; yet they feel that just like the other,
when again over the deep tumult
I improve their plight.                                        10

## EXE 5

My raiment is silent when I tread the ground,
or stay at home, or stir the waves.
   Sometimes my garments and this lofty air
raise me over men's houses,
and then the power of clouds                                    5
carries me widely over folk.
                     My attire
whistles loudly and makes music,

torhte singað,    þonne ic getenge ne beom
flode ond foldan,    ferende gæst.

## EXE 6

Ic þurh muþ sprece    mongum reordum,
wrencum singe,    wrixle geneahhe
heafod-woþe,    hlude cirme,
healde mine wisan,    hleoþre ne miþe.
5    Eald æfen-sceop,    eorlum bringe
blisse in burgum,    þonne ic bugendre
stefne styrme;    stille on wicum
sittað swigende.
                    Saga hwæt ic hatte,
þe swa scernicge    sceawend-wisan
10   hlude onhyrge,    hæleþum bodige
wil-cumena fela    woþe minre.

## EXE 7

Mec on þissum dagum    deadne ofgeafun,
fæder ond modor;    ne wæs me feorh þa gen,
ealdor in innan.
                    Þa mec an ongon,
wel-hold mege,    wedum þeccan,
5    heold ond freoþode,    hleo-sceorpe wrah,
swa arlice    swa hire agen bearn,
oþþæt ic under sceate,    swa min gesceapu wæron,
ungesibbum wearð    eacen gæste.

brightly sings, when I no longer touch
flood or field, a wayfaring spirit.


# EXE 6

I speak through my mouth with many voices,
sing in modulations, switch continually
the sounds in my head, cry out loud,
maintain my melody, do not hide my song.
  An ancient poet of evening, I bring to men                    5
bliss in the townships, when I call out
with varying voice; still in the buildings
they sit in silence.
Say what I am called,
                    who, like a lady actor, loudly mimics
the player's song, bids the fellows                             10
many welcomes with my voice.


# EXE 7

In these days they gave me up for dead,
father and mother; then I had no life yet,
spirit inside.
              But then a certain one began,
a kinswoman most constant, to cover me with clothes,
retained and maintained me, wrapped me in robes,             5
as kindly as she did her own young kin,
until under a bosom not of my blood,
I became increased in spirit, as was my fate.

Mec seo friþe-mæg    fedde siþþan,
10    oþþæt ic aweox,    widdor meahte
siþas asettan;    heo hæfde swæsra þy læs,
suna ond dohtra,    þy heo swa dyde.


## EXE 8


Neb wæs min on nearwe,    ond ic neoþan wætre,
flode underflowen,    firgen-streamum,
swiþe besuncen;    ond on sunde awox,
ufan yþum þeaht,    anum getenge
5    liþendum wuda    lice mine.
    Hæfde feorh cwico,    þa ic of fæðmum cwom
brimes ond beames    on blacum hrægle;
sume wæron hwite    hyrste mine,
þa mec lifgende    lyft upp ahof,
10    wind of wæge,    siþþan wide bær
ofer seolh-baþo.
                    Saga hwæt ic hatte.


## EXE 9


Hrægl is min haso-fag,    hyrste beorhte;
reade ond scire    on reafe hafu.
    Ic dysge dwelle    ond dole hwette
unræd-siþas;    oþrum styre
5    nyttre fore.    Ic þæs nowiht wat
þæt heo swa gemædde,    mode bestolene,
dæde gedwolene,    deoraþ mine
won wisan gehwam.
                    Wa him þæs þeawes,

That loving kinswoman fed me then
until I grew, and might more widely                                    10
make my way; she had fewer loved ones,
sons and daughters, because she did so.


# EXE 8

My beak was confined, and I, underwater,
flowed under by flood, in mighty currents,
surely sunk; and in the sea I grew,
covered above by waves, clinging with my body
to a single drifting spar.                                            5
　　I had a living spirit, when I came from the lap
of the beam and the brine in black array;
some of my garments were white,
when the living air lifted me aloft,
wind beyond wave, and afterward bore me wide               10
over the seal-baths.
　　　　　　　　　　　Say what I am called.


# EXE 9

My array is dusky colored, my accouterments bright;
red and gleaming garments I own.
　　I fool the foolish and stir up the stupid
on imprudent paths; others I steer away from
a useful track. I know not at all                                     5
why they, so maddened, bereft of mind,
deceived in deed, should glorify
my dark way to everyone.
　　　　　　　　　　Woe to them for that act,

siþþan heah bringað    horda deorast,
10   gif hi unrædes    ær ne geswicaþ.

## EXE 10

Fotum ic fere,    foldan slite,
grene wongas,    þenden ic gæst bere.
   Gif me feorh losað,    fæste binde
swearte Wealas,    hwilum sellan men.
5  Hwilum ic deorum    drincan selle
beorne of bosme;    hwilum mec bryd triedeð
fela-wlonc fotum;    hwilum feorran broht
won-feax Wale    wegeð ond þyð,
dol drunc-mennen    deorcum nihtum,
10  wæteð in wætre,    wyrmeð hwilum,
fægre to fyre;    me on fæðme sticaþ
hyge-galan hond,    hwyrfeð geneahhe,
swifeð me geond sweartne.
                 Saga hwæt ic hatte,
þe ic lifgende    lond reafige,
15  ond æfter deaþe    dryhtum þeowige.

## EXE 11

Ic seah turf tredan,    ·x· wæron ealra,
·vi· gebroþor    ond hyra sweostor mid;
hæfdon feorg cwico.    Fell hongedon
sweotol ond gesyne    on seles wæge
5  anra gehwylces.
              Ne wæs hyra ængum þy wyrs,

when they bring on high the most precious of treasures,
if they do not first refrain from imprudence.                    10

## EXE 10

I travel on foot, tear the earth,
green fields, while I carry my spirit.
     If I lose my life, I bind fast
the swarthy Welsh, sometimes finer folk.
Sometimes I give a drink from my breast                          5
to a bold warrior; sometimes, a bride treads me
proudly underfoot; sometimes, brought from afar,
a dark-haired Welsh girl grips and grasps me,
the dull drunk wench in the dark nights,
moistens me in water, sometimes warms me,                        10
favorably by the fire; a hand enflamed
thrusts in my lap, writhes rather much,
strokes me through the dark.
                              Say what I am called,
who, living, plunders the ground,
and, after death, gives service to mankind.                      15

## EXE 11

I saw them tread the turf; there were ten in all,
six brothers and their sisters too;
they had lively spirits. The skins
of every single one hung clearly visible
on the wall of a hall.
                         None of them was the worse,           5

ne siðe þy sarre,    þeah hy swa sceoldon,
reafe birofene,    rodra weardes
meahtum aweahte,    muþum slitan
haswe blede.    Hrægl bið geniwad
10  þam þe ær forð-cymene    frætwe leton
licgan on laste,    gewitan lond tredan.

## EXE 12

Ic wæs wæpen wigan;    nu mec wlonc þeceð
geong hago-steald-mon    golde ond sylfore,
woum wir-bogum.
                Hwilum weras cyssað;
hwilum ic to hilde    hleoþre bonne
5  wil-gehleþan;    hwilum wycg byreþ
mec ofer mearce;    hwilum mere-hengest
fereð ofer flodas    frætwum beorhtne;
hwilum mægða sum    minne gefylleð
bosm beag-hroden;    hwilum ic on bordum sceal,
10  heard, heafodleas,    behlyþed licgan;
hwilum hongige    hyrstum frætwed,
wlitig on wage,    þær weras drincað,
freolic fyrd-sceorp;    hwilum folc-wigan
on wicge wegað,    þonne ic winde sceal,
15  sinc-fag swelgan    of sumes bosme;
hwilum ic gereordum    rincas laðige
wlonce to wine;    hwilum wraþum sceal
stefne minre    forstolen hreddan,
flyman feond-sceaþan.
                Frige hwæt ic hatte.

nor their traveling more troublesome, even though,
robbed of robing, awakened by the powers
of heaven's guardian, they had to tear with their mouths
dusky crops. Their array will be renewed
for those who, having emerged, left their trappings          10
lying in their track, going to tread the land.


# EXE 12

I was a warrior's weapon; now a proud young fighting-man
covers me with gold and silver,
twisted wires.
                    Sometimes men kiss me;
sometimes with song I summon to war
familiar friends; sometimes a horse bears me               5
over the marches; sometimes a sea-stallion
ferries me over the flood, brightly attired;
sometimes one of the girls fills up
my bosom, ring-adorned; sometimes on boards,
hard, headless, I must lie, stripped bare;                 10
sometimes hang, arrayed with finery,
fair on the wall, where men drink,
a beautiful trapping of war; sometimes battle-warriors
bear me on a horse, when, treasure-adorned,
I must swallow breath from someone's breast;               15
sometimes with calls I summon men,
proud, to their wine; sometimes from hostile folk
with my voice I have to recover what is stolen,
put foemen to flight.
                    Find out what I am called.

# EXE 13

Hals is min hwit    ond heafod fealo,
sidan swa some.    Swift ic eom on feþe;
beado-wæpen bere.    Me on bæce standað
her swylce swe on hleorum.    Hlifiað tu
5  earan ofer eagum.    Ordum ic steppe
in grene græs.
                        Me bið gyrn witod,
gif mec onhæle    an onfindeð,
wæl-grim wiga,    þær ic wic buge,
bold mid bearnum,    ond ic bide þær
10  mid geoguð-cnosle;    hwonne gæst cume
to durum minum,    him biþ deað witod.
    Forþon ic sceal of eðle    eaforan mine
forht-mod fergan,    fleame nergan;
gif he me æfterweard    ealles weorþeð,
15  hine berað breost,    ic his bidan ne dear
reþes on geruman    —ne ic þæt ræd teale—
ac ic sceal fromlice    feþe-mundum
þurh steapne beorg    stræte wyrcan.
Eaþe ic mæg freora    feorh genergan,
20  gif ic mæg-burge mot    mine gelædan
on degolne weg    þurh dun-þyrel,
swæse ond gesibbe;    ic me siþþan ne þearf
wæl-hwelpes wig    wiht onsittan.
Gif se nið-sceaþa    nearwe stige
25  me on swaþe seceþ,    ne tosæleþ him
on þam gegn-paþe    guþ-gemotes,
siþþan ic þurh hylles    hrof geræce,

# EXE 13

My neck is white and head tawny,
sides the same. I am swift on my feet;
I bear battle-weapons. On my back stands
bristle, and likewise on my cheeks. There tower two
ears above my eyes. I step on tiptoe                                    5
in the green grass.
               Sorrow is decreed for me,
if someone uncovers me when I'm concealed,
a slaughter-grim warrior, where I have my house,
a home among my offspring, and there I wait
among my young brood; when an enemy comes                               10
to my doors, death is decreed for them.
   Wherefore in fear I must ferry from home
my children, save them by flight;
if he follows close afterward
on his belly, I dare not wait his fury
inside my den—I do not count that wise—                                15
but I must briskly with my front paws
create a street through a steep mountainside.
I can easily save my loved ones' lives,
if I may lead my entire family
on a hidden path through a hole in the hill,                           20
my kith and kin; then I need not
fear a jot the attack of the slaughter-hound.
If that harmful assailant pursues my path
down the narrow track, he will not lack
a warlike encounter on that hostile road,                              25
once I reach out through the hill's roof,

ond þurh hest hrino     hilde-pilum
lað-gewinnan,     þam þe ic longe fleah.


# EXE 14

Oft ic sceal wiþ wæge winnan     ond wiþ winde feohtan,
somod wið þam sæcce fremman,     þonne ic secan gewite
eorþan yþum þeaht;     me biþ se eþel fremde.
    Ic beom strong þæs gewinnes,     gif ic stille weorþe;
5   gif me þæs tosæleð,     hi beoð swiþran þonne ic,
ond mec slitende     sona flymað;
willað oþfergan     þæt ic friþian sceal.
    Ic him þæt forstonde,     gif min steort þolað,
ond mec stiþne wiþ     stanas moton,
10   fæste gehabban.
                Frige hwæt ic hatte.


# EXE 15

Ic eom mund-bora     minre heorde,
eodor wirum fæst,     innan gefylled
dryht-gestreona.     Dæg-tidum oft
spæte spere-brogan;     sped biþ þy mare
5   fylle minre.     Freo þæt bihealdeð,
hu me of hrife fleogað     hylde-pilas.
    Hwilum ic sweartum     swelgan onginne,
brunum beado-wæpnum,     bitrum ordum,
eglum attor-sperum.     Is min innað til,
10   womb-hord wlitig,     wloncum deore;
men gemunan     þæt me þurh muþ fareð.

and spitefully strike with darts of war
the hateful foe that I fled for long.


# EXE 14

Often I have to contend with wave and conflict with wind,
take them both on in battle, when, covered with breakers,
I go to seek the ground; that homeland is foreign to me.
    I am strong in that struggle, if I stay still;
if I fail in that, they are mightier than me,         5
and, tearing me up, they soon put me to flight:
they want to bear off what I must maintain.
    I stand up to them, if my tip endures,
and stones can secure me,
strongly firm.         10
        Find out what I am called.


# EXE 15

I am the protector of my flock,
an enclosure firm in wires, filled within
with noble treasures. Often in daytimes
I spit spear-terror; the gain is the greater
the fuller I am. The master beholds         5
how from my belly fly darts of war.
    Sometimes I begin to swallow swarthy things,
gleaming battle-weapons, bitter points,
painful poison-spears. My innards are fine,
a splendid womb-hoard, precious to the proud;         10
men remember what passes through my mouth.

## EXE 16

Ic eom wundorlicu wiht;    ne mæg word sprecan,
mældan for monnum,    þeah ic muþ hæbbe,
wide wombe ...
Ic wæs on ceole    ond mines cnosles ma.

## EXE 17

Ic on siþe seah · ᛋ ᚱ ᚩ ᚻ · hyge-wloncne,    heafod-beorhtne,
swiftne ofer sæl-wong    swiþe þrægan.
Hæfde him on hrycge    hilde-þryþe;
· ᚾ ᚩ ᛗ ·    nægledne rad,
5 · ᚪ ᚷ ᛖ ᚹ ·    Wid-last ferede,
ryne-strong on rade,    rofne · ᚳ ᚩ
ᚠ ᚩ ᚪ ᚻ ·    For wæs þy beorhtre,
swylcra siþ-fæt.    Saga hwæt hit hatte.

## EXE 18

Ic eom wunderlicu wiht,    on gewin sceapen,
frean minum leof,    fægre gegyrwed.
Byrne is min bleo-fag,    swylce beorht seomað
wir ymb þone wæl-gim    þe me waldend geaf,
5 se me wid-galum    wisað hwilum
sylfum to sace.    Þonne ic sinc wege
þurh hlutterne dæg,    hond-weorc smiþa,

## EXE 16

I am a curious creature; I cannot speak words,
declaim before men, though I have a mouth,
a wide belly . . .
I was on a ship with more of my kind.

## EXE 17

I saw *.sroh.* (a horse) proud in spirit, bright in head,
traveling swift over the lush plain, running strong.
He had on his back battle-force;
*.nom.* (a man) rode the nailed one,
*.agew.* (ways, waves). The wide-tracked one carried,        5
strong-running in riding, a bold *.co*
*foah.* (a hawk). The trip was that much the brighter,
the travel of such creatures. Say what it is called.

## EXE 18

I am a curious creature, created to strife,
dear to my lord, finely adorned.
My mail shirt is motley, and likewise bright wire
twines around the slaughter-gem my governor gave me,
and he, as I wander widely, sometimes himself        5
wields me in warfare. Then I wear treasure
throughout the clear day, the handiwork of smiths,

gold ofer geardas.
　　　　　Oft ic gæst-berend
cwelle comp-wæpnum;　cyning mec gyrweð
10　since ond seolfre　ond mec on sele weorþað,
ne wyrneð word-lofes,　wisan mæneð
mine for mengo,　þær hy meodu drincað,
healdeð mec on heaþore,　hwilum læteð eft,
rad-werigne　on gerum sceacan,
15　orleg-fromne.
　　　　　Oft ic oþrum scod,
frecne æt his freonde;　fah eom ic wide,
wæpnum awyrged.　Ic me wenan ne þearf
þæt me bearn wræce　on bonan feore,
gif me gromra hwylc　guþe genægeð;
20　ne weorþeð sio mæg-burg　gemicledu
eaforan minum　þe ic æfter woc,
nymþe ic hlafordleas　hweorfan mote
from þam healdende　þe me hringas geaf.
　　　Me bið forð witod,　gif ic frean hyre,
25　guþe fremme,　swa ic gien dyde
minum þeodne on þonc,　þæt ic þolian sceal
bearn-gestreona.　Ic wiþ bryde ne mot
hæmed habban,　ac me þæs hyht-plegan
geno wyrneð,　se mec geara on
30　bende legde;　forþon ic brucan sceal
on hagostealde　hæleþa gestreona.
　　　Oft ic wirum dol　wife abelge,
wonie hyre willan;　heo me wom spreceð,
floceð hyre folmum,　firenaþ mec wordum,
35　ungod gæleð:　ic ne gyme þæs compes . . .

gold over the courtyards.
                    Often I kill
soul-bearers with war-weapons; a king adorns me
with treasure and silver and honors me in the hall,                    10
spares not words of praise, spells out my nature
before the multitude, where they drink mead,
keeps me in confinement, sometimes lets me again,
weary of travel, wander free,
brave in battle.                                                       15
                    Often I harmed another,
fiercely in a friend's hand; I am widely outlawed,
cursed among weapons. I need not expect
that a son will avenge me on the life of my slayer,
if a certain foe should attack me in battle;
that family will not become increased                                 20
by sons of mine that I spawned from myself,
unless, lordless, I may depart
from the wielder who gave me rings.

     It is henceforth decreed, if I obey my lord,
wage war, as I have done so far                                       25
to please my prince, that I must lack
the riches of children. With a bride I may not
pursue my pleasure, but he still refuses me
that jolly sport, that one who long ago
laid bonds on me; therefore I must enjoy                              30
as a bachelor the riches of men.

     Often, dull-witted in wires, I stir up a woman,
take away what she wants; she speaks evilly to me,
smacks me with her hands, berates me with words,
screams ill will; I do not care for that conflict . . .              35

325

## EXE 19

Neb is min niþerweard;    neol ic fere
ond be grunde græfe,    geonge swa me wisað,
har holtes feond,    ond hlaford min
woh færeð    weard æt steorte,
5    wrigaþ on wonge,    wegeð mec ond þyð,
saweþ on swæð min.    Ic snyþige forð,
brungen of bearwe,    bunden cræfte,
wegen on wægne,    hæbbe wundra fela.
    Me biþ gongendre    grene on healfe,
10    ond min swæð sweotol    sweart on oþre.
Me þurh hrycg wrecen    hongaþ under
an orþonc-pil,    oþer on heafde,
fæst ond forðweard.    Fealleþ on sidan
þæt ic toþum tere,    gif me teala þenaþ
15    hindeweardre,    þæt biþ hlaford min.

## EXE 20

Ætsomne cwom    ·LX· monna
to wæg-stæþe    wicgum ridan;
hæfdon ·XI·    eored-mæcgas
frid-hengestas,    ·IIII· sceamas.
5    Ne meahton mago-rincas    ofer mere feolan,
swa hi fundedon,    ac wæs flod to deop,
atol yþa geþræc,    ofras hea,
streamas stronge.        Ongunnon stigan þa

326

# EXE 19

My beak points down; prone I go
and dig up the ground, travel as he guides me,
the gray forest-foe, and my master
walks bent over, a guard at my tail,
presses forward on the field, grips me and grasps,      5
sows in my track. I snuffle along,
brought from the grove, bound with skill,
fetched on a wagon: I have many wonders.
    As I travel there is green on one side of me,
and my track clear, black on the other.      10
Driven through my back, there hangs beneath
a single cunning spear, another in my head,
fixed and pointing forward. There falls to the side
what I tear with my teeth, if he serves me well
from behind, the one who is my lord.      15

# EXE 20

Together there came sixty men
to the seashore, riding horses;
eleven of the mounted men had
fine steeds, four grays.
    The warriors could not pass through the sea,      5
as they intended, but the flood was too deep,
the dread thrash of waves, steep shores,
strong streams.

       Then the men began

on wægn weras    ond hyra wicg somod
10  hlodan under hrunge;    þa þa hors oðbær,
eh ond eorlas,    æscum dealle,
ofer wætres byht    wægn to lande:
swa hine oxa ne teah,    ne esna mægen,
ne fæt-hengest,    ne on flode swom,
15  ne be grunde wod    gestum under,
ne lagu drefde,    ne of lyfte fleag,
ne under bæc cyrde;    brohte hwæþre
beornas ofer burnan    ond hyra bloncan mid
from stæðe heaum,    þæt hy stopan up
20  on oþerne,    ellen-rofe,
weras of wæge,    ond hyra wicg gesund.


# EXE 21

*Agof is min noma,    eft onhwyrfed.*
Ic eom wrætlic wiht    on gewin sceapen,
þonne ic onbuge,    ond me of bosme fareð
ætren onga;    ic beom eall-gearo
5  þæt ic me þæt feorh-bealo    feor aswape.
    Siþþan me se waldend,    se me þæt wite gescop,
leoþo forlæteð,    ic beo lengre þonne ær,
oþþæt ic spæte,    spilde geblonden,
eal-felo attor    þæt ic æror geap.
10    Ne togongeð þæs    gumena hwylcum,
ænigum eaþe    þæt ic þær ymb sprice,
gif hine hrineð    þæt me of hrife fleogeð:
þæt þone man-drinc    mægne geceapaþ,
full-wered fæste    feore sine.


328

to mount a wagon, and their steeds too
they loaded under the pole; then it bore off the horses,          10
mounts and men, exulting in spears,
the wagon across the watery bay to the land:
no ox drew it, or asses' strength,
or draft horse, nor did it swim in the flood,
nor wade on the ground under its guests,
nor stir up the sea, nor fly out of the sky,          15
nor turn back; yet it brought
warriors over the stream, and their chargers too,
from one high bank, so that they stepped up
onto the other, bold in spirit,
                                                          20
men from the wave, and their stallions safe.

# EXE 21

*UUOB is my name, turned backward.*
I am a quaint creature, created to strife,
when I bend, and from my bosom there goes
a poison dart; I am all set
to sweep that deadly evil far from me.          5
     Once my governor, who caused my torture,
loosens limbs, I am longer than before,
until I spit, corrupted with venom,
the dreadful poison that I swallowed previously.
     It does not leave behind any man,          10
easily, what I spoke of before,
if what flies from my belly strikes him:
he pays for that evil drink, very perilous,
with his strength, with his very life.

15     Nelle ic unbunden    ænigum hyran,
nymþe searo-sæled.
                 Saga hwæt ic hatte.

## EXE 22

Ic eom wunderlicu wiht:    wræsne mine stefne;
hwilum beorce swa hund;    hwilum blæte swa gat;
hwilum græde swa gos;    hwilum gielle swa hafoc;
hwilum ic onhyrge    þone haswan earn,
5    guð-fugles hleoþor;    hwilum glidan reorde
muþe gemæne;    hwilum mæwes song,
þær ic glado sitte.
                 · ᚷ · mec nemnað,
swylce · ᚠ · ond · ᚱ ·   · ᚷ · fullesteð,
· ᚻ · ond · ᛁ ·
          Nu ic haten eom,
10   swa þa siex stafas    sweotule becnaþ.

## EXE 23

Ic eom wunderlicu wiht:    wifum on hyhte,
neah-buendum nyt,    nængum sceþþe
burg-sittendra,    nymþe bonan anum.
    Stapol min is steap-heah;    stonde ic on bedde,
5    neoþan ruh nat-hwær.    Neþeð hwilum
ful cyrtenu    ceorles dohtor,
mod-wlonc meowle,    þæt heo on mec gripeð,

Unbound, I will not obey anyone,                                    15
unless I am strung with skill.

> Say what I am called.


# EXE 22

I am a curious creature: I vary my voice;
sometimes I bark like a dog; sometimes bleat like a goat;
sometimes cackle like a goose; sometimes shriek like a
    hawk;
sometimes I mimic the dusky eagle,
the sound of the war-bird; sometimes the kite's call          5
do I utter from my mouth; sometimes seagull's song,
as I sit glad.

> .*g.* they name me,
.*æ.* and .*r.* too; with the help of .*o.*
.*h.* and .*i.*

> Now I am named,
as these six symbols surely show.                              10


# EXE 23

I am a curious creature: what a woman wants,
at the service of neighbors, and harmful to none
of those at home, except the one who hurts me.
    My shaft is straight up; I stand in a bed,
more or less hairy beneath. Sometimes the very lovely         5
daughter of a churl takes a risk,
haughty girl, so that she grasps me,

331

ræseð mec on reodne,     reafað min heafod,
fegeð mec on fæsten.
                    Feleþ sona
10   mines gemotes,     seo þe mec nearwað,
wif wunden-locc:     wæt bið þæt eage.


# EXE 24

Mec feonda sum     feore besnyþede,
woruld-strenga binom,     wætte siþþan,
dyfde on wætre,     dyde eft þonan,
sette on sunnan,     þær ic swiþe beleas
5   herum þam þe ic hæfde.
                    Heard mec siþþan
snað seaxses ecg,     sindrum begrunden;
fingras feoldan,     ond mec fugles wyn
geondsprengde sped-dropum     spyrede geneahhe,
ofer brunne brerd,     beam-telge swealg,
10   streames dæle,     stop eft on mec,
siþade sweart-last.
                    Mec siþþan wrah
hæleð hleo-bordum,     hyde beþenede,
gierede mec mid golde;     forþon me glisedon,
wrætlic weorc smiþa,     wire bifongen.
15   Nu þa gereno     ond se reada telg
ond þa wuldor-gesteald     wide mære
dryht-folca helm     (nales dol wite).
       Gif min bearn wera     brucan willað,
hy beoð þy gesundran     ond þy sige-fæstran,
20   heortum þy hwætran     ond þy hyge-bliþran,

rubs me to redness, ravages my head,
stuffs me somewhere safe.
                She soon feels it,
her encounter with me, the one who confines me,        10
the curly-locked lady: one eye will be wet.


# EXE 24

A certain foe snatched away my life,
deprived me of earthly powers, then soaked me,
dipped me in water, drew me out again,
set me in sunlight, where I soon lost
those hairs I had.                             5
                  Then a hard knife's edge,
its roughness rubbed off, cut me up;
fingers folded me, and a bird's delight
spread on me serviceable drops, often made tracks
across a brown rim, swallowed wood dye,
in some solution, stepped back upon me,        10
and traveled, leaving a dark track.
                      Then a man
wrapped me with protective boards, bound me with hide,
adorned me with gold; and so there glistens upon me,
surrounded with wire, the wondrous work of smiths.
    Now those decorations, and that red dye,        15
and that fine fortune, spread wide the fame
of the protector of noble nations (let no fool find fault).
    If the children of men are willing to benefit from me,
they shall be the more sound and the more sure of victory,
the brisker in heart, the happier in mind,        20

ferþe þy frodran;   habbaþ freonda þy ma,
swæsra ond gesibbra,   soþra ond godra,
tilra ond getreowra,   þa hyra tyr ond ead
estum ycað   ond hy ar-stafum
25  lissum bilecgað   ond hi lufan fæþmum
fæste clyppað.
                  Frige hwæt ic hatte,
niþum to nytte;   nama min is mære,
hæleþum gifre   ond halig sylf.

# EXE 25

Ic eom weorð werum,   wide funden,
brungen of bearwum   ond of burg-hl eoþum,
of denum ond of dunum.   Dæges mec wægun
feþre on lifte,   feredon mid liste
5  under hrofes hleo;   hæleð mec siþþan
baþedan in bydene.
                  Nu ic eom bindere
ond swingere,   sona weorpe
esne to eorþan,   hwilum ealdne ceorl.
Sona þæt onfindeð,   se þe mec fehð ongean,
10  ond wið mægen-þisan   minre genæsteð,
þæt he hrycge sceal   hrusan secan,
gif he unrædes   ær ne geswiceð,
strengo bistolen,   strong on spræce,
mægene binumen,   nah his modes geweald,
15  fota ne folma.
                  Frige hwæt ic hatte,

the wiser in spirit; they will have the more friends,
more loved ones and kinsmen more loyal and close,
constant and true, who will gladly increase
their prosperity and honor, envelop them
with benefits and kindnesses, and enfold them                    25
in love's firm embrace.
                  Find out what I am called,
of service to men; my name is well known,
effective for folk, and holy itself.


# EXE 25


I am valued by men, widely found,
fetched from forests and mountain slopes,
from depths and heights. By day there bore me
wings in the air, carried me with cunning
under the shelter of a roof. Then men                            5
bathed me in a basin.
              Now I am a binder
and a beater; straightaway I cast down
a slave to the floor, sometimes an old churl.
Straightaway he perceives, who struggles against me,
and strives against my mighty force,                             10
that his back has to hit the ground,
if he does not first refrain from imprudence;
stripped of strength, strident in speech,
deprived of might, he has no power of mind,
nor feet nor hands.                                              15
              Find out what I am called

ðe on eorþan swa     esnas binde,
dole æfter dyntum     be dæges leohte.


## EXE 26

Biþ foldan dæl     fægre gegierwed,
mid þy heardestan     ond mid þy scearpestan,
ond mid þy grymmestan     gumena gestreona,
corfen, sworfen,     cyrred, þyrred,
5   bunden, wunden,     blæced, wæced,
frætwed, geatwed,     feorran læded
to durum dryhta.
                    Dream bið in innan
cwicra wihta;     clengeð, lengeð,
ær lifgende     longe hwile,
10   wilna bruceð     ond no wiht spriceð,
ond þonne æfter deaþe     deman onginneð,
meldan mislice.
                    Micel is to hycganne
wis-fæstum menn,     hwæt seo wiht sy.


## EXE 27

Ic wiht geseah     wundorlice,
hornum bitweonum     huþe lædan,
lyft-fæt leohtlic,     listum gegierwed,
huþe to þam ham     of þam here-siþe;
5   walde hyre on þære byrig     bur atimbran,
searwum asettan,     gif hit swa meahte.

who on the floor in this way binds slaves,
foolish after a battering by the light of day.

## EXE 26

There is a portion of the earth, richly provided
with the hardest, and with the sharpest,
and with the grimmest of the treasures of men;
sliced, leveled, twisted, made dry,
bound, wound, bleached, stretched,                    5
arrayed, attired, brought from far
to the doors of men.
      Joy will be within
of living creatures: it clings, it lingers,
where, of those previously living a long time,
it enjoys what they want, and does not speak at all,      10
and then after death begins to give judgment,
declaims variously.
      There is much to consider
for a wise person, what that creature may be.

## EXE 27

I saw a creature, a curious thing,
bringing booty between its horns,
a shining sky vessel artfully arrayed,
booty home from that journey of war;
she wanted to build her bower in that dwelling,       5
skillfully establish it, if only she could.

Ða cwom wundorlicu wiht     ofer wealles hrof,
seo is eallum cuð     eorð-buendum;
ahredde þa þa huþe     ond to ham bedraf
10  wreccan ofer willan,     gewat hyre west þonan,
fæhþum feran,     forð onette.
    Dust stonc to heofonum,     deaw feol on eorþan;
niht forð gewat.     Nænig siþþan
wera gewiste     þære wihte sið.

## EXE 28a

Ic eom leg-bysig,     lace mid winde,
bewunden mid wuldre,     wedre gesomnad,
fus forð-weges,     fyre gebysgad,
bearu blowende,     byrnende gled.
5  Ful oft mec gesiþas     sendað æfter hondum,
þæt mec weras ond wif     wlonce cyssað.
    Þonne ic mec onhæbbe,     ond hi onhnigaþ to me,
monige mid miltse;     þær ic monnum sceal
ycan up-cyme     eadignesse.

## EXE 28b

Ic eom lig-bysig,     lace mid winde,
wuldre bewunden     wedre gesomnad,
fus forð-weges,     fyre gemylted,
bearu blowende,     byrnende gled.
5  Ful oft mec gesiþas     sendað æfter hondum,

Then there came a curious creature over the roof-side,
she is familiar to every earth dweller;
recovered the booty, and drove the wanderer
back home against its will, took herself west from there,     10
passing in vengeance, she hastened on.
    Dust rose to the skies; dew fell on the ground;
night passed on. Afterward, no one
knew where that creature went.


# EXE 28a

I am flame-busy, play with the wind,
begirt with glory, by weather brought together,
eager for the journey forth, busied by fire,
a blooming grove, a burning ember.
Very often companions pass me from hand to hand,     5
where men and women proudly offer kisses.
    Then I raise myself up, and they bow down to me,
many with humility, where I must to men
increase the burgeoning of blessedness.


# EXE 28b

I am flame-busy, play with the wind,
begirt with glory, by weather brought together,
eager for the journey forth, melted by fire,
a blooming grove, a burning ember.
Very often companions pass me from hand to hand,     5

þær mec weras ond wif    wlonce gecyssað.

Þonne ic mec onhæbbe,    hi onhnigað to me,
modge miltsum;    swa ic mongum sceal
ycan up-cyme    eadignesse.

## EXE 29

*Is þes middan-geard    missenlicum*
*wisum gewlitegad,    wrættum gefrætwad.*
Ic seah sellic þing    singan on ræcede;
wiht wæs nower    werum on gemonge,
5  sio hæfde wæstum    wundorlicran.

Niþerweard onhwyrfed    wæs neb hyre,
fet ond folme    fugele gelice;
no hwæþre fleogan mæg    ne fela gongan,
hwæþre feþe-georn    fremman onginneð;
10  gecoren cræftum,    cyrreð geneahhe,
oft ond gelome    eorlum on gemonge,
siteð æt symble,    sæles bideþ,
hwonne ær heo cræft hyre    cyþan mote
werum on gemonge.    Ne heo þær wiht þigeð
15  þæs þe him æt blisse    beornas habbað.

Deor domes georn,    hio dumb wunað;
hwæþre hyre is on fote    fæger hleoþor,
wynlicu woð-giefu.    Wrætlic me þinceð,
hu seo wiht mæge    wordum lacan
20  þurh fot neoþan,    frætwed hyrstum.
Hafað hyre on halse,    þonne hio hord warað,
baru, beagum deall,    broþor sine,

where men and women proudly offer kisses.
When I raise myself up, they, in high spirits,
bow down to my humble self, where I must to many
increase the burgeoning of blessedness.


# EXE 29

*This middle-earth is in miscellaneous ways*
*made beautiful, with treasures made fair.*
I saw a strange thing sing in a hall:
nowhere was there a creature among men
that had a more spectacular shape.                               5
    Dropping down was her beak,
feet and hands like a bird;
yet she cannot fly, nor walk so much,
but, eager to step out, she begins to act;
chosen skillfully, she changes continually,                     10
often and again among men,
sits at the feast, bides her time,
until she can show her skill
among men. She tastes no part
of what the warriors have for delight.                          15
    Brave, eager for glory, she stays silent;
though there is from her foot a fine sound,
a graceful gift of song. It seems amazing to me,
how that creature can conjure sounds
through that downturned foot, fairly adorned.                   20
They have her by the neck, when she guards treasure,
bare, resplendent in rings, her own brothers,

mæg mid mægne.
             Micel is to hycgenne
wisum woð-boran,    hwæt sio wiht sie.

## EXE 30

*Is þes middan-geard    missenlicum*
*wisum gewlitegad,    wrættum gefrætwad.*
Siþum sellic   ic seah searo hweorfan,
grindan wið greote,   giellende faran.
5  Næfde sellicu wiht   syne ne folme,
exle ne earmas;   sceal on anum fet
searo-ceap swifan,   swiþe feran,
faran ofer feldas.   Hæfde fela ribba;
muð wæs on middan.   Mon-cynne nyt,
10  fereð foddur-welan,   folcscipe dreogeð,
wist in wigeð,   ond werum gieldeð
gaful geara gehwam   þæs þe guman brucað,
rice ond heane.
             Rece, gif þu cunne,
wis worda gleaw,   hwæt sio wiht sie.

## EXE 31

Wiht cwom æfter wege   wrætlicu liþan,
cymlic from ceole   cleopode to londe,
hlinsade hlude;   hleahtor wæs gryrelic,
egesful on earde,   ecge wæron scearpe.
5    Wæs hio hete-grim,   hilde to sæne,

kinsman among kinsman.
It is a great thing for a wise song-bearer
to think what that creature may be.


## EXE 30

*This middle-earth is in miscellaneous ways*
*made beautiful, with treasures made fair.*
On occasions I saw a strange contraption journey on,
grind against the gravel, travel screaming.
  That strange creature had no sight nor grip,     5
shoulder nor arms; on a single foot
the shaped contraption had to thrust and strongly go,
passing over fields. It had many ribs;
its mouth was in the midst. Useful to men,
it ferries a wealth of food, endures company,     10
bears sustenance, and grants to men
the tribute every year that folk enjoy,
rich and poor.
State, if you know,
you wise in words, what that creature may be.


## EXE 31

A creature came sailing, wondrous, over the waves,
splendid from the vessel, she called to the shore,
boomed loud; the laughter was terrible,
awesome on earth, the edges were sharp.
  She was hate-grim, slow to strife,     5

biter beado-weorca;    bord-weallas grof,
heard-hiþende,    hete-rune bond,
sægde searo-cræftig    ymb hyre sylfre gesceaft:
"Is min modor    mægða cynnes,
10   þæs deorestan,    þæt is dohtor min,
eacen uploden,    swa þæt is ældum cuþ,
firum on folce,    þæt seo on foldan sceal
on ealra londa gehwam    lissum stondan."

## EXE 32

Ic wiht geseah    in wera burgum;
seo þæt feoh fedeð.    Hafað fela toþa;
nebb biþ hyre æt nytte,    niþerweard gongeð,
hiþeð holdlice    ond to ham tyhð,
5   wæþeð geond weallas,    wyrte seceð.
    Aa heo þa findeð    þa þe fæst ne biþ,
læteð hio þa wlitigan,    wyrtum fæste,
stille stondan    on staþol-wonge,
beorhte blican,    blowan ond growan.

## EXE 33

Mec se wæta wong,    wundrum freorig,
of his innaþe    ærist cende;
ne wat ic mec beworhtne    wulle flysum,
hærum þurh heah-cræft,    hyge-þoncum min.
5   Wundene me ne beoð wefle,    ne ic wearp hafu,

bitter in battle-deeds; she dug into board-walls,
plundering hard, bound a hate-rune,
spoke, cunning-crafty, about her own creation:
 "My mother is, of all the maids there are,
the dearest, and she is my daughter,                                    10
grown up pregnant, as is well known to men,
to people among folk, when she has to stand with kindness
in the world, on every land."


## EXE 32

I saw a creature in the strongholds of men;
she feeds the cattle. She has many teeth;
her nose points down to serve her need,
she plunders fervently, and drags off home,
hunts out along the walls, seeks out roots.                              5
 She always finds ones that are not secure,
leaves behind the pretty ones, securely rooted,
standing still in a settled place,
shining brightly, glowing and growing.


## EXE 33

The wet ground, wondrously chilly,
first gave me birth from its innards;
I know that I was not produced from woolly fleeces,
or hairs, through lofty skill in thoughts.
 There are no twisted wefts for me, nor do I have warps,     5

ne þurh þreata geþræcu    þræd me ne hlimmeð,
ne æt me hrutende    hrisil scriþeð,
ne mec ohwonan    sceal am cnyssan.

    Wyrmas mec ne awæfan    wyrda cræftum,
10  þa þe geolo god-webb    geatwum frætwað;
wile mec mon hwæþre seþeah    wide ofer eorþan
hatan for hæleþum    hyhtlic gewæde.

    Saga soð-cwidum,    searo-þoncum gleaw,
wordum wis-fæst,    hwæt þis gewæde sy.

# EXE 34

Ic wiht geseah    on wege feran,
seo wæs wrætlice    wundrum gegierwed.
Hæfde feowere    fet under wombe
ond ehtuwe
5  *monn ·h·w·M· wiif ·m·x·l·kf wf· hors ·qxxs·*
             ufon on hrycge;
hæfde tu fiþru    ond twelf eagan
ond siex heafdu.
            Saga hwæt hio wære.

   *For flod-wegas;    ne wæs þæt na fugul ana,*
10 *ac þær wæs æghwylces    anra gelicnes:*
*horses ond monnes,    hundes ond fugles,*
*ond eac wifes wlite.*
            *Þu wast, gif þu const,*
*to gesecganne,    þæt we soð witan:*
*hu þære wihte    wise gonge.*

nor through a threat of violence does a thread resound in
    me,
nor does a humming shuttle slide in me,
nor does a slay beat me about at all.
   Nor did worms weave me with the skills of fate,
those who craftily decorate fine yellow cloth;           10
nonetheless, I will be called a desirable garment
widely over the earth among heroes.
   You who are clever in cunning thoughts, securely skilled
    in words,
say in truthful utterance what this garment might be.


# EXE 34


I saw a creature traveling along;
she was marvelously adorned with wonders.
She had four feet under her belly
and eight
*monn ·h·w·M· wiif ·m·x·l·kf wf· hors ·qxxs·*         5
        up on her back;
she had two feathers and twelve eyes
and six heads.
          Say what she was.
   *That creature traveled the waterways, nor was it only a bird,*
*but there was the likeness of every one of these:*      10
*horse and man, dog and bird,*
*and also the shape of a woman.*
             *You know,*
*if you know how to say it, what we know to be the truth:*
*how the track of that creature goes.*

347

## EXE 35

Ic þa wihte geseah:  womb wæs on hindan,
þriþum aþrunten.  Þegn folgade,
mægen-rofa man,  ond micel hæfde
gefered þæt hit felde,  fleah þurh his eage.
5    Ne swylteð he symle,  þonne syllan sceal
innað þam oþrum,  ac him eft cymeð
bot in bosme,  blæd biþ aræred;
he sunu wyrceð,  bið him sylfa fæder.


## EXE 36

Ic þa wiht geseah  wæpned-cynnes,
geoguð-myrþe grædig;  him on gafol forlet
ferð-friþende  feower wellan,
scire sceotan,  on gesceap þeotan.
5    Mon maþelade,  se þe me gesægde:
"Seo wiht, gif hio gedygeð,  duna briceð;
gif he tobirsteð,  bindeð cwice."


## EXE 37

Gewritu secgað  þæt seo wiht sy,
mid mon-cynne  miclum tidum
sweotol ond gesyne.  Sundor-cræft hafað
maran micle,  þonne hit men witen.
5    Heo wile gesecan  sundor æghwylcne
feorh-berendra;  gewiteð eft feran on weg.

348

## EXE 35

I saw that creature: its belly was in the back,
massively swollen. A servant stood behind,
a mighty powerful man, and he had in a big way
brought forth what filled it; that flew through its eyehole.

He does not keep on dying, when he has to give     5
his innards to that other, but again there comes
a betterment in the breast, breath is brought up;
he makes sons, and is his father himself.

## EXE 36

I saw a creature of the weaponed kind,
greedy with youth-glee; he took as tribute
four life-giving streams,
brightly spouting, spurting at his whim.

A man spoke, who said to me:     5
"That creature, if it survives, will break the fields;
if he is torn apart, he will bind the living."

## EXE 37

Writings say that that creature may be,
much of the time, plain and visible
among mankind. She has a special skill
much greater than people perceive.
She will seek out specially every one     5
of living creatures; then she travels back away again.

Ne bið hio næfre     niht þær oþre,
ac hio sceal wide-ferh     wreccan laste
ham-leas hweorfan;     no þy heanre biþ.
10    Ne hafað hio fot ne folme,     ne æfre foldan hran,
ne eagena hafað     ægþer twega,
ne muð hafaþ,     ne wiþ monnum spræc,
ne gewit hafað,     ac gewritu secgað
þæt seo sy earmost     ealra wihta,
15    þara þe æfter gecyndum     cenned wære.
      Ne hafað hio sawle ne feorh,     ac hio siþas sceal
geond þas wundor-woruld     wide dreogan.
Ne hafaþ hio blod ne ban,     hwæþre bearnum wearð
geond þisne middan-geard     mongum to frofre.
20    Næfre hio heofonum hran,     ne to helle mot,
ac hio sceal wide-ferh     wuldor-cyninges
larum lifgan.     Long is to secganne
hu hyre ealdor-gesceaft     æfter gongeð,
woh wyrda gesceapu;     þæt is wrætlic þing
25    to gesecganne.
                  Soð is æghwylc
þara þe ymb þas wiht     wordum becneð;
ne hafað heo ænig lim,     leofaþ efne seþeah.
      Gif þu mæge reselan     recene gesecgan
soþum wordum,     saga hwæt hio hatte.


# EXE 38

Ece is se scyppend,     se þas eorþan nu
wreð-stuþum wealdeð     ond þas world healdeð.

She is never there a second night,
but must journey evermore, homeless,
on an exile's path; she is no more miserable for that.
   She has neither foot nor hand, nor has ever touched the     10
    ground,
nor has even one of two eyes,
nor has a mouth, nor speaks with men,
nor has a mind, but writings say
that she is the most pitiful of all creatures
that are natural born.                             15
   She has no soul, nor life, but she has to endure
trials widely throughout this wonder-world.
She has no blood, nor bone, and yet has been a comfort
to many offspring throughout this middle-earth.
   She has never touched the sky, nor may she go to hell,     20
but she must evermore live in the teachings
of the king of glory. It is long to tell
how the fate of her life carries on,
the crooked shapes of events; that is a wondrous thing
to be told.                                       25
            Everything is true
that is mentioned in words about this creature;
she has no limbs, and nonetheless she lives.
   If you can quickly supply a solution
in true words, say what she is called.


# EXE 38

Eternal is the creator, who now controls
this earth with a guiding rod, and this world holds.

Rice is se reccend,   ond on ryht cyning,
ealra an-walda,   eorþan ond heofones:
5  healdeð ond wealdeð,   swa he ymb þas utan hweorfeð.

He mec wrætlice   worhte æt frymþe,
þa he þisne ymb-hwyrft   ærest sette,
heht mec wæccende   wunian longe,
þæt ic ne slepe   siþþan æfre,
10  ond mec semninga   slæp ofergongeþ:
beoð eagan min   ofestum betyned.

Þisne middan-geard   meahtig dryhten
mid his onwalde   æghwær styreð;
swa ic mid wealdendes   worde ealne
15  þisne ymb-hwyrft   utan ymbclyppe.

Ic eom to þon bleað,   þæt mec bealdlice mæg
gearu gongende   grima abregan,
ond eofore eom   æghwær cenra,
þonne he gebolgen   bid-steal giefeð;
20  ne mæg mec oferswiþan   segn-berendra
ænig ofer eorþan,   nymþe se ana god
se þisne hean heofon   healdeþ ond wealdeþ.

Ic eom on stence   strengre micle
þonne ricels   oþþe rose sy,
25  ... on eorþan tyrf
wynlic weaxeð;   ic eom wræstre þonne heo;
þeah þe lilie sy   leof mon-cynne,
beorht on blostman,   ic eom betre þonne heo;
swylce ic nardes stenc   nyde oferswiþe
30  mid minre swetnesse   symle æghwær,
ond ic fulre eom   þonne þis fen swearte,
þæt her yfle   adelan stinceð.

Powerful is that ruler, and rightly king,
monarch of all in heaven and earth:
he holds and controls, as he contains all these things.                     5

   He created me wondrously, right from the start,
when he first set up these surroundings,
had me wait, watching, for a long time,
so that ever after I may not sleep,
though sleep overcomes me suddenly:
my eyes are quickly covered.                                                10

   The mighty lord governs this middle-earth
everywhere with his power;
just so do I embrace these surroundings
entirely, at the commander's word.                                          15

   I am so timid that a quick-flitting ghost
can frighten me fully,
and yet I am in all ways braver than a boar,
when, bristling, he stands his ground;
no banner-bearer in the world                                               20
can overcome me, except the one God
who holds and controls this high sky.

   In scent I am much stronger
than incense or the rose,
. . . in the earth's turf                                                    25
gaily grows; I am more slender than she;
though the lily may be dear to mankind,
bright in blooming, I am better than she;
so too do I necessarily drown out nard's scent
with my sweetness, at all times everywhere,                                 30
and yet I am more stinking than this black fen,
which smells badly here with its stench.

Eal ic under heofones    hwearfte recce,
swa me leof fæder    lærde æt frymþe,
35 þæt ic þa mid ryhte    reccan moste
þicce ond þynne;    þinga gehwylces
onlicnesse    æghwær healde.
Hyrre ic eom heofone,    hateþ mec heah-cyning
his deagol þing    dyre bihealdan;
40 eac ic under eorþan    eal sceawige,
wom wrað-scrafu    wraþra gæsta.

Ic eom micle yldra    þonne ymb-hwyrft þes,
oþþe þes middan-geard    meahte geweorþan,
ond ic giestron wæs    geong acenned,
45 mære to monnum,    þurh minre modor hrif.
Ic eom fægerre    frætwum goldes,
þeah hit mon awerge    wirum utan;
ic eom wyrslicre    þonne þes wudu fula,
oððe þis waroð    þe her aworpen ligeð.

50 Ic eorþan eom    æghwær brædre,
ond wid-gielra    þonne þes wong grena;
folm mec mæg bifon    ond fingras þry
utan eaþe    ealle ymbclyppan.
Heardra ic eom ond caldra    þonne se hearda forst,
55 hrim heoru-grimma,    þonne he to hrusan cymeð;
ic eom Ulcanus    up irnendan
leohtan leoman    lege hatra.
Ic eom on goman    gena swetra
þonne þu beo-bread    blende mid hunige;
60 swylce ic eom wraþre    þonne wermod sy,
þe her on hyrstum    heasewe stondeþ.

Ic mesan mæg    meahtelicor
ond efnetan    ealdum þyrse,

I rule all things under the vault of the sky,
just as the dear father taught me from the start,
that I rightly be allowed to rule 35
both thick and thin; I held the likeness
everywhere, of everything.
I am higher than the sky; the high king himself
bids me secretly behold his hidden deeds;
I also spy out everything under the earth, 40
the evil pits of pain of wicked spirits.
I am much older than these surroundings are,
or this middle-earth may yet become,
and yet I was born young yesterday,
renowned among men, through my mother's womb. 45
I am more beautiful than ornaments of gold,
though they were covered all over with wires;
I am worse than this stinking wood,
or this seaweed that lies cast up here.
I am broader in every way than the earth, 50
and more vast than this green plain;
a hand can grasp me, and three fingers
easily enfold me utterly.
I am harder and colder than the hard frost,
the fiercely grim rime when it falls to the ground; 55
I am hotter than the flame of the fiery brightness
of Vulcan, flashing up high;
I am still sweeter in the mouth
than when you blend honeycomb with honey;
so too I am more bitter than wormwood is, 60
that stands here ashen in its array.
I can devour more powerfully
and match in munching an ancient giant,

     ond ic gesælig    mæg symle lifgan,
65   þeah ic ætes ne sy    æfre to feore.
     Ic mæg fromlicor    fleogan þonne *pernex*
     oþþe earn oþþe hafoc    æfre meahte;
     nis Zefferus,    se swifta wind,
     þæt swa fromlice mæg    feran æghwær;
70   me is snægl swiftra,    snelra regn-wyrm,
     ond fen-yce    fore hreþre;
     is þæs gores sunu    gonge hrædra,
     þone we wifel    wordum nemnað.

        Hefigere ic eom micle    þonne se hara stan
75   oþþe unlytel    leades clympre;
     leohtre ic eom micle    þonne þes lytla wyrm
     þe her on flode gæð    fotum dryge.
     Flinte ic eom heardre    þe þis fyr drifeþ
     of þissum strongan    style heardan,
80   hnescre ic eom    micle halsre-feþre,
     seo her on winde    wæweð on lyfte.

        Ic eorþan eom    æghwær brædre,
     ond widgelra    þonne þes wong grena;
     ic uttor eaþe    eal ymb-winde,
85   wrætlice gewefen    wundor-cræfte.
     Nis under me    ænig oþer
     wiht waldendre    on world-life;
     ic eom ufor þonne ealra gesceafta,
     þara þe worhte    waldend user,
90   se mec ana mæg    ecan meahtum,
     geþeon þrymme,    þæt ic onþunian ne sceal.

        Mara ic eom ond strengra    þonne se micla hwæl,
     se þe gar-secges    grund bihealdeð
     sweartan syne;    ic eom swiþre þonne he,

but I can live happily forever,
though I eat nothing ever more.                    65
I can fly faster than a *pernex*
or an eagle or a hawk ever might;
there is no Zephyr, that swift west wind,
that can travel faster anywhere;
a snail is swifter than me, an earthworm brisker,   70
and a fen frog can move more quickly;
that son of dung which we call the weevil
is also speedier to move.
   I am much heavier than the gray stone
or a mighty mass of lead;                           75
I am much lighter than this little insect
that walks here on water with dry feet.
I am harder than the flint that strikes this flame
from this strong hard steel,
I am much softer than the downy feather,            80
that floats in the sky on the breeze.
   I am broader in every way than the earth,
and more vast than this green plain;
I easily enfold all from afar,
marvelously woven with wondrous skill.              85
There is no other creature under me,
with more control in the life of the world;
I am above all created things,
those that our controller made,
and he alone can make my might more,                90
curb my power, so that I don't surpass myself.
   I am greater and stronger than the mighty whale,
that beholds the ocean bottom
with its black face; I am sturdier than he,

95   swylce ic eom on mægene     minum læsse
     þonne se hond-wyrm,     se þe hæleþa bearn,
     secgas searo-þoncle,     seaxe delfað.

     Ne hafu ic in heafde     hwite loccas,
     wræste gewundne,     ac ic eom wide calu;
100   ne ic breaga ne bruna     brucan moste,
     ac mec bescyrede     scyppend eallum;
     nu me wrætlice     weaxað on heafde,
     þæt me on gescyldrum     scinan motan
     ful wrætlice     wundne loccas.

105   Mara ic eom ond fættra     þonne amæsted swin,
     bearg bellende,     þe on boc-wuda,
     won wrotende     wynnum lifde,
     þæt he . . .


# EXE 39


     . . . edniwu;
     þæt is moddor     monigra cynna,
     þæs selestan,     þæs sweartestan,
     þæs deorestan     þæs þe dryhta bearn
5   ofer foldan sceat     to gefean agen.
     Ne magon we her in eorþan     owiht lifgan,
     nymðe we brucen     þæs þa bearn doð.

     Þæt is to geþencanne     þeoda gehwylcum,
     wis-fæstum werum,     hwæt seo wiht sy.

likewise I am less in my strength 95
than the tiny mite which the sons of men,
cunning folk, dig out with a knife.
    I do not have on my head blond hair,
tightly curled, but I am quite bald;
I have no use for eyelids or brows, 100
but the creator bereft me of all;
now, marvelously there grows on my head,
most marvelously, tight locks
that shine across my shoulders.
    I am bigger and fatter than a swine fed on mast, 105
a roaring boar, who has lived a fine life,
rooting away in a beech-wood,
so that he . . .

# EXE 39

. . . ever new;
that is the mother of many races,
the best, the blackest,
the dearest, which the sons of men
own joyfully across the surface of the ground. 5
We can in no way live here on earth,
unless we enjoy what those children do.
    It is something to ponder for every nation,
for men secure in wisdom, what that creature may be.

## EXE 40

Ic seah wyhte     wrætlice twa,
undearnunga,     ute plegan
hæmed-laces;     hwit-loc anfeng
wlanc under wædum,     gif þæs weorces speow,
5   fæmne fyllo.     Ic on flette mæg
þurh run-stafas     rincum secgan,
þam þe bec witan,     bega ætsomne
naman þara wihta.
                Þær sceal *nyd* wesan
twega oþer,     ond se torhta *æsc*
10   an an linan,     *acas* twegen,
*hægelas* swa some.
             Swa ic þæs hord-gates
cægan cræfte     þa clamme onleac
þe þa rædellan     wið ryne-menn
hyge-fæste heold,     heortan bewrigene
15   orþonc-bendum.
            Nu is undyrne
werum æt wine     hu þa wihte mid us,
heah-mode twa,     hatne sindon.

## EXE 41

Ic wat indryhtne     æþelum deorne
giest in geardum,     þam se grimma ne mæg
hungor sceððan     ne se hata þurst,
yldo ne adle.     Gif him arlice

## EXE 40

I saw two marvelous creatures,
unconcealed, playing at the sport of sex
out in the open; if that effort went well,
proud under clothing, the fair-haired female would get
a lady's belly-swelling. On the platform,     5
through rune-staves, I can tell those men
who know books, the names of both
of those creatures.
            There *need* shall be there
two times, as well as the bright *ash*
once in the line, two *oaks,*     10
and the same number of *hail.*
            In this way I have unlocked,
with the power of a key, the fastening of the hoard-door
that held the riddle mind-fast
against mystery-solvers, its heart concealed
with cunning bonds.     15
            Now is uncovered
to men at wine how those two
proud-minded creatures are called among us.

## EXE 41

I know a distinguished guest among the dwellings,
precious to nobles, that neither grim hunger
nor hot thirst can harm,
nor old age or illness. If the servant

5  esne þenað,    se þe agan sceal
on þam sið-fate,    hy gesunde æt ham
findað witode him    wiste ond blisse,
cnosles unrim;    care, gif se esne
his hlaforde    hyreð yfle,
10 frean on fore.    Ne wile forht wesan
broþor oþrum;    him þæt bam sceðeð,
þonne hy from bearme    begen hweorfað
anre magan    ellor-fuse,
moddor ond sweostor.
                        Mon, se þe wille,
15 cyþe cyne-wordum    hu se cuma hatte,
eðþa se esne,    þe ic her ymb sprice.


## EXE 42

Wrætlic hongað    bi weres þeo,
frean under sceate;    foran is þyrel.
Bið stiþ ond heard,    stede hafað godne,
þonne se esne    his agen hrægl
5  ofer cneo hefeð;    wile þæt cuþe hol
mid his hangellan    heafde gretan,
þæt he efen-lang    ær oft gefylde.


## EXE 43

Ic on wincle gefrægn    weaxan nat-hwæt,
þindan ond þunian,    þecene hebban;

that he has by him on his journey                                      5
attends him honorably, they will surely find,
safe at home, feasting and bliss,
countless kinsmen; but grief,
if the servant badly obeys his lord,
his master on the journey. Nor will one brother           10
fear another; it harms them both
when they both turn away from the bosom
of their one kinswoman, eager to be away,
their mother and sister.
                                    The one who wants to,
let them reveal in suitable words what that visitor is called,   15
or that servant, that I speak about here.


## EXE 42

A marvelous thing dangles by a man's thigh,
under its lord's clothing; ahead, a hole.
It is stiff and hard, stands in good stead,
when that servant lifts his own garments
over his knee; he wants to come upon                    5
a well-known hole with that dangling head:
one he has often filled full-length before.


## EXE 43

I heard that something or other was growing in a confined
        space,
swelling and surging, pushing up its covering;

on þæt banlease    bryd grapode,
hyge-wlonc hondum,    hrægle þeahte
5    þrindende þing,    þeodnes dohtor.


# EXE 44

Wer sæt æt wine    mid his wifum twam
ond his twegen suno    ond his twa dohtor,
swase gesweostor,    ond hyra suno twegen,
freolico frum-bearn;    fæder wæs þær inne
5    þara æþelinga    æghwæðres mid,
eam ond nefa.
                    Ealra wæron fife
eorla ond idesa    in-sittendra.


# EXE 45

Moððe word fræt.
                    Me þæt þuhte
wrætlicu wyrd,    þa ic þæt wundor gefrægn,
þæt se wyrm forswealg    wera gied sumes,
þeof in þystro,    þrym-fæstne cwide,
5    ond þæs strangan staþol.
                    Stæl-giest ne wæs
wihte þy gleawra,    þe he þam wordum swealg.

on that boneless thing a bride took a grip,
proud in her hands, a lord's daughter,
clothed with a covering that bulging thing.                    5


# EXE 44


A man sat at wine with his two wives
and his two sons and his two daughters,
sweet sisters, and their two sons,
fine-looking firstborn boys; and the father
of each of those princes was there inside,                    5
uncles and nephews together.
                                    In all, there were five
men and women sitting inside.


# EXE 45


A moth devoured words.
                            That seemed to me
a marvelous turn of events, when I heard about that
        wonder,
that that worm, a thief in the dark,
should swallow some man's song, his securely set speech,
and its strong foundation.                    5
                            The stealing guest was not
a whit the wiser, though he swallowed those words.

## EXE 46

Ic gefrægn for hæleþum    hring gyddian,
torhtne butan tungan,    tila þeah he hlude
stefne ne cirmde,    strongum wordum.
   Sinc for secgum    swigende cwæð:
5  "Gehæle mec    helpend gæsta."
   Ryne ongietan    readan goldes
guman galdor-cwide,    gleawe beþencan
hyra hælo to Gode,    swa se hring gecwæð.

## EXE 47

Ic wat eard-fæstne    anne standan,
deafne, dumban,    se oft dæges swilgeð
þurh gopes hond    gifrum lacum.
   Hwilum on þam wicum    se wonna þegn,
5 sweart ond salo-neb,    sendeð oþre,
under goman him,    golde dyrran,
þa æþelingas    oft wilniað,
cyningas ond cwene.
            Ic þæt cyn nu gen
nemnan ne wille,    þe him to nytte swa
10 ond to dugþum doþ    þæt se dumba her,
eorp unwita,    ær forswilgeð.

# EXE 46

I heard a ring singing in the presence of men,
bright, without a tongue, but well, with strong words,
though it did not call out with a loud voice.
    That treasure spoke silently before men:
"May the helper of souls heal me."                                    5
    Let men understand the enigma and the incantation
of red gold; let the wise entrust
their salvation to God, just as that ring said.


# EXE 47

I know a single creature, securely fixed to the ground,
deaf, dumb, that by day often swallows
useful gifts from a slave's hand.
    Sometimes in those dwelling places the dark servant,
swarthy and sallow-faced, produces others,                            5
more precious than gold, out of its mouth,
things which nobles, kings, and queens
often desire.
                I will not now just yet
name that sort of thing that is so useful to them
and converts to benefits whatever here                                10
that dumb, dusky, witless thing swallows before.

## EXE 48

Wiga is on eorþan     wundrum acenned
dryhtum to nytte,     of dumbum twam,
torht atyhted,     þone on teon wigeð
feond his feonde.
               Forstrangne oft
5   wif hine wrið;    he him wel hereð,
þeowaþ him geþwære,    gif him þegniað
mægeð ond mæcgas    mid gemete ryhte,
fedað hine fægre;    he him fremum stepeð,
life on lissum.
              Leanað grimme
10   þam þe hine wloncne    weorþan læteð.

## EXE 49

Ic seah wrætlice    wuhte feower
samed siþian;    swearte wæran lastas,
swaþu swiþe blacu.
             Swift wæs on fore,
fuglum framra;    fleag on lyfte,
5   deaf under yþe.
             Dreag unstille
winnende wiga,    se him wægas tæcneþ
ofer fæted gold    feower eallum.

## EXE 48

There is a warrior on earth, useful to mankind,
wondrously born from two dumb things,
brightly brought forth; and a foe hurls him
in hatred against his foe.
                    A woman often wraps round
the very strong one; he obeys them well,          5
serves them graciously, if maids and men
attend him rightly and in due measure,
feed him fairly, he plies them with benefits,
life's delights.
            He grimly repays those
who let him grow proud.          10

## EXE 49

I saw four marvelous creatures
traveling together; their tracks were black,
very dark traces.
            It was swift on its journey,
bolder than birds; it flew aloft,
dove under the wave.          5
              The working warrior
bustled busily, the one who teaches
all four their paths across precious gold.

## EXE 50

Ic seah ræpingas     in ræced fergan,
under hrof sales     hearde twegen,
þa wæron genumne,     nearwum bendum,
gefeterade     fæste togædre;
5     þara oþrum wæs     an getenge
won-fah Wale,     seo weold hyra
bega siþe     bendum fæstra.

## EXE 51

Ic seah on bearwe     beam hlifian,
tanum torhtne.     Þæt treow wæs on wynne,
wudu weaxende.     Wæter hine ond eorþe
feddan fægre,     oþþæt he frod dagum
5     on oþrum wearð     aglac-hade,
deope gedolgod,     dumb in bendum,
wriþen ofer wunda,     wonnum hyrstum
foran gefrætwed.
                Nu he fæcnum wæg
þurh his heafdes mægen     hilde-gieste
10     oþrum rymeð;     oft hy an yst strudon
hord ætgædre;     hræd wæs ond unlæt
se æftera,     gif se ærra fær
genamnan in nearowe     neþan moste.

## EXE 50

I saw captives brought into a building,
two hard creatures under the roof of a hall,
they were bound with restraining bonds,
fettered fast together;
close at hand to one of them                                    5
was a dark-skinned Welsh girl who controlled
them both in their journeying, secure in their bonds.

## EXE 51

I saw a tree trunk tower in a grove,
bright with branches. That tree was joyful,
wood growing. Water and soil
nourished it beautifully, until, experienced in days,
it fell into a monstrous state,                                 5
deeply injured, dumb in bonds,
its wounds wrapped round, adorned in front
with dark trappings.
                         Now for another
hostile battle-guest, it creates a path
through the power of its head; often in the tumult             10
they plundered hoards together; swift and unslack
the one who follows, if the one in front
was able to brave danger for a comrade in distress.

## EXE 52

Hyse cwom gangan,   þær he hie wisse
stondan in wincle;   stop feorran to,
hror hægsteald-mon,   hof his agen
hrægl hondum up,   hrand under gyrdels
5  hyre stondendre   stiþes nat-hwæt,
worhte his willan;   wagedan buta.

   Þegn onnette,   wæs þragum nyt
tillic esne,   teorode hwæþre
æt stunda gehwam   strong ær þon hio,
10  werig þæs weorces.   Hyre weaxan ongon
under gyrdelse   þæt oft gode men
ferðþum freogað   ond mid feo bicgað.


## EXE 53

Ic seah in healle,   þær hæleð druncon,
on flet beran   feower cynna;
wrætlic wudu-treow   ond wunden gold,
sinc searo-bunden,   ond seolfres dæl,
5  ond rode tacn,   þæs us to roderum up
hlædre rærde,   ær he hel-wara
burg abræce.          Ic þæs beames mæg
eaþe for eorlum   æþelu secgan:
þær wæs hlin ond acc   ond se hearda iw
10  ond se fealwa holen;   frean sindon ealle
nyt ætgædre.   Naman habbað anne:

## EXE 52

A young man came striding to where he knew
she was standing in a corner; the strapping lad
stepped up from afar, raised his own
clothing up with his hands, shoved something stiff
under her girdle as she was standing,                                    5
worked his will; they both shuddered.
      The freeman hurried, a splendid slave
was useful at times, but then grew tired
after a while, he who had been stronger than her
grew weary of that work. Under her girdle                               10
there began to grow what often good folk
love in their hearts and pay for with their purse.

## EXE 53

I saw in the hall, where warriors were drinking,
a fourfold thing borne onto the platform;
a wondrous wood-tree with twisted gold,
a treasure skillfully set with a portion of silver,
and the sign of the cross of him who raised                             5
a ladder for us up to heaven, before he stormed
the citadel of hell dwellers.
                        I can easily tell
that tree's lineage in the presence of men:
there was maple and oak and hard yew
and the tawny holly, all useful                                         10
to the lord together. They have one name:

wulf-heafed-treo,   þæt oft wæpen abæd
his mon-dryhtne,   maðm in healle,
gold-hilted sweord.
               Nu me þisses gieddes
15  ondsware ywe,  se hine on mede
wordum secgan  hu se wudu hatte.


## EXE 54

Ic wæs þær inne  þær ic ane geseah
winnende wiht  wido bennegean,
holt hweorfende;  heaþo-glemma feng,
deopra dolga.  Daroþas wæron
5  weo þære wihte,  ond se wudu searwum,
fæste gebunden.  Hyre fota wæs
biid-fæst oþer,  oþer bisgo dreag,
leolc on lyfte,  hwilum londe neah.
Treow wæs getenge  þam þær torhtan stod
10  leafum bihongen.
             Ic lafe geseah
minum hlaforde,  þær hæleð druncon,
þara flana,  on flet beran.


## EXE 55

Ðeos lyft byreð  lytle wihte
ofer beorg-hleoþa.  Þa sind blace swiþe,
swearte, salo-pade,  sanges rofe,
heapum ferað,  hlude cirmað,

wolf-head tree, that often provided a weapon
to its lord, a treasure in hall,
a gold-hilted sword.
                    Now show me
the answer to this song, whoever dares                              15
to say in words how that tree is called.


## EXE 54

I was inside there when I saw a single
struggling creature, stabbed by wood,
a darting beam; it received battle-blows,
deep wounds. Darts brought grief
to that creature, as did wood, with cunning                         5
firmly bound. One of its feet
was firmly attached, the other was busy,
flew in the air, sometimes close to the ground.
There was a tree nearby which stood there brightly
hung with leaves.                                                   10
                    I saw the remnant
of those arrows borne onto the platform
to my lord, where warriors were drinking.


## EXE 55

This air carries little creatures
over rolling hills. They are very black,
swarthy, sallow-coated, rich in song,
they travel in flocks, call out loudly,

5 tredað bearo-næssas,    hwilum burg-salo
niþþa bearna.    Nemnað hy sylfe.


## EXE 56

Ic wat an-fete    ellen dreogan
wiht on wonge.    Wide ne fereð,
ne fela rideð,    ne fleogan mæg
þurh scirne dæg,    ne hie scip fereð,
5 naca nægled-bord:    nyt bið hwæþre
hyre mon-dryhtne    monegum tidum.
    Hafað hefigne steort,    heafod lytel,
tungan lange,    toð nænigne;
isernes dæl,    eorð-græf pæþeð.
10    Wætan ne swelgeþ,    ne wiht iteþ,
foþres ne gitsað,    fereð oft swa
þeah lago-flod on lyfte;    life ne gielpeð,
hlafordes gifum,    hyreð swa þeana
þeodne sinum.
                        Þry sind in naman
15 ryhte run-stafas,    þara is *rad* foran.


## EXE 57

Ic seah in healle    hring gyldenne
men sceawian,    modum gleawe,
ferþþum frode.    Friþo-spede bæd
God nergende    gæste sinum

tread the woody promontories, sometimes the walled    5
    buildings
of the sons of men. They name themselves.


# EXE 56

I know a one-footed creature, working
mightily in a field. She does not travel far,
nor ride much, nor can she fly
throughout the bright day, nor does a ship,
a nail-planked vessel, ferry her: and yet many times    5
she provides a service to her lord.
    She has a heavy tail, a little head,
a long tongue, but not a single tooth;
partly of iron, she treads an earth-hole.
    She swallows no moisture, eats not at all,    10
does not seek out fodder, but often ferries
a flood of water aloft; she does not brag about her life,
her lord's gifts, but nevertheless must obey
her master.
            In her name there are
three straight rune-staves, of which *riding* is in front.    15


# EXE 57

I saw them examining a golden ring,
men in a hall, wise in mind,
experienced in spirit. The one who turned the ring
prayed to God the savior for happiness of heart

5  se þe wende wriþan;   word æfter cwæð,
hring on hyrede,   hælend nemde
till-fremmendra.

               Him torhte in gemynd
his dryhtnes naman   dumba brohte,
ond in eagna gesihð,   gif þæs æþelestan
10  goldes tacen   ongietan cuþe
ond dryhtnes dolg,   don swa þæs beages
benne cwædon.   Ne mæg þære bene
æniges monnes   ungefullodre
Godes ealdor-burg   gæst gesecan,
15  rodera ceastre.

            Ræde, se þe wille,
hu ðæs wrætlican   wunda cwæden
hringes to hæleþum,   þa he in healle
wæs wylted ond wended   wloncra folmum.

\* \* \*

# EXE Part 2

## EXE 58

Ic wæs be sonde,   sæ-wealle neah,
æt mere-faroþe:   minum gewunade
frum-staþole fæst;   fea ænig wæs
monna cynnes,   þæt minne þær

for his own soul; the ring then spoke words                    5
among the company, named the savior
of righteous men.
       The dumb thing brought
brightly to their minds the name of the Lord,
and to the sight of their eyes, if one could
understand the message of that noblest gold           10
and the Lord's wounds, and act as the scars
on the ring said. Nor can the soul of any man,
with his prayer unfulfilled,
seek out the chief city of God,
a dwelling in the heavens.                                      15
       Let him explain who will,
how the wounds of that marvelous ring
spoke to heroes, when it was in the hall
turned and twisted in the hands of the proud.

\*   \*   \*

# EXE Part 2

## EXE 58

I was by the sand, beside the seawall,
at the water's edge: I lived
secure in my first footing; few, if any,
there were of mankind who could see there

5    on anæde    eard beheolde,
    ac mec uhtna gehwam    yð sio brune
    lagu-fæðme beleolc.    Lyt ic wende
    þæt ic ær oþþe sið    æfre sceolde
    ofer meodu-bence    muðleas sprecan,
10   wordum wrixlan.

                 Þæt is wundres dæl,
    on sefan searolic    þam þe swylc ne conn,
    hu mec seaxes ord    ond seo swiþre hond,
    eorles in-geþonc    ond ord somod,
    þingum geþydan,    þæt ic wiþ þe sceolde
15   for unc anum twam    ærend-spræce
    abeodan bealdlice,    swa hit beorna ma
    uncre word-cwidas    widdor ne mænden.

* * *

# EXE Part 3

## EXE 59

Oft mec fæste bileac    freolicu meowle,
ides on earce;    hwilum up ateah
folmum sinum    ond frean sealde,
holdum þeodne,    swa hio haten wæs.
5    Siðþan me on hreþre    heafod sticade,
nioþan upweardne,    on nearo fegde.

my dwelling in solitude, 5
where every dawn and dusk the dark wave
enfolded me in its watery lap. I little thought
that sooner or later I should ever
speak across the mead bench without a mouth,
exchange words. 10
It is a kind of wonder,
a marvel for the mind that does not know such things,
how the point of a knife and a right hand,
a man's skill and the point together,
should have brought it about that I should to you
boldly announce an errand in speech 15
for the two of us alone, so that no more of men
should spread more widely the words that we share.

\* \* \*

# EXE Part 3

## EXE 59

Often a lovely lady locked me securely
in a box, a woman; sometimes she took me out
in her hands and gave me to her lord,
her gracious master, as she was told to do.
Then he would stick his head in my midst, 5
up from below, and fitted it in tight.

Gif þæs ondfengan    ellen dohte,
mec frætwedne    fyllan sceolde
ruwes nat-hwæt.

          Ræd hwæt ic mæne.


# EXE 60


Ic eom heard ond scearp,    hin-gonges strong,
forð-siþes from,    frean unforcuð,
wade under wambe    ond me weg sylfa
ryhtne geryme.

          Rinc bið on ofeste,
5  se mec on þyð    æftanweardne,
hæleð mid hrægle;    hwilum ut tyhð
of hole hatne;    hwilum eft fereð,
on nearo nat-hwær,    nydeþ swiþe,
suþerne secg.

          Saga hwæt ic hatte.


# EXE 61


Oft ic secga    sele-dreame sceal
fægre onþeon,    þonne ic eom forð boren
glæd mid golde,    þær guman drincað.
    Hwilum mec on cofan    cysseð muþe
5  tillic esne,    þær wit tu beoþ,
fæðme on folme    fingrum þyð,
wyrceð his willan    . . .ð lu. . .
. . . fulre,    þonne ic forð cyme

If the strength of the receiver was up to it,
something or other rough would fill me,
as I stood enhanced.

> Explain what I mean.

## EXE 60

I am hard and sharp, strong going hence,
firm heading forth, unafraid of my lord,
I plunge under the belly and the path itself
guides me right.

> The fighting-man is in a hurry

who shoves me in from behind,
a warrior working undercover; sometimes he tugs me out
hot from the hole; sometimes he puts me back in,
into some narrow place, really pushes,
the soldier from down south.

> Say what I am called.

## EXE 61

Often among the hall-joy of men I must
flourish fairly, when I am brought forth
bright with gold, where men drink.

> Sometimes a splendid servant in a closed room,

kisses me on the mouth, where we are two together,
with hand cupped on bosom, strokes me with fingers,
works his will . . .
. . . full, when I come forth

. . .
10    Ne mæg ic þy miþan . . .
    . . . siþþan on leohte
    . . .
    swylce eac bið sona    . . .
    torhte getacnad,    hwæt me to sohte,
15    receleas rinc,    þa unc geryde wæs.

## EXE 62

    Ic seah · ᚠ · ond · ᛁ ·     ofer wong faran,
    beran · ᛒ · ᛗ ·     bæm wæs on siþþe
    hæbbendes hyht    · ᚻ · ond · ᚠ · ;
    swylce þryþa dæl,    · ᚦ · ond · ᛗ ·.
5    Gefeah · ᚹ · ond · ᚪ ·     fleah ofer · ᛏ ·,
    · ᛋ · ond · ᚳ ·     sylfes þæs folces.

## EXE 63

    Cwico wæs ic, ne cwæð ic wiht,    cwele ic efne seþeah.
    Ær ic wæs, eft ic cwom;    æghwa mec reafað,
    hafað mec on headre,    ond min heafod scireþ,
    biteð mec on bær lic,    briceð mine wisan.
5    Monnan ic ne bite,    nymþe he me bite;
    sindan þara monige    þe mec bitað.

. . .
    I cannot conceal in this way . . .             10
. . . then in the light
. . .
so too it is straightaway . . .
clearly indicated, what he wanted from me,
that reckless man, when the way was cleared for us two.    15

## EXE 62

I saw .*w.* and .*i.* (*wicg,* "a horse") travel over the plain
carrying .*b.* and .*e.* (*beorn,* "a man"); for both on the trip
there was the hope of the one lifting up .*h.* and .*a.* (*hafoc,* "a
    hawk");
also a part of the force was .*þ.* and .*e.* (*þegn* or *þeow,* "a
    servant").
There rejoiced .*f.* and .*æ.* (*fælca,* "a falcon"), there flew over    5
    .*ea.* (*eard,* "the land"),
.*s.* and .*p.* (*spor,* "the track") of that very people.

## EXE 63

I was alive, but I said naught: nevertheless I die.
I was before; back I came: everyone ravages me,
keeps me in confinement and shears my head,
bites me on the bare body, bursts my stalk.
    I bite no man, unless he bites me;    5
there are many of those who bite me.

## EXE 64

Ic eom mare    þonne þes middan-geard,
læsse þonne hond-wyrm,    leohtre þonne mona,
swiftre þonne sunne.    Sæs me sind ealle
flodas on fæðmum    ond þes foldan bearm,
5    grene wongas.
                Grundum ic hrine,
helle underhnige,    heofonas oferstige,
wuldres eþel,    wide ræce
ofer engla eard,    eorþan gefylle,
ealne middan-geard    ond mere-streamas
10    side mid me sylfum.
                      Saga hwæt ic hatte.

## EXE 65

Ic on þinge gefrægn    þeod-cyninges
wrætlice wiht,    word-galdra . . .
. . . snyttro . . . hio symle deð
fira gehwylcum . . .
5    . . . wisdome.
                      Wundor me þæt . . .
. . . nænne muð hafað,
fet ne folme . . .
. . . welan oft sacað,
cwiþeð cy. . . wearð
10    leoda lareow.
                Forþon nu longe mæg

# EXE 64

I am greater than this middle-earth,
less than a tiny mite, brighter than the moon,
swifter than the sun. Seas and all the waters
are in my embrace, as well as this earth's bosom,
green fields.                                                          5
                    I touch the depths,
dive down under hell, climb above heaven,
the homeland of glory, roam widely
over the dwelling of angels, fill the world,
all middle-earth, and sea-streams
widely with myself.                                            10
                    Say what I am called.

# EXE 65

At the great king's council I learned
of a wondrous creature, word-spells' . . .
. . . insight . . . it always does
for every man . . .
. . . wisdom.                                                       5
                    It is a wonder to me that
. . . it has no mouth,
nor feet nor hands . . .
. . . often combats wealth,
says . . . became
the teacher of nations.                                      10
                    For that reason now I may

387

awa to ealdre     ece lifgan,
missenlice,    þenden menn bugað
eorþan sceatas.    Ic þæt oft geseah
golde gegierwed,    þær guman druncon,
15    since ond seolfre.
               Secge se þe cunne,
wis-fæstra hwylc,    hwæt seo wiht sy.

## EXE 66

Ic þa wiht geseah    on weg feran;
heo wæs wrætlice    wundrum gegierwed.
   Wundor wearð on wege;    wæter wearð to bane.

## EXE 67

Wiht is wrætlic    þam þe hyre wisan ne conn:
singeð þurh sidan.    Is se sweora woh,
orþoncum geworht;    hafaþ eaxle tua,
scearpan gescyldru.    His gesceapo dreogeð
. . .

## EXE 68

. . . þe swa wrætlice    be wege stonde
heah ond hleor-torht    hæleþum to nytte.

forever live eternal life,
in various ways, while men dwell
on the surface of the earth. I often saw it
adorned with gold, with treasure and silver,
where men drank.                                                15
                    Let anyone who knows,
any wise person, say what that creature is.


## EXE 66

I saw a creature traveling on the way;
it was marvelously adorned with wonders.
    There was a wonder in the wave: water became bone.


## EXE 67

A creature is marvelous to the one who knows not her ways:
she sings through her sides; her neck is bent,
cunningly wrought; she has two shoulders,
sharp shoulders.    It endures its fate
. . .


## EXE 68

. . . stands so marvelously by the way
tall and bright cheeked, useful to men.

## EXE 69

Ic eom rices æht,    reade bewæfed,
stið ond steap-wong.    Staþol wæs iu þa
wyrta wlite-torhtra;    nu eom wraþra laf,
fyres ond feole,    fæste genearwad,
5    wire geweorþad.
                Wepeð hwilum
for minum gripe    se þe gold wigeð,
þonne ic yþan sceal    . . .fe,
hringum gehyrsted.    Me . . .i. . .
. . . gold-dryhtne    min . . .
10    . . . wlite bete.

## EXE 70

Ic wæs lytel . . .
fo. . .
. . .te geaf . . .
. . .pe    þe unc gemæne . . .
5    . . . sweostor min
fedde mec fægre
                Oft ic feower teah
swæse broþor,    þara onsundran gehwylc
dæg-tidum me    drincan sealde
þurh þyrel þearle.    Ic þæh on lust,
10    oþþæt ic wæs yldra    ond þæt an forlet
sweartum hyrde,    siþade widdor,
mearc-paþas træd,    moras pæðde,

## EXE 69

I am the property of someone powerful, decked in red,
stiff and steep set. Previously, I was set up
among beautiful plants; now I'm what's left by my enemies,
fire and file, securely fastened,
adorned with wire.                                                    5
                              He sometimes weeps
because of my attack, the one who wears gold,
when I must destroy . . .
decked with rings. Me . . .
. . . to my gold-lord . . .
. . . better beauty.                                                 10


## EXE 70

I was little . . .
. . .
. . . gave . . .
. . . what we two together . . .
. . . my sister
brought me up . . .                                                   5
                              Often I tugged at four
beloved brothers, who each in turn
during the daytime gave me drink
briskly, through a hole. I drank with vigor,
until I was older, and left it all behind                             10
to the swarthy herdsman, traveled more widely,
trod march-paths, trekked over the moors,

bunden under beame,     beag hæfde on healse,
wean on laste     weorc þrowade,
15  earfoða dæl.
            Oft mec isern scod
sare on sidan;   ic swigade,
næfre meldade     monna ængum,
gif me ord-stæpe     egle wæron.


## EXE 71

Ic on wonge aweox,     wunode þær mec feddon
hruse ond heofon-wolcn,     oþþæt me onhwyrfdon
gearum frodne,     þa me grome wurdon,
of þære gecynde     þe ic ær cwic beheold,
5  onwendan mine wisan,     wegedon mec of earde,
gedydon þæt ic sceolde     wiþ gesceape minum
on bonan willan     bugan hwilum.
    Nu eom mines frean     folme bysigod,
. . . dlan dæl,   gif his ellen deag,
10  oþþe æfter dome   dri . . .
. . . ian     mærþa fremman,
wyrcan w. . .
. . . mec on þeode     utan we . . .
. . . ipe
15  ond to wroht-stæpe . . .
. . .eorp,   eaxle gegyrde,
wo . . .
ond swiora smæl,   sidan fealwe,
. . . þonne mec heaþo-sigel
20  scir bescineð,   ond mec . . .

bound under a beam, with a ring around my neck,
on a trail of grief, suffered pain,
a share of sorrows.                                    15
                    Often iron
struck me sorely in the side; I stayed silent,
never uttered at all to anyone,
even if the jabbing blows were awful to me.


## EXE 71

I grew up in a field, where there nurtured me
the ground and sky above, until those who hated me
removed me, mature in years,
away from the natural state I had looked at while alive,
changed my ways, took me from my home,           5
made it that I must, against my nature,
bend at times to a killer's will.
     Now I am busy in my lord's hand,
. . . part, if his courage keeps firm,
or for the sake of glory . . .                        10
. . . perform mighty deeds,
work . . .
me in a nation . . . abroad
. . .
and to cause harm . . .                               15
. . . girt shoulders
. . .
and tiny neck, tawny sides,
. . . when the sun of battle
shines clearly, and . . .                             20

fægre feormað ond on fyrd wigeð,
cræfte on hæfte.
                    Cuð is wide
þæt ic þristra sum    þeofes cræfte,
under brægn-locan . . .
25  hwilum eawunga    eþel-fæsten
forðweard brece,    þæt ær frið hæfde.
Feringe from,    he fus þonan
wendeð of þam wicum,    wiga se þe mine
siþas cunne.
                    Saga hwæt ic hatte.


# EXE 72


Ic wæs fæmne geong,    feax-har cwene,
ond ænlic rinc    on ane tid;
fleah mid fuglum,    ond on flode swom,
deaf under yþe,    dead mid fiscum,
5  ond on foldan stop,    hæfde ferð cwicu.


# EXE 73


Ic swiftne geseah    on swaþe feran;
        · ᛗ · ᚻ · ᚱ · ᚾ ·
Ic ane geseah    idese sittan.

brightly burnishes me, and bears me to battle,
craftily by the haft.
                It is widely known
that I, one among brave ones, with the skill of a thief,
under the skull . . .
sometimes openly breach the front                    25
of a homeland-fortress, which had peace before.
Suddenly emboldened, he turns away from there
eager from the dwellings, the warrior,
who knows my ways.
                  Say what I am called.

## EXE 72

I was a young woman, a gray-haired lady,
and a handsome man, all at once;
I flew with the birds, and swam in the flood,
dove under the wave, dead with the fishes,
and stepped on the earth, had a living soul.          5

## EXE 73

I saw a swift one travel on his path;
        *.dnlh.*
I saw a woman sitting alone.

## EXE 74

Sæ mec fedde,     sund-helm þeahte,
ond mec yþa wrugon     eorþan getenge,
feþelease.   Oft ic flode ongean
muð ontynde.
                  Nu wile monna sum
5   min flæsc fretan,     felles ne recceð,
siþþan he me of sidan     seaxes orde
hyd arypeð,     ond mec hraþe siþþan
iteð unsodene     eac ...

## EXE 75

Oft ic flodas ...
... leas     cynne minum
ond ...
dyde me to mose ...
5   ...   swa ic him ...
...   ne æt ham gesæt
... flote cwealde
þurh orþonc ...   yþum bewrigene.

## EXE 76

*Ic eom æþelinges     æht ond willa.*
Ic eom æþelinges     eaxl-gestealla,

## EXE 74

The sea nourished me, the covering of water cloaked me
    over,
and the waves concealed me close to the ground,
lacking a foot. Often in the face of the flood
I opened my mouth.
                  Now someone
wants to eat my flesh, does not care for my skin,       5
after with a knifepoint he plunders
the hide from my side, and then all at once
eats me uncooked . . .

## EXE 75

Often I . . . floods
. . . -less with my kin
and . . .
made me into food . . .
. . . likewise I . . . them       5
. . . nor did I sit at home
. . . killed afloat
through cunning . . ., concealed with waves.

## EXE 76

*I am a prince's possession and pleasure.*
I am a prince's close companion,

fyrd-rinces gefara,    frean minum leof,
cyninges geselda.    Cwen mec hwilum
5  hwit-loccedu    hond on legeð,
eorles dohtor,    þeah hio æþelu sy.
    Hæbbe me on bosme    þæt on bearwe geweox;
hwilum ic on wloncum    wicge ride
herges on ende;    heard is min tunge.
10  Oft ic woð-boran    word-leana sum
agyfe æfter giedde.    Good is min wise
ond ic sylfa salo.
                        Saga hwæt ic hatte.


# EXE 77


Ic eom bylged-breost,    belced-sweora,
heafod hæbbe    ond heane steort,
eagan ond earan    ond ænne foot,
hrycg ond heard-nebb,    hneccan steapne,
5  ond sidan twa,    sagol on middum,
eard ofer ældum.
                    Aglac dreoge,
þær mec wegeð    se þe wudu hrereð,
ond mec stondende    streamas beataö,
hægl se hearda,    ond hrim þeceð,
10  forst mec freoseð,    ond fealleð snaw
on þyrel-wombne,    ond ic þæt þolige
. . . mæg    won-sceaft mine.

a warrior's comrade, dear to my lord,
a king's colleague. A fair-haired lady
sometimes lays her hand upon me,                              5
a wellborn daughter, noble though she be.

   I have in my breast what grew in a grove;
sometimes I ride on a proud steed,
on the edge of an army; my tongue is harsh.
Often I give a songster some reward for words            10
after a song. My manner is good,
and I am myself sallow.

                   Say what I am called.

## EXE 77

I am bulging breasted and swollen throated,
have a head and tail held high,
eyes and ears and a single foot,
back and hard beak, steep neck,
and two sides, a stick in the middle,                          5
a domain above men.

                I put up with an awful assault,
when there touches me what stirs the woods,
and as I stand streams beat me,
the hard hail and rime covers
and frost freezes and snow falls on                            10
the one with a pierced belly, and I endure
my misery . . .

399

## EXE 78

Wiht is wundorlic . . .
. . . gongende,    greate swilgeð,
. . .
. . . fell ne flæsc,    fotum gonge. . .
5 . . .eð,
sceal mæla gehwam . . .

## EXE 79

Frod wæs min from-cynn    . . .
biden in burgum,    siþþan bæles weard
. . . wera    lige bewunden,
fyre gefælsad.
            Nu me fah warað
5 eorþan broþor,    se me ærest wearð
gumena to gyrne.    Ic ful gearwe gemon
hwa min from-cynn    fruman agette
eall of earde;    ic him yfle ne mot,
ac ic hæft-nyd    hwilum arære
10 wide geond wongas.    Hæbbe ic wunda fela,
middan-geardes    mægen unlytel,
ac ic miþan sceal    monna gehwylcum
degolfulne dom    dyran cræftes,
sið-fæt minne.
            Saga hwæt ic hatte.

# EXE 78

A creature is wondrous . . .
. . . walking, swallows dirt.
. . .
. . . skin nor flesh, walking on foot
. . .                                                    5
must every time . . .

# EXE 79

My ancestry was ancient . . .
brought up in enclosures, since I became by flame
. . . of men, enveloped in fire,
purified in a pyre.
                    Now earth's brother
guiltily guards me, who first brought me                    5
to grief among men. I remember full well
who first destroyed the beginning of my ancestry
wholly from the land; I cannot treat him badly,
though sometimes I cause captivity
widely throughout the world. I have many wounds,         10
no small power in middle-earth,
but I must hide from every man
the mysterious influence of precious power,
my experience.
                    Say what I am called.

## EXE 80

An wiht is on eorþan    wundrum acenned,
hreoh ond reþe,    hafað ryne strongne,
grimme grymetað    ond be grunde fareð.
    Modor is monigra    mærra wihta,
5  fæger ferende,    fundað æfre;
neol is nearo-grap.    Nænig oþrum mæg
wlite ond wisan    wordum gecyþan,
hu mislic biþ    mægen þara cynna,
fyrn forð-gesceaft;    fæder ealle bewat,
10  or ond ende,    swylce an sunu,
mære meotudes bearn,    þurh meahta sped,
ond þæt hyhste mægen    halges gæstes
. . . dyre cræft. . .
    . . .
15  þonne hy aweorp    . . .
. . .þe ænig þara    . . .
. . . æfter ne mæg    . . .
. . .a oþer cynn    eorþan . . .
. . . þon æror wæs
20  wlitig ond wynsum    . . .
    Biþ sio moddor    mægene eacen,
wundrum bewreþed,    wistum gehladen,
hordum gehroden,    hæleþum dyre.
Mægen bið gemiclad,    meaht gesweotlad,
25  wlite biþ geweorþad    wuldor-nyttingum,
wynsum wuldor-gimm    wolcnum getenge,
clæn-georn bið ond cystig,    cræfte eacen.

# EXE 80

One creature is wondrously born on earth,
rough and fierce: she has strong movement,
grimly roars and goes about the ground.
   She is the mother of many famous creatures;
passing peacefully, she always hastens;       5
her close embrace is deep. No one can make known to
      another
in words her beauty and her manner,
how manifold is the power of that kin,
ancient history; the Father knew it all,
beginning and end, likewise the one Son,       10
famous child of fate, through an abundance of virtues,
and the highest power of the Holy Spirit
. . . precious skill,
. . .
they cast away . . .       15
. . . any of them . . .
cannot afterward . . .
. . . another kin . . . earth . . .
. . . which was once
fair and beautiful . . .       20
   The mother is increased in strength,
wondrously enriched, laden with food,
adorned with hoards, dear to men.
Her power is made great, her might revealed,
her beauty is made precious by glorious favors,       25
a beautiful gem of glory, close to the clouds,
she is liberal and pure-seeking, swollen with power.

Hio biþ eadgum leof,     earmum getæse,
freolic, sellic;     fromast ond swiþost,
30   gifrost ond grædgost     grund-bedd trideþ,
þæs þe under lyfte     aloden wurde
ond ælda bearn     eagum sawe,
swa þæt wuldor wifeð,     world-bearna mægen,
þeah þe ferþum gleaw   ...
35   mon mode snottor     mengo wundra.
    Hrusan bið heardra,     hæleþum frodra,
geofum bið gearora,     gimmum deorra;
worulde wlitigað,     wæstmum tydreð,
firene dwæsceð   ...
40   oft utan beweorpeð     anre þecene,
wundrum gewlitegad,     geond wer-þeode,
þæt wafiað     weras ofer eorþan;
þæt magon micle   ...sceafte.
    Biþ stanum bestreþed,     stormum ...
45   ...len   ...timbred weall,
þrym. ..ed,
hrusan hrineð,     h. ..
...     eorþan gletenge,
oft searwum biþ   ...
50   ...     deaðe ne feleð,
þeah þe ...
...wudu hreren,     hrif wundigen,
...cneorisse.
    Hord-word onhlid,     hæleþum ge...
55   ...onwreoh,     wordum geopena,
hu mislic sy     mægen þara cynna.

She is precious to the rich, useful to the poor,
handsome, superb; she treads the earth,
the foremost and greatest, greediest and hungriest,                   30
of all that has sprung up under the sky
and the children of men may have seen with eyes,
so that she weaves glory, the power of worldly offspring,
even though he, smart at heart, has heard tell,
a man wise in mind, a multitude of wonders.                           35
    She is harder than the soil, more experienced than
       heroes,
readier than gifts, more precious than gems;
she beautifies the world, teems with produce,
washes sins away . . .
often encloses under a single roof,                                   40
wondrously beautified, throughout the nation,
so that men over the earth are amazed;
greatly are they able . . .
    She is hemmed in by stones, by storms . . .
. . . a timbered wall,                                                45
strength . . .
touches the earth . . .
close to the ground . . .
she is often cunningly . . .
. . . does not feel death,                                            50
even though . . .
the wood shaken, they may wound the womb,
. . . offspring.
    Reveal the hoarded word, unwrap to men,
. . . open up in words,                                               55
how manifold is the power of that kin.

## EXE 81

Nis min sele swige,    ne ic sylfa hlud;
ymb . . .    unc dryhten scop
siþ ætsomne.    Ic eom swiftre þonne he,
þragum strengra;    he þreohtigra.
5    Hwilum ic me reste;    he sceal rinnan forð.
Ic him in wunige    a þenden ic lifge;
gif wit unc gedælað,    me bið dead witod.

## EXE 82

Wiht cwom gongan    þær weras sæton
monige on mæðle,    mode snottre;
hæfde an eage,    ond earan twa,
ond ·ii· fet,    ·xii· hund heafda,
5    hrycg ond wombe,    ond honda twa,
earmas ond eaxle,    anne sweoran
ond sidan twa.
                Saga hwæt hio hatte.

## EXE 83

Ic seah wundorlice wiht:    wombe hæfde micle,
þryþum geþrungne.    Þegn folgade,
mægen-strong ond mund-rof;    micel me þuhte
godlic gum-rinc;    grap on sona
5    . . .    heofones toþe

## EXE 81

My hall is not silent, nor am I myself loud;
concerning the two of us . . . the Lord created
a common course. I am swifter than him,
at times stronger; he is more enduring.
   Sometimes I rest; he must run on.         5
I dwell in him always as long as I live;
if we two are divided, death is my lot.

## EXE 82

A creature came walking where men sat,
many in an assembly, wise at heart;
it had one eye, and two ears,
and two feet, twelve hundred heads,
a back and a belly, and two hands,         5
arms and shoulders, one neck
and two sides.
                Say what it is called.

## EXE 83

I saw an amazing creature: she had a big belly,
massively swollen. A servant stood behind,
strong in might and sturdy of hand; he seemed big to me,
a good and manly man; he suddenly grabbed
her and with heaven's tooth . . .         5

bleowe on eage;    hio boncade,
wancode willum;    hio wolde seþeah
niol. . .


# EXE 84


Ic weox þær ic stod . . .
. . . ond sumor    mi. . .
. . .me    wæs min ti. . .
. . .
5  stod ic on staðole . . .
. . .um geong,    swa . . .
. . .se þeana
oft geond . . . ofgeaf,
ac ic uplong stod,    þær ic ær aweox
10  ond min broþor;    begen wæron hearde.
    Eard wæs þy weorðra    þe wit on stodan,
hyrstum þy hyrra.    Ful oft unc holt wrugon,
wudu-beama helm    wonnum nihtum,
scildon wið scurum;    unc gescop meotud.
15    Nu unc mæran twam    magas uncre
sculon æfter cuman,    eard oðþringan
gingran broþor.    Eom ic gum-cynnes
anga ofer eorþan,    is min innaþ blæc,
wonn ond wundorlic.
                        Ic on wuda stonde
20  bordes on ende.    Nis min broþor her,
ac ic sceal broþorleas    bordes on ende
staþol weardian,    stondan fæste;
ne wat hwær min broþor    on wera æhtum

there blew from an eyehole; she stamped,
shuddered pleasurably; but she wanted nonetheless
the depths . . .

## EXE 84

I grew where I . . .
. . . and summer . . .
. . . was my . . .
. . .
I stood in place . . .                                                                          5
. . . young, as . . .
. . . nevertheless . . .
often gave up . . . throughout . . .
but I stood straight, where I had previously grown up
and my brother; both of us were hard.                                          10
    The ground became more valuable that we two stood on,
the loftier in adornments. Very often the forest hid us,
the covering of wooded beams in the dark nights,
shielded us from showers; the creator made us both.
    Now our kinsmen, splendid,                                            15
will come after the two of us, take our land,
younger brothers. I am among mankind
unique across the earth; my innards are black,
dark and marvelous.
                      I stand on wood
at the edge of the table. My brother is not here,                            20
but I, without my brother, must take my place
at the edge of the table, stand secure;
I do not know where on the earth's surface,

eorþan sceata eardian sceal,
25 se me ær be healfe heah eardade.
 Wit wæron gesome sæcce to fremmanne;
næfre uncer awþer his ellen cyðde,
swa wit þære beadwe begen ne onþungan.
 Nu mec unsceafta innan slitað,
30 wyrdaþ mec be wombe; ic gewendan ne mæg.
Æt þam spore findeð sped se þe se...
 ... sawle rædes.

# EXE 85

...
...se wiht wombe hæfde
...
...tne leþre wæs beg...
5 ... on hindan
grette wea...
 ... listum worhte
hwilum eft...
 ... þygan, him þoncade
10 siþþan...
 ... swæsendum swylce þrage.

# EXE 86

Mirum mihi videtur: lupus ab agno tenetur;
obcubuit agnus rupi et capit viscera lupi.

among the properties of men, my brother has to dwell,
he who once dwelt beside me on high.                                    25
We two together were to do battle;
neither of us ever demonstrated valor,
when we two were not both in conflict.
    Now monstrous creatures tear at my insides,
injure me in the belly; I cannot escape.                               30
Whoever looks for the profit of the counsel for the soul
finds it in those traces . . .

## EXE 85

. . .
. . . the creature had a belly
. . .
. . . was leather . . .
. . . behind                                                            5
greeted . . .
    . . . skillfully wrought . . .
again at times . . .
. . . press, thanked him
afterwards . . .                                                        10
. . . for deliciousness at such a time.

## EXE 86

A marvel appeared to me: a wolf captured by a lamb;
the lamb has lain down upon a rock and snatches the wolf's
        insides.

Dum starem et mirarem, vidi gloriam parem:
duo lupi stantes et tertium tribulantes;
5 ·IIII· pedes habebant, cum septem oculis videbant.

## EXE 87

Min heafod is     homere geþruen,
searo-pila wund,     sworfen feole.
Oft ic begine     þæt me ongean sticað,
þonne ic hnitan sceal,     hringum gyrded,
5 hearde wið heardum,     hindan þyrel,
forð ascufan     þæt mines frean
mod·ᚱ· freoþað     middel-nihtum.
    Hwilum ic under bæc     bregde nebbe
hyrde þæs hordes,     þonne min hlaford wile
10 lafe þicgan     þara þe he of life het
wæl-cræfte awrecan     willum sinum.

## EXE 88

Ic wæs brunra beot,     beam on holte,
freolic feorh-bora     ond foldan wæstm,
weres wynn-staþol     ond wifes sond,
gold on geardum.
                Nu eom guð-wigan
5 hyhtlic hilde-wæpen,     hringe be. . .
. . .e. . . byreð,
oþrum . . .

While I was standing and marveling, I saw an equal
    wonder:
two wolves standing and worrying a third;
they had four feet, and they looked with seven eyes.      5


## EXE 87

My head is beaten by a hammer,
wounded by skillful darts, ground by a file.
Often I swallow what sticks against me,
when, girded with rings, I have to thrust,
hard against a hard thing, pierced from behind,      5
shove forward what takes care of my master's
mind-*joy* in the middle of the night.
   Sometimes I draw back with my beak
the guardian of the hoard, when my lord wishes
to take what's left of those whom he had driven out of life    10
by the power of slaughter, according to his will.


## EXE 88

I was the boast of brown creatures, a tree in a forest,
a splendid life-bearer, and the fruit of the earth,
a man's joy-foundation, and a woman's message,
gold among the enclosures.
                         Now I am the trusty battle-weapon
of a fighting man, ring . . .      5
. . . bears,
to others . . .

# EXE 89

Frea min . . .
. . .de   willum sinum,
. . .
heah ond hyhtful;   hwilum . . .
5 . . . scearpne;   hwilum . . .
. . . hwilum sohte
frea. . . s wod,
dæg-rime frod,   deope . . .s,
hwilum stealc hliþo   stigan sceolde
10 up in eþel,   hwilum eft gewat
in deop dalu   duguþe secan
strong on stæpe,   stan-wongas grof,
hrimig-hearde,   hwilum hara scoc
forst of feaxe.   Ic on fusum rad
15 oþþæt him þone gleaw-stol   gingra broþor
min agnade,   ond mec of earde adraf.
   Siþþan mec isern   innanweardne
brun bennade;   blod ut ne com,
heolfor of hreþre,   þeah mec heard bite
20 stið-ecg style.   No ic þa stunde bemearn,
ne for wunde weop,   ne wrecan meahte
on wigan feore   wonn-sceaft mine,
ac ic aglæca   ealle þolige
þæt bord biton.
              Nu ic blace swelge
25 wuda ond wætre,   wombe befæðme
þæt mec on fealleð   ufan þær ic stonde,
eorpes nat-hwæt;   hæbbe anne fot.

414

# EXE 89

My master . . .
. . . according to his will,
. . .
high and hopeful . . . sometimes . . .
. . . sharp; sometimes . . .
. . . sometimes sought                                              5
master . . . waded,
old in the tally of days, deep streams,
sometimes had to climb steep slopes
up in its homeland, sometimes came back again          10
into deep valleys seeking out the company
strong in step, dug stone fields,
rime-hard, sometimes hoary frost
shook from its hair. I rode upon the eager one
until my younger brother took over                            15
the seat of joy, and drove me from my home.

   Then bright iron gave me wounds
inside; no blood came out,
gore from my heart, even though it cut me,
cruel, sharp-edged steel. I did not grieve for that time    20
nor did I weep at the wound, nor was I able to avenge
my miserable experience on that warrior's life,
but I endure all the torments
that have scarred shields.
                          Now I swallow
black wood and water, envelop in my belly                  25
what falls from above on me, where I stand,
something dark; I have a single foot.

415

Nu min hord warað    hiþende feond,
se þe ær wide bær    wulfes gehleþan;
30 oft me of wombe    bewaden fereð,
steppeð on stið bord,   ...
... deaþes d...    þonne dæg-condel,
sunne ...
...eorc    eagum wliteð
35 ond sped ...

## EXE 90

Smeþr ... ad,
hyrre þonne heofon ...
...     glædre þonne sunne,
... heardre þonne style,
5 smeare þonne sealt ry...
leofre þonne þis leoht eall,    leohtre þonne wyrm.

## EXE 91

Ic eom indryhten    ond eorlum cuð,
ond reste oft    ricum ond heanum,
folcum gefræge.    Fereð wide,
ond me fremdes ær    freondum stondeð,
5 hiþendra hyht,    gif ic habban sceal
blæd in burgum    oþþe beorhte god.
    Nu snottre men    swiþast lufiaþ
mid-wist mine;    ic monigum sceal
wisdom cyþan;    no þær word sprecan

Now a raiding enemy holds my hoard,
one that once carried widely the wolf's companion;
often, having dipped into my belly, it travels,                    30
steps on a stiff board, ...
... of death when the day-candle,
the sun ...
... deed looks with eyes
and success ...                                                    35

## EXE 90

Smoother than ...
higher than heaven ...
... brighter than the sun,
... stronger than steel,
sharper than salt...                                                5
lovelier than all this light, lighter than an insect.

## EXE 91

I am noble, and well known to men,
and I often remain among the powerful and the poor,
famed among folk. The pleasure of plunderers
travels widely and stands in a friendly fashion for me,
who was formerly a stranger's, if I am to have                      5
a reputation in the towns, or glittering wealth.
    Now wise men love most
my company; I shall show
wisdom to many, but not speak any words

10    ænig ofer eorðan.

Þeah nu ælda bearn,
lond-buendra,    lastas mine
swiþe secað,    ic swaþe hwilum
mine bemiþe    monna gehwylcum.

there on the earth.                                                                                10
                    Although now the sons of men,
living on the land, greatly seek out
my trails, my traces sometimes
I conceal from everyone.

# The Old English Rune Poem

## OER 1

·ᚠ· byþ frofur    fira gehwylcum;
sceal ðeah manna gehwylc    miclun hyt dælan,
gif he wile for drihtne    domes hleotan.

## OER 2

·ᚢ· byþ an-mod    and ofer-hyrned,
fela-frecne deor    (feohteþ mid hornum),
mære mor-stapa;    þæt is modig wuht.

## OER 3

·ᚦ· byþ ðearle scearp;    ðegna gehwylcum
an-feng ys yfyl,    ungemetun reþe
manna gehwylcun    ðe him mid resteð.

# The Old English Rune Poem

## OER 1

*f* is a comfort to all men;
but everyone must share it a lot,
if he wishes to gain glory in the presence of his lord.

## OER 2

*u* is determined and mighty horned,
a very bold beast (it fights with its horns),
a well-known moor-stalker; that is a brave creature.

## OER 3

*þ* is extremely sharp, bad to grasp
for any warrior, immeasurably fierce
for anyone who rests in its midst.

## OER 4

·ᚠ· byþ ord-fruma    ælcre spræce,
wisdomes wraþu    and witena frofur,
and eorla gehwam    eadnys and tohiht.

## OER 5

·ᚱ· byþ on recyde    rinca gehwylcum
sefte, and swiþ-hwæt    ðam ðe sitteþ on ufan
meare mægen-heardum    ofer mil-paþas.

## OER 6

·ᚳ· byþ cwicera gehwam    cuþ on fyre,
blac and beorhtlic;    byrneþ oftust
ðær hi æþelingas    inne restaþ.

## OER 7

·ᚷ· gumena byþ    gleng and herenys;
wraþu and wyrþ-scype,    and wræcna gehwam
ar and æt-wist    ðe byþ oþra leas.

## OER 4

*o* is the source of all speech,
the support of wisdom and a comfort of the wise,
and a blessing and delight to every noble.

## OER 5

*r* is a pleasure for every warrior in a hall,
and very brisk for the one sitting above
a powerful horse over long roads.

## OER 6

*c* is known to all of the living by its flame,
bright and shining; it burns most often
where princes are staying inside.

## OER 7

*g* of men is glory and praise;
support and honor, and grace and sustenance
for any exile who has a lack of them.

## OER 8

·ᚠ· ne bruceþ   ðe can weana lyt,
sares and sorge,   and him sylfa hæfþ
blæd and blysse   and eac byrga geniht.

## OER 9

·ᚺ· byþ hwitust corna;   hwyrft hit of heofones lyfte;
wealcaþ hit windes scuras;   weorþeþ hit to wætere syððan.

## OER 10

·ᚻ· byþ nearu on breostan,   weorþeþ hi ðeah oft niþa bearnum
to helpe and to hæle gehwæþre,   gif hi his hlystaþ æror.

## OER 11

·ᛁ· byþ ofer-ceald,   ungemetum slidor;
glisnaþ glæs-hluttur,   gimmum gelicust,
flor forste geworuht,   fæger ansyne.

## OER 8

*w* he does not enjoy who knows few woes,
sorrow and soreness, and has himself
happiness and plenty and the sufficiency of fortresses.

## OER 9

*h* is the whitest of grains; it tumbles from the air of heaven;
wind's showers send it billowing; then it turns to water.

## OER 10

*n* is tight in the breast, and yet it turns out often for the
        children of men
as help and healing likewise, if they only take heed ahead.

## OER 11

*i* is mighty cold, and immeasurably slippery;
glistening clear as glass, most like gems,
a floor wrought by frost, fair to behold.

## OER 12

·ᚷ· byþ gumena hiht,    ðon God læteþ,
halig heofones cyning,    hrusan syllan
beorhte bleda    beornum and ðearfum.

## OER 13

·ᛁ· byþ utan    unsmeþe treow,
heard, hrusan fæst,    hyrde fyres,
wyrtrumun under-wreþyd,    wyn on eþle.

## OER 14

·ᛈ· byþ symble    plega and hlehter
wlancum æt wine,    ðar wigan sittaþ
on beor-sele    bliþe ætsomne.

## OER 15

·ᛉ· eard hæfþ    oftust on fenne;
wexeð on wature;    wundaþ grimme,
blode breneð    beorna gehwylcne
ðe him ænigne    on-feng gedeð.

## OER 12

*j* is the hope of men, when God,
the holy king of heaven, allows the earth
to grant bright growth to the rich and the poor.

## OER 13

*i* is on the outside an unsmooth tree,
hard, firm in the ground, the guardian of flame,
underpinned by roots, a joy in the homeland.

## OER 14

*p* is always fun and laughter
for the proud at their wine-drinking, where warriors sit
happy together in the beer hall.

## OER 15

*x* has its home most often in a fen;
it grows in water; it gives grim wounds,
stains with blood each warrior
that takes any hold of it.

## OER 16

·ᚻ· se-mannum    symble biþ on hihte
ðonn hi hine feriaþ    ofer fisces beþ,
oþ hi brim-hengest    bringeþ to lande.

## OER 17

·ᛏ· biþ tacna sum,    healdeð trywa wel
wiþ æþelingas;    a biþ on færylde,
ofer nihta genipu;    næfre swiceþ.

## OER 18

·ᛒ· byþ bleda leas,    bereþ efne swa ðeah
tanas butan tudder,    biþ on telgum wlitig,
heah on helme,    hrysted fægere,
geloden leafum,    lyfte getenge.

## OER 19

·ᛗ· byþ for eorlum    æþelinga wyn,
hors hofum wlanc,    ðær him hæleþ ymbe
welege on wicgum,    wrixlaþ spræce,
and biþ unstyllum    æfre frofur.

## OER 16

*s* is for seafarers always a source of hope
when they travel over the fish's bath,
or the sea-steed brings them to land.

## OER 17

*t* is a particular token, it keeps faith well
with nobles; it is always in motion
above the clouds of night; it never fails.

## OER 18

*b* is fruitless, and yet nonetheless
bears twigs without seeds, but is beautiful in branches,
high in its crown, fairly adorned,
laden with leaves, reaching up to the sky.

## OER 19

*e* is the joy of nobles among men,
a horse proud in hooves, where warriors,
wealthy ones on stallions, speak among themselves,
and there is always comfort for those without rest.

## OER 20

·ᛗ· byþ on myrgþe,    his magan leof,
sceal þeah anra gehwylc    oðrum swican,
for ðam dryhten wyle    dome sine
þæt earme flæsc    eorþan betæcan.


## OER 21

·ᚱ· byþ leodum    langsum geþuht,
gif hi sculun neþan    on nacan tealtum,
and hi sæ-yþa    swyþe bregaþ,
and se brim-hengest    bridles ne gymeð.


## OER 22

·ᛉ· wæs ærest    mid East-denum
gesewen secgun,    oþ he siððan eft
ofer wæg gewat,    wæn æfter ran;
ðus heardingas    ðone hæle nemdun.


## OER 23

·ᚷ· byþ ofer-leof    æghwylcum men,
gif he mot ðær rihtes    and gerysena on
brucan on bolde    bleadum oftast.

## OER 20

*m* is full of mirth, dear to his kin,
though each individual must let down the other,
since by his own decree the Lord will
entrust that wretched flesh to the earth.

## OER 21

*l* seems interminable to folks,
if they have to take a chance on an unstable vessel,
and ocean waves terrify them greatly,
and that sea-steed does not care for the bridle.

## OER 22

*ng* was among the East Danes first
seen among men, until he went back
again over the wave, and his wagon followed;
thus did the hard ones name that hero.

## OER 23

*œ* is beyond dear to everyone,
if he can enjoy there what is right and proper
in his house most often in prosperity.

## OER 24

·ᛗ· byþ drihtnes sond,     deore mannum,
mære metodes leoht,     myrgþ and tohiht
eadgum and earmum,     eallum brice.

## OER 25

·ᚠ· byþ on eorþan     elda bearnum
flæsces fodor;     fereþ gelome
ofer ganotes bæþ;     garsecg fandaþ
hwæþer ac hæbbe     æþele treowe.

## OER 26

·ᚱ· biþ ofer-heah,     eldum dyre,
stiþ on staþule,     stede rihte hylt,
ðeah him feohtan on     firas monige.

## OER 27

·ᚾ· byþ æþelinga     and eorla gehwæs
wyn and wyrþ-mynd;     byþ on wicge fæger,
fæstlic on fær-elde,     fyrd-geatewa sum.

## OER 24

*d* is the Lord's messenger, dear to mankind,
the famed light of God, mirth and hope
to the blessed and the wretched, a boon to all.

## OER 25

*a* is on earth for the children of mankind
the fodder of flesh; it often travels
over the gannet's bath; the ocean tests
whether that oak keeps noble faith.

## OER 26

*æ* is very tall, precious to people,
stiff on its foundation, it holds its place straight,
even though many men fight against it.

## OER 27

*y* is for every prince and warrior
a joy and a distinction; it is beautiful on a horse,
reliable in motion, a piece of military gear.

## OER 28

·✲· byþ ea-fix,     and ðeah a bruceþ
fodres on foldan,     hafaþ fægerne eard,
wætre beworpen,     ðær he wynnum leofaþ.

## OER 29

·ᛏ· byþ egle     eorla gehwylcun,
ðonn fæstlice     flæsc onginneþ,
hraw colian,     hrusan ceosan
blac to gebeddan;     bleda gedreosaþ;
5   wynna gewitaþ,     wera geswicaþ.

## OER 28

*īa* is a river-fish, and yet it always enjoys
its food on the earth; it has a beautiful dwelling,
lapped about with water, where it lives in joy.

## OER 29

*ea* is loathsome to every man,
when unwaveringly the flesh begins,
the corpse to cool, the pale one
to choose the ground as its bedfellow;
fruits fall, joys fail, bonds are broken.                    5

# The Riddles of *Solomon and Saturn II*

## SOL 1

*Saturnus cwæð:*
"Ac hwæt is se dumba,    se ðe on sumre dene resteð?
Swiðe snyttrað,    hafað seofon tungan,
hafað tungena gehwylc    .xx. orda,
hafað orda gehwylc    engles snytro,
5  ðara ðe wile anra hwylc    uppe bringan,
ðæt ðu ðære gyldnan gesiehst    Hierusalem
weallas blican    ond hiera win-rod lixan,
soð-fæstra segn.    Saga hwæt ic mæne."

*Salomon cwæð:*
"Bec sindon breme,    bodiað geneahhe
10  weotodne willan    ðam ðe wiht hygeð,
gestrangað hie on gestaðeliað    staðol-fæstne geðoht,
amyrgað mod-sefan    manna gehwylces
of ðrea-medlan    ðisses lifes."

# The Riddles of *Solomon and Saturn II*

## SOL 1

*Saturn said:*
"But what is that dumb one, that rests in a certain valley?
It is very wise, has seven tongues,
each tongue has twenty points,
each point has the wisdom of an angel,
each one of which desires to enlighten                                       5
so that you will see the golden walls of Jerusalem
gleaming and their cross of joy shining,
banner of the righteous. Say what I mean."

*Solomon said:*
"Books are famous, they proclaim continually
the mastered will to him who thinks to any degree,                          10
they strengthen and fortify resolute thought,
amuse the mind of every man
away from the painful pondering of this life."

## SOL 2

*Saturnus cwæð:*
"Ac hwæt is ðæt wundor    ðe geond ðas worold færeð,
styrnenga gæð,    staðolas beateð,
aweceð wop-dropan,    winneð oft hider?
Ne mæg hit steorra ne stan    ne se steapa gimm,
5    wæter ne wil-deor,    wihte beswican,
ac him on hand gæð    heardes and hnesces,
micles ond mætes;    him to mose sceall
gegangan geara gehwelce    grund-buendra,
lyft-fleogendra,    lagu-swemmendra,
10    ðria ðreoteno    ðusend-gerimes."

*Salomon cwæð:*
"Yldo beoð on eorðan    æghwæs cræftig;
mid hiðendre    hilde-wræsne,
rumre racen-teage,    ręceð wide,
langre linan,    lisseð eall ðæt heo wile.
15    Beam heo abreoteð    and bebriceð telgum,
astyreð standendne    stefn on siðe,
afilleð hine on foldan;    friteð æfter ðam
wildne fugol.    Heo oferwigeð wulf,
hio oferbideð stanas,    heo oferstigeð style,
20    hio abiteð iren mid ome,    deð usic swa."

# SOL 2

*Saturn said:*
"But what is that wonder that travels throughout this
        world,
proceeds fiercely, smashes foundations,
stirs up tearful drops, often impinges here?
Neither star nor stone nor steep-sided gem,
not water nor wild beast can escape it at all,                    5
but into its domain go the hard and the soft,
the great and the small; into its maw
must travel every year thrice thirteen thousand
of those that dwell on earth
or fly in the sky or swim in the sea."                           10

*Solomon said:*
"Old age is on earth supremely powerful:
with plundering and battling bonds,
with shackles spreading, she takes wide control,
with her long line she subsumes all she will.
She shatters the tree and scatters the shrub,                    15
overturns the roots that stand in her way,
flattens them to the ground; then she chews up
the wild birds. She wears down the wolf,
outlasts the stones, surpasses steel,
consumes iron with rust, and does likewise with us."            20

# The Old English Prose Riddle

## OEP

*Nys þks frfgfn syllkc þknc to rædfnnf.*
Þu þe færst on þone weg, gret ðu minne broðor, minre
modor ceorl, þone acende min agen wif, and ic wæs mines
broðor dohtor, and ic eom mines fæder modor geworden,
and mine bearn syndon geworden mines fæder modor.

# The Old English Prose Riddle

## OEP

*This question is not a wondrous thing to explain.*
You who travel on the way, greet my brother, my mother's
man, the one to whom my own lady gave birth, and I was my
brother's daughter, and I have become my father's mother,
and my children have become my father's mother.

# SOURCES AND
ANALOGUES OF
THE TRADITION

# Symphosius

## SYM PR

*Haec quoque Symphosius de carmine lusit inepto:*
*sic tu, Sexte, doces; sic te deliro magistro.*
Annua Saturni dum tempora festa redirent,
perpetuo semper nobis sollemnia ludo,
5   post epulas laetas, post dulcia pocula mensae,
deliras inter vetulas puerosque loquaces,
cum streperet late madidae facundia linguae,
tum verbosa cohors studio sermonis inepti
nescio quas passim magno tentamine nugas
10  est meditata diu; sed frivola multa locuta est.
    Nec mediocre fuit, magni certaminis instar,
ponere diverse vel solvere quaeque vicissim.
Ast ego, ne solus foede tacuisse viderer,
qui nihil adtuleram mecum quod dicere possem,
15  hos versus feci subito discrimine vocis.
    Insanos inter sanum non esse necesse est:
da veniam, lector, quod non sapit ebria Musa.

# Symphosius

## SYM PR

*These bits of trifling verse Symphosius has also composed in sport:*
*just as you teach, Sextus; so, with you as my teacher, do I rave.*
When the annual festival season of Saturn was returning,
festivities that were always perpetual fun for us,
after the happy banquets, after the sweet drafts of the table,   5
among the raving crones and babbling boys,
when the eloquence of a drunken tongue clamored far and
    wide,
then the wordy throng in their zeal for senseless speech
pondered long some sort of random trifles with great effort:
but they uttered many a frivolous thing.   10
It was no small matter, but like a great contest,
variously setting and solving each in turn.
But I, who had brought nothing with me that I could say,
so that I alone not seem to be shamefully silent,
composed these verses with extemporized song.   15
Among the unwise there is no need to be wise:
forgive, reader, the fact that a drunken Muse makes no
    sense.

## SYM 1

De summo planus, sed non ego planus in imo;
versor utrimque manu, diverso munere fungor;
altera pars revocat quidquid pars altera fecit.

## SYM 2

Dulcis amica dei, ripae vicina profundae,
suave canens Musis; nigro perfusa colore,
nuntia sum linguae, digitis signata magistris.

## SYM 3

Corporis extremi non magnum pondus adhaesi;
ingenitum dicas, ita pondere nemo gravatur;
una tamen facies plures habitura figuras.

## SYM 4

Virtutes magnas de viribus affero parvis;
pando domos clausas, iterum sed claudo patentes;
servo domum domino, sed rursus servor ab ipso.

# SYM 1

I'm flat on top, but I'm not flat below;
I'm turned both ways in the hand, and perform opposite
   duties;
one part undoes what the other part has done.

# SYM 2

A god's sweet sweetheart, always close to a steep bank,
singing smoothly for the Muses; when dipped in black,
I am the tongue's herald, directed by guiding fingers.

# SYM 3

Of no great weight, I am stuck to the body's extremity;
you may say that I was born there, since no one is much
   burdened by my weight;
but one single facet will produce many more shapes.

# SYM 4

I offer great powers with little effort;
I open closed buildings, and again close open ones;
I guard the house for the householder, but again am
   guarded by him.

## SYM 5

Nexa ligor ferro, multos habitura ligatos;
vincior ipsa prius, sed vincio vincta vicissim;
et solvi multos, nec sum tamen ipsa soluta.

## SYM 6

Terra mihi corpus, vires mihi praestitit ignis;
de terra nascor, sedes est semper in alto;
et me perfundit qui me cito deserit umor.

## SYM 7

Sunt mihi, sunt lacrimae, sed non est causa doloris;
est iter ad caelum, sed me gravis impedit aer;
et qui me genuit, sine me non nascitur ipse.

## SYM 8

Nox ego sum facie, sed non sum nigra colore;
inque die media tenebras tamen affero mecum;
nec mihi dant stellae lucem nec Cynthia lumen.

## SYM 5

I am bound, fastened with iron, and I shall keep many
    bound;
I myself am tied up first, but when tied up I tie up in turn;
I have released many, but am not yet released myself.

## SYM 6

Earth gave me body, fire gave me strength;
I am born from earth, but my dwelling is always on high;
I am drenched by moisture that swiftly deserts me.

## SYM 7

With me it's tears, always tears, but no reason to cry;
there is a route to the sky, but the heavy air weighs me
    down;
the father who gave me life is not born without me.

## SYM 8

I look like night, but I am not black in color;
yet in the middle of the day I bring darkness with me;
neither the stars nor the moon grant me their light.

## SYM 9

Ex alto venio, longa delapsa ruina;
de caelo cecidi, medias transmissa per auras;
sed sinus excepit qui me simul ipse recepit.

## SYM 10

Unda fui quondam, quod me cito credo futuram;
nunc rigidi caeli duris connexa catenis;
et calcata pati possum nec nuda teneri.

## SYM 11

Pulvis aquae tenuis, modico cum pondere lapsus;
sole madens, aestate fluens, in frigore siccus;
flumina facturus totas prius occupo terras.

## SYM 12

Est domus in terris, clara quae voce resultat:
ipsa domus resonat, tacitus sed non sonat hospes;
ambo tamen currunt, hospes simul et domus una.

## SYM 9

I come from on high, after falling in a long descent;
I have dropped from the sky, having passed through midair;
but the same lap that received me straightaway sends me
    back.


## SYM 10

Once I was water, which I reckon I shall be again;
now I'm wrapped in the hard chains of harsh heaven;
I can bear to be trodden on, but not held naked.


## SYM 11

A light dusting of water, fallen without much weight;
melting in the sun, flowing in summer, dry in winter;
I, who will make rivers, beforehand cover whole lands.


## SYM 12

There is a home on earth which calls out with a clear voice:
the house itself resounds, but its silent guest makes no
    sound;
yet both flow together, the guest alongside the house.

## SYM 13

Longa feror velox, formosae filia silvae;
innumeris pariter comitum stipata catervis;
curro vias multas, vestigia nulla relinquens.

## SYM 14

Mira tibi referam nostrae primordia vitae:
nondum natus eram, nec eram genitricis in alvo;
iam posito partu natum me nemo videbat.

## SYM 15

Non possum nasci, si non occidero matrem;
occidi matrem, sed me manet exitus idem;
id mea mors patitur quod iam mea fecit origo.

## SYM 16

Littera me pavit, nec quid sit littera novi;
in libris vixi, nec sum studiosior inde;
exedi Musas, nec adhuc tamen ipsa profeci.

# SYM 13

I am carried along, the long, swift daughter of the beautiful
   forest;
I am likewise crammed with unnumbered throngs of
   companions;
I travel many paths, but leave no traces behind.

# SYM 14

I shall tell you the amazing origins of my life:
I had not yet been born, nor did I exist inside my mother's
   womb;
and so with my birth already taken care of, no one saw me
   born.

# SYM 15

I cannot be born, unless I have killed my mother;
I have killed my mother, but the same end waits for me;
my death endures what my beginning has already caused.

# SYM 16

A letter fed me, though I know not what a letter is;
I made my life in books, though I'm no smarter for that;
I've consumed the Muses, and yet I'm still no further on.

## SYM 17

Pallas me docuit texendi nosse laborem;
nec pepli radios poscunt nec licia telae;
nulla mihi manus est, pedibus tamen omnia fiunt.

## SYM 18

Porto domum mecum, semper migrare parata;
mutatoque solo non sum miserabilis exul;
sed mihi conchilium de caelo nascitur ipso.

## SYM 19

Rauca sonans ego sum media vocalis in unda;
sed vox laude sonat, quasi se quoque laudet et ipsa;
cumque canam semper, nullus mea carmina laudat.

## SYM 20

Tarda, gradu lento, specioso praedita dorso;
docta quidem studio, sed saevo prodita fato;
viva nihil dixi, quae sic modo mortua canto.

## SYM 17

Athena taught me to know the work of weaving;
my fabrics do not require shuttles, nor my webs threads;
I have no hands, but everything happens through my feet.

## SYM 18

I carry my house with me, always ready to move;
and when I have moved my place, I'm not a pitiful exile;
but my purple dye is born of heaven above.

## SYM 19

I sound croaking loud in the middle of the water;
but my voice sounds in praise, as if it were also praising
    itself;
and though I am always singing, no one praises my songs.

## SYM 20

Sluggish, and with slow step, furnished with a beautiful
    back;
well-taught indeed by study, but betrayed by cruel fate;
I said nothing when I was alive, but now that I am dead I
    sing like this.

## SYM 21

Caeca mihi facies, atris obscura tenebris;
nox est ipse dies nec sol mihi cernitur ullus;
malo tegi terra: sic me quoque nemo videbit.

## SYM 22

Provida sum vitae, duro non pigra labore,
ipsa ferens umeris securae praemia brumae;
nec gero magna simul, sed congero multa vicissim.

## SYM 23

Improba sum, fateor; quid enim gula turpe veretur?
Frigora vitabam, quae nunc aestate revertor;
sed cito submoveor falso conterrita vento.

## SYM 24

Non bonus agricolis, non frugibus utilis hospes;
non magnus forma, non recto nomine dictus;
non gratus Cereri, sed multa vivo sagina.

## SYM 21

My face is blind, hidden in dark shadows;
night and day are the same; nor do I see any sun;
I prefer to be covered by soil; that way no one will see me.

## SYM 22

I look after my life: I'm not shy of hard work,
as on my back I carry provisions for a winter free from care;
nor do I lift up mighty loads at once, but I collect a lot bit
    by bit.

## SYM 23

I'm filthy, I confess: what awful thing won't I eat?
I avoided the cold, and now I'm back in summer;
but I quickly disappear, scared by a phantom breeze.

## SYM 24

No good to farmers, not a useful visitor to crops;
not big in size, not even called by my right name;
not welcome to Ceres, but I live from much stuffing.

## SYM 25

Parva mihi domus est, sed ianua semper aperta;
exiguo sumptu furtiva vivo sagina;
quod mihi nomen inest, Romae quoque consul habebat.


## SYM 26

Littera sum caeli penna perscripta volantis;
bella cruenta gerens volucri discrimine Martis;
nec vereor pugnas, dum non sit longior hostis.


## SYM 27

Vivo novem vitas, si me non Graecia fallit;
nomen habens atrum nullo conpulsa dolore;
et non irascens ultro conuitia dico.


## SYM 28

Nox mihi dat nomen primo de tempore noctis;
pluma mihi non est, cum sit mihi penna volantis;
sed redeo in tenebris, nec me committo diebus.

## SYM 25

My house is humble, but the door is always open;
when I've taken a little, I live off the stolen stuffing;
the name which applies to me a consul in Rome also used to
      have.

## SYM 26

I am a letter written by the feather of a flying creature of
      the sky,
waging bloody battles in the swift conflict of Mars;
nor do I fear fighting, as long as my enemy is not taller.

## SYM 27

I live nine lives, if nets do not deceive me,
having a black name, even though I am not weighted down
      with any grief;
and even when I am not angry I utter insults anyway.

## SYM 28

Night gives me my name from the beginning of the night;
I have no feathers, though I have the wings of a flying
      creature;
but I return in darkness and do not trust myself to the day.

## SYM 29

Plena domus spinis, parvi sed corporis hospes;
incolumi dorso telis confixus acutis;
sustinet armatas segetes habitator inermis.

## SYM 30

Est nova nostrarum cunctis captura ferarum:
ut si quid capias, et tu tibi ferre recuses,
et quod non capias, tecum tamen ipse reportes.

## SYM 31

Vita mihi mors est, morior si coepero nasci;
sed prius est fatum leti, quam lucis origo;
sic solus Manes ipsos mihi dico parentes.

## SYM 32

Moechus eram regis, sed lignea membra sequebar;
et Cilicum mons sum, sed mons sum nomine solo;
et vehor in caelis, et in ipsis ambulo terris.

## SYM 29

A house full of prickles, but the guest inside is small;
transfixed with sharp points on an unharmed back;
an unarmed inhabitant upholds an armored crop.

## SYM 30

Strange to all is the hunt for wild creatures like us:
so that, if you were to capture anything, you'd refuse to
    bring it home,
and what you fail to capture, still you'd bring back with you
    anyway.

## SYM 31

Death is life to me; I die if I begin to be born;
Yet the fate of death occurs before the beginning of the
    light of life;
in this way do I alone call the very Shades my parents.

## SYM 32

I made a cuckold of a king, but I was chasing wooden limbs;
and I am a mountain in Cilicia, but a mountain in name
    alone;
and I ride in the heavens, and walk on the earth itself.

## SYM 33

Dentibus insanis ego sum qui vinco bidentes,
sanguineas praedas quaerens victusque cruentos;
multaque cum rabie vocem quoque tollere possum.

## SYM 34

Exiguum corpus sed cor mihi corpore maius;
sum versuta dolis, arguto callida sensu;
et fera sum sapiens, sapiens fera si qua vocatur.

## SYM 35

Alma Iovis nutrix, longo vestita capillo,
culmina de facili peragrans super ardua gressu,
custodi pecoris tremula respondeo lingua.

## SYM 36

Setigerae matris fecunda natus in alvo;
desuper ex alto virides expecto saginas;
nomine numen habens si littera prima periret.

## SYM 33

I am the one who crushes sheep with my ravenous teeth,
seeking bloody prey and gory food;
and with great madness I can also take away the voice.

## SYM 34

I have a tiny body, but my heart is bigger than my body;
I'm cunning at tricks, clever with keen sense;
I'm a wise beast, if any beast can be called wise.

## SYM 35

The nourishing nursemaid of Jove, clothed in long hair,
tripping over mountainous heights with an easy step,
with a bleating voice I answer the keeper of the flock.

## SYM 36

Born in the fertile womb of a bristly mother;
I wait for green forage to fall from up above;
if the first letter of my name were to perish I'd contain
    something divine.

## SYM 37

Dissimilis patri, matri diversa figura;
confusi generis, generi non apta propago,
ex aliis nascor, nec quisquam nascitur ex me.

## SYM 38

A fluvio dicor, fluvius vel dicitur ex me;
iunctaque sum vento, quae sum velocior ipso;
et mihi dat ventus natos nec quaero maritum.

## SYM 39

Quattuor insignis pedibus manibusque duabus,
dissimilis mihi sum, quia sum non unus et unus;
et vehor et gradior, quia me duo corpora portant.

## SYM 40

Grande mihi caput est, intus sunt membra minuta;
pes unus solus, sed pes longissimus unus;
et me somnus amat, proprio nec dormio somno.

## SYM 37

I am unlike my father, and look nothing like my mother;
of mixed breeding, a type unfit for breeding,
I am born from others, but no one is born from me.

## SYM 38

I am named from a river, or the river is named from me;
I am linked to the wind, although I am swifter than it;
and the wind gives me sons: I don't look for a mate.

## SYM 39

Distinguished by having four feet and two hands,
I am unlike myself, because I am one and yet not one;
I both ride and walk, because two bodies bear me.

## SYM 40

My head is large, though the bits within are tiny;
there is only one leg, but it is very long;
and sleep loves me, though I don't sleep a slumber of my
    own.

## SYM 41

Anseris esse pedes similes mihi, nolo negare;
nec duo sunt tantum, sed plures ordine cernis;
et tamen hos ipsos omnes ego porto supinos.

## SYM 42

Tota vocor Graece, sed non sum tota Latine;
ante tamen mediam cauponis scripta tabernam.
In terris nascor, lympha lavor, unguor olivo.

## SYM 43

Pendeo dum nascor, rursus dum pendeo, cresco;
pendens commoveor ventis et nutrior undis.
Pendula si non sim, non sum iam iamque futura.

## SYM 44

Mordeo mordentes, ultro non mordeo quemquam;
sed sunt mordentem multi mordere parati;
nemo timet morsum, dentes quia non habet ullos.

# SYM 41

I don't wish to deny that my feet are like those of a goose;
nor are there only two, but you see more in a row;
yet I carry all of these upside down.


# SYM 42

I am named fully in Greek, but I am not whole in Latin;
yet I am written before the middle of the pub owner's
    tavern.
I am born in the ground, washed in water, smeared with oil.


# SYM 43

I hang when I am born, and again when I hang I grow;
while hanging I am moved by the winds and fed by the
    waters.
If I don't dangle, I am no longer going to exist.


# SYM 44

I bite the biters, yet of my own accord I bite no one;
but there are many prepared to bite the one that bites;
no one fears the bite: it does not have any teeth.

## SYM 45

Purpura sum terrae, pulchro perfusa colore;
saeptaque, ne violer, telis defendor acutis.
O felix, longo si possim vivere fato!

## SYM 46

Magna quidem non sum, sed inest mihi maxima virtus;
spiritus est magnus, quamvis sim corpore parvo;
nec mihi germen habet noxam nec culpa ruborem.

## SYM 47

Dulcis odor nemoris, flamma fumoque fatigor,
et placet hoc superis, medios quod mittor in ignes;
nec mihi poena datur, sed habetur gratia danti.

## SYM 48

De lacrimis et pro lacrimis mea coepit origo;
ex oculis fluxi, sed nunc ex arbore nascor;
laetus honor frondis, tristis sed imago doloris.

## SYM 45

On earth I am crimson, drenched with a beautiful color;
hedged about so I am not violated, I am defended by sharp
    points.
Oh, I would be happy, if I could only live a long life!

## SYM 46

I am not great, for sure, but I have the greatest power;
my scent is great, although I have a small body;
my seed is harmless, nor does blame make me blush.

## SYM 47

I am a sweet scent from the grove, worn out by flame and
    smoke,
and it pleases the gods that I am put in the middle of the
    fire;
I am not punished, but grace is granted to the giver.

## SYM 48

My beginning started from tears and for tears;
I flowed from eyes, but now am born from a tree;
a lucky adornment on a leaf, but a sad picture of sorrow.

## SYM 49

Dens ego sum magnus populis cognatus Eois;
nunc ego per partes in corpora multa recessi;
nec remanent vires, sed formae gratia mansit.

## SYM 50

Herba fui quondam viridi de gramine terrae;
sed chalybis duro mollis praecisa metallo,
mole premor propria, tecto conclusa sub alto.

## SYM 51

Ambo sumus lapides, una sumus, ambo iacemus;
Quam piger est unus, tantum sed non piger alter;
hic manet inmotus, non desinit ille moveri.

## SYM 52

Inter saxa fui quae me contrita premebant;
vix tamen effugi totis conlisa medullis;
et nunc forma mihi minor est sed copia maior.

# SYM 49

I am a huge tooth, kindred of Eastern peoples;
but now I have withdrawn, split up into many bits;
none of my strength remains, but my basic beauty has
      endured.

# SYM 50

I was once the crop of the bright-green grass of the ground;
but when I was soft I was cut by a hard blade of steel,
and am pressed down by my own weight, closed in under a
      high roof.

# SYM 51

We are both stones, and we are together, and we both lie
      down;
and one is always moving, while the other does not move;
the one stands still, the other does not stay stationary.

# SYM 52

I spent time between stones that crushed and ground me;
yet I scarcely escaped with all my innards squeezed;
now I'm smaller in size, but greater in bountifulness.

## SYM 53

Nolo toro iungi, quamvis placet esse maritam;
nolo virum thalamo: per me mea nata propago est;
nolo sepulchra pati: scio me submergere terrae.

## SYM 54

Exiguum munus flexu mucronis adunci;
fallaces escas medio circumfero fluctu;
blandior, ut noceam; morti praemitto saginam.

## SYM 55

Longa sed exilis, tenui producta metallo;
mollia duco levi comitantia vincula ferro;
et faciem laesis et nexum reddo solutis.

## SYM 56

Maior eram longe quondam, dum vita manebat,
at nunc exanimis, lacerata, ligata, revulsa,
dedita sum terrae, tumulo sed condita non sum.

# SYM 53

I don't want to be joined in bed, although I am glad to be
    married;
I don't want a man to wed: my daughter is sprung from me;
I don't want to put up with a grave; I can bury myself in the
    earth.

# SYM 54

I'm a slight offering at the bend of a hooked point;
I carry tricky food in the midst of the stream;
I entice, so that I can give grief; I send food ahead of death.

# SYM 55

I am long and thin, drawn out in slender metal;
I go ahead of soft knots that follow the slender steel;
and I restore form to what's damaged and a fastening to
    what's been split.

# SYM 56

I was much larger once, when I had life,
but I am now expired, and cut, and bound, and torn apart,
and put on the ground, but not hidden in a tomb.

## SYM 57

In caput ingredior, quia de pede pendeo solo;
vertice tango solum, capitis vestigia signo;
sed multi comites casum patiuntur eundem.

## SYM 58

Findere me nulli possunt, praecidere multi;
sed sum versicolor, albus quandoque futurus;
malo manere niger: minus ultima fata verebor.

## SYM 59

Non sum cincta comis et non sum compta capillis;
intus enim crines mihi sunt quos non videt ullus;
meque manus mittunt manibusque remittor in auras.

## SYM 60

Dentibus innumeris sum toto corpore plena;
frondicomam sobolem morsu depascor acuto;
mando tamen frustra, quia respuo praemia dentis.

## SYM 57

I travel on my head, because I hang from a single foot;
my top touches the ground, and I engrave the marks of my
     head;
but many of my colleagues put up with the same position.

## SYM 58

No one can split me, though many cut me;
I have many colors, but one day I'll be white;
I would love to stay black; then I'll be less fearful of my final
     fate.

## SYM 59

I'm undecorated with locks, and I'm unadorned with
     tresses;
all my hair is inside, where no one ever sees it;
hands cast me, and by hands am I cast back into the air.

## SYM 60

My whole body is full of teeth without number;
and with a sharp bite I feast on whatever has leaves for hair;
but I chew in vain because I spit out the booty of my teeth.

## SYM 61

Mucro mihi geminus ferro coniungitur uno;
cum vento luctor, cum gurgite pugno profundo;
scrutor aquas medias, ipsas quoque mordeo terras.

## SYM 62

Stat nemus in lymphis, stat in alto gurgite silva;
et manet in mediis undis inmobile robur;
terra tamen mittit quod terrae munera praestat.

## SYM 63

Ipsa gravis non sum, sed aquae mihi pondus inhaeret;
viscera tota tument patulis diffusa cavernis;
intus lympha latet, sed non se sponte profundit.

## SYM 64

Tres mihi sunt dentes, unus quos continet ordo;
unus praeterea dens est et solus in imo;
meque tenet numen, ventus timet, aequora curant.

# SYM 61

My double point is joined by a single piece of iron;
I wrestle with the wind, I fight with the deep flood;
I search out the midst of the waters, and I also bite into the
  earth itself.

# SYM 62

A grove stands in the water, a forest stands in the deep
  stream,
and there remains in the midst of the flood an immovable
  oak;
but solid ground provides that which offers the benefits of
  solid ground.

# SYM 63

I am not heavy myself, but the weight of water adds to me;
all my innards swell, spread in gaping hollows;
liquid lurks inside, but does not pour out on its own.

# SYM 64

I have three teeth, contained in a single row;
in addition one tooth sticks out alone below;
a god holds me, the wind fears me, and the oceans pay heed.

# SYM 65

Saepta gravi ferro, levibus circumdata pinnis,
aera per medium volucri contendo meatu;
missaque discedens nullo mittente revertor.

# SYM 66

De pecudis dorso pecudes ego terreo cunctas,
obsequium reddens memorata lege doloris;
nec volo contemni, sed contra nolo nocere.

# SYM 67

Cornibus apta cavis, tereti perlucida gyro;
lumen habens intus divini sideris instar,
noctibus in mediis faciem non perdo dierum.

# SYM 68

Perspicior penitus nec luminis arceo visus,
transmittens oculos intra mea membra meantes;
nec me transit hiems, sed sol tamen emicat in me.

# SYM 65

Tipped with heavy iron, with a band of light feathers,
I make my way through midair in swift flight;
and, sent journeying, I return without anyone sending me
    back.

# SYM 66

I come from the back of cattle, and scare all cattle,
producing obedience through the well-known law of pain;
I don't want to be hated, but then again I don't want to
    harm.

# SYM 67

I am fitted with hollow horn, translucent in a smooth circle;
I have a light inside like a heavenly star,
and in the middle of the night I don't lose the appearance of
    day.

# SYM 68

I am looked deep into, and I do not completely impede the
    path of light,
allowing wandering eyes to peer into my inner parts;
and the cold does not pass through me, but the sun shines
    in me.

## SYM 69

Nulla mihi certa est, nulla est peregrina figura;
fulgor inest intus radianti luce coruscus,
qui nihil ostendit, nisi si quid viderit ante.

## SYM 70

Lex bona dicendi, lex sum quoque dura tacendi;
ius avidae linguae, finis sine fine loquendi,
ipsa fluens, dum verba fluunt, ut lingua quiescat.

## SYM 71

Mersa procul terris in cespite lympha profundo,
non nisi perfossis possum procedere rivis,
et trahor ad superos alieno ducta labore.

## SYM 72

Truncum terra tegit, latitant in cespite lymphae;
alveus est modicus, qui ripas non habet ullas;
in ligno vehitur medio, quod ligna vehebat.

# SYM 69

I have no fixed form, although none is a stranger to me;
there is a brightness inside, shining with brilliant light,
which reveals nothing, unless it has seen something first.


# SYM 70

A good guide for speaking, I am also a strict guide for being
    silent;
a judgment on an insatiable tongue, an end to endless
    talking:
I flow while words flow, until the tongue should be still.


# SYM 71

Liquid, submerged far off in the ground in the deep soil,
I cannot flow except where channels have been dug,
and I am dragged upward when drawn by the effort of
    another.


# SYM 72

The earth covers a tree-trunk, liquids lurk in the soil;
the channel is small and has no banks;
in the middle of the wood is borne what used to bear wood.

## SYM 73

Non ego continuo morior, dum spiritus exit,
nam redit adsidue, quamvis et saepe recedit;
et mihi nunc magna est animae nunc nulla facultas.

## SYM 74

Deucalion ego sum, crudeli sospes ab unda;
affinis terrae sed longe durior illa;
littera decedat: volucris quoque nomen habebo.

## SYM 75

Evasi flammas, ignis tormenta profugi;
ipsa medella meo pugnat contraria fato;
ardeo de lymphis, gelidis incendor ab undis.

## SYM 76

Semper inest intus, sed raro cernitur, ignis;
intus enim latitat, sed solos prodit ad ictus;
nec lignis ut vivat eget, nec ut occidat undis.

## SYM 73

I do not die immediately when my breath departs,
for it returns promptly, although it often goes away;
at one point there is a lot of breath, and at another none at
  all.

## SYM 74

I am a Deucalion, saved from a cruel wave;
akin to the earth, but far harder than that;
let one letter drop: I shall also have the name of a flying
  creature.

## SYM 75

I have escaped the flames, I have fled the torments of fire;
the antidote for that fights against my fate;
I am enflamed by liquids; I am ignited by cold waters.

## SYM 76

Fire is always inside me, but it is rarely seen;
for it lurks inside, but is brought out only in response to
  blows;
nor does it need wood to live, nor water to die.

## SYM 76a

Virtus magna mihi duro mollitur ab igne;
cessantique foco intus mihi virtus adhaeret;
semper inest in me, sed raro cernitur ignis.

## SYM 77

Quattuor aequales currunt ex arte sorores;
sic quasi certantes, cum sit labor omnibus unus;
et prope sunt pariter, nec se contingere possunt.

## SYM 78

Nos sumus ad caelum quae scandimus alta petentes;
concordi fabrica quas unus continet ordo,
ut simul haerentes per nos comitentur ad auras.

## SYM 79

Mundi magna parens, laqueo conexa tenaci;
iuncta solo plano, manibus conpressa duabus
ducor ubique sequens et me quoque cuncta sequuntur.

# SYM 76a

I have great power; it is softened by hard fire;
but when the flames die down, my power remains inside;
fire is always inside me, but it is rarely seen.

# SYM 77

Four equal sisters run craftily together
as if they were competing, although there is one task for all;
and they are equally close, but they cannot touch one
     another.

# SYM 78

We are the ones who climb to the sky, seeking the heights;
one sequence holds us together with well-crafted
     workmanship,
so that those who hang on are joined to the breezes through
     us.

# SYM 79

I am the great mother of cleanliness, bound by a tight
     noose;
grasped by two hands, and planted on the flat ground
I am led everywhere, following along, and everything comes
     along with me.

## SYM 80

Aere rigens curvo patulum componor in orbem;
mobilis est intus linguae crepitantis imago;
non resono positus, motus quoque saepe resulto.

## SYM 81

Mater erat Tellus, genitor est ipse Prometheus;
auriculaeque rigent, redimitae ventre cavato;
dum cecidi subito, mater mea me laniavit.

## SYM 82

Tres olim fuimus qui nomine iungimur uno;
ex tribus est unus, et tres miscentur in uno;
quisque bonus per se; melior qui continet omnes.

## SYM 83

Sublatum nihil est, nihil est extrinsecus auctum:
quod fuerat non est; coepit quod non erat esse;
nec tamen inveni quidquid prius ipse reliqui.

486

# SYM 80

Stiff with curved bronze, I am formed as an open circle;
inside there is the moving image of a rattling tongue;
I make no sound when set down, but when moved I often
   resound.

# SYM 81

My mother was Earth, my father is Prometheus himself;
and my little ears stick up, encircling a hollow belly;
when I fell, my own mother suddenly tore me to pieces.

# SYM 82

We were once three, joined by a single name;
out of the three there is one, and the three are mixed in the
   one;
each one is good in itself: better the one that contains us all.

# SYM 83

Nothing has been taken away, nothing added from outside;
what was is not; it begins to be what it was not;
and yet I have not found whatever I once left behind.

## SYM 84

Nomen ovis Graece, contentio magna dearum;
fraus iuvenis pulchri, multarum cura sororum;
hoc volo ne breviter mihi syllaba prima legatur.

## SYM 85

Nobile duco genus magni de gente Catonis;
una mihi soror est, plures licet esse putentur;
de fumo facies, sapientia de mare nata est.

## SYM 86

Non ego de toto mihi corpore vindico vires,
sed capitis pugna nulli certare recuso;
grande mihi caput est, totum quoque pondus in illo.

## SYM 87

Contero cuncta simul virtutis robore magno;
una mihi cervix, capitum sed forma duorum;
pro pedibus caput est, nam cetera corporis absunt.

# SYM 84

The name of a sheep in Greek; great conflict among
　　goddesses;
the cunning of a beautiful boy; the care of many sisters;
I do not want my first syllable to be read short.

# SYM 85

I have a noble lineage from the line of mighty Cato;
I have a single sister, although there are thought to be more;
my appearance comes from smoke, but my taste is born of
　　brine.

# SYM 86

I don't claim that I have strength in my whole body,
but as for battling with my head, I'll refuse no one that
　　fight;
my head is large, and also all my weight is there.

# SYM 87

I grind all things together with mighty force of strength;
I have one neck, but a double-headed form;
in the place of feet I have a head: the other body parts aren't
　　there.

## SYM 88

Rubida, curva, capax, alienis humida guttis,
luminibus falsis auri mentita colorem,
dedita sudori, modico subcumbo labori.

## SYM 89

Per totas aedes innoxius introit ignis;
est calor in medio magnus quem nemo veretur;
non est nuda domus, sed nudus convenit hospes.

## SYM 90

Dedita sum semper voto, non certa futuri;
iactor in ancipites varia vertigine casus;
non ego maesta malis, non rebus laeta secundis.

## SYM 91

Terra fui primo, latebris abscondita terrae;
nunc aliud pretium flammae nomenque dederunt;
nec iam terra vocor, licet ex me terra paretur.

## SYM 88

Reddish, curved, capacious, moist with drops from
     elsewhere,
with a false glitter, feigning the color of gold,
dedicated to sweat, I bow to modest toil.

## SYM 89

Throughout the whole building a harmless fire winds;
there is a great heat in the middle that no one fears;
the house is not naked, but it suits a naked guest.

## SYM 90

I am always given to a wish, uncertain of the future;
I am thrown with a different roll in dubious chances;
I am not sad at misfortune, nor happy at success.

## SYM 91

I was earth at first, hidden in earth's recesses;
now flames have given me another name and value;
I am no longer called earth, although earth may be bought
     with me.

## SYM 92

Plus ego sustinui quam corpus debuit unum;
tres animas habui, quas omnes intus habebam:
discessere duae, sed tertia paene secuta est.

## SYM 93

Bellipotens olim, semper metuendus in armis,
quinque pedes habui, quod numquam nemo negavit;
nunc mihi vix duo sunt; inopem me copia fecit.

## SYM 94

Cernere iam fas est quod vix tibi credere fas est:
unus inest oculus, capitum sed milia multa.
Qui quod habet vendit, quod non habet unde parabit?

## SYM 95

Inter lucifluum caelum terrasque iacentes,
aera per medium docta meat arte viator;
semita sed brevis est, pedibus nec sufficit ipsis.

# SYM 92

I have borne more than one body should;
I had three souls, and I used to have them all inside:
two departed, but the third almost expired.

# SYM 93

Once a mighty fighter, to be feared in savage arms,
I had five feet, and no one ever denied it;
now I have scarcely two: excess has left me lacking.

# SYM 94

Now you can see what you may scarcely believe:
there is one eye there, but many thousands of heads.
From where shall he, who sells what he has, get what he has
    not?

# SYM 95

Between the light-dripping sky and the earth that lies
    beneath,
a walker wanders in midair, after learning a skill;
but the path is narrow, and does not fit the feet.

## SYM 96

Nunc mihi iam credas fieri quod posse negatur:
octo tenes manibus, sed me monstrante magistro,
sublatis septem reliqui tibi sex remanebunt.

## SYM 97

Insidias nullas vereor de fraude latenti;
nam deus attribuit nobis haec munera formae,
quod me nemo movet, nisi qui prius ipse movetur.

## SYM 98

Virgo modesta nimis legem bene servo pudoris;
ore procax non sum, nec sum temeraria linguae;
ultro nolo loqui, sed do responsa loquenti.

## SYM 99

Sponte mea veniens, varias ostendo figuras;
fingo metus vanos nullo discrimine veri;
sed me nemo videt, nisi qui sua lumina claudit.

## SYM 96

Now you should believe me that a thing that can be denied
    in fact happens:
you hold eight in your hands, but after my instruction,
when seven are taken away, you will still have six.

## SYM 97

I fear no tricks from hidden cunning;
for God has given us this gift of form,
that no one moves me, unless he is moved himself first.

## SYM 98

As a modest maiden, I keep the rule of chastity well;
I am not shameful in speech, nor rash in talk;
I won't speak unprompted, but I reply when someone
    speaks.

## SYM 99

Coming of my own accord, I display different forms;
I feign empty fears with no distinction of truth;
but no one sees me, unless he closes his eyes.

## SYM 100

Nomen habens hominis post ultima fata relinquor;
nomen inane manet, sed dulcis vita profugit;
vita tamen superest morti post tempora vitae.

\* \* \*

## ps-SYM 1

Mater me genuit, eadem mox gignitur ex me.

## ps-SYM 2

Insidiis tacite dispono scandala mortis;
si faciem meam specient fugient cito mures;
paucos saltem nostros maxime et male timent.

## ps-SYM 3

Frigore digredior, redeunte calore revertor;
disero quod peperi; hoc tamen educat altera mater;
quid tibi vis aliud dicam? Me vox mea prodit.

## SYM 100

Having someone's name, I am left behind after death;
the empty name remains, but sweet life has fled;
but life survives death after a lifetime.

\* \* \*

## ps-SYM 1

A mother bore me, and the same is soon born from me.

## ps-SYM 2

I silently set traps with deadly obstacles;
if mice see my face they swiftly flee;
though we are few, they fear us, very much and very badly.

## ps-SYM 3

I depart in the cold, and return when heat comes back;
I abandon what I have borne, but another mother educates
    them;
what else do you want me to tell you? My own voice betrays
    me.

# ps-SYM 4

Candida supernis dilabor nubibus altis;
paulatim adcrescens acervos congero magnos;
tacens terris cado ullo nec murmure reddo.

# ps-SYM 4

White, I drop from the high clouds above;
growing, little by little I pile up great heaps;
I fall silent to the ground, and leave it without a sound.

# The Bern Riddles

## BER 1

Ego nata duos patres habere dinoscor:
prior semper manet; alter, qui vita finitur.
Tertia me mater duram mollescere cogit,
et tenera giro formam adsumo decoram.
5 Nullum dare victum frigenti corpore possum,
calida sed cunctis salubres porrego pastos.

## BER 2

Me mater novellam vetus de germine finxit,
et in nullo patris formata sumo figuram.
Oculi non mihi lumen ostendere possunt,
patulo sed flammas ore produco coruscas.
5 Nolo me contingat imber nec flamina venti;
sum amica lucis, domi delector in umbra.

# The Bern Riddles

## BER 1

I am a daughter distinguished by having two fathers:
the first always remains; the second is consumed by his life.
A third, my mother, compels me, the hard one, to be soft,
and, while tender, I am given a fine form on a wheel.
I can give no food from my chilly body,                              5
but when heated I offer healthy sustenance to all.

## BER 2

An aged mother produced me very fresh from a seed,
and when created I take on none of my father's form.
Eyes are unable to show me any light,
but from my gaping mouth I produce flashing flames.
I do not want a shower to touch me, nor gusts of wind;              5
I am a friend of light, enjoyed in the shadows at home.

## BER 3

Me pater ignitus ut nascar, creat urendo,
et pia defectu me mater donat ubique.
Is, qui dura solvit, hic me constringere cogit;
nullus me solutam, ligatam cuncti requirunt.
5  Opem fero vivis, opemque reddo defunctis,
patria me sine mundi nec ulla valebit.

## BER 4

Mollibus horresco semper consistere locis,
ungula nam mihi firma, si caute ponatur.
Nullum, iter agens, sessorem dorso requiro,
plures fero libens, meo dum stabulo versor.
5  Nulla frena mihi mansueto iuveni pendas:
calcibus et senem nolo me verberes ullis.

## BER 5

Pulchra mater ego natos dum collego multos,
cunctis trado quicquid libens in pectore gesto.
Oscula nam mihi prius qui cara dederunt,

# BER 3

An inflamed father causes me to be born from his burning,
and a kindly mother by disappearing makes me a gift
    everywhere.
He who dissolves hard things forces me to hold together;
no one needs me when I'm loose, but when I'm bound all
    do.
I am useful to the living, and render usefulness to the       5
    deceased,
nor will any land in the world prosper that is without me.

# BER 4

I always shudder standing in soft places,
but I have a steady hoof, if it's carefully placed.
When traveling, I need no one sitting on my back,
but happily carry many when I'm made stable.
Place no reins upon me, who am tamed when I am young:   5
I don't like it when you strike me with heels, when I am old.

# BER 5

When I, a beautiful mother, gather together my many
    children,
I happily grant to all whatever I bear in my breast.
But those who previously gave me their dear kisses

vestibus exutam turpi me modo relinquunt.
5 Nulli sicut mihi pro bonis mala redduntur:
quos lactavi, nudam me pede per angula versant.


# BER 6

Nullius ut meam lux solam penetrat umbram,
et natura vili miros postpono lapillos.
Ignem fero nascens, natus ab igne fatigor:
nulla me putrido tangit nec funera turbant;
5 pristina defunctus sospes in forma resurgo,
et amica libens oscula porrego cunctis.


# BER 7

Teneo liquentem, sequor membrana celatum;
verbero nam cursu, visu quem cernere vetor.
Impletur invisis domus, sed vacua rebus
permanet, dum civem nullo sub pondere gestat,
5 quae dum clausa fertur, velox ad nubila surgit;
patefacta nullum potest tenere manentem.

strip me of clothing and abandon me in a disgraceful
    fashion.
No one receives wickedness in return for good, as I do:      5
those whom I have nourished shove me naked into the
    corner with their foot.

## BER 6

Light passes through my likeness alone, like that of no one
    else,
and, though cheap by nature, I surpass small precious
    stones.
I bear fire being born, but once born am weakened by fire:
no rot affects me, nor does death distress me;
when my guest is gone, I appear again in the same form as     5
    before,
and I willingly offer friendly kisses to everyone.

## BER 7

I hold what is fluid; I follow, covered in a skin;
as I travel, I strike the one I am forbidden to see by sight.
My house is filled with what's unseen, but it remains
empty of anything, while it carries an inhabitant without
    weight,
and when it moves closed up, it swiftly rises to the clouds;     5
when opened, it can have no permanence.

## BER 8

Nati mater ego, natus ab utero mecum;
prior illo non sum, semper qui mihi coaevus.
Virgo nisi manens numquam concipere possum,
sed intacta meam infra concipio prolem.
5  Post si mihi venter disruptus ictu patescit,
moriens viventem sic possum fundere foetum.

## BER 9

Senior ab aevo; Eva sum senior ego;
et senectam gravem nemo currendo revincit.
Vitam dabo cunctis, vitam si tulero multis;
milia prosterno, manu dum verbero nullum.
5  Satura nam victum, ignem ieiuna produco,
et uno vagantes possum conprendere loco.

## BER 10

Singula si vivens firmis constitero plantis,
viam me roganti directam ire negabo;
gemina sed soror meo si lateri iungat,
coeptum valet iter velox percurrere quisquis.
5  Unde pedem mihi nisi calcaverit ille,
manibus quae cupit numquam contingere valet.

# BER 8

I am the mother of a son, a son with me from my womb;
I am no older than him, but he is always the same age as me.
Unless I remain a virgin I can never conceive,
but, while intact, I conceive my child inside.
If afterward my belly, broken by a blow, lies open,                    5
while dying I can nonetheless produce living offspring.

# BER 9

I am older, from the beginning of the world; I am older than
    Eve;
and no one surpasses in running my heavy old age.
I shall give life to all, once I have borne off life from many;
I lay low thousands, but strike none by hand.
When full, I bring forth food, but fire when I am hungry,            5
and I can keep those wandering ones together in one place.

# BER 10

If, while living alone, I stand on a firm footing,
I shall refuse the one asking me to go on a straight path,
but if a twin sister joins my side,
anyone can complete a swift journey once begun.
Unless that one will have taken a step on me,                         5
he can never reach what he wants with his hands.

## BER 11

Mortua maiorem vivens quam porto laborem;
dum iaceo, multos servo; si stetero, paucos.
Viscera si mihi foris detracta patescant,
vitam fero cunctis victumque confero multis.
5  Bestia defunctam avisque nulla me mordit;
et onusta currens viam nec planta depingo.

## BER 12

Mortem ego pater libens adsumo pro natis,
et tormenta simul, cara ne pignora tristent.
Mortuum me cuncti gaudent habere parentes,
et sepultum nullus parvo vel funere plangit.
5  Vili subterrena pusillus tumulor urna,
sed maiori possem post mortem surgere forma.

## BER 13

Uno fixa loco longinquis porrego victum;
caput mihi ferrum secat et brachia truncat.
Lacrimis infecta plura per vincula nector,
simili damnandos nece dum genero natos.

# BER 11

When dead I can bear a greater load than while alive;
lying flat I carry many, but few if I stand straight.
If what's inside me should be dragged out and revealed in
  full,
I bring life to all and convey food to many.
When I am deceased no beast or bird bites me;                    5
and when hastening under a heavy load I leave no footprint
  on the path.

# BER 12

As a father I willingly undergo death for my children,
tortures too, so that my dear offspring do not suffer.
All parents are happy to have me dead,
and no one weeps when I am buried or at my humble
  funeral.
I am tiny when entombed in a meager vessel underground,      5
but after death I can rise in a greater form.

# BER 13

Though fixed in one place I offer sustenance to those far
  away;
iron cuts my head and lops my limbs.
Drenched in tears I am tied up by many bonds,
while I produce offspring condemned to a similar death.

5  Sed defuncti solent ulcisci liberi matrem,
    sanguine dum fuso lapsis vestigia versant.


## BER 14

Nullam ante tempus inlustrem genero prolem,
annisque peractis superbos genero natos.
Quos domare quisquis valet industria parvos,
cum eos marinus iunctos percusserit imber.
5  Asperi nam lenes sic creant fili nepotes,
tenebris ut lucem reddant, dolori salutem.


## BER 15

Pulchra semper comis locis consisto desertis,
ceteris dum mihi cum lignis nulla figura.
Dulcia petenti de corde poma produco,
nullumque de ramis cultori confero fructum.
5  Nemo, qui me serit, meis de fructibus edit,
et amata cunctis flore sum socia iustis.


## BER 16

Me mater ut vivam spinis enutrit iniquis;
faciat ut dulcem, inter acumina servat.

But the deceased children often avenge their mother,                5
when with their spilled blood they confound the footsteps
    of those who slip up.

## BER 14

I produce no splendid offspring before the right time,
but when the years have passed I produce proud children,
little things which everyone can press with effort,
after a briny liquid has pierced them, packed together.
So the bitter children generate gentle grandchildren,                5
in such a way that they bring light to darkness, and a balm
    to pain.

## BER 15

Ever fair in foliage, I stand in desert places,
although I don't have a shape like other trees.
I produce sweet fruits from my heart for whoever seeks
    them,
but bring the cultivator no produce from my branches at all.
No one who plants me eats of my fruits,                               5
and in flower I am a dear companion to all just folk.

## BER 16

My mother raises me to live among cruel thorns;
to make me sweet, she guards me between sharp points.

Tereti nam forma ceram confingo rubentem,
et incisa nullam dono de corpore guttam.
5  Mellea cum mihi sit sine sanguine caro,
acetum eructant exta conclusa saporem.


## BER 17

Patulo sum semper ore nec labia iungo;
incitor ad cursum frequenti verbere tactus.
Exta mihi nulla; manu si forte ponantur,
quassa mitto currens, minuto vulnere ruptus:
5  meliora cunctis, mihi nam vilia servans;
vacuumque bonis inanem cuncti relinquunt.


## BER 18

Florigeras gero comas, dum maneo silvis,
et honesto vivo modo, dum habito campis.
Turpius me nulla domi vernacula servit;
et redacta vili solo depono capillos;
5  cuncti per horrendam me terrae pulverem iactant,
sed amoena domus sine me nulla videtur.

I create reddening wax in a smooth form,
and I grant no drop when my body is pierced.
Although my flesh is honeyed and bloodless,                    5
my bound-up innards belch forth a bitter flavor.


## BER 17

I always have a gaping mouth, and cannot close my lips;
knocked by frequent taps I am stirred to motion.
I have no innards; if such are by chance put there by hand,
by moving I emit them shaken, since I am punctured by
    tiny wounds:
granting the best bits to all, keeping the worst for myself;    5
all leave me vacant and empty of good.


## BER 18

I have luxuriant foliage, while I stand in the forest,
and live in a decent fashion, when I remain in the fields.
In the house, no serving girl does more degrading work
    than me;
when dragged down I put my tresses to the lowly ground;
everyone shoves me into the middle of the dreadful dust of     5
    the earth,
but without me no household seems clean.

## BER 19

Dissimilem sibi me mater concipit infra,
et nullo virili creta de semine fundor;
dum nascor sponte, gladio divellor a ventre;
caesa vivit mater, ego nam flammis aduror.
5  Nullum clara manens possum concedere quaestum;
plurem fero lucrum, nigro si corpore mutor.

## BER 20

Lucida de domo lapsus diffundor ubique,
et quali dimissus modo, non invenit ullus.
Bisque natus inde semel in utero cretus,
qualis in conceptu, talis in partu renascor.
5  Milia me quaerunt, ales sed invenit una,
aureamque mihi domum depingit ab ore.

## BER 21

Masculus qui non sum sed neque femina, coniunx;
filios ignoto patri parturio multos;
uberibus prolem nullis enutrio tantum,
quos ab ore cretos nulla de venere sumpsi;
5  nomen quibus unum natisque compar imago,
meos inter cibos dulci conplector amore.

## BER 19

My mother conceives me inside, unlike herself,
and I am produced and raised without any male seed;
while I am born of my own accord, I am torn from the
      womb by a sword;
my mother, cut, lives, but I am burned by flames.
While I remain clear I can offer no benefit:        5
I bring more advantage, if my body turns black.

## BER 20

Dropping from a translucent home I am spread out
      everywhere,
and no one discovers how I am sent forth.
Born twice, then once grown in a womb,
I am reborn in the same condition as I was when conceived.
Thousands seek me, but only one winged creature finds me,   5
and from its mouth adorns a golden home for me.

## BER 21

I am a spouse who is neither male nor female;
I bring forth many sons for a father unknown;
without breasts I nourish so great a brood,
the ones I acquired sprung from my mouth, without sex;
for my offspring there is one name and one similar      5
      appearance,
I enfold my own among nourishments with sweet love.

## BER 22

Exigua mihi virtus, sed magna facultas;
opes ego nulli quaero, sed confero cunctis.
Modicos oberrans cibos egena requiro,
et ieiuna saepe cogor exsolvere censum.
5  Nullus sine meo mortalis corpore constat,
pauperaque multum ipsos nam munero reges.


## BER 23

Durus mihi pater, dura me generat mater,
verbere nam multo huius de viscere fundor.
Modica prolatus feror a ventre figura,
sed adulto mihi datur inmensa potestas.
5  Durum ego patrem duramque mollio matrem,
et quae vitam cunctis, haec mihi funera praestat.


## BER 24

Lucrum viva manens toto nam confero mundo,
et defuncta mirum praesto de corpore quaestum.
Vestibus exuta multoque vinculo tensa,
gladio sic mihi desecta viscera pendent.
5  Manibus me postquam reges et visu mirantur,
miliaque porto nullo sub pondere multa.

# BER 22

I have little power, but I have great potential;
I look for benefit from no one, but offer it to all.
A poor wanderer, I require little nourishment,
and, hungry, I am often compelled to pay my dues.
No mortal survives without my body,                            5
and, though poor, I enrich kings themselves a lot.

# BER 23

My father is hard, and a hard mother makes me,
from whose innards I emerge after many a blow.
I am brought out first from the belly in tiny form,
but enormous power is given to me full-grown.
I soften my hard father and my hard mother,                    5
and what gives life to all brings an end to me.

# BER 24

While remaining alive, I bring benefit to the whole world,
but when deceased, I offer wondrous gain with my corpse.
When stripped of coverings and stretched by many a chain,
my innards, cut by a blade, dangle down.
Afterwards kings hold me and look at me with amazement,        5
and I support many thousands that weigh nothing at all.

## BER 25

Nascimur albenti loco sed nigrae sorores;
tres unito simul nos creant ictu parentes.
Multimoda nobis facies et nomina multa,
meritumque dispar vox et diversa sonandi.
5  Numquam sine nostra nos domo detenet ullus
nec una responsum dat sine pari roganti.

## BER 26

Me si visu quaeras, multo sum parvulo parvus,
sed nemo maiorum mentis astutia vincit.
Cum feror sublimi parentis humero vectus,
simplicem ignari me putant esse natura.
5  Verbere correptus saepe si giro fatigor,
protinus occultum produco corde saporem.

## BER 27

Amnibus delector molli sub caespite cretus,
et producta levi natus columna viresco.
Vestibus sub meis non queo cernere solem,
aliena tectus possum producere lumen.
5  Filius profundi dum fio lucis amicus,
sic quae vitam dedit mater, et lumina tollit.

# BER 25

We are born in a white place, but we are black sisters;
three parents together produce us at a single stroke.
We have many forms and many different names,
and unequal worth, and different-sounding voices.
No one ever holds onto us away from our house,                      5
nor does one of us answer an inquirer without another's
    help.

# BER 26

If you seek to see me, I am small, extremely so,
but nothing bigger surpasses me in sharpness of purpose.
When I am carried, borne on my parent's high shoulder,
the ignorant think that I am by nature simple.
But if I am often struck by a blow and ground down in a            5
    circling motion,
I immediately produce from my core a hidden flavor.

# BER 27

I delight in streams as I grow beneath the soft sod,
and, once born, I burgeon into a thin drawn-out stalk.
Beneath my own coverings I cannot see the sun,
but, when covered in that of another, I can produce
    illumination.
When I, a son of the deep, am made a friend of light,             5
so my mother, who gave me life, also takes away my
    illumination.

## BER 28

Arbor una, mihi vilem quae conferet escam,
qua repletus parva vellera magna produco.
Exiguos conlapsus foetos pro munere fundo,
et ales effectus mortem adsumo libenter.
5  Nobili perfectus forma me caesares ulnis
efferunt, et reges infra supraque mirantur.

## BER 29

Uterum si mihi praelucens texerit umbra,
proprios volenti devota porrego vultus.
Talis ego mater vivos non genero natos,
sed petenti vanas diffundo visu figuras.
5  Exiguos licet mentita profero foetos,
sed de vero suas videnti dirigo formas.

## BER 30

Nullo firmo loco manens consistere possum,
et vagando vivens nolo conspicere quemquam:
vita mihi mors est, mortem pro vita requiro,
et volventi domo semper amica delector.
5  Numquam ego lecto volo iacere tepenti,
sed vitale mihi torum sub frigora condo.

# BER 28

There is only one tree that provides my humble food;
when I am filled with this small morsel I produce great
   fleeces.
Collapsing, I send out slender offspring as a gift,
and, turned into a flying thing, I willingly accept death.
Caesars carry me on their shoulders when I am perfected in   5
   fine form,
and kings are amazed at me above and below.

# BER 29

If a shining shadow is spread across my womb,
I provide unerringly their own faces to those who wish it.
As such a mother I do not give birth to living children,
but I send forth empty images to whoever seeks to see.
Even if I am lying, I offer insubstantial offspring,   5
but in truth I send back their figures to the onlooker.

# BER 30

I am unable to stand still in any fixed spot,
and while I live wandering I don't want to see anyone:
life is death to me, and in place of life I ask for death,
and delight in a swirling home that is my friend.
I never want to lie on a warm couch,   5
but set up my vital bed where it is cold.

## BER 31

Ore mihi nulla petenti pocula dantur,
ebrius nec ullum reddo perinde fluorem.
Versa mihi datur vice bibendi facultas,
et vacuo ventri potus ab ima defertur.
5  Pollice depresso conceptas denego limphas,
et sublato rursum diffusos confero nimbos.

## BER 32

Dissimilem sibi dat mihi mater figuram:
caro nulla mihi, sed viscera cava latebris.
Sumere nihil possum, si non obsorbuero matrem,
et quae me concepit, hanc ego genero postquam.
5  Manu capta levis, gravis sum manu dimissa,
et quem sumpsi libens, mox cogor reddere sumptum.

## BER 33

Parvula dum nascor, minor effecta senesco,
et cunctas praecedo maiori veste sorores.

## BER 31

No drinks are given to me, when I seek them with my
    mouth,
nor, having drunk, do I then return any draft.
The ability to drink is granted to me when the tables are
    turned,
and a drink is brought from the depths to the empty belly.
When a thumb is pressed down I hold back the liquids     5
    inside,
and when it's raised again, I send out pouring rain.


## BER 32

My mother gave me a form very different from hers:
I have no flesh, just innards empty with dark places.
I can't take anything in, unless I have sucked up my mother,
and afterward I produce her who first gave birth to me.
Light when picked up by the hand, I am heavy when put     5
    down by the hand,
and the expense I took up willingly, I am soon compelled to
    repay.


## BER 33

While I am born very small, growing old, I become even
    smaller,
and I surpass all my sisters even with their bigger covering.

Extremos ad brumae me primo confero menses,
et amoena cunctis verni iam tempora monstro.
5 Me reddet inlustrem spiritus de corpore parvo,
et viam quaerendi docet, qui nulli videtur.


# BER 34

Pulchra in angusto me mater concipit alvo,
et hirsuta barbis quinque conplectitur ulnis;
quae licet parentum parvo sim genere sumpta,
honor quoque mihi concessus fertur ubique.
5 Utero cum nascor, matri rependo decorem,
et paturienti nullum infligo dolorem.


# BER 35

Nos pater occultus commendat patulae matri,
et mater onusta confixos porregit hasta.
Vivere nec umquam valemus tempore longo,
et leviter tactos incurvat aegra senectus.
5 Oscula si nobis causa figantur amoris,
reddimus candentes signa flaventia labris.

I first appear in the final months of winter,
and I show everyone the lovely time of spring.
The scent in my small body will make me glorious,          5
and, though no one sees it, it shows the way to whoever
          seeks me.


## BER 34

My beautiful mother conceives me in a narrow womb,
and, bristling with hairs, holds me in five arms,
and although I am brought forth from the small nature of
          my parents,
the honor accorded me is also mentioned everywhere.
When I am born from the womb, I pay back my mother          5
          with beauty,
and cause no pain to her who gives birth to me.


## BER 35

An unseen father entrusts us to an expansive mother,
and our mother, burdened, offers us up fixed on a spear.
Nor can we ever live for a long time,
and, softly touched, sickly old age bows us down.
If kisses are fixed on us for love's sake,          5
though white, we leave the lips with yellow marks.

# BER 36

Parvulus aestivas latens abscondor in umbras,
et sepulto mihi membra sub tellure vivunt.
Frigidas autumni libens adsuesco pruinas,
et bruma propinqua miros sic profero flores.
5  Pulchra mihi domus manet, sed pulchrior infra,
modica in forma clausus aromata vinco.

# BER 37

Pereger externas vinctus perambulo terras,
frigidus et tactu praesto sumenti calorem.
Nulla mihi virtus, sospes si mansero semper;
vigeo nam caesus, confractus valeo multum.
5  Mordeo mordentem morsu, nec vulnero dente;
lapis mihi finis, simul defectio lignum.

# BER 38

Corpore formata pleno de parvulo patre,
nec a matre feror, nisi feratur et ipsa.
Nasci vetor ego, si non genuero patrem,
et creata rursus ego concipio matrem.
5  Hieme conceptos pendens meos servo parentes,
et aestivo rursus ignibus trado coquendos.

## BER 36

When very small I hide concealed in summer shadows,
and my limbs live buried under the earth.
I willingly grow accustomed to the cold frosts of autumn,
and so when winter is close I put forth wonderful flowers.
I have a beautiful house, but am more beautiful below,     5
enclosed in a tiny form, I surpass all scents.

## BER 37

As a bound foreigner I wander through alien lands,
and, while cold to the touch, I give heat to the one
        consuming me.
There is no power in me, if I remain always whole;
for when struck I gain force, when crushed I become very
        strong.
I bite the biter with a bite, but I don't wound with teeth;     5
a stone causes my end; wood too grinds me down.

## BER 38

I am formed with a full body from my tiny father,
nor am I carried by my mother, unless she is carried too.
I am forbidden to be born, unless I give birth to my father,
and, once created, I conceive my mother again.
Hanging down, I keep my parents, who were conceived in     5
        winter,
and in summer I produce them again for cooking on flames.

## BER 39

Arbor mihi pater nam et lapidea mater,
corpore nam mollis duros disrumpo parentes.
Aestas me nec ulla, ulla nec frigora vincunt;
bruma color unus vernoque simul et aesto.
5   Propriis erecta vetor consistere plantis,
manibus sed alta peto cacumina tortis.

## BER 40

Vinculis extensa multos comprendo vagantes,
et soluta nullum queo comprendere pastum.
Venter mihi nullus, quo possim capta reponi,
sed multa pro membris formantur ora tenendi.
5   Opes mihi non sunt, sursum si pendor ad auras,
nam fortuna mihi manet, si tensa dimittor.

## BER 41

Velox curro nascens grandi virtute sonorus;
deprimo nam fortes, infirmos adlevo sursum.
Os est mihi nullum, dente nec vulnero quemquam,
mordeo sed cunctos silvis campisque morantes.
5   Cernere me quisquam nequit aut nectere vinclis;
Macedo nec Liber vicit nec Hercules umquam.

# BER 39

My father is a tree and my mother is made of stone,
and, while soft in body, I burst through my hard parents.
There is no summer's heat, nor any chill that beats me;
I keep the same color in winter, spring, and summer.
Though standing tall I cannot stand on my own feet,                5
but with twisted hands I seek the lofty heights.

# BER 40

When stretched out, I catch many wanderers in my clasp,
but when relaxed, I can't hold any food.
I have no belly where I can deposit what I catch,
but instead of limbs there are formed many mouths to grab.
There is no benefit to me, if I am hung up in the air,            5
but my luck remains within me, if I am set down taut.

# BER 41

I run swift and loud with great power, when I am born;
I strike down the strong, and lift the weak up on high.
I have no mouth, and do not harm anyone with my teeth,
though I bite everyone loitering in woods and in fields.
No one can see me, nor bind me with chains;                       5
neither Alexander nor Bacchus nor Hercules ever
        conquered me.

## BER 42

Arte me nec ulla valet durescere quisquam;
efficior dura, multosque facio molles.
Cuncti me solutam cara per oscula gaudent,
et nemo constrictam manu vel tangere cupit.
5  Speciem mi pulchram dat turpi rigidus auctor,
qui eius ab ira iubet turpescere pulchros.

## BER 43

Innumeros concepta mitto de nido volatus,
corpus et inmensum parvis adsumo de membris.
Mollibus de plumis vestem contexo nitentem,
et texturae sonum aure nec concipit ullus.
5  Si quis forte meo videatur vellere tectus,
protinus excussam vestem reicere temptat.

## BER 44

Conspicuum corpus arte mirifica sumpsi;
multis cava modis gemmarum ordine nector.

## BER 42

No one has the power by any craft to make me hard;
I am made hard, and make many soft.
Everyone rejoices with sweet kisses when I have been
    dissolved
and when I'm rigid, no one wants even to touch me with
    their hand.
A stiff creator gives a beautiful appearance to me, who am     5
    ugly,
and in his anger he wants the beautiful made ugly.

## BER 43

When I have conceived, I start innumerable flights from
    my nest,
and take on a vast body from little limbs.
From soft down I weave a shining cloak,
and no one hears the sound of weaving in their ears.
If by chance anyone should seem to be covered by my     5
    fleece,
he immediately tries to cast off the discarded cloak.

## BER 44

I have taken on a conspicuous body by marvelous artistry;
being perforated, I am woven in many ways in a string of
    gems.

Publicis concepta locis in abdito nascor;
vacua do lucem referta confero lucrum.
5    Nullum mihi frigus valet nec bruma valescit,
sed calore semper molli sopita fatigor.


## BER 45

Os est mihi patens crebroque tunditur ictu;
reddo libens omnes escas, quas sumpsero lambens.
Nulla mihi fames sitimque sentio nullam,
et ieiuna mihi semper praecordia restant.
5    Omnibus ad escam miros efficio sapores,
gelidumque mihi durat per saecula corpus.


## BER 46

Una mihi toto cervix pro corpore constat,
et duo libenter nascuntur capita collo.
Versa mihi pedum vice dum capita currunt,
lenes reddo vias, calle quas tero frequenti.
5    Nullus mihi comam tondet nec pectine versat:
vertice nitenti plures per oscula gaudent.

Though seen in public places, I am born in secret;
empty, I give light; full, I offer profit.
No cold overcomes me, nor does winter prevail,                    5
but I always grow weak when put to sleep with gentle heat.


## BER 45

My mouth is wide open, and struck by many a blow;
I willingly give back all the food that I have greedily
     consumed.
I have no hunger and feel no sense of thirst,
and my innards remain always empty.
I produce wondrous flavors for everyone's food,                  5
and my cold body endures for a long time.


## BER 46

I have a single neck that stands for my whole body,
and two heads are willingly born from that neck.
When in turn my heads become feet,
I render those paths smooth that I wear down on my
     regular route.
No one shaves my hair or styles it with a comb:                  5
many are made happy by the kisses of my shining head.

## BER 47

Aspera dum nascor cute producor a matre,
et adulta crescens leni circumdor amictu.
Sonitum intacta magnum de ventre produco,
et corrupta tacens vocem non profero ullam.
5   Nullus in amore certo me diligit umquam,
nudam nisi tangat vestemque tulerit omnem.


## BER 48

Quattuor has ego conclusa gero figuras,
pandere quas paucis deposcit ratio verbis:
humida sum sicca, subtili corpore crassa,
dulcis et amara, duro gestamine mollis.
5   Dulcis esse nulli possum nec crescere iuste,
nisi sub amaro duroque carcere nascar.


## BER 49

Mirantibus cunctis nascens infligo querelas;
efficior statim maior a patre qui nascor.
Me gaudere nullus potest, si terrae coaequor,
superas me cuncti laetantur carpere vias.
5   Inprobus amara diffundo pocula totis,
et videre quanti volunt tantique refutant.

## BER 47

When I am born I am produced by my mother with a rough
    outer coat,
but when I become an adult I am surrounded by a soft
    cloak.
When whole I produce a loud sound from my belly,
but when broken I am silent and make no sound.
No one ever adores me with true love,          5
unless he touches me when I am naked and has taken away
    all my clothes.

## BER 48

Closed up, I manifest these four qualities,
which reason seeks to explain in a few words:
I am both wet and dry, fat in a thin body,
sweet and bitter, soft with a hard covering.
I can be sweet to none, nor grow properly,          5
unless I am born in a harsh and bitter prison.

## BER 49

Being born, I cause all who wonder at me to complain;
and when I am born I immediately surpass my sire.
None can rejoice in me, if I become level with the earth,
all are happy when I take the higher path.
Wickedly I pour out bitter drafts for everyone,          5
and as many as want to see me don't.

## BER 50

Innumeris ego nascor de matribus unum
genitumque nullum vivum relinquo parentem.
Multa me nascente subportant vulnera matres,
quarum mihi mors est potestas data per omnes.
5    Laedere non possum, me si quis oderit, umquam,
et iniqua reddo me quoque satis amanti.

## BER 50a

Multimodo matris divellor opere membris,
et truncata multum reddor de minimo maior.
Fateor intacta firmis consistere plantis,
opera nullius virgo momenti relinquo.
5    Solida disiungor, rursum soluta reformor,
quo secura meis creduntur liquida membris.

## BER 51

Multiplici veste natus de matre producor,
Nec habere corpus possum, si vestem amitto.
Meos, unde nascor, in ventre fero parentes;
vivo nam sepultus, vitam et inde resumo.

## BER 50

I am born solitary from innumerable mothers,
and when produced I leave no living parent.
My mothers get many wounds while I am being born,
and through the death of all of them power is given to me.
If anyone hates me, I can never harm them,                    5
and I also render harm enough to the one who loves me.

## BER 50a

I am torn from my mother's limbs by different kinds of
    labor,
and, after being mutilated, I am made much bigger from
    being very small.
When intact I confess that I stand on firm feet;
as a virgin I leave behind works of no importance.
When solid I am broken up, when liquefied I am reformed    5
    again,
wherefore what is fluid is believed safe in my limbs.

## BER 51

I am produced from my mother, born with many layers of
    covering,
and I cannot have a body, if I lose my covering.
I carry my parents, from whom I am born, in my belly;
for I live while buried, and from there I resume my life.

5   Superis eductus nec umquam crescere possum,
dum natura caput facit succedere plantis.


## BER 52

Mollis ego duro de corde genero natos;
in conceptu numquam amplexu viri delector,
sed dum infra meis concrescunt filii latebris,
meum quisque nascens disrumpit vulnere corpus.
5   Postquam decorato velantes tegmine matrem,
saepe delicati frangunt acumine fortes.


## BER 53

Venter mihi nullus, infra praecordia nulla,
tenui nam semper feror in corpore sicca.
Cibum nulli quaero, ciborum milia servans;
loco currens uno lucrum ac confero damnum.
5   Duo mihi membra tantum in corpore pendunt;
similemque gerunt caput et planta figuram.


## BER 54

Duo generantur multo sub numero fratres,
nomine sub uno divisus quisque natura.
Pauper atque dives pari labore premuntur;

Brought out into the world above, I can never grow,          5
since nature places my head below my feet.


## BER 52

Though soft, I produce children from my hard heart;
in conceiving I am never pleasured by a man's embrace,
but while my sons grow within my hidden recesses,
each one bursts my body with a wound as it is born.
Afterwards, covering their mother with a decorative veil,          5
though delicate, they often break the strong with their
     sharpness.


## BER 53

I have no belly, nor any guts within,
for I am carried dry by a slender body;
I ask for food from no one, while observing a thousand
     kinds of food;
by traveling in one place I compare profit and loss.
Only two limbs hang on my body;          5
my head and foot bear the same shape.


## BER 54

Two brothers are produced out of a great number,
each divided by nature, carrying a single name.
The rich and the poor are oppressed by an equal labor;

pauper semper habet, divesque saepe requiret.
5  Caput illis nullum, sed et os cum corpore cingunt,
nam stantes nihil, iacentes sed plurima portant.

## BER 55

Semine nec ullo patris creatus renascor,
ubera nec matris suxi, quo crescere possem.
Uberibus ego meis reficio multos;
vestigia nulla figens perambulo terras.
5  Anima nec caro mihi nec cetera membra,
aligeras tamen reddo temporibus umbras.

## BER 56

Una mihi soror, unus et ego sorori;
coniunx illa mihi, huius et ego maritus.
Numquam uno simul toro coniungimur ambo,
sed a longe meam pregnantem reddo sororem,
5  quotquot illa suos gignit ex utero partus,
cunctos uno reddo tectos de peplo nepotes.

## BER 57

Prohibeor solus noctis videre tenebras,
et absconse ducor longa per avia fugiens.

the poor one always has and the rich one often seeks.
They have no head, but a body surrounds their mouth,     5
for while standing they carry nothing, but lying down a lot.


# BER 55

I am reborn, created without any father's seed,
nor have I suckled on a mother's breasts, so that I could
      grow.
I feed others with breasts of my own;
I plant no footsteps, but travel through the lands.
I have no soul or flesh or any other limbs,     5
but I produce flying shadows, following the seasons.


# BER 56

I have but one sister, and she has only me;
she is my wife, and I am her husband.
We are never both joined in the same bed,
but I make my sister pregnant from afar,
and as many births as she produces from her womb,     5
I cause all those descendants to be covered with one cloak.


# BER 57

Only I am stopped from seeing the darkness of night,
and fleeing through the vast and unfrequented places I am
      rendered hidden.

Nulla mihi velox avis inventa volatu,
cum videar nullas gestare corpore pennas.
5 Vix auferre praedam me coram latro valebit,
publica per diem dum semper compita curro.


# BER 58

Assiduo multas vias itinere currens,
corpore defecta velox conprendo senectam.
Versa vice rerum conpellor ire deorsum,
et ab ima redux trahor conscendere sursum.
5 Sed cum mei parvum cursus complevero tempus
infantia par est simul et curva senectus.


# BER 59

Quo movear gressum nullus cognoscere temptat,
cernere nec vultus per diem signa valebit.
Cotidie currens vias perambulo multas,
et bis iterato cunctas recurro per annum.
5 Imber, nix, pruina, glacies nec fulgora nocent,
timeo nec ventum forti testudine tecta.

No bird is found as fast in flight as me,
although I seem to wear no wings on my body.
A robber will scarcely be able to steal plunder in my            5
     presence,
since I run through public places all the day.

## BER 58

Running along many ways on a busy journey,
I am swift to gain old age, worn out in body.
Yet in turn I am forced to go below,
and then returning from the depths I am dragged back
     above.
But when I have completed the short time of my course,         5
my bent old age is likewise equal to my infancy.

## BER 59

No one tries to understand on what path I am drawn,
nor will any face see signs of me by day.
Running daily, I travel over many tracks,
and I travel them all again in twofold iteration each year.
Neither storm nor snow nor frost nor ice nor lightning          5
     cause me harm,
nor, covered by a thick protection, do I have any fear of the
     wind.

## BER 60

Promiscuo per diem vultu dum reddor amictus,
pulchrum saepe reddo, turpis qui semper habetur.
Innumeras ego res cunctis fero mirandas,
pondere sub magno rerum nec gravor onustus.
5   Nullus mihi dorsum, faciem sed cuncti mirantur,
et meo cum bonis malos recipio tecto.

## BER 61

Humili delector semper consistere loco,
et sine radice inmensos porrego ramos;
mecum iter agens nulla sub arte tenebit,
comitem sed viae ego conprendere possum.
5   Certum me videnti demonstro corpus a longe:
positus et iuxta totam me numquam videbit.

## BER 62

Milia conclusae domo sub una sorores:
minima non crescit, maior nec aevo senescit;
et cum nulla parem conetur adloqui verbis,
suos moderato servant in ordine cursus.
5   Pulchrior turpentem vultu non dispicit ulla;
odiuntque lucem, noctis secreta mirantur.

544

## BER 60

By day, when clothed, I am widely available to see,
and often render beautiful what is always thought vile.
I make available innumerable wonders to all,
nor, though heavily burdened, do I labor under a great
weight.
No one marvels at my back, but all marvel at my face,                    5
and I receive both evil and good beneath my roof.

## BER 61

I am happy always to stand in a low place,
and to proffer vast branches without having any root;
whoever takes a journey with me cannot catch me by any
cunning,
but I can catch my companion on the way.
I show a clear form to the one who sees me from afar:              5
the one close by will never see all of me.

## BER 62

There are a thousand sisters enclosed in a single home:
the least in age does not grow, nor does the elder age;
and though none attempts to engage her equal in words,
they keep their own course in strict succession.
None that is prettier sneers at one ugly in appearance;           5
they loathe the light, but wonder at the hidden aspects of
night.

\* \* \*

## ps-BER 1

Pulchrior me nullus versatur in poculis umquam,
Ast ego primatum in omnibus teneo solus,
Viribus atque meis possum decipere multos;
Leges atque iura per me virtutes amittunt.
5　Vario me si quis haurire voluerit usu,
Stupebit ingenti mea percussus virtute.

\* \* \*

## ps-BER 1

None more beautiful than me ever appears in cups,
but I alone hold primacy in all of them,
and I can deceive many by my powers;
laws and decrees lose their force because of me.
If anyone wants to exhaust me by much use,       5
he will be dumbstruck when struck by my mighty power.

# The Verses of a Certain Irishman
## on the Alphabet

## ALF A

Principium vocis veterumque inventio prima,
nomen habens domini sum felix voce Pelasga;
execrantis item dira interiectio dicor.

## ALF B

Principium libri, mutis caput, alter et ordo;
tertia felicis vere sum syllaba semper;
si me Graece legas, viridi tum nascor in horto.

## ALF C

Principium caeli, primis et luna figuris;
et me clerus amat, legeres si Graece, Latinus;
littera sum terrae pedibus perscripta quaternis.

# The Verses of a Certain Irishman
## on the Alphabet

### ALF A

The beginning of speech and the first invention of the
    ancients,
having the name of the Lord, I am blessed in Greek speech;
again, I am uttered as a dread cry by one cursing.

### ALF B

The beginning of "The Book"; the head of the mutes; the
    second in order;
I am always one of three syllables of the blessed;
if you read me in Greek, then I am born in a green garden.

### ALF C

The beginning of "celestial," and the moon in its first
    phases;
and if you were to read me in Greek, the Latin cleric loves
    me;
I am the letter written on the ground by four feet.

# ALF D

Ablati casus vox sum et pars septima linguae,
omnipotentis habens nomen, "us" bannita iuncta;
sum medium mille, et veterum mala nota deorum.

# ALF E

Pars ego mutarum, vere vocalis habebor;
altera deceptae quondam sum syllaba matris;
pars quoque sum plena, et vocis pars quinta Latinae.

# ALF F

Semisonus dicor liquidis ut muta ministro;
nescio quid causae est cur me sic Hebreus odit;
nox perit et tenebrae, si me de flumine tollas.

## ALF D

I am the sound of the ablative case and the seventh part of
    speech,
having the name of the almighty when the syllable "us" has
    been added;
I am half a thousand, and a wicked sign of ancient gods.

## ALF E

I am part of the mutes, but really I shall be reckoned to be a
    vowel;
I am one of two syllables of a mother deceived long ago;
I am also a full part, and the fifth part of Latin speech.

## ALF F

I am pronounced half-sounded, whenever, unvoiced, I am
    of service to liquids;
I don't know why it is that the Hebrew hates me so;
night disappears and darkness, if you remove me from
    "river."

## ALF G

Si solam legeres, tunc clarus Caesar habebor;
si duplicem legeres, Romanus praesul habebor;
post me quinta sonat parvum vocalis in ore.

## ALF H

Nomen habens vacuum, fragilem deporto figuram;
non nisi per versus in me manet ulla potestas;
hoc tantum valui: linguis spiramina ferre.

## ALF I

Sum numerus primus; iuvenum contentio magna;
spreta figura mihi est etiam, sed mira potestas;
me tamen haud Dominus voluit de lege perire.

## ALF K

Dux ego per primos primae vocalis habebar;
meque meo penitus pepulerunt iure moderni;
nunc caput Afrorum merui vel mensis habere.

## ALF G

If you were to read me once, I shall be reckoned a famous
   Caesar;
if you were to read me twice, I shall be reckoned a Roman
   prelate;
after me, the fifth vowel sounds only a little in the mouth.


## ALF H

Having an empty name, I sport a fragile figure;
nor does any force remain in me, except in verses;
this is all I can do: carry aspirations in languages.


## ALF I

I am the first number, a great contention of youngsters;
even my figure is slighted, but my power is amazing;
yet the Lord did not want me to perish from the Law.


## ALF K

I used to be reckoned a leader of the first vowel among the
   first men;
but modern folk have utterly expelled me from my rightful
   position;
now I have deserved to hold the headship of the Africans or
   of the month.

## ALF L

Si me Graece legas totum sine sorde videbis;
nec frustra quoniam per carmina saepe liquesco;
sed tamen agricola in curvo me vertice portat.

## ALF M

In metris iugiter cum sim vocalibus esca,
suadeo de musis tollas me non genitrice,
ne atra figura tuos tenebris offuscet ocellos.

## ALF N

Vox sum certa sonans, qua res monstratur adesse;
tollere me multi quaerunt de nomine frustra;
vim quoque sic solitam Pitheo de carmine perdens.

## ALF O

Littera saepe choris en sum signata canentum;
curro vias multas, manibus sed fixa manebo;
perque meam formam saeclorum vertitur ordo.

## ALF L

If you read me in Greek, you will see me completely
    spotless;
and not in vain, since I often make liquids in poems;
but yet a farmer carries me on a curved neck.

## ALF M

Although in poems I am continually a food for vowels,
I urge, in respect to the muses, that you don't take me away
    from "mother,"
lest a black figure hide your eyes in darkness.

## ALF N

I am a sure-sounding noise, by which a thing is shown to be
    present;
many seek in vain to take me from a "name";
so also I am losing my accustomed force in Pythian song.

## ALF O

Look: I am the letter often signaled by choirs of singers;
I run many ways, but I shall remain fixed to the hands;
and through my form the order of the ages revolves.

## ALF P

Me sine nulla potest hominum concordia cerni;
nota potentis eram plebis perscripta columnis;
sic quoque nota fui patrum, bis scripta, piorum.

## ALF Q

Sola mihi virtus vocalem vincere quintam,
qua sine non nascor ego; hanc occido nefande,
quapropter iuste memet respuere quaternae.

## ALF R

Est nomen durum, sed virtus durior illo,
idcirco placuit me nam mollire camenis;
nota tamen fueram populi vincentis et orbem.

## ALF S

Nota fui patrum; propriae et virtutis in odis;
sed modo iam melius Domini sum nota secunda,
et me Phoebus amat, posuitque in origine lucis.

## ALF P

Without me, no agreement of men can be seen;
I was written on columns as the mark of a powerful people;
twice written, I have been the abbreviation of holy fathers.

## ALF Q

My only power is conquering the fifth vowel,
without which I am not born; and I kill it unspeakably,
wherefore the four other vowels justly spurn me.

## ALF R

It is a harsh name, but it has a power harsher than that,
whereby it was pleasing to soften me in song;
yet I had been the mark of the people who conquered the
world.

## ALF S

I was a mark of the fathers, and in poems had my own
power;
but now I am better, the second mark of the Lord,
and Phoebus loves me and has placed me in the beginning
of "sunlight."

## ALF T

Angelus en voluit poni me in fronte gementum,
cetera turba neci misere dum tota dabatur;
te precor, haec legitans, proprio me nomine signa.

## ALF V

Forma manet semper, virtus mihi sed variatur:
utraque sum vere nullo discrimine formae;
nec me Graecus habet scriptam, sed me duo complent.

## ALF X

Forma mihi simplex, sed certe dupla potestas;
aere me puro perscribit penna volantis;
per me saepe patet numerus de lege sacratus.

## ALF Y

Nomine sum duplex, sed Graeco robore simplex;
ac typica in membris tribus, ut Samius bene sensit:
infima dans pueris, at dextra ac laeva sapitis.

## ALF T

Look: an angel wished me to be placed on the forehead of
    groaning ones,
while the whole other throng was given over to a wretched
    death;
I pray you, reading this, sign me by my own name.

## ALF V

The form remains always, but my power varies;
I am both truly, with no distinction of form;
nor did the Greek have me written, but two complete me.

## ALF X

My form is simple, but my force is surely double:
the wing of the flying one writes me on pure air;
through me the sacred number of the law is often revealed.

## ALF Y

I am double in name, but simple in Greek strength;
figurative in three limbs, as the Samian well sensed:
giving my bottom part to the boys, but the right and left to
    the wise.

# ALF Z

Littera sum Graeca, duplex, sed more liquentum
deficio currens per carmina sicuti simplex,
saepe etiam sibilans inter dentes morientum.

## ALF Z

I am a Greek letter, a double consonant, but in the manner
    of liquids
I become weak running through poems as a single one,
often also whistling through the teeth of the dying.

# The Old Icelandic Rune Poem

## OIR 1

·ᚠ· er frænda róg ok fyrða gaman
 ok grafseiðs gata.

## OIR 2

·ᚢ· er skýja grátr ok skára þverrir
 ok hirðis hatr.

## OIR 3

·ᚦ· er kvenna kvǫl ok kletta íbúi
 ok Valrúnar verr.

## OIR 4

·ᚬ· er aldingautr ok Ásgarðs jǫfurr
 ok Valhallar vísi.

# The Old Icelandic Rune Poem

## OIR 1

*f* is kinsman's strife; and people's delight;
and the path of the grave-fish.

## OIR 2

*u* is clouds' weeping; and diminisher of haycocks;
and hatred of herdsmen.

## OIR 3

*þ* is women's torment; and crags' inhabitant;
and Valrún's husband.

## OIR 4

*o* is ancient Gautr; and Ásgarðr's warrior;
and Valhǫll's leader.

## OIR 5

·R· er sitjandi sæla    ok snúðig ferð
   ok jórs erfiði.

## OIR 6

·ʏ· er barna bǫl    ok bardagi
   ok holdfúa hús.

## OIR 7

·✳· er kaldakorn    ok knappa drífa
   ok snáka sótt.

## OIR 8

·ʜ· er þýjar þrá    ok þungr kostr
   ok vássamlig verk.

## OIR 9

·ı· er árbjǫrkr    ok unnar þekja
   ok feigra manna fár.

## OIR 5

*r* is happiness of the seated; and swift journey;
  and horse's strain.

## OIR 6

*k* is pain and struggle of children;
  and the home of rotting flesh.

## OIR 7

*h* is cold corn; and driving sleet;
  and sickness of snakes.

## OIR 8

*n* is servant's longing; and tough choice;
  and dripping toil.

## OIR 9

*i* is river-bark; and wave's thatch;
  and trouble of doomed men.

## OIR 10

·I· er gumna gæði    ok gott sumar.
  ok algróinn akr.

## OIR 11

·I· er skýja skjǫldr    ok skínandi rǫðull.
  ok ísa aldrtregi.

## OIR 12

·I· er einhendr áss    ok úlfs leiðar.
  ok hofa hilmir.

## OIR 13

·B· er laufgat lim    ok lítit tré
  ok unsamligr viðr.

## OIR 14

·Y· er manns gaman    ok moldar auki
  ok skipa skreytir.

## OIR 10

*a* is men's gladness; and good summer;
    and fruitful field.

## OIR 11

*s* is clouds' shield; and shining rim;
    and turning wheel.

## OIR 12

*t* is the one-handed god; and wolf's leavings;
    and Baldr's brother.

## OIR 13

*b* is little branch; and leafy tree;
    and growing wood.

## OIR 14

*m* is man's delight; and earth's increase;
    and painter of ships.

# OIR 15

·ᚠ· er vellandi vimur    ok víðr ketill
ok glǫmmunga grund.

# OIR 16

·ᚢ· er bendr bogi    ok brotgjarnt járn
ok fífu fárbauti.

## OIR 15

*l* is bubbling Vimur; and broad cauldron;
and field of tiny fish.

## OIR 16

*y* is bent bow; and battle-help;
and arrow-slinger.

# The Riddles of Gestumblindi

## GES 1

Hafa ek þat vilda,
er ek hafða í gær,
vittu, hvat þat var.
Lýða lemill,
orða tefill,
ok orða upp-hefill.

## GES 2

Heiman ek fór,
heiman ek fǫr gerðak,
sá ek á veg vega.
Vegr var undir
ok vegr yfir
ok vegr á alla vega.

## GES 3

Hvat er þat drykkja,
er ek drakk í gær?

# The Riddles of Gestumblindi

## GES 1

I wish I had
what I had yesterday:
work out what it was.
Paralyzing to men,
slurring to words,
it also encourages speech.

## GES 2

I traveled from home;
I went traveling from home;
I saw a maze of ways:
there was a way under it,
and a way over it,
and a way every way.

## GES 3

What was the drink
that I drank yesterday?

Var-at þat vín né vatn,
né in heldr mungát
né matar ekki,
þó gekk ek þorsta-lauss þaðan.

## GES 4

Hverr er sá inn hvelli,
er gengr harðar gǫtur
ok hefir hann þær fyrr of farit?
Mjǫk fast kyssir
ok hefir munna tvá
ok á gulli einu gengr.

## GES 5

Hverr er sá inn mikli,
er ferr mold yfir,
svelgr hann vǫtn ok við?
Glygg hann óask,
en guma eigi
ok yrkir á sól til saka.

## GES 6

Hverr er sá inn mikli,
er mǫrgu ræðr
ok horfir til heljar hálfr?

It was not wine or water,
nor even strong beer,
nor any kind of food,
yet I went from there without thirst.

## GES 4

Who is that shrill one
who travels hard paths,
and has gone that way before?
He gives mighty kisses,
since he has two mouths,
and on gold alone he goes.

## GES 5

Who is that great one,
who passes over the earth,
and swallows both water and wood?
It trembles at the breeze,
but not at any man,
and wages war on the sun.

## GES 6

Who is that mighty one
who governs much,
but turns half to Hel?

Hǫlðum bergr,
en við jǫrð sakask,
ef hann hefir sér vel traustan vin.

## GES 7

Hverr byggir há-fjǫll?
Hverr fellr í djúpa dali?
Hverr anda-lauss lifir?
Hverr æva þegir?

## GES 8

Hvat er þat undra,
er ek úti sá
fyrir Dellings durum?
Hǫfði sínu
vísar heljar til,
en fótum til sólar snýr.

## GES 9

Hvat er þat undra,
er ek úti sá
fyrir Dellings durum?
Ókyrrir tveir
anda-lausir
sára lauk suðu.

He protects mankind
and battles against earth,
if he has a faithful friend.

## GES 7

Who dwells on the high fells?
Who falls in the deep dales?
Who lives without breathing?
Who is never silent?

## GES 8

What wonder is it,
that I saw outside,
just before Dellingr's door?
It points its head
down toward Hel,
but turns its feet to the sun.

## GES 9

What wonder is it,
that I saw outside,
just before Dellingr's door?
Two unquiet things,
devoid of breath,
cooked up a leek of wounds.

## GES 10

Hvat er þat undra,
er ek úti sá
fyrir Dellings durum?
Hvítir fljúgendr
hellu ljósta,
en svartir í sand grafask.

## GES 11

Hvat er þat undra,
er ek úti sá
fyrir Dellings durum?
Svartan gǫlt
ek sá í sauri vaða
ok reis-at honum burst á baki.

## GES 12

Hvat er þat undra,
er ek úti sá
fyrir Dellings durum?
Tíu hefr tungur,
tuttugu augu,
fjóra tigu fóta,
ferr hart sú vættr.

## GES 10

What wonder is it,
that I saw outside,
just before Dellingr's door?
White things flying
batter the stone,
black things are buried in the sand.

## GES 11

What wonder is it,
that I saw outside,
just before Dellingr's door?
I saw a dark-colored boar
wallowing in the filth,
but no bristles arose on his back.

## GES 12

What wonder is it,
that I saw outside,
just before Dellingr's door?
It has ten tongues,
twenty eyes;
that creature travels hard
with forty feet.

## GES 13

Hvat er þat undra,
er ek úti sá
fyrir Dellings durum?
Ofarliga flýgr,
alm-hljóð gellr,
harðar eru, hilmir.

## GES 14

Hvat er þat undra,
er ek úti sá
fyrir Dellings durum?
Fætr hefir átta,
en fjǫgur augu,
berr þat ofar kné en kvið.

## GES 15

Hvat er þat undra,
er ek úti sá
fyrir Dellings durum?
Lýðum lýsir,
en logi gleypir,
ok keppask um þat vargar ávallt.

## GES 13

What wonder is it,
that I saw outside,
just before Dellingr's door?
It flies overhead,
it screams an elm-sound;
they are hard, lord.

## GES 14

What wonder is it,
that I saw outside,
just before Dellingr's door?
It had eight legs,
and four eyes,
and bears its knees above its belly.

## GES 15

What wonder is it,
that I saw outside,
just before Dellingr's door?
It gives light to men,
it wolfs up flame,
and wolves always strive after it.

## GES 16

Hvat er þat undra,
er ek úti sá
fyrir Dellings durum?
Horni harðara,
hrafni svartara,
skafti réttara,
skjalli hvítara.

## GES 17

Báru brúðir
bleik-haddaðar,
ambáttir tvær,
ǫl-ker til skemmu;
var-a þat hǫndum horfit
né hamri klappat;
þó er fyrir eyjar útan
ǫrðigr, sá er ker gerði.

## GES 18

Hverjar eru þær rýgjar
á regin-fjalli?
Elr við kván kona,
mær við meyju
mǫg of getr,
ok eigut þær varðir vera.

## GES 16

What wonder is it,
that I saw outside,
just before Dellingr's door?
Harder than a horn
blacker than a raven,
straighter than a shaft,
brighter than egg white.

## GES 17

Bright-haired brides,
a pair of bondmaids,
bore off to the storehouse
a cask of ale;
no hand had turned it,
no hammer had forged it,
yet there was beyond the island
its maker standing straight.

## GES 18

Who are those great women
up on the mighty mountain?
A woman breeds with a woman,
and a girl with a girl
produces a son,
though they weren't with any man.

## GES 19

Hverjar eru þær snótir,
er um sinn dróttin
vápn-lausar vega?
Inar jǫrpu hlífa
um alla daga,
en inar fegri frýja.

## GES 20

Hverjar eru þær leikur,
er líða lǫnd yfir
at forvitni fǫður?
Hvítan skjǫld
þær um vetr bera,
en svartan um sumar.

## GES 21

Hverjar eru þær snótir,
er ganga syrgjandi
at forvitni fǫður?
Mǫrgum mǫnnum
hafa þær at meini orðit,
við þat munu þær aldr ala.

## GES 19

Who were those ladies
who are battling
weaponless around their lord?
The darker ones defend
all day long,
while the lighter ones mount a challenge.

## GES 20

Who are those playful women
who pass over the lands,
pursuing their father's curiosity?
They bear a white shield
throughout the winter,
but black throughout summertime.

## GES 21

Who are those ladies
who walk in sorrow,
pursuing their father's curiosity?
To many men
they have caused great harm,
and in that way they'll live out their lives.

## GES 22

Hverjar eru þær meyjar,
er ganga margar saman
at forvitni fǫður?
Hadda bleika
hafa þær inar hvít-fǫldnu
ok eigut þær varðir vera.


## GES 23

Hverjar eru þær brúðir,
er ganga brim-serkjum í
ok eiga eftir firði fǫr?
Harðan beð
hafa þær inar hvít-fǫldnu
ok leika í logni fátt.


## GES 23a

Hverjar eru þær ekkjur,
er ganga allar saman
at forvitni fǫður?
Sjaldan blíðar
eru þær við seggja lið
ok eigu í vindi vaka.

## GES 22

Who are those maidens
who travel in multitudes,
pursuing their father's curiosity?
They have pale hairstyles,
those white-hooded women,
though they weren't with any man.

## GES 23

Who are those brides
who travel in sea-shirts,
and plot a path along the fjord?
They have a hard bed
those white-hooded ones,
and they don't play much when it's calm.

## GES 23a

Who are those widows
who travel as a troop,
pursuing their father's curiosity?
They are seldom kind
to the troop of men,
and they have to wake up in the wind.

## GES 24

Fara ek sá
foldar mold-búa,
á sat nár á nái,
blindr reið blindum
brim-reiðar til,
jór er andar vanr.

## GES 25

Hvat er þat dýra,
er drepr fé manna
ok er járni kringt útan?
Horn hefir átta,
en hǫfuð ekki
ok rennr, sem renna má.

## GES 26

Hvat er þat dýra,
er Dǫnum hlífir,
berr blóðugt bak?
En bergr firum,
geirum mætir,
gefr líf sumum,
leggr við lófa
lík sitt gumi.

## GES 24

One who dwells in the earthy soil,
I saw traveling along:
a corpse sat on a corpse,
the blind rode the blind
down to the surging of the sea,
though the steed was lacking breath.

## GES 25

What is that animal
that kills men's wealth
and is surrounded with iron?
It has eight horns,
but no head at all,
and runs as much as it can.

## GES 26

What is that animal
that protects the Danes,
and bears a bloody back?
Yet it guards men,
encounters spears,
gives life to some,
lays its body
against a man's palm.

## GES 27

Næsta var forðum
nǫs-gás vaxin,
barn-gjǫrn sú er bar
bú-timbr saman,
hlífðu henni
hálms bit-skálmir,
þó lá drykkjar
dryn-hraun yfir.

## GES 28

Fjórir ganga,
fjórir hanga,
tveir veg vísa,
tveir hundum varða,
einn eftir drallar
ok oftast óhreinn.

## GES 29

Hverr er sá inn eini,
er sefr í ǫsku-grúa
ok er af grjóti einu gerr?
Fǫður né móður
áat sá inn fagr-gjarni,
þar mun hann sinn aldr ala.

## GES 27

Just some time ago,
a nose-goose grew up—
she was eager for offspring, that one—
who brought building timbers together;
biting-blades of straw
protected her,
although the sounding-lava
of drink lay above.

## GES 28

Four are walking,
four are hanging,
two point the way,
two keep off the dogs,
one dangles behind,
and that is mostly unclean.

## GES 29

Who is the one all alone
who sleeps in the ashpit
and is made from stone alone?
That one who wants brightness
has no father or mother,
but there he will live out his life.

## GES 30

Hest sá ek standa,
hýddi meri,
dúði dindil,
drap hlaun und kvið,
ór skal draga
ok gjǫfta at góða stund.

## GES 31

Hverir eru þeir þegnar,
er ríða þingi at
ok eru sextán saman?
Lýði sína
senda þeir lǫnd yfir
at byggja ból-staði.

## GES 32

Sá ek á sumri
sól-bjǫrgum í
verðung vaka
vilgi teita.
Drukku jarlar
ǫl þegjandi,
en æpanda
ǫl-ker stóð.

## GES 30

I saw a stallion
flogging a mare:
it tossed its tail
dropped buttocks under belly;
it must pull it out
and wave it for a while.

## GES 31

Who are those thegns,
who ride to the thing,
the ones all settled together?
They send their men
across the land,
to build up places to dwell.

## GES 32

I saw in summer
at the setting of the sun
how a household became
far from happy.
The earls were drinking
ale in silence,
but the ale cask stood,
screaming loudly.

## GES 33

Meyjar ek sá
moldu líkar,
váru þeim at beðjum bjǫrg,
svartar ok sámar
í sól-viðri,
en þess at fegri er færa of sér.

## GES 34

Sat ek á segli,
sá ek dauða menn
blóðs-hol bera
í bǫrk viðar.

## GES 35

Hverir eru þeir tveir,
er tíu hafa fætr,
augu þrjú
ok einn hala?

## GES EP

Hvat mælti Óðinn
í eyra Baldri,
áðr hann var á bál hafðr?

## GES 33

I saw some maidens
looking like dust:
they make their beds on stone;
they are black and dusky
in sunny weather,
but lighter, when they take themselves off.

## GES 34

| | | |
|---|---|---|
| I sat on a sail; | *or* | I sat on a wall; |
| I saw dead men | *or* | I saw a falcon |
| bearing a blood-hollow | *or* | bearing an eider duck |
| to tree bark. | *or* | to a cliff. |

## GES 35

Who are those two
who have ten legs,
three eyes,
and a single tail?

## GES EP

What did Odin say
in Baldr's ear,
before he was put on the pyre?

# Various Riddles

## XMS P1

Vulnere mucronis tam parvi pallidus exul,
tegmine substratus ramoso roboris alti
cacumen cuius conscendit corniger hospes
aera cum quadris remigans praepetis alis.
5 Ac senis pedibus suffultus soniger illic
amplectens ramum tum lassus longe volandi,
umbriferam noctem nitens pausare per horas.
Horridum hoc animal genuit Germanica tellus:
scrutetur sapiens, lector, quo nomine fungit.

## XMS P2

Prima sonat quartae, respondet quinta secundae,
Tertia cum sexta: nomen habebit avis.

# Various Riddles

## XMS P1

A pale exile, laid low by a wound of so small a sword,
stretched out beneath the covering branches of a tall oak,
to the top of which rises a beaked visitor,
as it rows through the air with the fourfold wings of a swift
    flier.
Perching there on six feet, the song-bearer,                5
tired from flying far, clasps a branch,
striving to rest for the shady night throughout the hours.
The Germanic land gave birth to this dreaded animal:
let the wise reader consider what name it goes by.

## XMS P2

The first echoes the fourth, the fifth matches the second,
the third the sixth: a bird has this name.

## XMS P3

Quod cernis, dicor. Tollatur littera prima:
  Scando polum calidum, curro solum gelidum.

\* \* \*

## XMS S1

Ad portam gemini se dedignantur egeni:
"Hospita sit sospes, non hospes ut hospita sospes."
"Hospes sit sospes, non hospita sospes ut hospes."
Hospes sit sospes, sic et hospita sospes ut hospes.

## XMS S2

Me tribus artificis compegit dextera membris
quae duo si demas, scito manere decem.

# XMS P3

I am called what you are looking at. Let the first letter be
    taken away:
  I travel the hot sky, I run on the cold ground.

\*   \*   \*

# XMS S1

At a gateway, twin wretches disdain each other:
"May the hostess be saved, but the guest not be saved like
    the hostess."
"May the guest be saved, but the hostess not be saved like
    the guest."
May the guest be saved, and the hostess saved too, like the
    guest.

# XMS S2

A craftsman's right hand has put me together from three
    members;
if you take two away, know that ten remain.

## XMS S3

Floribus et lignis quoddam mirabile vas fit
quod cum sit vacuum vel plenum ponderat aeque.

\* \* \*

## XMS X1

Vidi mortuum sedentem super vivum, et ex risu mortui moriebatur vivus.

## XMS X2

Vidi hominem ambulantem cum matre sua et pellis eius
pendebat in pariete.

## XMS X3

Vidi mulierem flentem et cum quinque filiis currentem,
cuius semita erat vita et pergebat valde plana campestria.

\* \* \*

# XMS S3

A certain amazing vessel is made from wood and flowers,
and it weighs the same whether it is empty or full.

\* \* \*

# XMS X1

I saw a dead man sitting on a live man, and the live man was
dying from the laughter of the dead man.

# XMS X2

I saw someone walking with his mother and his skin was
hanging on a wall.

# XMS X3

I saw a woman weeping, and running alongside five sons,
and her path was life, and she was traveling over very flat
fields.

\* \* \*

## XMS X4

Lucidus et placidus sedebant in quinque ramis: lucidus sedit, placidus pertransiit.

\* \* \*

## XMS Y1

Missus transmissus qui non loquebatur . . . Intellexit quoniam aquae recessissent a terris.

\* \* \*

## XMS Z1

Video et tollo: si vidissem, non tulissem. *Nxtz fbtxb.*

## XMS Z2

Portat animam et non habet animam: non ambulat super terram neque in caelo. *Nbxks.*

## XMS X4

A clear one and a pleasing one used to sit in five branches:
the clear one remains, the pleasing one has disappeared.

\* \* \*

## XMS Y1

A messenger was sent out who was unable to speak . . . He
knew then that the waters had receded from the earth.

\* \* \*

## XMS Z1

I see it and I take it up; if I had seen it properly, I would not
have taken it.
*Nux fatua* (a bad nut).

## XMS Z2

It carries life, and it has no soul: nor does it wander on the
land or in the air.
*Navis* (ship).

## XMS Z3

Quid est quod fuit et modo non est? Ambulat circa ignem et operatur obicem unum. *Pfdfm hbbfo.*

## XMS Z4

Volavit volucer sine plumis; sedit in arbore sine foliis; venit homo sine manibus; assavit illum sine igne; comedit illum sine ore. *Nxtz a Titane.*

## XMS Z5

Equitavit homo cum femina; mater eius matris meae socrus fuit. *Xktrkcxs.*

## XMS Z6

Porto filium filii mei, mariti mei fratrem, alterum unicum filium meum.

## XMS Z3

What is it that was and now is not? It wanders about the fire
and causes a block.
*Pedem habeo* (I have a foot).

## XMS Z4

A bird flew without feathers, sat in a tree without leaves; a
man came without hands, cooked it without fire, consumed
it without a mouth. *Nix a Titane* (snow melting from the
sun).

## XMS Z5

A man rode with his wife, and his mother was my mother's
mother-in-law.
*Vitricus* (stepfather).

## XMS Z6

I carry the son of my son, the brother of my husband, and
the second is my only son.

# Abbreviations

*AL* = Alexander Riese, ed., *Anthologia Latina, pars prior: Carmina in codicibus scripta,* 2nd ed., 2 vols. (Leipzig, 1894–1906)

ASPR = George Krapp and Elliot Van Kirk Dobbie, eds., *The Anglo-Saxon Poetic Records: A Collective Edition,* 6 vols. (New York, 1931–1953)

*BCLL* = Michael Lapidge and Richard Sharpe, *A Bibliography of Celtic–Latin Literature, 400–1200* (Dublin, 1985)

CCSL = *Corpus Christianorum, Series Latina* (Turnhout, 1953–).

*COEALRT* = Andy Orchard, *A Commentary on "The Old English and Anglo-Latin Riddle Tradition"* (Washington, D.C., 2021)

*CPL* = Eligius Dekkers and Aemilius Gaar, *Corpus Patrum Latinorum,* 3rd ed. (Steenbrugge, 1995)

*DMLBS* = R. E. Latham, D. R. Howlett, and R. K. Ashdowne, *Dictionary of Medieval Latin from British Sources* (Oxford, 1975–2013)

*DOE* = Angus Cameron, Ashley Crandell Amos, Antonette diPaolo Healey, and others, eds., *Dictionary of Old English: A–I* (Toronto, 2018). https://doe.utoronto.ca

G–L = Helmut Gneuss and Michael Lapidge, *A Bibliographical Handlist of Manuscripts and Manuscript Fragments Written or Owned in England up to 1100* (Toronto, 2014). Cited by entry number.

*ICUR* = Giovanni Battista de Rossi, ed., *Inscriptiones Christianae Urbis Romae,* 2 vols. (Rome, 1861–1888)

MGH = Monumenta Germaniae Historica

AA = Auctores Antiquissimi

ES = Epistolae Selectae

PLAC = Poetae Latini Aevi Carolini

*PN* = P. Mastandrea and Luigi Tessarolo, *PoetriaNova 2: A CD–ROM of Latin Medieval Poetry (650–1250 A.D.), with a Gateway to Classical and Late Antique Texts* (Florence, 2010)

*PSLMA* = H. Walther, *Proverbia Sententiaeque Latinitatis Medii Aevi*, 5 vols. (Göttingen, 1963–1969)

SK = Dieter Schaller and Ewald Könsgen, *Initia carminum Latinorum saeculo undecimo antiquiorum* (Göttingen, 1977)

SK Sup. = Dieter Schaller and Ewald Könsgen, with Thomas Klein, *Initia carminum Latinorum saeculo undecimo antiquiorum: Supplementband* (Göttingen, 2005)

## RIDDLES AND RIDDLE COLLECTIONS

ABI = *The Abingdon Riddle*

ALC = Alcuin, *Riddles*

　ALC D = Alcuin, *Debate between the Royal and Most Noble Youth Pippin and the Scholar Alcuin*

　ps-ALC = pseudo-Alcuin, *Riddle*

ALD = Aldhelm, *Riddles*

　ALD PR = Aldhelm, preface to the *Riddles*

ALF = *The Verses of a Certain Irishman on the Alphabet*

BED = Bede, *Riddles*

　ps-BED = pseudo-Bede, *Riddles*

BER = *The Bern Riddles*

　ps-BER = *The pseudo-Bern Riddle*

BIB = *The High-Minded Library*

BON = Boniface, *Riddles*

   BON PR = Boniface, preface to the *Riddles*

EUS = Hwætberht, *The Riddles of Eusebius*

EXE = *The Exeter Book Riddles*

FRA = *The Franks Casket Riddle*

GES = *The Riddles of Gestumblindi*

LEI = *The Leiden Riddle*

LOR = *The Lorsch Riddles*

OEP = *The Old English Prose Riddle*

OER = *The Old English Rune Poem*

OIR = *The Old Icelandic Rune Poem*

ONR = *The Old Norwegian Rune Poem* (found in notes to OIR)

SOL = *The Riddles of "Solomon and Saturn II"*

SYM = Symphosius, *Riddles*

   SYM PR = Symphosius, preface to the *Riddles*

   ps-SYM = pseudo-Symphosius, *Riddles*

TAT = Tatwine, *Riddles*

   TAT PR = Tatwine, preface to the *Riddles*

   TAT EP = Tatwine, epilogue to the *Riddles*

XMS = *Various Riddles*

   XMS P = riddles from P[5] (Paris, Bibliothèque nationale de France, lat. 8071 [tenth century]) and S[1] (London, British Library, Harley 3020, fols. 95–132 [provenance Glastonbury, tenth or eleventh century, Winchester?])

   XMS S = riddles from S (Edinburgh, National Library of Scotland,

Advocates 18.6.12 [provenance Thorney, end of the eleventh or beginning of the twelfth century])

XMS X = riddles from X (St. Gallen, Stiftsbibliothek 196 [middle of the tenth century]) and $X^1$ (St. Gallen, Stiftsbibliothek 446 [tenth century])

XMS Y = riddles from $P^2$ (Paris, Bibliothèque nationale de France, lat. 10861 [Canterbury Christ Church?; first half of the ninth century])

XMS Z = riddles from Z (Karlsruhe, Badische Landesbibliothek, Aug. perg. 205 [Reichenau, tenth century])

# Note on the Texts

The notes given here are not intended as an alternative to the various critical apparatuses found in the many editions, but rather as a lens or in some cases a supplement to the more authoritative readings to be found there. I have consulted a wide range of manuscripts at first hand, as well as in facsimile, focusing on those that were written or owned in England up to 1100, and although I am of course aware that such a perspective is necessarily skewed with regards to the authoritative readings considered by other editors scanning the whole range of available manuscripts, it seems also important in this context to stress the extant Anglo-Saxon evidence for the transmission of the riddle tradition. Throughout, I have attempted to highlight in particular those places where for one reason or another I have deviated from the received texts, or made conjectural emendations of my own, especially with regard to solutions: in such cases, given the commendably broad and general remit of the Dumbarton Oaks Medieval Library series, I have necessarily refrained from the kind of full analysis here that can be found in the complementary and fuller companion volume, *A Commentary on "The Old English and Anglo-Latin Riddle Tradition" (COEALRT),* to which the curious reader is referred.

## Aldhelm (ALD)

Manuscripts: ALD appears in whole or in part in two very different contexts, both as an independent verse collection and as part of a rather bigger compilation, the so-called *Epistola ad Acircium (Letter to Acircius)*, sent by Aldhelm to King Aldfrith of Northumbria (685–705) soon after his accession, where it appears as the third of four items, being preceded by treatises on the allegorical significance of the number seven and on meters *(De metris)*, and followed by another on the rules of metrical feet *(De pedum regulis)*. Such a context underlines the importance for Aldhelm of the use of ALD as an illustrative and didactic text focused on the teaching of Latin verse, as well as its likely existence as an independent collection before 685. Even so, that independent collection appears in two rather different recensions, with the earlier characterized by the use of nominative forms for the solutions and a number of metrical infelicities that are corrected in the later recension, which gives solutions in the ablative form, preceded by the preposition *de* (about, concerning). Indeed, the form of the solutions in the later recension may be a direct result of the incorporation of ALD into the *Epistola ad Acircium,* where the titles not only of the various sections but also of many of the subsections have an identical structure. The first recension is witnessed in three manuscripts: Saint Petersburg, Russian National Library, F. v. XIV. 1, and Paris, Bibliothèque nationale de France, lat. 13048, fols. 31–58 (R, or Ehwald and Lapidge's A); Brussels, Bibliothèque royale, 10615–10729 (F¹); and Brussels, Bibliothèque royale, 9799 (F²). The first of these (R) dates from the second quarter of the eighth century, while the others are from the twelfth century, F² simply being a direct copy of F¹. By contrast, there are over twenty manuscripts containing all or part of the second recension of ALD, five of which include it as part of the *Epistola ad Acircium,* with the rest containing ALD outside that context. The whole complex situation has been admirably described by Michael Lapidge, "Aldhelmus Malmesberiensis Abb. et Scireburnensis ep.," in *La trasmissione dei testi latini del medioevo/Medieval Latin Texts and Their Transmission: Te. Tra 4,* ed. P. Chiesa and L. Castaldi (Florence, 2012), 19–26. Here, I have consulted in particular the following Anglo-Saxon manuscripts, all from the second recension: Leiden, Universiteitsbibliotheek, Vossianus lat. Q. 106 (D), fols. 10v–25v; London, British Library, Royal 12. C. XXIII (L), fols. 83r–101v; Cambridge, University Library, Gg. 5. 35 (G), fols. 394v–407r; London, British Library, Royal 15. A. XVI (B), fols. 59v–73v; and Oxford, Bodleian Library, Rawlinson C. 697 (O), fols. 1r–16r. I have compared these with the recorded readings from the first-recension manuscripts noted above.

This edition has been adapted from Rudolph Ehwald, ed., *Aldhelmi Opera Omnia,* MGH AA 15 (Berlin, 1913–1919), 97–149, but incorporating many second-recension revisions, since these were clearly made by Aldhelm himself (see above). I have also consulted F. Glorie, ed., *Collectiones Aenigmatum Merovingicae Aeatis,* CCSL 133 (Turnhout, 1968), 377–539, and James H. Pitman, trans., *The Riddles of Aldhelm,* Yale Studies in English 67 (New Haven, 1925), 3–67.

## BEDE (BED AND PS-BED)

Manuscript: Cambridge, University Library, Gg. 5. 35 (G), fols. 418v–419r (BED).

This edition has been adapted from (BED) Frederick M. Tupper Jr., ed., "Riddles of the Bede Tradition: The *Flores* of pseudo-Bede," *Modern Philology* 2 (1905): 561–72; Michael Lapidge, *Bede's Latin Poetry* (Oxford, 2019), 316–24; and (ps-BED) Martha Bayless and Michael Lapidge, eds., *Collectanea Pseudo-Bedae,* Scriptores Latini Hiberniae 14 (Dublin, 1998).

## TATWINE (TAT)

Manuscripts: London, British Library, Royal 12. C. XXIII (L), fols. 121v–27r; Cambridge, University Library, Gg. 5. 35 (G), fols. 374v–77v.

This edition has been adapted from Mary Jane MacDonald Williams, "The Riddles of Tatwine and Eusebius" (PhD diss., University of Michigan, 1974), 101–56. I have also consulted Glorie, CCSL vol., 133, pp. 167–208.

## HWÆTBERHT, *THE RIDDLES OF EUSEBIUS* (EUS)

Manuscripts: London, British Library, Royal 12. C. XXIII (L), fols. 113v–21v; Cambridge, University Library, Gg. 5. 35 (G), fols. 370r–74v.

This edition has been adapted from Williams, "The Riddles of Tatwine and Eusebius," 157–249. I have also consulted Glorie, CCSL vol. 133, pp. 211–71.

## BONIFACE (BON)

Manuscripts: There are at least ten manuscripts of all or part of BON, with a number containing the texts in a radically different order; for a list and basic descriptions, see Glorie, CCSL vol. 133, pp. 276–77. Here, I have consulted the relevant Anglo-Saxon manuscripts: Aberystwyth, National Library of Wales, 735 C (A¹, not noted by Glorie), fols. 1r–2v; Cambridge, University Library, Gg. 5. 35 (G), fols. 382r–88v; London, British Library, Royal 15. B. XIX (L²), fols. 204r–5v (BON PR and 1–10.5 only).

This edition has been adapted from Ernst Dümmler, ed., *Aenigmata Anglica,* MGH PLAC 1 (Berlin, 1881), 3–15. I have also consulted Glorie, CCSL vol. 133, pp. 279–343.

## ALCUIN (ALC, PS-ALC, AND ALC D)

Manuscripts: As befits an important and widely read Latin author, the manuscript tradition for Alcuin is quite complex: see further Dümmler, MGH PLAC vol. 1, pp. 162–69 (ALC), and Lloyd William Daly and Walther Suchier, eds., *Altercatio Hadriani Augusti et Epicteti philosophi,* Illinois Studies in Language and Literature 24 (Urbana, 1939), 134–37 (ALC D).

This edition has been adapted from Dümmler, MGH PLAC vol. 1, pp. 223 and 281–83 (ALC), and Daly and Suchier, *Altercatio Hadriani,* 137–43 (ALC D). I have also consulted Martha Bayless, "Alcuin's *Disputatio Pippini and the Early Medieval Riddle Tradition,*" in *Humour, History and Politics in Late Antiquity and the Early Middle Ages,* ed. Guy Halsall (Cambridge, 2002), 157–78 (ALC D), and Paul Sorrell, "Alcuin's 'Comb' Riddle," *Neophilologus* 80 (1996): 311–18 (ALC 1).

## The Lorsch Riddles (LOR)

Manuscript: (Rome), Città del Vaticano, Biblioteca Apostolica Vaticana, Pal. lat. 1753 (U), fols. 115r–17v.

This edition has been adapted from Glorie, CCSL vol. 133, pp. 347–58.

## The Abingdon Riddle (ABI)

Manuscript: Antwerp, Plantin-Moretus Museum, M. 16. 2 (47) (Q), fol. 1r.

This edition has been adapted from David W. Porter, "A Double Solution to the Latin Riddle in Medieval Studies: Antwerp, Plantin-Moretus Museum M16.2," *American Notes and Queries* 9, no. 1 (1996): 3–9.

## The High-Minded Library (BIB)

Manuscript: Cambridge, University Library, Gg. 5. 35 (G), fols. 423v–25r.

This edition has been adapted from J. A. Giles, ed., *Anecdota Bedae Lanfranci, et aliorum* (London, 1851), 50–53.

## The Franks Casket Riddle (FRA)

There is, of course, no manuscript as such, but rather the front panel of the carved whalebone casket itself, from which the runes have been transcribed.

This edition has been adapted from R. I. Page, *Introduction to English Runes* (London, 1973), 174–77. I have also consulted Leslie Webster, *The Franks Casket* (London, 2012).

## The Leiden Riddle (LEI)

Manuscript: Leiden, Universiteitsbibliotheek, Vossianus lat. Q. 106 (D), fol. 25v.

This edition has been adapted from A. H. Smith, *Three Northumbrian Poems* (Exeter, 1978), 44–46, supplemented with reference to Richard Dance, "The Old English Language and the Alliterative Tradition," in *A Companion to Medieval Poetry,* ed. Corinne Saunders (Oxford, 2010), 40–42.

## The Exeter Book Riddles (EXE)

Manuscript: Exeter, Cathedral Library, 3501 (E), fols. 101r–15r, 122v–23r, and 124v–30v.

This edition has been adapted from George Philip Krapp and Elliot Van Kirk Dobbie, eds., *The Exeter Book,* ASPR 3 (London, 1936), 180–210, 224–25, and 229–43 (text) and 321–52, 361–62, and 366–82 (commentary). I have also consulted Bernard J. Muir, ed., *The Exeter Anthology of Old English Poetry,* 2 vols. (Exeter, 2nd rev. ed. 2006 with DVD), vol. 1, pp. 285–327, 352–53, and 359–79 (text), and vol. 2, pp. 606, 691–93, and 706–39 (commentary); Moritz Trautmann, *Die altenglischen Rätsel (die Rätsel des Exeterbuchs),* (Heidelberg, 1915), 1–56 (text) and 65–142 (commentary); Frank H. Whitman, *Old English Riddles,* Canadian Federation for the Humanities, Monograph Series 3 (Port Credit, ON, 1982), 161–224; Craig Williamson, ed., *The Old English Riddles of the "Exeter Book"* (Chapel Hill, 1977), 67–121 (text) and 127–402 (commentary); Alfred J. Wyatt, *Old English Riddles* (Boston, 1912), 1–64 (text) and 66–121 (commentary).

## The Old English Rune Poem (OER)

Manuscript: The original manuscript, London, British Library, Cotton Otho B. x, was destroyed in the fire of 1731, and the text that we have derives instead from the transcription by Humfrey Wanley that is printed in George Hickes, *Linguarum veterum septentrionalium thesaurus grammaticocriticus et archaeologicus* (Oxford, 1703–1705), vol. 2, p. 135, a text that combines material from another manuscript, London, British Library, Cotton Domitian A. ix.

This edition has been adapted from Bruce Dickins, *Runic and Heroic Poems of the Old Teutonic Peoples* (Cambridge, 1915), 12–23, and Maureen Halsall, *The Old English Rune Poem: A Critical Edition* (Toronto, 1981), 86–93. I have also consulted Page, *Introduction to Old English Runes,* 73–85.

## The Riddles of *Solomon and Saturn II* (SOL)

Manuscript: Cambridge, Corpus Christi College, 422 (C¹), pp. 16–18.

This edition has been adapted from Anlezark, *The Old English Dialogues of Solomon and Saturn* (Cambrdige, 2009), 80–85, where the two riddles appear at lines 52–64 and 104–23.

## THE OLD ENGLISH PROSE RIDDLE (OEP)

Manuscript: London, British Library, Cotton Vitellius E. xviii (C), fol. 16v.

This edition has been adapted from David Howlett, "*Tres linguae sacrae* and Threefold Play in Insular Latin," *Peritia* 16 (2002): 109–12. I have also consulted Max Förster, "Ein altenglisches Prosa-Rätsel," *Archiv für das Studium der neueren Sprachen und Literaturen* 115 (1905): 392–93, and "Die Lösung des Prosarätsels," *Archiv für das Studium der neueren Sprachen und Literaturen* 116 (1906): 267–71.

## SYMPHOSIUS (SYM)

Manuscripts: Earlier editions note more than thirty manuscripts; full details can be found in Manuela Bergamin, ed. and trans., *Aenigmata Symposii: La fondazione dell'enigmistica come genere poetico,* Per verba: Testi mediolatini con traduzione 22 (Florence, 2005), lxxiv–lxxxvii, and T. J. Leary, *Symphosius: The "Aenigmata": An Introduction, Text, and Commentary* (London, 2014), 32–37. I have consulted the following Anglo-Saxon manuscripts: Leiden, Universiteitsbibliotheek, Vossianus lat. Q. 106 (D), fols. 2v–8v; St. Gallen, Stiftsbibliothek 196 (X), pp. 374–87; London, British Library, Royal 12. C. XXIII (L), fols. 104r–13v; Cambridge, University Library, Gg. 5. 35 (G), fols. 389r–94r.

This edition has been adapted from Leary, *Symphosius: The "Aenigmata,"* 39–52 (text) and 53–247 (commentary). I have also consulted Bergamin, *Aenigmata Symposii,* 2–70 and 73–202 (commentary); Elizabeth Hickman du Bois, trans., *The Hundred Riddles of Symphosius* (Woodstock, Vt., 1912), 18–48 (text) and 61–86 (commentary); and Glorie, CCSL vol. 133, pp. 621–721.

## THE BERN RIDDLES (BER)

Manuscripts: There are nine relevant manuscripts, documented in *COEALRT;* here, I have consulted in particular (Rome), Città del Vaticano, Biblioteca Apostolica Vaticana, Reg. lat. 1553 (N), fols. 73r–80v.

This edition has been adapted from Karl Strecker, ed., *Aenigmata Hexasticha*, MGH PLAC vol. 4, part 2 (Berlin, 1923), 737–59, and Glorie, CCSL vol. 133A, pp. 547–610.

## THE VERSES OF A CERTAIN IRISHMAN ON THE ALPHABET (ALF)

Manuscripts: There are ten surviving manuscripts, documented in *COE-ALRT;* here, I have consulted London, British Library, Royal 12. C. XXIII (L), fols. 137v–38r (ALF A–L only); Cambridge, University Library, Gg. 5. 35 (G), fols. 381r–82r; Brussels, Bibliothèque royale, 10615–729 (F¹); Brussels, Bibliothèque royale, 9799–809 (F²); Oxford, Bodleian Library, Rawlinson C. 697 (O); Paris, Bibliothèque nationale de France, lat. 2773 (P³); Paris, Bibliothèque nationale de France, lat. 8071 (P⁵).

This edition has been adapted from Howlett, "*Versus cuiusdam Scotti de alphabeto:* An Edition, Translation, and Commentary," *Peritia* 21 (2010): 136–50. I have also consulted Glorie, CCSL vol. 133A, pp. 728–40.

## THE OLD ICELANDIC RUNE POEM (OIR)

Manuscript: Reykjavík, Stofnun Árna Magnússonar, AM 687d, 4° (Y), fol. iv.

This edition has been adapted from Page, "The Icelandic Rune-Poem," *Nottingham Medieval Studies* 42 (1998): 1–37, reprinted as a booklet by the Viking Society for Northern Research. I have also consulted Dickins, *Runic and Heroic Poems;* Hickes, *Linguarum veterum septentrionalium thesaurus;* Halsall, *The Old English Rune Poem,* 181–86.

## THE RIDDLES OF GESTUMBLINDI (GES)

Manuscripts: There are three main manuscript recensions, on which see Jeffrey Scott Love, *The Reception of "Hervarar saga ok Heiðreks" from the Middle Ages to the Seventeenth Century* (Munich, 2013), and Christopher Tolkien, ed. and trans., *The Saga of King Heidrek the Wise* (New York, 1960). Here, I have consulted the damaged Reykjavík, Stofnun Árna Magnússonar, AM 544, 4° (H¹, known as *Hauksbók*), pp. 235–37, as augmented by two

seventeenth-century paper manuscripts: Reykjavík, Stofnun Árna Magnússonar, AM 281 4° (H²), and Reykjavík, Stofnun Árna Magnússonar, AM
597b 4° (H³); I have also consulted Copenhagen, GKS 2845 4° (late four-
teenth or early fifteenth century) (R¹), and Uppsala, University Library,
R715 (paper, mid-seventeenth century) (U¹).

This edition has been adapted from Hannah Burrows, "Enigma Variations:
*Hervarar saga*'s Wave-Riddles and Supernatural Women in Old Norse Po-
etic Tradition," *Journal of English and Germanic Philology* 112 (2013): 194–216,
and Hannah Burrows, "Heiðreks gátur," in *Poetry in Fornaldarsögur,* ed.
Margaret Clunies Ross (Turnhout, 2017), 406–52; I have also consulted
Guðni Jónsson, *"Heiðreks saga,"* Fornaldar Sögur Norðurlanda, 4 vols.
(Reykjavík, 1954), vol. 2, pp. 1–71; Love, *Reception of "Hervarar saga ok
Heiðreks";* Tolkien, *The Saga of King Heidrek the Wise.*

## VARIOUS RIDDLES (XMS)

Manuscripts: Paris, Bibliothèque nationale de France, lat. 10861 (P²), fol.
123v; Paris, Bibliothèque nationale de France, lat. 8071 (P⁵), fol. 60v, col. 1;
Edinburgh, National Library of Scotland, Advocates 18. 6. 12 (S), fol. 35v;
London, British Library, Harley 3020, fols. 95–132 (S¹), fol. 95r; St. Gallen,
Stiftsbibliothek 196 (X), p. 389; St. Gallen, Stiftsbibliothek 446 (X¹), fol.
1r; Karlsruhe, Badische Landesbibliothek, Aug. perg. 205 (Z), fol. 70.

This edition has been adapted from *ICUR,* vol. 2, p. 245 (XMS P3 and
S1–3); Karl Müllenhof and Wilhelm Scherer, eds., *Denkmäler deutscher Poe-
sie und Prosa aus dem VIII.–XII. Jahrhundert* (Berlin, 1864), vol. 1, pp. 11–12
(XMS Z1–6); André Vernet, "Notice et extraits d'un manuscrit d'Edimbourg (Adv. Mss. 18.6.12, 18.7.8, 18.7.7)," *Bibliothèque de l'École des Chartres*
107 (1948): 33–51 (XMS P1–2 and S1); *AL* p. 235, nos. 770–71 (XMS P2–3);
Bayless and Lapidge, *Collectanea Pseudo-Bedae,* pp. 144–45 and 245, nos.
197–98 (XMS X1–3). In each case, I have consulted the relevant manuscripts.

# Notes to the Texts

6.4      cumulatus *R*: redundans *F¹F²*

12.2     replentur *other manuscripts*: redundant *AF¹F²*

14.1     pulcher et *other manuscripts*: sum namque *AF¹*

18.4     rescindere *GLR*: resistere *A*

19.4     constat *GLOR*: nitet *ABU*

30.1     denae *BL*: decem *other manuscripts*

34.4–5   *These lines appear* 34.6–7 *in most manuscripts and editions.*

34.5     plagas: plagae *most manuscripts and editions*

42.3     nam summa *other manuscripts*: summa dum *AF¹F²*

44.8     post haec *other manuscripts*: postmodum *AF¹F²*

52.7     extinguo: repello *AF¹F²*

53.2     esseda famoso: famosum nomen *L*; vulgo: vulgi *L*

53.8     cui pars *most second-recension manuscripts*: pars cuius *ROGL*

53.9     fundo . . . nigro *BL*: manibus . . . nigris *R*

54.1–2   tantarum foedera rerum . . . morum *BDGLO*: tantis spectacula
         causis . . . rerum *RF¹F²*

58.4     descendens *B*: relabens *F¹F²*

58.5     abscondens *BDGLO*: recondens *RF¹F²*

60.3     arciferi *BGLO*: arcister *R*

74.3     nam brachia loro *B*: retinacula filo *RF¹F²OGL*

78.7     hauserit *BDGLO*: auxerit *F¹F²*

82.1     curvas deflecto membra cavernas *most second-recension manu-
         scripts*: curvis conversor quadripes arvis *RF¹F²*

95.5     cruraque cum coxis *BDO*: femora cum coxis *GL*, femora cum
         cruribus *R*

## Bede (BED and ps-BED)

| | |
|---|---|
| 1.1 | nil: sic |
| 1.3 | titivillitium: titivicillium |
| 1.5 | oneris: honeris |
| 7.1 | tollit sine sanguine quod: sine sanguine quod tollit |
| 8.1 | manet: est |
| 11.1 | brevitatis: levitati |
| 13.2 | post hae maturae: he mature post |
| 14.1 | cornutam in celo: in celo cornutam |
| 14.2 | minime: minimum |
| 16.1 | tanto *not in the manuscript* |
| 17.3 | at: et |
| 18.4 | it: id; ubi: ibi |

## Tatwine (TAT)

| | |
|---|---|
| 1.2 | alta: alma *LG* |
| 1.3 | atque *G*: et *L* |
| 3.2 | sorores: sorori *LG* |
| 3.3 | diversis quae: diversisque *LG*; ornata *L*: ornamenta *G* |
| 6.5 | amor is: amoris *LG* |
| 11.3 | sine me iam: iam sine me *LG* |
| 20.1 | dulcifer: ducifer *LG* |
| 23.2 | nam *L*: iam *G*; perimo *L*: perunco *G* |
| 25.1 | eximiae: eximio *LG*; sedis: seclis *LG* |
| 25.5 | Parvulus *G*: Parvus *L* |
| 29.1 | multiferis: mulciferis *L* dulciferis *G* |
| 31.2 | iam *G* : nam *L* |
| 31.4 | ipse *L*: ipsa *G* |
| 32.2 | iubent: iuvant *LG* |
| 33.4 | haut sum *G*: sum haut *L* |
| 34.1 | Omnia: Omnis *L* Miles *G*; dirae: dire *L* diris *G*; flammae *L*: flammis *G* |
| 34.2 | acervis: acerbis *LG* |
| 36.4 | sola: solo *LG* |

| 37.1 | destino: destina *LG* |
| 37.4 | monte: mente *LG* |
| 38.1 | mutante: motante *LG* |
| 39.1 | natam: natum *LG* |
| EP. 1 | vates: vatem *LG* |

## HWÆTBERHT, *THE RIDDLES OF EUSEBIUS* (EUS)

| 3.3 | potenter: potentes *LG* |
| 4.3 | chelidrus: helidrum *LG* |
| 5.1 | avaris *L*: in arvis *G* |
| 10.4 | et *L*: non *G* |
| 11.4 | postea: post ego *LG* |
| 14.2 | vi: in *LG* |
| 22.1 | valde celer currens per inania: tam cito discurrens per aethera *L* |
| | valde celer discurrens per inania *G* |
| 24.1 | una: una sed *LG* |
| 26.2 | creatur: creator *LG* |
| 28.3 | possim *L*: possum *G* |
| 35.3 | vagabar: vagabor *LG* |
| 42.9 | cauda: cruda *LG* |
| 46.4 | nascitur: vescitur *LG*; ab ipsis *L* |
| 49.3 | oculos: animos *LG* |
| 49.4 | solam me: sola me *LG* |
| 51.4 | vocabar: vocabor *LG* |
| 54.3 | tantum: tamen *LG* |
| 55.6 | torpuerint: torpescerent *LG* |
| 56.4 | chelidrorum *L*: chelidri *G* |
| 57.4 | fotu: foetu *LG* |
| 59.1 | amoenum: amoenam *LG* |
| 59.6 | χαῖρε: care *LG* |

## BONIFACE (BON)

| PR.1 | nam: iure *G* |
| PR.11 | acervissmia: acerbissimia *GL²* |
| PR.15 | vipereo: viperea *L²*; saeve perlita: saepe maligna *L²* |

| | |
|---|---|
| PR.16 | Nitatur: Debuit *G* |
| PR.17 | quae: quem *L²* |
| PR.19 | frangantur: franguntur *G* |
| PR.20 | perdantur: perduntur *G* |
| 1.6 | degere nolo: degener erro *G* |
| 1.7 | tristis non: propria nunc *G*; sororem: sorore *GL²* |
| 2.3 | populo per mundum: populorum mundi *G*; labara: labere *L²* |
| 2.7 | terris: terrae *G* |
| 2.10 | qui: quia *G* |
| 2.12 | nullus: nullusque *G* |
| 2.13 | misero . . . fulget: miseros . . . fulcit *G* |
| 3.4 | fata: facta *GL²* |
| 4.4 | luerent: lustrent *GL²* |
| 4.10 | superi: superis *GL²* |
| 4.15 | ministra *L²*: ministro *G* |
| 7.4 | reorum: meorum *GL²* |
| 8.5 | dicor *G*: ditor *L²* |
| 9.9 | sorte sororum: iure sorores *G* forte sorores *L²* |
| 9.10 | sim: sit *GL²* |
| 9.19 | monarchus: manachus *L²* monachus *all other manuscripts and editions* |
| 10.12 | splendentia: splendentes *all other manuscripts and editions* |
| 13.17 | at *G*: et *L²* |
| 13.23 | at leges: atque; pares pariter *Dümmler*: patrias *all other manuscripts and editions* |
| 13.29 | monarchos: monachos *all other manuscripts and editions* |
| 13.32 | perpetuo *G*: perpetuae *all other manuscripts and editions* |
| 13.36 | nequiquam: nequicquam *all other manuscripts and editions* |
| 13.40 | dispergitur: disperditur *all other manuscripts and editions* |
| 13.57 | invitatur: vitatur *all other manuscripts and editions* |
| 14.11 | temptant: tendent |
| 16.5 | somnia: semina *other manuscripts and editions* |
| 16.11 | crudelis: crudeles |
| 18.5 | sanctorum facta: facta sanctorum *G* |
| 20.17 | pererrans: pervertens *G* |

## Alcuin (ALC, ps-ALC, and ALC D)

| | |
|---|---|
| 6.7 | aurum: taurum *all other manuscripts and editions* |
| ps-ALC 1.4 | necnon *not in either manuscript* |
| D20 | molae: mola; moles *are found in the manuscripts* |
| D30 | coctor: coquator *is found in most manuscripts* |
| D53 | fons: pons *both forms are found in the manuscripts, and both are feasible* |

## The Lorsch Riddles (LOR)

| | |
|---|---|
| 1.3 | consatus *U*: consistus *Glorie* |
| 1.5 | cum fine: sine fine |
| 2.9 | perpetue: perpetuae |
| 2.13 | fit: fio |
| 3.1 | aethera: aera |
| 5.6 | multifer: mulcifer |
| 6.1 | quandam: quondam |
| 6.4 | iosumque: dorsumque; manavit: cavavit |
| 6.5 | torum: terram |
| 12.6 | trusum: *the manuscript is damaged* |

## The High-Minded Library (BIB)

| | |
|---|---|
| 1.2 | genita: genito |
| 1.4 | nullo: ullo |
| 1.8 | pectore: pectora |
| 2.2 | amor *not in the manuscript* |
| 3.4 | numina: nomina |
| 3.8 | lucis: locis |
| 4.7 | metior at: meteoras |
| 5.2 | canora: corona |
| 5.7 | fuerit: sunt; cum: quid |
| 6.3 | sese dum tempora volvunt: se dudum tempora volutant |
| 12.5 | sollers: solers |

## The Leiden Riddle (LEI)

2b        cændæ *is invisible; the missing text is supplied from EXE 33.2b*

4b        *Only* hygi-ðonc *is visible; the missing text is supplied from EXE 33.4b.*

## The Exeter Book Riddles (EXE)

1.7        hlin: *altered to* hlyn *in the manuscript by a small superscript* i

1.10       heahum: heanū

1.11       wrecen: wrecan

1.19 (1b.4)  *The lacuna is supplied; there is no gap in the manuscript.*

1.32 (1c.2)  sal-wonges: sal wonge

1.33 (1c.3)  þone: *not in the manuscript*

1.35 (1c.5)  hæste: hætst; siteð *altered in the manuscript from* sited

1.37 (1c.7)  aglace: aglaca

1.38 (1c.8)  hrere: hrera

1.42 (1c.12)  aþringe: *altered in the manuscript from* þringe *in a different hand*

1.46 (1c.16)  tæcneð: *altered in the manuscript from* tacneð

1.48 (1c.18)  streamas *not in the manuscript*; þywan: þyran

1.49 (1c.19)  winneð *altered in the manuscript from* win/ned

1.51 (1c.21)  dun *altered in the manuscript from* dum

1.62 (1c.32)  bifohten *altered in the manuscript from* bifonten

1.64 (1c.34)  þær þe ic yrnan: þara / þe ic hyran

1.65 (1c.35)  gestilleð *altered in the manuscript from* gestilled

1.71 (1c.41)  sceor: sceo

1.75 (1c.45)  dreorgum: dreontum

1.77 (1c.47)  swinsendu: sumsen/du

1.81 (1c.51)  brogan *altered in the manuscript from* bratan

1.86 (1c.56)  læteð *altered in the manuscript from* lætað

1.87 (1c.57)  færende: ferende

1.92 (1c.62)  brunra: byrnan

1.95 (1c.65)  on *not in the manuscript*

1.96 (1c.66)  gemagnad: ge/manad

1.99 (1c.69)  hean: heah

2.2        hringum: hringan

2.8        hwilum *altered in the manuscript from* hwilcum

| | |
|---|---|
| 3.5 | guð-gewinnes *altered in the manuscript from* gudgewinnes |
| 3.6 | forwurðe: for wurde |
| 3.8 | hond-weorc: ꝼweorc |
| 4.10 | bete: betan |
| 6.8 | sittað: siteð |
| 6.9 | þe: þa; scernicge: scirenige |
| 6.11 | fela: *with the final letter over an erasure* |
| 7.1 | ofgeafun: ofgeafum |
| 7.3 | an *not in the manuscript* |
| 7.4 | þeccan: weccan |
| 7.6 | swa arlice: snearlice |
| 8.7 | hrægle: hrægl |
| 9.2 | hafu *not in the manuscript* |
| 9.9 | bringað: bringeð |
| 10.6 | beorne: beorn |
| 11.6 | siðe: side; sarre: sarra |
| 12.1 | wigan: wiga |
| 12.9 | on *not in the manuscript* |
| 12.14 | on *not in the manuscript* |
| 12.17 | wraþum: wraþþum |
| 13.2 | swift *altered in the manuscript from* swist |
| 13.4 | swe on hleorum: sweon leorum |
| 13.6 | grene: grenne |
| 13.9 | bold: blod |
| 13.14 | æfterweard *altered in the manuscript from* æfter wearð |
| 13.15 | breost berað: berað / breost; bidan: biddan |
| 13.16 | ne ic: nele |
| 13.21 | on degolne: *altered in the manuscript from* ondo / golne; dun-þyrel: dum þyrel |
| 13.24 | gif se: gifre |
| 13.29 | lað-gewinnan: laðgewin / num; fleah *altered in the manuscript from* flean |
| 14.2 | fremman *not in the manuscript* |
| 14.4 | strong: *altered in the manuscript from* strdng |
| 15.5 | frea: freo |
| 15.8 | brunum *altered in the manuscript from* brumum |

| | |
|---|---|
| 16.1 | wunderlicu *altered in the manuscript from* wundor licu |
| 16.3 | *The lacuna is supplied; there is no gap in the manuscript.* |
| 17.1 | on siþe *not in the manuscript* |
| 17.3 | swiftne: swist / ne |
| 17.8 | hit: ic |
| 18.3 | seomað *altered in the manuscript from* seo / mad |
| 18.7 | smiþa *altered in the manuscript from* smiþe |
| 18.8 | geardas *altered in the manuscript from* geardus |
| 18.29 | geara: gearo |
| 18.34 | firenaþ *altered in the manuscript from* firenuw |
| 18.35 | *a leaf is missing after* compes |
| 19.5 | wrigaþ: wriguþ |
| 19.7 | bearwe: bearme |
| 20.17 | ne under: neon der |
| 21.1 | onhwyrfed *altered in the manuscript from* onhwyrfeð |
| 21.9 | æror: ær |
| 21.14 | full-wered: full wer |
| 23.10 | seo: se |
| 24.3 | dyfde *altered in the manuscript from* difde |
| 24.6 | ecg: ecge |
| 24.8 | geondsprengde: geond |
| 24.12 | hyde: hyþe |
| 24.13 | glisedon: gliwedon |
| 25.7 | weorpe: weorpere |
| 25.8 | esne: efne |
| 25.9 | onfindeð *altered in the manuscript from* onfindet |
| 26.9 | þær þær: þara þeær |
| 26.10 | wiht: wið |
| 27.2 | hornum bitweonum: horna abitweonū |
| 27.5 | atimbran: atimbram |
| 27.9 | bedraf: bedræf |
| 27.11 | onette: o / netteð |
| 28a.7 | onhnigaþ: on hin gaþ |
| 29:4 | nower werum: onwerum |
| 29.6 | niþerweard: niþer wearð; onhwyrfed *not in the manuscript* |
| 29.15 | habbað: habbad |

| | |
|---|---|
| 29.18 | woðgiefu *altered in the manuscript from* wod giefu |
| 29.22 | baru: bær |
| 29.24 | sio *not in the manuscript* |
| 30.2 | wrættum *altered in the manuscript from* wrætum *in a different hand* |
| 30.8 | fela: fella |
| 30.10 | fereð: fere |
| 31.3 | hleahtor: leahtor |
| 31.9 | mægða: mæg / da |
| 31.11 | uploden: upliden |
| 33.8 | am: amas |
| 33.14 | gewæde: ge wædu |
| 35.4 | þæt: þær |
| 36.2 | geoguð-myrþe: geoguð myrwe |
| 37.2 | tidum *altered in the manuscript from* tilum |
| 37.4 | maran: maram |
| 37.10 | folme: folm |
| 37.11 | eagena hafað ægþer: eage neægþer |
| 37.21 | wuldor-cyninges: wuldor / cyninge |
| 37.24 | is *not in the manuscript* |
| 37.27 | heo ænig: hehænig |
| 38.2 | wealdeð *not in the manuscript* |
| 38.3 | rice: ric |
| 38.11 | betyned *altered in the manuscript from* betyneð |
| 38.23 | micle *not in the manuscript* |
| 38.25 | *The lacuna is supplied; there is no gap in the manuscript.* |
| 38.42 | þes: þæs |
| 38.49 | waroð *altered in the manuscript from* warod |
| 38.56 | Ic eom *not in the manuscript* |
| 38.61 | þe *not in the manuscript* |
| 38.63 | þyrse: þyrre |
| 38.70 | snelra: snel / ro þonne |
| 38.72 | is: Ic |
| 38.77 | on flode: onflonde |
| 38.78 | heardre *altered in the manuscript from* heardra; fyr *followed by an erasure* |
| 38.84 | eaþe *not in the manuscript* |

| | |
|---|---|
| 38.88 | þonne *not in the manuscript* |
| 38.91 | onþunian: onrinnan |
| 38.100 | brucan *altered in the manuscript from* brucam |
| 38.106 | bearg *altered in the manuscript from* bear; þe *not in the manuscript* |
| 38.108 | *A leaf is missing after* he; *the text resumes at 39.1.* |
| 40.4 | speow: speop |
| 40.11 | swa ic: hwylc; þæs: wæs |
| 42.7 | efenlang: efe lang |
| 43.1 | weaxan: weax |
| 44.1 | Wer: Wær |
| 44.3 | hyra: hyre |
| 46.1 | for: fer; hring gyddian: hringende an |
| 46.4 | swigende *altered in the manuscript from* swigend |
| 46.7 | beþencan: beþuncan |
| 47.4 | hwilum on þam: hwilū monþā |
| 47.11 | forswilgeð: fer swilgeð |
| 48.4 | forstrangne: fer strangne |
| 48.10 | þam *not in the manuscript* |
| 49.4 | fleag on: fleotgan |
| 49.6 | wegas: wægas |
| 50.3 | genumne: genamne |
| 51.9 | mægen: mæg |
| 52.2 | in wincle: Inwinc sele |
| 52.4 | hrand: rand |
| 52.9 | þon hio: þon hie ó |
| 53.1 | healle: heall |
| 54.7 | biid-fæst: biid fæft; dreag *altered in the manuscript from* dretg |
| 54.9 | torhtan *altered in the manuscript from* torhtun |
| 54.12 | flana: flan |
| 56.6 | mon-dryhtne: dryht / ne |
| 56.15 | foran: furum |
| 57.1 | gyldenne: gylddenne |
| 57.3 | friþo-spede: friþo spe / |
| 57.9 | æþelestan: æþelan |
| 57.11 | ond *not in the manuscript*; dryhtnes: dryht |
| 57.13 | ungefullodre: ungaful lodre |

57.17   þa *altered in the manuscript from* þe
58.1    sonde *altered in the manuscript from* sunde
58.9    meodu-bence: meodu
58.12   seaxes: seaxeð
58.15   twam: twan
59.8    mec: þemec
60.1    hin-gonges: Ingonges
60.7    fereð: fareð
60.9    hatte *altered in the manuscript from* natte
61.1    secga: secgan *altered in the manuscript from* secgun
61.7–13 *There is significant physical damage in the manuscript.*
61.7    willan: *only* willa *visible in the manuscript*
61.11   siþþan: *only* þþan *visible in the manuscript*
61.14   torhte: *only* r.te *visible in the manuscript*; sohte: *supplied; the manu-script is damaged*
61.15   receleas: *only* leas *visible in the manuscript*
62.1    faran *altered in the manuscript from* fanan
64.1    middan-geard: mindan geard
64.4    þes: þas
64.9    ealne: ealdne
64.10   me: mec
65.1    þinge: *only* þing *visible in the manuscript*
65.2–9  *There is significant physical damage in the manuscript.*
65.3    snyttro: *only* snytt *visible in the manuscript*
65.4    gehwylcum: *only* gehw *visible in the manuscript*
65.7    folme: *supplied; the manuscript is damaged*
65.11   awa to: *supplied; the manuscript is damaged*
67.1    hyre: hyra
67.4    dreogeð: *supplied; a leaf is missing after* gesceapo; *the text resumes at* 68.1
69.7–10 *There is significant physical damage in the manuscript.*
69.9    gold-dryhtne: *only* go..dryhtne *visible in the manuscript*
70.1–5  *There is significant physical damage in the manuscript.*
70.5    mec fægre: *only* me. *visible in the manuscript*
70.12   mearc-paþas træd: mearc paþas walas træd
71.1    wunode: wonode

| | |
|---|---|
| 71.2 | heofon-wolcn: heofon wlonc |
| 71.8 | bysigod: *only* bysigo *visible in the manuscript* |
| 71.9–20 | *There is significant physical damage in the manuscript.* |
| 71.10 | dri: *only* .ri *visible in the manuscript* |
| 71.11 | mærþa: *only* mær.a *visible in the manuscript* |
| 71.13 | mec: *only* ec *visible in the manuscript* |
| 71.15 | stæpe: *only* stæp *visible in the manuscript* |
| 71.23 | þristra: þrista |
| 71.24 | brægn-locan: hrægn / locan; *a half-line at least is missing, but there is no gap in the manuscript* |
| 71.29 | siþas: wisan |
| 72.5 | ferð: forð |
| 74.1 | Sæ: Se |
| 74.7–8 | *there is significant physical damage in the manuscript* |
| 74.7 | ond mec hraþe: *only* ec hr.þe *visible in the manuscript* |
| 75.1–8 | *there is significant physical damage in the manuscript* |
| 75.2 | leas cynne: *only* s cynn. *visible in the manuscript* |
| 75.5 | dyde me to mose: *only* . . .yde me to mos. . . *visible in the manuscript* |
| 77.1 | bylged-breost: by led breost |
| 77.4 | hneccan *altered in the manuscript from* neccan |
| 77.5 | sagol: sag |
| 77.10–12 | *there is significant physical damage in the manuscript* |
| 77.10 | forst mec freoseð: .orst . . .eoseð |
| 77.11 | on *not in the manuscript*; þolige: *only* .ol. . . *visible in the manuscript* |
| 78.1–6 | *there is significant physical damage in the manuscript* |
| 78.1 | wundorlic: *supplied; the manuscript is damaged* |
| 78.4 | fell: *only* ell *visible in the manuscript* |
| 79.1–3 | *There is significant physical damage in the manuscript.* |
| 79.1 | from-cynn: from cym |
| 79.3 | lige: life |
| 79.4 | gefælsad *altered in the manuscript from* gefælsað |
| 79.9 | hæft-nyd: onhæft nyd |
| 80.1 | on eorþan *not in the manuscript*; acenned: acenneð |
| 80.3 | fareð *altered in the manuscript from* farað |

80.11–20 *There is significant physical damage in the manuscript.*

80.11 mægen halges gæstes: *only* mæ. . .es gæ. . . *visible in the manuscript*

80.12 meahta sped: *only* ed *visible in the manuscript*

80.15 þonne: *only* onne *visible in the manuscript*

80.17 æfter: *only* fter *visible in the manuscript*

80.19 æror: ær

80.33 mægen: mæge

80.34 *The lacuna is supplied; there is no gap in the manuscript.*

80.39 *The lacuna is supplied; there is no gap in the manuscript.*

80.43–56 *There is significant physical damage in the manuscript.*

80.43 sceafte: *only* s.eafte *visible in the manuscript*

80.48 eorþan getenge: *only* etenge *visible in the manuscript*

80.52 wudu: *only* du *visible in the manuscript*

80.53 cneorisse: *only* risse *visible in the manuscript*

80.55 onwreoh: *only* wreoh *visible in the manuscript*

80.56 cynna: *only* cy *visible in the manuscript*

81.2 *The lacuna is supplied; there is no gap in the manuscript*; dryhten: dryht

81.3 swiftre: swistre

81.5 rinnan: yrnan

82.5 hrycg: hryc

82.7 hio: ic

83.3 mægen-strong: mẹgen / strong

83.5 *The lacuna is supplied; there is no gap in the manuscript.*

83.8–84.9 *There is significant physical damage in the manuscript.*

84.1 stod: *only* sto *visible in the manuscript*

84.5 stod: *only* d *visible in the manuscript*; staðole: *only* staðol *visible in the manuscript*

84.8 ofgeaf: *only* fgeaf *visible in the manuscript*

84.9 ær aweox: *supplied*

84.10 min: mine

84.18 innaþ *not in the manuscript*; blæc: bæc

84.22 stondan: stodan

84.29 nu: hu

84.31–85.11 *There is significant physical damage in the manuscript.*

| | |
|---|---|
| 86.1 | mihi videtur: uidetur mihi |
| 86.2 | rupi *not in the manuscript* |
| 86.3 | mirarem: misarem |
| 86.4 | parem: magnan; duo: dui; tribulantes: tribul |
| 87.1 | geþruen: geþuren |
| 88.3 | weres *not in the manuscript*; wynn-staþol: wym staþol |
| 88.5–89.8 | *There is significant physical damage in the manuscript.* |
| 89.4 | hyhtful: *only* hyht *visible in the manuscript* |
| 89.5 | scearpne: *only* rpne *visible in the manuscript* |
| 89.6 | hwilum: *only* wilum *visible in the manuscript* |
| 89.8 | deope: *only* deo *visible in the manuscript* |
| 89.14 | feaxe: feax; on: of |
| 89.15 | gingra: gingran |
| 89.31–90.5 | *There is significant physical damage in the manuscript.* |
| 89.35 | sped: *only* spe *visible in the manuscript* |
| 90.6 | wyrm: *only* w *visible in the manuscript* |
| 91.6 | beorhte: beorhtne |
| 91.9 | sprecan: sprecað |

## The Old English Rune Poem (OER)

| | |
|---|---|
| 8.2 | sorge: forge |
| 9.2 | scuras: scura |
| 11.3 | geworuht: ge worulit |
| 13.3 | wyn: wynan |
| 14.2 | æt wine: *supplied* |
| 15.1 | secg eard: seccard |
| 18.3 | heah: þeah |
| 19.2 | hæleþ ymbe: hæleþe ymb |
| 20.1 | man: an |
| 20.2 | oðrum: odrum |
| 21.2 | neþan: neþun |
| 21.4 | gymeð: gym |
| 22.2 | eft: est |
| 23.2 | rihtes: rihter |
| 23.3 | bolde: blode |

27.3    fyrdgeatewa: fyrd geacewa
28.1    ior: io; eafix: ea fixa
28.2    foldan: faldan

THE RIDDLES OF *SOLOMON AND SATURN II* (SOL)

1.10    willan: wilian
2.7     ond *not in the manuscript*
2.16    standendne: stan dene

SYMPHOSIUS (SYM)

PR.4    semper nobis: nec semper *most manuscripts*
PR.9    tentamine: de nomine *most manuscripts*
PR.15   discrimine: de carmine *most manuscripts*
1.2     utrimque: utrumque *GL*; diverso munere *GLX*: diverso et mu-
        nere *most manuscripts*
6.2     de terra nascor: est domus in alto *DGLX*
14.2    genetricis *DG*: matris *X*
17.2    pepli: telae *X*
18.3    conchilium *G*: *other manuscripts generally have either* concilium *or*
        consilium
24.3    sed multa vivo sagina *X*: non parvam sumo saginam *most manu-
        scripts*
27.1    Graecia: gratia *GL*
37.1    patri matri: patris matri *GL* matris patri *X*
48.3    frondis: frondi *DX*
79.2    iuncta: vincta *D*
81.2    rigent: cregunt *X*
81.3    dum cecidi subito: dum gaudii subito *D* dum misera cecidi *GLX*
83.3    inveni: invenio *X*
84.2    pulchri: functi *most manuscripts*
87.3    corporis: corpora *DGLX*
90.1    futuri: futuro *DGL*
91.1    terrae: diris *X*
92.3    peregit *X*: secuta est *most manuscripts*
93.2    quinque: quique *GLX*

633

## The Bern Riddles (BER)

| | |
|---|---|
| 1.3 | duram: dura *most manuscripts* |
| 2.6 | umbra: *most manuscripts read* umbras *or* umbris |
| 4.5 | nulla: nolo *most manuscripts* |
| 6.1 | nullius: nulli *most manuscripts*; solam: sola *most manuscripts* |
| 9.5 | satura nam victum: *most manuscripts have a selection of* satura(m) nam victu(m) |
| 9.6 | vagantes: *most manuscripts have variously* vacantes, cavantes, *or* cavantis |
| 14.5 | fili: filii *most manuscripts* |
| 21.4 | nulla de venere sumpsi: nullo de ventre resumpsi *most manuscripts* |
| 21.6 | quae: qui *most manuscripts* |
| 28.2 | repletus parva: *most manuscripts read* repleta parvus *or* repleta parvis |
| 28.3 | conlapsus: conlapsa *most manuscripts* |
| 28.4 | effectus: effecta *most manuscripts* |
| 32.6 | quem: quae *most manuscripts* |
| 33.5 | spiritus de corpore parvo: parvo de corpore spiritus *most manuscripts* |
| 36.6 | modica: *most manuscripts read* modicus *or* modicos |
| 37.5 | dente: dentem *most manuscripts* |
| 38.4 | creata: cretam *most manuscripts* |
| 42.1 | durescere: duriscere *most manuscripts* |
| 42.6 | turpescere: turpiscere *most manuscripts* |
| 44.5 | valescit: vilescit *most manuscripts* |
| 50.1 | unum: unus *most manuscripts* |
| 50.2 | genitum: genitus *most manuscripts* |
| 51.1 | natum: natus *most manuscripts* |
| 51.4 | sepultum: sepultus *most manuscripts* |
| 51.5 | eductum: eductus *most manuscripts* |
| 52.3 | filii: fili *most manuscripts* |
| 53.2 | sicca: *most manuscripts have variously* siccus, sicco, *or* siccum |
| 54.6 | sed: *not in the manuscripts* |
| 59.1 | Quo movear gressum nullus cognoscere temptat: *the manuscripts differ wildly* |
| 61.1 | humili . . . loco: humidis . . . locis *most manuscripts* |

## THE VERSES OF A CERTAIN IRISHMAN
## ON THE ALPHABET (ALF)

A.1    prima: mira $F^1LO$

A.3    dira: dura $P^3$

B.3    Si me grece legas: Littera greca manens $P^3$; horto: orto $G$

C.2    clarus clerus *corrected by means of superscript in* L

D.1    vox: mox $F^1O$

D.2    Omnipotentis habens nomen: Omnitenens nomen et habens
       $LG$; iuncta: vincta $F^1$

E.3    *the second* pars *is missing in* $F^2GLP^3$

F.2    Hebreus odit: odit Hebraeus $P^3$ ebrius odit $G$

G.1    legeres: recites $P^5$

G.1–2  tunc . . . legeres *is missing from* B *by eye-skip*

G.2    Si . . . legeres . . . habebor: has Si . . . vero . . . honorus $P^3$

H.2    manet: valet $P^3$

I.3    Me: Ne $P^3$

K.2    Meque meo: Denique me $O$ Deque meo $F^1F^2$; pepulerunt: pel-
       lerunt $L$

K.3    habebar: habebor $G$

M.2    tollas me non: ne tollas me $P^3$; genitrice: genitricis $G$

M.3    Ne atra: Neutra $L$

O.1    choris en sum: has chori sensum $P^3$ has choris sensum $G$ chori
       sensu $F^1L$

P.2    potentis: potens $P^3$

P.3    piorum: priorum $LG$

Q.3    quaternae: moderni $O$

R.2    nam: non $F^2GLP^3$

R.3    fueram populi: populi fueram $P^3$

S.3    origine: ordine $GP^3$

T.1    en voluit: assignat $P^5$

V.1    Forma manet: Formaret $F^1F^2$

## THE RIDDLES OF GESTUMBLINDI (GES)

1.1    hafa ek þat vilda: hafa vildak $R^1$ hafa vil ek dag $U^1$

1.2    er ek hafða í gær: þat í gær hafða(k) $R^1U^1$

| | |
|---|---|
| 1.3 | vittu: konungr gettu $H^1$ |
| 1.5 | orða: ok orða $H^1U^1$ |
| 2.1 | fór: fór *not in* $R^1$ |
| 2.4 | vegr var undir: var þeim (þar) vegr $R^1U^1$ |
| 3.1 | drykkja: drykki $R^1$ |
| 3.4 | né in heldr: mjǫðr né $H^1H^2$; mungát: mungatum $U^1$ |
| 4.3 | fyrr: fyrrum $R^1U^1$ |
| 5.2 | ferr: líðr $R^1U^1$ |
| 5.5 | guma: gumna $R^1U^1$ |
| 6.4 | hǫlðum: ýtum $U^1$ |
| 6.5 | við: við *not in* $R^1$ |
| 8.3 | Dellings: dǫglings $H^2H^3$ |
| 8.5 | heljar til: helju til $H^2H^3$ á helvega $R^1U^1$ |
| 9.3 | Dellings: dǫglings $H^2H^3$ |
| 9.4 | ókyrrir: ókvikvir $R^1$ |
| 10.3 | Dellings: dǫglings $H^2H^3$ |
| 11.3 | Dellings: dǫglings $H^2H^3$ |
| 12.3 | Dellings: dǫglings $H^2H^3$ |
| 12.7 | ferr: fram liðr $R^1$ fram gengr $U^1$ |
| 13.3 | Dellings: dǫglings $H^2H^3$ |
| 14.3 | Dellings: dǫglings $H^2H^3$ |
| 14.6 | þat: *not in* $R^1U^1$ |
| 15.3 | Dellings: dǫglings $H^2H^3$ |
| 16.3 | Dellings: dǫglings $H^2H^3$ |
| 16.6–7 | *reversed in* $R^1U^1$ |
| 16.7 | skjalli: skildi $R^1$ |
| 17.4 | ǫlker: ǫl $H^2H^3R^1$ áðr $U^1$ |
| 17.6 | hamri: hmri at $R^1$ |
| 17.8 | orðigr: konungr $U^1$ |
| 18.4 | mær við meyju: *not in* $R^1$ |
| 18.5 | mǫg of getr: þar til er mǫg of getr $R^1$ |
| 19.1 | snótir: brúðir $H^2H^3R^1$ drósir $U^1$ |
| 19.2 | um: *not in* $R^1$ |
| 19.3 | vápnlausar: vápnlausan $R^1$ |
| 19.4 | inar jǫrpu: jǫrpsku $H^2H^3$ jarpari $R^1$ *not in* $U^1$ |
| 20.3 | at forvitni fǫður: *not in* $R^1U^1$ |

20.5    þær um vetr bera: þær á við síðu vetrum bera $H^2H^3$ þær um haust bera $U^1$

21.2    ganga syrgjandi: ganga margar $R^1$

21.4    mǫrgum mǫnnum: mǫrgum hafr manni $H^2H^3U^1$

22.5    hvítfǫldnu: hvítfǫlduðu $R^1$

22.6    eigu-t: eigur $H^2H^3$ eigu $R^1$

23.2    brimserkjum í: í brimskerjum $R^1$ í brimserkjum $U^1$

23.3    eiga: eigu $U^1$

23.5    inar: konur $R^1U^1$; hvítfǫldnu: hvítfǫlduðu $R^1$

23a.4   blíðar: blíðir $R^1$

23a.6   eigu: eigu þær $R^1$

24.1    ek sá: søg $R^1$ sá ek $U^1$

24.3    nár: naðr $H^2H^3R^1U^1$

24.6    jór: þá jór $R^1$

25.3    kringt: kringr $R^1$

25.6    ok rennr sem renna má: ok fylgja því margir mjǫk $R^1$ ok fylgja margir $U^1$

26.6    sumum: firum $R^1$

26.8    gumi: guma $U^1$

27.1    næsta: mjǫk $H^2H^3R^1$ nær $U^1$

28.1–2  *reversed in* $R^1U^1$

28.6    ok oftast óhreinn: jafnan heldr saurugr $R^1U^1$

29.5    fagrgjarni: fjárgjarni $H^2H^3$ fárgjarni $U^1$

31.3    ok eru sextán saman: (all)sáttir allir saman $R^1U^1$

31.6    at byggja bólstaði: at sigra menn sérhverja $U^1$

32.2    sólbjǫrgum í: sólbjǫrg of á $R^1$ selbjǫrgum á $U^1$

32.3    verðung vaka: bað ek vel lifa $R^1$; vaka: vuka $U^1$

32.4    teita: teiti $R^1$

34.3    blóðshol: blóðshol $H^2H^3$ blóþ hold $R^1$ *not in* $U^1$

34.4    viðar: virðar $R^1$


## Various Riddles (XMS)

P1.7    per horas: *not in the manuscript*

S2.1    membris: menbris

S3.2    aeque: *not in the manuscript*

# Notes to the Translations

The notes given here are based on abbreviated and sim-
plified versions of those found alongside full introductions
to individual authors and texts, in the companion pages of
*COEALRT,* to which specific reference is sometimes given.
The focus here is on giving the preferred solutions to individual riddles and *aenigmata,* some (but by no means all) of
which are transmitted in the manuscripts themselves (see
further the *Index of Solutions* below). In explaining points of
detail and putative connections between successive texts
and giving brief explanatory notes of specific points of detail, as well as basic bibliographical information and suggestions for further reading, I have attempted to emphasize
potential links between texts, especially those in different
languages; where logographs, or letter games, are involved, I
have used the symbol "→" to highlight the putative (or, more
often, necessary) connection.

## ALDHELM (ALD)

I have consulted translations by James H. Pitman, *The Riddles of Aldhelm,*
Yale Studies in English 67 (New Haven, 1925), 3–67; Michael Lapidge and
James L. Rosier, *Aldhelm: The Poetic Works* (Cambridge, 1985), 70–94;
Nancy Porter Stork, *Through a Gloss Darkly: Aldhelm's Riddles in the British*

*Library MS Royal 12.C.xxiii,* Studies and Texts 98 (Toronto, 1990), 93–238; A. M. Juster, trans., *Saint Aldhelm's Riddles* (Toronto, 2015). See also the more detailed commentary in *COEALRT.*

For further reading, see in general Pitman, *Riddles of Aldhelm;* A. Campbell, "Some Linguistic Features of Early Anglo-Latin Verse and Its Use of Classical Models," *Transactions of the Philological Society* (1953): 1–20; V. M. Lagorio, "Aldhelm's *Aenigmata* in Codex Vaticanus Palatinus Latinus 1719," *Manuscripta* 15 (1971): 23–27; Nicholas Howe, "Aldhelm's *Enigmata* and Isidorian Etymology," *Anglo-Saxon England* 14 (1985): 37–59; Lapidge and Rosier, *Aldhelm: The Poetic Works;* M. L. Cameron, "Aldhelm as Naturalist: A Re-Examination of Some of His *Enigmata,*" *Peritia* 4 (1985): 117–33; Andy Orchard, "After Aldhelm: The Teaching and Transmission of the Anglo-Latin Hexameter," *Journal of Medieval Latin* 2 (1992): 96–133; Andy Orchard, *The Poetic Art of Aldhelm,* Cambridge Studies in Anglo-Saxon England 8 (Cambridge, 1994); Peter Dale Scott, "Rhetorical and Symbolic Ambiguity: The Riddles of Symphosius and Aldhelm," in *Saints, Scholars and Heroes: Studies in Medieval Culture in Honor of Charles W. Jones,* ed. Margot H. King and Wesley M. Stevens (Collegeville, Minn., 1979), vol. 1, pp. 117–44; Stork, *Through a Gloss Darkly;* Čelica Milanović-Barham, "Aldhelm's *Enigmata* and Byzantine Riddles," *Anglo-Saxon England* 22 (1993): 51–64; Emily Thornbury, "Aldhelm's Rejection of the Muses and the Mechanics of Poetic Inspiration in Early Anglo-Saxon England," *Anglo-Saxon England* 36 (2007): 71–92; Carin Ruff, "The Place of Metrics in Anglo-Saxon Latin Education: Aldhelm and Bede," *The Journal of English and Germanic Philology* 104 (2005): 149–70; Mercedes Salvador-Bello, "Patterns of Compilation in Anglo-Latin *Enigmata* and the Evidence of a Source-Collection in Riddles 1–40 of the Exeter Book," *Viator* 43 (2012): 339–74; Mercedes Salvador-Bello, "The Sexual Riddle Type in Aldhelm's *Enigmata,* the Exeter Book, and Early Medieval Latin," *Philological Quarterly* 90 (2012): 357–85; Michael Lapidge, "The Career of Aldhelm," *Anglo-Saxon England* 36 (2007): 15–69; Michael Lapidge, "Aldhelmus Malmesberiensis Abb. et Scireburnensis ep.," in *La transmissione dei testi latini del medioevo/Medieval Latin Texts and Their Transmission: Te. Tra 4,* ed. P. Chiesa and L. Castaldi (Florence, 2012), 14–38.

## ALD PR

As common in the medieval period, the *Preface* provides an opportunity for the author to showcase his talents, and in this elaborate *tour de force* Aldhelm displays both his breadth of learning and his metrical virtuosity. Aldhelm chooses the difficult acrostic-telestic form, where each line begins and ends with the same letters, reading in sequence yet another hexameter line of verse proclaiming with some exaggeration that "Aldhelm has sung songs in thousands of verses" *(ALDHELMUS CECINIT MIL-LENIS VERSIBUS ODAS)*, and intertwines various biblical and pagan classical stories of poetic inspiration in a manner that is clearly intended to show how those classical models are eclipsed; see further Thornbury, "Aldhelm's Rejection of the Muses."

The *Preface* is packed with biblical reference, beginning in the fourth line, where *Vehemoth* is the spelling used for the biblical *Behemoth*, a conflation of *b/v*-spellings that is characteristic of early Anglo-Saxon texts in both Latin and Old English. In the Bible, Behemoth is a massive creature of uncertain shape, emblematic of evil, that appears in the Old Testament in Job 40:15–24 and Enoch 60:7–8. The biblical story of Moses singing songs after the crossing of the Red Sea, as described in Exodus 15:1–18, is also referenced here; the reference to metrical songs here may refer to Christian Latin versifications of parts of the Bible that formed the backbone of Anglo-Saxon monastic schooling. Likewise, the bringing forth of water from the rock, especially in the context of King David, is found at Psalms 77:16 and 106:9 and Exodus 14:37–15:21. The phrasing from Psalms 77:16 seems closest, saying that "He brought forth water out of the rock: and made streams run down as rivers" *(et eduxit aquam de petra et deduxit tamquam flumina aquas)*. These biblical references to the Old Testament form a frame around some central lines (P. 10–13), referring to a variety of legends concerning poetic inspiration in antique pagan literature, each of which Aldhelm rejects in turn.

According to classical myth, Castalia was the name of a nymph whom Apollo, the god of poetry, turned into a spring and dedicated to the Muses; anyone who drank from this spring was filled with poetic inspiration. The notion of the honeyed words of poetry underlies this verse, which also seems to gesture toward a story about the early inspiration of the influential and famously eloquent fourth-century bishop of Milan, Ambrose (see Lapidge and Rosier, *Aldhelm: The Poetic Works,* 117).

Cynthus is a mountain on the Greek island of Delos, and was the birthplace of Apollo. Parnassus is a mountain that rises above the Greek shrine of Delphi, and was dedicated to Apollo. The Roman poet Persius, in a part of the *Prologue* to his *Satires* that Aldhelm is clearly echoing here, refers to the legend that anyone falling asleep on Parnassus and having the right dream would arise a poet.

## ALD 1

Solution: *TERRA* (earth).
For comparison, see EUS 6, ALC D47, OER 29, BER 45 (all solved "earth").

This *aenigma* celebrates the earth as the mother of all creatures, a commonplace notion that, however, also appears in the opening line of SYM 81. The reference to "nipples" here is striking, albeit emphasizing the poor treatment meted out to the earth, and Aldhelm may be alluding to the idea of *SAPIENTIA* (wisdom) as a woman from whose nipples pour the milk of wisdom, a theme that opens other riddle collections in the tradition, such as ps-BED 1, TAT 1, and BIB 1.

## ALD 2

Solution: *VENTUS* (wind).
For comparison, see EUS 8 (wind and fire); ALC D46 (wind); EXE 1 (wind and God); ps-BED 5, BER 41 (both solved "wind").

This *aenigma* follows the feminine solution of ALD 1 with a masculine one, and emphasizes the omnipresence and extraordinary power of its subject in a manner that seems to have been expanded considerably in EXE 1, which focuses not only on the might of its subject, but also on the power of the individual that controls it, presumably God, with many parallels to ALD 2, and to others of Aldhelm's works.

## ALD 3

Solution: *NUBES* (cloud).
For comparison, see ALC D45, SYM 8 (both solved "cloud").

The multicolored cloud mentioned here follows on naturally from the preceding *aenigma* and looks ahead to the more obviously spectacular ALD 5. The notion of a cloud as an endless traveling exile with no place on earth or in the sky, streaming tears, fits in well with the conception of exiles elsewhere in Old English poetry, notably in several of the so-called elegies in the Exeter Book.

## ALD 4

Solution: *NATURA* (nature).

This *aenigma,* like the previous ones, tends to focus on the most awe-inspiring aspects of the creature in question, and in this case the incomprehensible power of its subject harks back to ALD 2.

## ALD 5

Solution: *IRIS* (rainbow).

In classical myth, Thaumas (whose Greek name means "marvel"), a sea god who was the son of Pontus (sea) and Gaia (earth), was the father of Iris (rainbow); her mother was the sea nymph Electra. The references to wandering, clouds, and wind all link this *aenigma* back to those that precede it.

## ALD 6

Solution: *LUNA* (moon).
For comparison, see ALD 79 (sun and moon); EUS 11, ALC D42 (both solved "moon"); EXE 27 (moon and sun).

The connection with the sea, as well as with brightness, links this *aenigma* to the previous one; the reference to fate binds it to the one that follows.

## ALD 7

Solution: *FATUM* (fate).

Here, as in previous *aenigmata* and in ALD PR, Aldhelm is unafraid to flaunt his classical learning, here quoting a whole line from Virgil, who, despite being a pagan, is called "a skillful poet." The line quoted is from *Aeneid* 12.677, where a warrior doomed to die ruefully acknowledges the implacability of fate.

## ALD 8

Solution: *PLIADES* (Pleiades).

The Pleiades appear in classical myth as seven sisters, daughters of the Titan Atlas; they were immortalized as stars by the god Zeus, and while six of them are plainly visible, the seventh (known as Pleione) is distinctly fainter. Ælfric, writing in the late tenth century in his *De Temporibus Anni* 9.10.70, describes how: *Pliade sind gehatene ða seofon steorran, þe on hærfeste upagað, ond ofer ealne winter scinað* (those seven stars, which rise at harvest time and shine through the winter, are called the Pleiades). As in the previous *aenigma*, Aldhelm appeals here to classical authority, and in speaking of the connection of their name with springtime, acknowledges the fact that an alternative name for the Pleiades was *Vergiliae*, which begins with the Latin word for "spring" *(ver)*. Recollection of that alternative designation links this *aenigma* back to ALD 7, in which the poet Virgil is quoted.

## ALD 9

Solution: *ADAMAS* (diamond).

In Latin, the last line of the previous *aenigma* (ALD 8.5: *verno*) is echoed in the first line here (ALD 9.1: *vereor . . . ferro*), and of course diamonds sparkle like stars, so strengthening the connection; the rest of the largely fictitious diamond lore given here is taken from Isidore, *Etymologiae* 16.13.2, which describes how diamonds cannot be harmed by iron or fire, but can be shattered by iron if first soaked in fresh, warm goat's blood.

## ALD 10

Solution: *MOLOSUS* (mastiff).

The imagery of warfare in the previous *aenigma* is continued here, with the added twist that the fearsome dog is itself armed with fierce teeth (like the creature of ALD 56 [beaver]), but nonetheless, just as a diamond can (apparently) be softened unexpectedly by goat's blood, so too a mastiff can be cowed by a baby.

## ALD 11

Solution: *POALUM* (bellows).
For comparison, see EXE 35, 83, and 85; SYM 73; GES 9 (all solved "bellows"); BER 58–59 (both solved "moon").

The given solution, at least in its Latin form *(poalum)*, derives from confusion arising from a glossary entry; the depiction here, focusing on life and death through the theme of breath and lack of breath, seems to owe much to SYM 73 (bellows).

## ALD 12

Solution: *BOMBIX* (silkworm).
See too Kevin Leahy, *Anglo-Saxon Crafts* (Stroud, 2012), 62.
For comparison, see BER 28 and 43 (both solved "silkworm[s]").In his discussion of silkworms, Isidore, *Etymologiae* 12.5.8, speaks of them being emptied out in the course of spinning thread, a notion that seems to underlie the final line of this *aenigma,* and connects it to the preceding one.

## ALD 13

Solution: *BARBITA* (organ).

The conceptual link between an organ and a pair of bellows seems clear, so connecting this *aenigma* to ALD 11. There is a lengthy description by Wulfstan cantor of Winchester, lines 146–76 (Michael Lapidge, ed. and trans.,

*The Cult of St. Swithun* [Oxford, 2003], 382–87), of an enormous organ, comprising four hundred pipes, the twenty-six bellows of which were apparently worked by no fewer than seventy sweating men.

## ALD 14

Solution: *PAVO* (peacock).

In this *aenigma,* the creature in question is presented as a natural wonder, so beginning a sequence of similarly exotic topics (ALD 14–18). The idea that peacock flesh does not rot seems to derive from a passage in Augustine, *De civitate Dei* 21.4, a chapter that also mentions the salamander, the subject of the *aenigma* that immediately follows here.

## ALD 15

Solution: *SALAMANDRA* (salamander).

Just as the flesh of the peacock does not rot in ALD 14, so too the salamander is unharmed by flames, according to Isidore, *Etymologiae* 12.4.36. The insistently fiery language here is contrasted by the resolutely watery imagery of the two *aenigmata* that follow.

## ALD 16

Solution: *LULIGO* (flying fish).

After an *aenigma* that focuses on fire, this one turns to the elements of air and water, to describe another extraordinary creature, this time the flying fish. Aldhelm's immediate source is likely Isidore, *Etymologiae* 12.6.47.

## ALD 17

Solution: *PERNA* (ham, fan, mussel).

The double quality of the preceding *aenigma,* the subject of which both swims and flies, is here extended to another creature that can apparently supply both food and clothing. This *aenigma* turns on the recognition that, while the usual Latin term for a ham was *perna* (as in SYM 86), the same term could be used to describe a large ham-shaped shellfish, specifically a fan mussel (identified as the bivalve mollusk known scientifically as *pinna nobilis*); the double sense of *perna* also allows for a creature at home both on land and in the sea. The fan mussel is a Mediterranean species, and so continues the exotic flavor of the sequence (ALD 14–18). While it usually grows to a length of one or two feet, it can be twice that size, and it is anchored to the sea floor by fine excreted fibers that were used in antiquity to produce highly prized sea silk, which can be woven even more finely than its insect counterpart; the flesh of the fan mussel could also be eaten. Just as the previous *aenigma* combines the aerial and the marine, so here in the shape of *perna* we find a combination of the marine and the terrestrial; the *aenigma* that follows speaks of a creature that combines the terrestrial and the aerial.

## ALD 18

Solution: *MYRMICOLEON* (antlion).

The double qualities of the other *aenigmata* in this exotic sequence (ALD 14–18) are here taken into the area of etymology, one that is common within the Anglo-Saxon riddle tradition. The antlion is in fact well known to entomology as the ferocious larval stage of a large group of flying insects (mainly lacewing flies) from warmer climes that devour ants in great quantities and even set traps for them by digging holes in the dust. Aldhelm apparently derives his information from Isidore, *Etymologiae* 12.3.10.

## ALD 19

Solution: *SAL* (salt).

While at first glance the topic of this *aenigma* might seem mundane, especially when compared to the exotic qualities of the preceding sequence (ALD 14–18), here too the description makes clear that the creature in question, like its outlandish predecessors, is the product of the combination of two elements, namely fire and water, as if combining aspects of both ALD 15 (salamander) and ALD 16 (flying fish); one notes the verbal parallel in the Latin <u>*SALAMANDRA*</u> and <u>*SAL*</u>, a device employed several times in SYM.

## ALD 20

Solution: *APIS* (bee).
For comparison, see BER 21 (bee[s]).

After the double or exotic qualities of the preceding *aenigmata,* this and the *aenigma* that follows are focused on creatures that are somehow lacking: in this case, hands, in the next, a voice. In this *aenigma,* Aldhelm develops Isidore's (utterly erroneous) etymology, that bees (Latin *apes*) are so called because they are without feet (Latin *a-pes*).

## ALD 21

Solution: *LIMA* (file).
See too Leahy, *Anglo-Saxon Crafts,* 119–21; Dennis Riley, *Anglo-Saxon Tools* (Ely, 2014), 49–51.

Several factors link this *aenigma* to the preceding one, not least the reference to metallic craft; the voiceless nature of the subject here contrasts sharply with the incessantly multivoiced creature of the *aenigma* that follows.

## ALD 22

Solution: *ACALANTIS* (nightingale).
For comparison, see EXE 6 (nightingale).

This *aenigma* is connected to the preceding one by the harshness of voice mentioned in the opening two lines ("voice . . . harsh-sounding"), which picks up the same theme in the last line of ALD 21 ("voice[less] . . . harsh").

## ALD 23

Solution: *TRUTINA* (pair of scales).

Aldhelm tells us that among the subjects he studied at the Canterbury school of Theodore and Hadrian was law; here he introduces the twin ideas of justice and law while apparently describing a simple pair of scales. It is clear that Boniface at least picked up on the hint: he echoes this *aenigma* in his own on both "mercy" (BON 4) and "justice" (BON 6.9). The third line seems to allude to Acts 10:34: "God is no respecter of persons" *(non est personarum acceptor Deus)*.

## ALD 24

Solution: *DRACONTIA* (dragon stone, draconite).

Aldhelm returns to the theme of the exotic in this *aenigma,* which describes a magical gemstone plucked from the head of a dragon. The most detailed account available to Aldhelm would have been in Isidore, *Etymologiae* 16.14.7 (where the stone in question is called *dracontites*); there, Aldhelm would have found the following: *"Dracontites* is snatched from a dragon's brain, and it does not develop into a gemstone, unless it has been cut from a living creature; and so magicians extract it from sleeping dragons. So brave men seek out the caves of dragons, and sprinkle drugged herbs there to cause the dragons to fall asleep, and then they cut off their heads when they are fast asleep and take out the gemstones: they are translucent white. The kings of the East especially glory in their use." Note, however, that Aldhelm evidently believed that the stone in question was bright red; extended versions of the solution state that the stone is so called from dragon's blood.

## ALD 25

Solution: *MAGNES FERRIFER* (magnet).

This *aenigma* links back to the previous one, since, according to Isidore, both the "dragon stone" and the "magnet" *(Etymologiae* 16.4.1) were stones that came from the East, in the case of the magnet, specifically India. The opposition of the magnet to the diamond is explored in ALD 9 *(ADAMAS,* "diamond"), although it is unclear why the diamond should be specified here as coming from Cyprus.

## ALD 26

Solution: *GALLUS* (cock).

There is an obvious pun here on the homonyms *gallus* (cock) and *Gallus* (Gaul, Frank): the latter are the "famous folk" of the third line; the opening line also offers another linguistic clue for those sensitive enough to see an echo of the solution in the very first word of the Latin, *Garrulus* (chatty).

## ALD 27

Solution: *COTICULUS* (whetstone).
For comparison, see TAT 39 (whetstone).

The martial and heroic language of the last few lines of the preceding *aenigma* presumably leads on to this one, which speaks of sharpening iron, most likely weapons. In 27.4 Aldhelm uses a rare spelling variant of the (itself rather infrequent) name *Mulciber* (here *Mulcifer,* using the same alternation witnessed in *Vehemoth* for *Behemoth* at P. 4), instead of Vulcan to signify the smith-god. In any case, the name of the god stands metonymically for "fire."

## ALD 28

Solution: *MINOTAURUS* (Minotaur).

The hybrid Minotaur, part man, part bull, was the product of the union of Pasiphaë, queen of Crete (the capital of which was then at Knossos), with a bull sent by Poseidon, the god of the sea. The watery associations of the gift may connect this *aenigma* to the one that follows.

## ALD 29

Solution: *AQUA* (water).
For comparison, see ALC D50, LOR 3, EXE 39 and 80, OER 21 (all solved "water").

This *aenigma* makes mention of the land and sea and air, and that is presumably why the creature in question can claim a third of the dominion of the world. The "thousand oaks of the forests" are ships (see further EXE 72 and OER 25 below); presumably the "slender point" in question is some hidden rock that might catastrophically breach a ship's hull.

## ALD 30

Solution: *ELEMENTUM* (a letter of the alphabet).
For comparison, see TAT 4, EUS 7, ALC D1, EXE 55, BER 25 (all solved "letter[s]").

Isidore, *Etymologiae* 1.4.10, explains that there were seventeen "letters" (*litterae,* grammatically feminine, hence "sisters") in the original Latin alphabet, *A, B, C, D, E, F, G, I, L, M, N, O, P, R, S, T,* and *U,* and that these were called "legitimate" *(legitimus);* in Latin *I/J* and *U/V* were interchangeable. The other letters (*H, K, Q, X, Y,* and *Z*) were added later, and since they were not "legitimate," are here designated "bastards." Next, Aldhelm refers to two writing tools, namely the stylus (on which see SYM 1) and the quill pen (on which see ps-BED 11, EUS 35, LOR 9, and XMS X3). Toward the end of the *aenigma,* there is a description of the act of writing itself, involving two fingers and a thumb (the Latin for "finger," *digitus,* is masculine, as is that for "thumb," *pollex,* which is why there is a reference to "three brothers"), as well as a writing implement, in this case a quill pen (Latin *penna,* which is why there is a reference to "an unknown mother"); see further EXE 49 (quill pen and fingers).

## ALD 31

Solution: *CICONIA* (stork).
For comparison, see EUS 56 (stork).

Much of the information given here is also found in Isidore, *Etymologiae* 12.7.16. This *aenigma* connects to the last through the shared notion of voicelessness and feathers, as does the specific contrast of black and white noted in the opening line here, which is also common in riddles dealing with script (see further ALD 59). The same association with writing continues in the next *aenigma*.

## ALD 32

Solution: *PUGILLARES* (writing tablets).
For comparison, see XMS S3 (writing tablets).

Folded wooden writing tablets filled with wax were standard equipment in the ancient and early medieval worlds; they could easily be written on with the sharp point of a stylus, and mistakes smoothed over by using the flattened opposite end (see further SYM 1 [stylus]). The Latin name given here *(pugillares)* derives from one meaning a "handful" or a "fistful" *(pugilla)*, so emphasizing the essentially portable nature of the object.

## ALD 33

Solution: *LORICA* (armor).
See too Leahy, *Anglo-Saxon Crafts,* 131–33.

The martial, indeed pugilistic, overtone of the previous *aenigma* is continued here, in the paradox of an item of clothing that is not woven or made of wool or silk. This *aenigma* is the source for both EXE 33 and LEI, and with its reference to "Chinese worms" opens a further exotic sequence that covers Egypt, Greece, and Rome (ALD 33–37).

## ALD 34

Solution: *LOCUSTA* (locust).
See further Erika von Erhardt-Siebold, *Die lateinischen Rätsel der Angelsachsen: Ein Beitrag zur Kulturgeschichte Altenglands,* Anglistische Forschungen 61 (Heidelberg, 1925; repr., Amsterdam, 1974), 221–22.

The reference to the plagues of Egypt connects this *aenigma* to ALD 36 *(SCNIFES,* "gnat," "midge"); for the biblical story, see Exodus 10:4–16.

## ALD 35

Solution: *NYCTICORAX* (night raven).

The hybrid Latin-Greek name emphasizes the twin nature of this creature, whose precise identity is difficult to determine; Isidore, *Etymologiae* 12.7.39–42 distinguishes a *nycticorax* from a *strix* (screech owl) and a *noctua* (night owl), and the word also appears in the Vulgate Psalms 101:7.

## ALD 36

Solution: *SCNIFES* (gnat, midge); alternative spellings are *SCIPHES, SCINIPHES,* and *CINIFES.*

Isidore, *Etymologiae* 12.8.14, says that "*Sciniphes* are very tiny flies, very irritating with their stinging. The proud people of Egypt were struck down by these in the third plague." The reference to the plagues of Egypt connects this *aenigma* back to ALD 34 (*LOCUSTA,* "locust"); the biblical tale is told in Exodus 8:16–18 and Psalms 104:31.

## ALD 37

Solution: *CANCER* (crab).
For comparison, see EXE 75 and 78 (crab).

The Latin word *nepa* usually refers to a scorpion, although it is clear here that a crab is intended, and that the reference is also to the constellation of Cancer. The association of the creature in question with all three of the elements of earth, sea, and sky is a theme common in the riddle tradition; the antipathy of crabs and oysters, described by Isidore, *Etymologiae* 12.6.51–52 (who makes it clear that the crab does not smash the oyster's shell with stones, but simply props open the already open shell and feasts on the exposed flesh) is explored further in consecutive riddles in EXE 74 and 75.

## ALD 38

Solution: *TIPPULA* (water strider).

Just as the crab in the previous *aenigma* traverses different elements (in that case, land and sea and sky), so here the creature in question travels over water as if it were dry land.

## ALD 39

Solution: *LEO* (lion).

This *aenigma,* connected conceptually and verbally to the preceding one by a lack of fear, is unusual in tallying up four different kinds of quintessentially fierce and masculine animal that are emphatically *not* the subject, namely boars, stags, bears, and wolves. Aldhelm evidently derives much of his information from Isidore, *Etymologiae* 12.2.3–5.

## ALD 40

Solution: *PIPER* (pepper).
For comparison, see BER 37 (pepper).

The exotic nature of the lion that is the subject of the previous *aenigma* is repeated here, since in Anglo-Saxon England pepper was very much a luxury item; here Aldhelm uses the creature in question as a springboard for describing a variety of foods.

## ALD 41

Solution: *PULVILLUS* (pillow).
For comparison, see ALC D96 (pillow).

This *aenigma* at first glance looks like an extension of the exotic topics covered in the previous *aenigmata,* but the language of disbelief in the opening lines is evidently a mask for rather a mundane subject, albeit one also considered in ALC D83.

## ALD 42

Solution: *STRUTIO* (ostrich).
For comparison, see EUS 57 (ostrich).

This *aenigma* returns to the exotic, with its reference to the "African land of the Phoenicians," albeit a theme that is both biblical (Job 39:13–18) and found in the usual encyclopedic sources, notably Pliny, *Naturalis Histo-*

*ria* 10.1, and Isidore, *Etymologiae,* 12.7.20. The same topic is addressed in EUS 57.

## ALD 43

Solution: *SANGUISUGA* (leech).

The bloodthirsty, fen-dwelling creature seems at first to evoke the notion of a Grendel, but Aldhelm's immediate source was more likely Isidore, *Etymologiae* 12.5.3, where it is noted that "the leech is a kind of water-dwelling vermin, so called because it sucks blood. It lies in wait for creatures when they are drinking, and when it slips into their throat, or attaches itself somewhere, it gorges on their blood. When it is drenched by too much blood, it vomits out what it has gorged so that it may again suck fresher blood." The apparent reference in the final lines to the medicinal use of leeches is backed up by the fact that "leech" (Old English *læca*), and other compounds, routinely refer to the craft of a healer.

## ALD 44

Solution: *IGNIS* (fire).
For comparison, see TAT 31 and 33, ALC D51 and D73, EXE 48, GES 29 (all solved "fire").

This *aenigma* celebrates the awesome if destructive power of its subject, with its frightening consumption linking back to the previous *aenigma.* The precise identities of the "father and mother" in the opening line are somewhat opaque; it does not help that the Latin word for "flint" (as at SYM 76 and 76a) occurs with both genders.

## ALD 45

Solution: *FUSUM* (spindle).

The description here is of a wooden, stone-weighted spindle, evidently drawing out a very lengthy thread. The reference to the Fates (Latin *Parcae*) is to the mythical three sisters who wove the fates of men.

## ALD 46

Solution: *URTICA* (nettle).

This *aenigma* has several resemblances to SYM 44 (onion), and is a further example of the "biter-bitten" motif that is prevalent in the Anglo-Saxon riddle tradition.

## ALD 47

Solution: *HIRUNDO* (swallow).

The rather startling lore recounted here derives ultimately from Isidore, *Etymologiae* 17.9.36, who notes of the plant celandine that: "the celandine (*chelidonia*) is so called either because it seems to burgeon with the coming of swallows (χηλιδών, in Greek, transliterated as *chelidon* in Latin) or because if the eyes of swallow chicks are picked out, their mothers are said to heal them with this herb." Note that in combining reference to more than one element (here the earth-bound plant and the airborne swallow), this *aenigma* introduces a sequence of creatures at home in such combinations.

## ALD 48

Solution: *VERTICO POLI* (sphere of the heavens).

This is the spelling of the solution found in the manuscripts; the usual spelling is *VERTIGO* (compare ALD 63 below). This all-embracing *aenigma* covers earth, sea, and sky, so leading on naturally from the preceding one, which combined only two of those areas. For a similar topic, see ALD 53.

## ALD 49

Solution: *LEBES* (cauldron).
For comparison, see ps-BED 10, ALC D76, XMS X1 (all solved "cauldron").

This *aenigma* considers the conflict between fire and water; the same subject is addressed in different ways in ps-BED 10 and ALC D76. For a similar topic, see ALD 54.

## ALD 50

Solution: *MYRIFYLLON* (milfoil yarrow).

The phrase "thousand-leafed one" essentially translates the Latin solution for what is generally called the yarrow plant; the reference to both Greek and Latin languages aligns this *aenigma* with the preceding hybrid forms.

## ALD 51

Solution: *ELIOTROPUS* (heliotrope).

The reference to both Latin and Greek names here links this *aenigma* to the one immediately preceding, the subject of which is another plant; this is one of several *aenigmata* that play explicitly on perceived Greek etymology (see further ALD 18, 35, and 60).

## ALD 52

Solution: *CANDELA* (candle).
For comparison, see EUS 28 (candle).

This *aenigma* leads on from the last through its focus on light and burning; just as the flower is associated with daylight, so too the candle is linked to night. There is a subtle nudge toward the solution in the second line, in the Latin for "my innards shine" *(interiora mihi candescunt)*.

## ALD 53

Solution: *ARCTURUS* (Arcturus).

Following on from the heat of the preceding *aenigma,* this one focuses on its opposite. The Latin Arcturus is ultimately derived from the Greek word for "bear" (ἄρκτος), and is associated with the larger constellation usually known as the "Great Bear" (Latin *Ursa Major*), a constituent part of which is the so-called "Big Dipper" or "Wagon" (here ironically designated "in common speech" by the distinctly uncommon Latin word *esseda*), consisting of seven stars, the same number as make up the Pleiades. There seems little that is meant to be specific in the reference to the Rhipaean mountains of Scythia, presumably a shorthand for some bleak, cold, and remote place, famously the birthplace of the biting north winds. For a riddle on the same topic, see EXE 20 (Charles's Wain), and ALC D66–71 on the classical motif of the wagon of the heavens; on the Pleiades, see ALD 8 above.

## ALD 54

Solution: *COCUMA DUPLEX* (double boiler).

After the extreme cold of the previous *aenigma,* there is a return here both to the heat of ALD 52, and to the hybrid mixtures of ALD 50 and 51, while the general topic of the clash between fire and water in a cooking vessel is also echoed in ALD 50, so lending a tight structure to this sequence as a whole.

## ALD 55

Solution: *CRISMAL* (chrismal).

In Anglo-Saxon churches, a chrismal was used to house the eucharist, and the description given here is a of a square box, somewhat in the shape of a house, the lid of which needed to be removed to grant access to the wafer of the host. There are broad parallels between this *aenigma* and TAT 12 (paten).

## ALD 56

Solution: *CASTOR* (beaver).
For comparison, see OER 28 (beaver).

The beaver was only made extinct in Britain during the sixteenth century, though such animals were becoming progressively rare from the twelfth century on. While Aldhelm may well have seen beavers at first hand, it is also likely that he was working from written sources. The mock-heroic style here is found commonly elsewhere in the riddle tradition, where animals are often endowed with "weapons": here the "axes" wielded by the creature in question are of course the teeth used to fell trees (for another "armed" creature, see ALD 10 [mastiff]). As a concomitant to such martial language, we are also told that the beaver (or more correctly the castoreum it secretes) was used for treating a range of conditions.

## ALD 57

Solution: *AQUILA* (eagle).

The *aenigma* begins with a reference to the beautiful Trojan shepherd boy Ganymede, snatched up and carried off by the pagan (and so "accursed") Greek god Zeus, who had transformed himself into an eagle. Although the story is given as if in the form of a series of quoted phrases, there are not always precise parallels to be identified. The last few lines recall the myth of the rejuvenated phoenix, and, in the imagery of being dipped in rejuvenating streams, link forward to the *aenigma* that follows.

## ALD 58

Solution: *VESPER SIDUS* (evening star).

The "early hours of the night" are, of course, in monastic terms, "vespers" (Latin *vesper,* "evening"), so lending a broad hint as to the solution. The way the evening star dips into the cooling waters recalls the language of the previous *aenigma.*

## ALD 59

Solution: *PENNA* (pen).
For comparison, see TAT 6 (pen).

The pelican imagery that opens this *aenigma* may connect it to the previous one, through a shared Christological theme: according to ancient tradition, pelicans wound themselves in the breast and use their own blood to rejuvenate their dead young, and Early Christian writers pick up on this image as a symbol of Christ's own self-sacrifice. Such a tradition is preserved alongside other christianizing interpretations of the animal world in the so-called *Physiologus*, versions of which are certainly found in both Latin and Old English in Anglo-Saxon England. The black-on-white theme also found here is likewise a commonplace of riddles on writing within the tradition.

## ALD 60

Solution: *MONOCERUS* (unicorn).

The creature in question fears no battles ("the contests of cruel Mars," since Mars is the Roman god of war), nor human hunters, and can even face up to an elephant unafraid, yet crumples before a maiden. Aldhelm's source is undoubtedly Isidore, *Etymologiae* 12.2.12–13, albeit there talking about a rhinoceros: "The rhinoceros (*rhinoceron*) is named by the Greeks; in Latin it means 'horn on the nose.' The same creature is a *monoceron*, that is, a unicorn (*unicornus*), because it has a single horn four feet long in the middle of its forehead, so sharp and strong that whatever it attacks it tosses in the air or impales. It often fights with the elephant and after wounding it in the belly throws it down to the ground. It has such strength that it can be captured by no hunter's ability, but, as those who have written about the natures of animals claim, if a virgin girl is placed before it, as the beast approaches, she may open her lap and it will lay its head there with all its fierceness set aside, and thus lulled and disarmed it may be captured."

## ALD 61

Solution: *PUGIO* (dagger).

Misdirection is in evidence throughout this *aenigma*, which never mentions metal, but instead seems rather to come from the natural world rather than that of human craftsmanship; for a similar strategy, compare EXE 20 (sword, man), which may have been inspired in that regard by this very *aenigma*. Indeed, more space is given to the sheath, made of wood and leather from bulls and goats, rather than to the deadly blade itself.

## ALD 62

Solution: *FAMFALUCA* (bubble).
For comparison, see BER 7 (bubble).

The solution preferred for this *aenigma* is the ultimately Latin version of the Greek πομφόλυξ, presumably via some garbled form of *pomfalux*. It is in any case an extremely rare term, and an Old English gloss, meaning "froth" or "foam," is perhaps more helpful.

## ALD 63

Solution: *CORBUS* (raven).

This is the spelling of the solution found in the manuscripts; the usual spelling is *CORVUS* (see further the note at ALD PR above). The watery sense of the previous *aenigma* leads into one of the most obvious sequences in this collection: ALD 63 and 64 retell the story of the Flood, through the release of first a black raven and then a white dove from the ark. The raven fails to return, but instead was held to feed on carcasses, so proving faithless to Noah ("refusing to submit to patriarchal authority"), while the dove at first returns, having failed to find dry land, but when sent again a week later does not, signaling that the Flood is receding. The biblical references are to Genesis 8:6–7 and 8:8–9, respectively. The direct quotation in the seventh line is from the Christian-Latin poet Caelius Sedulius (*Carmen paschale* 1.175), whose works were widely studied in Anglo-Saxon schools, and contrasts the faithless behavior of the raven on the water with the later feeding of the prophet Elijah on land (1 Kings 17:1–6). The final line is a letter riddle or logogriph: removing the first letter from *corbus* (raven) produces *orbus* (bereaved, childless). The usual spelling of the Latin word is *corvus*, the *b/v*-spelling conflation is typical of early Anglo-Saxon texts, and is found in both Latin and Old English.

## ALD 64

Solution: *COLUMBA* (dove).
For comparison, see XMS Y1 (Noah and the dove).

This *aenigma* is closely connected to the preceding one: see the note there.

## ALD 65

Solution: *MUSIO* (mouser); the various manuscripts give, with various degrees of glossing, *MURICEPS* (mouse catcher) and *DE CATTO VEL MURICIPE VEL PILACE* (on a cat or a mouse catcher or a kitty).

By comparison with the spelling riddle, or logograph, in the last line of ALD 63, another type of word game is evident in the last line here, where the enemy of the cat, a "mouse" (Latin *mus*), is literally contained in the solution, hence "mouser" (Latin *musio*).

## ALD 66

Solution: *MOLA* (mill, millstone).
For comparison, see SYM 51, BER 9 (both solved "millstone").

This *aenigma* seems closely based on SYM 51, of which it seems a simple elaboration.

## ALD 67

Solution: *CRIBELLUS* (sieve).
For comparison, see BER 17 (sieve).

The connection between this *aenigma* and the last is obvious. The sieved flour (here described as "snow"; the same term is used of flour in ALD 70 [loaf of bread]) would have been used in baking and brewing; the last lines here, referring to the paradoxical effect of fire on this "snow," which does not melt but rather hardens, evidently describes baking.

## ALD 68

Solution: *SALPIX* (trumpet).

This *aenigma* divides easily into three parts: the opening couplet stresses the martial context of the item in question, but is then followed by three lines emphasizing the thing's essential emptiness, expanding on the opening words *(sum cava);* the final three lines inject a rather learned note, and link back to the earlier *aenigma* on the nightingale (ALD 22 [nightingale]).

## ALD 69

Solution: *TAXUS* (yew).
For comparison, see OER 13, OIR 16 (both solved "yew tree").

With another kind of misdirection, Aldhelm's description of the poisonous yew focuses not on the tree that is the subject, but on the various winds that batter it (as, in reverse, ALD 2, on "wind," focuses on the oak that is battered). The specific winds mentioned here come from broadly similar directions: Circius from the northwest, Boreas from the north or northeast, and Caurus from the northeast or northwest.

## ALD 70

Solution: *TORTELLA* (loaf of bread).

The shape of the loaf here is clearly round, to judge from the repeated reference to shields, given that Anglo-Saxon shields were always of that shape; the Latin *tortella* (compare the modern "tortilla") is likewise shaped like a flat pancake. The references to Vulcan, the god of fire, but also the god of smithying and weapon forging, and Hades, the god of death, only add to the martial flavor of this otherwise mundane subject.

## ALD 71

Solution: *PISCIS* (fish).
For comparison, see EUS 40, BER 30 (both solved "fish").

The idea that the creature in question represents both a mundane creature and a constellation is matched elsewhere, notably ALD 37 (*CANCER,*
"crab"), ALD 86 (*ARIES,* "ram"), and SYM 32 (*TAURUS,* "bull"), while the
combined ideas of flying, swimming, and breathing are also explored in
ALD 16 (flying fish).

## ALD 72

Solution: *COLOSUS* (Colossus).

The massive statue known as the Colossus of Rhodes was noted as one of
the Seven Wonders of the Ancient World. In focusing resolutely on its essential emptiness here, Aldhelm very clearly places the manmade world as
essentially inferior to the natural one.

## ALD 73

Solution: *FONS* (spring).

This rather elegant *aenigma* again covers all of the dominions of earth, sea,
and sky, and introduces a version of what is sometimes known as the "inex-
pressibility topos" to describe something that is as numberless as (for example) the stars in the sky or the grains of sand on a beach.

## ALD 74

Solution: *FUNDIBALUM* (sling).

The primary source for this *aenigma* is evidently the biblical tale of David
and Goliath, as told in 1 Samuel 17:40–50.

## ALD 75

Solution: *CRABRO* (hornet).

The heightened martial and aggressive tone so much in evidence in this
*aenigma* matches the nature of its subject, even with regard to the mention
of hornet honey, which is so inimical to human taste.

## ALD 76

Solution: *MELARIUS* (apple tree).

Since the Fall of Man was caused in Eden through an apple, there grew a legend that the Crucifixion, which paid for that Fall, took place at the site of Eden (now named Golgotha), with the Cross itself made in part from the wood of the original tree. The well-known hymn *Pange lingua* by Venantius Fortunatus popularizes this perspective. Toward the end of the *aenigma*, we find the designation "the Thunderer" (Latin *tonans*), which began as a pagan designation of Jupiter, but for metrical reasons as much as anything else was widely adopted by Christian-Latin poets.

## ALD 77

Solution: *FICULNEA* (fig tree).

The biblical subject matter links this *aenigma* to the one that precedes. For the background and possible sources, see Genesis 3:7; 1 Kings 4:25; Matthew 21:18–22; and Caelius Sedulius, *Carmen paschale* 4.45–56. In the last two examples, the reference is to Christ cursing the fig tree. The "Carian fruit" mentioned in the sixth line is a kind of dried fig.

## ALD 78

Solution: *CUPA VINARIA* (wine cask).
For comparison, see LOR 5, EXE 9, XMS X4 (all solved "wine cup").

Bacchus was the Roman god of wine, and his name could be used for wine itself. The Christological themes of the preceding two *aenigmata* may have suggested this extended meditation on the benefits of the vine, given Christ's statement in John 15:1 that "I am the true vine" (*Ego sum vitis vera*).

## ALD 79

Solution: *SOL ET LUNA* (sun and moon).
For comparison, see ALD 6 (moon); EUS 10 (sun) and 11 (moon); ALC D41 (sun) and D42 (moon); EXE 4 (sun) and 27 (moon and sun); BER 55–57 (all

solved "sun") and 58–59 (both solved "moon"); OIR 11, GES 15 (both solved "sun"); XMS Z4 (snow and sun).

This *aenigma* offers a wide range of classical references, which are nonetheless presented in a generally negative light and roundly rejected; Aldhelm denies the validity of classical myths, while demonstrating his knowledge of those traditions. So, for example, Saturn, who gave his name to the festival of Saturnalia during which SYM was supposed to have been composed, was considered an ancient Roman god, born of Chaos at the beginning of time, and identified with the Greek god Chronos (whose name means "time"); Saturn was considered Jupiter's predecessor, and therefore by some his father. Likewise, Jupiter fathered Apollo and his sister Cynthia on Latona at Delos, just as described here; Apollo and Cynthia were reckoned to be personifications of the sun and the moon. A further classical reference is found at the end of this *aenigma:* Erebus was a primordial god, born of Chaos, and was the very embodiment of darkness itself, so giving the whole *aenigma* a circular shape moving from one son of Chaos to another. By contrast, Aldhelm co-opts a final classical reference, namely Olympus, the home of the gods, to follow the rest, and implicitly replaces them all with Christ.

## ALD 80

Solution: *CALIX VITREUS* (glass cup).
See too Leahy, *Anglo-Saxon Crafts,* 106–7.
For comparison, see EXE 61, BER 50a (both solved "glass beaker").

There is an obvious sense of sensual pleasure pervading this *aenigma,* which explores the tactile and even erotic pleasures of what would undoubtedly have been a luxury item in the period, concluding with a warning of the dangers inherent in such pleasures, especially the dangers of alcohol. This *aenigma* inspired many imitations in the tradition: see especially BON 6; LOR 5; EXE 12, 28, and 61; among the analogues, one might also consult BER 5–6, 35, 42, and 46; GES 4.

## ALD 81

Solution: *LUCIFER* (morning star).

The fact that Lucifer, the morning star, was widely identified with Venus, the classical god of love and sex, connects this *aenigma* to the preceding one; the exoticism and classical references certainly link it back to the preceding two. Phoebus is another name for Apollo, the sun, while in pre-Copernican astronomy there were seven planets: the sun, the moon, Mercury, Venus, Mars, Jupiter, and Saturn, so providing the context for the "six friends" of Venus mentioned here. Note that five of the seven feature in ALD 79 and 81 alone. It is intriguing that Aldhelm does not make explicit here the usual identification of Lucifer with the fallen angel Satan (on which see Isaiah 14:3–20 and 2 Peter 1:19), but his general disapproval, running throughout the sequence ALD 79–81, is perfectly clear.

## ALD 82

Solution: *MUSTELA* (weasel).

Aldhelm's source here is most likely Isidore, *Etymologiae* 12.3.3: "The weasel *(mustela)* is so called as if it were a long mouse *(mus)*, for a dart *(telum)* is so called due to its length. This creature, by its nature, practices deceit in the houses where it nurses its pups, and it moves and changes its dwelling. It hunts snakes and mice. There are two kinds of weasels: one, which the Greeks call ἴκτις, lives in the wild and is different in size, while the other wanders into houses. Those people are mistaken who suppose that the weasel conceives through its mouth and bears its young through its ear." The idea in the closing lines that one weasel can revive another weasel, even at the point of death, is found elsewhere both in the French *Eliduc* of Marie de France, and in the Old Norse *Vǫlsunga saga;* see further Carol Clover, "*Vǫlsunga saga* and the Missing Lai of Marie de France," in *Sagnaskemmtun: Studies in Honour of Hermann Pálsson on His 65th Birthday,* ed. Rudolf Simek, Jónas Kristjánsson, and Hans Bekker-Nieldsen, Philologica Germanica 8 (Vienna, 1986), 79–84.

## ALD 83

Solution: *IUVENCUS* (bullock).
For comparison, see ps-BED 7, EUS 37, LOR 11, EXE 36 (all solved "bullock").

This *aenigma* is the first of several within the Anglo-Saxon riddle tradition dealing with the same or similar themes, namely the suffering of bullocks and oxen, and the use made of their leather after death. See too, for example, ps-BED 8, EUS 37, LOR 11, EXE 12 and 36. While the four springs here naturally refer to the udders of a cow, it is worth noting that patristic sources note the four rivers of Paradise, and connect this with the idea of drinking from the streams of the four Gospels, especially since Luke, one of the Evangelists, is himself identified as a bullock or ox. In this respect, see EUS 37 in particular.

## ALD 84

Solution: *SCROFA PRAEGNANS* (pregnant sow).
For comparison, see GES 12 (sow and nine piglets).

This extraordinary *aenigma* conceals its solution (itself a highly unusual one) by various kinds of misdirection: the second half offers a litany of six different trees in four lines, while the first half is an arithmetical puzzle based on body parts, the solution to which is ninety-six, described here as "the total tally of metrical feet" (so employing another body-part term in a technical sense). Aldhelm may have derived this notion from Isidore, *Etymologiae* 1.17.1; certainly, he repeats it at Aldhelm, *De pedum regulis* 112 (Rudolf Ehwald, ed., *Aldhemi Opera*, MGH AA 15 [Berlin, 1913–1919], pp. 150–51). There is a close analogue in the Norse GES 12 (sow and piglets).

## ALD 85

Solution: *CAECUS NATUS* (man born blind).

This *aenigma* leads on smoothly from the last, inasmuch as both deal with natural bodies with unusual qualities; it is notable here that the solution, namely that a man born blind can father sighted children, is barely hinted at.

## ALD 86

Solution: *ARIES* (ram).
For comparison, see XMS P3 (*PARIES* → *ARIES*).

This is another *aenigma* playing on the conceit of creatures at home in several domains, here the earth and the sky, as well as on the double meaning of "ram" as both an animal and a weapon of war. In terms of the first of these characteristics, Aldhelm offers here a further riddle on those constellations that are also creatures of the land or sea or both, as earlier at ALD 37 (*CANCER,* "crab") and ALD 71 (*PISCIS,* "fish"). Line 8 alludes to a common logograph, or letter riddle: the fifteenth letter of the medieval roman alphabet is *p,* so adding it to *aries* produces *paries* (wall); there is a precise parallel at XMS P3.

## ALD 87

Solution: *CLIPEUS* (shield).
For comparison, see EXE 3, GES 26 (both solved "shield").

This *aenigma* amply describes the horrors of war and the sufferings of the creature in question, in this case the shield; there are broad parallels to be drawn with EXE 3 (shield, chopping board). *Orcus* is the Latin name for the underworld and also an alternative name for its lord, Pluto; as such, it can also stand simply for "death."

## ALD 88

Solution: *BASILISCUS* (serpent).

This *aenigma* has a fascinating bilingual connection with ALD 87 (shield), which immediately precedes, since while Latin *aspis* commonly means "serpent," and rarely "shield," in Greek, ἀσπίς generally means "shield," and rarely "serpent." The reader is required to recognize that both of the solutions to ALD 87–88 (*CLIPEUS* and *BASILISCUS;* note the Greek derivation of the latter) have a synonym in *ASPIS.*

## ALD 89

Solution: *ARCA LIBRARIA* (book chest, a box filled with books).

Given the common notion of snakes or dragons guarding various kinds of hoards, and their association with wisdom, there seems a connection between this *aenigma* and the one that precedes it. The idea that the creature in question is filled with books, but derives no benefit from them, is echoed and brilliantly developed in EXE 45 (book moth). For the Fates (Latin *Parcae*), see the note at ALD 45.

## ALD 90

Solution: *PUERPERA GEMINAS ENIXA* (woman bearing twins).
For comparison, see ps-BED 12, SYM 93 (both solved "woman bearing twins").

This *aenigma,* in which the creature in question has an unusual number of eyes, ears, and digits, links back to the previous one, and is clearly based on the similar SYM 92 (mother of twins). Likewise, ALD 84 (pregnant sow) is largely made up of the same kind of enumeration of body parts.

## ALD 91

Solution: *PALMA* (palm).
For comparison, see BER 15 (palm tree).

There are parallels and potential sources in John 12:13, and (especially) Isidore, *Etymologiae* 17.7.1, part of which states that "the tree is the symbol of victory, with lofty and luxuriant growth, clothed in long-lasting leaves, and preserving its leaves without any succession of foliage."

## ALD 92

Solution: *FARUS EDITISSIMA* (very tall lighthouse).
For comparison, see EXE 68 (lighthouse).

Although the well-read, well-traveled, and well-connected Aldhelm could have come across lighthouses either secondhand or on his own travels, it is notable both that Bede, *Historia ecclesiastica* 1.11, mentions a Roman lighthouse surviving to his day, and that there may have been a lighthouse in Aldhelm's time at the chapel at Worth Matravers in Dorset.

## ALD 93

Solution: *SCINTILLA* (spark).

This *aenigma* presents an extended meditation on the hugely destructive power of fire, and as such has much in common with ALD 44 (fire), even down to the coldness of the parent, here a mother and presumably a reference to flint.

## ALD 94

Solution: *EBULUS* (dwarf elder).

There is no clear source for this *aenigma,* and no indication elsewhere that it was used in the treatment of leprosy, or whatever other ailment Aldhelm understood by the term. In later terminology, the dwarf elder (in scientific classification, *Sambucus ebulus*) is also known as Danewort, with the explanation either that it grew on the bloody battlefield of slaughtered Vikings or was even introduced by them, though they are not otherwise known for their horticultural interests.

## ALD 95

Solution: *SCILLA* (Scylla).

There is a full account of the ancient myth of the monster Scylla and the whirlpool Charybdis given in Ovid, *Metamorphoses* 14.248–308, a text that Aldhelm appears to have known in some form, although here his most immediate source is more likely Isidore, *Etymologiae* 11.3.32: "They say that Scylla is a woman girt about with the heads of dogs and their mighty barking, since sailors, scared by whirlpools dashing against each other in the straits of the sea of Sicily, reckon that the waves, which the cleft of the sucking tide forces together, are barking." In Ovid's version, Scylla was originally a beautiful sea nymph beloved by Glaucos. She was transformed into a monster by the witch Circe, a daughter of Titan, in a fit of jealous rage. The reference to dogs derives from the fact that the Greek σκύλαξ *(skylax)* means "puppy."

## ALD 96

Solution: *ELEFANS* (elephant).

This rather exotic *aenigma* follows on naturally from the one that precedes it. The heroic language of the battlefield in the early part of this *aenigma* seems something of a set piece. Aldhelm seems to have drawn not only on Isidore, *Etymologiae* 12.2.14 *(elephans)* and *Etymologiae* 18.4.5 *(classica,* "trumpets") but also on medieval *Physiologus* traditions, where elephants are described as notoriously light sleepers that sleep only standing up.

## ALD 97

Solution: *NOX* (night).

Although at first glance the solution to this *aenigma* might seem mundane, the flurry of classical references that it contains renders it quite as exotic as the other riddles in this closing sequence (ALD 95–99); the parallel closing sequence of Symphosius (SYM 92–95) is likewise outlandish, and supplies a likely model. Strikingly, the *aenigma* quotes six whole lines from Virgil that in context refer to the monstrous figure of "rumor" *(fama),* which was spread at night *(Aeneid* 12.846, 4.177 [itself repeated at 10.767], and 4.181–84). The Furies, also known as the Eumenides, were the goddesses of vengeance, while Tartarus was a primordial god who also gave his name to the entire underworld, and "The Titan torch of Phoebus" is a poetic circumlocution for the sun, the natural enemy of the night.

## ALD 98

Solution: *ELLEBORUS* (hellebore).

In classical texts, the plant hellebore was associated with inducing and curing various kinds of frenzy and madness, and while such a solution fits much of this *aenigma,* it has been argued that Aldhelm is conflating his book learning with firsthand knowledge of woody nightshade, which shares many of the same qualities; Alaric Hall, "Madness, Medication—and Self-Induced Hallucinogen? *Elleborus* (and Woody Nightshade) in Anglo-Saxon England, 700–900," *Leeds Studies in English* n.s. 44 (2013): 43–69.

## ALD 99

Solution: *CAMELLUS* (camel).

There is a terrible pun here on the name of the Roman Marcus Furius Camillus, who was a consular tribune and dictator many times between the 380s and 360s BCE, apparently following on (and in terms of date outdoing) the model of the equally dreadful puns in SYM 25 (*MUS*, "mouse") on another famous Roman, namely Publius Decius Mus, who was consul in 340 BCE, and again in SYM 32 (*TAURUS*, "bull") on the Roman general and twice consul (37 and 26 BCE), Titus Statilius Taurus.

## ALD 100

Solution: *CREATURA* (creation).
See further Erin Sebo, *In Enigmate: The History of a Riddle, 400–1500* (Dublin, 2018), 71–91.
For comparison, see EXE 38, 64, and 90 (all solved "creation"), all of which ALD 100 has inspired in different ways.

The closing and by far the longest *aenigma* of this collection, which draws together many of the strands of individual texts within it, concludes with the kind of challenge to the would-be solver that is more characteristic of the Old English texts in the Anglo-Saxon riddle tradition. It has been observed that this *aenigma* is quite heavily glossed when compared to others in ALD, and it was very clearly the ultimate source of the three riddles from EXE noted above.

## BEDE (BED AND PS-BED)

I have consulted translations by Frederick M. Tupper, Jr., "Riddles of the Bede Tradition: The *Flores* of Pseudo-Bede," *Modern Philology* 2 (1905): 561–72; Lapidge, *Bede's Latin Poetry* [BED]; and Martha Bayless and Michael Lapidge, eds., *Collectanea Pseudo-Bedae,* Scriptores latini Hiberniae 14 (Dublin, 1998) [ps-BED]. See also the more detailed commentary in *COEALRT.*

It is important to note that since many of the *aenigmata* in BED turn on specific Latin words and their spellings, even more is necessarily lost in translation than usual; I have attempted to unpack the concomitant details here, and the reader is especially encouraged to consult both the intertexts noted and *COEALRT*.

## BED 1

Solution: *LIBRA* (scales).

This *aenigma* plays on the idea of the rising and the falling of the respective pans of the scales weighing up various objects and concepts; for others on a similar theme, see ALD 23 and BER 53 (both *TRUTINA*, "scales"), although the treatment there is quite different. The weighing described here seems a matter of metrics, and appears to refer to the number of beats *(tempora)*, periods *(morae)*, and syllables *(syllabae)* that various words take up. If a short syllable (◡) is reckoned to comprise one beat, and a long syllable (–) two, then "nothing" (here *nīl*, so two beats) does indeed weigh less than "Hell" (here *Hĕrĕbō,* so four beats), and is therefore "better," in the sense that it rises in the scales, while "nothing" (*nil* again, with a single syllable) is by the same measure worse than "heaven" (*celo* has two). By contrast, a "scintilla" (*tĭtĭvīcĭlĭŭm,* so eight beats) is twice as heavy as "lead" (*plūmbūm,* so four) on one measure, but, given that Latin *plumbum* has only two syllables, while *titivicilium* has six, is three times greater on another. The grammatical theme continues in the subsequent *aenigmata*.

## BED 2

Solution: *F LITTERA* (the letter *f* ).
For comparison, see ALF F (letter *f* ).

This *aenigma* introduces an extended sequence dealing with word games of one kind or another (BED 2–13). The gloss explains: "*fel* (gall) has a bitter taste; change the *f* to *m* and you will change the taste, since it will be *mel* (honey)."

## BED 3

Solution: *OS* (mouth, bone).
For comparison, see ALC D19, OER 4 (both solved "mouth" or "bone").

The gloss explains the likely solution: "*Os* is a monosyllable, whether you mean *os, oris* (mouth) or *os, ossis* (bone), and it does not change its spelling in the nominative, but its sense." In other words, the same two-letter sequence *os* means both "mouth" and "bone" in Latin.

## BED 4

Solution: *AMOR* (love) → *ROMA* (Rome).
For comparison, see TAT 14, BON 5 (both solved "love").

The gloss explains the likely solution: "*Amor* (love) is disyllabic: reverse the syllables and it will become *Roma* (Rome). The reverse spelling produces the alternative sense."

## BED 5

Solution: *NEMO* (no one) → *OMEN* (omen).

As with the previous *aenigma*, the reverse spelling of the relevant Latin word produces the alternative sense: an omen is literally ominous in this context. One gets a similar effect in Modern English with the words "live" (which is positive) and its mirror image, "evil" (which is not). There may be a secondary sense in which *nemo* here can be read as *nullus*, so giving the interpretation that "no almighty one loves anyone backward, nor those who do," so aligning this with other double-entendre riddles in the tradition, where the sexual meaning arises from misreading; I am grateful to Bob Babcock for the suggestion.

## BED 6

Solution: *SEGES* (field of grain).

Here, in distinction to the previous two *aenigmata*, the reverse spelling of the relevant Latin word does not change the meaning at all.

## BED 7

Solution: *A LITTERA* (the letter *a*)
For comparison, see ALF A (letter *a*).

Note that BED 7–10 deal with four of the five vowels in sequence (it seems likely that another on the letter *e* has dropped out). There appears to be a reference here and in the gloss to Isidore, *Etymologiae* 12.8.1, where the etymology of "bees" *(apes)* is traced to the fact that they are "without a foot" *(a-pes)*.

### BED 8

Solution: *I LITTERA* (the letter *i*).
For comparison, see EUS 39, ALF I (both solved "letter *i*").

The gloss explains the likely solution: "*i* is the only upright letter in the alphabet."

### BED 9

Solution: *O LITTERA* (the letter *o*).
For comparison, see ALF O (letter *o*).

The gloss explains the likely solution: "The *culus* is the backside of the anus, which hardly sees; put the letter *o* in front and it will see just like an eye, since it will be *oculus* (eye)."

### BED 10

Solution: *V LITTERA* (the letter *u/v*).
For comparison, see EUS 19, ALF V (both solved "the letter *u/v*").

If we accept the preceding sequence of vowel-solutions to imply this is another, then it is indeed true that when the letter *u* appears at the beginning of words (in other words, has lost its head), it is written with straight lines as *v* and becomes a consonant (so taking up the burden of producing sound in conjunction with other letters, as consonants do).

### BED 11

Solution: *ONUS* (load, burden).

Taking away the "head of shortness" (in other words, the beginning of the word *brevitatis,* namely *b*-) turns *bonus* (good) to *onus* (burden); the stubborn are assuredly a burden.

## BED 12

Solution: *NAVIS* (ship).
For comparison, see ALC D61, SYM 13, BER 11 (all solved "ship"); GES 24 (where "ship" is one possible solution); XMS Z2 (ship), where, however, the treatment is in all cases quite different.

The gloss explains the likely solution: "The prow and the stern of a ship will be dry when they swim upon the sea."

## BED 13

Solution: *OVA* (eggs).
For comparison, see BER 8 (egg[s]), where, however, the treatment is quite different.

The gloss explains the likely solution: "This is the construction: three joined sisters, that is, the three letters *o, v,* and *a,* begot three swimming children, that is, three chicks, and in turn the mature chicks begot 'the same,' that is, the letters *o, v,* and *a,* which signify the joined eggs." The third line alludes to the common prognostic idea that dreaming of eggs betokens bad luck: see further *COEALRT.*

## BED 14

Solution: *SAGITTA* (arrow).
For comparison, see TAT 32, ALC D85, SYM 65, GES 13 (all solved "arrow").

The gloss explains the likely solution: "A missile seeks a bird with a beak flying in the air, which it could not reach at all, if the missile itself were not lifted up by its feathers."

## BED 15

Solution: *MARE* (sea).
For comparison, see ALC D48 (sea), where, however, the treatment is quite different.

The gloss explains the likely solution: "The sea always ebbs and flows; when it stops on Doomsday that will be a mighty portent."

## BED 16

Solution: *AETAS HOMINIS* (the age of man).
For comparison, see ps-BED 4, SOL 2 (both solved "age of man").

The gloss explains the likely solution: "Man's age will come the closer to death the more it grows."

## BED 17

Solution: *CETUS* (a whale).

Whale oil is used for lighting, and while a whale is fed mysteriously (its ingestion of plankton is all but invisible), it can clearly feed a multitude.

## BED 18

Solution: *DIGITI SCRIBAE* (a scribe's fingers).
For comparison, see EXE 29 and 49 (quill pen and fingers). The positive and negative aspects of the written word are stressed here, in an *aenigma* that is the most heavily glossed of the entire collection.

## ps-BED 1

Solution: *SAPIENTIA* (wisdom).
For comparison, see BIB 1 (wisdom). Note that in this case, the solution is plainly given.

## ps-BED 2

Solution: *PULLUS* (chick)
For comparison, see EUS 38, XMS X2 (both solved "chick").

The various parallels and analogues seem to make the suggested solution certain; the skin referred to here is the membrane that remains on the edge of the eggshell, which is the "wall" in question.

## ps-BED 3

Solution: *EQUI PICTURA* (a drawing of a horse?).

Tupper suggests the solution given here, considering the "mother" to be the pen (*penna* in Latin is feminine), although it is tempting to suggest instead "ship," given the common association within the Anglo-Saxon riddle tradition of ships and horses; in that case the "unborn" creature would be the tree from which the ship was fashioned, and the "mother" would then be another wooden object, either an oar or the tiller.

## ps-BED 4

Solution: *AETAS HOMINIS* (age of man)
For comparison, see BED 16, SOL 2 (both solved "age of man").

The parallels make the suggested solution seem certain.

## ps-BED 5

Solution: *VENTUS* (wind)
For comparison, see EUS 8 (wind and fire); ALC D46 (wind); EXE 1 (wind and God); BER 41 (wind).

This is obviously a prose version of ALD 2, sharing the same solution.

## ps-BED 6

Solution: *GLACIES* (ice).

For comparison, see ALC D53, LOR 4, EXE 31 and 66, OER 11, BER 38 and 42, OIR 9 (all solved "ice").

This is obviously a prose version of ps-SYM 1, sharing the same solution, and with the introductory phrase *Quid est quod* (What is it?) added.

## ps-BED 7

Solution: *IUVENCUS* (bullock).
For comparison, see ALD 83, EUS 37, LOR 11, EXE 36 (all solved "bullock").

The parallels make the solution clear.

## ps-BED 8

Solution: *HOMO SEDENS SUPER TRIPODEM* (man sitting on a three-legged stool).

This *aenigma* plays on the same conceit as other body-part riddles, but seems somewhat literal-minded.

## ps-BED 9

Solution: *CUCULUS* (cuckoo).
For comparison, see EXE 7 (cuckoo), with which it shares a number of key features.

## ps-BED 10

Solution: *LEBES* (cauldron).
For comparison, see ALD 49, ALC D76, XMS X1 (all solved "cauldron"), which together make precise parallels.

The underlying notion is that of a cauldron of water boiling over on a fire and of the water putting out the fire.

## ps-BED 11

Solution: *PENNA* (quill pen).
For comparison, see EUS 35, LOR 9, XMS X3 (all solved "quill pen").

This *aenigma* has particularly close affinities with LOR 9 and XMS X3: the "girl weeping and muttering" is the (grammatically feminine) quill pen, whose tears are ink, and whose muttering produces the words on the page; the fact that "her ways are the paths of life" suggests that what is at issue is a religious text (in other words, *scriptura*, "writing," is understood as *sacra scriptura*, "sacred scripture"). The pun on *virga* (rod, twig, stalk) and *virgo* (girl) hints at the solution.

## ps-BED 12

Solution: *PUERPERA GEMINAS ENIXA* (woman bearing twins).
For comparison, see ALD 90, SYM 93 (both solved "woman bearing twins"); this is evidently essentially a prose rendering of the latter, a version of which follows in the original text.

## ps-BED 13

Solution: *CUPA* (clay beer mug).

This seems a fairly straightforward *aenigma,* with the notion of a creature with but a single foot a feature found frequently in the wider tradition: see further, for example, the notes to TAT 10 (lectern) and 12 (paten), SYM 57 (hobnail).

## TATWINE (TAT)

I have consulted translations by Mary Jane MacDonald Williams, "The Riddles of Tatwine and Eusebius" (PhD diss., University of Michigan, 1974), 101–56. I have also consulted F. Glorie, ed., *Collectiones aenigmatum Merovingicae aetatis,* CCSL 133, and 133A (Turnhout, 1968), vol. 133, pp. 167–208. See also the more detailed commentary in *COEALRT.* For further reading, see in general Karl Wilhelm Adolf Ebert, "Die Räthselpoesie der

Angelsachsen, inbesondere die *Aenigmata* des Tatwine und Eusebius," *Berichte über die Verhandlung der königlich sächsischen Gesellschaft der Wissenschaften zu Leipzig, philologisch-historische Classe* 79 (1877): 20–56; Heinrich Hahn, "Die Rätseldichter Tatwin und Eusebius," *Forschungen zur deutschen Geschichte* 26 (1886): 601–31; Williams, "The Riddles of Tatwine and Eusebius"; Frank H. Whitman, "Aenigmata Tatwini," *Neuphilologische Mitteilungen* 88 (1987): 8–17; Orchard, "After Aldhelm."

## TAT PR

Tatwine takes the whole idea of prefacing a collection of *aenigmata* to a vastly more complicated level, surpassing the relatively simple acrostic-telestich of ALD PR, which merely produced a single hexameter by reading the first and (identical) last letters of each line. In this case, Tatwine produces two lines of hexameters that explain how to read the whole collection by reading the first letters of every opening line of the forty *aenigmata* that make up TAT in order (given here in italics) and the last letters of the opening lines of the same *aenigmata* in reverse (also given here in italics). This arrangement, incidentally, fixes the order of the texts, since any deviation would spoil the acrostic-telestich. In fact, there is clear corruption to the transmitted text in both manuscripts (the readings of which appear quite closely related): TAT PR is given in both as the opening two lines of TAT 1 (still more confusingly, in reverse, despite the obvious disruption of sense, and there is also disruption to the order; see notes below).

## TAT 1

Solution: *SAPIENTIA* (Wisdom); the solution given is *DE PHILOSOPHIA* (about Philosophy).

The opening three *aenigmata* of this collection form a clearly related sequence concerning interpretation and the world of learning. The idea that "wisdom" should begin a riddle-collection is echoed at ps-BED 1 and BIB 1, as well as (more obliquely) at ALD 1. This *aenigma* certainly combines elements and echoes of other texts: reference to the "seven encompassing wings" in the opening line has been related to the literally proverbial seven pillars of Wisdom (Proverbs 9:1) but seems equally likely to comprise a combination of the threefold and fourfold solutions to the two *aenigmata* that follow. The following two lines emphasize that the domain of the creature in question is the earth, sea, and sky; the string of comparatives in the subsequent lines (TAT 1.4–7: "wiser . . . swifter . . . brighter . . . more precious . . . more pleasant . . . sweeter") readily recalls similar sequences elsewhere, notably in the lengthy passage at ALD 100.25–67, and its various derivatives in both Latin and Old English. There then follows the assertion that "No hand can touch nor eye fall upon me" (TAT 1.8), a line that readily recalls the similar boast of "wind" (ALD 2.1) that "No one can see me or hold me in their hands." The litany of quotation is continued in TAT 1.11 ("Happy the one who can learn my laws"), which seems an obvious echo of Virgil, *Georgics* 2.490 ("Happy the one who can understand the reasons for things").

## TAT 2

Solution: *SPES, FIDES, CARITAS* (Hope, Faith, and Charity).
For comparison, see BON 3, ALC D68 (both solved "hope").

The biblical triad of faith, hope, and charity (1 Corinthians 13:13) was also considered a trio of saintly martyred sisters, whose "wise mother" was Sophia (Greek for "wisdom"). It is through that mother (whose Latin name would be *Sapientia*) that one connection between this *aenigma* and the previous one is made; another is the fact that in both the creatures in question are said to be invisible in ways that recall the opening line of Aldhelm's *aenigma* on "wind" (ALD 2.1: "No one can see me or hold me in their hands"), here "No one will be able to see."

## TAT 3

Solution: *HISTORIA ET TROPOLOGIA ET ALLEGORIA ET ANA-GOGE* (historical, tropological, allegorical, and anagogical meaning); the solution given is *DE HISTORIA ET SENSU ET MORALI ET ALLEGO-RIA,* which makes no sense, and is obviously incomplete.

This *aenigma* continues the theme of sisters, again presumably the offspring of "wisdom," who guard the entrance to correct interpretation. Aldhelm again provides a succinctly relevant summary (*De virginitate* 4;

Ehwald, *Aldhelmi Opera,* p. 232): "Now [we mention] the fourfold methods of interpreting the Gospels . . . according to history, allegory, tropology, and anagogy." These four methods concentrate in turn on the literal meaning of a passage (also known as the past or historical interpretation), the moral (present or tropological) interpretation, the allegorical (or future) interpretation, and the spiritual (or anagogical) interpretation.

## TAT 4

Solution: *APICES* (letters); the solution given is *DE LITTERIS* (about letters).
For comparison, see ALD 30, EUS 7, ALC D1, EXE 55, BER 25 (all solved "letter[s]").

The rather lofty and learned tone of the opening sequence of three *aenigmata* (TAT 1–3) is carried on here in an *aenigma* that introduces a further sequence of three (TAT 4–6) dealing broadly with the theme of writing. The solution "letters" is plain from the "black-on-white" motif found here and widely elsewhere in the tradition, while written texts are described as food and drink; the inclusion of a spelling riddle, or logograph (on which see the note on ALD 63 above) in the final line (as often), however, renders impossible the usual Latin form for "letters" *(litterae),* despite what the manuscripts say; it is appropriate that Tatwine, the grammarian, should require the elevated grammarian's term *apices* instead: the removal of the first letter of *apices* would give *pices,* the first syllable of which is shared with *pix, picis* (pitch), a word that assuredly "does not shine."

## TAT 5

Solution: *MEMBRANUM* (parchment).
See too Leahy, *Anglo-Saxon Crafts,* 89–93.
For comparison, see EUS 32, EXE 24, BER 24 (all solved "parchment").

In describing the various grim and painful stages by which a living creature was turned first into parchment and then into a book, Tatwine characterizes the humans involved in very evocative terms, first as "ravager," then "artisan," then "cultivator" (Latin *populator . . . auctor . . . cultor*). As such, this *aenigma* is a good example of the so-called "suffering servant" motif, also witnessed in (for example) EUS 12 (bull) and 28 (candle); EXE 24 (Gospel book), 26 (parchment), and 77 (weathercock); SYM 56 (boot) and 66 (whip); BER 5 (table), 13 (vine), 18 (broom), 26 (mustard seed), and 37 (pepper).

## TAT 6

Solution: *PENNA* (pen).
For comparison, see ALD 59 (pen).

As in the previous *aenigma,* the human agents here are viewed in rather negative terms by the creature in question: "cheated by an enemy" and "thrice bound" (by the thumb and two fingers that grip the pen, as at ALD 30 and EXE 49).

## TAT 7

Solution: *TINTINNABULUM* (bell).
See too Leahy, *Anglo-Saxon Crafts,* 132.
For comparison, see ALC D74, EXE 2 and 67, SYM 80 (bell[s]).

This *aenigma* again follows on from the previous one, with its monastic and ecclesiastical associations, and opens a sequence describing various items of church furniture (TAT 7–10 and 12). It is connected to the preceding *aenigma* by the shared themes of an object bemoaning its transformed fortunes, although whereas the pen was once a creature of the air it is now the bell that hangs on high. The reference to Caesar is unclear.

## TAT 8

Solution: *ALTARE* (altar).

This *aenigma* links back to TAT 5, by focusing on a man-made quadruped that serves the church, as opposed to a four-legged living creature that is slaughtered in its service. It also connects to the previous two *aenigmata* in its relation to height, since in the "lofty task" (Latin *alta . . . re*) mentioned in the final line, it reveals its Latin name: *altare.*

## TAT 9

Solution: *CRUX CHRISTI* (Christ's cross).
For comparison, see EUS 17 (cross).

This is the third of five items of church furniture in the themed sequence (TAT 7–10 and 12). Several commentators, such as Whitney F. Bolton, "Tatwine's *De cruce Christi* and *The Dream of the Rood*," *Archiv für das Studium der neueren Sprachen und Literaturen* 200 (1963): 344–46, have connected this *aenigma* with the celebrated Old English poem *The Dream of the Rood;* see further Andy Orchard, "*The Dream of the Rood:* Cross-References," in *New Readings in the Vercelli Book,* ed. Samantha Zacher and Andy Orchard, Toronto Old English Series (Toronto, 2009), 225–53.

## TAT 10

Solution: *RECITABULUM* (lectern).

This description of what is evidently an eagle-shaped lectern plugs into a recurring pattern of body-part riddles within the tradition, often predicated on the idea that the feature focused on is essentially a lack of the usual faculty: here, the tongue cannot speak, the wings cannot fly, and the single foot is unable to move.

## TAT 11

Solution: *ACUS* (needle).
See too Leahy, *Anglo-Saxon Crafts,* 76–78.
For comparison, see SYM 55 (needle).

This *aenigma,* while it continues the body-part imagery of the previous one by speaking of the single eye of the creature in question, appears to interrupt the themed sequence of church furniture in TAT 7–10 and 12, but is obviously connected by subject with TAT 13 (embroidery needle). It seems likely, given the importance of ecclesiastical vestments, many of which would have been embroidered, that Tatwine considered the entire sequence (TAT 7–13) to be part of the same broader theme.

## TAT 12

Solution: *PATENA* (paten).
For comparison, see EXE 46 (paten).

The last two lines (TAT 12.4–5) seem to refer to the paradox of a paten, standing on a single foot (just like the lectern of TAT 10), but adorned with an image containing six legs (Christ, Mary, and John? Christ and the two thieves?). I am grateful to Bob Babcock for the suggestion. There are broad parallels between this *aenigma* and ALD 55 (chrismal).

## TAT 13

Solution: *ACUS PICTILIS* (embroidery needle).

For the connection of this *aenigma* to the ones that precede it, see the note to TAT 11 (needle) above.

## TAT 14

Solution: *CARITAS* (love).
See further Leslie Lockett, *Anglo-Saxon Psychologies in the Vernacular and Latin Traditions* (Toronto, 2011), 273–74.
For comparison, see BED 4, BON 5 (both solved "love").

The same essential paradox of freeing that which is bound and binding that which is free is found in SYM 55.2–3 ("I go ahead of soft knots that follow the slender steel; / and I restore form to what's damaged and a fastening to what's been split"); the solution to which ("needle") connects this *aenigma* to the preceding one.

## TAT 15

Solution: *NIX, GRANDO, ET GLACIES* (snow, hail, and ice).
For comparison, see ps-BED 6, ALC D53 (both solved "ice"); ALC D54 (snow); LOR 4 (ice) and 6 (snow); EXE 31 and 66 (both solved "ice"); OER 11 (ice); SYM 10 (ice) and 11 (snow); BER 38 and 42 (both solved "ice"); OIR 9 (ice); XMS Z4 (snow and sun).

The proverbial heat of love in the previous *aenigma* is turned to extreme cold here; the father here is presumably "wind" (Latin *ventus* is grammatically masculine), the mother "water" (Latin *aqua* is grammatically feminine), just as they also seem to be in the very similar LOR 4 (ice).

## TAT 16

Solution: *PREPOSITIONES UTRIUSQUE CASUS* (prepositions that take two cases).
See further Lockett, *Anglo-Saxon Psychologies,* 262–63.

This *aenigma* highlights the role of riddles in general as teaching texts: the solution is of little interest outside the classroom. In his grammar Tatwine notes that while most Latin prepositions take either the accusative or ablative case, there are four that take both (*Ars Tatuini* 7.4); the prepositions in question signify "in," "under," "above," and "beneath" *(in, sub, super, and subter)*. The difference between the senses is whether what is intended is motion or rest, and the fact that these four "sisters" are differently influenced by and the product of both motion and rest may link this *aenigma* back to the previous one, where three "sisters" are the product of a father in motion and a mother at rest.

## TAT 17

Solution: *SCIURUS* (squirrel).

This *aenigma* at first glance seems to disrupt the sequence, but may, like the previous, be the result of a grammatical nicety: the Latin word for "womb" *(alvus)* has the normal *-us* ending generally associated with masculine nouns but is in fact feminine, as the feminine adjective *fecunda* makes clear. The reference to Mars (the Roman god of war) lends this *aenigma* a mock-heroic feel, and echoes, for example, ALD 60 (unicorn).

## TAT 18

Solution: *OCULI* (eyes).
See further Erhardt-Siebold, *Die lateinsichen Rätsel,* 240.

This *aenigma* begins a short sequence of three on eyes (TAT 18–20: eyes, squinting eyes, and a one-eyed man). The plodding meter of this *aenigma* contrasts with the skipping rhythm of the preceding one, presumably according to the perceived appropriateness of the topics.

## TAT 19

Solution: *STRABI OCULI* (squinting eyes).

This is the second of a tightly knit series of three *aenigmata* on eyes (TAT 18–20); see the note on the previous *aenigma*.

## TAT 20

Solution: *LUSCUS* (one-eyed man).
For comparison, see EXE 82, SYM 95 (both solved "one-eyed garlic-seller").

Although the Latin term *luscus* refers to a "one-eyed man," it is clear that the creature in question here is the single eye itself, in the third of a tightly knit series of three *aenigmata* on eyes (TAT 18–20). There seems a close parallel in ALD 85 (man born blind).

## TAT 21

Solution: *MALUM* (evil).
For comparison, see ALC 2 (*MALUM*, "evil," "apple" → *MULAM*, "mule").

The repetition of "the good" in three different cases (*bono . . . bonum . . . boni*) in TAT 21.3–5 again underlines Tatwine's main interests in Latin grammar and offers a broad clue to the solution.

## TAT 22

Solution: *ADAM* (Adam).
For comparison, see ALC D84 (Adam, Enoch/Elias, and Lazarus).

The juxtaposition of Adam and evil, while clearly biblical, is not exploited either in TAT 21 or 22; if the suggested connection between TAT 22 and 23 seems fruitful, there seems also to be an implicit link between an "apple" (Latin *mālum*) and "evil" (Latin *mălum*), alluding to the eating of the fateful apple in Eden (Genesis 2:16–17). See too ALC 2, which comprises a logogriph, *MALUM* (evil, apple) → *MULAM* (mule), and SYM 84 (apple).

## TAT 23

Solution: *TRINA MORS* (threefold death).

The motif of the threefold death is common in Celtic sources but here has a parallel in the pseudo-Bede *Collectanea* 77: "Tell me, how many deaths are reckoned for sinners? Death in sin, and the separation of the soul and body, and the death of torment" (Bayless and Lapidge, *Collectanea Pseudo-Bedae*, 130–31 and 218). Presumably, the notion of the threefold death is linked implicitly to Adam, the subject of the preceding *aenigmata*, through the motif of the Fall.

## TAT 24

Solution: *HUMILITAS* (humility).
For comparison, see BON 9 (humility).

This *aenigma* harks back to TAT 1 in its motif of the creature in question being lower than the earth and higher than heaven; both seem to derive ultimately from ALD 100.

## TAT 25

Solution: *SUPERBIA* (pride).
For comparison, see BON 14 (pride).

This *aenigma* follows on smoothly from the previous one; the father of Pride is of course Satan. In giving Pride seven sisters, Tatwine seems influenced here by Aldhelm, who, following Cassian, concludes his *Carmen de virginitate* with an extended passage that in some later manuscripts is given the separate title *De octo vitiis principalibus* (On the eight principal vices; *Carmen de virginitate* 2446–2761). The *parvulus* (little boy) of line 5 is perhaps best taken as Christ, but might just as easily refer to David (himself a type of Christ), as slayer of Goliath.

## TAT 26

Solution: *QUINQUE SENSUS* (the five senses).

Presumably the previous enumeration of Pride and her seven sisters sparks off this *aenigma* on the five senses *(odor, gustatus, tactus, visus, auditus)*, here depicted as brothers (all are masculine nouns in Latin) and presented in the order smell, taste, touch, sight, and hearing (the last of which seems more focused on speech).

## TAT 27

Solution: *FORCEPS* (pair of tongs).
See too Leahy, *Anglo-Saxon Crafts,* 117; Dennis Riley, *Anglo-Saxon Tools* (Ely, 2014), 46–48.

This *aenigma* is obviously connected to the one that follows and introduces a loose sequence focused on the art of the smith, specifically the weaponsmith.

## TAT 28

Solution: *INCUS* (anvil).
See too Leahy, *Anglo-Saxon Crafts,* 117; Riley, *Anglo-Saxon Tools,* 44–45.

See the note to the previous *aenigma.* The clearly masculine forms *fixus . . . siniturus* seem to belie the title/solution *incus,* which is grammatically feminine; the only other word for "anvil" that is masculine, *stithus,* is both rare and late, being derived from Old Norse. It is possible that Tatwine was misled by the *-us* ending of the nominative of *incus,* although the noun is third declension and in any case that would be an odd error for a grammarian.

## TAT 29

Solution: *MENSA* (table).
For comparison, see BER 5 (table).

There is a conceptual parallel between this and the previous *aenigma,* although the language of plunder also links it to TAT 5 (parchment). The closest general parallel here is with BER 5 (table), and indeed several specific details (notably those of clothing, nakedness, and ingratitude) seem to correspond quite closely.

## TAT 30

Solution: *ENSIS ET VAGINA* (sword and sheath).
For comparison, see EUS 36 (sword); EXE 18 and 69 (both solved "sword" or "man").

The closest parallel is found in ALD 61 (dagger), to the extent that in both cases the sheath is described as a "house" or "hall," although the speakers change perspective: here the sheath speaks, there the blade. While it is undeniable that Tatwine was familiar with ALD as a collection, this and the following *aenigma* amply demonstrate the difference in outlook between the two authors.

## TAT 31

Solution: *IGNIS* (fire), based on the masculine gender of several forms; the solution given is *DE SCINTILLA* (about a spark). The problem is that there is the same solution for TAT 33 (fire).
For comparison, see ALD 44, TAT 33, ALC D51 and D73, EXE 48, GES 29 (all solved "fire").

There is a parallel in ALD 93 (spark), although here the focus is rather on the contrast between life and death, while there it is on the contrast between the tiny spark and the vast devastation of a raging fire. The "mother's chilly innards" here presumably refers to flint.

## TAT 32

Solution: *SAGITTA* (arrow).
For comparison, see BED 14, ALC D85, SYM 65, GES 13 (all solved "arrow").

The *aenigma* explains the threefold role of archery in war, hunting, and (presumably) target practice. Compare BED 14, ALC D98, and SYM 65 (all "arrow"). There is a natural link with TAT 34 (quiver).

## TAT 33

Solution: *IGNIS* (fire).
For comparison, see ALD 44, TAT 31, ALC D51 and D73, EXE 48, GES 29 (all solved "fire").

See further the note to TAT 31 above; the threefold nature of fire (volcanic from the earth, meteorological from the sky in the form of lightning, and mundane from human kindling) links this *aenigma* to the preceding one.

## TAT 34

Solution: *FARETRA* (quiver).
For comparison, see EXE 15 (quiver).

The language of fire and flame here connects this *aenigma* to the preceding one, as well as to the one that follows. The flames in question here are arrows (so linking this *aenigma* also to TAT 32), through the association of the burning pain of arrow wounds.

## TAT 35

Solution: *PRUNA* (ember).
For comparison, see GES 33 (ember[s]).

The solution given is *DE PRUINA* (about rime, about hoarfrost). The given solution confuses the direction of travel of the spelling riddle, or logo-griph, of the final two lines: the "ninth letter" is *i,* and adding it to the true solution turns heat to cold; heat is what connects this *aenigma* to the preceding one.

## TAT 36

Solution: *VENTILABRUM* (winnowing fan).

The link to the *aenigma* that follows is very clear.

## TAT 37

Solution: *SEMINANS* (sower).

The notion of seeds and sowing and living and dying is enshrined centrally in biblical passages such as John 12:24–25 and, more succinctly, 1 Corinthians 15:36: "Senseless man, that which thou sowest is not quickened, except it die first" *(insipiens tu quod seminas non vivificatur nisi prius moriatur)*.

## TAT 38

Solution: *CARBO* (charcoal).

The "enemy" *(hostis)* in TAT 38.2 is "fire" (compare TAT 33 [fire]). See further Erhardt-Siebold, *Die lateinischen Rätsel,* 150–53.

## TAT 39

Solution: *COS* (whetstone); the given solution is *DE COTICULO* (whetstone).
For comparison, see ALD 27 (whetstone).

Given the reference to a city in TAT 39.2, as well as the feminine forms *sordida* (39.3) and (by emendation) *natam* (39.1), the transmitted title/solution *DE COTICULO* cannot be correct: the capital city of the island Cos has the same name, and the correct solution must be *COS* (whetstone).

## TAT 40

Solution: *RADII SOLIS* (sun's rays).
Compare Lockett, *Anglo-Saxon Psychologies,* 264–65.

It is tempting to emend the given solution to the singular form *(radius solis),* but perhaps unnecessary. In its closing challenge, the final line of this *aenigma* clearly echoes the final line of Aldhelm's *aenigmata* (ALD 100.83), and again underlines the necessary connection between the collections.

## TAT EP

It is far from clear that these closing four lines, which are syntactically very difficult and essentially repeat the directions of the opening couplet (which is established by the acrostic-telestich itself) are the work of Tatwine himself.

## HWÆTBERHT, *THE RIDDLES OF EUSEBIUS* (EUS)

I have consulted translations by Williams, "The Riddles of Tatwine and Eusebius," 157–249. I have also consulted Glorie, CCSL vol. 133, pp. 211–71. See also the more detailed commentary in *COEALRT*. For further reading, see in general Ebert, "Die Räthselpoesie der Angelsachsen"; Hahn, "Die Rätseldichter Tatwin und Eusebius"; Michael Tangl, *Die Briefe des heiligen Bonifatius und Lullus,* MGH ES 1 (Berlin, 1916), 158–59 (no. 76); Williams, "The Riddles of Tatwine and Eusebius."

## EUS 1

Solution: *DEUS* (God).

Eusebius begins his collection in a novel fashion, compared with his predecessors, but also establishes a sequence that is followed in the *aenigmata* that follow.

## EUS 2

Solution: *ANGELUS* (angel). See further Lockett, *Anglo-Saxon Psychologies,* 266–68.

The opening word drops a heavy hint about the answer: the Greek form of *nuntius* is ἄγγελος, which essentially supplies the solution. The connection with the previous *aenigma* is clear.

## EUS 3

Solution: *DAEMON* (demon).

Eusebius continues his cosmological sequence with "demon," really a fallen angel, whose interaction with mankind was to prove so fatal.

## EUS 4

Solution: *HOMO* (mankind).
See further Lockett, *Anglo-Saxon Psychologies,* 266–68.
For comparison, see ALC D7, LOR 1 (both solved "mankind").

The double substance *(substantia bina)* of mankind, comprising both body and soul, aligns this *aenigma* with a number of other riddles. Man is the last and lowest in the opening cosmological sequence EUS 1–4.

## EUS 5

Solution: *CAELUM* (heaven); the given solution in L is *DE CAELO,* although the scribe of G rather extraordinarily prefers *DE CAMELO* (about a camel).
For comparison, see ALC D38 (heaven).

The general pairing of "heaven" and "earth" in EUS 5–6 leads on naturally from the previous cosmological sequence. There is a broad parallel to this *aenigma* in ALD 48 (sphere of the heavens). The opening line seems to echo 1 Corinthians 6:10: "nor covetous . . . shall possess the kingdom of God" *(neque avari . . . regnum Dei possidebunt).*

## EUS 6

Solution: *TERRA* (earth).
For comparison, see ALD 1, ALC D47, OER 29, BER 45 (all solved "earth").

This *aenigma* is obviously linked to the last, and it connects well with EUS 8 (wind and fire); there is a general parallel with ALD 1 (earth).

## EUS 7

Solution: *LITTERAE* (letters); the given solution is *DE LITTERA* (about a letter).

For comparison, see ALD 30, TAT 4, ALC D1, EXE 55, BER 25 (all solved "letter[s]").

This *aenigma* links well with EUS 9 (alpha), and demonstrates the familiar "black-on-white" theme of many riddles on letters and writing (see, for example, TAT 4 above, and the note there). Otherwise, however, this *aenigma* demonstrates a rather original approach. There is a clear interleaving of topics between EUS 6 and 8 and EUS 7 and 9.

## EUS 8

Solution: *VENTUS ET IGNIS* (wind and fire).
For comparison, see ALD 2, ALC D46 (both solved "wind"); EXE 1 (wind and God); BER 41, ps-BED 5 (both solved "wind").

This is one of the *aenigmata* in which Eusebius takes his penchant for paradox to its natural conclusion, and it requires a double solution involving opposites; see further EUS 15 (fire and water), 18 (iniquity and justice), 21 (land and sea), 24 (life and death), 27 (humility and pride), and 48 (day and night).

## EUS 9

Solution: *ALPHA* (alpha).
See further Erhardt-Siebold, *Die lateinischen Rätsel,* 249–52; Patrick J. Murphy, *Unriddling the Exeter Riddles* (University Park, Pa., 2011), 100.

This is the first of several *aenigmata* in this collection focusing on individual letters: see further EUS 14 (the letter *x*), 19 (the letter *v/u*), and 39 (the letter *i*); also compare ALF A. Just as it is preceded by a double *aenigma* on "wind and fire," this *aenigma* is separated from the next one on an individual letter by two sets of paired *aenigmata,* on "sun" and "moon" and "bull" and "cow," respectively, in the sequence EUS 10–13. The *aenigma* incorporates a considerable amount of lore relating to *alpha.* In the second line, the use of Greek *alpha* (marked with strokes above and below) to stand for the numbers one and one thousand, respectively is generally known, but its claimed use for five hundred (for which the normal letter used is *phi*) is highly unusual. In the third line, the allusion is to the fact that the first letter of *Adam* is *A,* while the source of the final line is Isidore, *Etymologiae* 1.4.16: "But *A* is the first letter among all peoples for the reason that it is the first to open the voice for those being born." Presumably, that is why the creature is called "the lady of language."

## EUS 10

Solution: *SOL* (sun).
For comparison, see ALD 79 (sun and moon); ALC D41, EXE 4, BER 55–57 (all solved "sun"); EXE 27 (moon and sun); GES 15, OIR 11 (both solved "sun"); XMS Z4 (snow and sun).

For the positioning of this *aenigma* (which obviously connects to the one that follows) within the wider sequence, see the note at EUS 9 above.

## EUS 11

Solution: *LUNA* (moon).
See further Erhardt-Siebold, *Die lateinischen Rätsel,* 247–49.
For comparison, see ALD 6 (moon) and 79 (sun and moon); ALC D42, BER 58–59 (all solved "moon"); EXE 27 (moon and sun). For the positioning of this *aenigma* (which obviously connects to the one that precedes) within the wider sequence, see the note at EUS 9 above; Phoebus here stands simply for the sun, as at (for example) ALD 26.2 and 57.8, and EUS 58.2.

## EUS 12

Solution: *BOS* (bull).
See further Erhardt-Siebold, *Die lateinischen Rätsel,* 170–73; Dieter Bitterli, *Say What I Am Called: the Old English Riddles of the Exeter Book and the Anglo-Latin Riddle Tradition* (Toronto, 2009), 34.
For comparison, see SYM 32 (bull).

For the positioning of this *aenigma* (which obviously connects to the one that follows) within the wider sequence, see the note at EUS 9 above. This *aenigma* continues the wider theme of the "suffering servant," widely attested within the Anglo-Saxon riddle tradition, but in its final line alludes to the idea of a portentous speaking ox, bringing cities to a standstill, on which see further *COEALRT.* The fact that in one case such a portent, occurring in the reign of Augustus, announces the birth of Christ may connect this *aenigma* to EUS 14 below.

## EUS 13

Solution: *VACCA* (cow).
For comparison, see GES 28 (cow).

For the positioning of this *aenigma* (which obviously connects to the one that precedes) within the wider sequence, see the note at EUS 9 above.

## EUS 14

Solution: *X LITTERA* (the letter *x*). See further Erhardt-Siebold, *Die lateinischen Rätsel,* 249–53.
For comparison, see ALF X (letter *x*).

For the positioning of this *aenigma* within the wider sequence, see the notes at EUS 9 and 12 above. In the opening line, the word *augustus* hides a reference to the emperor Augustus, whose connection with the letter *X* is described by Isidore, *Etymologiae* 1.4.14, who notes that "the letter *X* did not exist until the time of Augustus."

## EUS 15

Solution: *IGNIS ET AQUA* (fire and water).
See further Erhardt-Siebold, *Die lateinischen Rätsel,* 245.

The double solution here links back both to EUS 8 (wind and fire) and to the immediately preceding *aenigma,* given that the letter *x,* which stands for the number ten, was itself held to be a double letter, as the final line makes clear. The final line appears to refer to a cooking pot, separating fire and water.

## EUS 16

Solution: *PHLASCA* (flask); the given solution in both G and L is in fact *DE PLASCA*.
See further Erhardt-Siebold, *Die lateinischen Rätsel,* 39–41.

This *aenigma,* which focuses through repetition on the joys to be had through drinking, has connections with other riddles in the tradition. There is a strong biblical echo with Psalms 103:15.

## EUS 17

Solution: *CRUX* (cross).
See further Erhardt-Siebold, *Die lateinischen Rätsel,* 107–15.
For comparison, see TAT 9 (Christ's cross).

This *aenigma* represents an original take on its topic: the parallels with TAT 9 (Christ's cross) are utterly commonplace.

## EUS 18

Solution: *INIQUITAS ET IUSTITIA* (iniquity and justice).

As with EUS 8 (about wind and fire) and EUS 15 (fire and water), there is an essential antipathy between the two elements.

## EUS 19

Solution: *V LITTERA* (the letter *u/v*).
See further Erhardt-Siebold, *Die lateinischen Rätsel,* 249–51 and 253–54; Murphy, *Unriddling the Exeter Riddles,* 94.
For comparison, see BED 10, ALF V (both solved "the letter *u/v*").

The first word, *Quinta* (fifth), provides a broad clue to the solution, since of course the letter *v* signifies "five" in the Roman alphabet; the notion that it is "the fifth of the vowels and the first" again highlights that fact that the subject is also the fifth vowel and that it derives its particular power from its position at the head of the key words *vox* (voice, speech), *verbum* (word), and *vocalis* (vowel). The idea that when it stands between *q* and a vowel, *u* is "nothing," stems from the usual spelling conventions: the letter itself has no force in that position. It is not clear what is meant by the statement that the third-century North African heretic Arius "banishes me from the rule of faith": the opening of John 1:1 ("In the beginning was the word: and the word was with God: and the word was God"; *In principio erat verbum et verbum erat apud deum et deus erat verbum*) seems in the poet's mind and lies behind the reference to the heretic Arius in EUS 19.4.

## EUS 20

Solution: *DOMUS* (house).
See further Erhardt-Siebold, *Die lateinischen Rätsel*, 156.

The first line presumably refers to the roofers who cover the house, and then dwell inside.

## EUS 21

Solution: *TERRA ET MARE* (land and sea).
See further Erhardt-Siebold, *Die lateinischen Rätsel*, 241–43.

This is another of the seven *aenigmata* in this collection requiring a double solution; see further the note to EUS 8 above.

## EUS 22

Solution: *SERMO* (speech).
See further Murphy, *Unriddling the Exeter Riddles*, 97.

There are numerous parallels that seem to connect this intriguing *aenigma* with some of the more puzzling and baffling riddles in the entire riddle tradition, notably EXE 37.

## EUS 23

Solution: *AEQUOR* (ocean).
See further Erhardt-Siebold, *Die lateinischen Rätsel*, 243–45.

The playful paradoxes of the previous *aenigma* are continued here; the final line is rather obscure and presumably refers to the contrast between the relatively small number of ships on the sea, when compared with the large number of waves that cover it. Alternatively, and given the subject of the *aenigma* that follows, the contrast is between the small number of ships on the surface of the sea, compared with the wrecked multitudes it contains.

## EUS 24

Solution: *MORS ET VITA* (life and death).
For comparison, see ALC D5 (life).

This is another of the seven *aenigmata* in this collection requiring a double solution; see further the note to EUS 8 above.

## EUS 25

Solution: *ANIMA* (soul); the solution given in G is *DE ANIMO* (about the mind), but *DE CORDE* (about the heart) in L.
See further Lockett, *Anglo-Saxon Psychologies*, 273–74.

This *aenigma* leads smoothly on from the previous one.

## EUS 26

Solution: *DIES BISSEXTILIS* (bissextile day).
See further Erhardt-Siebold, *Die lateinischen Rätsel*, 258–61.

This *aenigma* refers to the medieval science of calendar reckoning, known as *computus;* see too EUS 29. The bissextile day is the one added every leap year to regularize the calendar. In modern times, this produces a February 29 every four years, but in the Julian calendar the extra day was inserted at February 24, which in Roman reckoning was the sixth *(sextus)* day before the kalends of March; in a leap year that sixth day would therefore occur twice, producing a second sixth day *(bissextilis)*.

## EUS 27

Solution: *HUMILITAS ET SUPERBIA* (humility and pride).

This is another of the seven *aenigmata* in this collection requiring a double solution; see further the note to EUS 8 above.

## EUS 28

Solution: *CANDELA* (candle).
See further Erhardt-Siebold, *Die lateinischen Rätsel*, 26–29.
For comparison, see ALD 52 (candle).

This *aenigma* seems clearly aligned to the theme of "the suffering servant" that is so widespread in the tradition.

## EUS 29

Solution: *AETAS ET SALTUS LUNAE* (the age and the leap of the moon); the given solution is *DE AETATE ET SALTU*. On grounds of sense, it seems clear that a reference to the moon has dropped out, hence the preferred solution.
See further Erhardt-Siebold, *Die lateinischen Rätsel*, 258–61.

This *aenigma* seeks to square the circle with regard to the disparity between solar and lunar calendars, a problem that is at the heart of the issue of determining the date on Easter from the point of view of a solar calendar, when the Jewish festival of Passover, to which Easter is scripturally tied, is based on a lunar one; the medieval science is called *computus*. A solar year comprises 365.2422 days, a lunar month 29.3506 days; there are therefore 12.3683 lunar months in a solar year. The extra 0.3683 months over the standard twelve-month year can be variously expressed in fractions, but the one Bede chooses, namely 7/19 (= 0.3684), is astonishingly accurate: if seven extra lunar months are added (the technical term is "intercalated") over every nineteen years, the cycles remain closely in sync. The *momenta* (intervals) in question (EUS 29.3) are equivalent to one-fortieth of an hour, according to Bede, *De temporum ratione* 3, so "twenty times forty-eight *momenta*" equates to a normal twenty-four-hour day.

## EUS 30

Solution: *ATRAMENTORIUM* (inkhorn).
See further Erhardt-Siebold, *Die lateinischen Rätsel,* 68–71; Patrizia Lendinara, "Aspetti della società germanica negli enigmi del Codice Exoniense," in *Antichità germaniche,* ed. Vittoria Dolcetti Corazza and Renato Gendre, vol. 1, *I Seminario avanzato in Filologia germanica,* Bibliotheca Germanica, Studi e Testi 10 (Alessandria, 2001), 3–41; Bitterli, *Say What I Am Called,* 151–52.
For comparison, see EXE 84 and 89 (both solved "inkhorn").

This *aenigma* begins a sequence that is clearly focused on writing and scribal activity (EUS 30–33 and 35; see too the note on EUS 34). The "bitter gall" of the third line refers to ink, which was formed from oak gall.

## EUS 31

Solution: *PUGILLARES* (writing tablets); the given solution is *DE CERA* (about wax).
See further Erhardt-Siebold, *Die lateinischen Rätsel,* 63–67.
For comparison, see BER 19 (wax).

This *aenigma* leads on smoothly from the last, in that what is being described is not simply wax *per se,* but a wax tablet: the former certainly dispels darkness literally, but the latter does so with more force figuratively, by purging the darkness of ignorance. Once again, there seems doubt about whether the title/solution in both manuscripts is the correct one. The final line is evidently influenced by the opening words of John 1:1. See further the note to EUS 19 above.

## EUS 32

Solution: *MEMBRANA* (pieces of parchment); the given solution is *DE MEMBRANO* (about parchment). The subject speaks in the plural, hence the preferred solution; for a similar disparity, compare EUS 7.
See further Erhardt-Siebold, *Die lateinischen Rätsel,* 67–68; Murphy, *Unriddling the Exeter Riddles,* 86 and 94.

See too Leahy, *Anglo-Saxon Crafts,* 89–93.

For comparison, see TAT 5, BER 24, EXE 24 (all solved "parchment").

## EUS 33

Solution: *SCETHA* (book satchel).

This *aenigma* plays upon the idea of a creature that contains wisdom but cannot comprehend it; compare ALD 89 (book chest), EXE 45 (book moth), and SYM 16 (bookworm); ALD 89 may be the direct source here.

## EUS 34

Solution: *ATRAMENTUM* (ink); most previous commentators take *FLU-MEN* (river) as the answer, supported by the title (and marginal gloss) *DE FLUMINE* in both manuscripts.

See further Erhardt-Siebold, *Die lateinischen Rätsel,* 243–45.

For comparison, see ALC D49 (river[s]), LOR 12 (ink).

This *aenigma* is an oddity in several ways, interrupting as it does a sequence on books and writing (EUS 30–33 and 35), as well as being the only *aenigma* among the first forty in EUS to comprise more than four lines. As they stand, lines 3 and 4 simply repeat themselves, while line 5 explains that the Latin words *flūmen* and *flŭvius* (both meaning "river") share an opening syllable distinguished only by vowel length, with the "real" solution revealed in the final line through another spelling riddle, or logogriph, with *FLU-MEN* → *LUMEN* (light) by subtraction; the same logogriph appears at ALF F. It is tempting to regard lines 4 and 6 as interpolations, which is why I have tentatively italicized them here. In that case, a better solution might be *ATRAMENTUM* (ink), with the current fifth line (on this argument, the fourth and final line of the original) explained by the fact that the word can be scanned in verse as both *ătramentum* and *ātramentum,* given the dual nature of vowels followed by combinations of mute and liquid. The entire *aenigma* would then be a comment on how fluid ink is contained on parchment.

## EUS 35

Solution: *PENNA* (quill pen).
For comparison, see ps-BED 11, LOR 9, XMS X3 (all solved "quill pen").

This *aenigma* returns to the general sequence of writing and books found in EUS 30–33 and also returns to the "black-and-white" theme of writing. For rather similar *aenigmata*, see ALD 59, TAT 6, and LOR 9.

## EUS 36

Solution: *GLADIUS* (sword).
See further Erhardt-Siebold, *Die lateinischen Rätsel,* 77–85; Murphy, *Unriddling the Exeter Riddles,* 209.
For comparison, see TAT 30 (sword and sheath); EXE 18 and 69 (both solved "sword" or "man").

The final line is problematic. It looks as if the transmitted phrase *tot pene* may mask an infinitive, as *possum* seems to require; *torquere* (twist) or *torpere* (be still) are the right shape but confound both meaning and meter; perhaps one should read *tangere* (touch) instead. As it stands, the final line is simply baffling.

## EUS 37

Solution: *VITULUS* (bullock).
See further Erhardt-Siebold, *Die lateinischen Rätsel,* 170–73; Andy Orchard, "Enigma Variations: The Anglo-Saxon Riddle-Tradition," in *Latin Learning and English Lore: Studies in Anglo-Saxon Literature for Michael Lapidge,* ed. Katherine O'Brien O'Keeffe and Andy Orchard (Toronto, 2005), vol. 1, pp. 297–99; Bitterli, *Say What I Am Called,* 26–30.
For comparison, see ALD 83, ps-BED 7, LOR 11, EXE 36 (all solved "bullock").

This is another in a series of *aenigmata* on very similar topics; see, for example, ALD 83, EUS 12 and 13, and EXE 36 (all "bullock"). The broad themes of life and death here link this *aenigma* to the next one. For a further connection to the four rivers of Paradise and to the four Gospels, see ALD 83 in particular.

## EUS 38

Solution: *PULLUS* (chick).
See further Bitterli, *Say What I Am Called*, 115–21; Murphy, *Unriddling the Exeter Riddles*, 54–55.
For comparison, see ps-BED 2, XMS X2 (both solved "chick").

Just as the previous *aenigma* represents a variation on a familiar theme, so too does this one: for other riddles on similar topics, see ps-BED 2, LOR 8, EXE 11, SYM 14, BER 8.

## EUS 39

Solution: *I LITTERA* (the letter *i*).
See further Erhardt-Siebold, *Die lateinischen Rätsel*, 249–51 and 255–56.
For comparison, see BED 8, ALF I (both solved "letter *i*").

In the opening line, the suggestion seems to be that *i* can stand for Latin *imperator* (emperor) or *imperium* (empire) or perhaps *Iulius* (Julius [Caesar]). In the third line, the word *sola* (alone) gives a clue to the solution, when it is remembered that in the Roman alphabet the number one is signified by an *I;* the two letters are either *IC* or *IX,* abbreviations of *Iesus Christus* or *Iesus Xristus* ( Jesus Christ).

## EUS 40

Solution: *PISCIS* (fish).
See further Erhardt-Siebold, *Die lateinischen Rätsel*, 198–99.
For comparison, see ALD 71, BER 30 (both solved "fish").

The identification of the fish as a symbol for Christ connects this *aenigma* to the last, while it also continues the theme of earth/sea/sky found elsewhere. This *aenigma* seems notably similar to ALD 71, which has an identical solution. This is the first *aenigma* in a sequence of three (EUS 41–43) the solutions of which, *PISCIS* (for *PISCES*), *HYDRA*, and *DRACO*, are all constellations.

## EUS 41

Solution: *HYDRA* (Hydra); the given solution is *DE CHELIDRO SERPENTE* (on the demonic serpent).
See further Erhardt-Siebold, *Die lateinischen Rätsel*, 233–35.

Note that the unusual form *scedra* found in 41.2 represents a variant spelling (through aphaeresis) of the terms *excetra* or *excedra*, both of which signify a snake, indeed a hydra. Whereas in the previous *aenigma* mention is made of the earth/sea/sky, here the haunts of the watery creature in question are earth and water, since a hydra is defined as a water snake. The source is Isidore, *Etymologiae* 11.3.34–35, which describes how the Hydra has nine heads (rather than the seven specified here), and that whenever one is cut off, three grow back; Isidore also mentions that Hercules destroyed the Hydra, and that it is also the name of a place spewing waters that devastated the nearby city. In this *aenigma*, the seven heads seem to reflect the seven-headed dragon of Revelation 12:3: *draco magnus rufus habens capita septem* (a great red dragon, having seven heads), and may explain why this *aenigma*, describing a Satanic dragon (as does EUS 42), follows immediately after EUS 40, which deals with the Christological fish. This *aenigma* depicts another constellation (see the note at EUS 40); Hercules, another constellation, is mentioned at EUS 41.6.

## EUS 42

Solution: *DRACO* (dragon).
See further Erhardt-Siebold, *Die lateinischen Rätsel*, 231–32.

The source is clearly Isidore, *Etymologiae* 12.4.4, which describes how the dragon is bigger than all other serpents, dwells in a cave, can be driven into the air, has a crest and a small mouth, and its most dangerous part is its tail. This *aenigma* depicts yet another constellation in the series (see the note at EUS 40).

## EUS 43

Solution: *TIGRIS* (tigress); the given solution is *DE TIGRI BESTIA* (on the animal the tiger).
See further Erhardt-Siebold, *Die lateinischen Rätsel*, 224–25.
For comparison, see SYM 38 (tigress).

The source is clearly Isidore, *Etymologiae* 12.2.7, which describes how the creature in question is distinctive by its various markings and derives its name from the Persian word for an arrow, which it also shares with the name of the River Tigris. This *aenigma*, like many others, associates its subject with earth, air, and water.

## EUS 44

Solution: *PANTER* (panther); the given solution is *DE PANTHERA,* presumably influenced by the feminine form of the solution for the *aenigma* that precedes this one.
See further *COEALRT,* and Erhardt-Siebold, *Die lateinischen Rätsel*, 225–26.

The given solution for this *aenigma* cannot be correct as it stands, in view of the clearly masculine form of *alium* in EUS 44.3. The source is clearly Isidore, *Etymologiae* 12.2.8–9, which describes the panther as friendly to all creatures save the dragon and claims that the female of the species can only give birth once. The final line is a logograph in Latin: PANTER → PATER (father).

## EUS 45

Solution: *CAMELEON* (chameleon); the given solution is *DE CAME-LEONTE.*

Once again, the given solution cannot as it stands be strictly correct. This *aenigma* conflates two consecutive descriptions given by Isidore, *Etymologiae* 12.2.18–19, namely that of the *chamaeleon* (chameleon) and the *cameleopardus* (giraffe), a confusion explicable by the fact that Isidore compares both the chameleon and the giraffe to a creature known in Latin as a *pardus* (a term usually denoting a male panther), so linking this *aenigma* to the two that precede and follow. Isidore speaks of both creatures as being variegated in color, but while the chameleon adapts to its surroundings, the giraffe has a horse's neck, the feet of an ox or a buffalo, and a camel's head.

## EUS 46

Solution: *LEOPARDUS* (leopard).
See further Erhardt-Siebold, *Die lateinischen Rätsel,* 226–28.

The connection with the previous *aenigma* is through the *pardus.* The source is clearly Isidore, *Etymologiae* 12.2.10–11, which describes how leopards take their compound name from both the "filthy mating" of a kind of panther (here called *pardus*) and a lion *(leo),* with variations deriving from which of the two parent species is a male and which female. The use of the Latin term *lena* in the opening line highlights the disapproving sexualized imagery here: *lena* (seductress, whore) and *leaena* (lioness) seem deliberately conflated.

## EUS 47

Solution: *SCITALE* (piebald serpent); the given solution is *DE SCITALI SERPENTE.*
See further Erhardt-Siebold, *Die lateinischen Rätsel,* 235–36.

The variegated coloring of the creature in question in this *aenigma* links it back to the two previous *aenigmata,* while its celebrated lack of speed contrasts sharply with the immediately preceding leopard. The source is clearly Isidore, *Etymologiae* 12.4.19, which describes how the creature's mesmerizing markings compensate for its slowness by deluding victims and also notes that it generates enough of its own heat to thrive in winter.

## EUS 48

Solution: *DIES ET NOX* (day and night).

This is the only *aenigma* within the last group of twenty (EUS 41–60) that has a solution that is not an animal, however fantastic, is not largely or wholly reliant on Isidore, and in both its length (four lines) and its subject matter matches more closely the first group of forty *aenigmata,* from which it may well have been displaced. This is one of seven *aenigmata* in EUS with a double solution (see further the note at EUS 8 above, and note that all the others are in the sequence EUS 1–40), and yet its double aspect might also connect it to the *aenigma* that follows here (though see the note below). One might also suggest that, given the reference to winter in the previous *aenigma,* the true solution here might be "summer and winter," the one for work, the other for rest, although the transmitted solution certainly fits just as well.

## EUS 49

Solution: *AMPHISBAENA* (two-headed serpent); the given solution is *DE ANFIBINA SERPENTE* (on the serpent *amphisbaena*).

The double aspect of the "two-headed serpent" at first glance connects it to the preceding *aenigma,* although in fact the source, which is clearly Isidore, *Etymologiae* 12.4.20 (and note, for example, that it has heads at both ends, has blazing eyes, and does not shun the cold), links it still more securely with EUS 47, so again suggesting that EUS 48 has been displaced.

## EUS 50

Solution: *SAURA* (lizard); the given solution is *DE SAURA LACERTO* (on the lizard called *saura*).
See further Erhardt-Siebold, *Die lateinischen Rätsel,* 213–14.

The source is clearly Isidore, *Etymologiae* 12.4.37, which describes a type of lizard that grows blind with age and loves to gaze through cracks at the rising sun (here designated as "Titan").

## EUS 51

Solution: *SCORPIO* (scorpion).
See further Erhardt-Siebold, *Die lateinischen Rätsel,* 210.

The source is clearly Isidore, *Etymologiae* 12.5.4, which places the scorpion among worms (or "vermin": the Latin *vermis* signified both) rather than serpents and notes the fearsome "bite" of its tail and how it cannot attack the palm of the hand when placed there.

## EUS 52

Solution: *CYMERA* (Chimera).
See further Erhardt-Siebold, *Die lateinischen Rätsel*, 238–40.

The source here is evidently Isidore, *Etymologiae* 11.3.36 and 1.40.4, which describes the chimera as a tripartite creature, part lion, part dragon, part goat, sharing its name with a mountain in Cilicia, and slain by the famous monster slayer Bellerophon.

## EUS 53

Solution: *HIPPOPOTAMUS* (hippopotamus); the given solution is *YPOTAMA* (note the absence here of *DE*).
See further Erhardt-Siebold, *Die lateinischen Rätsel*, 228–29.

This *aenigma* begins a sequence of water-dwelling creatures, all broadly categorized as "fish" (EUS 53–55). The source is clearly Isidore, *Etymologiae* 12.6.21, which gives the Greek etymology for hippopotamus (river horse) and describes its hybrid existence both on land and in the water, as well as the mixed appearance, part horse, part boar, that links this *aenigma* to the one that immediately precedes it.

## EUS 54

Solution: *ECHENEIS* (remora); the given solution is *DE OCEANO PISCE* (about an ocean fish).
See further Erhardt-Siebold, *Die lateinischen Rätsel*, 99.

The source is clearly Isidore, *Etymologiae* 12.6.34, which describes a small sea creature (also known as a *remora,* a word connected to the Latin word for "delay," *mora*), some six inches long, which has the power to stick to a ship and hold it back.

## EUS 55

Solution: *TORPEDO* (electric ray); the given solution is *DE TURPEDO PISCE* (on the *torpedo* fish).
See further Erhardt-Siebold, *Die lateinischen Rätsel,* 199–200.

The source is clearly Isidore, *Etymologiae* 12.6.45, which describes this "fish" as being native to India and having the power to cause anyone who comes in contact with it to grow numb suddenly. In the second line, it is ambiguous whether *infandum* refers to *nomen* or *opus,* and so whether it is the "name" or the "deed" that is "unspeakable." I am grateful to Bob Babcock for the suggestion that what is at stake is the root *pedo,* which signifies both a verb (to fart, to break wind) and a noun (a farter, one who breaks wind): in either case, such an action is literally "unspeakable," and also "foul" and "offensive" (*turpis,* also spelled *torpis*), if we assume an invented etymology formed on *torp-pedo.*

## EUS 56

Solution: *CICONIA* (stork); the given solution is *DE CICONIA AVI* (on the bird the stork).
See further Erhardt-Siebold, *Die lateinischen Rätsel,* 186–89; Murphy, *Unriddling the Exeter Riddles,* 83.
For comparison, see ALD 31 (stork).

After the previous set of *aenigmata* dealing with creatures whose main domain is in the water (EUS 53–55), this *aenigma* opens the closing sequence, where all the creatures concerned are birds of one sort or another (EUS 56–60); for a similar sequence of bird riddles, compare EXE 5–8; note that while Symphosius often has *aenigmata* on living creatures, very few relate to birds: EUS and EXE may be filling a perceived gap. The source is clearly Isidore, *Etymologiae* 12.7.16–17, which describes the cracking sound of their cry, Asian origin, antipathy to snakes, role as harbingers of spring, and extraordinary devotion to their chicks.

## EUS 57

Solution: *STRUTIO* (ostrich).

See further Erhardt-Siebold, *Die lateinischen Rätsel,* 195–97.
For comparison, see ALD 42 (ostrich).

This *aenigma* is linked to the one preceding it by the theme of care for off-spring (or, in this case, the lack of it). The source is clearly Isidore, *Etymologiae* 12.7.20, which speaks about the creature's Greek name, feathers, flight-lessness, and abandonment of its eggs in the dust.

## EUS 58

Solution: *NOCTUA* (owlet).
See further Erhardt-Siebold, *Die lateinischen Rätsel,* 190–92.

The source is clearly Isidore, *Etymologiae* 12.7.40, which notes the antipathy of the creature in question to the sun (here designated as both "Phoe-bus" and "Titan"), its absence from Crete, and the fact that it would die if it ever came there. The precise description of the wind that kills it as coming from the south seems opaque.

## EUS 59

Solution: *PSITTACUS* (parrot).
See further Erhardt-Siebold, *Die lateinischen Rätsel,* 197–98.

The observation that a parrot naturally makes sounds that mimic greet-ings in both Latin and Greek derives from Isidore, *Etymologiae* 12.7.24, which also specifies its green and red coloring, its Indian origin, and its talent for mimicking human speech. I have restored the Greek in the bi-lingual penultimate line, as sanctioned by the source, Isidore, *Etymologiae* 12.7.24 (see further *COEALRT*); the Latin term transmitted in both manu-scripts, *care,* which on the face of it could be construed as "darling," is an evident transmission error of the possible transliterations *chaire* or *xaire;* the further form *kere* is found in manuscripts of Isidore.

## EUS 60

Solution: *BUBO* (horned owl); the given solution is *DE BUBALO* (about a buffalo).

See further Erhardt-Siebold, *Die lateinischen Rätsel,* 190; Murphy, *Unriddling the Exeter Riddles,* 83.

The gloomy connections with tombs and caves and darkness here all stem from the immediate source, Isidore, *Etymologiae* 12.7.39 and 42, two sections that deal, respectively, with the "horned owl" *(bubo)* and the "screech owl" *(strix).* The funereal sense of the final *aenigma* here matches similarly dolorous conclusions to other collections: compare OER 29 (grave) and SYM 100 (tombstone).

## BONIFACE (BON)

I have consulted the German translation in Glorie, CCSL, vol. 133, pp. 278–342. See also the more detailed commentary in *COEALRT.* For further reading, see in general Ernst Dümmler, ed., *Aenigmata Bonifatii,* MGH PLAC 1 (Berlin, 1881), 1–15; Chauncey E. Finch, "The Text of the *Aenigmata* of Boniface in Codex Reg. Lat. 1553," *Manuscripta* 6 (1962): 23–28.

## BON PR

The fundamental problem regarding the addressee is compounded by the fact that there are several "sisters" who figure in Boniface's extensive extant letter collection; see in particular Fell, "Some Implications of the Boniface Correspondence," in *New Readings on Women in Old English Literature,* ed. Helen Damico and Alexandra Hennessey Olsen (Bloomington, 1990), 29–43. Otherwise, however, the verse preface is a relatively straightforward piece of poetry: the twenty lines of verse break easily into two groups of ten, each dealing with the groups of ten virtues, "golden apples" produced from the "tree of life," and ten vices, "bitter apples" from the "tree of death," that follow. Some manuscripts and edition therefore distinguish BON 1–10 with the subtitle *De virtutibus* (on the virtues) and 11–20 *De vitiis* (on the vices).

## BON 1

Solution: *VERITAS* (truth); the acrostic reads *VERITAS AIT* (truth speaks).

This *aenigma* represents an extended meditation on the nature of truth, whose "sister" is unspecified, but could be any of the other virtues listed here. It is notable that in some manuscripts BON 5 (love, charity) follows immediately after BON PR, and this *aenigma* appears sixth in the series, so creating a sequence of "charity," "faith," and "hope," in the reordered first three *aenigmata,* but with the repositioned BON 1 splitting what seems an obvious link between "mercy" and "justice" (now BON 4 and 6). The notion that "truth" should come first seem strong, but it is tempting to reorder the sequence. See further *COEALRT.* The apparent reference to the Psalms in line 8 ("As the ancient poet David sang in song") seems opaque: Psalm 5:10 perhaps comes nearest (*Quoniam non est in ore eorum veritas; cor eorum vanum est;* "For there is no truth in their mouth; their heart is vain"), but does not seem particularly apposite.

## BON 2

Solution: *FIDES* (faith); the acrostic reads *FIDES CATHOLICA* (catholic faith).

One might wish for a sequence "faith," "hope," and "charity" or "love," followed by a contrast between "mercy" and "justice," but none such appears in the extant record. There seems a clear contrast in the final lines of this *aenigma* and the one that precedes it: "truth" belongs in heaven, to which "faith" is not destined to ascend.

## BON 3

Solution: *SPES* (hope); the acrostic reads *SPES FATUR* (hope declares). For comparison, see TAT 2 (Hope, Faith, Charity); ALC D68 (hope).

The motif of ascending to heaven, from which "faith" is sadly barred, links this *aenigma* to the preceding one. The middle lines of the *aenigma* contrast the true hope of heaven with the false hopes of this world.

## BON 4

Solution: *MISERICORDIA* (mercy); the acrostic reads *MISERICORDIA AIT* (mercy speaks).

This *aenigma* is clearly a companion piece to BON 6 (*IUSTITIA,* "justice"), and "justice" is evidently the sister in question. If BON 5 is misplaced, then BON 4 and BON 6 would be contiguous, as they indeed appear in several manuscripts. The theme of this *aenigma* is in any case that justice must always be tempered with mercy.

## BON 5

Solution: *CARITAS* (love, charity).
For comparison, see BED 4, TAT 14 (both solved "love").

The double acrostic reads *CARITAS AIT* (love speaks), with *CARITAS* spelled out twice, both forward at the beginning of the odd-numbered hexameters and in reverse in the even-numbered hexameters. This poem follows on immediately from BON PR in several manuscripts, including ones from Anglo-Saxon England, so emphasizing the primacy of love, the boundless power of which is emphasized throughout this *aenigma*. The "thought, word, and deed" triad found in line 12 represents a theme found commonly in early Anglo-Saxon literature, including at *Beowulf* 1844–45a, where Hrothgar tells Beowulf, *Þu eart mægenes strang ond on mode frod, / wis word-cwida* (You are strong in might and wise in mind, / clever in utterances); see further Andy Orchard, *A Critical Companion to "Beowulf "* (Cambridge, 2007), 55.

## BON 6

Solution: *IUSTITIA* (justice); the acrostic reads *IUSTITIA DIXIT* (justice has said).
This *aenigma* is clearly a companion piece to BON 4 (*MISERICORDIA AIT,* "mercy speaks").

There is a considerable focus here on the punishing aspects of "justice," and it is notable that although Christ appears in line 11 it is in his forbidding role as "the Thunderer," while there are rather more references to pagan myth, in the form of Jupiter the sky-god in the first line and Erebus and Pluto of the underworld in the concluding lines.

## BON 7

Solution: *PATIENTIA* (patience); the acrostic reads *PATIENTIA AIT* (patience speaks).

The long-suffering nature of patience contrasts sharply with the swift and summary aspects of justice emphasized in the preceding *aenigma*, while the persistence of patience is also highlighted by the threefold repetition of "through me" *(Per me . . . per me . . . per me)*.

## BON 8

Solution: *PAX* (peace); the acrostic reads *PAX VERA CRISTIANA* (true Christian peace), followed by five further and more enigmatic letters H2C22

In the third line there is an apparent reference to the angelic *Gloria in excelsis* from the greater doxology in the Mass, for which the Vulgate equivalent is *Gloria in altissimis Deo* (Luke 2:14). There is a broad clue to the solution (as if the acrostic were not enough) in the opening word, *Pacificum* (literally, "peace-bearing," "peace-bringing").

## BON 9

Solution: *HUMILITAS* (humility); the acrostic reads *HUMILITAS CRISTIANA FATETUR* (Christian humility confesses), although in G the acrostic is spoiled.

This *aenigma* is linked to the preceding one by the shared *CRISTIANA* in their respective acrostics. The manuscripts and previous editions all read "monk" *(monachus)* in line 19, though there seems no particular reason to single out monks as lacking humility; here I emend to "monarch" *(monarchus)* and note that the same evident error appears at the end of BON 13.29, translated there as "leaders" *(monarchos)*.

## BON 10

Solution: *VIRGINITAS* (virginity); the acrostic reads *VIRGINITAS AIT HUMILIUM* (the virginity of the humble speaks), although in G the acrostic is spoiled.

The complete acrostic connects this *aenigma* specifically with the one that precedes it. For the theme of mothers giving birth to their own parent, specified here in the fourth line and common throughout the riddle tradition as a whole, see the Introduction on shared themes across the collections.

## BON EP

Note that the sequence dealing with the virtues has its own epilogue, while that for the vices (and the entire set of poems as a whole) has none. The opening lines stress the fact that even among the pious elect, the virtues have their own special song to sing. In the manuscripts, this epilogue appears as the concluding lines to BON 10.

## BON 11

Solution: *NEGLEGENTIA* (negligence); the acrostic reads *NEGLE-GENTIA AIT* (negligence speaks).

In some manuscripts, this *aenigma* and the next one appear as the final two in the sequence on vices, with the much longer and more elaborate BON 13 occupying first place on the list. In the sequence as it stands, the opening and closing lines of this *aenigma*, with their emphasis on virginity, link it back to the subject matter of BON 10.

## BON 12

Solution: *IRACUNDIA* (anger); the acrostic reads *IRACUNDIA LOQUI-TUR* (anger declares).

For the different sequence found in some manuscripts, see the note on BON 11 above. The idea that anger travels looking back (BON 12.15) is a curious one; the phrase *spatior retrograda* is evidently borrowed from ALD 37.2–3, where it describes the motion of the crab.

## BON 13

Solution: *CUPIDITAS* (greed); the acrostic reads *CUPIDITAS AIT* (greed speaks), in BON 13.1–12.

Following the acrostic in 13.1–12 are a further fifty-five lines of explanation, mostly consisting of boasting about how greed has conquered a great variety of people. It is particularly striking that BON 13.39–43 should appear to refer by name to no fewer than seven of the virtues as adversaries (justice, faith, peace, Christ's humility, patience of the saints, mercy, and holy charity; *Iustitiaeque fidem et pacem . . . et Christi humilitas . . . sanctorum . . . patientia . . . misericordia . . . dilectio sancta,* with the last taken as a synonym for *caritas*). For the sequence of this *aenigma* in some manuscripts, see the note on BON 11 above. Note that the opening word *Cernebam* aligns this *aenigma* with a whole range of riddles, mostly in Old English, that begin with some form of "I saw" (see further *COEALRT*).

## BON 14

Solution: *SUPERBIA* (pride); the acrostic reads *SUPERBIA LOQUITUR* (pride speaks).
For comparison, see TAT 25 (pride).

In traditional theology, pride (which cause the temptation of Satan and the Fall of Angels) is the first of the sins, but here it is rather relegated down the list, albeit that its prime importance in sacred history is emphasized throughout. In BON 14.15 ("with hateful force I strike the holy in the heel"), the word translated here as "hateful" *(invisis)* might equally be rendered "unseen," while the notion of striking in the heel might allude to Genesis 3:15, when God curses the serpent in Eden, saying of Eve: "She shall crush thy head, and thou shalt lie in wait for her heel" *(ipsa conteret caput tuum, et tu insidiaberis calcaneo eius).*

## BON 15

Solution: *CRAPULA* (overindulgence); the acrostic reads *CRAPULA GULAE* (overindulgence of the gullet).

The Medieval Latin term *crapula* refers both to "gluttony" and to "intoxication" or "inebriation"; while the former is evidently the central topic here, the latter sense very clearly links this *aenigma* to the next.

## BON 16

Solution: *EBRIETAS* (drunkenness); the acrostic reads *EBRIETAS DICE-BAT* (drunkenness used to utter).

It is notable that only here and at BON 6 *(IUSTITIA)* does the acrostic employ a verb in the past tense. The link between the excesses of this *aenigma* and the one that precedes seems clear; a similar connection ties it to the next.

## BON 17

Solution: *LUXORIA* (lust); the acrostic reads *LUXORIA AIT* (lust speaks).

Mention of Sodom in its closing lines links this *aenigma* to the excesses of BON 15, where Sodom appears in the opening line. Here, the first line, describing the seductive brilliance of lust, contains a very obvious echo of ALD 100.53 *(Limpida sum, fateor;* "I am good-looking, I confess"), where the subject is creation itself.

## BON 18

Solution: *INVIDIA* (envy); the acrostic reads *INVIDIA AIT* (envy speaks).

In this *aenigma*, envy is explicitly linked in lines 3–4 back to pride (BON 14), through the description of the serpent that entered Eden, and caused the expulsion of Adam and Eve from Paradise. The closing lines of this *aenigma*, in which envy says of herself that "I am called the wicked devastator of virtues" *(virtutum vastatrix impia dicor)* connect to the opening line of the next, where ignorance announces of herself that "For a long time now I shall be described as a fool and nurse of errors" *(Iam dudum nutrix errorum et stulta vocabor)*.

## BON 19

Solution: *IGNORANTIA* (ignorance); the acrostic reads *IGNORANTIA AIT* (ignorance says).

The connection between this *aenigma* and the preceding one has been discussed above; it is connected to the one that follows by the notion in BON 19.12 that "wise Greece calls me 'unperceived'" *("invisam," vocitat me Grecia prudens)*, which is echoed at BON 20.14 where we are told by vainglory that those who seek heaven "name me a wicked virgin" *(vocitant me "virgo maligna")*. The geographical range of the poem is notable, contrasting the ignorance of the Germans, Slavs, and Scythians in BON 19.4–5 with the wisdom of the Greeks in BON 19.12.

## BON 20

Solution: *VANA GLORIA* (vainglory); the acrostic reads *VANA GLORIA IACTANTIA* (vainglory boastfulness).

This *aenigma* extends still further the geographical range of the previous one, adding here a reference to China in BON 20.21. Vainglory concludes the sequence of vices by proclaiming that of all her sisters (the other vices) "none . . . is proved to be more false" *(falsior . . . probatur nulla)*.

## ALCUIN (ALC, PS-ALC, AND ALC D)

I have consulted translations by Martha Bayless, "Alcuin's *Disputatio Pippini* and the Early Medieval Riddle Tradition," in *Humour, History and Politics in Late Antiquity and the Early Middle Ages*, ed. Guy Halsall (Cambridge, 2002), 157–78 (ALC D), and Paul Sorrell, "Alcuin's 'Comb' Riddle," *Neophilologus* 80 (1996): 311–18 (ALC 1). See also the more detailed commentary in *COEALRT*. For further reading, see in general Helga Reuschel, "Kenningar bei Alcuin: Zur 'Disputatio Pippini cum Albino,'" *Beiträge zur Geschichte der deutschen Sprache und Literatur* 62 (1938): 143–55; W. Wilmanns, ed., "Disputatio regalis et nobilissimi iuvenis Pippini cum Albino scholastico," *Zeitschrift für deutsches Altertum* 14 (1869): 530–55; Walther Suchier, ed., "Disputatio Pippini cum Albino," in *Die Altercatio Hadriani Augusti et Epicteti philosophi, nebst einigen verwandten Texten*, ed. L. W. Daly and Walther Suchier, Illinois Studies in Language and Literature 24 (Urbana, 1939), 134–46; Julián Solana Pujalte, "Análisis métrico-prosódico de la poesía de Alcuino de York," (PhD diss., University of Seville, 1987); Menso Folkerts, "Die Alkuin zugeschriebenen *Propositiones ad acuendos iuvenes*," in *Science in*

*Western and Eastern Civilization in Carolingian Times,* ed. P. L. Butzer and D. Lohrmann (Basel, 1993), 273–81; John Hadley and David Singmaster, "Problems to Sharpen the Young: An Annotated Translation of *Propositiones ad acuendos iuvenes,* the Oldest Mathematical Problem Collection in Latin, Attributed to Alcuin of York," *Mathematical Gazette* 76 (1992): 102–26; Sorrell, "Alcuin's 'Comb' Riddle"; David Singmaster, "The History of Some of Alcuin's Propositions," in *Karl der Grosse und sein Nachwirken: 1200 Jahre Kultur und Wissenschaft in Europa,* vol. 2, *Mathematisches Wissen,* ed. P. L. Butzer, M. Kerner, and W. Oberschelp (Turnhout, 1998), 11–29; Dieter Bitterli, "Alkuin von York und die angelsächsische Rätseldichtung," *Anglia* 128 (2010): 4–20; Andy Orchard, "Alcuin's Educational Dispute: The Riddle of Teaching and the Teaching of Riddles," in *Childhood and Adolescence in Anglo-Saxon Literary Culture,* ed. Susan Irvine and Winfried Rudolf (Toronto, 2018), 167–201.

## ALC 1

Solution: *PECTEN* (comb).

See further Sorrell, "Alcuin's 'Comb' Riddle"; Andy Orchard, "Wish You Were Here: Alcuin's Courtly Verse and the Boys Back Home," in *Courts and Regions in Medieval Europe,* ed. Sarah Rees Jones, Richard Marks, and A. J. Minnis (Woodbridge, 2000), 21–43; and Leahy, *Anglo-Saxon Crafts,* 55–58.

The circumstances behind this *aenigma,* which was sent along with a letter of thanks to Archbishop Riculf of Mainz (787–813), are known with some precision and are discussed by Sorrell and Orchard in the articles noted above.

## ALC 2

Solution: *MALUM* (evil, apple) → *MULAM* (mule).

For comparison, see TAT 21 (evil); SYM 37 (mule).

This *aenigma* begins a sequence of logographs (ALC 2–6) that might easily be considered part of one long poem; the sequence ends (ALC 6.7) with a challenge of the type found at ALC 1.8 (see note there). This *aenigma* opens with a reference to the eating of the fateful apple in Eden (Latin *mālum*, Genesis 2:16–17), but also to the fact that the word *mălum* (with a short *a*) also means "evil"; when reversed, the word *malum* (whether meaning "evil" or "apple") produces *mulam* (mule). See too TAT 22 (Adam) and SYM 84 (apple).

## ALC 3

Solution: *VIRTUS* (power) → *TUS* (incense) → *VIR* (man) → *VIRUS* (venom).

The only difficulty here lies in the third line, where the two halves of the key word *VIRTUS* are transposed, to give *TUS* (incense) and *VIR* (man), presumably to put the words for "God" *(deum)* and "man" *(hominem)* next to each other in the Latin.

## ALC 4

Solution: *CANUS* (white-haired man) → *ANUS* (old woman) → *SUS* (swine).

Earlier editors have *SANUS* (healthy man) as the first element of the solution, but this seems unlikely, given that the word appears in the opening line. I am grateful to Bob Babcock for the suggestion that if the numeration in the riddle is progressive, and entails the removal of first one letter, then two, then three, there may also be a bilingual pun on the Greek word ὗς (pig, wild boar), which is grammatically both masculine and feminine.

## ALC 5

Solution: *MAGNUS* (mighty) → *AGNUS* (lamb) → *MANUS* (hand) → *MAGUS* (magician) → *MUS* (mouse) → *ANUS* (old woman).

The fact that the opening line denoting *MAGNUS* contains the word *presbyter,* a synonym of *sacerdos* (priest) is presumably a reference through allusion to the antiphon and responsory from the common of confessors, which begins "Behold: a great priest" *(Ecce sacerdos magnus)*. In the last line, the rare word *dolabra* usually means "pickax," but here uniquely seems to be used in the sense "old woman," perhaps through confusion with the word for a "handmaid" *(abra)*, which appears, for example in the biblical Judith 8:32.

## ALC 6

Solution: *SIC ET NON* (yes and no) → *MEUM ET TUUM* (mine and yours) → *EGO ET TU* (I and you) → *NOS ET VOS* (we and you [?]). The first solution could also be *EST ET NON,* with essentially the same meaning.

## ALC 7

Solution: *FORNAX* (furnace).

This *aenigma* opens a sequence of three (ALC 7–9) that all share the same solution; a similar strategy is found in several of the other analogous collections: see, for example, SYM 76 and 76a (both "flint"), BER 55–59 (all "sun," "moon," or "sun and moon"), and GES 21–23a (all "waves," with different formulations). This *aenigma,* unlike the ones preceding and the one that follows, is in elegiac couplets.

## ALC 8

Solution: *FORNAX* (furnace).

Although previous editors understand this as part of the *aenigma* that follows, it is taken here as a separate two-line text because it is in hexameters, rather than the elegiac couplets of the *aenigmata* that precede and follow.

## ALC 9

Solution: *FORNAX* (furnace).

This is the last of the sequence of three *aenigmata* with the same solution. This *aenigma* returns to the elegiac couplets of ALC 7.

## ps-ALC 1

Solution: *IHC* ( Jesus), though this solution is far from certain.

This *aenigma* follows after ALC 6 in two manuscripts but is so garbled and stylistically distinct that it seems highly unlikely to be by Alcuin. Even though there is clear reference to God the Creator and the Trinity, the precise solution seems opaque: in Latin, the word for God *(deus)* is usually abbreviated as *ds*, with the two vowels "changed," but the word itself appears in the final line, so it is unlikely to offer the correct answer. A three-letter solution seems called for, and a common abbreviation for Jesus derived ultimately from the Greek, namely *IHC*, may be required instead; the solution offered here is tentative at best, given the faulty nature of the text.

## ALC D1

Solution: *LITTERA* (letter).
For comparison, see ALD 30, TAT 4, EUS 7, EXE 55, BER 25 (all solved "letter[s]").

The Latin word *historia* covers both "story" and "history"; both seem appropriate here.

## ALC D2

Solution: *VERBUM* (word).

## ALC D3

Solution: *LINGUA* (tongue).

## ALC D4

Solution: *AER* (air, breath).

Whereas Latin *aer* generally means "air," the positioning of this term invites rather the solution "breath"; it is notable that the Old English word *æðm* carries both senses.

## ALC D5

Solution: *VITA* (life).
For comparison, see EUS 24 (life and death).

## ALC D6

Solution: *MORS* (death).
For comparison, see EUS 24 (life and death); EXE 37 (death).

## ALC D7

Solution: *HOMO* (mankind).
For comparison, see EUS 4, LOR 1 (both solved "mankind"). Note that in this case there are nine separate questions combining to supply the solution; the last word of ALC D6 and the first word of ALC D8 seem to set the limits for the topic.

## ALC D8

Solution: *SOMNUS* (sleep).
For comparison, see SYM 99 (sleep).

## ALC D9

Solution: *INNOCENTIA* (innocence).

Presumably what links the themes of "sleep" and the body parts that follow is the notion that innocent sleep is not concerned with the body, but rather with the soul.

## ALC D10–37

This extended sequence contains no fewer than twenty-eight *aenigmata* on body parts:

ALC D10 (*CAPUT,* "head").
ALC D11 (*CORPUS,* "body").

ALC D12 (*COMAE*, "hair"; for comparison, see too SYM 58 [hair]).
ALC D13 (*BARBA*, "beard").
ALC D14 (*CEREBRUM*, "brain").
ALC D15 (*OCULI*, "eyes").
ALC D16 (*NARES*, "nostrils").
ALC D17 (*AURES*, "ears").
ALC D18 (*FRONS*, "face").
ALC D19 (*OS*, "mouth," "bone"; for comparison, see too BED 3, OER 4 [both solved "mouth" or "bone"]).
ALC D20 (*DENTES*, "teeth").
ALC D21 (*LABIA*, "lips").
ALC D22 (*GULA*, "throat").
ALC D23 (*MANUS*, "hands").
ALC D24 (*DIGITI*, "fingers").
ALC D25 (*PULMO*, "lung").
ALC D26 (*COR*, "heart"; for comparison, see too LOR 2 [heart]).
ALC D27 (*IECUR*, "liver").
ALC D28 (*FEL*, "gallbladder").
ALC D29 (*SPLEN*, "spleen").
ALC D30 (*STOMACHUS*, "stomach").
ALC D31 (*VENTER*, "belly").
ALC D32 (*OSSA*, "bones").
ALC D33 (*COXAE*, "hips").
ALC D34 (*CRURA*, "shins").
ALC D35 (*PEDES*, "feet").
ALC D36 (*SANGUIS*, "blood").
ALC D37 (*VENAE*, "veins").

## ALC D38–43

This sequence of six *aenigmata* on celestial bodies and calendrical features comprises the following:

ALC D38 (*CAELUM*, "sky"; for comparison, see too EUS 5 [heaven]).
ALC D39 (*LUX*, "light").
ALC D40 (*DIES*, "day"; for comparison, see too OER 24 [day]).

ALC D41 (*SOL,* "sun"; for comparison, see too ALD 79 [sun and moon]; BER 55–57, EXE 4 [all solved "sun"] and 27 [moon and sun]; OIR 11, GES 15 [both solved "sun"]; XMS Z4 [snow and sun]).

ALC D42 (*LUNA,* "moon"; for comparison, see too ALD 6 [moon] and 79 [sun and moon]; EUS 11, BER 58–59 [all solved "moon"]; EXE 27 [moon and sun]).

ALC D43 (*STELLAE,* "stars"; for comparison, see too OER 16, BER 62 [both solved "star(s)"]).

## ALC D44–54

This sequence of eleven *aenigmata* on natural phenomena comprises the following:

ALD D44 (*PLUVIA,* "rain"; for comparison, see too SYM 9 [rain]).

ALC D45 (*NEBULA,* "cloud"; for comparison, see too ALD 3, SYM 8 [both solved "cloud"]).

ALC D46 (*VENTUS,* "wind"; for comparison, see too ALD 2 [wind]; EUS 8 [wind and fire]; EXE 1 [wind and God]; ps-BED 5, BER 41 [both solved "wind"]).

ALC D47 (*TERRA,* "earth"; for comparison, see too ALD 1, EUS 6, OER 29, BER 45 [all solved "earth"]).

ALC D48 (*MARE,* "sea"; for comparison, see too BED 15 [sea]).

ALC D49 (*FLUMINA,* "rivers"; for comparison, see too EUS 34 [river(s)]).

ALC D50 (*AQUA,* "water"; for comparison, see too ALD 29, LOR 3, EXE 39 and 80, OER 21 [all solved "water"]).

ALC D51 (*IGNIS,* "fire"; for comparison, see too ALD 44, TAT 31 and 33, ALC D73, EXE 48, GES 29 [all solved "fire"]).

ALC D52 (*FRIGUS,* "cold").

ALC D53 (*GELU,* "ice"; for comparison, see too ps-BED 6, LOR 4, EXE 31 and 66, OER 11, SYM 10, BER 38 and 42, OIR 9 [all solved "ice"]).

ALC D54 (*NIX,* "snow"; for comparison, see too TAT 15 [snow, hail, and ice]; LOR 6, SYM 11 [both solved "snow"]; XMS Z4 [snow and sun]).

## ALC D55–59

This sequence of five *aenigmata* on the seasons culminates with the year itself:

ALC D55 (*HIEMS*, "winter").
ALC D56 (*VER*, "spring").
ALC D57 (*AESTAS*, "summer").
ALC D58 (*AUTUMNUS*, "autumn").
ALC D59 (*ANNUS*, "year"; for comparison, see too OIR 10 [year]). The twelve palaces of the year are evidently the astrological houses of the relevant signs.

## ALC D60

Solution: *CURIOSITAS* (curiosity).

## ALC D61

Solution: *NAVIS* (ship).
For comparison, see SYM 13, BED 12, BER 11 (all solved "ship"); GES 24 (solved "iceberg" or perhaps "ship"); XMS Z2 (ship).

## ALC D62

Solution: *HARENA* (sand).

## ALC D63

Solution: *HERBA* (grass).

## ALC D64

Solution: *OLERA* (herbs).

## ALC D65

Solution: *FAMES* (hunger).

## ALC D66

Solution: *LUCRUM* (wealth).
For comparison, see OER 1, OIR 1 (both solved "wealth").

## ALC D67

Solution: *SOMNUS* (sleep).

## ALC D68

Solution: *SPES* (hope).
For comparison, see BON 3 (hope); TAT 2 (Hope, Faith, Charity).

## ALC D69

Solution: *AMICITIA* (friendship). One wonders whether a better solution might be *CARITAS* (love) to fit more smoothly with the preceding and following questions, and so provide the familiar triad of hope, faith, and charity.

## ALC D70

Solution: *FIDES* (faith).

## ALC D71

Solution: *IMAGO IN AQUA* (reflection in water).

## ALC D72

Solution: *SOMNIUM* (dream); perhaps a better solution would be *HOMO IN SOMNIO VISUS* (man seen in a dream).

## ALC D73

Solution: *IGNIS* (fire).

For comparison, see ALD 44, TAT 31 and 33, ALC D51, EXE 48, GES 29 (all solved "fire").

## ALC D74

Solution: *TINTINNABULA* (bells).
See too Leahy, *Anglo-Saxon Crafts,* 132.
For comparison, see TAT 7, EXE 2 and 67, SYM 80 (all solved "bell[s]").

## ALC D75

Solution: *SILEX* (flint).
For comparison, see SYM 76 and 76a (both solved "flint").

## ALC D76

Solution: *LEBES* (cauldron).
For comparison, see ALD 49, ps-BED 10, XMS X1 (all solved "cauldron").

## ALC D77

Solution: *PEDICULI* (lice).
For comparison, see SYM 30 (lice).

## ALC D78

Solution: *PULLUS IN OVO* (chick in egg).
For comparison, see SYM 14 (chick in egg).

## ALC D79

Solution: *ECHO* (echo).
For comparison, see SYM 98 (echo).

## ALC D80

Solution: *PISCIS ET FLUMEN* (fish and river).
For comparison, see EXE 81, SYM 12 (both solved "river and fish").

## ALC D81

Solution: *HOMO IN SOMNIO* (figure in a dream).

## ALC D82

Solution: *FLEXUS DIGITORUM* (finger counting).
For comparison, see SYM 96 (finger counting).

## ALC D83

Solution: *PULVILLUS* (pillow).
For comparison, see ALD 41 (pillow).

## ALC D84

Solution: *ADAM, ENOCH/ELIAS, LAZARUS* (Adam, Enoch/Elijah, Lazarus).
For comparison, see TAT 22 (Adam).

The roman numerals at the end of this *aenigma* must be understood as equating to the Greek system, where numbers equate to letters, in these cases α (I), ε (V), and λ (XXX), which are indeed (whether understood in Greek or in Latin) the first letters of the solutions. The Hebrew meaning of Adam is "earth," as was widely understood in the period, and both Enoch and Elijah are identified as types of Christ, since they were assumed directly into heaven without dying; the biblical Lazarus of Luke 16:19–31 was likewise explicitly a poor man, contrasted in Christ's parable with a rich man (and a distinct figure from Lazarus of Bethany, who was raised from the dead in John 11).

## ALC D85

Solution: *SAGITTA* (arrow).
For comparison, see BED 14, TAT 32, SYM 65, GES 13 (all solved "arrow").

## ALC D86

Solution: *MILES* (soldier).

## ALC D87

Solution: *NIHIL* (nothing).

The whole philosophical notion of "nothingness" was a hot topic in late eighth-century philosophy, partly promoted by one of Alcuin's own students, Fredegesius, who suggested that "nothing" must exist because there was a word for it. See further John Marenbon, *From the Circle of Alcuin to the School of Auxerre* (Cambridge, 1981), 63.

## ALC D88

Solution: *EPISTOLA* (letter).

## THE LORSCH RIDDLES (LOR)

I have consulted the German translation in Glorie, CCSL vol. 133, pp. 347–58. See also the more detailed commentary in *COEALRT.* For further reading, see in general Ernst Dümmler, "Lörscher Rätsel," *Zeitschrift für deutsches Altertum* 22 (1878): 258–63; Ernst Dümmler, *Aenigmata Anglica,* MGH PLAC 1 (Berlin, 1881), 20–23; Ludwig Bieler, "Some Remarks on the *Aenigmata Laureshamensia,*" *Romanobarbarica* 2 (1977): 11–15; Patrizia Lendinara, "Gli Aenigmata Laureshamensia," *PAN: Studi dell'Istituto di Filologia Latina* 7 (1981 for 1979): 73–90.

## LOR 1

Solution: *HOMO* (mankind).
For comparison, see EUS 4, ALC D7 (both solved "mankind").

This *aenigma* breaks easily into two parts: the first four lines deal with the double birth of mankind, with "God" (*deus*) as the father and "earth" (*terra*) as the mother, while the final eight form a long and complex single sentence bewailing what happens next.

## LOR 2

Solution: *ANIMUS VEL ANIMA* (mind or soul). Suggested solutions include *ANIMA/CORS* (soul/heart).

See further Lockett, *Anglo-Saxon Psychologies,* 275–78, who suggests *BREOST-COFA* (breast-coffer) as another possibility.
For comparison, see ALC D26 (heart).

This *aenigma* leads on naturally from the one that precedes (LOR 1 [mankind]). A likely partial source is Song of Songs 5:2 ("I sleep and my heart watcheth").

## LOR 3

Solution: *NIMBUS* (storm cloud); other suggestions include *AQUA* (water).
For comparison, see ALD 29, ALC D50, EXE 39 and 80, OER 21 (all solved "water").

Given the possibility that the previous *aenigma* refers both to the body and to the soul that it contains, it is tempting here too to prefer a similar kind of solution: both "storm cloud" and the rain it contains.

## LOR 4

Solution: *GELU* (ice).
For comparison, see ps-BED 6, ALC D53, EXE 31 and 66, OER 11, SYM 10, BER 38 and 42, OIR 9 (all solved "ice").

This *aenigma* continues the theme of the previous sequence of discussing both a container and its contents; the same theme continues in the *aenigma* that follows. The father here is presumably *ventus* (wind), the mother *aqua* (water), as they also appear to be in the rather similar TAT 15 (snow, hail, and ice). The third line seems to refer to the production of great sheets of ice or icebergs on the surface of the water (the mother) through the influence of the freezing wind (the father). The final lines of the *aenigma* repeat the common riddling theme of the daughter who gives birth to her own mother, on which see the Introduction, on shared themes across the riddle collections.

## LOR 5

Solution: *CUPA VINARIA* (a wine cup).
For comparison, see ALD 78, EXE 9, XMS X4 (all solved "wine cup").

This *aenigma* again seems to refer both to a container and what it contained, with the "five branches" the fingers that cup the wine vessel, and the wine itself also referred to here.

## LOR 6

Solution: *NIX* (snow).
For comparison, see TAT 15 (snow, hail, and ice); ALC D54, SYM 11 (both solved "snow"); XMS Z4 (snow and sun).

There are several textual problems in this *aenigma* (on which see in detail *COEALRT*); the general sense, however, is clear enough.

## LOR 7

Solution: *CASTANEA* (chestnut).
For comparison, see BER 48 (chestnut tree).

The last two lines turn on a logograph (for this kind of word riddle, see the note at ALD 63): when the last three letters of *castanea* are removed, the result is *casta* (a chaste woman), here cynically and misogynistically declared a rarity.

## LOR 8

Solution: *FETUS* (fetus), or *OVUM* (egg), or *PULLUS IN OVO* (chick in egg).

The skin hanging on the wall of a cell is the membrane left behind in the broken eggshell.

## LOR 9

Solution: *PENNA* (quill pen).
See further Murphy, *Unriddling the Exeter Riddles,* 86.
For comparison, see ps-BED 11, EUS 35, XMS X3 (all solved "quill pen").

## LOR 10

Solution: *LUCERNA* (lamp).
For comparison, see BER 2 (lamp).

This *aenigma* is connected to the previous one by the contrast between light and darkness.

## LOR 11

Solution: *IUVENCUS* (bullock); other suggestions include *TAURUS* (bull), *VITULUS* (bullock), or *BOS* (bull).
For comparison, see ALD 83, ps-BED 7, EUS 37, EXE 36 (all solved "bullock").

There seems to be a potential connection between this *aenigma* and the one preceding it, in terms of the cruel binding of limbs.

## LOR 12

Solution: *ATRAMENTUM* (ink).
For comparison, see EUS 34 (ink).

### THE ABINGDON RIDDLE (ABI)

Solution: *SCALAE* ("bowls," "scales").
I have consulted the translations by David W. Porter, "A Double Solution to the Latin Riddle in MS. Antwerp, Plantin-Moretus Museum M16.2," *American Notes and Queries* 9.1 (1996): 3–9. See also the more detailed commentary in *COEALRT*. See further: Max Förster, "Die altenglische Glossenhandschrift Platinus 32 (Antwerpen) und Additional 32246 (London)," *Anglia* 41 (1917): 155; David W. Porter, "Æthelwold's Bowl and *The Chronicle of Abingdon*," *Neuphilologische Mitteilungen* 97 (1996): 163–67.

While the general subject has been identified as Æthelwold's bowl, a measure introduced by Abbot Æthelwold as the official measure for the amount of beer to be drunk daily in the monastery, it has also been argued that there is a double solution, and that while the singular "bowl" *(scala)* refers to a drinking measure, the plural can also refer to a set of scales.

## THE HIGH-MINDED LIBRARY (BIB)

See further *COEALRT.* BIB is the least studied and least annotated of the collections that make up the Anglo-Saxon riddle tradition; for the general context, see A. G. Rigg and G. R. Wieland, "A Canterbury Classbook of the Mid-Eleventh Century (The 'Cambridge Songs' Manuscript)," *Anglo-Saxon England* 4 (1975): 113–30; Martin Irvine, *The Making of Textual Culture*: "Grammatica" and Literary Theory (350–1100) (Cambridge, 1994).

## BIB 1

Solution: *SAPIENTIA* (wisdom).
For comparison, see ps-BED 1 (wisdom).

BIB opens with a reference to "wisdom," as do ps-BED 1 and TAT 1 (the given solution of the latter is *PHILOSOPHIA* [philosophy]). The source of this *aenigma* is probably Isidore, *Etymologiae* 2.24.3, which explains that "wisdom" or "philosophy" is divided into "natural science" (BIB 2), "ethics" (BIB 7), and "logic" (BIB 9), each of which is further subdivided as explained in the relevant notes below. In the final line, the word *lota* (the past participle of the verb *lavo,* "wash") is understood in its poetic and figurative sense, "glorious," "well-scrubbed," "noble."

## BIB 2

Solution: *PHYSICA* (natural science).

The ultimate source seems to be Isidore, *Etymologiae* 2.24.3–4, where we are told that physics is divided into four, namely arithmetic, geometry, music, and astronomy, which are the subjects of the four *aenigmata* that follow (BIB 3–6). See too the note at BIB 10 below.

## BIB 3

Solution: *ARITHMETICA* (arithmetic).

The ultimate source seems to be Isidore, *Etymologiae* 2.24.14–15, where "arithmetic" is described as the discipline of counting. For another possible rationale behind the sequence BIB 3–6, see the note at BIB 10.


## BIB 4

Solution: *GEOMETRIA* (geometry); G has *DE GEOMETRICA.*

For the likely ultimate source, see Isidore, *Etymologiae* 2.24.15 above, where "geometry" is described as the discipline of shapes and unmoving size; lines 7–8 comprise an allusion to the traditional etymology of *geometria* (measuring earth), found in Isidore, *Etymologiae* 3.10.3.


## BIB 5

Solution: *MUSICA* (music).

According to Isidore, *Etymologiae* 3.18, music is divided into three, namely *harmonicus* (vocal song), *organicus* (music from wind instruments), and *rhythmicus* (music from plucked or struck instruments).


## BIB 6

Solution: *ASTRONOMIA* (astronomy).

For the likely ultimate source, see Isidore, *Etymologiae* 2.24.15, above; this is the final *aenigma* of the sequence BIB 3–6, as explained in the note to BIB 2 above.


## BIB 7

Solution: *ETHICA* (ethics).

For the likely ultimate source, see Isidore, *Etymologiae* 2.24.5. The "two sisters" are physics (BIB 2) and logic (BIB 9); see further the note at BIB 1 above. According to Isidore, *Etymologiae* 2.24.5–6, ethics is divided into four (the "forms," "eyes" and "children" noted here), namely prudence (*prudentia*, the difference between good and bad), justice (*iustitia*), fortitude *(fortitudo)*, and temperance *(temperantia)*, which together make up the "four virtues" of the *aenigma* that follows.

## BIB 8

Solution: *QUATUOR VIRTUTES* (the four virtues).

As described in the previous *aenigma*, the four virtues are temperance *(temperantia*, described in lines 3–4), prudence *(prudentia,* lines 5–6), fortitude *(fortitudo,* lines 7–8), and justice *(iustitia,* lines 9–12).

## BIB 9

Solution: *LOGICA* (logic).

For the likely ultimate source, see Isidore, *Etymologiae* 2.24.7, which describes how Plato divided logic into rhetoric and dialectic, which follow in BIB 11–12 below. Presumably the three "forms," "eyes," and "children" noted here also include grammar, which follows in BIB 10.

## BIB 10

Solution: *GRAMMATICA* (grammar).

The reference to "The Greek for letter" *(gramma)* offers the broadest of hints as to the solution. For the likely ultimate source, see Isidore, *Etymologiae* 1.2.1–3, which describes the seven liberal arts as grammar, rhetoric, dialectic, arithmetic, music, geometry, and astronomy. The first three of these provide the closing sequence BIB 10–12; the latter four the earlier sequence BIB 3–6.

## BIB 11

Solution: *RHETORICA* (rhetoric).

For the likely ultimate source, see Isidore, *Etymologiae* 2.23 (*De differentia dialecticae et rhetoricae artis;* "The difference between the arts of rhetoric and dialectic"). See the note at BIB 9 above for the arrangement of the final sequence BIB 10–12 here.

## BIB 12

Solution: *DIALECTICA* (dialectic).

The likely ultimate source is Isidore, *Etymologiae* 2.22, which explains that dialectic is a sub-branch of logic (BIB 9 above) and that it rightly follows rhetoric, as here. The "twin sisters" are presumably grammar and rhetoric, the subjects of the previous two *aenigmata;* all three are considered as the "children" of logic (see BIB 9 above).

## THE FRANKS CASKET RIDDLE (FRA)

See also the more detailed commentary in *COEALRT.* For further reading, see in general Leslie Webster, *The Franks Casket* (London, 2012).

My translation assumes that *flodu* (sea) is the subject and *fisc* (fish) the object, but in fact the terms could be reversed: "The fish raised up the sea onto the towering cliff" also works both grammatically and conceptually.

## THE LEIDEN RIDDLE (LEI)

Solution: *BYRNE* (mailcoat).
See also the more detailed commentary in *COEALRT.* For further reading, see in general M. B. Parkes, "The Manuscript of the Leiden Riddle," *Anglo-Saxon England* 1 (1972): 207–17; Rolf H. Bremmer, Jr. and Kees Dekker, "Leiden, Universiteitsbibliotheek, Vossianus Lat. Q. 106," in *Anglo-Saxon Manuscripts in Microfiche Facsimile,* vol. 13, *Manuscripts in the Low Countries,* ed. A. N. Doane (Tempe, 2006), 107–11; Andy Orchard, "Old English and Latin Poetic Traditions," in *A companion to Medieval Poetry,* ed. Corinne Saunders (Oxford, 2010), 65–82.

This is one of two Old English renderings of ALD 33 (*LORICA,* "armor"); the other is EXE 33. See the appropriate notes there. See too Leahy, *Anglo-Saxon Crafts,* 131–33. The indentation here reflects the capitalization found in the unique manuscript; see in particular Parkes, "The Manuscript of the Leiden Riddle."

## The Exeter Book Riddles (EXE)

There is an extensive body of translations and commentary, widely scattered; I have consulted the complete translations by H. H. Abbott, *The Riddles of the Exeter Book* (Cambridge, 1968), 1–57; Kevin Crossley-Holland, *The Exeter Book Riddles* (Harmondsworth, 1993); Paul F. Baum, *The Anglo-Saxon Riddles of the Exeter Book* (Durham, N.C., 1963), 4–63; Kevin Crossley-Holland, trans., *The Exeter Book Riddles* (Harmondsworth, 1993), 3–122; John Porter, trans., *Anglo-Saxon Riddles* (Hockwold-cum-Wilton, 1995), 11–98; Louis J. Rodrigues, trans., *Anglo-Saxon Riddles* (Felinfach, 1990), 91–115; Craig Williamson, *A Feast of Creatures: Anglo-Saxon Riddle-Songs* (Philadelphia, 1982), 59–154 and 157–219; Megan Cavell, Victoria Symons, and Matthias Ammon, eds., "The Riddle Ages: Old English Riddles, Translations and Commentaries," https://theriddleages.wordpress.com, accessed November 15, 2019. See also the more detailed commentary in *COEALRT.* Excellent and highly specific commentary is to be found in the various editions and translations of EXE listed in the bibliography, especially Williamson, *Old English Riddles of the "Exeter Book,"* and Hans Pinsker and Waltraud Ziegler, ed. and trans., *Die altenglischen Rätsel des Exeterbuchs*, Anglistische Forschungen 183 (Heidelberg, 1985). The most useful monographs on the subject are, most notably, John D. Niles, *Old English Enigmatic Poems and the Play of the Texts,* Studies in the Early Middle Ages 13 (Turnhout, 2006); but also Bitterli, *Say What I Am Called;* Reinhard Gleissner, *Die "zweideutigen" altenglischen Rätsel des "Exeter Book" in ihrem zeitgenössischen Kontext,* Sprache und Literatur: Regensburger Arbeiten zur Anglistik und Amerikanistik 23 (Bern, 1984); Helga Göbel, *Studien zu den altenglischen Schriftwesenrätseln,* Epistemata: Würzburger wissenschaftliche Schriften, Reihe Literaturwissenschaft 7 (Würzburg, 1980); Murphy, *Unriddling the Exeter Riddles;* and Antje Rügamer, *Die Poetizität der altenglischen Rätsel des Exeter Book* (Hamburg, 2008). For earlier general studies, see Nigel F. Barley, "Structural Aspects of the Anglo-Saxon Riddle," *Semiotica* 10 (1974): 143–75; Marie Nelson, "The Rhetoric of the Exeter Book Riddles," *Speculum* 49 (1974): 421–40; Marie Nelson, "Time in the Exeter

Book Riddles," *Philological Quarterly* 54 (1975): 511–18; Ann Harleman Stewart, "Kenning and Riddle in Old English," *Papers on Language and Literature* 15 (1979): 115–36; Donald K. Fry, "Exeter Book Riddle Solutions," *Old English Newsletter* 15, no. 1 (1981): 22–33; Lendinara, "Aspetti della società germanica negli enigmi del Codice Exoniense"; Wim Tigges, "Signs and Solutions: A Semiotic Approach to the Exeter Book Riddles," in *This Noble Craft*, ed. Erik Kooper (Amsterdam and Atlanta, 1991), 59–82; Wim Tigges, "Snakes and Ladders: Ambiguity and Coherence in the Exeter Book Riddles and Maxims," in *Companion to Old English Poetry*, ed. Henk Aertsen and Rolf H. Bremmer, Jr. (Amsterdam, 1994), 95–118; Patrick W. Conner, "Structure of the Exeter Book Codex," in *Anglo-Saxon Manuscripts: Basic Readings*, ed. Bichael Swanton (London, 2001), 301–15; Susanne Kries, "*Fela í rúnum eða í skáldskap:* Anglo-Saxon and Scandinavian Approaches to Riddles and Poetic Disguises," in *Riddles, Knights and Cross-Dressing Saints: Essays on Medieval English Language and Literature*, ed. Thomas Honegger, Sammlung Variations 5 (Bern, 2005), 139–64; Anita R. Riedinger, "The Formulaic Style in the Old English Riddles," *Studia Neophilologica* 76 (2004): 30–43; Richard Gameson, "The Origin of the Exeter Book of Old English Poetry," *Anglo-Saxon England* 25 (1996): 135–85; Matthew Marino, "The Literariness of the Exeter Book Riddles," *Neuphilologische Mitteilungen* 79 (1978): 258–65; John C. Pope, "Palaeography and Poetry: Some Solved and Unsolved Mysteries of the Exeter Book," in *Medieval Scribes, Manuscripts and Libraries: Essays Presented to N. R. Ker*, ed. M. B. Parkes and Andrew G. Watson (London, 1978), 25–65; Peter Orton, "The Technique of Object-Personification in *The Dream of the Rood* and a Comparison with the Old English Riddles," *Leeds Studies in English* n.s. 11 (1980): 1–18; Russell Poole, *Old English Wisdom Poetry*, Annotated Bibliographies of Old and Middle English Literature 5 (Cambridge, 1998); Salvador-Bello, "Patterns of Compilation"; Salvador-Bello, "Sexual Riddle Type."

## EXE 1

Solution: *GODES WIND* (wind of God); other suggested solutions include: "storm," "wind," "atmosphere," "power of Nature," "apocalyptic storm," "the Stoic cosmological concept of *pneuma*." For EXE 1.1–15, when edited as a separate riddle, suggested solutions include: "fire," "raiding party," "army," *storm* (storm). For EXE 1.16–30, when taken as a separate riddle, suggested solutions include: "anchor," "submarine earthquake." For EXE 1.16–104, if taken as a separate riddle, a suggested solution is "sun." For EXE 1.31–104 taken as a separate riddle, suggested solutions include: "hurricane," "revenant," *god* (God).

See too Elinor Bartlet Teele, "The Heroic Tradition in the Old English *Riddles*" (PhD diss., Cambridge University, 2004), 123–29; Brian McFadden, "Raiding, Reform, and Reaction: Wondrous Creatures in the Exeter Book Riddles," *Texas Studies in Literature and Language* (2008): 329–51.

For comparison, see ALD 2, ps-BED 5 (both solved "wind"); EUS 8 (wind and fire); ALC D46, BER 41 (both solved "wind").

The opening *hwylc* ("what," EXE 1.1) is taken here as a question, though other editors have assumed that it is an exclamation. At EXE 1.68b, other translations prefer to read *lagu-streama full* (the cup of liquid streams) as adjectival, "full of liquid streams," although the parallel kenning *yþa full* ("cup of the waves," signifying the sea) is found at *Beowulf* 1208b.

## EXE 2

Solution: *BELLE* (bell); other suggested solutions include: "millstone," "revenant," "flail," "lock," "handmill," "quill," "penis," "bucket of water," "bucket on chain or rope in cistern or well," "watchdog," "a devil," "plow team," "water bucket," "sword."

See further Murphy, *Unriddling the Exeter Riddles,* 71–77; Mercedes Salvador-Bello, "The Compilation of the Old English Riddles of the *Exeter Book*" (PhD diss., University of Seville, 1997), 103–5.

See too Leahy, *Anglo-Saxon Crafts,* 132.

For comparison, see TAT 7, ALC D74, EXE 67, SYM 80 (all solved "bell[s]").

The chief difficulty in the interpretation of this riddle stems from the significance of the "rings" in EXE 2.2a *(hringum)* and 2.8a *(bæg)*, as well as the number of unique compounds.

## EXE 3

Solution: *BORD* (chopping board, shield); other suggested solutions include: "chopping block," "guilt," "whetstone," "shield."
See further E. G. Stanley, "Heroic Aspects of the Exeter Book Riddles," in *Prosody and Poetics in the Early Middle Ages: Essays in Honour of C. B. Hieatt,* ed. M. J. Toswell (Toronto, 1995), 197–218; Salvador-Bello, "Compilation of the Old English Riddles," 105–7; Teele, "The Heroic Tradition," 74–81; Murphy, *Unriddling the Exeter Riddles,* 68–70.
See too Leahy, *Anglo-Saxon Crafts,* 128–29.
For comparison, see ALD 87, GES 26 (both solved "shield").

The runic ·ᚻ· *(S)* that follows this riddle in the manuscript supports the generally held solution "shield," both in Old English *(scyld)* and Latin *(scutum),* although here I would argue that the more likely solution is the broader and ambiguous *BORD*.

## EXE 4

Solution: *SUNNE* (sun); other suggested solutions include: "guilt and conscience."
See further Salvador-Bello, "Compilation of the Old English Riddles," 107–9; Teele, "The Heroic Tradition," 129–32; Murphy, *Unriddling the Exeter Riddles,* 126–27.
For comparison, see ALD 79 (sun and moon); ALC D41, BER 55–57, EUS 10 (all solved "sun") and 27 (moon and sun); GES 15, OIR 11 (both solved "sun"); XMS Z4 (snow and sun).

The runic ᚻ *(S)* that follows this riddle in the manuscript supports the generally held solution *sigel, sunne* (sun), though as with the previous riddle, a Latin solution *(sol)* would also fit. Just as EXE 3 and 4 may be connected by the circular shape of their solutions ("shield" and "sun," respectively), so too EXE 4 and 5 may be connected through the idea of a swan, like the sun, moving through the sky.

## EXE 5

Solution: *SWAN* (swan); other suggested solutions include: either "swan" or "soul," "soul," both "swan" and "soul," "mute swan."
For comparison, see GES 17 (female swans).

A poorly formed letter, likely written after the main text and variously read as Roman *n* or runic ᚾ *(U)* or ᚲ *(C)* follows this riddle in the manuscript and has been used to support the Latin solutions *cygnus* (swan) or *ulula* (owl) for this riddle, or Old English *nihte-gale* (nightingale) or *ule* (owl). Most commentators accept the general solution "swan," a creature that fulfills the necessary conditions of being at home on land and in the water and in the air, and such an answer is all the more appealing if it is supposed that the riddle also refers to the whistling sounds made by the swan's wings both in flight while alive and by the swan's wing bones in the form of flutes after death. This whole riddle turns on the paradox of silence on land and water, contrasted with sound in the sky, and emphasized with a series of verbs *(swigað . . . swogað . . . swinsiað . . . singað)* that offer aural clues to the solution, *SWAN*. This is the opening riddle in a sequence (EXE 5–8) with bird solutions, all connected in various ways; see further Salvador-Bello, "Compilation of the Old English Riddles," 109–11; Bitterli, *Say What I Am Called,* 38–46; Andy Orchard, "Performing Writing and Singing Silence in the Anglo-Saxon Riddle-Tradition," in *Or Words to That Effect: Orality and the Writing of Literary History,* ed. Daniel F. Chamberlain and J. Edward Chamberlin (Amsterdam, 2016), 73–91. A similar sequence is found at EUS 56–60, while SYM, despite a plethora of *aenigmata* relating to life on sea and land (see especially the extended sequence SYM 15–39), contains notably few relating to birds.

## EXE 6

Solution: *NIHTE-GALE* (nightingale); other suggested solutions include: "pipe," "jay," "reed pipe," "chough" or "jackdaw," "song thrush," either "nightingale" or "frog," "crying baby," "owl," "flute."
See further Salvador-Bello, "Compilation of the Old English Riddles," 111–

14; Teele, "The Heroic Tradition," 231–35; Bitterli, *Say What I Am Called*, 46–56; Orchard, "Performing Writing and Singing Silence."
For comparison, see ALD 22 (nightingale).

Given what seems a clear sequence of bird solutions for EXE 5–8, it seems most reasonable to read this as some nocturnal bird or other, given the reference to an "ancient poet of evening" in EXE 6.5; "nightingale" or "owl" both seem feasible, and the former is preferred here because the Old English *æfen-sceop* (literally, "evening-poet") seems closest to the sense of *nihte-gale* (literally, "night-singer"). The description of the bird as a "lady actress" stems from the fact that *nihte-gale* is feminine in gender (as is *ule*, "owl").

## EXE 7

Solution: *GEAC* (cuckoo); other suggested solutions include: "conception and birth/revenant/soul." Bitterli, *Say What I Am Called*, points out a good parallel in ps-BED 9.
See further Salvador-Bello, "Compilation of the Old English Riddles," 114–16.
For comparison, see ps-BED 9 (cuckoo).

Most commentators accept the solution "cuckoo," given the widespread bird-lore surrounding cuckoos as unwelcome visitors fostered on unsuspecting others. For the notion in the first three lines that while incubating in the egg, the bird is "unliving," compare Lockett, *Anglo-Saxon Psychologies*, 44.

## EXE 8

Solution: *BYRNETE* (barnacle goose); other suggested solutions include: "ocean furrow," "bubble," "water lily," "anchor," "alchemy/baptism."
See further Salvador-Bello, "Compilation of the Old English Riddles," 117–21.

This is another bird riddle; the notion that the barnacle goose was part fish, part bird was known in Anglo-Saxon England is witnessed in the *Ant-*

*werp Glossary* (7.1): *lolligo, id est piscis maritimus uno anno piscis alio avis hoc est byrnete* (cuttlefish: a sea fish that is one year a fish and the next a bird, namely a *byrnete* or barnacle goose).

## EXE 9

Solution: *WIN-FÆT* (cup of wine); other suggested solutions include: "night," "gold," "wine," "penis," "wine and beaker of wine."
See further Salvador-Bello, "Compilation of the Old English Riddles," 121–24; Teele, "The Heroic Tradition," 178–80.
For comparison, see ALD 78, LOR 5, XMS X4 (all solved "wine cup").

## EXE 10

Solution: *OXA* (ox); other suggested solutions include: "leather," "oxhide," "hide or skin," "ox, and female masturbation with a leather dildo," "an ox and its hide."
See further Edith Whitehurst Williams, "What's So New about the Sexual Revolution? Some Comments on Anglo-Saxon Attitudes toward Sexuality in Women Based on Four Exeter Book Riddles," *Texas Quarterly* 18 (Summer 1975): 46–55; Elizabeth Stevens Girsch, "Metaphorical Usage, Sexual Exploitation, and Divergence in the Old English Terminology for Male and Female Slaves," in *The Work of Work: Servitude, Slavery, and Labor in Medieval England*, ed. Allen J. Frantzen and Douglas Moffat (Glasgow, 1994), 30–54; John W. Tanke, "*Wonfeax wale*: Ideology and Figuration in the Sexual Riddles of the Exeter Book," in *Class and Gender in Early English Literature*, ed. Britton J. Harwood and Gillian R. Overing (Bloomington and Indianapolis, Ind., 1994), 21–42; Salvador-Bello, "Compilation of the Old English Riddles," 124–26; Lendinara, "Aspetti della società germanica negli enigmi del Codice Exoniense"; Nina Rulon-Miller, "Sexual Humor and Fettered Desire in Exeter Book Riddle 12," in *Humour in Anglo-Saxon Literature*, ed. Jonathan Wilcox (Cambridge, 2000), 99–126; Teresa Fiocco, "Gli animali negli enigmi anglo-sassoni dell'*Exeter Book*," in *Simbolismo animale e letteratura*, ed. Dora Faraci, Memoria bibliografica 42 (Rome, 2003), 133–57; Sarah L. Higley, "The Wanton Hand: Reading and Reaching into Grammars and Bodies in Old English *Riddle 12*," in *Naked before God: Uncovering*

*the Body in Anglo-Saxon England,* ed. Benjamin C. Withers and Jonathan Wilcox, Medieval European Studies 3 (Morgantown, W.Va., 2003), 29–59; Peter Robson, "'Feorran Broht': Exeter Book Riddle 12 and the Commodification of the Exotic," in *Authority and Subjugation in Writing of Medieval Wales,* ed. Ruth Kennedy and Simon Meecham-Jones (New York, 2008), 71–84; Bitterli, *Say What I Am Called,* 26–34; Murphy, *Unriddling the Exeter Riddles,* 176–77 and 195–98.

For comparison, see EXE 70 (ox).

## EXE 11

Solution: *TEN CICCENU* (ten chickens); other suggested solutions include: "aurelia of the butterfly, and its transformations," "letters of the alphabet," "looper caterpillar," "ten fingers (with gloves)," "twelve chickens," "hatchling chicks."

See further Salvador-Bello, "Compilation of the Old English Riddles," 127–31; Fiocco, "Gli animali negli enigmi anglo-sassoni dell'*Exeter Book*"; Bitterli, *Say What I Am Called,* 115–21; Murphy, *Unriddling the Exeter Riddles,* 53–60 and 91–95.

The "wall" in question is the eggshell.

## EXE 12

Solution: *HORN* (horn); other suggested solutions include: "an ox and its horns."

See further Stanley, "Heroic Aspects of the Exeter Book Riddles"; Lendinara, "Aspetti della società germanica negli enigmi del Codice Exoniense"; Salvador-Bello, "Compilation of the Old English Riddles," 131–34; Teele, "The Heroic Tradition," 50–54; Bitterli, *Say What I Am Called,* 124–31 and 166–67.

For comparison, see EXE 76, OER 27 (both solved "horn").

A later hand seems to have added a capital *H* or perhaps a variant form of runic ᚻ *(H),* so suggesting the solution "horn" that is so widely favored by most commentators.

## EXE 13

Solution: *IGIL* (hedgehog, porcupine); other suggested solutions include: "weasel," "badger," "fox," "fox and hound."
See further Megan Cavell, "The *Igil* and Exeter Book *Riddle 15*," *Notes and Queries* 64, no. 2 (2017): 206–10; Lendinara, "Aspetti della società germanica negli enigmi del Codice Exoniense"; Salvador-Bello, "Compilation of the Old English Riddles," 134–39; Fiocco, "Gli animali negli enigmi anglosassoni dell'*Exeter Book*"; Teele, "The Heroic Tradition," 149–58.
For comparison, see SYM 29 (hedgehog).

The precise identity of this creature remains a source for conjecture: "fox" and "badger" are the usual choices. Here, although "weasel" is attractive, I prefer "hedgehog," based partly on the description in Isidore, *Etymologiae* 12.3.7.

## EXE 14

Solution: *ANCOR, ANCRA* (anchor, anchorite).
See further Salvador-Bello, "Compilation of the Old English Riddles," 139–40; Teele, "The Heroic Tradition," 52–55.
For comparison, see SYM 61, GES 6 (both solved "anchor").

## EXE 15

Solution: *COCER* (quiver); other suggested solutions include: "ballista," "forge," "inkwell," "fortress" and "soul," "oven," "town," "penis," "plaited beehive," "fortress," "quiver," "bee skep," "Samson's lion and bees." See further Stanley, "Heroic Aspects of the Exeter Book Riddles"; Salvador-Bello, "Compilation of the Old English Riddles," 140–42; Teele, "The Heroic Tradition," 201–6.
For comparison, see TAT 34 (quiver).

The sheer number of solutions proposed for this riddle suggests something of its complexity; the two most compelling seem to be "quiver" and "beehive." The former suggestion turns on some neat verbal parallels with EXE 21, universally accepted as having the solution "bow" (*BOGA*), the latter on recognizing that Anglo-Saxons kept bees in skeps of upturned wickerwork or plaited straw.

## EXE 16

Solution: *CROG* (amphora, vessel); other suggested solutions include: "leather bottle," "cask," "inkwell," "jug (amphora)," "penis," "jug of wine." See further Lendinara, "Aspetti della società germanica negli enigmi del Codice Exoniense"; Salvador-Bello, "Compilation of the Old English Riddles," 142–44.

Physical damage to the manuscript obscures the possibility of determining a clear solution to this riddle; the notion that many such items are carried in the hold of a ship supports the idea of amphorae or jugs and helps connect this riddle to the next.

## EXE 17

Solution: *SNAC* (light warship); other suggested solutions include: "horse, man, wagon, and hawk"; "sun"; "falconry"; "man upon horseback with a hawk on his fist"; "horseman, servant, and hawk"; "writing"; "hand writing on manuscript sheet with pen"; "ship."
On this riddle in particular, see Jonathan Wilcox, "Mock-Riddles in Old English: Exeter Riddles 86 and 19," *Studies in Philology* 93 (1996): 180–87; Salvador-Bello, "Compilation of the Old English Riddles," 144–46; Teele, "The Heroic Tradition," 59–61; Bitterli, *Say What I Am Called*, 86–91; Mark Griffith, "Riddle 19 of the Exeter Book: *Snac*, an Old English Acronym," *Notes and Queries* n.s. 39 (1992): 15–16; Shu-han Luo, "Prosody and Literary Play: A Metrical Study of the Exeter Book Riddles" (MSt diss., University of Oxford, 2011), 12–13 and 28–32; Douglas P. A. Simms, "Exeter Book *Riddle 19:* Its Runes and Transmission," *Notes and Queries* 261 (2016): 351–54.

Most of the earlier attempts to solve this riddle have focused on the rather obvious collections of runes that spelled out backward the words *HORS* (horse), *MON* (man), *WEGA* ("ways" or "waves" or perhaps "warrior," if *wiga* is intended), and *HAOFOC* (hawk). The problem is that attempting to incorporate the runes leads to a range of metrical and alliterative difficulties, and it may be, as Simms, "Exeter Book *Riddle 19*," suggests, that they are interpolations hinting at a solution. Unfortunately, removing the runic groups leads to other problems: it is unclear how to fill the resulting gaps.

Williamson noted that much of the riddle plays on the common Old English kenning of a ship as a horse of the sea and suggested that the proper solution was "ship." Other kennings are found at EXE 3.7b (*homera lafe*, "hammers' leavings") and EXE 71.19b (*heapo-sigel*, "sun of battle"). Griffith took the argument still a stage further and offered a completely convincing solution that also explained why the runes spell out these words backward, by taking the final runes of each group to produce *SNAC*, the name of a swift, light kind of warship mentioned in the *Anglo-Saxon Chronicle* entry for 1052.

On the use of runes in the riddles, see René Derolez, *Runica Manuscripta: The English Tradition* (Brugge, 1954); René Derolez, "*Runica Manuscripta* Revisited," in *Old English Runes and Their Continental Backgrounds*, ed. A. Bammesberger, Anglistische Forschungen 217 (Heidelberg, 1991), 85–106; Raymond Edward Gleason, "*Per speculum in enigmate*: Runes, Riddles and Language in Anglo-Saxon Literature" (PhD diss., Northwestern University, 1997); Christine E. Fell, "Runes and Riddles in Anglo-Saxon England," in *"Lastworda betst": Essays in Memory of Christine E. Fell with Her Unpublished Writings,* ed. Carole Hough and Kathryn A. Lowe (Donington, 2002), 264–77; Roberta Dewa, "The Runic Riddles of the Exeter Book: Language Games and Anglo-Saxon Scholarship," *Nottingham Medieval Studies* 39 (1995): 26–36; Robert DiNapoli, "Odd Characters: Runes in Old English Poetry," in *Verbal Encounters: Anglo-Saxon and Old Norse Studies for Roberta Frank,* ed. Antonina Harbus and Russell Poole, Toronto Old English Series (Toronto, Buffalo, and London, 2005), 145–61; Victoria Symons, *Runes and Roman Letters in Anglo-Saxon Manuscripts* (Berlin, 2016); Tom Birkett, *Reading the Runes in Old English and Old Norse Poetry* (London, 2017).

## EXE 18

Solution: *SECG* (sword, man); other suggested solutions include: "hawk and sword"; *heoru-swealwe* (a uniquely attested compound, meaning "fierce swallow," "taloned swallow," signifying some bird of prey); "hawk, falcon"; "penis"; "falcon"; "sword," with wordplay on "weapon."
See further Stanley, "Heroic Aspects of the Exeter Book Riddles"; Lendinara, "Aspetti della società germanica negli enigmi del Codice Exoniense";

Salvador-Bello, "Compilation of the Old English Riddles," 146–50; Teele, "The Heroic Tradition," 58–62; Bitterli, *Say What I Am Called*, 124–31; Murphy, *Unriddling the Exeter Riddles*, 206–15.

For comparison, see TAT 30 (sword and sheath); EUS 36 (sword); EXE 69 ("sword" or "man").

This is a problematic riddle, with two main schools of thought: those who would solve it as some kind of bird of prey promote some rather strained readings, but equally those who believe that the solution is "sword" cannot easily account for what looks like obviously sexual overtones toward the end of the text. Combining the basic "sword" solutions with suggestions of phallic aggression, Niles offers his compromise: "*sweord*, 'sword,' with wordplay on *wæpen*, 'weapon,'" since grammatically masculine items were designated as *wæpned-men*. It seems more likely in such a context that a preferable solution is *SECG*, denoting both "sword" and "man." Both the martial and avian solutions link back to the previous riddle, depending on whether one focuses on the third or fourth of the runic groups.

## EXE 19

Solution: *SULH* (plow); other suggested solutions include: "penis."
See further Salvador-Bello, "Compilation of the Old English Riddles," 150–52; Murphy, *Unriddling the Exeter Riddles*, 175–76.

The solution "plow," first suggested by Franz Eduard Dietrich, is generally accepted, though given the common sexual associations of the activity of plowing, the secondary sense "penis" is by no means unlikely. For a description of Anglo-Saxon plows and the various tools associated with them, see Riley, *Anglo-Saxon Tools*, 113–17.

## EXE 20

Solution: *CARLES WÆN* (Charles's Wain, *Ursa Major*); other suggested solutions include: "days of the month," "bridge," "rite of passage," "ice bridge."
See further Salvador-Bello, "Compilation of the Old English Riddles," 152–

56; Teele, "The Heroic Tradition," 54–59; Bitterli, *Say What I Am Called,* 59–68; Murphy, *Unriddling the Exeter Riddles,* 111–23.

This riddle fits an astronomical solution best, and several commentators point to the constellation variously known as the Plow or the Great Bear *(Ursa Major),* which has the useful information about the eleven stars of the *Canes Venatici* that sit under the pole of the Wain, of which four are noticeably brighter than the others.

## EXE 21

Solution: *BOGA* (bow); other suggested solutions include: "crossbow," "penis."
See further Salvador-Bello, "Compilation of the Old English Riddles," 156–58; Teele, "The Heroic Tradition," 98–106; Elena Afros, "Linguistic Ambiguities in Some Exeter Book Riddles," *Notes and Queries* n.s. 52 (2005): 431–37; Murphy, *Unriddling the Exeter Riddles,* 158–59; Winfried Rudolf, "Riddling and Reading: Iconicity and Logographs in Exeter Book *Riddles* 23 and 25," *Anglia* 130 (2012): 499–525.
For comparison, see OER 27 (bow).

The opening line offers the solution *boga* (bow) backward, employing the nonce-form *agof,* and with the substitution of *f* for *b,* a phonological and orthographical variant that may point to an early date of composition. Given that this line is entirely self-contained, and that the riddle functions well without it, it may well be an interpolated solution (which is why I print it in italics). To emulate the effect, I employ a similarly archaized nonce-form, *UUOB,* in the translation, with *UU* standing for more usual *W.*

## EXE 22

Solution: *HIGORA* (jay, magpie); other suggested solutions include: "magpie," "woodpecker," "actor specializing in animal and bird noises," "jay" or "green woodpecker."
See further Stanley, "Heroic Aspects of the Exeter Book Riddles"; Salvador-Bello, "Compilation of the Old English Riddles," 158–59; McFadden, "Raiding, Reform, and Reaction"; Bitterli, *Say What I Am Called,* 91–97.

This riddle carries its solution (*higora*, "jay," "magpie") embedded in runes and in the form of an anagram (*garohi*). The unusual form of the *G*-rune suggests a scribe unused to copying runes, or an exemplar that was similarly problematic, or both.

## EXE 23

Solution: *CIPE* (onion); other suggested solutions include: "hemp," "mustard," "leek," "onion," "rosehip," "penis."
See further Williams, "What's So New about the Sexual Revolution?"; Salvador-Bello, "Compilation of the Old English Riddles," 160–62; Orchard, "Enigma Variations," 295–97; Murphy, *Unriddling the Exeter Riddles,* 176–77 and 221–34.
For comparison, see EXE 63, SYM 44, BER 51 (all solved "onion").

Following two somewhat self-evident riddles, this one employs a form of misdirection through double entendre, with what seems an obvious solution, "penis," masking the "true" one, *cipe-leac* (onion). This is the first of the undoubted so-called double-entendre riddles, on which see further Gleissner, *Die "zweideutigen" altenglischen Rätsel des "Exeter Book";* Ann Harleman Stewart, "Double-entendre in the Old English Riddles," *Lore and Language* 3, no. 8 (1983): 39–52; Glenn Davis, "The Exeter Book Riddles and the Place of Sexual Idiom in Old English Literature," in *Medieval Obscenities,* ed. Nicola McDonald (York, 2006), 39–54; Jorge Luis Bueno Alonso, "Actitudes anglosajonas hacia el humor: L caracterización del humor obsceno y sexual en los acertijos del *Exeter Book*," *Cuadernos del CEMYR* 12 (December 2004): 17–36; Julie Coleman, "Sexual Euphemism in Old English," *Neuphilologische Mitteilungen* 93 (1992): 93–98; Roberta Frank, "Sex in the *Dictionary of Old English*," in *Unlocking the Wordhord: Anglo-Saxon Studies in Memory of Edward B. Irving, Jr.,* ed. Mark C. Amodio and Katherine O'Brien O'Keeffe (Toronto, 2003), 302–12; Salvador-Bello, "Sexual Riddle Type."

## EXE 24

Solution: *CRISTES BOC* (Gospel book); other suggested solutions include: "book," "hide," "holy scripture."

See further Lendinara, "Aspetti della società germanica negli enigmi del Codice Exoniense"; Jennifer Neville, *Representations of the Natural World in Old English Poetry,* Cambridge Studies in Anglo-Saxon England 27 (Cambridge, 1999), 113–14; Salvador-Bello, "Compilation of the Old English Riddles," 162–65; Teele, "The Heroic Tradition," 110–20; Richard Marsden, "'Ask What I Am Called': The Anglo-Saxons and Their Bibles," in *The Bible as Book: The Manuscript Tradition,* ed. John L. Sharpe III and Kimberly Van Kampen (London, 1998), 145–76; Bitterli, *Say What I Am Called,* 171–78; Murphy, *Unriddling the Exeter Riddles,* 90–91.

See too Leahy, *Anglo-Saxon Crafts,* 89–93.

For comparison, see TAT 5, EUS 32, BER 24 (all solved "parchment").

This violent and graphic riddle offers the most comprehensive description of the whole process of bookmaking, from the death of the unwitting donor of the raw material through to its ultimate adornment; there is a likely source (at least for EXE 24.1–6) in TAT 5 (*MEMBRANUM,* "parchment"). The connection of this to both the preceding and the following riddles is striking, although later riddles also exploit the juxtaposition between the sacred and the profane. This is the first of a scattered series of riddles relating to writing, many of which are discussed in detail by Göbel, *Altenglischen Schriftwesenrätseln:* this one is considered at pp. 182–224.

## EXE 25

Solution: *MEDU* (mead); other suggested solutions include: "whip," "sleep" (?), "mead (and its source)."

See further Neville, *Representations of the Natural World,* 200–201; Salvador-Bello, "Compilation of the Old English Riddles," 166–68; Teele, "The Heroic Tradition," 181–87; Murphy, *Unriddling the Exeter Riddles,* 164–65.

This riddle offers a full account of the making and power of mead (or perhaps beer, which in Anglo-Saxon England was often made with fruit and honey), from the production of honey by bees to the binding and punishing effects of the mead when made.

## EXE 26

Solution: *BOC-FELL* (parchment); other suggested solutions include: "harp," "John Barleycorn," "stringed instrument," "wine cask," "beer," "tor-

toise," "malt liquor," "trial of the soul," "barrow," "yew horn" (?), "pattern-welded sword," "woman," "ale (and its source)."
See further Bitterli, *Say What I Am Called*, 178–90.

This is a somewhat perplexing riddle, though perhaps those suggested solutions that point to associations with brewing, such as "beer" or "ale," come closest to catching the flavor of the elongated process by which the end product is made.

## EXE 27

Solution: *MONA OND SUNNE* (moon and sun); other suggested solutions include: "sun and moon," "bird and wind" or "swallow and sparrow," "cloud and wind."
See further Salvador-Bello, "Compilation of the Old English Riddles," 139–40 and 172–75; Teele, "The Heroic Tradition," 52–55 and 132–36; Charles D. Wright, "The Persecuted Church and the *Mysterium Lunae*," in *Latin Learning and English Lore: Studies in Anglo-Saxon Literature for Michael Lapidge*, ed. Katherine O'Brien O'Keeffe and Andy Orchard (Toronto, 2005), vol. 2, pp. 293–314; Murphy, *Unriddling the Exeter Riddles*, 123–39.
For comparison, see ALD 6 (moon) and 79 (sun and moon); EUS 10 (sun) and 11 (moon); ALC D41 (sun) and D42 (moon); EXE 4, GES 15 (both solved "sun"); BER 55–57 (sun) and 58–59 (moon); OIR 11 (sun); XMS Z4 (snow and sun).

Dietrich's early solution was based on the perceived parallel between the opening lines of this riddle and *Boethius* 4.10–11a, *hwilum eac þa sunnan sines bereafað / beorhtan leohtes* (sometimes [the moon] also robs the sun of its bright light); other suggested solutions are more or less fanciful.

## EXE 28a and 28b

Solution: *BEAM* (beam, tree, wood, beam of light, cross, gallows); other suggested solutions include: "rainwater," "cornfield," "penis," "cross/sun," "birch," "cross as vehicle of salvation," "snow," "fire," *treow* (a tree/grove/firewood/wooden objects).
See further Roy Michael Liuzza, "The Texts of the Old English *Riddle 30*," *Journal of English and Germanic Philology* 87 (1988): 1–15; Salvador-Bello,

"Compilation of the Old English Riddles," 175–80 and 263–66; Afros, "Linguistic Ambiguities."

This riddle appears in slightly different forms on fols. 108r and 122v of E and is generally solved either as "wood" (or some kind of wooden object) or "fire," with the former preferred by the majority. A solution such as *BEAM,* covering all of the possibilities "beam," "tree," "wood," "beam of light," and "gallows," especially with the supplementary sense "cross" witnessed in the *Dream of the Rood,* might cover all objections, and at the same time emphasize the necessity to think in terms of potential wordplay.

## EXE 29

Solution: *SALTERE* (psaltery); other suggested solutions include: "bagpipe(s)"; "fiddle"; "musical instrument"; "portable organ"; "organistrum"; "harp," in Gregory K. Jember, trans., *The Old English Riddles: A New Translation* (Denver, 1976); "feather pen"; "cithara."
See further Lendinara, "Aspetti della società germanica negli enigmi del Codice Exoniense"; Salvador-Bello, "Compilation of the Old English Riddles," 139–40 and 180–81; Teele, "The Heroic Tradition," 52–55; Orchard, "Performing Writing and Singing Silence."
For comparison, see EXE 49 (quill pen and fingers).

The opening lines of this and the following riddle are very close and suggest a link. The creature in question in EXE 29 is generally taken to be some kind of musical instrument, and, taking the various parts described to refer to spread drones and a downward-pointing chanter, most commentators have accepted the solution "bagpipe," despite the rather obvious difficulty that no bagpipes from the period are attested. Given, however, the various parallels to other riddles dealing with writing, detailed most fully by Fry, the solution "quill pen and fingers" (as at EXE 49) is certainly in play; see Donald K. Fry, "Exeter Riddle 31: Feather-Pen," in *De Gustibus: Essays for Alain Renoir,* ed. John Miles Foley, J. Chris Womack, and Whitney A. Womack, Albert Bates Lord Studies in Oral Tradition 11 (New York, 1992), 234–49.
An elegant way to deal with the tension between a solution involving a musical instrument and the practice of writing may be a psaltery, a stringed instrument shaped like an inverted delta and plucked with a quill rather

than strummed with the fingers; I am grateful to Chris Laprade for this inventive suggestion, which has the added advantage of linking this riddle to the next (with which it is in any case verbally connected): the inverted delta shape of a psaltery also fits the most plausible suggested solutions there, namely "wheelbarrow," "cart," and "ship."

## EXE 30

Solution: *CEAP-SCIP* (merchant ship); other suggested solutions include: "wagon," "millstone," "ship," "wheel," "wheelbarrow," "merchant ship."
See further Teresa Fiocco, "Il viaggio della nave nell'enigma 32 dell'*Exeter Book*," *Blue Guitar* 7–8 (1984–1987): 80–89; Salvador-Bello, "Compilation of the Old English Riddles," 181–82.

Like the preceding riddle, with which it shares both opening and closing formulas, EXE 30 describes a one-footed, open-mouthed creature, in this case capable of carrying food across a distance. The solutions "wheelbarrow," "cart," and "ship" all seem feasible, with the last perhaps the most likely.

## EXE 31

Solution: *IS* (ice, ice floe); other suggested solutions include: "ice floe," "archetypal feminine," "iceberg," and "hatred."
See further Salvador-Bello, "Compilation of the Old English Riddles," 139–40; Teele, "The Heroic Tradition," 52–55; Afros, "Linguistic Ambiguities." For comparison, see ps-BED 6, ALC D53, LOR 4, EXE 66, OER 11, SYM 10, BER 38 and 42, OIR 9 (all solved "ice"); GES 24 (ice floe).

If the solution "ship" is accepted for the preceding EXE 30, then that of "iceberg" here makes a likely connection. In the second line, there is a possibility of deliberate confusion here between *ceol* (ship, seagoing vessel) and *ceole* (throat, gorge).

## EXE 32

Solution: *RACA* (rake); other suggested solutions include: "rake," "bee," "harrowing of Hell" or "penis."

See further Salvador-Bello, "Compilation of the Old English Riddles," 185–86.
See too Riley, *Anglo-Saxon Tools,* 126.

The painful and fearsome marine scraping of the iceberg connects the previous EXE 31 to the strictly earthbound EXE 32; the early suggested solution "rake" is generally accepted.

## EXE 33

Solution: *BYRNE* (mailcoat); there are no other suggested solutions.
See further Parkes, "The Manuscript of the Leiden Riddle"; Johan Gerritsen, "Leiden Revisited: Further Thoughts on the Text of the Leiden Riddle," in *Medieval Studies Conference, Aachen 1983,* ed. Wolf-Dietrich Bald and Horst Weinstock, Bamberger Beiträge zur englischen Sprachwissenschaft 15 (Bern, Frankfurt am Main, and New York, 1984), 51–59; Stanley, "Heroic Aspects of the Exeter Book Riddles"; Salvador-Bello, "Compilation of the Old English Riddles," 187–89; Bremmer and Dekker, "Leiden, Universiteitsbibliotheek, Vossianus Lat. Q. 106"; Steen, *Verse and Virtuosity: The Adaptation of Latin Rhetoric in Old English Poetry* (Toronto, 2008), 91–98; Murphy, *Unriddling the Exeter Riddles,* 3–4.
See too Leahy, *Anglo-Saxon Crafts,* 131–33.

It was noticed long ago that EXE 33 (largely an updated version of LEI) translates closely ALD 33 (*LORICA,* "mailcoat"), with each of Aldhelm's hexameters being translated into two long lines of Old English verse. The word order suggests that the original Latin text from which the Old English translator was working had lines 4 and 5 transposed. The final line of ALD 33 is not translated in EXE 33, which instead substitutes a pair of lines that constitute a form of the standard concluding challenge.

## EXE 34

Solution: *BAT* (boat); other suggested solutions include: "two men, woman, horses, dog, bird on ship"; "pregnant woman"; "ship" or "man, woman, and horse"; "waterfowl hunt"; "pregnant horse with two pregnant women on its back" (lines 1–8 only) and "ship"; "monster."

See further Salvador-Bello, "Compilation of the Old English Riddles," 139–40 and 189–93; Niles, *Old English Enigmatic Poems,* 85–89; Teele, "The Heroic Tradition," 52–55; Bitterli, *Say What I Am Called,* 68–74.

This riddle looks to be a composite text, with an interpolated "solution" (printed as line 5 in most editions), and six further lines later added. The "solution" appears as the evidently interpolated and garbled *monn ·h·w·M· wiif ·m·x·l·kf wf hors ·qxxs·,* likely the product of a series of misreadings. The Old English words *monn* (man), *wiif* (woman), and *hors* (horse) are relatively transparent, and their Latin equivalents *homo, mulier,* and *equus* can ultimately be derived from the remaining jumble, by applying the common Latin substitution cipher that replaces vowels with the consonants that follow them in the Roman alphabet (see further Levison, *England and the Continent in the Eighth Century,* 290–94).

## EXE 35

Solution: *BLÆST-BELG* (bellows); other suggested solutions include: "wagon," "penis."
See further Marie Nelson, "Plus Animate: Two Possible Transformations of Riddles by Symphosius," *Germanic Notes* 18 (1987): 46–48; Salvador-Bello, "Compilation of the Old English Riddles," 193–94; David Hill, "Anglo-Saxon Mechanics: 1. *Blæstbel(i)g*—The Bellows. 2. *Ston mid stel*—The Strikealight," *Medieval Life* 13 (2000): 9–13; Murphy, *Unriddling the Exeter Riddles,* 215–19.
For comparison, see ALD 11, EXE 83 and 85, SYM 73, GES 9 (all solved "bellows").

Though this riddle, like EXE 23, uses the device of misdirection by giving what is crying out to be seen as a graphic description of sexual activity, the "true" solution is more mundane: "bellows" seems most plausible, though "wagon" would better connect it to the preceding riddle.

## EXE 36

Solution: *HRYÐER* (bullock); other suggested solutions include: "young bull," "man," *bulluc* (bull calf [young ox]).

See further Salvador-Bello, "Compilation of the Old English Riddles," 194–96; Fiocco, "Gli animali negli enigmi anglo-sassoni dell'*Exeter Book*"; Orchard, "Enigma Variations," 297–99; Bitterli, *Say What I Am Called,* 26–34; Murphy, *Unriddling the Exeter Riddles,* 186–87.

For comparison, see ALD 83, ps-BED 7, EUS 37, LOR 11 (all solved "bullock").

The translation of the final two lines reflects a change in grammatical gender in the referents, from feminine *(Seo wiht . . . hio)* to masculine *(he).*

## EXE 37

Solution: *DEAÐ* (death); other suggested solutions include: "day," "moon," "time," "cloud," "revenant," "speech," "dream," "dream" or "cloud," "comet," "creature death," "auspicious dream."
See further Bello, "Compilation of the Old English Riddles," 196–200.
For comparison, see ALC D6 (death).

The evidently Christian tone and anaphoric style of this highly puzzling riddle connects it with EXE 38 (creation), which follows, and it may also share with that riddle a learned, literate, and Latinate motivation; some have even suggested shared authorship.

## EXE 38

Solution: *GESCEAFT* (creation); other suggested solutions include: "nature," "primordial matter: water."
See further Katherine O'Brien O'Keeffe, "The Text of Aldhelm's *Enigma* no. c in Oxford, Bodleian Library, Rawlinson C.697 and Exeter Riddle 40," *Anglo-Saxon England* 14 (1985): 61–73; Salvador-Bello, "Compilation of the Old English Riddles," 200–209; Janie Steen, *Verse and Virtuosity: The Adaptation of Latin Rhetoric in Old English Poetry* (Toronto, 2008), 98–109; Afros, "Linguistic Ambiguities"; Murphy, *Unriddling the Exeter Riddles,* 154–56; Sebo, *In Enigmate,* 92–116.
For comparison, see ALD 100, EXE 64 and 90 (all solved "creation").

This riddle, the longest in the Exeter Book, has as its direct source Aldhelm's longest and final *aenigma* (ALD 100 [creation]), and to that extent its solution is not in doubt. Even in the manuscript, EXE 38 is distinctive, with an extra blank line inserted before its opening, something that is unique in the formatting of the Exeter Book riddles.

## EXE 39

Solution: *WÆTER* (water); other suggested solutions include: "earth"; "fire"; "wisdom"; "barm, a dough starter."
See further Salvador-Bello, "Compilation of the Old English Riddles," 210–11.
For comparison, see ALD 29, ALC D50, LOR 3, EXE 80, OER 21 (all solved "water").

The beginning of this riddle is missing, through the loss of a leaf between fols. 111v and 112r, and so several of the suggested solutions seem feasible; "water" is perhaps the likeliest.

## EXE 40

Solution: *HANA OND HÆN* (cock and hen); there are no other suggested solutions.
See further Salvador-Bello, "Compilation of the Old English Riddles," 211–16; Fiocco, "Gli animali negli enigmi anglo-sassoni dell'*Exeter Book*"; McFadden, "Raiding, Reform, and Reaction"; Mercedes Salvador-Bello, "The Key to the Body: Unlocking Riddles 42–46," in *Naked before God: Uncovering the Body in Anglo-Saxon England,* ed. Benjamin C. Withers and Jonathan Wilcox, Medieval European Studies 3 (Morgantown, 2003), 63–72; Orchard, "Enigma Variations," 287–88; Bitterli, *Say What I Am Called,* 121–24; Murphy, *Unriddling the Exeter Riddles,* 40–41.

EXE 40 and 41 appear in the manuscript as if they were one, but while both have double solutions, the tone of each is quite different. EXE 40 is unabashedly sexual, a celebration of the "the sport of sex" *(hæmed-lac)* of two creatures who are identified as a cock and a hen by the rearrangement of the initial letters of the runes, presented here by their names given in italics, which spell out *HANA* (cock) and *HÆN* (hen).

## EXE 41

Solution: *GAST OND LIC-HAMA* (soul and body); there are no other suggested solutions.

See further Williams, "What's So New about the Sexual Revolution?"; Salvador-Bello, "Compilation of the Old English Riddles," 216–20; James E. Anderson, "Two Spliced Riddles in the Exeter Book," *In Geardagum* 5 (1983): 57–75; Salvador-Bello, "The Key to the Body," 72–76; Lockett, *Anglo-Saxon Psychologies,* 28–30.

This riddle clearly depicts life as a journey in a way that makes the solution "soul and body" so widely accepted. It is evidently presented in the manuscript as a spiritual contrast to the rather earthly EXE 40 that precedes it, although in fact they are copied as if coupled; the argument that both should indeed be read together is a powerful one, but it undercuts the idea that within the Anglo-Saxon riddle traditions contiguous riddles (and *aenigmata*) in specific manuscripts were intended to be read together. This is the first of three riddles to begin with the "I know" formula (the others are EXE 47.1a and 56.1a).

## EXE 42

Solution: *CÆG* (key); other suggested solutions include: "dagger sheath," "penis," *cæg ond loca* (key and lock).

See further Salvador-Bello, "Compilation of the Old English Riddles," 220–21; D. K. Smith, "Humor in Hiding: Laughter between the Sheets in the Exeter Book Riddles," in *Humour in Anglo-Saxon Literature,* ed. Jonathan Wilcox (Cambridge, 2000), 88–94; Salvador-Bello, "The Key to the Body," 76–82; Murphy, *Unriddling the Exeter Riddles,* 176–81.

See too Leahy, *Anglo-Saxon Crafts,* 130–31.

For comparison, see EXE 87, SYM 4 (both solved "key").

This riddle introduces a sequence of three with more or less overt sexual elements (EXE 42–44). The generally accepted solution is "key," although given the clearly phallic language it is worth pointing out that the Old English word *cæg(e)* is usually feminine (as is the Latin *clavis*).

## EXE 43

Solution: *DAG* (dough); other suggested solutions include: "bee," "penis." See further Salvador-Bello, "Compilation of the Old English Riddles," 222–23; Smith, "Humor in Hiding," 97–98; Salvador-Bello, "The Key to the Body," 82–86; Salvador-Bello, "Sexual Riddle Type," 358; Rudolf, "Riddling and Reading."

Like the preceding EXE 41, this one too is evidently intended as employing misdirection through double entendre, although "dough" (*dag, dah:* the noun is grammatically either masculine or neuter) is generally accepted as the solution.

## EXE 44

Solution: *LOTH OND HIS BEARN* (Lot and his children); other suggested solutions include: "Adam and Eve with two sons and a daughter." See further Salvador-Bello, "Compilation of the Old English Riddles," 223–27; Salvador-Bello, "The Key to the Body," 86–93; Bitterli, *Say What I Am Called,* 58–59; Murphy, *Unriddling the Exeter Riddles,* 143–44.

The generally accepted solution is "Lot and his children," based on the account in Genesis 19:32–38, in which Lot's daughters have sex with him after getting him drunk, and each has a son. The riddle plays on the conflation and confusion of kinship relationships shared by the five key players.

## EXE 45

Solution: *\*BOC-MOÐÐE* (book moth); other suggested solutions include: "demon," "writing on vellum," *mapa ond sealm-boc* (maggot and psalter). See further Ann Harleman Stewart, "The Diachronic Study of Communicative Competence," in *Current Topics in English Historical Linguistics,* ed. Michael Davenport, Erik Hansen, and Hans Frede Neilsen (Odense, 1983), 123–36; Salvador-Bello, "Compilation of the Old English Riddles," 227–31; Fiocco, "Gli animali negli enigmi anglo-sassoni dell'*Exeter Book*"; Göbel, *Altenglischen Schriftwesenrätseln,* 226–55; Bitterli, *Say What I Am Called,* 191–93; Orchard, "Performing Writing and Singing Silence."
For comparison, see SYM 16 (bookworm).

NOTES TO THE TRANSLATIONS

The solution "bookworm" or "book moth" has been widely accepted ever since Dietrich pointed out the parallel with SYM 16 (*TINEA,* "bookworm"), although the differences in treatment are striking. Fred C. Robinson, "Artful Ambiguities in the Old English 'Book-Moth' Riddle," in *Anglo-Saxon Poetry: Essays in Appreciation, for John C. McGalliard,* ed. Lewis E. Nicholson and Dolores Warwick Frese (Notre Dame, 1975), 355–62, points out the skillful use of ambiguity on the part of the Old English poet. So, for example, we might note an apparent play on words between *wyrd* (fate) and *gewyrd* (speech, sentence), especially since *wyrd* here is back-linked alliteratively to *word* (words) in the previous line. The "darkness" may also of course be metaphorical, and denote ignorance; likewise, some pun on *cwide* (speech, sentence) and *cwidu* (cud, what is chewed) seems likely, especially given the prominence of the latter term in phrases such as *cwudu ceowan* (to chew the cud), so emphasizing the notion of *ruminatio* (rumination). The "support" may likewise signify both a physical and an intellectual foundation, while the verb "to swallow" again covers both corporeal and mental consumption.


## EXE 46

Solution: *HUSEL-DISC* (paten); other suggested solutions include: "chrismal," "chalice," "bell/sacramental vessel," "gospel book or book of offices" (?), "inscription ring on a chalice."
See further Marie Nelson, "The Paradox of Silent Speech in the Exeter Book Riddles," *Neophilologus* 62 (1978): 609–15; Teele, "The Heroic Tradition," 162–65; Orchard, "Performing Writing and Singing Silence."
For comparison, see TAT 12 (paten).


If the words that are so unprofitably consumed by the subject of the preceding EXE 45 are taken to be the edifying words of scripture or sacred study, the evidently Christian tone of EXE 46 may well maintain or indeed reclaim the pious tone and feel. The most likely solution is some item of church furniture, with "paten," the small plate used to hold the Eucharistic wafer during the Mass, perhaps the most likely solution.

## EXE 47

Solution: *BÆC-OFEN* (baking oven); other suggested solutions include: "falcon cage"; "bookcase"; "oven"; "books"; "barrow, sacrificial altar"; "altar"; "millpond and its sluice"; *hlaf ond ofen* (bread and oven).

See further Adam Davis, "*Agon* and *Gnomon:* Forms and Functions of the Anglo-Saxon Riddles," in *De Gustibus: Essays for Alain Renoir,* ed. John Miles Foley, J. Christ Womack, and Whitney A. Womack, Albert Bates Lord Studies in Oral Tradition 11 (New York, 1992), 110–50; Salvador-Bello, "Compilation of the Old English Riddles," 234–36; For the notion that this is one of the riddles that focus on the scriptorium and the process of writing, see in particular Göbel, *Altenglischen Schriftwesenrätseln,* 256–83.

This riddle continues to resist interpretation, partly due to some obscure vocabulary. So, for example, the word *gifre* in the sense "useful" is found only here and at EXE 24.28a, and there may also be a play on the homograph *gifre* (greedy), coming so close after the word "swallows" (*swilgeð*) in the previous line.

## EXE 48

Solution: *FYR* (fire); other suggested solutions include: "dog," "penis," and "fire and anger."

See further Salvador-Bello, "Compilation of the Old English Riddles," 236–39; Jennifer Neville, "The Unexpected Treasure of the 'Implement Trope': Hierarchical Relationships in the Old English Riddles," *Review of English Studies* 62 (2011): 505–19. There are some broad parallels to be found in *Hisperica famina* A426–51 ("on fire"); see further Michael W. Herren, ed. and trans., *The "Hisperica famina" I: The A-Text* (Toronto, 1974); Andy Orchard, "The *Hisperica famina* as Literature," *Journal of Medieval Latin* 10 (2000): 1–45.

For comparison, see ALD 44, TAT 31 and 33, ALC D51 and D73, GES 29 (all solved "fire").

The solution "fire" seems to fit best all the requirements of this riddle, being produced from two dumb creatures, namely flint and iron.

## EXE 49

Solution: *FEÐER OND FINGRAS* (quill pen and fingers); other suggested solutions include: "dragon," "alchemy," "horse and wagon," and "quill pen" or "pen and three fingers."
See further Salvador-Bello, "Compilation of the Old English Riddles," 239–40; Bitterli, *Say What I Am Called*, 145–50; Murphy, *Unriddling the Exeter Riddles*, 85–86.
For comparison, see EXE 29 (quill pen and fingers).

This riddle is widely agreed to depict the act of writing, a combined effort of three fingers and (in this case at least) a quill pen.

## EXE 50

Solution: *ÞERSCEL* (flail); other suggested solutions include: "two buckets," "well buckets," "broom," "yoke of oxen led into barn or house by female slave."
See further Lendinara, "Aspetti della società germanica negli enigmi del Codice Exoniense"; Salvador-Bello, "Compilation of the Old English Riddles," 241; Murphy, *Unriddling the Exeter Riddles*, 198–200.

This riddle, like the one that precedes it, speaks of collaborative work, and the solution "flail" is generally accepted.

## EXE 51

Solution: *GEALGA* (gallows, cross); other suggested solutions include: "spear," "battering ram," "penis," *gealg-treow* (gallows/cross).
See further Stanley, "Heroic Aspects of the Exeter Book Riddles"; Lendinara, "Aspetti della società germanica negli enigmi del Codice Exoniense"; Salvador-Bello, "Compilation of the Old English Riddles," 241–43; Teele, "The Heroic Tradition," 85–90.

There is a certain amount of misdirection here through double entendre, which links this riddle to the one that follows.

## EXE 52

Solution: *CYRN* (churn); other suggested solutions include: "baker's boy and oven," "penis/intercourse," "butter-churning servant," "churn and butter," "male masturbation."
See further Salvador-Bello, "Compilation of the Old English Riddles," 243–44; Smith, "Humor in Hiding," 94–97; Rudolf, "Riddling and Reading."

In this riddle, the stratagem of misdirection through double entendre is so overt that scholars have sometimes struggled to identify alternatives: if the activity described is not simply sexual, then the churning of butter or cheese seems the most likely solution; verbal parallels with other riddles employing double entendre only strengthen the supposition that the author of this riddle feels part of a wider tradition.

## EXE 53

Solution: *WÆPEN-HENGEN* (weapon rack); other suggested solutions include: "shield," "scabbard," "harp," "sword stand," "cross," "tetractys," "reliquary (containing a splinter of the True Cross)," "wooden liturgical cross," "cross reliquary," "mead barrel and drinking bowl."
See further Seth Lerer, *Literacy and Power in Anglo-Saxon Literature* (Norman, 1991), 113. Stanley, "Heroic Aspects of the Exeter Book Riddles"; Salvador-Bello, "Compilation of the Old English Riddles," 245–51; Teele, "The Heroic Tradition," 147–57; Niles, *Old English Enigmatic Poems*, 61–84; Bitterli, *Say What I Am Called*, 124–31; Murphy, *Unriddling the Exeter Riddles,* 61–67.

This riddle is one of the most perplexing in the Exeter Book, with suggested solutions vacillating between the martial, the mundane, and the marvelous.

## EXE 54

Solution: *RID-ROD* (riding pole, pole lathe); other suggested solutions include: "lathe," "loom," "flail"; "web in the loom," "execution," *webb ond webbeam* (tapestry and loom).

See further Lendinara, "Aspetti della società germanica negli enigmi del Codice Exoniense"; Salvador-Bello, "Compilation of the Old English Riddles," 251–55; Teele, "The Heroic Tradition," 157–61.
See too Leahy, *Anglo-Saxon Crafts*, 30–35; Riley, *Anglo-Saxon Tools*, 80–82.
For comparison, see EXE 56 (well sweep).

This riddle also seems to focus on the domestic, and some solution involving weaving has been suggested, on the basis that similarly martial and violent imagery is found in other weaving songs, such as the Old Norse *Darraðarljóð* (found in chapter 157 of the fourteenth-century Icelandic *Njáls saga*). Here I prefer the suggestion of Pinsker and Ziegler, building on a second thought of Dietrich, namely that what is at issue here is instead a wood-turning lathe, also known as a pole lathe, whereby a sappy branch is drawn up and down by a treadle, rotating a piece of wood that can be carved both outside and in by one or more metal points or blades (the "arrows" mentioned at 54.12a).

## EXE 55

Solution: *STAFAS* ("letters," likely "neumes," though the Old English is in the latter case unclear); other suggested solutions include: "martins," "gnats," "swallows," "starlings," "storm clouds," "a somewhat mysterious brown bird," "hailstones," "raindrops," "rooks" or "crows," "midges," "swifts," "jackdaw," "bees," "musical notes as notated in manuscripts," "damned souls," "blackbirds," "crows," "letters."
See further Salvador-Bello, "Compilation of the Old English Riddles," 255–58; Orchard, "Performing Writing and Singing Silence."
For comparison, see ALD 30, TAT 4, EUS 7, ALC D1, BER 25 (all solved "letter[s]").

This riddle seems at first sight somewhat out of place in the sequence, which otherwise appears to be concerned with man-made objects and processes; few of the solutions proposed so far move beyond the natural world, and the notion that the solution might be a kind of bird is supported by the verbal parallel to EXE 5.4b (swan) and 6.3b (nightingale) at EXE 55.1a and 55.4b, but this may be a form of misdirection: the much closer conceptual parallels with *aenigmata* such as TAT 4 (letters) and EUS

7 (letters) support the suggested solution, with the proviso that musical notes or "neumes" would also fit well and maintain the link with the singing birds. A very similar kind of misdirection seems to be involved in the equally musical EXE 29 (psaltery), where a musical instrument is also figured as a form of writing.


## EXE 56

Solution: *RAD-ROD (well sweep); other suggested solutions include: "well," "penis," *rid-rod (moving pole, pole lathe), "drawing well" (?), R-RⱮM (*rad-rod, "well sweep").
See further Lendinara, "Aspetti della società germanica negli enigmi del Codice Exoniense"; Salvador-Bello, "Compilation of the Old English Riddles," 258–60; Niles, *Old English Enigmatic Poems,* 89–92; Bitterli, *Say What I Am Called,* 98–105.
See too Leahy, *Anglo-Saxon Crafts,* 30–35; Riley, *Anglo-Saxon Tools,* 80–82.
For comparison, see EXE 54 (pole lathe).

The notion of naming connects this riddle with the one preceding, EXE 55, although it also seems very concerned with defining the creature in question in relation to a whole slew of characteristics, both positive (being earthbound, being one footed, being useful, having particular body parts) and negative (it needs neither food nor drink) that effectively characterize so many of the previous riddles. The notion that this is a summary text from a knowing poet seems strengthened by the paradox of an earthbound item bearing water into the air, the solution to which is given a runic solution that can be summarized as signifying something beginning with *r* (or at least R [*r*] or maybe just *rad* ). Both *rid-rod (moving pole, pole lathe) and *rad-rod (well sweep) have been suggested, and both seem possible, with the latter more likely as being able to be written with three runes and a creature that "often ferries a flood of water aloft."


## EXE 57

Solution: *CALIC* (chalice); other suggested solutions include: "inscription ring on a chalice."

See further Salvador-Bello, "Compilation of the Old English Riddles," 260–62; Teele, "The Heroic Tradition," 166–70; Orchard, "Performing Writing and Singing Silence."

This is one of the few riddles for which there exists a generally accepted solution, in this case "chalice." Certainly, the emphasis on visual wounds combines nicely with the idea of an engraved chalice that symbolizes the suffering of Christ.

## EXE PART 2

### EXE 58

Solution: *HREOD* (reed). See, in particular, Göbel, *Altenglischen Schrift-wesenrätseln,* 306–68; other suggested solutions include: "letter beam cut from stump of old jetty," "reed pen," "yew tree," "reed flute," "reed pipe," "kelp weed," "revenant," *hreod* (reed/reed pipe/reed pen).
See further Nelson, "The Paradox of Silent Speech"; Gregory K. Jember, "A Generative Method for the Study of Anglo-Saxon Riddles," *Studies in Medieval Culture* 11 (1977): 33–39; Neville, *Representations of the Natural World,* 114–15; Salvador-Bello, "Compilation of the Old English Riddles," 266–69; Afros, "Linguistic Ambiguities"; Bitterli, *Say What I Am Called,* 137–45; Murphy, *Unriddling the Exeter Riddles,* 140–41; Orchard, "Performing Writing and Singing Silence."
For comparison, see SYM 2 (reed).

This riddle, which appears on fols. 122v–23r, follows EXE 28b, the solution to which seems to be *BEAM* (beam, tree, wood, beam of light, cross, gallows). Likewise, it is not at all clear that this poem is not part of *The Husband's Message,* which certainly contains enigmatic runes, nor that the text that follows *The Husband's Message* in the Exeter Book, namely *The Ruin* (which also contains a not very enigmatic rune) was not perceived as part of a wider pattern. Just as the first batch of riddles in the Exeter Book is bracketed by two enigmatic texts, namely *Wulf and Eadwacer* and *The Wife's Lament,* so too the second batch, which ends in physical damage to the manuscript, is introduced by two others, namely *The Husband's Message* and *The Ruin,* that the compiler may have thought were simply part of the whole sequence, preceded as they are by EXE 28b and 58.

## EXE PART 3

### EXE 59

Solution: *CYRTEL* (shirt, garment); other suggested solutions include: "shirt," "helmet," "mail shirt," "vagina," "hood."
See further Williams, "What's So New about the Sexual Revolution?";
Salvador-Bello, "Compilation of the Old English Riddles," 269–71; Higley, "The Wanton Hand," 48–48; Murphy, *Unriddling the Exeter Riddles,* 178–79 and 197–98.

Perhaps the marital difficulties regaled in *The Husband's Message* and the internal seething implied in *The Ruin,* both of which precede this group (see further the note on EXE 58 above), have informed the more or less overtly sexual impetus that opens what is generally seen as the second set of riddles in the Exeter Book. Certainly, EXE 59 and 60 are both firmly in the double-entendre camp, as may also be the fragmentary EXE 61, and all three have many similarities with several double-entendre riddles in EXE part 1; see further Peter Orton, "The Exeter Book *Riddles:* Authorship and Transmission," *Anglo-Saxon England* 44 (2016): 131–62; and Andy Orchard, "The Riddle of Anglo-Saxon Lewdness and Learning," *Anglo-Saxon England,* forthcoming.

### EXE 60

Solution: *SPURA* (spur); other suggested solutions include: "gimlet," "poker," "borer," "burning arrow," "oven rake," "penis," *nafu-gar* (auger).
See further Dieter Bitterli, "Spur, a New Solution to Exeter Book *Riddle 62,*" *Notes and Queries* 66 (2019): 343–47; Salvador-Bello, "Compilation of the Old English Riddles," 271–72; Murphy, *Unriddling the Exeter Riddles,* 202–4.
See too Riley, *Anglo-Saxon Tools,* 68–70 and 78.

The frankly phallic language here limits the range of possible solutions, of which "auger," "borer," and "poker" are the most commonly proposed, though "spur," as suggested by Bitterli, is preferred here.

## EXE 61

Solution: *GLÆS-FÆT* (glass beaker); other suggested solutions include: "beaker," "flute," "can or flask."
See further Salvador-Bello, "Compilation of the Old English Riddles," 272–75; Bitterli, *Say What I Am Called,* 124–31; Murphy, *Unriddling the Exeter Riddles,* 204–6.
See too Leahy, *Anglo-Saxon Crafts,* 106–7.
For comparison, see ALD 80, BER 50a (both solved "glass beaker").

This badly damaged riddle supplies enough tantalizing information to make it worth hazarding a guess, especially since it follows two riddles relying on double entendre, and there is a close parallel for the central lines of a creature whose body is pressed with fingers and kissed on the mouth (EXE 61.4–6) in Aldhelm's *aenigma* on a "glass cup" (ALD 80.5–9).

## EXE 62

Solution: *BRIM-HENGEST* (sea-steed or ship); other suggested solutions include: "ring-tailed peacock"; "snake-eating bird of prey and ring-shaped adder"; "horseman and hawk"; "horseman, hawk, and servant"; "falconry"; "writing."
See further Salvador-Bello, "Compilation of the Old English Riddles," 275–77; Teele, "The Heroic Tradition," 59–61; Karin Olsen, "Animated Ships in Old English and Old Norse Poetry," in *Animals and the Symbolic in Mediaeval Art and Literature,* ed. L. A. J. R. Houwen, Mediaevalia Groningana 20 (Groningen, 1997), 53–66; Bitterli, *Say What I Am Called,* 86–91.

This riddle is unique in containing runes in every line, and several commentators have compared it to EXE 17, which also appears to offer a description of a kind of horse bearing both a man and a bird on a journey. Many of the suggested solutions rely on the assumption that the groups of runes spell out the initial letters of other elements of the solution. Typical is Williamson, *Old English Riddles of the "Exeter Book,"* 326, who takes the runes to indicate *wicg* (horse), *beorn* (warrior), *hafoc* (hawk), *þegn* (servant), *fælca* (falcon) and *\*ea-spor* (water track). At all events, and again relying on the perceived parallel with EXE 17, this would seem to be another ship riddle, playing on the many ship kennings based on some term for "horse."

## EXE 63

Solution: *CIPE* (onion); other suggested solutions include: "chives, leek"; "revenant, spirit."

See further Kries, *"Fela í rúnum eða í skáldskap";* Salvador-Bello, "Compilation of the Old English Riddles," 277–78; Orchard, "Enigma Variations," 295–97; Murphy, *Unriddling the Exeter Riddles,* 223–24.

For comparison, see EXE 23, SYM 44, BER 51 (all solved "onion").

This is the second of two "onion" riddles in the Exeter Book (the other is EXE 23), both of which derive ultimately from an *aenigma* of Symphosius (SYM 44 [onion]).

## EXE 64

Solution: *GESCEAFT* (creation); other suggested solutions include: "divine power," "nature," "water."

See further Salvador-Bello, "Compilation of the Old English Riddles," 278–81; Sebo, *In Enigmate,* 92–116.

For comparison, see ALD 100 and EXE 38 and 90 (all solved "creation").

This riddle, like the one preceding it, has links both with a Latin *aenigma* (in this case ALD 100) and with an earlier riddle in the Exeter Book (in this case EXE 38).

## EXE 65

Solution: *CRISTES BOC* (Gospel book); other suggested solutions include: "bible," "bible" or "cross," "holy book."

See further Salvador-Bello, "Compilation of the Old English Riddles," 282–83; Marsden, "'Ask What I Am Called': The Anglo-Saxons and Their Bibles"; Bitterli, *Say What I Am Called,* 124–31. See, in particular, Göbel, *Altenglischen Schriftwesenrätseln,* 284–305.

Another fragmentary riddle, which in its celebration of a mouthless creature who nonetheless dispenses wisdom, has parallels in two of the *aenigmata* of Eusebius, EUS 7 (letters) and EUS 33 (parchment), as well as many other features in common with EXE 24 (Gospel book). For both these reasons, the likely solution seems to be "Gospel book."

## EXE 66

Solution: *IS* (ice); other suggested solutions include: "winter," "petrifaction," "Christ walking on the sea," "running water," "iceberg," and "ice" or "frozen pond."

See further Salvador-Bello, "Compilation of the Old English Riddles," 283–84; Davis, "*Agon* and *Gnomon*"; Orchard, "Enigma Variations," 290–91; Dieter Bitterli, "The One-Liners among the Exeter Book *Riddles*," *Neophilologus* 103 (2019): 419–34.

For comparison, see ps-BED 6, ALC D53, LOR 4, EXE 31, OER 11, SYM 10, BER 38 and 42, OIR 9 (all solved "ice").

In the manuscript, this riddle is presented as if it were two, comprising lines 1–2 and line 3, respectively. There are several other apparently single-line riddles in this part of the Exeter Book (see the notes to EXE 73 and 76), but they too can be explained as part of longer structures, and here too it seems simplest to consider this a three-line riddle, with "iceberg" as the most feasible solution. Part of the rationale for considering these lines together is that EXE 67.1–2 can be matched closely in EXE 34.1–2, where they seem simply an introductory formula for a riddle that depicts another waterborne creature.

## EXE 67

Solution: *BELLE* (bell); other suggested solutions include: "harp"; "shawm, shepherd's pipe"; "rye flute"; "shawm"; "organistrum"; "shuttle"; "church bell."

See further Salvador-Bello, "Compilation of the Old English Riddles," 285–88; Niles, *Old English Enigmatic Poems,* 92–96.

See too Leahy, *Anglo-Saxon Crafts,* 132.

For comparison, see TAT 7, ALC D74, EXE 2, SYM 80 (all solved "bell[s]").

John C. Pope, "An Unsuspected Lacuna in the Exeter Book: Divorce Proceedings for an Ill-Matched Couple in the Old English Riddles," *Speculum* 49 (1974): 615–22, argued persuasively that a folio is missing between fols. 125 and 126, so rendering what previous editors had thought to be one riddle as most likely fragments of two. The first fragmentary riddle seems to depict some kind of musical instrument that "sings through its sides" (EXE 67.2); either "harp" or "bell" seems feasible. Given the preferred solution for EXE 68 (lighthouse), it is tempting to consider this as a similarly lofty construction: perhaps *BELLE-TORR (bell tower) is more fitting.

## EXE 68

Solution: *BEACEN-STAN* (lighthouse); other suggested solutions include: "nose," *candel* (candle), "twin-piped flute."
For comparison, see ALD 92 (lighthouse).

This fragmentary two-line riddle depicts a towering and bright-cheeked creature that stands at the water's edge and is useful for men. Of the solutions suggested so far, that of "lighthouse" at least has a parallel in ALD 92 ("very tall lighthouse": see the note there), while "candle" seems less convincing, and the other solutions proposed seem to require special pleading to a greater or lesser extent. The phrase *be wege* in the opening line can be translated both as "by the way" and as "by the water"; the preferred solution fits both.

## EXE 69

Solution: *SECG* (sword, man); other suggested solutions include: "cupping glass"; "iron helmet"; "sword, dagger"; "iron weapon or ore"; "iron shield"; "revenant"; "sword."
See further Stanley, "Heroic Aspects of the Exeter Book Riddles"; Salvador-Bello, "Compilation of the Old English Riddles," 288–90; Teele, "The Heroic Tradition," 84–85.
For comparison, see TAT 30 (sword and sheath); EUS 36 (sword); EXE 18 (sword or man).

This riddle has several parallels with EXE 18, which is generally solved as "sword," the solution that most commentators have accepted here too. The problematic lines EXE 69.2–3 introduce the notion of a foundation "set up among beautiful plants," that seems to run contrary to the usual answer. If, however, we contemplate the solution *secg* (sword, man, sedge), that part of the answer that pertains to plants may be satisfied.

## EXE 70

Solution: *OXA* (ox); other suggested solutions include: "axle and wheel," "slave" (?).

See further Lendinara, "Aspetti della società germanica negli enigmi del Codice Exoniense"; Salvador-Bello, "Compilation of the Old English Riddles," 290–91; Bitterli, *Say What I Am Called,* 26–34.

For comparison, see EXE 10 (ox).

Just as the previous riddle has a parallel in the first batch of riddles in the Exeter Book, so does this match two in the same group (EXE 10 and EXE 36). In particular, the motif of being fed from four fountains is found in EXE 36.3–4, as well as in two Latin *aenigmata* (ALD 83 and EUS 37).

## EXE 71

Solution: *ÆSC* (spear made of ash); other suggested solutions include: "lance"; "spear"; "battering ram"; "revenant, spirit"; "cross"; "writing" or "pen"; "lance" or "javelin"; "bow and incendiary arrow"; "bow."

See further Stanley, "Heroic Aspects of the Exeter Book Riddles"; Lendinara, "Aspetti della società germanica negli enigmi del Codice Exoniense"; Salvador-Bello, "Compilation of the Old English Riddles," 291–93; Teele, "The Heroic Tradition," 90–97.

See too Leahy, *Anglo-Saxon Crafts,* 125–28.

Among the many solutions for what seems clearly a weapon made of wood, that of "spear" held the day until Niles pointed out that the solution *æsc* (ash, ash spear) covered all the options. Griffith went even further, connecting this riddle with the one that follows it and suggesting instead the runic solution ᚫ (*Æ* or *æsc,* "ash").

## EXE 72

Solution: *AC* (ship made of oak); other suggested solutions include: "swan," "nature" or "life," "cuttlefish," "siren," "water," "hyena," "rain," "pen," "diving bird," "ship's figurehead," "sun," "whooper swan," "barnacle goose."

For the notion that this is one of the riddles that deal with the scripto-

rium and the act of writing, see Göbel, *Altenglischen Schriftwesenrätseln,*
390–420.

See further Davis, "*Agon* and *Gnomon*"; Salvador-Bello, "Compilation of
the Old English Riddles," 293–97; Paul Sorrell, "Oaks, Ships, Riddles and
the Old English *Rune Poem*," *Anglo-Saxon England* 19 (1990): 103–16; Mercedes Salvador-Bello, "Direct and Indirect Clues: Exeter Riddle No. 74,"
*Neuphilologische Mitteilungen* 99 (1998): 17–29; Fiocco, "Gli animali negli
enigmi anglo-sassoni dell'*Exeter Book*"; Niles, *Old English Enigmatic Poems,*
11–54; Murphy, *Unriddling the Exeter Riddles,* 13–18.

This has long been considered one of the most frustrating and perplexing
of all the riddles, as the great range of suggested solutions makes clear. The
latest solution, that by Griffith, seems entirely the most satisfying, building as it does on an earlier suggestion. What is intended is a creature that
is both masculine and feminine, a condition filled by the word *ac,* which in
its feminine form signifies a tree, but in its masculine form equates to the
rune ᚪ (*ac,* "oak"), specifically in its role as an oaken ship, as outlined rather
precisely in OER 25 (see too the note to ALD 29 above).


## EXE 73

Solution: *AC* (oak); other suggested solutions include: "piss," "cock and
hen," *hund ond hind* (hound and hind). Suggested solutions for EXE 73.1
(taken as a separate riddle) include: "dog," *hælend* (savior), "elk hunter"; a
suggested solution for EXE 73.3 (taken as a separate riddle) is "hen."
See further Salvador-Bello, "Compilation of the Old English Riddles,"
297–300; Davis, "*Agon* and *Gnomon*"; Niles, *Old English Enigmatic Poems,*
96–100; Bitterli, *Say What I Am Called,* 105–10; Bitterli, "The One-Liners
among the Exeter Book *Riddles*."

Here again there is debate about whether one riddle or two is intended, as
well as about the precise status (not to mention the meaning) of the runes
· ᚾᛏᚱᚻ · *(DNLH)* that, if one considers two riddles to be involved, come as
the second line of the first, or as the middle line of a single combined riddle. Elsewhere, any runes that appear as an integral part of the text also
partake of the structural alliteration, and so it seems safest to take these
runes as an interpolated attempt at a solution; such is certainly the route

taken by those who also assume that the solution is given in some sort of code. If one or other of the runic solutions offered here is accepted, then there is a further link with the riddle that follows; alternatively, one might make the still more dramatic suggestion that the two lines of this riddle are a set of clues to the one that follows, with two "I saw" perspectives on the "I am" riddle that follows, and that the solution "oyster," generally accepted for EXE 74, fits this combined one too. Or, perhaps, this is another *AC* (oak) riddle, playing on the fact that the creature in question is both male and female, and both moves (when a boat) and stands still (when a tree or rune).

## EXE 74

Solution: *OSTRE* (oyster); other suggested solutions include: "female genitalia," "flatfish."
See further Salvador-Bello, "Compilation of the Old English Riddles," 300–302; Fiocco, "Gli animali negli enigmi anglo-sassoni dell'*Exeter Book*"; Mercedes Salvador-Bello, "The Oyster and the Crab: A Riddle Duo (nos. 77 and 78) in the *Exeter Book*," *Modern Philology* 101 (2004): 400–419.

Like the preceding, this riddle too seems to speak of a stationary female creature matched with a moving male, in this case a creature that is brutally skinned at knifepoint and eaten raw.

## EXE 75

Solution: *CRABBA* (crab); other suggested solutions include: "water-dwelling creature," "oyster," "lamprey."
See further Salvador-Bello, "Compilation of the Old English Riddles," 302–5; Salvador-Bello, "The Oyster and the Crab."
For comparison, see ALD 37, EXE 78 (both solved "crab").

This is another riddle that damage to the manuscript has rendered more or less unintelligible, although the repetition of the words "floods" (EXE 75.1a) and "waves" (EXE 75.8b) with similar forms in the preceding EXE 74 (at 74.3b and 74.2a) have led some to suggest that this is another "oyster" riddle, but Salvador-Bello in particular has noted the association between crab and oyster in such authors as Isidore and Aldhelm, not to mention Ælfric.

## EXE 76

Solution: *HORN* (horn); other suggested solutions include: "spear," "sword," "penis." Suggested solutions for EXE 76.1, considered as a separate riddle, include: "falcon," "hawk," "sword in its scabbard."
See further Stanley, "Heroic Aspects of the Exeter Book Riddles"; Salvador-Bello, "Compilation of the Old English Riddles," 305–7; Davis, "*Agon* and *Gnomon*"; Bitterli, *Say What I Am Called*, 167–69; Bitterli, "The One-Liners among the Exeter Book *Riddles*."
For comparison, see EXE 12, OER 27 (both solved "horn").

Like EXE 73.2, EXE 76.1 appears as a single stray short line in the manuscript, and here again a single riddle seems to have been split into two in the manuscript, what several earlier editors, based on manuscript layout, have considered another one-line riddle by analogy with the equally pithy and puzzling EXE 73 (again, following the manuscript). It seems more reasonable, given the similar structure and close sound patterning, to assume that lines 1 and 2 are in fact variants (perhaps produced by oral/aural confusion?) and that the combined riddle is not only a noble's "comrade-in-arms" *(eaxl-gestealla)* but his "property and pride" *(æht ond gewilla)*. The solution "horn" seems to fit best.

## EXE 77

Solution: *WEDER-COC* (weathercock); other suggested solutions include: "ship," "helmet with visor."
See further Salvador-Bello, "Compilation of the Old English Riddles," 307–9.

This riddle, like the preceding one, carries a riddle within a riddle: any solution must also be able to explain "what stirs the woods" *(se þe wudu hhereð,* EXE 77.7b). In this case, the answer occurs earlier in the same manuscript, when the creature of EXE 1 (wind of God) claims that "I shake up the woods" *(ic wudu hrere,* EXE 1.8), an association that might seem tenuous, except that fully three consecutive lines of this riddle have parallels with what some earlier commentators considered three separate texts, but which on this evidence seems to be a single coherent whole.

## EXE 78

Solution: *CRABBA* (crab); other suggested solutions include: "harrow."
See further Salvador-Bello, "Compilation of the Old English Riddles," 309–10.
For comparison, see ALD 37, EXE 75 (both solved "crab").

This is another badly damaged riddle for which most commentators have effectively despaired of offering a solution. The creature travels on feet and consumes greatly, but it is unclear whether the reference to neither "skin nor flesh" *(fell ne flæsc)* refers to the creature itself or to what it consumes.

## EXE 79

Solution: *GOLD* (gold); other suggested solutions include: "ore"; "metal" or "money"; "revenant, spirit"; "ore/metal/coins."
See further Lendinara, "Aspetti della società germanica negli enigmi del Codice Exoniense"; Salvador-Bello, "Compilation of the Old English Riddles," 310–12; Teele, "The Heroic Tradition," 197–200; Murphy, *Unriddling the Exeter Riddles,* 139–51.

This riddle describes a creature born of earth, purified by fire, and capable of bestowing power; the language is not particularly spiritual, and so most commentators have opted for concrete solutions along the lines of "ore" or "gold" or even specifically "coinage," which in Anglo-Saxon England would have been predominantly silver.

## EXE 80

Solution: *WÆTER* (water); there are no other suggested solutions.
See further Salvador-Bello, "Compilation of the Old English Riddles," 312–13; McFadden, "Raiding, Reform, and Reaction."

For comparison, see ALD 29, ALC D50, LOR 3, EXE 39, OER 21 (all solved "water").

Most commentators have accepted the solution "water," based on the parallel between EXE 80.4, where the creature is described as "mother of many famous creatures" *(Modor . . . monigra mærra wihta),* and EXE 39.2 (also generally solved as "water"), where the creature in question is described as "mother of many races" *(moddor monigra cynna).*

## EXE 81

Solution: *FISC OND EA* (fish and river), *GAST OND LICHAMA* (soul and body); other suggested solutions include: "body and soul," *fisc ond flod* (fish and river).

See further Nelson, "The Paradox of Silent Speech"; Salvador-Bello, "Compilation of the Old English Riddles," 313–15; Fiocco, "Gli animali negli enigmi anglo-sassoni dell'*Exeter Book*"; Orchard, "Enigma Variations," 293–94; Bitterli, *Say What I Am Called,* 14–18.

For comparison, see ALC D80, SYM 12 (both solved "river and fish").

Ever since the similarities between this riddle and the *aenigma* by Symphosius on "fish and river" (SYM 12) were first noted, it has become conventional simply to adopt the Latin solution for the Old English riddle too. But EXE 81.3b–7 introduce a number of elements that are entirely original and draw the vernacular riddle into a whole new area of interpretation, where indeed there are several useful parallels to be drawn with the widespread "soul and body" literature of Anglo-Saxon England, a point first made in unpublished comments by Irina Dumitrescu, to whom I am grateful.

## EXE 82

Solution: *AN-EAGEDA GAR-LEAC-MONGER* (one-eyed garlic seller); other suggested solutions include: "organ."

See further Hans Pinsker, "Ein verschollenes altenglisches Rätsel?" in *A Yearbook of Studies in English Language and Literature,* ed. Siegfried Korninger, Beiträge zur englischen Philologie 78 (Vienna, 1981), 53–59; Wilcox, "Mock-Riddles"; Salvador-Bello, "Compilation of the Old English Riddles," 315–17; Robert DiNapoli, "In the Kingdom of the Blind, the One-Eyed Man Is a Seller of Garlic: Depth-Perceptino and the Poet's Perspective in the Exeter Book Riddles," *English Studies* 81 (2000): 422–55; Bitterli, *Say What I Am Called*, 68–74 and 124–31; Murphy, *Unriddling the Exeter Riddles*, 42–43.

For comparison, see TAT 20 (one-eyed man); SYM 95 (one-eyed garlic seller).

Like the preceding riddle, this one has been conventionally associated with an *aenigma* by Symphosius (SYM 95), which also describes a creature with many heads but only one eye. The solution given in the Latin manuscripts is "one-eyed garlic seller" *(luscus alium vendens)*, without which this riddle would surely seem obscure indeed.

## EXE 83

Solution: *BLÆST-BELG* (bellows); other suggested solutions include: "cask and cooper," "penis."
See further Salvador-Bello, "Compilation of the Old English Riddles," 317–19; David Hill, "Anglo-Saxon Mechanics"; Davis, *"Agon* and *Gnomon"*; Murphy, *Unriddling the Exeter Riddles*, 216–17.
For comparison, see ALD 11, EXE 35 and 85, SYM 73, GES 9 (all solved "bellows").

This is one of the more obviously sexualized of the double-entendre riddles, and again, like several in this batch of the Exeter Book, contains a riddle within a riddle: the phrase "heaven's tooth" *(heofenes tope)* in EXE 83.5 presumably refers to the wind, at least to judge by the perceived parallels to BER 41 (wind).

## EXE 84

Solution: *BLÆC-HORN* (inkhorn); other suggested solutions include: "horn," "antler," "staghorn," *heortes horn* (inkwell [made from an antler]).
See in particular Göbel, *Altenglischen Schriftwesenrätseln*, 422–59.
See further Lendinara, "Aspetti della società germanica negli enigmi del

Codice Exoniense"; Salvador-Bello, "Compilation of the Old English Riddles," 319–21; Teele, "The Heroic Tradition," 106–9; Bitterli, *Say What I Am Called*, 152–57.
For comparison, see EUS 30, EXE 89 (both solved "inkhorn").

Most commentators agree that the solution here should be "inkhorn," as at EXE 89; both contain (as do so many of the riddles) a description of both the "former life" of the object in question and its current manifestation.

## EXE 85

Solution: *BLÆST-BELG* (bellows); other suggested solutions include: "bellows or leather bottle," "penis."
See further Salvador-Bello, "Compilation of the Old English Riddles," 321–22; Teele, "The Heroic Tradition," 50–54.
For comparison, see ALD 11, EXE 35 and 83, SYM 73, GES 9 (all solved "bellows").

This is another riddle so fragmentary as not easily to permit of a solution; there are vague parallels with EXE 35 and 83 that support the one suggested here.

## EXE 86

Solution: *AGNUS DEI* (Lamb of God); other suggested solutions include: "Lamb of God who overcame the devil," *lupus* (wolf), "Cyn(e)wulf," "pike," an allusion to some person whose name contained the element *wulf*, "web and loom," "Augustine and Tertullian."
See further Leslie Whitbread, "The Latin Riddle in the Exeter Book," *Notes and Queries* 190 (1946): 156–58, and 194 (1949): 80–82; Stanley, "Heroic Aspects of the Exeter Book Riddles"; Salvador-Bello, "Compilation of the Old English Riddles," 322–27; Davis, "*Agon* and *Gnomon*"; Bitterli, *Say What I Am Called*, 74–79.

This is the only Latin *aenigma* in the Exeter Book, and it is enigmatic indeed. Even the form of the text is problematical, and the lines can be viewed as rhythmical hexameters somewhat similar to those found in BER, but only by emending several lines. If some form of medial rhyme is assumed, five long lines of between fourteen and seventeen syllables can be produced; the usual number of lines in BER is six, and it is possible that a line has been omitted altogether.

## EXE 87

Solution: *CÆG* (key); other suggested solutions include: "sickle," "keyhole," "penis."
See further Salvador-Bello, "Compilation of the Old English Riddles," 327–28; Teele, "The Heroic Tradition," 193–97.
See too Leahy, *Anglo-Saxon Crafts*, 130–31.
For comparison, see EXE 42, SYM 4 (both solved "key").

This is another riddle from the second group in the Exeter Book that matches one in the first. In this case, while EXE 42 (key) is a highly sexualized text making much use of double entendre, the language is at least slightly more subtle, although still pretty fruity; the further resemblances between both Old English riddles and SYM 4 (key) are relatively slight. The arguments put forward by Williams, "What's So New about the Sexual Revolution?" that the solution here should be "keyhole," rather than "key," and that the creature in question is the feminine counterpart to the masculine "key," with the corresponding sexual switch, is a very tempting one.

## EXE 88

Solution: *BOC* (book, beech); other suggested solutions include: "ash tree," "beech," "book," "beechwood shield," "beechwood battering ram," "yew (Yggdrasil)," *boc* (beech tree/book/objects made of beech wood). See, in particular, Göbel, *Altenglischen Schriftwesenrätseln*, 460–85.
See further Salvador-Bello, "Compilation of the Old English Riddles," 328–30; Davis, "*Agon* and *Gnomon*."
For comparison, see EXE 91 (book).

The badly damaged ending of this poem has not prevented commentators from attempting to solve this riddle. The suggestion that the solution may turn on the Old English homonym *boc,* meaning both "book" and "beech tree," as well as (less certainly on the evidence beyond this riddle) "beech-nuts" (though compare below) is an intriguing one, made still more attractive by the similarly homonymic tree-based solutions *ac* and *æsc* for EXE 71 and 72. In both those cases a rune is involved, however, whereas the ᛒ-rune, while it does indeed signify a tree, generally stands for "birch" (*berc* or *beorc*) rather than "beech" (*boc*). Both of the main suggested meanings for *boc* connect this riddle to the one that follows.

## EXE 89

Solution: *BLÆC-HORN* (inkhorn). See, in particular, Göbel, *Altenglischen Schriftwesenrätseln,* 486–537; other suggested solutions include: "inkwell fashioned from an antler," "antler or horn."
See further Stanley, "Heroic Aspects of the Exeter Book Riddles"; Lendinara, "Aspetti della società germanica negli enigmi del Codice Exoniense"; Salvador-Bello, "Compilation of the Old English Riddles," 330–32; Teele, "The Heroic Tradition," 106–9; Bitterli, *Say What I Am Called,* 157–63; Murphy, *Unriddling the Exeter Riddles,* 69–70.
For comparison, see EUS 30, EXE 84 (both solved "inkhorn").

This riddle, like EXE 84, is generally solved "inkhorn," and indeed there are certain parallels to be drawn, more so than with the *aenigma* on the same topic by Eusebius (EUS 30 [inkhorn]). If the solutions *boc* (beech, book) for the previous riddle and "inkhorn" for this are accepted, the past and present lives of the current creature as a beechnut-eating animal and object crucial for book production make a pleasing pair.

## EXE 90

Solution: *GESCEAFT* (creation); other suggested solutions include: "nature."
See further Salvador-Bello, "Compilation of the Old English Riddles," 333–34; Sebo, *In Enigmate,* 92–116.
For comparison, see ALD 100, EXE 38 and 64 (all solved "creation").

Even in its badly damaged state, the fact that the six presumed lines of this riddle seem to contain six comparative adjectives has led most commentators to draw parallels with EXE 38 and EXE 64, both of which are generally solved as "creation."

## EXE 91

Solution: *BOC* (book). See, in particular, Göbel, *Altenglischen Schriftwesenrätseln*, 538–606; other suggested solutions include: "word of God"; "thought"; "wandering singer"; "riddle"; "moon"; "soul, spirit"; "quill pen"; *halig gewrit* (holy text); "prostitute"; "book with gilding"; "riddle book"; "holy scriptures"; *mona* (moon).
See further Stanley, "Heroic Aspects of the Exeter Book Riddles"; Salvador-Bello, "Compilation of the Old English Riddles," 334–37; Davis, "*Agon* and *Gnomon*."
For comparison, see EXE 88 (book and beech tree).

The precise interpretation of this riddle is problematic, as the number and range of suggested solutions makes clear. Here, I understand "the pleasure of plunderers" to refer to the ink that "travels widely" over the page; see further the more extensive note in *COEALRT*.

## The Old English Rune Poem (OER)

I have consulted the editions and translations of Bruce Dickins, *Runic and Heroic Poems of the Old Teutonic Peoples* (Cambridge, 1915), and Maureen Halsall, *The Old English Rune Poem: A Critical Edition* (Toronto, 1981). See also the more detailed commentary in *COEALRT*. For further reading, see in general Margaret Clunies Ross, "The Anglo-Saxon and Norse *Rune Poems: A Comparative Approach*," *Anglo-Saxon England* 19 (1990): 23–39; R. I. Page, *An Introduction to Old English Runes* (London, 1973), 73–85; R. I. Page, "The Icelandic Rune-Poem," *Nottingham Medieval Studies* 42 (1998): 1–37, reprinted as a booklet by the Viking Society for Northern Research.

## OER 1

Solution: *FEOH* (wealth).
For comparison, see ALC D66, OIR 1 (both solved "wealth").

The primary meaning of *feoh* (livestock, cattle) was extended early on to signify any kind of moveable wealth, and hence ultimately "money": the same semantic trajectory is found in the movement from Latin *pecus* (cattle) to *pecunia* (money).

## OER 2

Solution: *UR* (aurochs).

This stanza has several parallels with the "ox" riddles found widely elsewhere in the tradition: see especially the headnotes to EXE 12 and 76 (both "horn"), as well as OER 27 below.

The aurochs (*Bos primogenius*) was an enormous wild ox, native to Europe, Asia, and North Africa, standing as much as six feet high at the shoulder and with impressive and massive horns. The horns could likewise be up to six feet in length and, when fashioned into drinking horns, hold as much as a gallon. In Europe the auroch only became extinct in the seventeenth century, but in Britain it died out in the Bronze Age, so its survival here presumably reflects continuity from the Continental tradition. The solution offered for the parallel rune at OIR 2 (*ÚR*, "shower") is strikingly different; see the note there.

## OER 3

Solution: *ÞORN* (thorn).

This rune was introduced early alongside eth into the Roman alphabet to represent the dental fricative, both voiced and voiceless (ð and θ). Note the variance here from the parallel rune in OIR 3 (giant), where the solution is quite different, and the treatment altogether more mythological; see the headnote there.

## OER 4

Solution: *OS* (god or mouth).

For comparison, see BED 3, ALC D19 (both solved "mouth" or "bone").

The original sense of the Germanic rune seems to have been "god," and indeed the pagan god Woden is associated with the invention of runes, and hence written language. Here, the idea that it is the mouth that produces language seems to sanitize the pagan associations, by offering the Christian-Latin interpretation instead.

## OER 5

Solution: *RAD* (riding).

This stanza has evident links to OER 19, which also celebrates the horse that is the other partner in the pleasures of riding. The parallel rune in OIR 5 (*REIÐ*, "riding") is rather similar, but also emphasizes the labor of the horse.

## OER 6

Solution: *CEN* (torch).

The word *cen* is attested only as the rune name and appears ten times in total in surviving Old English, in four of which cases it contributes to the enigmatic runic signature of the poet Cynewulf. The positive picture painted here contrasts sharply with that in the parallel rune in OIR 6 (*KAUN*, "ulcer"), where naturally the outlook is unremittingly bleak.

## OER 7

Solution: *GYFU* (gift).

The aspects of consolation stressed here are in line with the generally more positive, Christianizing, and moralizing attitudes that are found in OER when compared with OIR, where there is no parallel rune; see further, for example, OER 10 below. In the Anglo-Saxon riddle tradition, the *n*-rune also appears, for example, in both EXE 15 and 22.

## OER 8

Solution: *WYNN* (joy) or perhaps *WEN* (hope, expectation).

The earliest attestation of the use of runic *wynn* instead of the spelling <*uu*> is in a charter dated 742–43, but it soon became ubiquitous.

## OER 9

Solution: *HÆGL* (hail).

The parallel rune in OIR 7 (*HAGALL,* "hail") offers a very similar set of perspectives, on which see the note there; both are also associated by further parallels between them and the linked parallels between OER 11 (*IS,* "ice") and OIR 9 (*ÍS,* "ice").

## OER 10

Solution: *NYD* (need, oppression, conflict).

The final line here emphasizes from a Christian and moral perspective the spiritual benefits of suffering; by contrast, see the wholly negative outlook offered by the parallel rune in OIR 8 (*NAUÐ,* "need").

## OER 11

Solution: *IS* (ice).
For comparison, see ps-BED 6, ALC D53, LOR 4, EXE 31 and 66, SYM 10, BER 38 and 42, OIR 9 (all solved "ice").

See in particular the notes at OIR 9 (*ÍS,* "ice") below and OER 9 above, where the chain of connections is clearest. The seasonal link between this stanza and the next is likewise obvious. Unlike the majority of the descriptions of ice offered in the various texts noted above, the perspective given here is again largely positive.

## OER 12

Solution: *GER* (year).

The connection between this stanza and the previous one is made clear in *Beowulf* 1132b–34a (*winter yþe beleac / isgebinde, opðæt oþer com / gear in geardas;* "winter locked the waves, / icebound, until another year came / into the home fields"). The Christian emphasis here on the role of God in bringing the fruitfulness of the earth out of the icy winter is also emphasized elsewhere in *Beowulf*, for example at 1608–11.

## OER 13

Solution: *EOH* (yew).
For comparison, see ALD 69 and OIR 16 (both solved "yew tree"), both of which take very different approaches to describing the tree in question, emphasizing on the one hand its lethal potential through poison (ALD 69) and its role as the main wood used in making bows, as a "battle-help" (OIR 16).

## OER 14

Solution: *PEORÐ* (gaming piece).
For comparison, see GES 25 (board-game piece), which emphasizes the extent to which board games can cause men to lose money.

Here, in keeping with the generally positive attitudes expressed in OER, the happy aspects of gaming are emphasized as part of the general joy to be had in the hall.

## OER 15

Solution: *EOLH-SECG* (elk-sedge).

The Old English word *secg* signifies not only the sedge plant, which flourished in damp and fenland environments, but also "man" and "warrior," as well as "sword," with the last sense being restricted to poetry.

## OER 16

Solution: *SIGEL* (sun).
For comparison, see ALC D43, BER 62 (both solved "star[s]").

This stanza emphasizes the importance of the sun in a seafaring context, so linking it to the one that follows, which also speaks of a star or constellation. There are two kennings in this stanza, namely "fish's bath" (for "sea") and "sea-steed" (for "ship"), but both are quite conventional; the latter also appears at OER 21.


## OER 17

Solution: *TIR* (honor).

In addition to being the common noun for "honor" or "glory," the proper name Tir or Tiw belongs to a star or constellation and a god identified with Roman Mars (both as a god and a planet: compare English "Tuesday" with French *mardi*), so explaining why the creature in question "is always in motion / above the clouds of night." Such a connection also provides a link to the preceding stanza.


## OER 18

Solution: *BEORC* (birch).
For comparison, see OIR 13 (birch); note that both stanzas emphasize the leafiness of the birch, when compared with other trees, as well as the splendor of its branches.


## OER 19

Solution: *EOH* (horse).
See too OER 5 (riding), which also celebrates the aristocratic aspects of horses and horse riding.


## OER 20

Solution: *MANN* (man).

The "kin" here seem to be the body and soul, which are dear to each other while man lives, though the body is doomed to die and let down the soul, as the last line explains.

## OER 21

Solution: *LAGU* (liquid).
For comparison, see ALD 29, ALC D50, LOR 3, EXE 39 and 80 (all solved "water").

## OER 22

Solution: *ING* (Ing).

This stanza refers unequivocally to a Germanic deity whose name is enshrined both in the tribe of the Ingvaeones (who are mentioned in the first century CE by Tacitus, *Germania* 40) and in the Swedish royal family of the Ynglings (who are documented by the Icelander Snorri Sturluson in the thirteenth century, in his *Ynglinga saga* 20).

## OER 23

Solution: *EÞEL* (homeland).

## OER 24

Solution: *DÆG* (day).
For comparison, see ALC D40 (day).

## OER 25

Solution: *AC* (oak).
For comparison, see EXE 73 (oak).

The phrase "the fodder of flesh" refers to the feeding of acorns to pigs to fatten them up for meat.

## OER 26

Solution: *ÆSC* (ash).
For comparison, see EXE 71 (spear made of ash).

## OER 27

Solution: *YR* (horn, bow).
For comparison, see EXE 12 (horn), 21 (bow), and, perhaps especially, 76 (horn).

## OER 28

Solution: *IOR* (beaver [?]).
For comparison, see ALD 56 (beaver).

## OER 29

Solution: *EAR* (grave).
For comparison, see ALD 1, EUS 6, ALC D47, BER 45 (all solved "earth").

## THE RIDDLES OF *SOLOMON AND SATURN II* (SOL)

I have consulted translations by Daniel Anlezark, ed. and trans., *The Old English Dialogues of Solomon and Saturn* (Cambridge, 2009), 81–85. See also the more detailed commentary in *COEALRT*. For further reading, see in general Anlezark, *The Old English Dialogues;* Thomas D. Hill, "Saturn's Time Riddle: An Insular Latin Analogue for *Solomon and Saturn II* lines 282–91," *Review of English Studies* 39 (1988): 273–76; Charles D. Wright, *The Irish Tradition in Old English Literature,* Cambridge Studies in Anglo-Saxon England 6 (Cambridge, 1993), 233–48 and 255–67.

## SOL 1

Solution: *BEC* (books).

In discussing SOL 1, Anlezark notes its "eschatological flavour" (*Old English Dialogues,* 121) and highlights some general biblical parallels.

## SOL 2

Solution: *YLDO* (old age).
For comparison, see BED 16, ps-BED 4 (both solved "age of man").

## The Old English Prose Riddle (OEP)

Solution: *EVA* (Eve).

I have consulted the translation by David Howlett, "*Tres linguae sacrae* and Threefold Play in Insular Latin," *Peritia* 16 (2002): 109–12. See also the more detailed commentary in *COEALRT*. For further reading, see in general Max Förster, "Ein altenglisches Prosa-Rätsel," *Archiv für das Studium der neueren Sprachen und Literaturen* 115 (1905): 392–93; Max Förster, "Die Lösung des Prosarätsels," *Archiv für das Studium der neueren Sprachen und Literaturen* 116 (1906): 267–71; Phillip Pulsiano, "Abbot Ælfwine and the Date of the Vitellius Psalter," *American Notes and Queries* 11 (1998): 3–12.

This is one of a number of incest riddles, of which the best known in Old English is EXE 44 (*LOTH OND BEARN*, "Lot and his children"), and the solution suggested by Förster, "Die Lösung des Prosarätsels," here, namely *EVA* (Eve), gives this prose riddle an equally Old Testament theme. The riddle turns on the twin facts that Adam, whose name means "earth" in Hebrew, was produced from earth and that in turn Eve, produced from his rib, was therefore herself produced from earth. In that sense, Adam and Eve are simultaneously father and daughter (since she was produced from him), brother and sister (since both were produced from both earth and God), and husband and wife, from whom the rest of the human race was eventually produced. Since the Virgin Mary is both the daughter of Eve and the mother of God, Eve can ultimately be considered as the mother of her own father. Finally, mankind, born of Adam and Eve, all return in death to the earth from which they came.

## Symphosius (SYM)

I have consulted the translation by Raymond Theodore Ohl, *The Enigmas of Symphosius* (Philadelphia, 1928), and the Italian one by Manuela Bergamin, ed. and trans., *Aenigmata Symposii: La fondazione dell'enigmistica come genere poetico,* Per Verba: Testi mediolatini con traduzione 22 (Florence, 2005). See also the more detailed commentary in *COEALRT*. For further reading, see in general Chauncey E. Finch, "Codex Vat. Barb. Lat. 721 as a Source for the Riddles of Symphosius," *Transactions and Proceedings of the American Philological Association* 98 (1967): 173–80; Chauncey E. Finch, "Symphosius in Codices Pal. lat. 1719, 1753, and Reg. lat. 329, 2078," *Manuscripta* 13 (1969): 3–11; Peter Goolden, ed., *The Old English "Apollonius of Tyre,"* Oxford English Monographs (London, 1958); Scott, "Rhetorical and Symbolic Ambiguity"; Salvador-Bello, "The Compilation of the Old English Riddles," 17–19; Bergamin, *Aenigmata Symposii.*

## SYM PR

The remarkable Preface clearly mentions the rather riotous Roman festival of Saturnalia, which was originally a one-day event at midwinter (December 19), but which was expanded over time to be a three-, five-, and even sometimes seven-day feast, at which large quantities were drunk, gifts were exchanged, and, apparently, riddles set and solved. Here, Symphosius (whose name is clearly related to the notion of a *symposium,* "drinking party") claims to be at one such revel, with nothing to say, but is inspired to what seems extemporized performance, even if the final line clearly mentions an implied "reader" *(lector),* asking the indulgence of such a reader, since his inspiration derives from a drunken Muse.

## SYM 1

Solution: *GRAPHIUM* (stylus), as in the majority of manuscripts.
See further Orchard, "Performing Writing and Singing Silence."

The stylus, usually made of metal, was used to inscribe on a wax tablet; one end was pointed to write, the other was flat to smooth over the wax and make corrections.

## SYM 2

Solution: *HARUNDO* (reed), as in the majority of manuscripts.
See further Bitterli, *Say What I Am Called,* 137; Orchard, "Performing Writing and Singing Silence."
For comparison, see EXE 58 (reed).

This *aenigma* can be linked to the preceding one by the similar shapes of the stylus and reed, as well as by the use of sharpened reeds in writing. Here, again, a double function is suggested: reeds were used both to make flutes and to make pens. The general reference is to the myth of the attempted rape of the wood nymph Syrinx (her Greek name, σῦριγξ, means "reed," "pipe") by the lusty and drunken Pan, who was a satyr (half man, half goat). Syrinx runs to the side of a river and is transformed into reeds, so escaping his attentions.

## SYM 3

Solution: *ANULUS CUM GEMMA* (ring with gem), as in the majority of manuscripts.

Presumably it is the hollow reed of the preceding *aenigma* that prompts the association here with a finger ring, most likely a signet ring of some kind; the gem produces multiple images of itself when pressed in wax, as the final line describes.

## SYM 4

Solution: *CLAVIS* (key).
For comparison, see EXE 42 and 87 (both solved "key").

The specific kind of key mentioned here seems to be a ring key, of a type that appears to be Roman innovation, so linking this riddle back to SYM 3, and ahead to SYM 5.

## SYM 5

Solution: *CATENA* (chain).
See further Murphy, *Unriddling the Exeter Riddles*, 40.

Here again, the binding and loosing motif provides a connection between successive *aenigmata*, in this case linking back to the preceding one.

## SYM 6

Solution: *TEGULA* (roof tile).

The connection here with the preceding *aenigma* is presumably derived from the resemblance of interlinked curved terracotta tiles to a chain.

## SYM 7

Solution: *FUMUS* (smoke).
See further Murphy, *Unriddling the Exeter Riddles*, 219.

From the roof tile of the previous *aenigma* it is a short conceptual step to the smoke that rises from rooftops.

## SYM 8

Solution: *NEBULA* (cloud).
For comparison, see ALD 3, ALC D45 (both solved "cloud").

This *aenigma* follows immediately on from the last and in turn links neatly to the next. Note that the moon is called here by her classical name, Cynthia.

## SYM 9

Solution: *PLUVIA* (rain).
For comparison, see ALC D44 (rain).

This *aenigma* follows smoothly on in sequence from the last and introduces a meteorological element that continues in SYM 10–11.

## SYM 10

Solution: *GLACIES* (ice).
For comparison, see ps-BED 6, ALC D53, LOR 4, EXE 31 and 66, OER 11, BER 38 and 42, and OIR 9 (all solved "ice").

The connection of cloud, rain, ice, and snow in SYM 8–11 examines water in its various states.

## SYM 11

Solution: *NIX* (snow).
For comparison, see TAT 15 (snow, hail, and ice); ALC D54 (snow); LOR 6 (snow); XMS Z4 (snow and sun).

The self-evident association of snow and ice connects this *aenigma* to the previous one.

## SYM 12

Solution: *FLUMEN ET PISCIS* (river and fish). See further Orchard, "Enigma Variations," 293–94; Murphy, *Unriddling the Exeter Riddles,* 19–20. For comparison, see ALC D80, EXE 81 (both solved "fish and river").

Presumably the fact that the subject of the previous *aenigma* concludes with a reference to the rivers *(flumina)* that snow creates leads to the association here, although in this case the wintry weather implied by SYM 8–11 gives way to flowing water, an association continued in SYM 13. Note that this is one of only ten *aenigmata* in SYM that are couched in the third person: SYM 12, 29, 62, 72, 76–77 (76a is in the first person), 89, and 94–96.

## SYM 13

Solution: *NAVIS* (ship).
For comparison, see BED 12, ALC D61, BER 11 (all solved "ship"); GES 24 (ship [?]); XMS Z2 (ship).

Following on from an *aenigma* with the given solution of *FLUMEN ET PISCIS* (river and fish), this riddle focuses instead on a different water-dwelling creature. Given the speed and the length of the ship as described, it may well be a warship that is intended, and the "unnumbered throngs of companions" may refer to the rowers who propel it, along with the waves. Such an interpretation connects this *aenigma* with both SYM 12 and SYM 14, in that all three refer to dwellings and their inhabitants.

## SYM 14

Solution: *PULLUS IN OVO* (chick in egg).
See further Murphy, *Unriddling the Exeter Riddles*, 39.
For comparison, see ALC D78 (chick in egg).

This *aenigma* introduces a lengthy sequence (SYM 14–25), all dealing with small creatures of one kind or another. Here, the paradox of the unborn chick speaking before it is hatched introduces elements of the themes of birth, life, and death that run through the sequence.

## SYM 15

Solution: *VIPERA* (viper).

The traditional etymology for the Latin form of "viper" *(vipera)* was considered to derive from the words for "I am born by force" *(vi pario);* unlike other snakes, vipers do not lay eggs (in itself, a further connection to SYM 14), but instead they give live birth, with the young appearing to burst out of their mother's side. Needless to say, the mother survives, but that is no bar to folk etymology.

## SYM 16

Solution: *TINEA* (bookworm).
Compare Bitterli, *Say What I Am Called*, 191–93.
For comparison, see EXE 45 (book moth).

SYM 15 describes the violent nature of the viper, while SYM 16 describes another wormlike creature in mock-heroic mode: the Latin term *tinea* certainly refers to the kinds of bookworms that damaged papyrus rolls throughout antiquity, as well as to the moth that consumes clothing, but can also mean any kind of worm or grub. The metaphorical sense of a reader devouring books was, however, a commonplace in the ancient world too, and here the twin idea of a human and a worm deriving no benefit from the words consumed seems clear. This *aenigma* seems clearly to have inspired EXE 45; see the note there. The reference to the classical

Muses here seems to refer to poetry, as it certainly does elsewhere, and may be the poet's way of downplaying any benefit to be had from his own verse, as he also seems to do in SYM PR. This *aenigma* begins a sequence of three (SYM 16–18) where the solutions offer a loosely rhyming group (*TINEA, ARANEA,* and *COCLEA*).

## SYM 17

Solution: *ARANEA* (spider).
For comparison, see GES 14 (spider).

The technical language of weaving employed here is echoed in ALD 33 (*LORICA,* "mail shirt") and its Old English equivalent, EXE 33 (*BYRNE,* "mail shirt"). While continuing the general theme of small creatures that characterizes SYM 14–25, this *aenigma* introduces an interleaved sub-sequence (SYM 17–20), partly verbal (SYM 17 *ARANEA* links to SYM 19 *RANA,* "frog"), partly conceptual (SYM 18 and 20 both describe creatures with shells). Note that the Latin Pallas is another name for Athena, the goddess of learning and wisdom, so providing a link back to SYM 16. In myth, Arachne was taught to weave by Athena, but then she foolishly challenged her teacher to a weaving contest and of course lost; her punishment was to be turned into a spider.

## SYM 18

Solution: *COCLEA* (snail).
For comparison, see BER 47 (snail).

The reference to the creature in question and its house recalls SYM 12–14; for its position here in sequence, see the previous note. The final line has a number of problems of transmission (on which see *COEALRT*); the reading given here—with its apparent reference to the kind of sumptuous crimson dye, also called "purple," produced from certain snail-like whelks—links this *aenigma* back to the previous one, which speaks of weaving.

## SYM 19

Solution: *RANA* (frog).

The Latin word for "frog" *(rana)* was considered onomatopoeic in classical literature, and etymological connection was made with such forms as *racco* (I cry out, roar, croak) and *raucus* (raucous, croaking); the link is made explicit in the opening phrase, *rauca sonans* (croaking loud).

## SYM 20

Solution: *TESTUDO* (tortoise).

The (non)musical theme of the preceding *aenigma* is continued here, with the living tortoise contrasted with the lyre that the Greek god Hermes is said to have first made from the shell of a dead one.

## SYM 21

Solution: *TALPA* (mole).

Although clearly part of the wider sequence SYM 14–25, with its focus on small creatures, this *aenigma* introduces a further sub-sequence: the final five (SYM 21–25) all deal with pests and vermin of one kind or another, and indeed four of them (the exception is SYM 23) appear in close succession in a description of agricultural pests in Virgil, *Georgics* 1.181–86, where the order is mouse . . . mole . . . weevil . . . ant (Latin *mus . . . talpa . . . curculio . . . formica*).

## SYM 22

Solution: *FORMICA* (ant).
See further Marilina Cesario, "Ant-Lore in Anglo-Saxon England," *Anglo-Saxon England* 40 (2012): 273–91.

As the second in the sub-sequence of agricultural pests (SYM 21–25), this *aenigma* also introduces a further sub-sequence of interleaved riddles, with links, in a reversal of SYM 17–20 above, that are partly conceptual (SYM 22 and 24 are both tiny scavengers), partly verbal (SYM 23 [*MUSCA*, "fly"] links to SYM 25 [*MUS*, "mouse"]).

## SYM 23

Solution: *MUSCA* (fly).

For the position of this *aenigma* within the wider sequence(s), see the notes at SYM 21 and 22 above. The "phantom breeze" referred to here is presumably produced by the fans used to keep flies off food during banquets.

## SYM 24

Solution: *CURCULIO* (weevil).

For the position of this *aenigma* within the wider sequence(s), see the notes at SYM 21 and 22 above. There are well-attested variant spellings (including in manuscripts of SYM) that spell the Latin word *gurgulio* (also with the sense "gullet"), and so link back to the disgusting eating habits of the fly, as described in the previous *aenigma;* the litany of negatives used to describe this creature only emphasizes its role as a pest. Ceres was the goddess of grain and the harvest (her name underlies the Modern English word "cereal"), and the weevil was certainly an unwelcome guest in a granary.

## SYM 25

Solution: *MUS* (mouse).

For the position of this *aenigma* within the wider sequence(s), see the notes at SYM 21 and 22 above. The opening line refers to an open mousehole; the final line probably refers to Publius Decius Mus, who was consul in 340 BCE, and, according to Livy, *Ab urbe condita* 8.9, died in a distinctly unmouselike manner at the Battle of Vesuvius the same year.

## SYM 26

Solution: *GRUS* (crane).
See further Murphy, *Unriddling the Exeter Riddles*, 95.

This *aenigma* connects to the previous through the Latin rhyme *mus/grus*, and, given that at this point there is some confusion in the various manuscripts as to the precise order of texts, may also introduce a sequence of flying creatures (SYM 26–28; Leary would also include SYM 31, his 29). The opening line refers not only to the legend that Palamedes invented (or, in some versions, simply supplemented) the Greek alphabet by watching the flight of cranes, based on their *v*-formation, but also presumably to the use of quill pens. The final lines allude to the legendary hostility, culminating in annual battles, between cranes and pygmies, mentioned by, for example, Ovid, *Metamorphoses* 6.90–93; Mars is the Roman god of war. The fighting prowess of the crane contrasts sharply with the timidity of the mouse in the preceding *aenigma*.

## SYM 27

Solution: *CORNIX* (crow).

This *aenigma* is linked to the last by the association of birds, and to the one that follows by blackness and the fact that the bat is also a flying creature. In the classical tradition, crows are proverbially long lived, with different authorities giving different numbers for how many human lifespans a crow might survive. Likewise, according to classical legend, crows were originally white but were turned black after a terrible deception. As in many countries and cultures, black is the color of mourning. The final line likely alludes to the resemblance between the repeated sound of the cawing of a crow (*ca*) with the Latin verb for defecating (*caco, cacare*).

## SYM 28

Solution: *VESPERTILIO* (bat).

The whole *aenigma* plays on the problematic categorization of bats, which are flying creatures, like birds, but without feathers. The beginning of night, evening (Latin *vesper*), also supplies the beginning of the Latin name for a bat *(vespertilio)*.

## SYM 29

Solution: *ERICIUS* (hedgehog).
For comparison, see EXE 13 (hedgehog, porcupine).

This *aenigma* is one of only ten in SYM that lack a first-person reference; for the others, see the note at SYM 12. The word *sustinet* (translated here as "upholds") could also be rendered "withstands."

## SYM 30

Solution: *PEDICULI* (lice).
For comparison, see ALC D77 (lice).

This *aenigma* is a traditional one, reported by Heraclitus, and, according to legend, the riddle that annoyed Homer so much at being unable to solve that he died. See further the note to ALC D77 (*PEDICULI,* "lice").

## SYM 31

Solution: *PHOENIX* (phoenix).

This *aenigma* describes the mythical phoenix, a bird that, according to classical tradition, is reborn every five hundred years after building a pyre and immolating itself. The phoenix was soon adopted by Christian writers as a symbol of resurrection, but that is not to say that SYM should be considered a Christian collection; here, the paradox turns simply on notions of life and death. The word "Shades" (Latin *Manes,* "spirits of the dead") is used here metonymically for death itself.

## SYM 32

Solution: *TAURUS* (bull).
For comparison, see EUS 12 (bull).

This *aenigma* begins a sequence describing larger animals (SYM 32–39); it is notable that this run begins and ends with verbal parallels: SYM 32 *(TAURUS)* is echoed by SYM 39 *(CENTAURUS)*. This *aenigma* relies on offering three different perspectives on the same creature, by focusing in turn on the story of Pasiphaë, wife of King Minos, who was impregnated by a bull after concealing herself in a wooden cow made by the craftsman Daedalus (the deception is alluded to in the opening line). She subsequently gave birth to the Minotaur; the other lines refer to the Taurus mountain chain in Asia Minor and the sign of the zodiac. See further Sebo, *In Enigmate*, 67–68.

## SYM 33

Solution: *LUPUS* (wolf).

This *aenigma* is perhaps connected to the next by the traditional etymologies of both "wolf" and "fox": "wolf" *(lupus)* is considered a corruption of "lion-foot" *(leo-pes)*, while "fox" *(vulpes)* is reckoned to derive from "shifty-foot" *(volu-pes)*. Compare Isidore, *Etymologiae* 12.2.23, as well as Pliny, *Naturalis Historia* 8.80, which describes the belief that if a wolf saw someone before they saw him, they would be struck dumb.

## SYM 34

Solution: *VULPES* (fox).

See the note to the previous *aenigma*. This *aenigma* plays on the proverbially cunning nature of the fox. Compare Isidore, *Etymologiae* 12.2.29.

## SYM 35

Solution: *CAPRA* (she-goat).

This *aenigma* begins a sub-sequence (SYM 35–38) focusing on birth and upbringing. In the opening line, the she-goat in question is Amalthea, who nursed the young Zeus in Crete.

## SYM 36

Solution: *PORCUS* (pig).

This *aenigma* divides easily into two parts: the first two lines describe the birth and upbringing and nurturing of the creature in question, while the third is the first example in SYM of the kind of spelling puzzle known as a logograph, discussed above (see the note to ALD 63). In this case, the logograph itself is highlighted by further wordplay on the Latin terms "name" and "the divine" *(nomine numen)*, explaining how the word "pig" *(porcus)* becomes "divine," specifically "the underworld" *(Orcus)*; the same Latin term *(Orcus)* is also used as an alternative name for Pluto, the god of the underworld, as well as a term for "death." In the second line, the "green forage . . . from up above" is mast or acorns.

## SYM 37

Solution: *MULA* (mule).
For comparison, see ALC 2 *(MALUM → MULAM)*.

In Latin usage, the "mule" *(mula)* is the offspring of a he-ass and a mare; the product of a she-ass and a stallion is called a "hinny" *(hinnus)* instead. Both the mule and the hinny are sterile. It is notable that SYM 37–39 all describe creatures that are the product of mixed parentage of one sort or another.

## SYM 38

Solution: *TIGRIS* (tigress).
For comparison, see EUS 43 (tigress).

SYM is notable among riddle collections for generally avoiding overly exotic subjects, but SYM 38–39, which conclude the sequence on birth and upbringing, supply exceptions and are both based on more or less arcane lore. The idea in the opening line that the Persian word for "arrow" was *tigris* and that both the river and the beast were named from there is found in Pliny, *Naturalis Historia* 7.127. The notion mentioned in the second line that swift creatures are impregnated by the wind is discussed by Pliny, *Naturalis Historia* 8.166.

## SYM 39

Solution: *CENTAURUS* (centaur).

This *aenigma* concludes the sequence describing larger animals (SYM 32–39) and the bookending by the obviously verbally related "bull" *(TAURUS)* and "centaur" *(CENTAURUS)*, which are also connected by the fact that both Taurus and Sagittarius, one of the most celebrated of the centaurs, are star signs, while the fact that Sagittarius is a celebrated archer (the Latin for "arrow" is *sagitta*) connects this *aenigma* with the immediately preceding one. Another celebrated centaur is Chiron, who, according to tradition, taught the Greek hero Achilles how to use a bow but was also closely connected with medicine, so linking this *aenigma* to the one immediately following.

## SYM 40

Solution: *PAPAVER* (poppy).

This *aenigma* begins a sequence (SYM 40–48) of plants and flowers and vegetables and vegetable products. The connection with the preceding *aenigma* may be made either through the narcotic and medicinal properties of the poppy or through the reference to body parts in the first two lines.

## SYM 41

Solution: *MALVA* (mallow).

Ideas of hybridity and monstrosity in the unexpected number and disposition of body parts link this *aenigma* with those immediately preceding; a different kind of hybridity (in that case linguistic) likewise connects it to the *aenigma* that follows.

## SYM 42

Solution: *BETA* (beet).

For the connection with the preceding *aenigma*, see the note there. The conceit of the opening line turns on the fact that the whole of *beta* is the name of a Greek letter, while only half of it *(be)* is the name of the equivalent Latin letter. Similarly, the second line refers to the fact that in the middle of the word *tabernam* (tavern) we find *be*, preceded by *ta* (with *ta–be* being also obviously a reversal of *be–ta*).

## SYM 43

Solution: *CUCURBITA* (gourd).

This *aenigma* continues the vegetable theme of SYM 42, which is extended in SYM 44; in each case the vegetables in question are rather commonplace, and a far cry from the exotic tone of SYM 38–39. Note the insistent wordplay on hanging and dangling, derived directly from the Latin *(Pendeo ...pendeo...pendens...Pendula)*.

## SYM 44

Solution: *CAEPA* (onion).
See further Orchard, "Enigma Variations," 295–97; Murphy, *Unriddling the Exeter Riddles,* 166 and 223–24.
For comparison, see EXE 23 and 63, BER 51 (all solved "onion").

The insistent wordplay on hanging and dangling in the preceding *aenigma* is expanded and paralleled here by the extended language of biting; the Latin, which uses soundplay impossible to replicate in translation, is still more spectacular *(Mordeo mordentes ... mordeo ... mordentem ... mordere ... morsum dentes)*.

## SYM 45

Solution: *ROSA* (rose).
For comparison, see BER 34 and 52 (both solved "rose").

The "biting" motif of the previous *aenigma* is matched here by the sharp weapons in the shape of thorns that protect the rose; the crimson (Latin *purpura*) is a sign of high status: compare SYM 18 above.

## SYM 46

Solution: *VIOLA* (violet).
For comparison, see BER 33 (violet).

This *aenigma* is linked to the previous one in a number of ways, not least the high status of both in the floral world; it is linked to the *aenigma* that follows through the strong scent of both violets and incense. In the second line, the violet's "scent" *(spiritus)* is indeed strong and plays on the primary meaning of the Latin word as "spirit"; there is a clear contrast here between body and spirit in this line. The third line alludes to a contrast with the harmful thorns of the rose, the subject of the preceding *aenigma.*

## SYM 47

Solution: *TUS* (incense).

The theme of perfume connects this *aenigma* to the one immediately preceding, just as the notion of an exotic resinous extract links it to the next.

## SYM 48

Solution: *MURRA* (myrrh).

The reference here is to the mythical origin of myrrh as the resinous teardrops of the metamorphosized Myrrha, the mother of Adonis, bewailing her incestuous relationship with her father, Cinyras. The exoticism of this *aenigma* connects it directly with the one that follows. See further Sebo, *In Enigmate,* 68–69.

## SYM 49

Solution: *EBUR* (ivory).

The "Eastern peoples" mentioned here are likely from India, and the ivory is therefore a rather exotic import; see further ALD 96 (elephant).

## SYM 50

Solution: *FAENUM* (hay).

There is a clear contrast between the exoticism of SYM 47–49 and the rather workaday topics that follow, beginning with the sequence SYM 50–52. The enclosure mentioned in the third line is presumably the barn.

## SYM 51

Solution: *MOLA* (millstone).
For comparison, see ALD 66, BER 9 (both solved "millstone").

While the usual Latin solution *mola* refers to a single millstone, the whole sense of this *aenigma* is that there are two millstones grinding, with the top stone being rotated over the fixed lower stone, so turning the grain to flour, the subject of the *aenigma* that follows.

## SYM 52

Solution: *FARINA* (flour).

The connection between this *aenigma* and the preceding one is obvious; the language spoken by the anthropomorphized flour, especially in the second line, highlights the grim reality of the original grain, broken down into tiny but inevitably more numerous grains of flour.

## SYM 53

Solution: *VITIS* (vine).
For comparison, see BER 13 (vine).

This *aenigma* leads on from the grinding that links the preceding two, perhaps through the association of the eventual crushing of grapes to provide wine. It is notable chiefly for the repetition of the sense "I don't want to" (*nolo*) at the beginning of each line. The grafting of the vine onto a tree described here was generally reckoned a form of marriage, and the metaphor is exploited here to the full.

## SYM 54

Solution: *HAMUS* (hook).
See too Riley, *Anglo-Saxon Tools*, 127–29.

This *aenigma* retains the rural sense of the previous sequence, SYM 50–53, but begins a mixed sequence of its own, broadly outlined as SYM 54–61 and describing pointed or sharp-edged tools or instruments, interspersed with other items that connect either backward or forward to these main themes. In this case, there is a fairly straightforward description of the hook's role in angling. The second line offers a description of the fishing line, with *levi* carrying the twin senses "light" and "agile."

## SYM 55

Solution: *ACULA* (needle).
For comparison, see TAT 11 (needle).

Just as the hook of the previous *aenigma* needs to be connected to a fishing line to function, so too here the needle is only useful when tied to thread; the notion of stitching presumably also links this *aenigma* with the one that follows. There is an interesting connection between this *aenigma* and TAT 14 (love); see the note there.

## SYM 56

Solution: *CALIGA* (boot).
See further Bitterli, *Say What I am Called*, 32.

In describing the suffering of the original living creature in question, and the torments visited on its dead body to produce the subject of this *aenigma,* the poet firmly aligns it with the widespread theme of the "suffering servant" in the Anglo-Saxon riddle tradition, on which see the note at TAT 5. The whole *aenigma* is thick with the language of burial and epitaph.

## SYM 57

Solution: *CLAVUS CALIGARIS* (hobnail).

The connection between this *aenigma* and the previous one is obvious; it is also clear that in inverting the usual arrangement, and having the head pressing down on the ground, hanging from a single foot, that this is another of the body-part riddles, on which see the notes at SYM 39–41.

## SYM 58

Solution: *CAPILLUS* (hair).
For comparison, see ALC D12 (hair).

The previous *aenigma* spoke of the many inverted heads of the hobnails, and that connection allows the segue here to hair, which will be a constituent part of the subject of the next *aenigma,* which, like the boot itself, is also fashioned from leather.

## SYM 59

Solution: *PILA* (ball).

The connection between this *aenigma* and the previous one is the hair with which the ball is stuffed. The language of the opening line plays on the feminine gender of "ball" in Latin *(pila),* as if the creature in question were a playful woman or a girl.

## SYM 60

Solution: *SERRA* (saw).

Once again, the link with the preceding *aenigma* is hair, in this case the metaphorical hair of trees, using the extremely rare compound, *frondicomas* (which literally means "having leafy tresses").

## SYM 61

Solution: *ANCORA* (anchor).
For comparison, see EXE 14 (anchor, anchorite); GES 6 (anchor).

There seems a self-conscious attempt here to cover earth, sea, and sky in this *aenigma,* a feature that is found widely elsewhere in the tradition. This *aenigma* begins a sequence concerned with the water (SYM 61–64) and presumably links back to the previous one through the resemblance of the serrated edge of a saw to choppy waters. The last line might equally refer to the use of anchors on dry land, to protect tents against the rising wind, though given the sequence that this *aenigma* introduces, it seems safest to assume a maritime use throughout, and that "earth" here refers to the sea-bed.

## SYM 62

Solution: *PONS* (bridge).
For comparison, see GES 2 (bridge).

This *aenigma* leads on from the previous one by also supplying a subversion of earth and water: trees, especially oak trees, should grow on the land. This is another of the few *aenigmata* in SYM that do not have a first-person referent (see the note at SYM 12). The sense of the third line seems to be that just as the trees that supply the wood for the bridge come out of the ground, so too they give a good grounding for those traveling over the bridge.

## SYM 63

Solution: *SPONGIA* (sponge).
For comparison, see BER 32 (sponge).

The watery associations of the previous two *aenigmata* presumably prompt this one, a sequence maintained in the *aenigma* that follows.

## SYM 64

Solution: *TRIDENS* (trident).
See too Riley, *Anglo-Saxon Tools,* 127.

See the note to the previous *aenigma;* this is the fourth in a sequence of *ae-nigmata* (SYM 61–64) linked with water. It also begins a sequence of three

815

*aenigmata* (SYM 64–66) on weapons of various kinds, associated with earth, sea, and sky (or, in order, sea, sky, and earth). Presumably, the second line describes a further spike at the far end of the handle; in the third line, the god in question is the trident-wielding Neptune.

## SYM 65

Solution: *SAGITTA* (arrow).

For comparison, see BED 14, TAT 32, ALC D85, GES 13 (all solved "arrow").

This *aenigma* is the second in a sequence on various weapons (SYM 64–66). The first line contrasts the heavy iron and light feathers that decorate each end of the arrow; the final line refers to the fact that an arrow is shot forcefully from a bow but falls back to earth of his own accord.

## SYM 66

Solution: *FLAGELLUM* (whip).

This *aenigma* concludes the sequence on weapons of different kinds (SYM 64–66), and in its language of the pain of the original animal as it is made into an instrument for inflicting further pain on its own kind fits perfectly into the widespread theme of the "suffering servant" in the tradition, on which see the note at TAT 5.

## SYM 67

Solution: *LANTERNA* (lantern).

Ancient lanterns consisted of a frame made from any number of substances, such as wood, metal, or ceramic, to which were fitted "windows" made of some translucent material, such as horn, glass, or stretched skin, usually bladder. It is perhaps the potential use of horn as a window that might link this *aenigma* back to the previous one, which deals with another thing that cattle provide, the leather for making whips. This *aenigma* introduces a sequence of three *aenigmata* dealing with light and vision (SYM 67–69).

## SYM 68

Solution: *VITREUM* (windowpane).

Leahy argues that the given solution is too general (*VITREUM* simply signifies anything made of glass) and that a more correct one would be *SPECULAR,* which has the specific sense of a "windowpane." That a glass pane is in question is not in doubt, however, and while *SPECULAR* would connect this *aenigma* more firmly to the one that follows (*SPECULUM,* "mirror"), both are clearly part of the same sequence dealing with light and vision (SYM 67–69).

## SYM 69

Solution: *SPECULUM* (mirror).
For comparison, see BER 29 (mirror).

This *aenigma* follows on naturally from the last and concludes the sequence dealing with light and vision (SYM 67–69).

## SYM 70

Solution: *CLEPSYDRA* (water clock).

In the ancient world, water clocks, in which the regular draining of liquid from a large vessel might be measured, were regularly used in the law courts to ensure equal time for each speaker, silencing those who would talk for too long. Whereas the previous sequence was concerned with light and vision (SYM 67–69), and indeed in a sense with the containment and release of that light, this *aenigma* introduces a further sequence concerned with the containment and release of water (SYM 70–71).

## SYM 71

Solution: *PUTEUS* (well).
See further Bitterli, *Say What I Am Called,* 103–5.

This *aenigma* seems to refer to a man-made well and fits into the sequence identified in the note on the previous *aenigma*.

## SYM 72

Solution: *TUBUS* (pipe).

It is clear from the description that what is intended here are wooden water pipes of a kind far from rare in the ancient world, though of course lead pipes lasted longer in the archaeological record (our Modern English word "plumber" derives from the Latin word for "lead," *plumbum*). This *aenigma* concludes the brief sequence, begun at SYM 70, dealing with the containment and release of water. This is another of the few *aenigmata* in SYM that do not have a first-person referent (see the note at SYM 12). The last line presumably refers to the way logs were floated down rivers, or perhaps to the way water supports wooden boats and ships.

## SYM 73

Solution: *UTER FOLLIS* (bellows).
See further Murphy, *Unriddling the Exeter Riddles*, 216.
For comparison, see ALD 11; EXE 35, 83, and 85; GES 9 (all solved "bellows").

The wooden (or perhaps metal) pipe that forms part of a bellows connects this *aenigma* both to the one that immediately precedes and to the two earlier sequences by dealing with the containment and release of light on the one hand (SYM 67–69), and of water on the other (SYM 70–72). Here, by contrast, it is air that is first contained and then released; the whole theme is presented as a constant cycle of life and death, with life being presented as the breath of air.

## SYM 74

Solution: *LAPIS* (stone).

This *aenigma* opens a sequence of three (or four: see the note on SYM 76 below) that deal with the mineral world, and perhaps specifically the architectural world. Two (or three) of these are concerned with fire, and so link back to the *aenigma* that immediately precedes, given that there is a clear link between bellows and flames. Here, by contrast, the connection appears to be with the water sequence that comes immediately before that (SYM 70–72), through the mechanism of the mythical flood that the god Zeus unleashed on the earth as punishment, and which was survived only by Deucalion (named here in the first line) and his wife, Pyrrha. Deucalion was the son of Prometheus, who stole fire from the gods and was warned by him to build a chest and escape the rising waters. After the flood, Pyrrha and Deucalion were instructed by the goddess Themis in appropriately enigmatic fashion to throw the bones of their mother over their shoulders; the scene is described by Ovid, *Metamorphoses* 1.381–83. They understood their mother to be the earth, and her bones stones, so threw them backward: those that Deucalion threw became men, those that Pyrrha threw, women. Here, Deucalion has apparently been identified with the stones he cast. Such is the complex background to the first two lines; the third is a word riddle, or logogriph (another example is found at SYM 36): removing a letter from Latin *lapis* (stone) produces *apis* (bee), a creature that was classified by the ancients among birds and other flying creatures. See further Sebo, *In Enigmate*, 62–65.

## SYM 75

Solution: *CALX* (lime, quicklime).

This *aenigma* leads on naturally from the last by the association with water; it connects to the next through fire. For the use of lime in the Roman world, mostly for building, see Pliny, *Naturalis Historia* 36.173–79. Lime was produced by burning limestone or sometimes seashells, both of which are rich in calcium carbonate; the resulting compound was unstable, and when put in contact with water, it reacts violently, with the production of great heat. Lime was a key ingredient for both mortar and plaster in the Roman building trade.

## SYM 76 and 76a

Solution: *SILEX* (flint).
For comparison, see ALC D75 (flint).

There are two *aenigmata* on the same subject that appear adjacent in one class of manuscripts and as alternatives in two others, apparently part of a sequence that deals with the mineral world; the link with the preceding *aenigma* focuses on the intimate association of both lime and flint with fire. SYM 76 is another of the few *aenigmata* in SYM that is couched in the third person, though it does have a first-person referent (see the note at SYM 12).

## SYM 77

Solution: *ROTAE* (wheels).

While the given solution seems perfectly feasible, the fact that the opening line specifies "Four equal sisters" means that, in effect, what is being envisioned is rather in the nature of a four-wheeled vehicle, like a wagon or a cart. It is possible to connect this *aenigma* with the one preceding through the fact that roads were often covered with hard stone or flint. This is another of the few *aenigmata* in SYM that do not have a first-person referent (see the note at SYM 12).

## SYM 78

Solution: *SCALAE* (ladder, steps).

This *aenigma* is connected to the preceding one by the fact that, just as the four wheels of a cart or a ladder are sisters separated from each other but acting in tandem, so too both the sides and the rungs of a ladder or a set of steps can function only in combination.

## SYM 79

Solution: *SCOPA* (broom).
For comparison, see BER 18 (broom).

This *aenigma* links back to the previous one, since both brooms and ladders are single objects that comprise multiple components connected together. The opening line employs wordplay on Latin *mundus,* which as an adjective means "clean," and as a noun "world"; both are applicable here; the alternative translation "great mother of the world" is therefore also applicable.

## SYM 80

Solution: *TINTINNABULUM* (bell).
See further Murphy, *Unriddling the Exeter Riddles,* 72.
For comparison, see TAT 7, ALC D74, and EXE 2 and 67 (all solved "bell[s]").

This *aenigma* seems connected to the preceding one by the general bell shape of a broom and by the way in which both are swung back and forth to operate; it is presumably the same generally swollen shape that likewise links this *aenigma* to the one that follows.

## SYM 81

Solution: *LAGENA* (earthenware jar, flask).

The Roman *lagena* had a narrow neck, a wide body ("hollow belly"), and handles ("little ears") and was used to bring both wine and water to the table. It was made of fired clay, hence the reference to the earthen mother and to Prometheus, who stole fire from the gods, as father. Such a jar, when dropped to the ground, would inevitably shatter, so explaining the third line. This *aenigma* begins a sequence on food and drink, specifically wine (SYM 81–85). The mention of Prometheus in the opening line links this *aenigma* back to those that are connected by fire, such as SYM 73 and 75–76, as well as to SYM 74, which mentions Deucalion, the son of Prometheus, and also has an oblique reference to Earth (here *Tellus*), Deucalion's mother. See further Sebo, *In Enigmate,* 65–66.

## SYM 82

Solution: *CONDITUM* (spiced wine).

This *aenigma* sits easily between the ones that precede and follow and fits well with the general sequence on food and drink (SYM 81–85). There are a number of recipes for spiced wine available from ancient times, but the three ingredients specified here are likely to be wine, honey, and pepper, each of which individually is certainly "good in itself," to the extent that while all three were highly prized individually, it is their combination that is deemed best of all.

## SYM 83

Solution: *VINUM IN ACETUM CONVERSUM* (wine turned to vinegar). For comparison, see BER 50 and ps-BER 1 (both solved "wine").

The connection of this *aenigma* to the previous one seems obvious, with the bitterness of the vinegar contrasting with the sweetness of the spiced wine noted previously. Unlike the subject of the previous *aenigma,* where three ingredients are blended to produce a more flavorsome whole, the emphasis here is on the fact that while nothing has been added or taken away, the subject itself has simply changed. The key point is contained in the last line, where the speaker notes that "I have not found whatever I once left behind." Time, in short, has oxidized the wine, and turned it sour.

## SYM 84

Solution: *MALUM* (apple).

This *aenigma* adopts a studiously linguistic, even philological, perspective, beginning with a bilingual approach: the Greek word μῆλον means both "apple" and "sheep"; the further reference is to the tale of the apple inscribed "to the fairest" that was the focus of dispute between the goddesses Hera, Athena, and Aphrodite (Juno, Minerva, and Venus in the Roman tradition). The middle line is also packed with mythological lore, since both "the cunning of a beautiful boy" and "the care of many sisters" refer to episodes in which women were again deceived by men. The first alludes either to the manner in which Hippomanes cast a golden apple to distract Atalanta in the middle of their footrace, after she decreed that she would only wed the one who outran her, or to the way in which Acontius threw into Cydippe's lap an apple inscribed with an inviolable oath to wed him, which she innocently read out loud and so bound herself. The final line plays on the fact that in Latin *mālum* (apple) has a long vowel, while *mălum* (evil) has a short one. It is tempting to see here a reference to the Fall of Man in the Garden of Eden, when Adam and Eve (in this case reversing the order of male and female folly referred to above) brought evil into the world by eating the fateful apple. See too TAT 22 (Adam) and ALC 2 (*MALUM*, "evil" or "apple" → *MULAM*, "mule").

## SYM 85

Solution: *PERNA* (ham).

This *aenigma* concludes the sequence on food and drink (SYM 81–85) and connects to the one that follows, which focuses on aspects of work and leisure (SYM 86–91). The reference in the opening line is presumably to Marcus Porcius Cato, whose middle name recalls the Latin word for "pig" *(porcus),* though the name is shared both by Cato the Elder (also known as Cato the Censor, 234–149 BCE), who, among other things, composed the treatise *De agri cultura (On Agriculture)* and by his grandson Cato the Younger (95–46 BCE), the Stoic, who clashed famously with Julius Caesar. The "sister" in the second line is presumably the ham from the other back leg.

## SYM 86

Solution: *MALLEUS* (hammer).
For comparison, see GES 4 (hammer).

This *aenigma* is presumably linked to the previous one by the similar shapes of a ham and a hammer; both have a slender shaft in the shape of a leg bone or a handle, respectively, with the other end significantly bigger and heavier. The same idea of an oversized head likewise connects this *aenigma* to the one that follows.

## SYM 87

Solution: *PISTILLUS* (pestle).
For comparison, see BER 46 (pestle).

Some conceptual link between this *aenigma* and the preceding one seems likely; the fact that it is a body-part riddle not only connects it to others earlier in the collection (see the notes at SYM 39–41, 57, and 87) but also forms a segue to the two *aenigmata* that follow, which focus on various aspects of bodily care.

## SYM 88

Solution: *STRIGILIS AENEA* (bronze strigil).

This *aenigma* introduces a series that focuses on leisure, with two on athletic activities (SYM 89–90) and two on gambling (SYM 91–92). The Romans used a curved metal strigil to scrape off accumulated sand and sweat after exercise; the second line, describing this particular implement as golden in color yet not itself gold, makes it clear that it is made of bronze.

## SYM 89

Solution: *BALNEUM* (bathhouse).

The connection of this *aenigma* with the preceding one is obvious, since strigils were widely used to scrape away the sweat inevitably produced in the steamy atmosphere of the bathhouse. This is another of the few *aenigmata* in SYM that do not have a first-person referent (see the note at SYM 12).

## SYM 90

Solution: *TESSERA* (die).

The late antique association of gambling and the bathhouse connects this *aenigma* to the previous one. This *aenigma* refers repeatedly and ruefully to the role of luck, including in the first line the speaking of prayers and vows before the dice are thrown, and it leads on easily to the one that follows.

## SYM 91

Solution: *PECUNIA* (money).

The link between this *aenigma* and the previous one is presumably through the gambler's dream of winnings, although again the focus is on the transformation involved in using flame to turn base ore from the ground into valued metal that can be used in turn to purchase other ground for itself.

## SYM 92

Solution: *MULIER QUAE GEMINOS PARIEBAT* (mother of twins).
For comparison, see ALD 90, ps-BED 12 (both solved "woman bearing twins").

This *aenigma* begins a sequence of four dealing with wonders or marvels (SYM 92–95), all in the human sphere, but their increasingly bizarre nature contributes to an end-of-(drinking)-party feel, and, coming hard after a sequence focusing on wine (SYM 81–83), links back to the conceit of a progressively more drunken Saturnalian revel introduced in the Preface (SYM PR). The stated combination of three in one harks back to SYM 82, and this *aenigma* resembles a number of the body-part riddles found widely elsewhere, including in the *aenigma* that immediately follows.

## SYM 93

Solution: *MILES PODAGRICUS* (gouty soldier).

This *aenigma* is connected to the ones preceding and following not only by its rather wondrous and unusual solution but also by the fact that it aligns easily with the other body-part riddles in the wider tradition. The "feet" in question refer, on the one hand (as it were), to height (according to Bergamin, *Aenigmata Symposii*, 194) and, on the other, to the difficulty the afflicted infantryman now has in walking; or for a different suggestion about the "feet," see Erin Sebo, "Symphosius 93.2: A New interpretation," *Harvard Studies in Classical Philology* 106 (2011): 315–20. The common association of gout and alcoholic overindulgence only emphasizes the sense in which, according to the framing tale promoted in SYM PR and enshrined in Symphosius's name, we are coming to the end of a long party.

## SYM 94

Solution: *LUSCUS ALIUM VENDENS* (one-eyed garlic seller).
See further Bitterli, *Say What I Am Called,* 68–69; Murphy, *Unriddling the Exeter Riddles,* 42–43.
For comparison, see TAT 20 (one-eyed man); EXE 82 (one-eyed garlic seller).

This *aenigma* is evidently the source of EXE 82 and stretches the conceit of the body-part riddle to breaking point. The suggestion that this one-eyed individual is, like the subject of the previous *aenigma,* a former soldier, is attractive but unnecessary: the sequence of oddities in SYM 92–95 is in any case undoubtedly maintained. This is another of the few *aenigmata* in SYM that do not have a first-person referent (see the note at SYM 12).

## SYM 95

Solution: *FUNAMBULUS* (tightrope walker).

It is clear from the multiplicity of references that tightrope walking was a popular entertainment in antiquity, and the focus here on the tightrope walker's suspension between earth and sky ties this *aenigma* back to others in SYM that focus similarly on creatures caught between the contrasting worlds of earth, sea, and sky. This is another of the few *aenigmata* in SYM that do not have a first-person referent (see the note at SYM 12).

## SYM 96

Solution: *VERBA* (words), although most manuscripts have some form of *DE VIII TOLLAS VII ET REMANET VI* (take seven from eight and six remain), usually itself solved as a reference to some form of *FLEXUS DIGITORUM* (finger counting), with increasingly elaborate explanations.

See further J. Hilton Turner, "Roman Elementary Mathematics: The Operations," *The Classical Journal* 47 (1951): 63–74 and 106–8; Bayless, "Alcuin's *Disputatio Pippini*," 172–73.

This *aenigma* is omitted from SYM in several manuscripts, perhaps owing to its difficulty; more likely it is an interpolation. This is in any case the most perplexing of the *aenigmata* in SYM, not least because at least one Anglo-Saxon, namely Alcuin, clearly thought that "finger counting" was the proper solution; see ALC D82 *(FLEXUS DIGITORUM)*. The alternative and elegant solution by Leahy turns on noticing that, uniquely in SYM, the three lines of SYM 96 contain eight, seven, and six words, respectively, so mirroring precisely the figures given in the *aenigma* itself. Read in this way, this *aenigma* forms a link between the marvelous body-part counting of the preceding sequence and introduces an increasingly incorporeal sequence dealing with illusions of one sort or another (SYM 96–99). In this case, the poem itself is the subject, being in the first line the eight (words) that the reader holds in the hand (compare ALC D88), and in the second line the seven (words) that are taken away while being read, leaving only the six (words) of the final line. This is another of the few *aenigmata* in SYM that do not have a first-person referent (see the note at SYM 12).

## SYM 97

Solution: *UMBRA* (shadow).
For comparison, see BER 61, XMS Z3 (both solved "shadow").

If the suggested solution (*VERBA*, "words") to the previous *aenigma* is accepted, there is a clear connection to this one, and certainly a much more obvious one than could be imagined if the alternative (*DE VIII TOLLAS VII . . .*," take seven from eight") is preferred. In either case, this *aenigma* is very evidently linked to the one that follows. Indeed, one wonders whether what is at issue here is not so much a shadow as a reflection, and whether what links this *aenigma* with the next is the legend of Echo and Narcissus, as outlined in Ovid, *Metamorphoses* 3.356–401.

## SYM 98

Solution: *ECHO* (Echo).
For comparison, see ALC D79 (echo).

This *aenigma* follows on naturally from the preceding one and is in turn linked conceptually to the next. Underlying this *aenigma* is the tragic legend of the mountain nymph Echo who falls in love with the self-obsessed Narcissus (who prefers his own reflection), as Ovid, *Metamorphoses* 3.339–510, among others, explains.

## SYM 99

Solution: *SOMNUS* (sleep); an alternative solution, *SOMNIUM* (dream), is also found.
For comparison, see ALC D8 (sleep).

Although the latter would make a stronger connection between this *aenigma* and the two that precede, given the common thematic bond between sleep and death, it is clear that the more generally accepted solution makes a much closer link with the *aenigma* that follows. The language of the *aenigma* itself is ambiguous and could fit either solution.

## SYM 100

Solution: *MONUMENTUM* (tombstone).

The subject is a fitting one to conclude the collection, especially if viewed as the death of the drinking party that forms the back narrative to the collection as a whole. The conscious manipulation of the language of life and death that is found elsewhere in SYM is in full evidence here.

## ps-SYM 1

Solution: *GLACIES* (ice).

The fact that this *aenigma* is only one line long militates against the likelihood that it is genuinely part of SYM, although Aldhelm certainly believed that it was and directly attributes it to "Simfosius" in the metrical treatises that are attached to ALD. Undoubtedly, the high reputation and wide circulation of SYM as a riddle collection caused other stray *aenigmata* to be attached to it, as the following three examples attest.

## ps-SYM 2

Solution: *PILAX* (cat), as in the manuscripts.

This *aenigma* is found only in the Anglo-Saxon manuscripts LG, where it follows directly on from SYM 25 (mouse), through an obvious association of subject matter.

## ps-SYM 3

Solution: *CUCULUS* (cuckoo).

This *aenigma* is itself something of a cuckoo, having been wished on SYM by earlier editors, presumably on account of its form and the perceived echo of the opening line (*Frigore digredior, redeunte calore revertor;* "I depart in the cold, and return when heat comes back") to SYM 23.2 (*Frigora vitabam, quae nunc aestate revertor;* "I avoided the cold, and now I'm back in summer"), when in fact it is not found in any manuscripts containing any part of SYM.

## ps-SYM 4

Solution: *NIX* (snow).

There are a number of metrical difficulties with this *aenigma,* which appears to be a weak imitation of SYM 12 (river and fish).

## THE BERN RIDDLES (BER)

I have consulted the German translation in Glorie, CCSL, vol. 133A, pp. 547–610. See also the more detailed commentary in *COEALRT.* For further reading, see in general, Alexander Riese, ed., "Bern Riddles," in *Anthologia Latina,* part 1, fasc. 1 (Leipzig, 1894; repr., Amsterdam, 1964),

351–70; Karl Strecker, ed., *Aenigmata Hexasticha,* MGH PLAC 4, no. 2 (Berlin, 1923), 732–59; Chauncey E. Finch, "The Bern Riddles in Codex Vat. Reg. Lat. 1553," *Transactions and Proceedings of the American Philological Association* 92 (1961): 145–55.

## BER 1

Solution: *OLLA* (earthenware jar).

The two fathers are presumably *limus* (clay, earth) and *ignis* (fire), both of which are grammatically masculine: the former endures, while the latter is consumed as its fuel is used up. The harsh mother is presumably the grammatically feminine *manus* (hand) that throws the clay on a potter's wheel, or perhaps the *rota* (wheel) itself.

## BER 2

Solution: *LUCERNA* (lamp); the solution given is *DE LUCERNA.*
For comparison, see LOR 10 (lamp).

This *aenigma* seems connected both to the previous one and to the next by fact that the fathers are in each case the same: *ignis* (fire). The "aged mother" here may be *lux* (light), whence, according to Isidore, *Etymologiae* 20.10.2, the word *lucerna* derives.

## BER 3

Solution: *SAL* (salt).

As with the previous two *aenigmata,* the "father" here is *ignis* (fire); the "mother" is presumably *aqua* (water). The language of binding and loosing *(solvit . . . solutam ligatam),* focused on salt in solution and when crystallized, here recalls the biblical language of the Sermon on the Mount, in which Christ first addresses "the salt of the earth" *(sal terrae,* Matthew 5:13) and subsequently promises not to "destroy the law" (literally, "loosen the law": *solvere legem,* Matthew 5:17). There is a further connection to the preceding *aenigma* through the words of the intervening biblical verses, which speak of being "the light of the world" *(lux mundi,* Matthew 5:14) and that "Neither do men light a candle" *(Neque accendunt lucernam,* Matthew 5:15).

## BER 4

Solution: *SCAMNUM* (bench).

The continued conceit that the object is metaphorically quite a different kind of quadruped, namely a horse, is extremely well sustained. The comparable four-legged shapes of a bench and a table link this *aenigma* to the next, which indeed elaborates on the idea voiced in the last few lines here of mistreatment of the creature in question by mankind.

## BER 5

Solution: *MENSA* (table).
For comparison, see TAT 29 (table).

The connection between this *aenigma* and the previous one seems clear, even down to the use of a second solution heavily hinted at, but ultimately misleading. This *aenigma* is intimately linked to those immediately preceding and following, since both "benches" and "glass cups" are the children of this particular "beautiful mother" when it comes to being decked out for a feast. But when the feast is finished, and the "kisses" have been given to the glasses full of drink, the table itself is stripped of cloth and everything else that covered it and just kicked into a corner until required again.

## BER 6

Solution: *CALIX VITREUS* (glass cup); the solution given is *DE CALICE*.

This *aenigma* is evidently linked to the preceding one through the themes of shared kisses and to the one that follows through the theme of transparency.

## BER 7

Solution: *VESICA* (bubble).
For comparison, see ALD 62 (bubble).

This *aenigma* moves from the manmade and rounded clearness of the glass cup described in the previous *aenigma* to the natural world, where the innate fragility of a see-through bubble formed from liquid is depicted. The shape of the bubble leads on equally clearly to the egg that is the subject of the *aenigma* that follows.

## BER 8

Solution: *OVUM* (egg).
For comparison, see BED 13 (egg[s]).

This *aenigma* gestures back to the mother-daughter theme found first in ps-SYM 1 and widely imitated within the tradition. It is here adapted to a mother-son motif that is further augmented by a series of paradoxes.

## BER 9

Solution: *MOLA* (millstone).
For comparison, see ALD 66, SYM 51 (both solved "millstone").

It seems likely that the fire mentioned in the fifth line is one produced by sparks through friction when the grain is gone, while "those wandering ones" in the final line are presumably the draft animals who turn the quern-stones, or perhaps the stones themselves.

## BER 10

Solution: *SCALA* (ladder).

Just as the individual millstone of the preceding *aenigma* requires a sister to function (and so *molae,* "millstones," is usually found in the plural), so too here the same conceit is repeated: a ladder requires twin verticals to be of genuine use, and likewise the plural *scalae* is the usual form.

## BER 11

Solution: *NAVIS* (ship).
For comparison, see BED 12, ALC D61, SYM 13 (all solved "ship"); GES 24 (ship [?]); XMS Z2 (ship).

There is a clear contrast with the previous *aenigma*, where a ladder is of less use horizontal than vertical; here, the vertical living tree, nibbled at by birds and beasts, is of less utility to mankind that the dead tree's horizontal planking when built as a ship.

## BER 12

Solution: *GRANUM* (grain).

The term "parents" in the third line presumably refers to mankind in general, who profit from the demise of the kernel of grain by feeding children of their own.

## BER 13

Solution: *VITIS* (vine).
For comparison, see SYM 53 (vine).

This *aenigma* is linked to the previous one, since just as crushed grains go to make food, as explained in BER 9 (millstone), so too do crushed grapes make wine.

## BER 14

Solution: *OLIVA* (olive tree).

## BER 15

Solution: *PALMA* (palm tree).
For comparison, see ALD 91 (palm tree).

## BER 16

Solution: *CEDRUS* (cedar tree).

The opening two lines describe the berry (or rather berry-like cone) of the cedar or juniper, while the rest refer to the resin of the cedar tree and its fragrant wood.

## BER 17

Solution: *CRIBRUS* (sieve); the solution given is *DE CRIBRO*.
For comparison, see ALD 67 (sieve).

## BER 18

Solution: *SCOPA* (broom).
For comparison, see SYM 80 (broom).

It is hard to recreate in English the sense that in Latin the terms *comas* and *capillos* in BER 18.1 and 18.3 can serve for both human hair and foliage.

## BER 19

Solution: *LINEA CEREA* (candlewick); the solutions given are *DE CERA* (on wax) and *DE PICE* (on pitch).
For comparison, see EUS 31 (wax).

The first two lines again seem to point to Christological narrative, while the third line points to caesarean section, with the added etymological clue of *caesa* (cut) at BER 19.4. Either of the solutions "on wax" and "on pitch" given in the manuscripts can fit the sequence of *aenigmata,* with the former pointing forward to BER 20 (honey) and BER 21 (bee), and the latter pointing back to a sappy and resinous tree such as BER 16 (cedar tree). Both solutions offered, it will be noted, suggest that those transmitted in manuscript, if indeed they were, were not always accepted as authoritative as well as that putative solutions often looked to proximate riddles for support. If we reject both transmitted suggestions and go back to the *aenigma* itself, a better solution for BER 19, linking it both back and forward, might be "candlewick." The usual term, *linum* (literally, "linen") is grammatically neuter, but the feminine form *linea* (linen thread) might suffice, and would seem to fit.

## BER 20

Solution: *MEL* (honey).
See further Murphy, *Unriddling the Exeter Riddles,* 168–69.

## BER 21

Solution: *APIS* (bee); the solution given is *DE APIBUS* (on bees) in most of the manuscripts, although the subject is certainly singular; one manuscript has *APIS*.
See further Murphy, *Unriddling the Exeter Riddles*, 165.
For comparison, see ALD 20 (bee[s]).

The notion of the asexual generation of bees alluded to in 21.4 is a commonplace of the Middle Ages, where the virginal nature of bees is a byword: see Augustine Casiday, "St. Aldhelm's Bees (*De virginitate prosa*, cc. iv–vi): Some Observations on a Literary Tradition," *Anglo-Saxon England* 33 (2004): 1–22.

## BER 22

Solution: *OVIS* (sheep).

## BER 23

Solution: *IGNIS* (fire).

## BER 24

Solution: *MEMBRANUM* (parchment).
See further Bitterli, *Say What I Am Called*, 178–90.
For comparison, see TAT 5, EUS 32, EXE 24 (all solved "parchment").

This *aenigma* seems to follow on more appropriately from BER 22 (*OVIS*, "sheep") and evidently describes a chained-up book, whose contents, presumably of a sacred sort, are of benefit even to kings. The "many thousands" in the sixth line are letters.

## BER 25

Solution: *LITTERAE* (letters).
See further Murphy, *Unriddling the Exeter Riddles*, 85.
For comparison, see ALD 30, TAT 4, EUS 7, ALC D1, EXE 55 (all solved "letter[s]").

The connection between this *aenigma* and the preceding one is obvious; it is also connected to the one following by the notion of small objects having extraordinary power.

## BER 26

Solution: *SINAPIS* (mustard seed).

## BER 27

Solution: *PAPIRUS* (papyrus).

The mother mentioned here is presumably "water" (in Latin, the grammatically feminine *aqua*), which both extinguishes flames and damages papyrus and its written contents.

## BER 28

Solution: *BOMBIX* (silkworm); the solution given is *DE SERICO* (on silk). For comparison, see ALD 12, BER 43 (both solved "silkworm[s]").

The reference to kings being amazed at the product of the silkworm "above and below" in the sixth line work presumably describes silk being worn royally all over.

## BER 29

Solution: *SPECULUM* (mirror).
For comparison, see SYM 69 (mirror).

## BER 30

Solution: *PISCIS* (fish).
For comparison, see ALD 71, EUS 40 (both solved "fish").

## BER 31

Solution: *SIPHO* (siphon); the solution given is *DE NYMPHA* (on a nymph). The masculine gender of *ebrius* in 31.2 supports the former.

## BER 32

Solution: *SPONGIA* (sponge).
For comparison, see SYM 63 (sponge).

The mother in the first line is presumably water (*aqua*); the spontaneous generation of sponges is implied.

## BER 33

Solution: *VIOLA* (violet).

Note that the sequence BER 33–34 (*VIOLA*, "violet," and *ROSA*, "rose") is matched in reverse by SYM 45–46 (*ROSA*, "rose," and *VIOLA*, "violet").

## BER 34

Solution: *ROSA* (rose).
For comparison, see SYM 45, BER 52 (both solved "rose").

This *aenigma* follows naturally on from the last and connects again to the one following. Compare SYM 45 (rose), and see the note for BER 33 (violet).

## BER 35

Solution: *LILIA* (lilies).

The "spear" in the second line is presumably the stamen, the anther at the tip of which is indeed packed (*onusta*) with bright orange pollen that is released easily on contact, leaving the stamen wilting. An alternative suggestion, put to me by Bob Babcock, is that the "spear" is the long stalk, packed with leaves and flowers, and easily wilting under the burden.

## BER 36

Solution: *CROCUS* (saffron crocus).

## BER 37

Solution: *PIPER* (pepper).
For comparison, see ALD 40 (pepper).

The sixth line presumably describes the grinding of peppercorns by wood or stone.

## BER 38

Solution: *GLACIES* (ice).
For comparison, see ps-BED 6, ALC D53, LOR 4, EXE 31 and 66, OER 11, SYM 10, ps-SYM 1, BER 42, OIR 9 (all solved "ice").

## BER 39

Solution: *HEDERA* (ivy).

## BER 40

Solution: *MUSCIPULA* (mousetrap).

## BER 41

Solution: *VENTUS* (wind).
For comparison, see ALD 2, ps-BED 5 (both "wind"); EUS 8 (wind and fire); ALC D46 (wind); EXE 1 (wind and God).

The heroic trio of Bacchus *(Liber)*, Alexander, and Hercules mentioned in the sixth line comprise those popularly supposed in their respective times to have conquered the known world.

## BER 42

Solution: *GLACIES* (ice).
For comparison, see ps-BED 6, ALC D53, LOR 4, EXE 31 and 66, OER 11, SYM 10, BER 38, OIR 9 (all solved "ice").

This *aenigma* follows on neatly from the preceding one. The final lines are perplexing as they stand, turning as they do on the contrast between forms of *turp-* in the apparent sense "ugly," with an apparent pun on *torp-* (stiff); the same thing is found in BER 62.5. For other *aenigmata* sharing similar themes, see SYM 10, BER 38 (both "ice"); TAT 15 (snow, hail, and ice); LOR 4 (ice). For the theme of kissing in the third line, see the note to ALD 80.

## BER 43

Solution: *BOMBYCES* (silkworms); the solution given is *DE VERMIBUS BOMBYCIBUS SERICAS VESTES FORMATIS* (on the insects called silkworms that create silk clothing).
For comparison, see ALD 12, BER 28 (both solved "silkworm[s]").

The "flights" mentioned in the opening line presumably refer to strands of silk or web, sprayed out from the center. The apparent revulsion expressed in the last two lines presumably refers to raw silk in its natural state being perceived as akin to walking into a spider web, before it is spun into fine silk cloth.

## BER 44

Solution: *MARGARITA* (pearl).

This *aenigma* is another that does not seem to fit the given solution; could the real solution be "oyster"?

## BER 45

Solution: *PILA* (mortar); the solution given is *DE TERRA* (on earth).
For comparison, see ALD 1, EUS 6, ALC D47, OER 29 (all solved "earth").

This *aenigma* is another that does not seem to fit the given solution. Since the one that follows has the solution "pestle," which fits it well, this one would seem to suit the solution "mortar."

## BER 46

Solution: *PILUM* (pestle); the solution given is *DE PISTILLO* (on a pestle).
For comparison, see SYM 88 (pestle).

This *aenigma* leads on very naturally from the last, with a closer verbal link to the solution of the preceding *aenigma* if the solution *pilum* is preferred to the given *pistillum,* which carries the same sense.

## BER 47

Solution: *CONCHA* (conch); the solution given is *DE COCHLEA* (on a snail).
For comparison, see SYM 18 (snail).

Given that BER 47.3–4 appears to suggest that the creature in question is employed as some kind of horn (as in Virgil, *Aeneid* 6.171 and 10.209), the solution "conch" is preferred to the given "snail," especially if BER 47.5–6 is taken to refer to the deliciousness of shelled conch meat.

## BER 48

Solution: *CASTANEA* (chestnut tree).
For comparison, see LOR 7 (chestnut tree).

This *aenigma* is linked to the last by the idea of a delicious foodstuff hidden inside a hard shell.

## BER 49

Solution: *PLUVIA* (rain).

## BER 50

Solution: *VINUM* (wine).
For comparison, see SYM 84 (wine turned to vinegar); ps-BER 1 (wine).

## BER 50a

Solution: *CALIX VITREUS* (glass beaker); Glorie prefers *DE CHARTA* (on paper).
For comparison, see ALD 80, EXE 61 (both solved "glass beaker").

The somewhat convoluted description appears to chart the creation of glass from sand snatched from the earth (the "mother" of BER 50a.1) and the production of a glass beaker, which can itself be re-formed, and which carries liquid.

## BER 51

Solution: *ALIUM* (garlic).
For comparison, see EXE 23 and 63, SYM 44 (all solved "onion").

There seems a reference in the third line to the notion of a child giving birth to their parent, as commonly elsewhere.

## BER 52

Solution: *ROSA* (rose).
For comparison, see SYM 45, BER 34 (both solved "rose").

If the solution *ALIUM* (garlic) is accepted for the preceding *aenigma,* then the one given here may be strengthened; certainly, a connection may be made between the individual cloves that make up a bulb of garlic and the constituent parts of a rose hip.

## BER 53

Solution: *TRUTINA* (pair of scales).

## BER 54

Solution: *INSUBULUM* (weaver's heddle, treadle on a weaver's loom). No solution is given in the manuscripts.

The *aenigma* seems to describe a horizontal loom that, operated by trea-dles and working through pulleys, lifts and drops multiple heddles through which the shuttle could be passed. Although such horizontal looms are at-tested from the fifth or sixth century on the continent, there is no evi-dence for them in Anglo-Saxon contexts before the eleventh century; see further Leahy, *Anglo-Saxon Crafts*, 72–74.

### BER 55

Solution: *SOL* (sun).
For comparison, see ALD 79 (sun and moon); EUS 10, ALC D41, EXE 4 (all solved "sun") and 27 (moon and sun); BER 56 (sun and moon) and 57 (sun); OIR 11, GES 15 (both solved "sun"); XMS Z4 (snow and sun).

### BER 56

Solution: *SOL ET LUNA* (sun and moon); the solution given is *DE SOLE* (on sun). Other suggested solutions include *CAELUM ET TERRA* (heaven and earth), *VERBUM* (word), *ANNUS* (year).
For comparison, see ALD 79 (sun and moon); EUS 10, ALC D41, EXE 4 (all solved "sun") and 27 (moon and sun); BER 55 and 57, OIR 11, GES 15 (all solved "sun"); XMS Z4 (snow and sun).

### BER 57

Solution: *SOL* (sun).
For comparison, see ALD 79 (sun and moon); EUS 10, ALC D41, EXE 4 (all solved "sun") and 27 (moon and sun); BER 55 (sun) and 56 (sun and moon); OIR 11, GES 15 (both solved "sun"); XMS Z4 (snow and sun).

### BER 58

Solution: *LUNA* (moon).
For comparison, see ALD 6 (moon) and 79 (sun and moon); EUS 11, ALC D42 (both solved "moon"); EXE 27 (moon and sun); BER 59 (moon).

This *aenigma* follows on naturally from the preceding ones that seem to focus on the sun. The sixth line seems to refer to the fact that the new moon and the old moon share the same crescent shape.

## BER 59

Solution: *LUNA* (moon).

For comparison, see ALD 6 (moon) and 79 (sun and moon); EUS 11, ALC D42 (both solved "moon"); EXE 27 (moon and sun); BER 58 (moon).

The "twofold iteration" in the fourth line seems to refer to the four main phases that follow the new moon: crescent, half, gibbous, and full.

## BER 60

Solution: *CAELUM* (sky); the solution given is *DE CAELO*.

## BER 61

Solution: *UMBRA* (shadow).
For comparison, see SYM 97, XMS Z3 (both solved "shadow").

## BER 62

Solution: *STELLAE* (stars). See further Murphy, *Unriddling the Exeter Riddles*, 115.
For comparison, see ALC D43, OER 16 (both solved "star[s]").

## ps-BER 1

Solution: *VINUM* (wine).
For comparison, see SYM 84 (wine turned to vinegar); BER 50 (wine).

This poem is of a very different pattern from those that precede and is clearly not of the same fourteen-syllable rhythmical form; it is attached to the collection in only a single manuscript, but nonetheless in its evident subject matter speaks well to the Anglo-Saxon riddling tradition in general. The evident acrostic *PAULUS* presumably identifies the author (and it has been suggested that the "Paul" in question is the Carolingian poet Paul the Deacon), who cannot, however, be saddled with the whole collection.

## THE VERSES OF A CERTAIN IRISHMAN
## ON THE ALPHABET (ALF)

I have consulted the translation by David Howlett, *"Versus cuiusdam Scotti de alphabeto:* An Edition, Translation, and Commentary," *Peritia* 21 (2010): 136–50. See also the more detailed commentary in *COEALRT.* For further reading, see in general Halsall, *The Old English Rune Poem;* Ross, "The Anglo-Saxon and Norse *Rune Poems"*; Page, "The Icelandic Rune-Poem."

### ALF A

For comparison, see BED 7 (letter *a*).

The letter *a* is obviously the first in the alphabet, and it was considered the first sound uttered by babies, as well as an interjection (also spelled *ah*) often used in cursing. The Greek name *alpha* is blessed as part of the name of the Lord in Revelation 1:8.

### ALF B

As well as being the first in the Latin word *biblia* (bible), the letter *b* begins both the Hebrew book of Genesis (*b'reshit*, Genesis 1:1) and the Latin book of Psalms (*Beatus vir,* Psalms 1:1); it is also the first letter in the prefatory letter to Pope Damasus that precedes the Vulgate Gospels *(Beatissimo papae Damaso)*. Latin grammarians define mute letters as those whose names end in -*e*, of which *b*, although the second letter of the alphabet, is the first. The Latin word *beatus* (blessed) has the Latin name of the letter *(be)* as one of its three syllables, while the equivalent Greek name *(beta)* signifies the vegetable beet in Latin.

### ALF C

The letter *c* is the first of the Latin word for "heaven" *(caelum)* and of the Latin word for "cleric" *(clerus);* the Greek equivalent (κλῆρος) begins with the same sound. The shape of the letter *c* suggests both the crescent moon and the hoof marks made by horses.

## ALF D

The name of the letter *d* in Latin *(de)* is also a preposition (meaning "about," "concerning") that takes the ablative case, while Latin grammarians considered prepositions as the seventh of the eight parts of speech. When *-us* is added to the name, the resulting word *(deus)* is the Latin word for "God," while a capital *D* stood for the number five hundred in Roman reckoning. The "ancient gods" mentioned here presumably are the devilish or demonic deities that preceded Christianity, since the Latin words for "devil" *(diabolus)* and "demon" *(daemon)* both begin with the relevant letter. Note likewise that Latin inscriptions, particularly on gravestones and including written spells, often employ the abbreviation *D. M.,* for *Diis Manibus* (meaning "to the gods of the dead," or "to the gods of the underworld").

## ALF E

The letter *e* is both a mute and a vowel, according to the reckoning of Latin grammarians, and is the first syllable of the Latin name for "Eve" *(Eva),* deceived by the serpent long ago. As the fifth letter of the alphabet, as well as one of the five vowels, the letter *e* is indeed "the fifth part of Latin speech," while as a word in its own right (the Latin preposition *e,* an alternative spelling of *ex,* meaning "out of," "from") it is certainly "a full part."

## ALF F

For comparison, see BED 2 (letter *f*).

The letter *f* is, according to the Latin grammarians, a semivowel (literally "half-sounded") when it precedes the liquids, the letters *l* and *r;* in that position, a preceding short vowel in poetry can be scanned either long or short (in technical terms, such a vowel is "common," *communis*). The second line draws on the erroneous notion, propagated by Jerome, that there is no equivalent letter to *f* in the Hebrew alphabet; see further the commentary in *COEALRT.* The final line alludes to a common logogriph, whereby removing the initial *f* from *flumen* (river) produces *lumen* (light).

## ALF G

In Latin epigraphy, a single *G* stood for *Gaius:* the "famous Caesar" would therefore be Gaius Julius Caesar or his heir, Gaius Julius Caesar Octavianus. By the same token, *GG* was used epigraphically in other contexts to stand for Pope Gregory the Great. The fifth vowel is *u,* before which (in Latin words such as *lingua*) *g* is indeed not sounded with full force.

## ALF H

The letter *h* in Latin was regarded by the grammarians as the weakest guttural and seems not always to have been sounded, to judge from the fact that it was frequently omitted in writing: to that extent, it does indeed have "an empty name." In Greek, there is no such letter at all, and the sound is simply represented by a sign to represent an aspirate breathing. In Latin poetry, however, an *h* could easily affect the relevant syllable, such as when a word beginning with *h* caused the preceding syllable of a word ending in a vowel, diphthong, or *m* to be elided; in such cases, the letter does undoubtedly demonstrate its residual "force."

## ALF I

For comparison, see BED 8, EUS 39 (both solved "letter *i*").

Capital *I* stands for the numeral one in Roman reckoning and in shape represents the sticks that the young use in their play fights as well as the rod with which they are punished. In both Hebrew (as *yod*) and Greek (as *iota*), it is the slightest of letters, and yet, according to Matthew 5:18, the Lord did not wish even a single one of these letters to be lost from the Law.

## ALF K

The "first vowel" is *a,* and in early Latin *k* appears only before *a,* and then simply in a few words, notably *Karthago* (Carthage), the capital of the Carthaginian empire based in Africa, and *kalendae* (the calends), the beginning of the month. Later Latin spelled both words with *c,* so rendering the letter *k* obsolete.

### ALF L

The Greek name for the letter *l* was *lam(b)da* (λάμ[β]δα), and the poet here has evidently identified that form with the Latin word *lauta* (washed, cleansed). On the power of the liquids (the letters *l* and *r*) in poetry, see the note on ALF F above. The concluding agricultural reference presumably refers to the shape of the Greek capital letter (Λ), which resembles a plowshare.

### ALF M

In Latin poetry, final *-m* was generally elided (or "swallowed," hence the reference to "food" here) when the following word began with a vowel, diphthong, or *h.* The Latin for "mother" is *mater;* if *m* is removed, the remaining word, *ater,* means "dark" or "black."

### ALF N

The name of the letter *n* in Latin is an exclamation *(en!),* variously translated as "look!" or "see there!" or "here it is!" and one that is certainly "a sure-sounding noise, by which a thing is shown to be present." Removing the *n-* from "name" in Latin *(nomen)* produces the word for an "omen" *(omen),* often replicated as a kind of oracular prophecy of the sort that were routinely delivered in a special Delphic meter known as "Pythian song." The association between Pythian meter and the Delphic oracles is outlined in Isidore, *Etymologiae* 1.39.13.

### ALF O

For comparison, see BED 9 (letter *o*).

The reference to choirs seems to signify the common choral singing of the so-called "O antiphons" or "great Os" performed at Vespers on the seven final evenings of Advent, between December 17 and 23. Each of them begins with an address prefaced by the vocative *O* (Oh). The letter *o* also recalls the shape of a wheel, as well as a ring "fixed to the hands," and the cycle of the years and successive ages.

## ALF P

The "agreement of men" referred to here is "peace" (Latin *pax*), impossible without the letter *p*. The *SPQR (Senatus PopulusQue Romanus)* that constituted the official mark of the Roman Republic is mentioned in ALF P, R, and S; its lack in ALF Q may signify the lesser status of *-que*. The abbreviation *PP* stood for *papa* (pope) and *pater patriae* (father of the fatherland).

## ALF Q

The power of "conquering the fifth vowel" refers to the fact that the letter *q* is routinely followed by *u*, which is sounded less strongly in that context; none of the four other vowels ever follows *q*.

## ALF R

The letter *r* would have been rolled, to produce a rather harsh sound, but in poetry had its idiosyncratic features; on the power of the liquids (the letters *l* and *r*) in poetry, see the note on ALF F above. As for "the mark of the people who conquered the world," see the note to ALF P above.

## ALF S

For the "mark of the fathers," see the note to ALF P above. The noted special power of *s* in poetry seems to refer to the fact that, in certain conditions, short vowels before *s*-groups, particularly (-)*sp*- and (-)*st*-, could be scanned either long or short; see too the note at ALF F above. Since both *Dominus* (Lord) and *Deus* (God) can be written *DS*, the letter is rightly designated as "the second mark of the Lord"; likewise, it is the first letter of *sol* (sun), beloved of Phoebus, the sun god.

## ALF T

There seems a clear reference here to Ezekiel 9:4: "And the Lord said to him: Go through the midst of the city, through the midst of Jerusalem: and mark Thau upon the foreheads of the men that sigh, and mourn for all the abominations that are committed in the midst thereof" (*Et dixit Dominus ad eum: Transi per mediam civitatem, in medio Jerusalem, et signa thau super frontes virorum gementium et dolentium super cunctis abominationibus quae fiunt in medio eius*). The last line plays on the fact that the name of the letter, *te,* also signifies the accusative form of the second-person singular pronoun.

## ALF V

For comparison, see BED 10, EUS 19 (both solved "the letter *u/v*").

In Latin, the letter *v* can signify both a vowel and a consonant, while in Greek, by contrast, there is no equivalent single letter, since while *upsilon* covers the vowel, the consonantal equivalent would be the obsolete *digamma,* or *beta.* The last line seems to refer to the fact that the letter is formed of two strokes; an alternative explanation, suggested to me by Bob Babcock, is that when Latin names beginning *v-* (and pronounced as if *w-*) were transliterated into Greek, they were spelled with two letters (οὐ-).

## ALF X

For comparison, see EUS 14 (letter *x*).

The double power of *x* represents *cs,* while its shape is imagined here as the combination of a bird's wings beating both up and down; ((since it also signifies the number ten, it represents the Decalogue, through which "the sacred number of the law is often revealed."

## ALF Y

The double power mentioned here is the twin pronunciation of Greek *upsilon* as both /u/ and /i/. The Samian mentioned here is Pythagoras, who, as Isidore, *Etymologiae* 1.3.7 explains, based part of his philosophy of the stages of human life on the shape of the letter Υ.

## ALF Z

The double power of *z* represents *ds;* for its ability to influence the meter of poetry, compare the notes on ALF F and S above.

## The Old Icelandic Rune Poem (OIR)

I have consulted the translations by Page, "The Icelandic Rune-Poem," and Dickins, *Runic and Heroic Poems.* See also the more detailed commentary in *COEALRT.* For further reading, see in general Ross, "The Anglo-Saxon and Norse *Rune Poems*"; Page, *Introduction to Old English Runes,* 73–85. Page, "The Icelandic Runic Poem," 1, makes the important observation that "the text commonly called the Icelandic rune-poem is only a poem by courtesy. It consists of a series of stanzas of common pattern." Here too, as for ALF and OER (where the same observation is less uniformly applicable), I consider individual stanzas as riddles in their own right. For much of the Norse mythological lore included here, see, for example, Andy Orchard, *Dictionary of Norse Myth and Legend* (London, 1997).

## OIR 1

Solution: *FÉ* (wealth).
For comparison, see ALC D66, OER 1 (both solved "wealth").

The term "grave-fish" is a poetic periphrasis, or kenning, for a snake or a serpent, whose "path" is gold and other forms of treasure guarded by a dragon. In effect, however, all three elements of the stanza are mini-riddles in the forms of kennings, a model followed throughout.

## OIR 2

Solution: *ÚR* (shower).

Like the previous stanza, this one ends with the most difficult kenning, in this case "hatred of herdsmen," for whom showers were evidently a particular bugbear. It is notable that the parallel rune in OER 2 is solved *UR* (aurochs), since the transfer of sense from an extinct and exotic creature to a meteorological phenomenon seems to indicate the comparative antiquity of the Anglo-Saxon tradition. See further the note to the succeeding stanza, where the reverse trajectory appears to apply.

## OIR 3

Solution: *ÞURS* (giant).

The parallel rune in OER 3 is solved *ÞORN* (thorn), which seems much more mundane. Here, the threefold definition of a "giant" as a scourge of women and a rock dweller plays into Norse mythological commonplaces; we can infer that Valrún (literally, "slaughter-rune") is the name of a giantess; elsewhere, we find giantesses and other supernatural female creatures, notably Valkyries (slaughter-selector, chooser of the slain) named, for example, Guðrún (battle-rune), Sigrún (victory-rune), Úlfrún (rune-rune), and Varðrún (rune-keeper, keeper of secrets).

## OIR 4

Solution: *ÓSS* (god).

Each of the three designations given here aligns extremely with titles and periphrastic expression for the god Óðinn. Note that the parallel rune in OER 4 (*OS,* "god" or "mouth"), mentions the solution as "the source of all speech," as well as "the support of wisdom and a comfort of the wise, and a blessing and delight to every noble," all attributes equally applicable to the aristocratic Anglo-Saxon god Woden and his Norse equivalent, Óðinn.

## OIR 5

Solution: *REIÐ* (riding).

Both here and in the parallel rune in OER 5 (*RAD,* "riding"), there is emphasis on the contrast between the exhilaration of the seated human rider and the speed of the journey; only the Norse emphasizes the "horse's strain."

## OIR 6

Solution: *KAUN* (ulcer).

The parallel rune in OER 6 (*CEN*, "torch") emphasizes the living, while here there is a sharp focus on disease and death.

## OIR 7

Solution: *HAGALL* (hail).

The parallel rune in OER 9 (*HÆGL*, "hail") also emphasizes the similarity of its subject to grain: there, hail is described as "the whitest of grains," while here it is "cold corn," "cold grain"; there is a notable parallel with the Old English poem *The Seafarer* 33a, which describes one aspect of a wintry landscape, presumably hail, as *corna caldast* (coldest of corns, coldest of grains). The description here of hail as "sickness of snakes" emphasizes the sluggishness of snakes in cold weather.

## OIR 8

Solution: *NAUÐ* (need).

The parallel rune in OER 10 (*NYD*, "need," "oppression," "conflict") tempers the unremittingly negative outlook given here, apparently admitting the beneficial effect of want and trauma on the soul, albeit after describing its more negative aspects.

## OIR 9

Solution: *ÍS* (ice).
For comparison, see ps-BED 6, ALC D53, LOR 4, EXE 31 and 66, OER 11, SYM 10, BER 38 and 42 (all solved "ice").

As with the other stanzas of OIR, the three designations that make up this one comprise a series of poetic periphrases: ice on a river or on the sea does indeed act like bark on a tree or the thatch on a wave, and causes trouble for doomed men. Once again, the final line takes a pessimistic turn.

## OIR 10

Solution: *ÁR* (year).

For comparison, see ALC D59 (year), which offers a quite different perspective.

The parallel rune in OER 12 (*GER*, "year") is given the customarily positive set of designations, while the utterly optimistic tone here is relatively unusual for OIR.

## OIR 11

Solution: *SÓL* (sun).

For comparison, see ALD 79 (sun and moon); EUS 10, ALC D41, EXE 4, BER 55 and 57 (all solved "sun"); EXE 27 (moon and sun); BER 56 (sun and moon); GES 15 (sun); XMS Z4 (snow and sun).

The circular shape of Germanic shields is echoed in each of the three designations given here; for a similar series of poetic circumlocutions for the sun, compare *Alvíssmál* 16.

## OIR 12

Solution: *TÝR* (Týr).

The three designations in this stanza require some knowledge of Norse mythology, as it is laid out in its most systematic form by the thirteenth-century Icelander, Snorri Sturluson, who describes how Týr lost his hand when he placed it in the mouth of the mighty wolf Fenrir, as a pledge, before the wolf consented to be bound. Such a narrative accounts for the first two designations at least; Snorri nowhere explicitly describes Týr as the brother of the god Baldr. The parallel rune in OER 17 (*TIR*, "honor") is quite differently explained, and effectively demythologized.

## OIR 13

Solution: *BJARKAN* (birch).
For comparison, see OER 18 (birch).

The form *bjarkan* is rare indeed and all but restricted to the name of the rune; *bjǫrk* is the common alternative.

## OIR 14

Solution: *MAÐR* (man).

## OIR 15

Solution: *LÖGR* (liquid).

The Vimur is a mighty river in Norse myth, separating the domains of the giants and the gods, famously waded by the god Thor on his giant-slaying exploits.

## OIR 16

Solution: *ÝR* (yew).
For comparison, see ALD 69, OER 13 (both solved "yew tree").

### The Riddles of Gestumblindi (GES)

I have consulted the translations by Burrows, "Heiðreks gátur"; by Christopher Tolkien, ed., *The Saga of King Heidrek the Wise* (New York, 1960), 32–44; and by Jeffrey Scott Love, *The Reception of "Hervarar saga ok Heiðreks" from the Middle Ages to the Seventeenth Century* (Munich, 2013), 190–238. See also the more detailed commentary in *COEALRT*. For further reading, see in general E. Matthias Reifegerste, *Die Hervarar Saga: Eine kommentierte Übersetzung und Untersuchungen zur Herkunft und Integration ihrer Überlieferungsschichten* (Berlin, 1999); Alaric Hall, "Changing Style and Changing Meaning: Icelandic Historiography and the Medieval Redactions of *Heiðreks saga*," *Scandinavian Studies* 77 (2005): 1–30; Love, *Reception of "Her-*

*varar saga ok Heiðreks,"* 190–238; Hannah Burrows, "Enigma Variations: *Hervarar saga*'s Wave-Riddles and Supernatural Women in Old Norse Poetic Tradition," *Journal of English and Germanic Philology* 112 (2013): 194–216.

## GES 1

Solution: *MUNGÁT* (ale).

Note that while other collections begin with riddles on creation or wisdom or God, this one is unashamed about its boozy origins, a conceit that links this collection back to the *Saturnalia* celebrated at the beginning of SYM. The saga has King Heiðrekr begin by praising the quality of the conundrum: "your riddle is good, Gestumblindi, but I have guessed it," as he does for GES 1–11, 13, 15, 17–19, 24, 28, 31, and 33. The king goes on to explain: "Bring him some ale! That paralyzes the wits of many, and many are the more loose lipped when ale kicks in, but for some the tongue gets tied, so that no words get out."

## GES 2

Solution: *BRÚ* (bridge).
For comparison, see SYM 62 (bridge).

King Heiðrekr explains: "You went over a bridge on a river, and the river's path was beneath you, but birds flew over your head and on both sides of you, and that was their path." One of the manuscripts (H) includes the supplementary observation by Heiðrekr that "you saw a salmon in the river, and that was its way," as if the fish in the river perceives the various ways that are to be traveled on land, in the water, and even (presumably) in the air.

## GES 3

Solution: *DǪGG* (dew).

King Heiðrekr explains: "You lay in the shade, and dew had fallen on the grass, and so your lips were refreshed and your thirst was quenched." This riddle returns to the opening theme of drink, this time not of the intoxicating variety. One of the manuscripts (H), includes a suspicious observation by Heiðrekr that Gestumblindi is "wiser than I thought," an early sign of the actual identity of his opponent.

## GES 4

Solution: *HAMARR* (hammer).
See too Leahy, *Anglo-Saxon Crafts*, 117–19; Riley, *Anglo-Saxon Tools*, 42–43.
For comparison, see SYM 87 (hammer).

King Heiðrekr explains: "That is the hammer that is used in the craft of goldsmithing; it calls out shrilly, when it beats on the hard anvil, and that is its path." The reference to the "way" the creature travels ties it back to GES 2; the final lines specify that a craftsman's hammer is in question, specifically that of a goldsmith.

## GES 5

Solution: *MYRKVI* (fog).

King Heiðrekr explains: "That is fog; it travels over the earth, so that one can see nothing ahead, not even the sun, but it goes away, as soon as the wind gets up." There are multiple variants for this riddle, but in each case the creature in question is associated with the land, the sea (or other water), and the air, just like in GES 1.

## GES 6

Solution: *AKKERI* (anchor).
For comparison, see SYM 61 (anchor); EXE 14 (anchor, anchorite).

King Heiðrekr explains: "That is an anchor with a strong rope; if the anchor's fluke is in the ground, then it will be secure." As with the previous riddle, there are multiple variants found here, and again the emphasis is on a creature at home in more than one element, here being buried in the earth (of the river or sea bottom) and washed by the water. GES 8 plays on a similar pairing, in that case earth and air.

## GES 7

Solution: *FOSS* (waterfall).

King Heiðrekr explains: "The raven always lives on the high fells, the dew always falls in the deep dales, the fish lives without breathing, and the crashing waterfall is never silent." In giving his explanation, in a form that is highly alliterative in the original, the king effectively gives four separate answers. It seems preferable to take the creature in question as a single entity, and "waterfall" seems to fit all the relevant clues. This *aenigma* introduces a different structure, and in its suggested solution, which seems particularly Icelandic (given the comparative frequency of waterfalls in Iceland when compared with other Scandinavian countries), again embodies elements of land, and water, and air.

## GES 8

Solution: *LAUKR* (leek); an alternative solution given in one manuscript is *GEIR-LAUKR* (garlic).
See the note on GES 6 above.

King Heiðrekr explains: "It is a leek; its head is securely fastened in the ground, but it forks, as it grows upward." The three main versions appear to differ significantly in the third line of the three-line formula: the reading *Dǫglings* refers ultimately to the legendary king Dagr, whose name means "day," and signifies any king; the lowercase form *dǫglings* would signify any princeling. The alternative reading *Dellings* relates instead to the name of the dwarf Dellingr (dayspring?), the father of another more literal *dagr* (day). Despite the discrepancy of names, the sense may in fact be similar: the riddle contest occurs at night, presumably in a court setting, and before the coming of dawn; the difference lies in whether the background is the human world or that of mythology.

## GES 9

Solution: *SMIÐ-BELGIR* (bellows).

For comparison, see ALD 11; EXE 35, 83, and 85; SYM 73 (all solved "bellows"). The elements of lifelessness and lack of breath here link this riddle to the other "bellows" riddles in the tradition.

King Heiðrekr explains: "Those are the bellows of a smith; they have no breath, unless they are blown, and they are as dead as any other aspect of the smith's craft, but with them one can as easily forge a sword as anything else." A "leek of wounds" is a kenning for a sword, and links this riddle back to the previous one.

## GES 10

Solution: *HAGL OK REGN* (hail and rain).

King Heiðrekr notes that "your riddles become petty" (as he does again at GES 16) and goes on to explain: "That is hail and rain, since hail beats on the street, but raindrops sink into the sand and penetrate into the earth." The black-and-white theme here looks ahead to the later sequence on "waves" at GES 20–23a.

## GES 11

Solution: *TORD-ÝFILL* (dung beetle).

King Heiðrekr gives the simple answer but goes on to say that "the chatter has gone on too long, when dung beetles are the subject of the questions of powerful men." The description of the creature in question here as a "boar" looks ahead to the solution of the riddle that follows.

## GES 12

Solution: *SÚ OK NÍU GRÍSIR* (sow and nine piglets).
For comparison, see ALD 84 (pregnant sow).

King Heiðrekr expresses his unease at the riddle, saying: "If you are the Gestumblindi that I thought, then you are wiser than I reckoned; you are now talking about the sow out in the yard." The prose goes on: "Then the king had the sow killed, and it had nine piglets inside, just as Gestumblindi said. Now the king starts to suspect who that person might be."

## GES 13

Solution: *QR* (arrow).
For comparison, see BED 14, TAT 32, ALC D85, SYM 65 (all solved "arrow").

King Heiðrekr simply states: "That is an arrow."

## GES 14

Solution: *KǪNGUR-VÁFA* (spider).
For comparison, see SYM 17 (spider).

King Heiðrekr simply states: "That is a spider."

## GES 15

Solution: *SÓL* (sun).
For comparison, see ALD 79, BER 56 (both solved "sun and moon"); EUS 10, ALC D41, EXE 4, BER 55 and 57, OIR 11 (all solved "sun"); EXE 27 (moon and sun); XMS Z4 (snow and sun).

King Heiðrekr explains: "That is the sun; it illuminates all lands and shines over all men, but Skalli and Hati are the names of those wolves, and one of those wolves goes before the sun, and the other follows afterward." This seems a reference to the myth that eventually wolves will swallow both the sun and the moon.

## GES 16

Solution: *HRAFN-TINNA* (obsidian).

King Heiðrekr notes that "your riddles become petty" (as he did before at GES 10), and goes on to explain: "What need is there to spend any more time on this? That is obsidian, with a sunbeam shining on it." Obsidian is a shiny black form of volcanic glass, found in parts of Iceland, which is presumably the origin for this riddle.

## GES 17

Solution: *SVAN-BRÚÐIR* (female swans).
For comparison, see EXE 5 (swan[s]).

King Heiðrekr explains: "Female swans go to their nests and lay eggs; the eggshell is not made by hand or forged by a hammer; and the male swan, with whom they created the eggs, stands straight, beyond the island." The focus is very much on the role of the female swan; the male swan (also known as a "cob," in contrast to the female "pen") appears as the aloof "maker" of the "cask of ale" (the egg), only in the last two lines.

## GES 18

Solution: *HVANNIR* (angelica); $U^1$ gives *FJALL-HVANNIR* (mountain angelica).

King Heiðrekr explains: "Those are two angelica stalks, and a fresh angelica sprout between them."

## GES 19

Solution: *HNEFA-TAFL* (board game).
For comparison, see GES 31 ("board game").

King Heiðrekr explains: "This is a game of *hnefa-tafl;* the darker ones defend the *hnefi,* and the white ones attack." The rules of *hnefa-tafl* are somewhat opaque, but it seems to be a board game based on the idea of one team (in this case "white") attempting to corner or surround the king-piece (*hnefi,* meaning "fist"), which is defended by its own side (here "darker").

## GES 20

Solution: *RJÚPUR* (ptarmigans) or *UNNIR* (waves); $U^1$ gives *SKÓGAR-RJÚPUR* (wood ptarmigans).

King Heiðrekr explains: "Those are ptarmigans . . . They are white in winter, but black in summer." While all three versions agree with the avian solution, the appearance of this riddle at the beginning of a sequence that is otherwise solved "waves" may suggest that the given solution is not the only one: while ptarmigans do indeed change their plumage according to the season, so too do waves, buffeted to whitecaps in a windy winter and dark in the summer's calm.

## GES 21

Solution: *BYLGJUR* (waves).
For comparison, see GES 22–23a (all solved "waves").

King Heiðrekr explains: "Those are the brides of Hlér, who are named in that way." Hlér is another name of the sea giant Ægir, who has nine daughters, whose various names all mean "wave." This is the first of a sequence of (depending on the manuscript) three or four consecutive riddles with the same general solution. See further Burrows, "Enigma Variations."

## GES 22

Solution: *BÁRUR* (waves).
For comparison, see GES 21 and 23 (both solved "waves").

King Heiðrekr explains: "Those are waves, that are named in that way."

## GES 23

Solution: *ÆGIS MEYJAR* (waves, literally, "Ægir's girls").
For comparison, see GES 21–22 (both solved "waves").

King Heiðrekr explains: "Those are waves, and their beds are skerries and shingle, and they are seen little in calm weather." Ægir is the sea giant and his daughters are the waves.

## GES 23a

Solution: *ÆGIS EKKJUR* (waves, literally "Ægir's women").

King Heiðrekr explains: "Those are Ægir's women." See the notes above.

## GES 24

Solution: *ÍS-JAKA* (ice floe) or *SKIP* (ship)
See further Olsen, "Animated Ships in Old English and Old Norse Poetry,"
especially 54–64.
For comparison, see BED 12, ALC D61 (both solved "ship"); EXE 31 (ice
floe); SYM 13, BER 11, XMS Z2 (all solved "ship").

King Heiðrekr explains: "You came upon a dead horse on an ice floe, and
there was a dead snake on the horse, and they all floated down the river
together." This solution seems overly elaborate, and if the creature "who
dwells in the earthy soil" is solved as a tree, which when felled is made into
a ship, it seems possible to construe the whole riddle as an elaborate description of a ship.

## GES 25

Solution: *HÚNN* (gaming piece, die).
For comparison, see OER 14 (board-gaming piece); SYM 90 (die).

King Heiðrekr explains: "That is the *húnn* in *hnefa-tafl.*" The riddle turns
on two puns: the *húnn* (in the sense "bear cub") is indeed an "animal,"
but the term also seems to designate a "gaming piece" or "die"; likewise,
*horn* (translated here as "horn") also has the sense "corner." A die, like all
cuboids, has eight corners. For *hnefa-tafl,* see the note to GES 19.

## GES 26

Solution: *SKJÖLDR* (shield).
For comparison, see ALD 87, EXE 3 (both solved "shield").

King Heiðrekr explains: "That is a shield; it often becomes bloody in battle, and defends those men well, who are shield-nimble." The "Danes" here
are warriors in general.

## GES 27

Solution: *QND Í MILLI NAUT-SKJÁLKA* (a duck in an ox skull's jaws).

King Heiðrekr explains: "A duck has built its nest in the jawbones of an ox, and the skull has covered it over." The term "nose-goose" is evidently construed as another name for a duck, though it is somewhat opaque, while "biting-blades of straw" signify teeth and the "sounding-lava of drink" is a kenning for an ox skull, given the fact that the horns of the skull would have served as drinking horns. Such a bizarre and specific solution, built on a combination of kennings, is not unparalleled in the Anglo-Saxon riddle tradition; see further *COEALRT.*

## GES 28

Solution: *KÝR* (cow).

For comparison, see EUS 13 (cow).

King Heiðrekr simply states: "That is a cow."

## GES 29

Solution: *ELDR* (fire).

For comparison, see ALD 44, TAT 31 and 33, ALC D51 and D73, EXE 48 (all solved "fire").

King Heiðrekr explains: "That is fire hidden in the hearth, and it is struck from flint."

## GES 30

Solution: *SKEIÐ OK LÍN-VEF* (heddle and weft).

No answer is given for this riddle in the saga (which one would think would negate the terms of the contest, although Óðinn, in the guise of Gestumblindi, raises no objections); rather, Heiðrekr offers the same kind of further clue that is found in ALC D76, D79, and D82, saying: "My courtiers ought to solve this riddle." The prose continues: "They made many guesses, but they were not very pretty. When the king saw that they could make nothing of it, he said: 'You call that horse a weft, and the heddle his mare, and the web is shaken up and down.'" As in the so-called "rude riddles" (also known as "double-entendre riddles") of EXE, the more obviously filthy solution is misleading and masks one that is mundane.

## GES 31

Solution: *TAFL* (board game).
For comparison, see GES 19 (board game).

King Heiðrekr explains: "That is Ítrekr and Andaðr, sitting at their board game." Elsewhere, Ítrekr is another name for Óðinn (and so looks ahead to the closing sequence), while Andaðr is found as the name of a giant, so suggesting a wisdom contest not unlike the riddle contest here.

## GES 32

Solution: *SÚ OK GRÍSUR* (sow and piglets).

King Heiðrekr explains: "Piglets were suckling at a sow, and she was squealing."

## GES 33

Solution: *GLÆÐUR* (embers).
For comparison, see TAT 35 (ember[s]).

King Heiðrekr explains: "Those are embers that have grown pale on the hearth."

## GES 34

Solution: *SKÁLDSKAPR* (poetry).

King Heiðrekr explains: "You sat on a wall there and saw a falcon carrying an eider duck to the crags." The riddle turns on the complicated kind of poetic wordplay known ironically as "extra clear" *(ofljóst)*, whereby a homonym is used to suggest a synonym. Here, the Norse *segl* (sail) first suggests the poetic equivalent *veggr*, which in prose means "wall"; "dead men" *(dauða menn)* suggests "the slain" *(valr)*, while the same form also means "falcon"; another name for a "blood-hollow" is a "vein" *(æðr)*, which can also signify "eider duck"; the final equivalence is opaque: here, I rely on the king's explanation.

# GES 35

Solution: *ÓÐINN OK SLEIPNIR* (Óðinn and Sleipnir).

King Heiðrekr explains: "That is when Óðinn rides Sleipnir." The god Óðinn has only one eye, while Sleipnir, his horse, has eight legs. Perhaps the main point to be made is that while this seems at first glance a body-part riddle (on which see the notes at SYM 39–41), it is in fact a simple description that requires only specialized mythological knowledge. As such, it effectively identifies Óðinn as Gestumblindi and prepares the way for the final, unanswerable GES EP that follows.

# GES EP

The prose conveys the king's frustration at such an essentially underhand trick as asking an unanswerable riddle (since only Óðinn can possibly know the answer): "Only you know that, you wicked creature" (a rather toned-down translation of an utterly offensive slur). The prose goes on to state that he drew his celebrated sword, Tyrfing, but Óðinn changed himself into a falcon and flew off, while the king slashed at its tail feathers. For that reason, we are told, falcons have had short tail feathers ever since.

## VARIOUS RIDDLES (XMS)

I have translated all these *aenigmata* afresh, based on parallels from elsewhere in the Anglo-Saxon riddle tradition. See also the more detailed commentary in *COEALRT.*

# XMS P1

Solution: UNKNOWN.

This is a genuinely puzzling *aenigma,* which nonetheless clearly fits within the tradition.

# XMS P2

Solution: *TURTUR* (turtledove).

This is another bird riddle, this time in the form of a further letter game, or logogriph: the presumably onomatopoeic repetition of *tur*, echoing the cooing of the dove, supplies the solution.

## XMS P3

Solution: *PARIES* → *ARIES* (wall → ram).
For comparison, see ALD 86 (ram).

Another logogriph, which has a good parallel in ALD 86 *(ARIES);* see the note there. The manuscript P⁵ simply has the single word *pariete,* presumably the remnant of a title or a solution: the text printed here is reproduced from the fuller versions found in other manuscripts and presented in AL.

## XMS S1

Solution: *CORPUS ET ANIMA* (body and soul).

Vernet offers a banal solution, based on the notion of three disgruntled students emerging from an inn. In fact, this *aenigma* seems better to fit the soul-and-body nexus exemplified by EXE 41 (soul and body) and 81 (fish and river), with the second and third lines taking up antagonistic positions, while the last expresses the pious hope for the salvation of both. The "gateway" in question is presumably death. See further the notes to EXE 41 and 81 above.

## XMS S2

Solution: *REX* (king).

This *aenigma* brilliantly brings together a number of aspects of the Anglo-Latin riddle tradition and how they are often combined: if the solution "king" is accepted, then it is a simple logogriph, where reducing the constituent letters of Latin *REX* to a single element does indeed render *X* (representing the number ten in Roman numerals).

866

## XMS S3

Solution: *PUGILLARES* (writing tablets, wax tablets).
For comparison, see ALD 32 (writing tablets).

As noted by André Vernet, "Notice et extraits d'un manuscrit d'Edimbourg (Adv. Mss. 18.6.12, 18.7.8, 18.7.7), *Bibliothèque de l'École des Chartres* 107 (1948): 33–51, there are variant forms of this *aenigma,* but the general close similarity of theme to ALD 32 suggests the same solution, with the necessary emendation in the second line; see the note there. The idea seems to be that, when bees visit flowers, a by-product is wax, and from wax and wood writing tablets are made. The wax is written on with a stylus, but a tablet full of writing weighs the same as one that is empty.

## XMS X1

Solution: *LEBES* (cauldron).
For comparison, see ALD 49, ps-BED 10, ALC D76 (all solved "cauldron").
There is a particularly close parallel in ps-BED 10; see the note there.

## XMS X2

Solution: *PULLUS* (chick).
For comparison, see ps-BED 2, EUS 38 (both solved "chick"). There is a particularly close parallel in ps-BED 2; see the note there.

## XMS X3

Solution: *PENNA* (quill pen).
For comparison, see ps-BED 11, EUS 35, LOR 9 (all solved "quill pen"). There is a particularly close parallel in ps-BED 11; see the note there.

## XMS X4

Solution: *CUPA VINARIA* (wine cup).
For comparison, see ALD 78, LOR 5, EXE 9 (all solved "wine cup"). There is a particularly close parallel at LOR 5; see the note there.

## XMS Y1

Solution: *NOE ET COLUMBA* (Noah and the dove).
For comparison, see ALD 64 (dove).

## XMS Z1

Solution: *NUX FATUA* (a bad nut). Note that the solution given is garbled: in the substitution cipher it should be *Nxx fbtxb.*

This is the first of the so-called "Reichenau riddles," on which see in general Arno Schmidt, "Die Reichenauer Rätsel," *Zeitschrift für deutsches Altertum und deutsche Literatur* 73 (1936): 197–200; Bitterli, *Say What I Am Called,* 74–75. These six riddles appear in sequence in the single manuscript Z, immediately following a version of Alcuin's mathematical puzzles, *Propositiones ad acuendos iuvenes* (propositions for sharpening up young men), on which see Hadley and Singmaster, "Problems to Sharpen the Young"; Orchard, "Enigma Variations," 284–89. These *aenigmata* share many aspects of the Anglo-Saxon riddle tradition, including the use of the same basic substitution cipher as found in EXE 34. The cipher is exemplified in a title in the manuscript, reading *Aenigmata rkskbklkb* (for *Aenigmata risibilia,* "funny riddles"), although this collection is not notably funnier than the rest.

## XMS Z2

Solution: *NAVIS* (ship).
For comparison, see BED 12, ALC D61, SYM 13, BER 11 (all solved "ship"); GES 24 (ship [?]).

## XMS Z3

Solution: *UMBRA* (shadow). Note that the "solution" given seems to offer a further clue: "I have a foot."
For comparison, see SYM 97, BER 61 (both solved "shadow").

## XMS Z4

Solution: *NIX ET SOL* (snow and sun). Note that the solution given here in italics is garbled: in the substitution cipher it should perhaps be *Nkx ft Tktbn* (for *nix et Titan,* with Titan as another term for "sun").

For comparison, see ALD 79 (sun and moon); TAT 15 (snow, hail, and ice); EUS 10, ALC D41 (both soved "sun") and D54 (snow); LOR 6 (snow); EXE 4 (sun) and 27 (moon and sun); SYM 11 (snow); BER 55 (sun), 56 (sun and moon), and 57 (sun); OIR 11, GES 15 (both solved "sun").

## XMS Z5

Solution: *VITRICUS* (stepfather).

Note that this and the *aenigma* that follows are self-evidently linked by the themes of family relationships, marking them out as different from the incest riddles found elsewhere in the tradition.

## XMS Z6

Solution: *FILIUS PRIVIGNI* (the son of a stepson).

This *aenigma* is clearly linked thematically to the one that precedes.

# Bibliography

### EDITIONS AND TRANSLATIONS

Abbott, H. H. *The Riddles of the Exeter Book.* Cambridge, 1968.

Alexander, Michael. *The Earliest English Poems.* Harmondsworth, 1966.

Anlezark, Daniel, ed. and trans. *The Old English Dialogues of Solomon and Saturn.* Cambridge, 2009.

Baum, Paul F. *The Anglo-Saxon Riddles of the Exeter Book.* Durham, N.C., 1963.

Bayless, Martha. "Alcuin's *Disputatio Pippini* and the Early Medieval Riddle Tradition." In *Humour, History and Politics in Late Antiquity and the Early Middle Ages,* edited by Guy Halsall, 157–78. Cambridge, 2002.

Bayless, Martha, and Michael Lapidge, eds. *Collectanea Pseudo-Bedae.* Scriptores Latini Hiberniae 14. Dublin, 1998.

Bergamin, Manuela, ed. and trans. *Aenigmata Symposii: La fondazione dell'enigmistica come genere poetico.* Per Verba: Testi mediolatini con traduzione 22. Florence, 2005.

Burrows, Hannah. "Heiðreks gátur." In *Poetry in Fornaldarsögur,* edited by Margaret Clunies Ross, 406–52. Turnhout, 2017.

Cavell, Megan, Victoria Symons, and Matthias Ammon, eds. "The Riddle Ages: Old English Riddles, Translations and Commentaries." https://theriddleages.wordpress.com (accessed November 15, 2019).

Crossley-Holland, Kevin, trans. *The Exeter Book Riddles.* Harmondsworth, 1993.

Daly, Lloyd William, and Walther Suchier, eds. *Altercatio Hadriani Augusti et Epicteti philosophi.* Illinois Studies in Language and Literature 24. Urbana, 1939.

Derolez, René. *Runica Manuscripta: The English Tradition.* Brugge, 1954.

Dickins, Bruce. *Runic and Heroic Poems of the Old Teutonic Peoples.* Cambridge, 1915.

du Bois, Elizabeth Hickman, trans. *The Hundred Riddles of Symphosius.* Woodstock, Vt., 1912.

Dümmler, Ernst, ed. *Aenigmata Anglica.* MGH PLAC 1, 20–23. Berlin, 1881.

——, ed. *Aenigmata Bonifatii.* MGH PLAC 1, 1–15. Berlin, 1881.

——. "Lörscher Rätsel." *Zeitschrift für deutsches Altertum* 22 (1878): 258–63.

Ehwald, Rudolph, ed. *Aldhelmi Opera.* MGH AA 15. Berlin, 1913–1919.

Erhardt-Siebold, Erika von. *Die lateinischen Rätsel der Angelsachsen: ein Beitrag zur Kulturgeschichte Altenglands.* Anglistische Forschungen 61. Heidelberg, 1925; repr., Amsterdam, 1974.

Folkerts, Menso. "Die Alkuin zugeschriebenen *Propositiones ad acuendos iuvenes.*" In *Science in Western and Eastern Civilization in Carolingian Times,* edited by P. L. Butzer and D. Lohrmann, 273–81. Basel, 1993.

——. *Die älteste mathematische Aufgabensammlung in lateinischer Sprache: Die Alcuin zugeschriebenen "Propositiones ad acuendos iuvenes."* Österreichische Akademie der Wissenschaften, Mathematisch-naturwissenschaftliche Klasse, Denkschriften, vol. 116, part 6. Vienna, 1978.

Förster, Max. "Ein altenglisches Prosa-Rätsel." *Archiv für das Studium der neueren Sprachen und Literaturen* 115 (1905): 392–93.

Giles, J. A., ed. *Anecdota Bedæ, Lanfranci, et Aliorum.* London, 1851.

Glorie, F., ed. *Collectiones aenigmatum Merovingicae aetatis.* 2 vols. CCSL 133 and 133A. Turnhout, 1968.

Hadley, John, and David Singmaster. "Problems to Sharpen the Young: An Annotated Translation of *Propositiones ad acuendos iuvenes,* the Oldest Mathematical Problem Collection in Latin, Attributed to Alcuin of York." *Mathematical Gazette* 76 (1992): 102–26.

Halsall, Maureen. *The Old English Rune Poem: A Critical Edition.* Toronto, 1981.

Howlett, David. "*Versus cuiusdam Scotti de alphabeto*: An Edition, Translation, and Commentary." *Peritia* 21 (2010): 136–50.

Jember, Gregory K., trans. *The Old English Riddles: A New Translation.* Denver, 1976.

Juster, A. M., trans. *Saint Aldhelm's Riddles.* Toronto, 2015.

Krapp, George Philip, and Elliot Van Kirk Dobbie, eds. *The Exeter Book.* ASPR 3. London, 1936.

Lapidge, Michael. *Bede's Latin Poetry.* Oxford, 2019.

Leary, T. J. *Symphosius, The "Aenigmata": An Introduction, Text, and Commentary.* London, 2014.

Muir, Bernard J., ed. *The Exeter Anthology of Old English Poetry.* 2 vols. Exeter, 1994; rev. ed., 2000; 2nd rev. ed. with DVD, 2006.

Ohl, Raymond Theodore. *The Enigmas of Symphosius.* Philadelphia, 1928.

Page, R. I. "The Icelandic Rune Poem." *Nottingham Medieval Studies* 42 (1998): 1–37. Reprinted as a booklet by the Viking Society for Northern Research.

Pinsker, Hans, and Waltraud Ziegler, ed. and trans. *Die altenglischen Rätsel des Exeterbuchs.* Anglistische Forschungen 183. Heidelberg, 1985.

Pitman, James H., trans. *The Riddles of Aldhelm.* Yale Studies in English 67. New Haven, 1925.

Porter, David W. "A Double Solution to the Latin Riddle in Mediaeval Studies: Antwerp, Plantin-Moretus Museum M16.2." *American Notes and Queries* 9.1 (1996): 3–9.

Porter, John, trans. *Anglo-Saxon Riddles.* Hockwold-cum-Wilton, 1995.

Riese, Alexander, ed. "Bern Riddles." In *Anthologia Latina,* part 1, fascicle 1, pp. 351–70. Leipzig, 1894; repr., Amsterdam, 1964.

Stork, Nancy Porter. *Through a Gloss Darkly: Aldhelm's Riddles in the British Library MS Royal 12.C.xxiii.* Studies and Texts 98. Toronto, 1990.

Strecker, Karl., ed. *Aenigmata Hexasticha.* MGH PLAC vol. 4, no. 2, pp. 732–59. Berlin, 1923.

Suchier, Walther, ed. 'Disputatio Pippini cum Albino.' In *Die Altercatio Hadriani Augusti et Epicteti philosophi, nebst einigen verwandten Texten,* edited by L. W. Daly and W. Suchier, 134–46. Illinois Studies in Language and Literature 24. Urbana, 1939.

Tangl, Michael, ed. *Die Briefe des heiligen Bonifatius und Lullus.* MGH ES 1. Berlin, 1916.

Tolkien, Christopher, ed. and trans. *The Saga of King Heidrek the Wise.* New York, 1960.

Trautmann, Moritz. *Die altenglischen Rätsel (die Rätsel des Exeterbuchs), herausgegeben, erläutert und mit Wörterverzeichnis versehen.* Heidelberg, 1915.

Tupper, Frederick M., Jr. "Riddles of the Bede Tradition: The *Flores* of pseudo-Bede." *Modern Philology* 2 (1905): 561–72.

———, ed. *The Riddles of the Exeter Book.* Boston, 1910; repr., 1968.

Whitman, Frank H. *Old English Riddles.* Canadian Federation for the Humanities, Monograph Series 3. Port Credit, ON, 1982.

Williams, Mary Jane MacDonald. "The Riddles of Tatwine and Eusebius." PhD diss., University of Michigan, 1974.

Williamson, Craig. *A Feast of Creatures: Anglo-Saxon Riddle-Songs, Translated with Introduction, Notes and Commentary*. Philadelphia, 1982.

——, ed. *The Old English Riddles of the "Exeter Book."* Chapel Hill, 1977.

Wilmanns, W., ed. "Disputatio regalis et nobilissimi iuvenis Pippini cum Albino scholastico." *Zeitschrift fur deutsches Altertum* 14 (1869): 530–55.

Wyatt, Alfred J. *Old English Riddles*. Boston, 1912.

## FURTHER READING

Archibald, Elizabeth. *Apollonius of Tyre: Medieval and Renaissance Themes and Variations: Including the Text of the 'Historia Apollonii Regis Tyri' with an English Translation*. Cambridge, 1991.

Athenaeus of Naucratis. *The Learned Banqueters*. Edited and translated by S. Douglas Olson. 8 vols. Loeb Classical Library 204, 208, 224, 235, 274, 327, 345, 519. Cambridge, Mass., 2007–2012.

Barney, Stephen A., W. J. Lewis, J. A. Beach, and Oliver Berghof, trans. *The "Etymologies" of Isidore of Seville*. Cambridge, 2006.

Cavell, Megan. *Weaving Words and Binding Bodies: The Poetics of Human Experience in Old English Literature*. Toronto, 2016.

Cook, Eleanor. *Enigmas and Riddles in Literature*. Cambridge, 2006.

Fell, Christine E. "Runes and Riddles in Anglo-Saxon England." In *"Lastworda Betst": Essays in Memory of Christine E. Fell with Her Unpublished Writings*, edited by Carole Hough and Kathryn A. Lowe, 264–77. Donington, 2002.

Forster, Edward Seymour. "Riddles and Problems from the Greek Anthology." *Greece and Rome* 14 (1945): 42–47.

Goolden, Peter, ed. *The Old English "Apollonius of Tyre."* Oxford English Monographs. London, 1958.

Green, R. P. H., ed. *The Works of Ausonius*. Oxford, 1991.

Herren, Michael W., ed. and trans. *The Hisperica Famina I: The A-Text*. Toronto, 1974.

Irvine, Martin. *The Making of Textual Culture: "Grammatica" and Literary Theory (350–1100)*. Cambridge, 1994.

Kries, Susanne. "*Fela í rúnum eða í skáldskap*: Anglo-Saxon and Scandinavian Approaches to Riddles and Poetic Disguises." In *Riddles, Knights and*

*Cross-Dressing Saints: Essays on Medieval English Language and Literature,* edited by Thomas Honegger, 139–64. Sammlung Variations 5. Bern, 2005.

Lindsay, W. M., ed. *Isidorii Etymologiarum Sive Originum Libri XX.* 2 vols. Oxford, 1911.

Lockhart, Jessica. "Everyday Wonders and Enigmatic Structures: Riddles from Symphosius to Chaucer." PhD diss., University of Toronto, 2017.

Milanović-Barham, Čelica. "Aldhelm's Enigmata and Byzantine Riddles." *Anglo-Saxon England* 22 (1993): 51–64.

Orchard, Andy. "Enigma Variations: The Anglo-Saxon Riddle-Tradition." In *Latin Leraning and English Lore: Studies in Anglo-Saxon Literature for Michael Lapidge,* edited by Katherine O'Brien O'Keeffe and Andy Orchard, vol. 1, pp. 284–304. Toronto, 2005.

———. "The *Hisperica famina* as Literature." *Journal of Medieval Latin* 10 (2000): 1–45.

Orton, Peter. "The Exter Book Riddles: Authorship and Transmission." *Anglo-Saxon England* 44 (2016): 131–62.

Paton, W. P., ed. *The Greek Anthology.* 5 vols. London, 1916–1918.

Pavlovskis, Zoja. "The Riddler's Microcosm: From Symphosius to St. Boniface." *Classica et Mediaevalia* 39 (1988): 219–51.

Porter, David W. "Æthelwold's Bowl and *The Chronicle of Abingdon.*" *Neuphilologische Mitteilungen* 97 (1996): 163–67.

Salvador-Bello, Mercedes. *Isidorean Perceptions of Order: The Exeter Book Riddles and Medieval Latin Enigmata.* Medieval European Studies 17. Morgantown, 2015.

Schmidt, Arno. "Die Reichenauer Rätsel." *Zeitschrift für deutsches Altertum und deutsche Literatur* 73 (1936): 197–200.

Sebo, Erin. *In Enigmate: The History of a Riddle, 400–1500.* Dublin, 2018.

Stanley, E. G. "Riddling: A Serious Pursuit through the Ages and in Many Languages." In *Proceedings of the Sixth International Conference, "Language, Culture, and Society in Russian/English Studies,"* edited by Jane Roberts and Emma Volodarskaya, 16–36. London, 2016.

Vernet, André. "Notice et extraits d'un manuscrit d'Edimbourg (Adv. Mss. 18.6.12, 18.7.8, 18.7.7)." *Bibliothèque de l'École des Chartes* 107 (1948): 33–51.

Wilcox, Jonathan. "'Tell Me What I Am': The Old English Riddles." In *Readings in Medieval Texts: Interpreting Old and Middle English Literature,* edited by David F. Johnson and Elaine Treharne, 46–59. Oxford, 2005.

# Index of Solutions

The symbol † marks riddles where the solution is one that has sometimes been suggested, but for which another is preferred.